AF601789

Concise Critical Comments of the New Testament

Concise Critical Comments of the New Testament

Robert Young, LL. D.

Sovereign Grace Publishers, Inc.
P.O. Box 4998
Lafayette, IN 47903
2001

Concise Critical Comments of the New Testament

ISBN 1-58960-261-7

Printed In the United States of America
By Lightning Source, Inc.

THE NEW COVENANT

THE NEW COVENANT is contained in twenty-seven books, written by eight persons, and divided into three classes, viz., five Historical, twenty-one Doctrinal, and one Prophetic.

I. HISTORICAL—containing the history of JESUS CHRIST:

1.) *In Himself*—his genealogy, birth, life, teaching, miracles, death, resurrection, and ascension, as viewed in four distinct relationships—in four 'Gospels,' by MATTHEW, MARK, LUKE, and JOHN.

2.) *In His Church*—whose primitive planting, state, and progress among Jews and Gentiles—are set forth in the 'Acts of the Apostles,'—by LUKE.

II. DOCTRINAL—setting forth the principles of the Gospel of The Christ to primitive Believers, whether *Jews* or *Gentiles*, viewed either as Communities or as Individuals, e.g.

1.) *For Believing Gentile Communities*—Letters to the 'Romans, Corinthians (i. ii), Galatians, Ephesians, Philippians, Colossians, Thessalonians (i. ii),'—by PAUL.

2.) *For Believing Gentile Individuals*—Letters to 'Timothy (i. ii), Titus, Philemon,'—by PAUL.

3.) *For Believing Jewish Communities*—Letter to the 'Hebrews'—by PAUL; to the 'Twelve Tribes and strangers scattered abroad,'—by JAMES, PETER (i. ii), JUDE, JOHN (i).

4.) *For Believing Jewish Individuals*—Letters to the 'The Lady Electa,' and to 'Gaius,'— by JOHN (ii. iii).

III. PROPHETICAL—describing the future trials and triumphs of the Gospel, in the 'Revelation' of Jesus Christ made to his servant JOHN.

THE FOUR GOSPELS are not designed to be merely supplementary or corroborative of each other, but rather to exhibit JESUS THE CHRIST in four distinct aspects of his Character and Work; MATTHEW viewing Him chiefly as the 'Son of Abraham and David,' the long-promised and long-expected 'Messiah, and king of Israel;' MARK chiefly as the Delegated 'Servant of God,' who came not to do his own will, but the will of Him who sent Him; LUKE chiefly as the 'Son of Man, or the Son of Adam,' whose mission was to ALL MEN, Jew and Gentile alike; and JOHN chiefly as the 'SON OF GOD,' who is in the bosom of the Father, and who alone can and doth declare Him. In the *first* he is the 'born king,' in the *second*, but the 'shepherd,' of Israel; in the *third*, he is 'the glad tidings of great joy that shall be to all people,' and in the *fourth*, he is 'the Word become flesh He who hath seen me hath seen the Father.'

Four Gospels, and four only, have been received by the Christian Church generally from the earliest ages, as is testified by Ignatius (A.D. 107), Justin Martyr (A.D. 100—165), Tatian (A.D. 158), Irenaeus (A.D. 202,) and Origen (A.D. 185—250), not to speak of later writers. All these Gospels were written in GREEK, which was at that time not only the language of science and literature, but of religion, commerce, and every-day life, in Palestine, Syria, Asia Minor, Egypt, and throughout the civilized Roman empire, hence not only did Paul write to the 'Romans' in Greek,—not in Latin,—but also in the same language to the 'Hebrews' to whom Matthew had shortly before addressed his 'Gospel.'

The following important FACTS are found in all the Four Evangelistic Writers, viz.:—

Ministry of John, his fore-runner,—in Mat. 3. 1—12; Mark 1. 1—8; Luke 3. 1—18; John 1. 15—31. Baptism of Jesus Christ by John,—in Mat. 3. 13—17; Mark 1. 9—11; Luke 3. 21, 22; John 1. 32—34. John the Baptist in Prison,—in Mat. 4. 12; 14. 3; Mark 1. 14; 6. 17; Luke 3. 19, 20; John 3. 4. Jesus' Return to Galilee after Baptism,—in Mat. 4. 12; Mark 1. 14, 15; Luke 4. 14, 15; John 4. 43—5. He feeds the Five Thousand,—in Mat. 14. 13—21; Mark 6. 30—44; Luke 9. 10—17; John 6. 1—15. Peter's Profession of Faith in Him,—in Mat. 16. 13—19; Mark 8. 27—29; Luke 9. 18—20; John 6. 61—71. He is anointed before his suffering,—in Mat. 26. 6—13; Mark 14. 3—9; Luke 7. 36—50; John 12. 1—11. He enters Jerusalem in triumph,—in Mat. 21. 11; Mark 11. 1—10; Luke 19. 29—44; John 12. 12—19. He cleanses the Temple at Jerusalem,—in Mat. 21. 12—16; Mark 11. 15—18; Luke 19. 45—48; John 2. 13—22. He partakes of the Passover Feast,—in Mat. 26. 17—29; Mark 14. 12—25; Luke 22. 7—23; John 13. 1—35. He foretells Peter's Fall,—in Mat. 26. 30—35; Mark 14. 26—31; Luke 22. 31—39; John 13. 36—38. He enters into Gethsemane,—in Mat. 26. 36—46; Mark 14. 32—42; Luke 22. 40—46; John 18. 1. He is betrayed by one of his Disciples,—in Mat. 26. 47—56; Mark 14. 43—52; Luke 22. 47—53; John 18. 2—11. He is brought before the High Priest,—in Mat. 26. 57, 58; Mark 14. 53, 54; Luke 22. 54; John 18. 13. He is brought before Pilate,—in Mat. 26. 1, 2, 11—14; Mark 15. 1—5; Luke 23. 1—3; John 18. 28. He is denied by Peter,—in Mat. 26. 69—75; Mark 14. 66—72. Luke 22. 54—62; John 18. 15—27. He is Accused and Condemned,—in Mat. 27. 15—26; Mark 15. 6—15; Luke 23. 13—25; John 18. 29—40. He is abused by the Soldiers,—in Mat. 27. 27—31; Mark 15. 16—20; Luke 23. 36, 37; John 19. 2, 3. He is crucified,—in Mat. 27. 32—38; Mark 15. 21—28; Luke 23. 26—34; John 19. 17—24. He dies,—in Mat. 27. 50; Mark 15. 37; Luke 23. 46; John 19. 28—30. He is buried,—in Mat. 27. 57—61; Mark 15. 42—47; Luke 23. 50—56; John 19. 38—42. He rises again,—in Mat. 28. 1—10; Mark 16. 1—11; Luke 24. 1—12; John 20. 1—18.

MATTHEW

THE GOSPEL OF MATTHEW was the first published of all the Gospels, according to the uniform testimony of all who have examined the subject. It was written most probably about A.D. 40, that is, seven years after the ascension of Christ; others date it as late as A.D. 60. It was written in Greek, like the other Gospels, though almost all the ancient fathers thought it was written in Hebrew, confounding it perhaps with the Hebrew 'Gospel of the Nazarenes,' or of 'the Hebrews,' which was probably a corrupted, interpolated, castrated, copy of it. Its author was a Jew, writing for Jews, and hence it is full of references to Old Testament passages bearing upon the Messiahship of Jesus. His other name was Levi, and his call (recorded in ch. 9. 9.) to be one of the personal followers and apostles of Christ fitted him, as an eye-witness, to write this Gospel, aided, as he doubtless was, by the Divine Spirit who was promised to lead the disciples into 'all truth' necessary for salvation, and to 'bring all things to their remembrance' that Jesus had said and done. The special object of this Gospel is to present to the reader 'Jesus Christ as the promised seed of Abraham and son of David, who as the Messiah of Jehovah, was the true king of Israel.' It may be divided as follows ;—

I. Genealogy & Childhood of Jesus, ch. i. ii.
II. John's Preaching, and Jesus' Baptism, iii.
III. Jesus in the Wilderness, and in Galilee, iv.
IV. Jesus' teaching on the Mount, v—vii.
V. Jesus' doings in Galilee, viii—xii.
VI. Jesus' Similes or Parables, &c. xiii—xiv.
VII. Jesus about Tyre and Sidon, xv—xviii.
VIII. Jesus' return to Judea, xix—xxi. 27.
IX. Jesus' Similes, xxi. 28—xxiv. 1. 2.
X. Jesus on the Mount of the Olives, xxiv. 3—xxvi. 5.
XI. Jesus in Bethany and Gethsemane, xxvi. 6—56.
XII. Jesus before his judges, xxvi. 57—xxvii. 31.
XIII. Jesus on Calvary, xxvii. 32—56.
XIV. Jesus in the Grave, xxvii. 57—66.
XV. Jesus risen and in Galilee, xxviii. 1—20.

Chapter I. may be divided into two parts; v. 1—17 containing Christ's genealogy; and v. 18—25 His birth and its incidents.

1. BOOK,] *lit.* 'birth-roll of Jesus Christ, son of David, son of Abraham;' that is, descendant of these ancient patriarchs, the former being he whose 'seed' was to sit on his throne for ever, as in 2 Sa. 7. 12, 13; and the latter he in whose seed all nations of the earth should bless themselves, as in Ge. 22. 18. The 'born-king' must have his royal lineage recorded and proved; but now that the tribal distinctions are for ever lost—how will the Jews be able to ascertain the descent of the Messiah they yet expect from the royal seed of David and the tribe of Judah? This first verse is the title to v. 2—17 only, not to the Gospel generally.

8. JORAM,] between whom and Ozias (Uzziah) come properly Ahaziah, Joash & Amaziah.

16. JACOB BEGAT JOSEPH,] who espoused Mary, daughter of Heli (Luke 3. 23), and is hence called 'his son,' i.e. son-in-law; Matthew gives the genealogy through Joseph, Luke through Mary.

17. FOURTEEN GENERATIONS.] Probably taken from the public registers at Beth-Lehem: see Luke 2. 4.

18. OF THE HOLY GHOST,] *lit.* 'out of (or by) a holy spirit,' or influence, proceding from God the Father; probably the influence, not the person, of the Spirit is here indicated; the Greek text has no definite article, as it has in 4. 1; 12. 31, 32; 28. 19, &c.

18. WITH CHILD,] *lit.* 'having in the womb.'

19. HER HUSBAND,] by law and courtesy; being a 'just' man, anxious to keep himself pure and act according to law, he 'was counselled,' or advised by others 'to loose her from (him) privately.'

20. THE ANGEL,] *lit.* 'a messenger (or worker) of the Lord,' said, thou mayest not fear to 'take along with thee' Mary thy (espoused) wife, for that which is 'begotten' (not 'conceived' merely) in her is 'out of (or by) a holy spirit or influence' from God; as in v. 18.

21. JESUS,] in Hebrew 'Joshua,' a saviour, one who 'eases' another from any burden or affliction, such as 'sins,' especially 'omissions or failures in duty,' seeing 'perfection' is required by law, not merely 'sincerity.'

22. WAS DONE,] *or* 'happened, came to pass.'

FULFILLED,] *or* 'filled out fully,' realized, exemplified, completed.

OF,] *lit.* 'by the Lord through the prophet.'

23. A VIRGIN,] *lit.* 'the virgin (as in Isa. 7. 14) shall have in the womb..and they (i.e. men) shall call his name Emanuel (i.e. with us [he is] God, or a mighty one).'

24. BEING RAISED,] *lit.* 'having risen from the sleep,' did as the messenger of the Lord 'set before' him, and 'took along' with him his espoused wife.

25. TILL,] which naturally, if not necessarily, implies later knowledge. The 'first-born;' as in Luke 2. 17.

Chapter II. may be divided into four parts; v. 1—12 visit of magi; v. 13—15 flight into Egypt; v. 16—18 Herod's cruelty; and v. 19—23 return to Israel and Nazareth.

1. BETH-LEHEM,] i.e. 'house of bread;' six

miles from Jerusalem, birth-place of David, and of Joseph, Mary's husband (see Luke 2. 4), who came hither from Nazareth in Galilee to be 'enrolled,' not 'taxed.' There was another Bethlehem in Zebulun, as in Jos. 19. 15.

WISE MEN,] *lit.* 'mages,' a philosophic sect in the east, see Jer. 39. 3.

HEROD THE KING,] an Edumean by birth, and a proselyte, who greatly enlarged and beautified the temple, but of whom it was too truly said, 'Better be Herod's hog than his son.' Like his grandson Agrippa (Acts 25. 13), he was a 'king' by courtesy chiefly.

JERUSALEM,] i.e. 'possession of peace;' anciently called Jebus, chosen by God to be his dwelling place (Ps. 78. 68), surrounded by hills (Ps. 125. 2), yet often captured (2 Ch. 12. 9; 25. 23); 'the joy of all the land,' (Ps. 48. 2).

2. WHERE IS] 'the born-king of the Jews?' he is so, not by election like Saul (1 Sa. 10. 24), nor by violence like Herod; His right it is to reign (Eze. 21. 27).

WE HAVE SEEN,] *lit.* 'we saw' his star when we were in the east (Nu. 24. 17), but not now; and 'we came' from the east to 'kiss (the hand) before or towards him,' as in Job 31. 27; civil respect, not religious 'worship,' alone was intended.

3. TROUBLED,] as in 14. 26; Mark 6, 50, &c.

4. GATHERED TOGETHER,] *lit.* 'made a synagogue' of the 'chief priests,' who were changed often at the will of the king, (there being lay-patronage in those days in all civil establishments of religion as at present,) together with the 'scribes,' that is, writers or copyists and expounders of the Scriptures, grammarians, and teachers of the people; he was 'inquiring' (not 'demanding') from them where 'the Christ' (not 'Christ,' of whom he knew nothing) or the Messiah, that is, 'the Anointed one,' whom the prophet had spoken of, and the people expected, may (or might) be born or is (already) born.

5. IT IS,] *lit.* 'it has been written through the prophet,' (Micah 5. 2; compare John 7. 42).

6. PRINCES,] *lit.* 'leaders..for out of thee shall come forth a leader, who shall feed my people—Israel.'

7. DILIGENTLY,] *or* 'exactly, accurately.. the time of the appearing star.'

8. WORSHIP,] *lit.* 'may kiss (the hand) before or towards him;' as in v. 2. 11, &c.

9. DEPARTED,] *lit.* 'went on' ..and the star 'led them forward,' or went before them.

11. THEY SAW.] Some MSS. read 'they found,' and 'opened up' their treasures, and 'brought before him gifts.'

12. OF GOD,] *lit.* 'having been oracularly warned not to return..they withdrew.'

13. DEPARTED,] *lit.* 'and they having withdrawn, lo, a messenger of the Lord..saying, Having arisen, take with (thee) the young child..till that I say to thee, for Herod is about to seek.'

14. WHEN,] *lit.* 'and having arisen, he took with (him)..and withdrew to Egypt,' as Jacob had done for a time, see Ge. 45, 28.

15. DEATH,] *lit.* 'end of Herod..by the Lord through the prophet (Hosea 11. 1), saying..I did call,' not 'I have called,' as in C. V.

16. WHEN,] *lit.* 'having seen that he was treated as a child by the mages..slew all the male-children..in all its borders, from two years and downward....he enquired accurately from the mages.

17. FULFILLED,] *or* 'filled out;' as in v. 15.

18. RAMA,] *lit.* a 'high' place; near Beth-Lehem, as in Jer. 31. 15; great or rather 'much' mourning; Rachel (who was buried near it, see Ge. 48. 7), 'bewailing her children, and did not wish to be comforted,' or rather 'called on;' as in 5. 4, &c.

19. WAS DEAD,] *lit.* 'ended;' as in 9. 18, &c

28. ARISE,] *lit,* 'having arisen, take with (thee)..seeking the soul of the young child.'

22. DID REIGN,] *lit.* 'doth reign *or* is king over Judea instead of, ..to go away thither, and having been oracularly warned..he withdrew to the parts of the Galil,' or 'circuit' around the lake of Tiberias.

23. FULFILLED,] *or* 'filled out..through the prophets, that.' The general testimony of the prophets was that he should be 'despised,' as he was in John 1. 46, 'out of Nazareth is any good thing able to be?'

Chapter III. may be divided into two parts; v. 1—12, John's preaching and baptism; v. 13—17, 'Jesus' baptism and anointing.

1. IN THOSE DAYS,] when Jesus dwelt in Nazareth (as in 2. 23), A.D. 26, there 'came alongside of' him John (i.e. Jah is gracious) the Baptist, proclaiming (as a herald) in the wilderness (or pasture land) of Judea.

2. REPENT,] *or* 'Have another (or a new) mind, for come nigh has the reign of the heavens,' that is, the Gospel dispensation.

3. PREPARE,] *or* 'make ready..make straight.'

4. LEATHERN,] *lit.* a 'skin zone about his loin.'

5. WENT,] *lit.* 'were going forth,' that is day by day, continuously, to 'the Jordan,' the great and almost solitary river of Palestine, running from north to south through the centre of the whole land.

6. BAPTIZED,] in the Jordan by him, *lit.* 'under him,' i.e. received as his disciples. There is now no real dispute among biblical scholars about the true meaning of the word translated 'baptize;' it simply signifies to cause an object some way or other to be in or under some liquid, such as water, which may be done either by dipping or pouring out, or shedding forth, as in Acts 2. 2, 3. where the Holy Spirit 'came down' and 'sat upon' each, where 'dipping' is entirely out of the question; so in 1 Cor. 10. 2, 'were baptized in the cloud and in the sea,' where the two modes are conjoined, the cloud coming *down* upon them, and they going down *into* the hollow of the sea.

CONFESSING,] that is, acknowledging their shortcomings and failures of duty brought against them by John.

PHARISEES..SADDUCEES.] The first were so called because of their keeping themselves 'separate,' as if better than others, and the second because of their being followers of one Sadoc, who taught that men ought to serve God without any hope of a reward which degenerated into a denial of the resurrection and a future life.

COME TO,] *lit.* 'coming upon' his baptism.

GENERATION,] *or* 'brood, offspring, progeny;' who 'did shew you' the duty or the way of fleeing from the 'coming (*lit* about-to-be) wrath' of God on the Jewish nation, which issued in its ruin and rejection, so that 'the city and the nation are no longer his,' see Dan. 9. 26.

8. BRING FORTH,] *lit.* 'make fruits (or fruit) worthy of the new mind' you profess to have.

9. WITHIN,] *or* 'among yourselves,' that God will accept us because of our parentage. 'every man must bear his own burden' (Gal. 6. 5), and 'out of these stones,' lying on the edge, or at the bottom of the Jordan, God can raise up a spiritual seed to Abraham as he promised, see Gal. 3. 29; Heb. 11. 11, &c.

10. IS LAID.] The *present* tense in Greek (as in Hebrew and all other languages) is used rhetorically for the *future* to express the certainty and habituality of the action; so 'bringeth not forth, *lit.* maketh not,..is hewn down, and to fire (not 'the' fire) is being cast.'

11. WITH,] *or* 'in water, with a view to a new mind,' such as you propose to have and wish to have; he who after me 'is coming' as the Messiah and King of Israel, shall baptize you 'with (in *or* by) a holy spirit *or* influence' (communicated by *the* Holy Spirit) and with (in *or* by) 'fire,' that is, afflictions and trials.

12. BURN UP,] *lit.* 'burn down' utterly with (*or* by) fire 'unquenched,' i.e. 'sufferings or trials' (as in v. 11.) unalleviated, as at the destruction of Jerusalem; figuratively it may be applied to the final lot of sinners. 'Unquenched' not 'unquenchable;' it is not that He *cannot*, but that He *does* not, interfere to quench it till the whole heap of chaff is burnt down to the ground.

13. GALILEE,] or Nazareth, 'upon (not *to*) the Jordan,' sailing down, it may be, in some fishing boat, to the place where John was baptizing.

14. FORBAD,] *lit.* 'was forbidden *or* keeping him thoroughly back.'

15. ANSWERING,] *lit.* 'having judged himself of' the matter, says, 'Leave *or* let go now,' for the present, this opinion of yours, for thus it is 'distinguishing or eminent' to us (you and I) to 'fill up *or* out every just *or* righteous' state or act of God's appointment.

16. WHEN,] *lit.* 'having been baptized, went up' the banks of the Jordan, away 'from the water,' not 'out of' it, as in C.V.

OPENED,] *or* 'cleft *or* rent asunder,' as in Acts 7. 56; and 'he saw,' probably John is meant as a witness-bearer; see John 1. 32.

THE SPIRIT OF GOD,] *lit.* 'the Spirit of the (true) God, coming down as if (it were, in the manner of) a dove, and coming upon him,' that is, Jesus.

17. FROM,] *lit.* 'out of the heavens, saying, This is the Son of Me, the dearly-beloved one, in whom I was well-pleased,' up to the present moment, when he is commencing a new career; or by whom I 'thought well' of all things, as in Ge. 1. 21.

IV. may be divided into *seven* parts; v. 1—4, Jesus' first trial; v. 5—7 second trial; v. 8—11 third trial and issue; v. 12—16, Jesus goes to Galilee and its result; v. 17. Jesus' text and theme; v. 18—22, call of four apostles; v. 23—25, Jesus teaching, preaching, healing, and their results.

1. LED UP,] from the banks of the Jordan to the mountain range north of the road from Jerusalem to Jericho, 'under' the influence of the Spirit (of God, as in 3. 16), to be 'tested *or* tried under' the suggestions of the Devil, *lit.* one who 'throws (anything) through' another; in the N.T. the word is always in the singular number, never in the plural, except in 1 Tim. 3. 11. The C.V. injuriously confounds it with 'Demons;' as in v. 24, &c.

2. 40 DAYS..40 NIGHTS,] like Moses and Elijah, (see Ex. 24. 18; 1 K. 19. 8) as a preparation for the great work before him. He submitted to all the *sinless* infirmities of man.

3. THE TEMPTER,] *or* 'trier, tester,' i.e. the Devil, 'If Son thou be of the (true) God,' not 'a son' merely, like any and every created being, but 'Son' in a special manner, (see Ps. 2. 7), for though the definite article is omitted, yet the power suggested to be employed was not at the will of any mere created son.

COMMAND,] *lit.* 'speak *or* say the word in order that these stones (lying around) loaves may become,' to satisfy his natural hunger. The *first* thurst was: Distrust the general providence of God,—be impatient!

4. ANSWERED.] See note on 3. 15.

IT IS WRITTEN,] *lit.* 'it has been written, ages ago for direction in De. 8. 3. He uses 'the sword of the Spirit—which is—a saying of God,' any 'saying' and every one, not merely 'the word of God' that is, the Scriptures, as is commonly supposed. Not upon bread alone doth Man live, but upon every word (*or* thing) coming out through the mouth of God, that is, through every thing ordained by God; he who gave the greater will give the less, see 6. 25, &c. The great thing taught us here is: *Know* the will of God.

5. TAKETH HIM UP,] *or* 'taketh him along with' himself to the 'holy city,' that is, Jerusalem, which had been 'set apart' by God from the other cities of Israel, and setteth him on 'the little wing' or corner of the temple.

6. IN THEIR HANDS,] *lit.* 'on hands they shall lift thee up,' lest thou 'mayest strike forward towards a stone thy foot.' Jesus having manifested his regard for God's law, the Devil tries to pervert its promises into a snare. The second thrust is: Presume on the general providence of God!

7. SAID,] *lit.* 'brought to light' by speech.

AGAIN.] The position of the Greek word is ambiguous: it may mean, 'Jesus said to him again, It hath been written:' *or* 'Jesus said to him, Again, it hath been written.'

TEMPT,] *lit.* 'try out,' that is, excessively, to the full, beyond measure; as in Luke 4. 12; 10. 25; 1 Cor. 10. 9. The great truth taught us here is: *Understand* the will of God.

8. MOUNTAIN,] perhaps Nebo; the 'world' (Gr. *kosmos*) is in Luke 4. 5, the 'inhabited' land, as in 2. 1, and it *may* refer to Palestine only.

9. WORSHIP,] *lit.* 'kiss (the hand) before *or* to me;' as in v. 10; 2. 3, &c.

10. SAITH,] *lit.* 'layeth *or* layeth down,' his wish and will, as it were.

GET THEE HENCE,] *lit.* 'go away under' *or* in silence or shame.

SATAN.] A Hebrew word signifying simply an 'adversary,' applied in Nu. 22. 22, 32, even to 'the angel of the Lord,' who personated Jehovah, and is supposed to have been Christ himself.

ONLY.] This word is not expressed in De. 9. 13, but of course it is plainly understood.

11. LEAVETH,] *or* 'letteth him alone,' and 'messengers came forward (being probably spectators) and were acting-as-deacons to him;' he who performs any act of service—secular or sacred—is a 'deacon' in N.T. language, and there is no N.T. authority whatever for making it the name of an 'official.'

12. WAS CAST INTO PRISON,] *lit.* 'was given up,' that is, 'betrayed,' as in 10. 4.

DEPARTED,] *or* rather, 'withdrew towards Galilee.'

13. LEAVING,] *lit.* 'having utterly left' Nazareth, where he was brought up (never returning), 'having come he settled down (that is, utterly) at Capernaum (i.e. village of Nahum) along aside of the sea' of Tiberias, in or within the borders or territory of the two tribes of Zabulon and Naphthalim.

14. BY,] *lit.* 'through' the instrumentality of Isaiah (9. 1, 2), who was only the instrument in the hand of the Spirit.

15. GENTILES,] *lit.* 'nations,' in opposition to the 'Jews;' most of the inhabitants of Upper Galilee being non-Israelites.

16. SAT,] *lit.* 'is sitting down in (moral and spiritual) darkness saw (and some of them rejected) a great light, and to those sitting down in a region (or space) and a shadow of death, light arose to them.'

17. JESUS,] *lit.* 'the Jesus,' i.e. the Saviour, 'to preach *or* cry, *or* proclaim as a herald, and to say, Have a new (*or* another) mind, for come nigh hath the kingdom (*or* reign) of the heavens;' as in 3. 2.

18. WALKING,] *lit.* 'walking round about' saw two brothers (not 'brethren' merely) Simon (i.e. heard), named Peter (i.e. a rock), casting a drag (or large enfolding net) into the sea, because they were fishers, *lit.* salt-men, i.e. mariners.

19. FOLLOW,] *lit.* 'come ye after me, and I will make you fishers (i.e. salt-men, mariners) of men.'

20. LEFT,] *lit.* 'having let alone the nets.'

21. GOING ON,] *or* 'forward,' he saw other two brothers (not 'brethren' merely), James (i.e. Jacob, one who takes by the heel) the son (or perhaps merely the step-son) of Zebedee (i.e. my dowry), and John (i.e. Jah is gracious) his brother, in the (not *a*) boat.. making throughly perfect their nets.'

22. LEFT,] *lit.* 'having let alone the boat.'

23. WENT,] *lit.* 'was going round about' all Galilee..crying (or proclaiming-as-a-herald) the good news of the reign (of the heavens), and healing (*lit.* cherishing any afflicted with) every disease (or pain), and every weakness among the people.'

24. FAME,] *lit.* 'hearing went forth to all Syria, and they brought before him all having ailment, with manifold diseases and trials held close, and demonized, and moon-struck, and paralyzed, and he healed (*lit.* cherished) them.'

25. GREAT MULTITUDES,] *or* 'many crowds,' in different places, one after another, from Galilee and Decapolis, i.e. 'ten cities,' as in Mark 5. 20; 7. 31), Jerusalem, (the dual form is used, to express the two parts of the city), and Judea (generally), and (from Iturea and Petrea) beyond the Jordan eastward.

Chapter V. may be divided into various parts; v.1, 2, The occasion of the following discourse; v. 2—12, Who are truly happy v. 13—16, Their duties to others; v. 17—48, Opening up of the Moral Law in four special particulars; 1) murder; 2) unchastity; 3) oaths; 4) retaliation.

1. MULTITUDES,] *or* 'crowds,' he went up to 'the mountain' (not *a* mountain), probably Tabor, and 'he having sat down,' his disciples 'came forward' to him.

2. OPENED] his mouth; a Hebrew mode of speaking, he 'was teaching' them as the 'prophet like unto' Moses; see De. 18. 15.

SAYING,] *lit.* 'laying down' the following teachings.

3. BLESSED,] *lit.* 'happy,' (because arising from 'within' rather than from 'without,') the 'poor (*lit.* bent, folded) in the spirit,' because 'of them' (not 'to them') is the reign of the heavens, i.e. the gospel church is composed of such.

4. MOURN,] suffering afflictions, because they shall be 'comforted,' *lit.* 'called near,' or invited by God, to Himself.

5. MEEK,] that is, mild or gentle, for they shall 'have by lot' the 'land' of their sojournings, not the 'earth;' see Ps. 37. 11, &c.

6. HUNGER AND THIRST,] that is long as it were instinctively to be in a 'right state' towards God and Man, because they shall be 'fed' and abundantly 'satisfied.'

7. MERCIFUL,] *lit.* 'kind,' having reference to the unfortunate rather than to the guilty, because they shall 'have kindness' from God and man.

8. PURE,] *or* 'clean,' i.e. 'unsoiled, unalloyed in the heart,' because they shall 'see' that is, enjoy God, being admitted into his favour.

9. PEACE-MAKERS,] because they shall be called 'sons (as the more honourable gender) of God,' having his nature in this respect.

10. PERSECUTED,] *lit.* 'caused to flee,' because of being in a 'right state' towards God

or men, because 'of them' is the reign of the heaven; as in v. 3, &c.

11. REVILE,] *lit.* 'make a fame, name, or report' of you, and 'may cause (you) to flee, and may say any evil thing (or word) against you (speaking) falsely (*or* being liars), because of me.'

12. REJOICE,] *or* 'hail ye (it),' and 'leap much or greatly' because your 'hire *or* wage is abundant in the heavens, for so they 'caused the prophets to flee—those before you.'

13. YE ARE,] *or* 'Be ye' the salt of the 'land,' (not of the 'earth') in which ye live, but if the salt may become insipid, (*lit.* foolish), in *or* by what shall it be salted, for nothing 'is it powerful' except to be cast without *or* outside, and to be trodden down by (*or* under the feet of) the men and women passing by.

14. WORLD.] *Gr.* kosmos, *lit.* 'order, adornment,' applied to the universe, the globe, the land (of Israel), and the people thereon. A city (that is, a place inhabited by 'many') is not able to be hid (*or* to hide itself, i.e. be kept secret or concealed), being set or placed upon a hill (or visible object).

15. MEN,] *lit.* 'they light a lamp, and put *or* set it under the measure,' (kept by oriental families for measuring grain, containing about a peck), but upon 'the lampstand,' and it shineth to all those in the house.'

17. THINK NOT,] *lit.* 'let it not be (a thing) allotted' to me in your minds, that I come to 'loose down the law (*lit.* 'thing allotted') and the prophets,' that is, the things written by them; 'I did not come to loose down, but to fill out,' so as to bring to a climax—their design being accomplished.

18. VERILY,] *lit.* 'amen (i.e. stedfast!) I say to you, till the heaven and the earth may go away, one iota (the smallest letter) may not go away from the law (of Moses in particular) till that all may happen.'

19. BREAK,] *lit.* 'may loose one of these precepts (i.e. instructions, charges, commands, commissions, directions),..shall be called least in the reign of the heavens,' i.e. the gospel church.

20. EXCEED,] *lit.* 'be not over and above that of the scribes..ye may not enter into the reign of the heaven.'

21. YE HAVE HEARD,] *lit.* 'ye did hear that it was said to the ancients (*lit.* first ones), thou shall not do murder, and who ever may murder, shall be held in the judgment.'

22. WHOSOEVER,] *lit.* 'every one who is made angry at his brother [without a purpose] shall be held in the judgment, and whosoever may say to his brother, Raka, (a Hebrew word signifying vain, empty one) shall be held in the sanhedrim (or court of 70 members), and whosoever may say, More (in *Heb.* a Rebel) shall be held with a view to the Gehenna (i.e. valley of Hinnom) of the fire.'

23. BRING,] *lit.* 'bear forward thy gift upon (not 'to') the place of sacrifice.'

24. LEAVE,] *lit.* 'let alone there thy gift.. and go away, first, change thyself thoroughly to thy brother, and then, having come, bear forward thy gift.'

25. AGREE.] *lit.* 'be of a good mind to thine opponent quickly..give thee up to the judge, and the judge give thee up to the officer, and into ward thou mayest be cast.'

26. VERILY,] *lit.* 'Amen (i.e. stedfast).. thou mayest not go forth thence, till that thou mayest give back the last farthing (*Gr.* kodran).'

27. YE HAVE HEARD,] as in v. 21. Most MSS. omit 'to the ancients.'

28. WHOSOEVER,] *lit.* 'every one who is beholding (perseveringly and continuously) a women *or* wife to be hot upon her, already did commit adultery (with) her in (with or by) his heart.'

29. OFFEND,] *lit.* 'cause thee to stumble, lift it out and cast from thee, for it is preferable for thee, in order that one of thy members may utterly perish, and not thy whole body be cast to Gehenna (i.e. valley of Hinnom).'

31. IT HAS BEEN SAID,] *lit.* 'It was said' (in De. 24. 1), that whosoever may loose from (him) his wife, let him give to her a 'release' (*lit.* a 'letting go').

32. PUT AWAY,] *lit.* 'may loose from (him) his wife, beyond the matter of whoredom, maketh her to commit adultery, and whosoever may marry her who has beenloosed from (her husband,) committeth adultery.'

33. YE HAVE HEARD,] as in v. 21.

FORSWEAR THYSELF,] *lit.* 'take oath upon thyself, but thou shall give back to the Lord thine oaths.'

34. SWEAR,] *lit.* 'Not to swear at all; neither in *or* by the heaven, because it is God's throne.'

35. NEITHER BY,] *lit.* 'in the earth *or* land, because it is his footstool, neither towards Jerusalem, because it is a (or the) city of the great king,' that is the Messiah. Compare James 5. 12; solemn appeals to God are not forbidden; see Matt. 26. 23, 24; Rom. 1. 9.

36. NEITHER BY,] *lit.* 'in thy head mayest thou swear, because thou art not able one hair to make light (i.e. shining) or black.'

37. COMMUNICATION,] *lit.* 'word be, Yes, Yes, No, No, and that which is over and above these is of the evil' that is in the heart of man.

38. YE HAVE HEARD,] *lit.* 'ye did hear that it was said, Eye instead of (*or* over-against) eye, tooth instead of (*or* over-against) tooth;' the old law of retaliation permitted by God in ancient times.

39. THAT YE RESIST NOT,] *lit.* 'Not to stand up over-against the evil, but whoever shall slap thee on the right cheek (*or* jaw), turn round also the other,' i.e. manifest the utmost forbearance; a bold orientalism taught only by Jesus.

40. IF ANY MAN WILL,] *lit.* 'he who is wishing to bring thee to judgment, and to take thy coat, let go to him also the mantle (*or* cloak).'

41. COMPEL,] *or* 'impress thee one mile, go on with him two.'

42. GIVE,] *lit* 'to him who is asking (of)

thee be giving, and he who is wishing to ask-a-gift from thee thou mayest not turn away from,' i.e. reject utterly.

43. YE HAVE HEARD,] *lit.* 'ye did hear, that it was said, Thou shalt dearly-love thy neighbour, and hate thine enemy.' No such passage is in the Old Testament; traditional teaching must here be alluded to, yet no distinction is made in the formula of quotation.

44. LOVE,] *lit.* 'dearly-love your enemies; speak well of those imprecating curses against you; do good to (*or* deal well with) those hating you; and pray (*or* speak out more) for those bitter against you, and causing you to flee.'

45. THAT,] *lit.* 'so that ye may become sons of your Father who is in the heavens, because his sun he doth cause to rise up upon evil and good, and he rains upon just and unjust.'

46. LOVE,] *lit* 'love-dearly those loving you dearly, what hire (wage *or* reward) have ye? do not also the tax-gatherers (many MSS. read 'nations') so *or* thus.'

48. BE,] *lit.* 'ye shall therefore—ye—be complete, even as your Father who is in the heavens is complete.'

Chapter VI. may be divided into six parts: v. 1—4 of alms; v. 5—15 of prayer; v. 16—18 of fasting; v. 19—21 of treasures; v. 22, 23 of single-mindedness; v. 24—34 of anxiety for the future.

1. TAKE HEED,] *lit.* 'have it forward (in your minds) not to do your kindness before (the) men, to be seen (*or* to shew themselves) to them; and if not, a hire (wage *or* reward) ye have not from (or along-side of) your Father who is in the heavens.'

2. WHEN,] *or* 'whenever thou mayest do kindness (*or* deal kindly), thou mayest not trumpet it before thee, even as the hypocrites do in the synagogues (*lit.* 'bringings together' of people to worship God), and in the lanes, so that they may have glory from (*lit.* under) the men; Amen (i.e. stedfast!) I say unto you, they hold off their hire (wage *or* reward,) so as not to obtain it at all.'

3. BUT WHEN,] *lit.* 'but thou, doing kindness, let not thy left (hand) know what thy right (hand) doeth, so that thy kindness may be in the secret (hidden, *or* concealed place of thine own mind), and thy Father who is beholding in the secret (place), he shall give from (himself) to thee in the light.'

5. WHEN,] *lit.* 'whenever ye may pray (*lit.* 'speak out before' God) thou shalt not be as the hypocrites, because they love in the synagogues and in the corners (*or* angles) of the broad places standing to pray (i.e. 'speak out before' God), so that they may be seen to the men.'

6. WHEN,] *lit.* 'whenever ye may pray (*lit.* 'speak out before' God), enter into thy inner (or store) chamber, and having closed thy door, pray (*or* 'speak out') before thy Father who is in the secret (hidden *or* concealed) place, and thy Father who is beholding in the secret (hidden or concealed) place, shall give from (himself) to thee in 'the light.'

7. WHEN,] *lit.* 'but ye praying, ye may not speak emptily, like the nations, for they think, that in their abundant speech they shall be hearkened to.'

8. KNOWETH,] *lit.* 'hath himself known.. before your asking him.'

9. AFTER THIS MANNER,] *lit.* 'thus, therefore, be ye praying.'

OUR FATHER.] By *creation* primarily God is the '*father*' of all his creatures, in the strictest sense of the word; by *preservation* he is figuratively so, as also by *redemption*.

IN HEAVEN,] *lit.* 'in the heavens.'

HALLOWED,] *lit.* 'let thy name (i.e. character) be set-apart' from all others, and reckoned as such by men.

10. KINGDOM,] *or* 'let thy reign (i.e. authority) come; let thy wish (*or* will, i.e, God's revealed will, never his secret will) happen (*or* come to pass), as in heaven also upon the earth (or land).'

11. GIVE,] *lit.* 'our bread—the appointed (*or* needful)—give to us to day.'

12. FORGIVE,] *lit.* 'let go to us our debts as also we let go to our debtors.'

13. LEAD,] *lit.* 'and mayest thou not bring us into trial, but free us from the evil (that is in the world)..because, of thee is the reign, and the power, and the glory—with regard to the ages (past, present, and to come). Stedfast (is the word now spoken)!' Many MSS., Versions, and Critics omit this doxology entirely, as an interpolation.

14. FORGIVE,] *lit.* 'may let go to the men their fallings from (duty), let go also to you will your heavenly Father.'

16. MOREOVER,] *or* 'but (and, now) whenever ye may fast, become ye not as the hypocrites—scowling-faced, for they make their (own true) faces to disappear, so that they may appear to the men fasting. Stedfast! I say (*or* lay it down) to you, that they hold off their hire (wage or reward)' as in v. 2.

17. WHEN,] *lit.* 'but thou, fasting, anoint (*or* besmear) thy head, and thy face wash.'

18. THAT,] *lit.* 'so that thou mayest not appear to the men fasting, but to thy Father who is in the secret (hidden or concealed) place, and thy Father, who is beholding in the secret (hidden or concealed) place, shall give from (himself) to thee in the light.'

19. LAY,] *lit.* 'treasure not up to yourselves upon the earth, where moth and corrosion cause to disappear, and where thieves dig through and steal;' so also in next verse.

22. LIGHT,] *or* 'lamp ..be single (i.e. may not be complex) thy whole body shall be lightened up.'

23. BE EVIL,] *lit.* 'may be evil, thy whole body shall be darkened.'

24. NO MAN,] *lit.* 'no one is able to serve two lords *or* masters,..or of one he will lay hold, and of the other he will think less (*or* down upon). You are not able to do service to God and to Mammon,' i.e. the Syriac god of riches.

25. THEREFORE,] *lit.* 'because of this I say to you, be not parted (in your mind) as to your soul (or life), what ye may eat, and

what ye may drink, neither as to your body, what ye shall go in (or envelope yourself); is not the soul (or life) more than the fattening (or nourishment), and the body (than) the thing gone into (*or* envelope) ?'

26. BEHOLD,] *lit.* 'look in on the flying things of the heaven, that they do not sow (seed), nor do they make hot, nor do they bring together into a place of putting away (grain), and your heavenly Father fatteneth them: are not ye more borne through than they ?'

27. WHICH,] *lit.* 'but who of you parting (your minds) is able to put forward upon his age (not 'stature') one cubit ?' comp. Ps. 39. 5.

28. TAKE YE THOUGHT,] *lit.* 'and about the thing gone into, why are ye parted (in your minds) ? be ye thorough disciples (as to) the lilies of the field; how do they increase (or become great) ? they are not beaten out (or wearied), nor do they spin.'

29. YET,] *lit.* 'but I say to you, that not even Solomon in (or among) all his glory, was wrapped about as (is) one of these.'

30. WHEREFORE,] *lit.* 'but if the fodder of the field, which to-day is, and to-morrow into an oven is being cast, God doth thus surround,—not much more you—ye of little stability (or stedfastness) ?'

31. WHEREFORE,] *lit.* 'therefore, ye may not be parted (in your minds), saying, what may we eat, or what may we drink, or what may we cast around (us) ?'

32. GENTILES,] *lit.* 'nations are seeking after (*or* zealous upon); for your heavenly Father has known that ye have need of all these.'

33. SEEK,] *or* 'desire ye first the reign of the (true) God, and of his right (or just) state, and all these shall be put forward to you.'

34. TAKE NO THOUGHT,] *lit.* 'ye may not be parted (in your minds) in reference to the morrow, for the morrow will be parted (in its mind) for the things of itself. Sufficient to the day is the evil of it.'

Chapter VII. may be divided into seven parts; v. 1—4 of rash judgments; v. 5. 6 of holy prudence; v. 7—12 of perseverance in seeking good; v. 13, 14 of the strait and the wide gates; v. 15—20 of false teachers and their fruits; v. 21—27 of the hearers and the doers of duty; v. 28, 29 of the result and manner of Jesus' teaching.

1. JUDGE,] *lit.* separate ye not, that ye may not be separated.'

2. FOR WITH,] *lit.* 'in (or by) what judgment (or separation) ye do judge (or separate) ye shall be judged; and in (by or with) what measure ye measure, it shall be measured again to you.'

3. MOTE,] *lit.* 'dry splinter..and the beam ..dost not mind thoroughly.'

4. LET ME PULL OUT,] *lit.* 'let alone, let me cast forth the splinter from thine eye, and lo, the beam is in thine (own) eye.'

5. SEE CLEARLY,] *or* 'behold thoroughly.'

6. GIVE,] *lit.* 'ye may not give that which is set-apart (to God) to the dogs, neither may ye cast your pearls before the swine, lest they tread (them) down with (in *or* by) their feet, and having turned about, may rend you.'

7. ASK,] *lit.* 'be asking..be seeking (or desiring), .be knocking. opened up;' perseverance is here specially taught.

8. ASKETH,] *lit.* 'is asking..is seeking..is knocking, it shall be opened up;' as in v. 7.

9. WHAT,] *or* 'which man..if his son may ask..will he give over to him ?'

10. ASK,] *or* 'he may ask..will he give over to him ?'

11. KNOW,] *lit.* 'have known..in the heaven..to those asking him.'

12. WHATSOEVER,] *or* 'as many as ye may wish that the men may do to you, so also ye, do ye, to them, for this is (the design of the law of Moses) and (of) the prophets,' who declared the will of God after him.

13. ENTER,] *lit.* 'go ye in through the strait gate, because broad is the gate, and wide the way, which is leading away to (the) loss (of truth and virtue), and many there are who are going in through it.'

14. NARROW] *or* 'pressed the way which is leading away to the life (and happiness of the soul),and few there are who are finding it.

15. BEWARE,] *lit.* 'but hold forward from the false-prophets, who come toward you in (the) clothing of sheep, but from within are ravening wolves.'

16. BY,] *lit.* 'from their fruits ye shall know them fully (*or* further); do they i.e. (men) bring together from thorns grapes, or from thistles figs ?'

17. EVEN SO,] *lit.* 'so (*or* thus) every good tree good fruits doth make, but the rotten tree evil fruits doth make,' naturally and habitually.

18. CANNOT,] *lit.* 'is not able evil fruits to make, nor a rotten tree good fruits to make,' without an interference from without on the part of others.

19. THAT BRINGETH,] *lit.* 'not making good fruit is cut off, and to fire is cast,' as cumbering the ground, and good for nothing else.

20. WHEREFORE,] *lit.* 'therefore, then, (*or* at least) from their fruits ye shall know them fully:' and may beware of them accordingly.

21. THAT SAITH,] *lit.* 'who is saying to me, Lord, (*lit.* 'powerful one') Lord, shall enter (really) into the reign of the heavens (or gospel dispensation), but he who is doing the wish of my Father who is in the heavens,' and which accordingly he has *revealed* to man for his guidance; we have nothing to do with his *secret* will whatever.

22. HAVE,] *lit.* 'did we not prophesy (that is, declare publicly before men), in (by or with) thy name, and in (by or with) thy name cast forth demons, and in (by or with) thy name done many mighty (not 'wonderful' merely), things,' such as Jesus himself had done, and even 'greater,' (John 5. 20), at least in their effects.

23. PROFESS,] *or* 'confess (at the same time) to them, that not even at any time did I know (i.e. approve of) you, give farther

place (i.e. withdraw) from me ye who are working the lawlessness,' or thing unauthorized by law; see Isa. 1. 12.

24. SAYINGS,] *lit.* 'words..a thoughtful man, who built his house upon the rock.'

25. RAIN,] i.e. wet *or* moisture, and 'come did the streams, and blew upon (it) did the winds, and they fell towards that house, and it did not fall, for it had been founded upon the rock.'

26. HEARETH,] *lit.* 'is hearing these words of mine, and not doing them, shall be likened to a foolish (*or* rebellious) man.'

27. BLEW,] *lit.* 'did blow upon (it), and struck towards that house.'

28. ENDED,] *lit.* 'fully ended these words, the crowds were greatly struck at his teaching, for he was teaching them as (one) having authority, and not as the scribes,' or writers, who gave forth merely the contradictory and vacilating opinions of men.

Chapter VIII. may be divided into eight parts; v. 1—4 cure of a leper; v. 5—13 of a centurion's servant; v. 14, 15 of Peter's wife's mother: v. 16, 17 a fulfilment of prophecy; v. 18—20 a forward scribe; v, 21, 22 a backward disciple; v. 23—27 a quieting of the sea; v. 28—34 two demonized ones and a herd of swine.

1. GREAT MULTITUDES.] *lit.* 'many crowds.'

2. WORSHIPPED,] *lit.* 'kissed (the hand) towards him;' as in 2. 2, &c.

LORD,] *or* 'Sir,' an ordinary title of respect, as in 13. 27; 21. 30, &c.

IF THOU WILL,] *or* 'if thou mayest wish, thou art able to cleanse me,' i.e. make me unsoiled *or* unalloyed.

3. PUT FORTH,] *lit.* 'having stretched forth the hand.'

I WILL,] *or* 'I wish; be thou cleansed.'

4. NO MAN,] *lit.* 'see, to no one may thou say (anything), but go away (*lit.* under). and bring forward the gift that Moses set forth (Lev. 14. 3, 4, 10) for a witness to them,' that he had been cleansed, and was now free to go about among men, as before.

5. CAME,] *lit.* 'there came forward to him a centurion (*lit.* head or chief of a hundred) calling him near, and saying.' *lit.* laying it down.

6. LORD,] *or* 'Sir, my lad (*or* boy) has been cast (down) in the house paralytic, fearfully tried,' with suffering.

7. HEAL,] *lit.* 'attend (*or* nourish) him;' as in v. 16; 4. 23, 24; 9. 35; 10. 1, 8; 12. 10, &c.

8. WORTHY,] *or* 'sufficient,' that under my 'covering' thou 'mayest enter,' but only say 'a word,' and my boy (or lad) shall be cured *or* healed.'

9. FOR I AM,] *lit.* 'for I also am' a man.. having under 'myself' soldiers,..Be going on, and he goeth on, Be coming, and he cometh.'

10. MARVELLED,] i.e. 'wondered *or* admired..Amen, I lay it down to you, not even in (i.e. among) the Israel such stedfastness did I find,' as in this man.

11. EAST,] *lit.* 'eastern and western (parts) shall come, and shall recline (at meat) with Abraham..in (*or* during) the reign of the heavens,' the gospel dispensation.

12. CHILDREN,] *lit.* 'sons of the reign' those to whom it was first offered, shall be 'cast forth into the darkness—the outer, there shall be the weeping (*or* wailing) and the gnashing of the teeth,' with rage and cold.

13. GO THY WAY,] *lit.* 'go away,' and as 'thou didst remain stedfast (in thy trust in me), let it be (*or* happen) to thee; and his boy (*or* lad) was healed in that hour.'

14. WIFE'S MOTHER,] *or* 'mother-in-law cast down (on the bed) and fevered.'

15. LEFT,] *lit.* 'let her go, and she was raised, and ministered (*lit.* was becoming a deacon) to them.'

16. THE EVEN,] *lit.* 'late' time..they 'brought before him many (who were) demonized (i.e. made to act as demons,) and he cast forth the spirits with (or by) a word, and all those having ills he attended (*or* cherished), so that it might be (said to be) fulfilled that was spoken through (the medium of) Isaiah the prophet (53. 4), laying (it) down: Himself our infirmities (*lit.* powerlessnesses) took up, and our unsoundnesses he bare away.'

18. GREAT MULTITUDES,] *lit.* 'many crowds about him, he commanded (or perhaps simply 'named') to go from (thence) to the further side,' of the lake of Genneseret.

19. SCRIBE,] *or* 'writer having come forward..Teacher, I will follow (or go along with) thee, wherever thou mayest go away to.'

20. THE FOXES,] *lit.* 'deceivers of sight.'

HOLES,] *lit.* 'loss of light.'

BIRDS,] *lit.* 'flying things of the heaven places of settling-down. but the Son of the Man (perhaps Adam is meant,) has not where he may lay down the head.' He had no worldly advantages to offer.

21. DISCIPLES,] *or* scholars, learners,.. 'Lord *or* Sir, suffer (*lit.* turn it over upon) me first to go away, and to bury my father,' that is, remain with him till he die in the ordinary course of nature, and then I will follow thee. Had his father been really dead already Jesus *could* not have refused the filial request.

22. FOLLOW,] *lit.* 'be following me (even now), and let the dead (in spirit) go to bury their own dead' (in spirit), when they die.

23. A SHIP,] *lit.* 'the boat' belonging to Peter, (Luke 5. 3) which he always used in crossing the sea of Galilee.

24. TEMPEST,] *or* 'commotion, in the sea (of Galilee), so that the boat was being covered (*or* hidden) under the swellings (of the sea), but himself was sleeping fast.'

25. CAME,] *lit.* 'having come forward raised him, saying, Sir, save us, we are lost.'

26. LITTLE FAITH,] *or* 'little stability (*or* stedfastness), then having risen he rebuked (*lit.* set a weight upon) the winds (or blowings), and the sea (*lit.* disturber), and it became a great calm' *lit.* smile.

27. MARVELLED,] *or* 'wondered, saying, Of what kind (*or* sort) is this one, that both the winds and the sea do hearken to (*lit.* under) him?'

28. OTHER,] *lit.* 'further side, to the place of the Gergesenes (*or* Gadarenes), there came away to him two demonized ones out of the tombs (*lit.* places of memorial) coming forth, fierce (*or* rough) exceedingly, so that no one had power to go along through that way.'

29. WHAT HAVE WE,] *lit.* 'what to us and to thee (in common), Jesus, Son of the (true) God; thou hast come hither before the time (*or* season) to torment (*or* try) us;' an affirmation, not a question, as in C.V.

30. A GREAT WAY OFF,] *or* 'far off' from them a herd (*or* drove).

31. DEVILS,] *lit.* 'demons were calling upon him.'

SUFFER,] *lit.* 'turn over upon us to go away to.'

32. GO,] *lit.* 'go away; and having come forth, they went away to..went impetuously down the steep (*lit.* 'hanging' place) to the sea, and died utterly in (or among) the waters.'

33. KEPT,] *lit.* 'those feeding (them) did flee, and having gone away to the city, they declared all things fully, and the matter of the demonized ones,' to the inhabitants.

34. TO MEET,] *lit.* 'to come together against Jesus (the Saviour),..they called upon (him) so that he might go (away) again from their border.'

Chapter IX. may be divided into ten parts; v. 1—8 cure of a paralytic, and authority of the Son of Man; v. 9 call of Matthew; v. 10—13 eating with tax-gatherers and sinners; v. 14—17 of fasting; v. 18, 19 application of a chief man; v. 20—22 cure of an issue of blood; v. 23—26 raising of the chief's daughter; v. 27—31 cure of two blind men; v. 32—34 cure of a dumb man; v. 35—38 Jesus' teaching, proclaiming, healing, and compassion.

1. A SHIP,] *lit.* 'the boat' belonging to Peter, or the regular 'ferry boat.'

HIS OWN CITY,] that is, Capernaum, as in 4. 13.

2. BROUGHT,] *lit.* 'bare forward to him a paralytic, laid down upon a couch, and Jesus having seen their faith (*or* stedfastness) said to the paralytic, Have courage, child, let go to thee have been thy failures,' of duty, or 'missings' of the mark.

3. WITHIN,] *or* 'among themselves, This one speaks hurtfully' of God.

4. THOUGHTS,] *or* 'inner minds said, Wherefore mind ye inwardly evil in your hearts?'

5. WHETHER,] *or* 'which is more laborious, to say, Let go to thee have been the failures (of duty), or to say, Rise and be going (*lit.* tramping) about.'

6. POWER,] *lit.* 'the Son of the Man hath authority upon the earth to let failures (of duty) go,..thy couch, and go away.'

8. MULTITUDES,] *or* 'crowds,..who gave such authority to the men.'

9. PASSED FORTH,] *or* 'went along..sitting over the custom-office..be following me.'

10. SAT,] *lit.* 'lay back (or down) in the house..tax-gatherers and sinners (i.e. those 'missing' the mark) were lying down with him,' to take food or rest.

11. PHARISEES,] *lit.* those 'separated' from others.

WHY,] *or* 'wherefore with the tax-gatherers and sinners (as in v. 10) doth your Teacher eat?'

12. WHOLE,] *lit.* 'the strong have no need (and feel not the necessity) of a healer, but those having ills,' need one.

13. GO,] *lit.* 'having gone on learn ye (i.e. learn ye further) what is (the meaning of these words of God); Kindness I wish, and not sacrifice,' (Hos. 6. 6; Mic. 6. 6, 8; Prov. 31. 3. that is, he would rather have the one than the other, but both were required,) 'for I did not come to call just men but (rather) sinners to a new mind' regarding God and themselves. Scripture is not afraid to speak of some men as 'righteous,' but of course it is only *relatively* so, 'for there is no man that sinneth not.'

14. CAME,] *lit.* 'come forward to him do the disciples of John (i.e. some of those who had been baptized by him),..fast much,' not 'oft,' as in C.V.

15. CAN,] *lit.* 'are the sons of the bride-chamber (i.e. those admitted into it) able to mourn..but days shall come, whenever the bridegroom may be taken away (or lifted up) from them.'

16. PUTTETH,] *lit.* 'patcheth a patch of undressed cloth upon an old garment, for that which fills it up (*lit.* its filling up) taketh away from the garment, and a worse rent happens.'

17. MEN,] *lit.* 'do they put (*lit.* cast) new wine into old bottles (made of skin), and if not so, the (skin) bottles are burst, and the wine is poured forth, and the bottles are utterly lost, but they put (*lit.* cast) new wine into new bottles, and both are preserved together' till they are required.

18. RULER,] *lit.* 'a certain head (or chief) man having come, kissed forward to him (the hand), saying thus (*lit.* that), My daughter did just now die, but having come put up thy hand upon her.'

20. A WOMAN,] 'having a running of blood twelve years, having come forward from behind, touched the hem (or fringe, *lit.* that which trails on the ground) of his garment.'

21. FOR SHE SAID,] *lit.* 'laid it down within herself, If only I might touch his garment I shall be saved' from this disease.

22. TURNED HIM ABOUT,] *lit.* 'having turned round upon (her), and having seen her, said, Have courage, daughter, thy stedfastness hath saved thee; and the woman was saved from that hour'—from her harassing sufferings. 'Salvation,' in SS. is either temporal, or spiritual, or both.

23. RULER,] *lit.* 'head *or* chief' man.

MINSTRELS,] playing on 'pipe *or* flute.'

PEOPLE,] *lit.* 'crowd tumultuous.'

24. GIVE PLACE,] *lit.* 'withdraw, for the little damsel did not die entirely, but she sleeps fast, and they were laughing him down.'

25. PEOPLE,] *lit.* 'crowd was cast forth, having gone in, he seized her hand, and the

little damsel arose,' at once in health, and strength from the very gates of death, if not from death itself.

27. DEPARTED,] *lit.* 'and Jesus going a-long.'

HAVE MERCY,] *or* 'Deal kindly with us, Son of David;' a well-known title of the expected Messiah; see 15. 22; 20. 30, 31, &c.

28. CAME,] *lit.* 'came forward to him.. believe ye,' which may be regarded either as a *command*, or as an *enquiry*, as in the C.V.

29. FAITH,] *lit.* 'stedfastness let it happen to you.'

30. OPENED,] *lit.* 'opened again,' as if they had formerly seen, and had become blind.

STRAITLY CHARGED,] *or* 'charged them sadly,' as if with groans.

31. DEPARTED,] *lit.* 'having gone forth spake it everywhere in all that land.'

32. WENT OUT,] *lit.* 'going forth, lo, they brought forward to him a man dumb (*or* deaf), demonized.'

33. DEVIL.] *lit.* 'demon;' a class of beings, supposed to consist of the spirits of 'the mighty dead,' whether good or bad, who in their disembodied state had power to enter into the body of a living man, and reduce it to subjection; they were accordingly feared and worshipped as 'heroes and demi-gods;' see Acts 17. 18, 22; 25. 19; 1 Cor. 10. 20, 21; 1 Tim. 4. 1; James 2. 19: Rev. 9. 20.

MULTITUDES,] *or* 'crowds, wondered, saying, No even at any time was it seen thus in the Israel' of God.

34. CASTETH OUT,] *lit.* 'In (by *or* with) the head (*or* chief) of the demons he casteth forth the demons.'

35. WENT ABOUT,] *lit.* 'was going round about..teaching (*lit.* showing, i.e. causing to see) in their synagogues, (that is, places for 'bringing together' the people 'to meet' with God, as in Ex. 25. 22, and more systematically established after the captivity wherein any one present might address the audience), and preaching (*or* proclaiming-as-a-herald) the good news of the reign (of the heavens), and attending (*or* cherishing those troubled with any or) every unsoundness and every weakness.'

36. MULTITUDES,] *or* 'crowds, his bowels were moved for them, because they were let loose (*or* loosed out) and thrown away as if (they were) a flock not having a shepherd,' *lit.* 'feeder.'

37. THE HARVEST,] *lit.* 'the reaping (whether used of the crop or of the work) indeed is much, but the workers few.'

38. PRAY,] *or* 'beseech (*lit.* let be wanted) therefore, (from) the Lord of the reaping that he may cast forth workers for his reaping.'

Chapter X. may be divided into various parts; v. 1 the general power given to the twelve sent; v. 2—4 their names; v. 5, 6 to whom they were to go; v. 7, 8 what to do; v. 9, 10 what not to provide; v. 11—15 how to behave to all; v. 16 what to be; v. 17 what to beware of; v. 18 what to expect; v. 19—22 not to be anxious; v. 23 speedy comfort; v. 24, 25 not to wonder at sufferings; v. 26—31 to fear God not men; v. 32, 33 mutual avowals; v. 34—36 result of his coming; v. 37, 38 who is worthy of him; v. 39 losing and finding; v. 40 recompense of reward.

1. CALLED,] *or* 'and having called forward ..authority (over) unclean spirits, so as to cast them forth, and to attend every unsoundness, and every softness,' or weakness, among the people.

2. FIRST] in order, not in dignity.

SIMON,] i.e. 'hearing;' Peter, a 'rock;' Andrew, 'manly;' James, a 'supporter;' Zebedee, a 'dowry;' John, 'Jah is gracious.'

3. PHILIP,] i.e. 'lover of horses;' Bartholomew, 'son of Tolmi;' Thomas, a 'twin;' Matthew, 'gift of Jah;' James, the (son or step-son) of Alpheus, 'taught of Jah;' Lebbeus, 'lion of Jah;' who was surnamed Thaddeus, i.e. 'breast of Jah.'

4. SIMON,] the Cananite (not Canaanite), from 'Cana' of Galilee, (John 2. 1), and Judas Iscariot, i.e. 'the man of Carioth' or 'the man of the city,' who also 'gave him over' into the hands of the Jews. 'Betrayed,' is much too strong a word for the Greek or the unimpassioned character of the Sacred Writers.

5. SENT FORTH,] *or* 'away,' having at the same time spoken or laid down to them, saying, 'To a way of the nations ye may not go away, and to a city of Samaritans ye may not go in.'

6. GO,] *lit.* 'be going on rather towards the lost sheep,' (who have been 'loosed away,' or have 'loosed themselves' from the fold) of the 'house of Israel,'—to whom the offer of the gospel was to be made first.

7. AS YE GO,] *lit.* 'and going on, proclaim (as heralds), saying, That the reign of the heavens has drawn nigh;' as in 3. 2: 4. 17,&c.

8. HEAL,] *lit.* 'powerless ones be ye attending; lepers be cleansing; dead ones be raising, (but this clause is omitted by many critics); demons be casting forth, freely (*lit.* givingly) ye received, givingly give ye;' they were to be under no fear of lacking sufficiency or ability.

9. PROVIDE,] *or* 'prepare not gold, nor silver (so called from its whiteness), nor copper for your girdles,' around their wrists, wherein the orientals carry their money.

10. NOR SCRIP,] *or* 'no bag for (the) way, nor two coats, nor anything bound under (the feet), nor a staff (*or* rod); for worthy is the worker of his nourishment.' Comp. 1 Cor. 9. 6—14, &c.

11. INQUIRE,] *lit.* 'set out..till that ye may go forth.'

12. AN HOUSE,] *lit.* 'the house' set out in v. 11, salute it, *lit.* 'draw it together,' to you.

13. IF,] *lit.* 'if indeed..your peace (or word bringing into unity) come upon it..turn round upon you.'

14. SHALL,] *lit.* 'may not receive you, nor hear (*lit.* sharpen *or* be sharp at) your words, ye coming out of that house,' shake off, &c.

15. VERILY,] *lit.* 'Amen,' (a Hebrew word signifying 'stedfast,') in 'a (*or* any, not the) day of judgment.'

16. SEND FORTH,] *or* 'away' as sheep or as a flock.

BE,] *lit.* 'become ye mindful as the serpents (*lit.* seers), and harmless (*lit.* un-horned, un-mixed, or un-hurtful) as the doves,' *lit.* abundant lovers.

17. BEWARE,] *lit.* 'hold off from the men (of the world), for they will give you up to sanhedrims, and in their synagogues they will scourge you,' with forty lashes, save one, as in 2 Cor. 11. 25.

18. GOVERNORS,] *lit.* 'leaders.. ye shall be led.. because of me.. for witness to (not *against*) them and the nations.'

19. DELIVER,] *lit.* 'give you up, ye may not be parted (in your minds) how or what ye may speak.'

20. SPEAKETH,] *lit.* 'is speaking in (or by) you.'

21. THE BROTHER,] *lit.* 'and brother shall give up brother to death, and father child, and children shall stand up against parents, and shall put them to death,' by bearing witness against them.

22. OF ALL,] *lit.* 'under (by) all, because of my name, but he who has endured to (the) end, he shall be saved,' from temporal or spiritual loss.

23. PERSECUTE,] *lit.* 'cause you to flee in this city, flee to the other; amen, I say to you, ye may not have ended (going over) the cities of (the) Israel, till that the Son of the Man may come,' in glory and terrible majesty, as at the Mount of Transfiguration, the Day of Pentecost, the Destruction of Jerusalem, &c.

24. THE DISCIPLES,] *lit.* 'a learner is not above the teacher, nor a servant above his lord,' or master, that he should be more regarded.

25. ENOUGH,] *or* 'sufficient to the learner that he may become as his teacher,.. did call the master (*lit.* despot) of the house Beelzebub,' i.e. lord of flies, or Beelzeboul i.e. lord of dung.

26. REVEALED,] *lit.* 'uncovered, and hid (or secret) that shall not be known.'

27. TELL,] *lit.* 'lay down to you in the dark, speak ye (or lift ye up) in the light, and what at the ear ye hear, proclaim (as-a-herald) upon the roofs,' *lit.* 'built places.'

28. FEAR,] *or* 'be afraid of those killing (utterly) the body, but the soul are not able to kill (utterly).. able to loose utterly both soul and body in Gehenna,' i.e. the valley of the Son of Hinnom.

29. SPARROWS,] *lit.* 'little sparrows sold for an assar, (about three farthings), and one of them doth not fall upon the land without the assent of your Father.'

30. VERY HAIRS,] *lit.* 'but of you even the hairs of the head are all numbered.'

31. OF MORE VALUE,] *lit.* 'than many little sparrows ye are borne through.'

32. CONFESS ME,] *lit.* 'speak the same thing with me.. I also will speak the same thing with him.. in the heavens.'

33. DENY,] *lit.* 'may not lift up (the hand with) me.'

34. THINK NOT,] *lit.* 'make it not a law (in your reasonings) that I came to cast peace upon the land (of Israel), I came not to cast peace but a sword,' foreknowing their rejection of him.

35. I AM COME,] *lit.* 'I came to divide a man with regard to his father, and a daughter with regard to her mother, and a daughter-in-law (*or* bride) with regard to her mother-in-law.'

36. HOUSE,] *or* 'household.'

37. LOVETH,] *lit.* 'is loving.. above me.'

38. TAKETH,] *or* 'receiveth not his cross (i.e. affliction or burden sent him by God) and followeth after me,' in the same spirit of submission.

39. FINDING,] *lit.* 'is finding (by unlawful compliances) his life (soul or breath), shall loose it from (himself), and he who has loosed from (himself) his soul because of me, shall find it.'

40. RECEIVETH,] *lit.* 'is receiving.. is receiving.. him who sent me from (himself),' as his servant.

41. A PROPHET,] that is, a 'public preacher,' one who proclaims publicly the will or the praises of God; see Ge. 20. 7; Ex. 7. 1; 15. 20; 1 Sa. 10. 5, 10, 11; 18. 10; 19. 23, 24; 1 Ch. 25. 1; Acts 21. 9; Rom. 12. 6; 14. 1, 24, 31; John 11. 51; 1 Cor. 11. 5; 14. 3, 4, 5, &c.

IN THE NAME,] *or* 'with a regard to the name (*or* character) of a prophet, (the) hire (wage or reward) of a prophet shall receive.

RIGHTEOUS,] *or* 'just, right,' used often in Scripture to denote a man 'right' in the eye of the law, irrespective of his moral character.

42. SHALL GIVE,] *lit.* 'may cause one of these little ones to drink a cup of cold (water) only with a respect to the name of a learner (of mine), may not loose away from (himself) his hire,' wage *or* reward.

Chapter XI. may be divided into five parts; v. 1—6 John's enquiry at Jesus and the answer; v. 7—15 Jesus' testimony to John; v. 16—19 His simile about that generation; v. 20—24 His reproof of three cities; v. 25—30 His thanksgiving and his invitation to men.

1. OF COMMANDING,] *or* 'thoroughly setting in order to his twelve disciples, he went afterwards (*or* on) from thence, to teach and to proclaim (as-a-herald) in their cities.'

2. OF CHRIST,] *lit.* 'of the Christ,' the promised Messiah.

3. ART THOU HE,] *lit.* 'Thou, art thou The Coming One, or another do we look for? The present tense is rhetorically used for the future in Greek, as in English, Hebrew, and all other languages.

4. SHEW AGAIN,] *lit.* 'tell thoroughly' to John.

5. THE BLIND,] *lit.* 'blind ones behold again (*or* look up), and lame ones walk about, lepers are cleansed, and deaf hear, dead ones are raised, and poor ones are having good news proclaimed, and happy (in his own soul, not 'blessed' as in C.V.) is he whosoever may not be stumbled in (*or* by) me.'

6. DEPARTED,] *lit.* 'and these going on (to John's prison), Jesus began to say (*lit.* 'lay down') to the crowds concerning John (thus):

What went ye forth to the wilderness to view? a reed by wind shaken (*or* tossed)? but what went ye forth to see? a man in soft garments arrayed? behold, those bearing the soft things are in the house of the kings' of the earth.

9. MORE,] *lit.* 'and very much more.'

10. OF WHOM,] *lit.* 'concerning whom it has been written (in Mal. 3. 1): Behold, I send from (myself) my messenger (or announcer) before thy face (*or* presence), who shall thoroughly make ready thy way before thee.'

11. VERILY,] *lit.* 'Amen,' i.e. stedfast.

KINGDOM,] *or* 'reign of the heavens,' that is, the gospel dispensation.'

12. TAKE IT BY FORCE,] *or* 'seize, snatch or lay hold of it.'

14. YE WILL,] *lit.* 'ye wish to receive (him) he is Elijah who is about to come.'

16. CHILDREN,] *lit.* 'little children in market-places sitting, and sounding forth to their comrades, and saying.'

17. WE HAVE PIPED,] *lit.* 'we piped to you, and ye did not dance (*or* leap), we shrieked to you, and ye did not smite (the breast).'

18. DEVIL,] *lit.* 'demon;' as in 7. 22; 9. 33.

19. SON OF MAN,] *lit.* 'Son of the Man.. wine-drinker, of tax-gatherers a friend, also of sinners; and the wisdom (of God) was declared right by (*lit.* from) her children,' that is, those to whom it was taught, and who received it.

UPBRAID,] *lit.* 'reproach..the most.. they had not a new mind.'

21. CHORAZIN,] 12 miles N. E. of Tiberias, now Gerasi.

BETHSAIDA,] *lit.* 'house of hunting *or* fishing,' afterwards called Julias.

TYRE,] *lit.* a 'rock *or* sharp place;' bordering on the tribe of Asher.

SIDON,] *lit.* 'place of hunting *or* fishing;' now called Sayde.

REPENTED,] *lit.* 'had a new or another mind.'

22. BUT,] *lit.* 'fully I lay down to you, To Tyre and Sidon it shall be more tolerable (or bearable) in a (not *the*) day of judgment than to you.'

23. CAPERNAUM,] *lit.* 'village (*or* covering) of Nahum, which unto the heaven was exalted (by Christ's residence and works within it), unto Hades (the 'unseen' world) thou shalt be brought down,' (so as to be ruined and desolate as it now is), because if among (they of) Sodom (had) happened the mighty works that (have) happened in thee, they (had) remained till to-day.'

24. BUT,] *lit.* 'fully I lay down to you, that to the land of Sodom it shall be more tolerable (*or* bearable) in a day of judgment that to thee.'

25. AT,] *lit.* 'in (*or* during) that time (*or* season)..I thank (*lit.* speak out of the same thing to) thee, Father, Lord of the heaven and of the earth, that thou didst hide these (things) from wise (i.e. skilful) and prudent (those 'bringing things together' for observation), and didst reveal them to babes.'

26. EVEN SO,] *lit.* 'Yes, Father, that thus it became a good thought before thee.'

27. ALL THINGS,] *or* 'all were given over to me by (*lit.* under) my Father, and no one knows fully the Son, except the Father, neither the Father doth any one know except the Son, and he to whom the Son may take (or give) counsel to reveal (him),' by sending the Gospel to him.

28. LABOUR,] *lit.* 'are struck *or* tried.'

ARE HEAVY-LADEN,] *lit.* 'have been burdened.'

GIVE YOU REST,] *or* 'let you cease again.'

29. TAKE,] *or* 'lift up..learn from me (that is, my example), because (*or* that) I am meek (mild or gentle), and lowly in (*or* as to) the heart, and ye shall find rest again to your souls.'

30. EASY,] *lit.* 'useful.'

Chapter XII. may be divided into six parts; v. 1—8 kindness better than sacrifice; v. 9—13 cure of a withered hand; v. 14—21 plot against Jesus, his work and character; v. 22—37 cure of a blind and dumb man, and reproof of idle words; v. 38—45 a sign sought and given with a warning; v. 46—50 his true brethren and friends.

1. AT,] *lit.* 'during that time (*or* season) Jesus passed on in the sabbaths (from time to time) through the sown places, and..to pluck ears (of corn).'

2. DISCIPLES,] *or* 'learners..to do in (*or* during) the sabbath.'

3. HAVE YE NOT READ,] *lit.* 'did ye not know thoroughly (from the SS.) what David did..himself and those with him?'

4. OF GOD,] *lit.* 'of the God, and the loaves of the presence did eat,' which were sacred to God's table.

5. READ,] *lit.* 'did ye not know thoroughly in (*or* by) the law that on the sabbaths the priests in the temple make common the sabbath, and are guiltless?' the greater law of necessity sets aside the lesser one.

6. THAT] 'something greater than the temple is here.'

WHAT THIS MEANETH,] *lit.* 'what is (the meaning of the following passage of Scripture in Hos. 6. 6): 'Kindness I wish (from men,) and not sacrifice, (that is, rather than sacrifice,) ye had not condemned the guiltless.'

8. THE SON OF MAN,] not Christ merely, but every descendant of Adam, the sabbath and the other ordinances of religion being made for their behoof, and not men for them. See Mark 2. 28; Rev. 1. 13, &c.

9. THEIR SYNAGOGUE,] there being only one probably in that place.

10. WITHERED,] *or* 'dried up, and they asked at him, saying, Is it lawful on the sabbaths to attend (*or* cherish such), in order that they might make (it) public against him.'

11. WHAT,] *or* 'which man shall there be of you..and if this may fall on the sabbaths into a deep place, will he not seize it and raise (it)?'

12. BETTER,] *lit.* 'borne through,..so that it is lawful on the sabbaths to do well.'

13. STRETCH FORTH,] *or* 'extend, make long.'

WAS RESTORED,] *lit.* 'stood thoroughly forth sound as the other.'

14. HELD A COUNSEL,] *lit.* 'took united counsel.'

DESTROY,] *or* 'loose him from' them by excommunication or otherwise.

15. WITHDREW,] *lit.* 'gave place again.. many crowds..and he attended (*or* cherished) them all.'

16. SHOULD NOT,] *lit.* 'might not make it manifest.'

17. FULFILLED,] filled out, i.e. realized.. 'through Isaiah,' (Ch. 42. 1.)

18. SERVANT,] *lit.* 'lad *or* boy, whom I did chuse. (*or* 'lift up for myself,') my dearly-beloved, in reference to whom my soul thought well; I will put my spirit upon him, and judgment to the nations he will tell thoroughly.'

19. STREETS,] *lit.* 'broad places' of the city.

20. BRUISED,] *or* 'crushed together he will not bring down,..he may cast forth (with a view) to victory (or unyieldingness) the judgment.'

21. THE GENTILES,] *lit.* 'nations.'

22. BROUGHT,] *lit.* 'brought forward to him one demonized,..and he attended (or cherished) him.'

23. MULTITUDES,] *lit.* 'crowds stood out and said, Is (not) this the Son of David,' i.e. the expected Messiah.

24. THIS FELLOW,] *lit.* 'this one doth not cast forth the demons except by (*lit.* in) the Beelzeboul, chief of the demons.'

25. THOUGHTS,] *or* 'inner minds.'

26. SATAN,] *lit.* 'the Adversary cast forth the Adversary, he was divided about himself.'

27. BY,] *lit.* 'in Beelzeboul cast forth the demons, your sons by (*or* in) whom do they cast forth? because of this of you they shall be judges.'

28. BY,] *lit.* 'in (the) spirit of God do cast forth the demons, then come first upon you did the reign of the (true) God.'

29. A STRONG,] *lit* 'the strong..seize thoroughly..seize thoroughly his house.'

30. GATHERETH,] *lit.* 'is not bringing together with me disperseth.'

31. WHEREFORE,] *lit.* 'because of this I lay (it) down to you, Every sin (*or* 'missing' of the mark) and injurious-speech shall be let go to (the) men, but the injurious speech of (that is, *about*) the Spirit shall not be let go to (the) men.'

32. SPEAKETH,] *lit.* 'may say a word against the Son of the Man (or perhaps simply *a human being*, as in v. 8) it shall be let go to him, but whosoever may say (an injurious-word) against the Holy Spirit, it shall not be let go to him neither in this age (i.e. Jewish dispensation), nor in the one about to be,' that is, the Christian.

33. CORRUPT,] *or* 'rotten,.. rotten, for from (*lit.* out of) the fruit is the tree known.'

34. GENERATION,] *or* 'brood, offspring, progeny,' as in 3. 7.

ABUNDANCE,] *or* 'over-abundance;' as in Mark 8. 8; Luke 4. 5, &c.

35. A GOOD MAN,] *lit.* 'the good man.. casteth forth the good things, and the evil man..casteth forth evil things.'

36. WORD,] *or* 'saying, which the men (of the world) may speak, they shall give back for it a word in a day of judgment.'

37. FOR,] 'by (*lit.* out of or from) thy words thou shalt be declared just, and from (or out of) thy words thou shalt be declared unjust.'

38. MASTER,] *lit.* 'teacher, we wish to see.'

39. BUT,] *lit.* 'except.'

ADULTEROUS,] *lit.* 'contemptibly adulterous.'

40. WHALE,] *lit.* 'fish,'—as in Jonah 1. 17.

41. THE MEN,] *lit.* 'men, Ninevites, shall stand up in the judgment with this generation, and shall condemn it (*lit.* judge it down,) because they had a new mind at the proclamation of Jonah, and behold something more than Jonah is here.'

42. THE QUEEN,] *lit.* 'a queen.. and shall judge it down, because she came out of the ends.. something greater than Solomon is here.'

43. IS GONE OUT,] *lit.* 'may go both from the man (as in v. 22) it goeth through waterless places seeking a rest again,' or 'a thorough rest.'

44. RETURN,] *lit.* 'turn round upon my house..schooled, swept, and adorned.'

45. GOETH,] *lit.* 'goeth on, and taketh along with itself..and maketh a house there, and the last (troubles) of that man..evil generation.'

46. PEOPLE,] *lit.* 'crowds,..his brothers (Mat. 1. 25) had stood without seeking.'

47. ONE,] *lit.* a 'certain one.'

49. TOWARD,] *lit.* 'upon.'

50. SHALL,] *lit.* 'may do the wish (or will) of my Father who is in the heavens, he is my brother, &c.

Chapter XIII. may be divided into various parts; v. 1—10 Simile of various kinds of soil; v. 11—17 reasons for teaching by similes; v. 18—23 explanation of the simile; v. 24—30 simile of the tares; v. 31, 32 of the mustard-seed; v. 33 of the leaven; v. 34, 35 reason for so teaching; v. 36—43 explanation of the tares; v. 44 simile of the hid treasure; v. 45, 46 of pearl of great price; v. 47—50 of the net; v. 51 of the householder; v. 53—58 Jesus rejected by his townsmen.

1. THE SAME DAY,] *lit.* 'and in that day Jesus having gone forth from the house (probably his mother's) was sitting near (or along-side of) the sea' of Galilee.

2. GATHERED,] *lit.* 'brought together toward him were many crowds,..the boat (belonging to Peter)..crowd on the break-water had stood' or stationed themselves.

3. IN PARABLES,] *or* 'similes,' *lit.* a 'thing laid long-side' of another for the sake of comparison; it was, and still is, a common oriental mode of teaching, hence Christ used it, as had been foretold in Ps. 78. 2; see v. 35 below.

A SOWER,] *lit.* 'the sower,' one accustomed to it.

4. BY THE WAY SIDE,] *lit.* 'along (or near) the way, and the flying creatures came.'

5. SOME,] *lit.* 'but others fell upon the rocky places.'

6. WAS UP,] *lit.* 'the sun having risen.'
7. SOME,] *lit.* 'but others fell upon the thorns (or briers)..came up, and choked them thoroughly.'
8. INTO,] *lit.* 'upon the good land, and were giving fruit.'
10. CAME,] *lit.* 'having come forward, said.'
11. BECAUSE,] *or* 'that,' i.e. thus, in the following manner.
IT IS GIVEN,] *lit.* 'it has been given (by this request) to know the secrets of the reign of the heavens, and to them (i.e. the crowds) it has not been given,' for many of them had probably gone away without asking any explanation.
13. THEREFORE,] *lit.* 'because of this in similes spake I to them, because beholding they do not behold (clearly), and hearing they do not hear (distinctly), neither do they send (their hearts) with it;' the fault was entirely their own.
14. IN THEM,] *lit.* 'and filled up upon them ..with hearing (of the ear) ye shall hear, and ye may not send (your heart) with it, and beholding (with the eye) ye shall behold, and ye may not see.'
15. FOR WAXED,] *or* 'made fat (by themselves) was the heart of this people, and with (the) ears they heard heavily, and their eyes they did close thoroughly, lest at any time they might see with the eyes, and might send together with the heart, and might turn round upon (me,) and I might heal them,' which he was most willing to do.
16. BLESSED,] *lit.* 'happy your eyes that they behold, and your ears that they hear' intelligently, and with self-application.
17. HAVE DESIRED,] *lit.* 'had a mind upon seeing what ye behold, and did not see, and to hear what ye hear, and did not hear;' the set time being not then come.
18. HEAR,] *lit.* 'ye, therefore, hear ye (so as to understand) the simile of the sower.'
19. WHEN,] *lit.* 'every one hearing the word of the reign (of the heavens), and not sending (his heart) with it, the Evil One cometh, and snatcheth away that which has been sown in his heart; this is that sown along (or near) the way.'
20. BUT,] *lit.* 'and that sown upon the rocky places, this is he who is hearing the word, and straightway with joy (or leaping) is receiving it.'
21. DURETH,] *lit.* 'is for a time (*or* season) but tribulation or a cause of flight having happened because of the word, straightway he is stumbled.'
22. HE,] *lit.* 'and that sown towards the thorns (or briers), this is he who is hearing the word, and the partings (of mind) of this age, and the deceitfulness of the riches (or fulness) choketh thoroughly the word, and it becometh unfruitful.'
23. BUT,] *lit.* 'and that sown upon the good land, this is he who is hearing the word, and is sending (his heart) with it, who indeed, beareth fruit, and maketh, some indeed, a hundred, and some sixty, and some thirty-*fold*.'
24. PARABLE,] *or* 'simile,' as in v. 3, 10, 13.
KINGDOM,] *or* 'reign of the heavens (that is, the exercise of its rule) was likened to (the conduct of) a man sowing good seed in his field.'
25. SLEPT,] *lit.* 'are sleeping fast..darnel through the midst of the wheat.'
26. BLADE,] *or* 'herb,..made fruit. the darnel.'
27. HOUSE-HOLDER,] *lit.* 'house-despot came forward..the darnel.'
28. ENEMY,] *lit.* 'an enemy, a man (not an accident) did this..Dost thou wish,..lay them together?'
29. LEST,] *lit.* 'lest at any time laying together the darnel.'
30. LET,] *lit.* 'let alone, let both increase together until the reaping, and in the time of the reaping I will say to the reapers, Lay together first the darnel, and bind them into bundles to burn them thoroughly, but the wheat bring together into my storehouse.'
31. PARABLE,] *or* 'simile;' as in v. 3, &c.
KINGDOM,] *or* 'reign of the heavens (in its influence) is like to a grain of mustard.'
32. ALL SEEDS,] *lit.* 'all the seeds (used in gardens), but whenever it may increase, it is greatest of the dug-herbs,..the flying things of the heaven..settle down in its branches,' *lit.* clefts or breaches.
33. PARABLE,] *or* 'simile;' as in v. 3, &c.
KINGDOM,] *or* 'reign of the heavens (in its influence) is like to leaven (*lit.* a hot, boiling, fermenting thing),..of ground-flour.'
34. MULTITUDE,] *lit.* 'crowds,' coming and going.
SPAKE HE NOT,] *lit.* 'he was not speaking,' that is, habitually.
35. THAT,] *or* 'so that it might be filled out (that is, illustrated) that was spoken through the prophet (David, in Ps. 78. 2), saying, I will belch forth..from the foundation (*lit.* laying down) of the world,' *lit.* 'order, arrangement,' either of the physical or spiritual world.
36. SENT,] *lit.* 'having let the crowds go, went into the house (as in v. 1), and his disciples came forward to him, Explain (to our minds) the simile of the darnel of the field,' given in v. 24—30.
37. SOWETH,] *lit.* 'is sowing..the son of the man,' i.e. a human being, himself and all his preachers.
38. CHILDREN,] *lit.* 'sons of the reign (of the heavens, i.e. those who submit to it), and the darnel the sons of the evil' that is, in the world.
39. THE DEVIL,] *lit.* one who is 'casting (something) through' another, as in Mat. 4. 1, &c.
HARVEST,] *lit.* 'reaping is the full end of the (Jewish) age, and the reapers are messengers,' such as wars, pestilences, &c. See Ps. 78. 49, &c.
40. TARES,] *lit.* 'darnel are laid together. and by fire burnt down, so shall it be in the full end of this (Jewish) age.'
41. THE SON] of 'the Man shall send from (him) his messengers, and they shall lay together out of the kingdom all the stumbling blocks, and those doing the unlawlessness.
42. A FURNACE,] *lit.* 'the furnace of the

fire; there shall be the weeping and the gnashing of the teeth;' as in v. 50, &c.

43. RIGHTEOUS,] *or* 'just ones..in (during or by) the reign of their Father.'

44. KINGDOM,] *or* 'reign of the heavens (in its value) is like to (a) treasure hid in the field..did hide, and from the joy of it goeth (under secresy), and selleth (*lit.* worketh, plougheth, turneth up) all as much as he hath, and buyeth (*lit.* attends the market for) that field.'

45. KINGDOM,] *lit.* 'reign of the heavens (in its value) is like unto a man, a merchant,' or traveller.

46. GREAT PRICE,] *or* 'much prized (or priced) pearl, having gone away, used all as much as he had, and bought (*lit.* attended the market for) it.'

47. KINGDOM,] *lit.* 'reign of the heavens (in its working) is like to a drag cast into the sea, and brought together of all kinds.'

48. THEY DREW,] *lit.* 'having brought up upon the breakwater,..they laid together the good into the vessels, but the rotten they cast forth without.'

49. AT,] *lit.* 'in the full end of the (Jewish) age, the messengers shall come forth, and shall bear off the evil out of the midst of the just,' as when the first Christians fled to Pella, and escaped the destruction of Jerusalem; see Rev. 17. 1—8.

50. FURNACE,] of 'the fire (prepared for them); there shall be the weeping and the gnashing of the teeth,' with rage and disappointment; the destruction of Jerusalem only made the Jews more bitter against Christ and Christians.

51. UNDERSTOOD,] *lit.* 'sent (your hearts) with all these.'

52. THEREFORE,] *lit.* 'because of this, every writer having been discipled (or taught) with a view to the reign of the heavens, is like to a man, a house-despot,' not merely an *owner*, but a *ruler*.

53. DEPARTED,] *or* 'took himself away from thence.'

54. HIS OWN COUNTRY,] *or* 'father's place, he was teaching them in their synagogues, so that they were exceedingly struck and said, Whence to this one this wisdom and the mighty works?'

55. CARPENTER,] or simply, 'workman.'

MARY.] *Gr.* Mariam, *Heb.* Miriam.

BRETHREN,] *or* 'brothers;' see Mat. 1. 25.

JAMES,] i.e. 'one who takes by the heel.'

JOSES,] i.e. 'saviour.'

SIMON,] i.e. 'hearing.'

JUDAS,] i.e. 'confession, praise.'

57. OFFENDED,] *lit.* 'stumbled in (or by) him,' appearing thus humble.

A PROPHET,] that is, one who 'proclaims publicly' the will and praise of God, 'is not unhonoured (or dishonoured) except in his father's place and in his (own) house.'

58. UNBELIEF,] *or* 'unstedfastness,' in not adhering to his person and teaching.

Chapter XIV. may be divided into four parts; v. 1—12 imprisonment and death of John the Baptist; v. 13—21 Jesus feeds five thousand men; v. 22—33 He and Peter walk on the waters; v. 34—36 Jesus at Gennesaret.

1. AT,] *lit.* 'in (or during) that time (or season) Herod the Tetrarch,' governor of a 'fourth' part of the country.

2. SERVANTS,] *lit.* 'lads or boys;' as in 2 16; 8. 6, 8, 13, &c.

HE IS RISEN,] *lit.* 'he rose from the dead, and because of this the mighty powers are working in him.'

3. PRISON,] *or* 'ward, because of Herodias.'

4. SAID,] *lit.* 'was saying,' habitually.

5. WOULD HAVE,] *lit.* 'wished to..the crowd, because as a prophet (or public preacher) they held him.'

6. BIRTH-DAY] festivals 'were led on.. danced in the midst.'

7. WHEREUPON,] *lit.* 'whence.'

PROMISED,] *lit.* 'said at the same time to her to give whatever she might ask.'

8. BEING BEFORE INSTRUCTED,] *or* 'instigated *or* put forward by (*lit.* under) her mother, Give to me (says she) here upon a plate the head of John the Baptist.'

9. SORRY,] *or* 'vexed, but because of the oaths, (having probably repeated his promise), and of those reclining with (him).'

10. PRISON,] *or* 'ward;' as in v. 3. 25, &c.

11. IN A CHARGER,] *lit.* 'on a plate.'

12. CAME,] *lit.* 'came forward..told (it) thoroughly to Jesus.'

13. DEPARTED,] *or* 'withdrew from thence in a boat..the crowds.'

14. MULTITUDE,] *or* 'crowd, and his bowels were moved upon them and he attended (or cherished) their infirm.'

15. AND WHEN,] *lit.* 'and evening having come,..came forward to him, saying, The place is a desert, and the hour (of taking food) did now go by, let loose the crowds.'

17. BRING,] *lit.* 'bear' ye them to me.

19. MULTITUDE,] *lit.* 'crowds to reline..to the heaven, he blessed (*lit.* spake well)..to the crowds.'

20. TOOK,] *or* 'lifted up the superabundance of the broken pieces, twelve wicker-baskets full.'

21. HAD EATEN,] *lit.* 'and those eating were men, as it were five thousand, apart from women and children.'

22. TO GET,] *lit.* 'to go into the boat,..till he might let the crowds away.'

23. SENT AWAY,] *lit.* 'having let the crowds go..into the hill by himself to pray before (God).'

24. SHIP,] *or* 'boat..tried by (*lit.* under) the waves *or* billows,..wind was adverse.'

25. WENT,] *lit.* 'went away towards them, walking about upon the sea.'

26. WALKING,] *lit.* 'walking about..an apparition (*lit.* phantasm), and from the fear they called out.'

27. GOOD CHEER,] *lit.* 'have courage!'

28. LORD,] *or* 'Sir, command me to come.'

29. OUT OF THE SHIP,] *lit.* 'from the boat, he walked about upon the water to go towards Jesus'

30. HE SAW,] *lit.* 'beholding the wind strong.'

31. IMMEDIATELY,] *or* 'straightway..he took hold of him, and says to him, Little

faith! for what didst thou waver?' *lit.* 'stand on two things' at once.

32. SHIP,] *lit.* 'boat, the wind was wearied.'

33. SHIP,] *lit.* 'boat,..kissed forward to him (the hand), saying, Truly, God's Son thou art!' that is, the constituted King of Israel; as in Ps. 2. 7; 82. 6; Heb. 1. 9, &c.

34. GENNESARET,] i.e. 'garden of help.'

35. COUNTRY,] *lit.* 'space *or* place round about, and brought forward to him all those having ills.'

36. BESOUGHT,] *lit.* 'were calling him near,' *or* alongside of him.

HEM,] *or* 'fringe,' *lit.* that which trails on the ground, and 'as many as touched (him) were saved' from their ailments.

Chapter XV. may be divided into four parts; v. 1—20 Jesus and the tradition of the presbyters; v. 21—28 cure of a Canaanitess' daughter; v. 29—31 cure of many others; v. 32—39 feeding of four thousand men, &c.

1. CAME,] *lit.* 'came forward to Jesus the Scribes and Pharisees from Jerusalem,' who were more bigoted than others and anxious to entrap him.

2. TRANSGRESS,] *lit.* 'go beyond the traditions (*lit.* things 'given forth' by *or*) of the elders,' *Gr.* presbyters, belonging either to the Jewish Church or State or both.

3. BY,] *lit.* 'through or because of.'

4. HONOUR,] *lit.* 'make heavy, weighty;' see Ex. 20. 12, &c.

THAT CURSETH,] *lit.* 'who is speaking evil of..let him be ended by death;' see Ex. 21. 17.

5. SHALL SAY,] *lit.* 'may say..a gift (to God) is whatever thou mayest be profited out of mine.'

6. HONOUR,] *lit.* 'and he may not honour (that is, it is lawful for him not to do so).. and ye did make powerless (*lit.* lordless) the command of the (true) God through (*or* because of) your tradition.'

7. HYPOCRITES,] *lit.* 'judges under (a pretence).'

8. IS FAR,] *lit.* 'holds far off from me.'

9. WORSHIP,] *lit.* 'fear (or venerate) me, teaching teachings, commands of men.'

10. CALLED,] *lit.* 'called forward the crowd,..and send (your heart) with it.'

11. DEFILETH,] *or* 'maketh common the man.'

12. CAME,] *lit.* 'came forward..hast thou known..the word were stumbled?'

13. HATH NOT,] *lit.* 'did not plant shall be rooted out.'

14. THE DITCH,] *lit.* 'a deep place.'

15. DECLARE,] as in 13. 36.

17. UNDERSTAND,] *lit.* 'have in the mind ..in the belly (*lit.* hollow place) findeth place, and at a seat far off is cast forth.'

18. DEFILE,] *or* 'make common,' as in v. 11.

19. THOUGHTS,] *lit.* 'things laid thoroughly together.'

BLASPHEMIES,] *lit.* 'injurious speakings.'

20. DEFILE,] *lit.* 'make common the man.'

21. WENT,] *lit.* 'having gone forth from thence, withdrew into the parts of Tyre and Sidon,' near the Great Sea.

22. OF CANAAN,] *lit.* a 'woman, a Canaanitess, from those borders having come forth, called out to him, saying, Be kind to me, Son of David! my daughter is badly demonized.'

23. CAME,] *lit.* 'having come forward were requesting him, saying, Loose her from (thee, by granting her request).'

24. I AM,] *lit.* 'I was not sent from (God) except to the loosed away sheep of the house of Israel;' that is, *primarily* and *personally* I was so sent. Much of the strongly *positive* language of Scripture is to be understood as merely *comparative;* as in v. 6; 9. 13: 12. 7, &c.

25. WORSHIPPED,] *lit.* 'kissed forward (the hand) to him, saying, Sir, be helping me!'

26. MEET,] *lit.* 'good or beautiful..the little dogs.'

27. TRUTH,] *lit.* 'yes, sir, for even the little dogs do eat from the little crumbs falling from the table (*lit.* thing with four feet) of their lord,' or master.

28. FAITH,] *lit.* 'stedfastness (in clinging to me), let it be (become, happen) to thee, as thou dost wish.'

29. DEPARTED,] *lit.* 'having gone on from thence, came near (or along-side of) the sea of the Galil, and having gone up to the hill, was sitting there.'

30. MULTITUDES,] *lit.* 'many crowds come forward,..near Jesus' feet, and he attended (or cherished) them.'

31. MULTITUDE,] *lit.* 'crowds wondered, beholding dumb ones speaking, maimed ones whole (or healthy), lame ones walking about, and blind ones beholding.'

32. CALLED,] *lit.* 'called forward his disciples, said, My bowels are moved for the crowd, because already three days they remain before me,..and to send them from (me) fasting I wish not, lest at any time they may be loosed out in (or by) the way.'

33. WHENCE,] *lit.* 'whence to us in a desert place so many loaves so as to feed so great a crowd?'

35. MULTITUDE,] *lit.* 'crowds..to sit down (*or* again) on the earth.'

36. GAVE THANKS,] *lit.* 'having leaped well for joy.'

37. FILLED,] *or* 'fed, and they lifted up the superabundance of the broken pieces.'

39. SENT AWAY,] *lit.* 'having let loose the crowds, he went up into the boat, and came into the borders of Magdala,' whence Mary Magdalene came, a little south of which was Dalmanutha, see Mark 8. 10.

Chapter XVI. may be divided into five parts; v. 1—4 a sign sought and given; v. 5—12 tendency of the teachings of the Pharisees and Sadducees; v. 13—20 Jesus confessed by Peter; v. 21—23 avows his sufferings, and rebukes Peter; v. 24—28 announces profit and loss.

1. CAME,] *lit.* 'came forward, trying, asked him a sign out of the heavens to show to them over and above' what he had done already.

2. WHEN,] *lit.* 'evening having come, ye say, Fair weather (*lit.* 'well or good of

Jupiter'), for the heaven burns-with-fire.'

3. FOUL WEATHER,] *lit.* 'winter! for the heaven burns-with-fire and is glooming. Hypocrites (*lit.* 'judges under' a pretence), the face of the heaven indeed ye know to judge thoroughly, but the signs of the times (*or* seasons) ye are not able! A generation evil and adulterous (i.e. departing from God) a sign do seek for (or after),..and having left them utterly, he went from (thence).'

5. THEY HAD FORGOTTEN,] *lit.* 'they forgot over (it) to take loaves,' being in haste to embark with Jesus, who had left the Pharisees so abruptly.

6. TAKE HEED,] *lit.* 'see and hold off from.'

7. REASONED,] *or* 'were reasoning in themselves.'

HAVE TAKEN.] *lit.* 'we took no loaves.'

8. PERCEIVED.] *lit.* 'known..little stedfastness,..in yourselves, because ye took no loaves.'

9. UNDERSTAND,] *or* 'bear in mind..wicker-baskets.'

11. UNDERSTAND,] *or* 'bear in mind that not concerning loaves did I say to you to hold off from the leaven,' &c.

12. UNDERSTOOD,] *lit.* 'then they sent (or brought their minds) together, that he said not to hold off from the leaven of the loaf, but from the teaching, of the Pharisees and Sadducees.'

13. COASTS,] *lit.* 'parts..was asking.'

16. THE CHRIST,] *lit.* 'the anointed' one.

THE SON OF THE LIVING GOD,] as in 14. 33: 26. 63, 64; John 1. 49; 6. 69; 11. 27; 1 John 4. 15; 5. 5; the constant omission of the *conjunction* between this and the preceding clause shews that the one is explanatory of the other; see also Ps. 2. 2, 7, &c.

17. BLESSED,] *lit.* 'happy art thou, Simon bar Jonah (i.e. son of a dove), that flesh and blood (i.e. any worldly inducement) did not uncover it to thee, but My Father who is in the heavens,' from whom cometh down every perfect gift, as in James 1. 17; comp. John 6. 45; Isa. 54. 13.

18. PETER,] i.e. 'a rock and upon this rock (viz. that I am '*the Christ the Son of the Living God*,') I will build up (or bind together) my house—the church.' How fully the apostles felt this to be the case, see 1 John 2. 22; 3. 23; 4. 2, 3, 15; 5. 1, 5; 2 John 1. 7, 9; Acts 2. 36; 4. 11; 8, 37; 9. 20, 22; 13. 33; 17. 3; 18. 28; Rom. 1. 3, 4, &c. It is THE testing article of a standing or of a falling church; other articles may be *useful*, but they are not *necessary*, for a Christian to believe, and hold to.

AND THE GATES OF HELL,] *lit.* 'of hades (the 'unseen' world, where all go to, good and bad alike) shall not be powerful against it,' that is, so powerful as to overturn it. The simple meaning is, that *the Church* will always exist, and cannot by any hostile power ever be brought into *non-existence*, though individual churches may.

19. AND I WILL GIVE TO THEE,] that is, to Peter, as the spokesman of his companions, 'the keys (as a symbol of trust) of the reign of the heavens (i.e. the Gospel dispensation), and whatsoever thou mayest bind upon the earth shall be that which has (already) been bound in the heavens, and whatsoever thou mayest loose upon the earth shall be that which has (already) been loosed in the heavens.' So far from granting power to Peter and the other apostles, it expressly *limits* their right of forbidding or allowing things to be done in the church below to things that *have been bound* in the heavens, and a knowledge of which is only in the BIBLE. Any attempt therefore of Pope, Council, Convocation or Assembly, to extend their powers beyond this standard is truly ANTI-Christian. See Acts 10. 15, 20, 28, &c.

20. CHARGED,] *or* 'gave a thorough message to his disciples, that they might say to no one, that he is the Christ,' i.e. the Messiah.

21. HE MUST GO,] *lit.* 'he is bound to go away to Jerusalem, and to suffer many things from the presbyters and head priests and writers, and to be killed utterly, and the third day to rise.'

22. TOOK,] *lit.* 'took him forward (*or* off, aside), and began to put a weight upon him, saying, Be kind to thyself, Sir.'

23. GET,] *lit.* 'get away behind me! adversary!'

OFFENCE,] *lit.* 'my stumbling-block thou art!'

SAVOUREST,] *lit.* 'dost not mind.'

24. WILL COME,] *lit.* 'wisheth to come after me, let him renounce himself thoroughly, and lift up his cross;' as in 10. 38, &c.

25. WILL SAVE,] *lit.* 'may wish to save his life (*lit.* soul) shall loose it from (him self), and whosoever may loose from (him self) his life (*lit.* soul) shall find it.'

26. LOSE HIS OWN SOUL,] that is, 'of his life suffer loss; or what shall a man give (in) exchange for his life?' i.e. nothing earthly can benefit a man after his death, and he then is unable to offer any thing sufficient to regain his life.

27. SHALL COME,] *lit.* 'is about to come,' in 40 years.

IN,] *or* 'with (or by) the glory of his Father.'

ANGELS,] *or* 'messengers,' rational and irrational; as in John 1. 51, &c.

REWARD,] *or* 'give from (himself) to each according to his work,' or act, of receiving or rejecting Christ.

28. VERILY,] *lit.* 'Amen, I lay (it) down to you, there are certain of those standing here, ..till they may see the Son of the Man coming in his reign,' as at the mount of transfiguration, the day of Pentecost, the destruction of Jerusalem, &c; as in Mark 9. 1.

Chapter XVII. may be divided into five parts; v. 1—8 Jesus is transfigured; v. 9—13 the true Elijah; v. 14—21 expulsion of demoniac, and power of prayer; v. 22, 23 suffering foretold; v. 24—27 tribute paid.

1. TAKETH,] *lit.* 'taketh along with himself.'

BRINGETH,] *lit.* 'beareth them up.'

TRANSFIGURED,] *lit.* 'had another form'

RAIMENT,] *lit.* 'garments became white.'

3. TALKING,] *lit.* 'speaking together with him.'

4. WILT,] *lit.* 'if thou dost wish, we may make here three booths (*lit.* places for settling down).'

5. BRIGHT,] *or* 'light, shining.'

OVERSHADOWED,] *lit.* 'settled down upon' them.

BELOVED,] *lit.* 'dearly beloved;' as in 3. 17; 12. 18, &c.

I AM,] *lit.* 'I was well-pleased;' as in 3. 17.

6. WERE SORE AFRAID,] *or* 'feared exceedingly.'

7. CAME,] *lit.* 'came forward.'

8. LIFTED UP,] *lit.* 'lifted up upon (him) their eyes.'

9. VISION,] *or* 'sight *or* appearance..may stand up out of the dead.'

10. ASKED,] *lit.* 'asked him also.'

MUST,] *lit.* 'is bound to come first.'

11. TRULY SHALL,] *lit.* 'indeed doth come rst..cause all things to stand thoroughly ck.

12. IS COME,] *lit.* 'came..did not fully know him, but did on (*lit.* in) him as many things as they wished..so also the Son of the Man is about to suffer under them.

13. SPAKE,] *lit.* 'said (this) to them.

14. TO,] *lit.* 'towards the crowd, then came forward to him a man, falling on the knee to him.

15. LORD,] *or* 'Sir, be kind to my son, because he is lunatized, and suffers evilly.'

16. BROUGHT,] *lit.* 'brought him forward to..not able to attend (*or* cherish) him,' so as to relieve him.

17. FAITHLESS,] *lit.* 'unstedfast and thoroughly overturned generation till when..till when shall I hold you up? bear him to me here.'

18. CHARGED,] *lit.* 'put a weight upon the demons, and he went forth from him, and the lad (*or* boy) was cherished from that hour.'

19. CAME,] *lit.* 'came forward.'

20. BECAUSE OF,] *or* 'through your unstedfastness.'

YE HAVE,] *lit.* 'ye may have stedfastness as a grain of mustard. Let it be cast forward from hence thither, and it shall be cast forward.'

21. BY,] *or* 'in prayer (*lit.* a 'pouring forth abundantly before' God), and fasting,' *lit.* a not-eating.

22. WHILE THEY ABODE,] *lit.* 'they turning round again in the Galil..is about to be given over.'

23. KILL,] *lit.* 'kill him utterly.'

24. TRIBUTE,] *lit.* 'the didrachms (or two drachms 7½d. each), came forward..your teacher end (or complete) the didrachms,' required for the temple.

25. PREVENTED,] *lit.* 'anticipated .. or census (i.e. poll-tax)? from their sons, or from those of others?'

26. OF STRANGERS,] *lit.* 'from those of others; Jesus said to him, Then, indeed, are the sons freed.'

27. NOTWITHSTANDING,] *lit.* 'but that we may not stumble them..to the sea' of Galilee.

PIECE OF MONEY,] *lit.* a 'stater,' worth about half-a-crown.

Chapter XVIII. may be divided into seven parts; v. 1—6 the great one in the kingdom; v. 7—9 wo to the stumbling-block; v. 10—14 value of a lost sheep; v. 15—18 how to deal with a stumbling brother; v. 19, 20 unity of desire; v. 21, 22 extent of forgiveness; v. 23—35 mutual forgiveness.

1. AT,] *lit.* 'in that hour came forward.. who indeed is great..reign of the heavens,' or gospel church.

2. CALLED,] *lit.* 'called forward.'

3. CONVERTED,] *lit* 'turned round,..as the little children, ye may not enter into the reign of the heavens,' in *reality*, though they may *nominally*.

4. SHALL,] *lit.* 'may humble himself.'

5. SHALL,] *lit.* 'may receive..upon (i.e. in consideration of) my name,' or character.

6. SHALL,] *lit.* 'may stumble..who are remaining stedfast to me..a mill-stone—a weighty one (*lit.* one driven by an 'ass') may be hung upon his neck, and he may sink down in the depths of the sea.'

7. BECAUSE OF,] *lit.* 'from the stumbling-blocks, for there is a necessity for the stumbling-blocks to come..through whom the stumbling-block cometh.'

8. OFFEND,] *lit.* 'cause thee to stumble.. into the life lame..into the fire—the age-during!' not *necessarily* 'everlasting,' as in C.V. The simple meaning is that it should last as long as 'the age,' whatever that may be, whether it be the *age* (i.e. existence) of the offender, or of the Jewish or Christian dispensations. See also 19. 16, 29; 25. 41.

9. OFFEND,] *lit.* 'cause thee to stumble.. into the life one-eyed..into the gehennah of the fire;' that is, the worst part of it.

10. TAKE HEED,] *lit.* 'see that ye may not think down..their messengers in the heavens throughout all (time) behold the face of my Father who is in the heavens;' compare 1 K. 10. 8. *Messengers* (or angels) here mean most probably disembodied spirits, as in Acts 12. 15; in which case this passage expressly proves *infant* salvation, which however rests on the broader considerations of the justice and 'philanthropy of God our Saviour.'

11. IS COME,] *lit.* 'came..loosed (itself) away.' Many critics reject this whole verse as an interpolation.

12. HOW,] *lit.* 'what..if there may be to a certain man 100 sheep, and one of them may be led astray..let alone..upon the hills,..is led astray.'

13. AND IF] he 'may happen to find it..he leapeth with joy over it, more than over.. were not led astray.'

14. IT IS NOT,] *or* 'there is not a wish before your Father who is in the heavens, that ..may be lost *or* destroy itself.'

15. TRESPASS,] *lit.* 'sin (*or* 'miss' the mark) in reference to thee, go away (*lit.* 'under' secresy), and convict him..if he may hear.' See Lev. 19. 17; De. 19. 15.

16. WILL,] *lit.* 'may not hear, take along with thee yet one or two, that upon the mouth of two witnesses or of three, every matter may stand.' See De. 19. 15; John 8. 17; 2 Cor. 13. 1.

17. SHALL,] *lit.* 'may not hear them, say it to the assembly (of the brethren around him), and if also the assembly he may not hear,..as the Gentile and the publican *or* custom-house officer.'

18. SHALL,] *lit.* 'may bind upon the earth, shall be those which have (already) been bound in the heavens,..may loose..those which have been loosed in the heavens,' i.e. revealed to be so in the Scriptures; as in 16. 19, &c.

19. SHALL AGREE,] *lit.* 'may agree (*lit.* sound forth) together upon the earth concerning any matter, whatsoever they may ask, it shall happen to them from my Father.'

20. FOR,] where 'there are two or three brought together, with a reference to my name.'

21. CAME,] *lit.* 'came forward..sin (or 'miss' the mark) with reference to me, and shall I let (it) go to him?'

23. THEREFORE,] *lit.* 'because of this was the reign of the heavens (in its rule) likened to a man, a king, who wished to take up at once a reckoning with his servants.'

24. TO RECKON,] *lit.* 'take it up, there was brought forward to him one debtor of a myriad of talents,' i.e. an immense sum.

25. PAY,] *lit.* 'give back..to be carried away (for sale), also his wife and children, and (the money) to be given back.'

26. WORSHIPPED,] *lit.* 'kissed forward (the hand) to him, saying, Sir,..and I will give all back to thee.'

27. WAS MOVED,] *lit.* 'having the bowels moved, loosed him from (the charge), and the loan (or gift) let go to him.'

28. PENCE,] *lit.* 'denaries (worth 7½d. each), and having seized him, he throttled him, saying, Give back to me whatever thou owest.'

29. BESOUGHT,] *lit.* 'called upon him,..I will give back to thee.'

30. WOULD NOT,] *lit.* 'did not wish, but having gone away, cast him into ward till he might give back that which was owing.'

31. WAS DONE,] *lit.* 'had happened,.. shewed fully..that had happened.'

32. CALLED,] *lit.* 'called him near, says to him, Evil servant! all that debt I let go to thee, since thou did call upon me (so to do).'

33. SHOULDST,] *lit.* 'is it not binding also on thee to be kind to thy fellow-servant, as I also was kind to thee?'

34. WROTH,] *or* 'angry, and give him over to those testing (criminals), till he might give back all that was owing to him (self),' viz., 10,000 talents.

35. LIKEWISE,] *lit.* 'so also..let not go each to his brother their fallings aside (from duty.)'

Chapter XIX. may be divided into seven parts; v. 1, 2 Jesus' return to Judea; v. 3—9 law of divorce; v. 10—12 when marriage is necessary; v. 13—15 He blesses little children; v. 16—22 a rich young ruler; v. 23—26 earthly riches a hindrance; v. 27—30 rewards of fidelity.

1. FINISHED,] *lit.* 'ended these words, he removed from the Galil, and came to the borders of the Judea beyond the Jordan.'

2. GREAT MULTITUDES,] *lit.* 'many crowds, ..he attended (or cherished) them there.'

3. CAME,] *lit.* 'came forward..trying..to loose from (him) his wife.'

4. HAVE YE NOT READ,] *lit.* 'did ye not know fully that he who made (them), from the beginning a male and a female made them?'

5. FOR THIS CAUSE,] *lit.* 'because of this shall a man leave utterly father and mother, and shall be joined (*lit.* glued) to his wife, and the two shall be with a view to one flesh.'

6. WHEREFORE,] *lit.* 'so that they are no more two, but one flesh,..did yoke together, ..man make a space' between them.

7. WRITING,] *lit.* 'roll *or* scroll of putting away, and to loose (oneself) from her?'

8. BECAUSE OF,] *or* 'towards your stiffness of heart turned over to you to loose away your wives,..it did not happen so.'

9. SHALL,] *lit.* 'may loose away his wife, except upon whoredom, and may marry another,..married her who has been loosed away.'

10. CASE,] *or* 'cause..with the woman.'

11. ALL,] have 'not room for this word, but those to whom it has been given.'

12. EUNUCHS,] *lit.* 'keepers (i.e. guardians) of the bed,' in large harems.

WOMB,] *or* 'belly,' *lit.* 'hollow place.'

OF MEN,] *lit.* 'under the men.'

MADE,] i.e. 'kept themselves eunuchs because of the reign of the heavens.' Origen's misapprehension of this passage is well known.

13. BROUGHT,] *lit.* 'brought forward.. might put..might pour forth (prayer) for them,..laid a weight upon them.'

14. SUFFER,] *lit.* 'let alone the little children, and forbid them not to come toward me.'

16. CAME,] *lit.* 'came forward..Teacher, good one!'

ETERNAL,] *lit.* 'life age-during.'

17. WILT ENTER,] *lit.* 'dost wish to enter into the life.'

18. WHICH,] *lit.* 'what kind?'

FALSE WITNESS,] *or* 'a lying testimony.'

19. HONOUR,] *lit.* 'make weighty.'

LOVE,] *lit.* 'dearly love thy neighbour.'

20. HAVE I KEPT,] *lit.* 'did I observe..do I fall short of?'

21. WILT,] *lit.* 'dost wish to be perfect (*or* finished, complete), go away, sell (*lit.* work *or* use up) the things thou hast,..be following me.'

22. THAT SAYING,] *lit.* 'the word..for he was having many possessions.'

23. REIGN OF THE HEAVENS,] *or* gospel church.

24. CAMEL.] Some critics read a 'cable.'

EYE,] *lit.* 'hole' of a needle.

GO,] *lit.* 'go thoroughly through.'

25. AMAZED,] *lit.* 'struck.'

26. BEHELD,] *lit.* 'beheld them earnestly.

27. HAVE FORSAKEN,] *lit.* 'we let go all.. what then shall be to us?

28. HAVE,] *lit.* 'did follow me.'

REGENERATION,] or new state of things introduced by the preaching of Christ and his apostles; hence the ancient fathers unanimously speak of all who have been admitted into the church by baptism as being 'regenerated,' not as implying any *spiritual* change, but only a *legal*, forensic one, in the eye of law (see Tit. 3. 5). So Josephus (Ant. 11. 3, 9) applies the word to the *return* from Babylon, and Cicero (ad Att. 6. 6) to the *restoration* of his dignity and fortune.

SHALL,] *lit.* 'may sit upon the throne of his glory,' that is, after his ascension; as in 25. 31; Acts 2. 30, 33; 5. 31, &c.

YE ALSO SHALL SIT,] as co-workers with Christ in converting the world and guiding the church, by example, precept, &c.

TWELVE TRIBES] of 'the Israel' of God, the spiritual seed of Abraham, to whom James and Peter addressed their Letters. Compare Luke 22. 30; 1 Cor. 6. 2; Rev. 2. 26.

HATH FORSAKEN,] *lit.* 'let go..or fields, because of my name..and life age-during shall have by lot.'

30. FIRST,] in point of time shall be last in receiving their reward, as is manifest from the following simile, in chap. 20. 10.

Chapter XX. may be divided into five parts; v. 1—16 simile of the dissatisfied workmen; v. 17—19 Jesus foretells his suffering; v. 20—23 reasons with the sons of Zebedee; v. 24—28 and with his disciples; v. 29—34 cures two blind men.

1. KINGDOM,] *lit.* 'reign of the heavens is like to (the conduct of) a man, a house-despot, who went forth with the morning to hire workers for his vineyard.'

2. LABOURERS,] *lit.* 'workers for (*lit.* out of) a denary (worth 7½d.) the day, he sent them away into his vineyard.'

3. IDLE,] *lit.* 'not working.'

4. THEM,] *lit.* 'unto these, Go away, also ye, into.'

RIGHT,] *or* 'just..they went away' into it.

6. STAND YE,] *lit.* 'have ye stood.'

7. HATH HIRED,] *lit.* 'did hire us. Go away, also ye,..just.'

8. STEWARD,] *lit.* one on whom a thing is 'turned over.'

LABOURERS,] *lit.* 'workers, and give away to them the hire.'

9. PENNY,] *lit.* 'denary,' as in v. 2.

10. SUPPOSED,] *lit.* 'they made it a law (in their own minds) that they shall receive more.'

11. MURMURED,] *lit.* 'they were murmuring.'

12. WROUGHT,] *lit.* 'made..didst make.. the heat (*or* the hot one, i.e. the sun) of the day.'

13. FRIEND,] *or* 'comrade..no injustice (*or* unrighteousness)..for a denary?'

14. TAKE,] *lit.* 'lift up..go away; I wish to give.'

15. I WILL,] *or* 'I wish in the things of my own?'

16. SO,] *or* 'thus..called (to work for Christ), but few are chosen,' *lit.* 'elect or select,' that is, of a *choice* character and disposition, so as to see others receiving an equal reward with themselves without murmuring or repining. *Choice, excellent, approved* is the pervading acceptation of the Greek word throughout the Septuagint and the New Testament. See Luke 23. 35; Rom. 16. 13; 1 Tim. 5. 21; 1 Pet. 2. 4, 6, 9, (Isa. 28. 16; 42. 1; 43. 20), &c.

17. TOOK,] *lit.* 'took along with him.'

18. BETRAYED,] *lit.* 'given over..judge him down to death.'

19. DELIVER,] *lit.* 'give him over..to treat as a child, and to lash,..shall stand up.'

20. CAME,] *lit.* 'came forward,..mother of Zebedee's sons (i.e. Salome)..kissing forward (the hand), and asking (not 'desiring' merely) something from him.'

21. WILT,] *lit.* 'what dost thou wish?'

GRANT,] *lit.* 'say (the word) in order that they may sit (*or* set themselves) down, one on thy right, and one on thy left, in thy reign.'

22. KNOW NOT,] *lit.* 'ye have not known what ye ask for yourselves..that I am about to drink?'

23. BUT,] *or* 'except to those for whom it has been prepared by (*lit.* under) my Father.'

24. INDIGNATION,] *lit.* 'much displeased at.'

25. CALLED,] *lit.* 'called them forward.. ye have known that the chiefs of the nations lord it over them, and the great ones exercise authority over them.'

26. WILL,] *lit.* 'may wish to become great, let him be your minister,' *lit.* 'deacon,' as in 22. 13; 23. 11; Mark 9. 35; 10. 43; John 2. 5.

27. WILL,] *lit.* 'may wish to be first.'

28. MINISTERED UNTO,] *lit.* 'to be served by deacons, but to serve as a deacon;' as in 4. 11; 8. 15; 25. 44; 27. 55, &c.

LIFE,] *lit.* 'soul a ransom (*lit.* a 'thing loosing,' setting free) over against many;' most expositors take '*many*' here in the sense of '*all*,' but in that case it would require the definite article, as in Rom. 5. 15, 19. See, however, 1 Cor. 10. 33; Rom. 12. 5; John 5. 28, compared with Dan. 12. 2, &c.

29. MULTITUDE,] *lit.* 'crowd..cometh along ..deal kindly.'

31. REBUKED,] *lit.* 'laid a weight upon them, that they might be silent.'

32. CALLED,] *lit.* 'sounded to them..what do ye wish.'

33. OPENED,] *lit.* 'opened up *or* thoroughly.'

34. COMPASSION,] *lit.* 'and Jesus having his bowels moved..straightway their eyes beheld again.'

Chapter XXI. may be divided into six parts; v. 1—11 Jesus enters Jerusalem amid hosannahs; v. 12—17 cleanses the temple, cures the people, and defends the children; v. 18—22 the barren fig-tree; v. 23—27 He silences the priests and elders; v. 28—32 parable of two sons; v. 33—46 of the wicked husbandmen.

1. BETHPHAGE,] i.e. 'house of figs.'

UNTO,] *lit.* 'towards the mount of the olives.'

SENT,] *lit.* 'sent away.'

2. GO,] *lit.* 'go on..an ass bound.'

3. ANY MAN,] *lit.* 'any one may say anything..that the master..will send them away.'

4. WAS DONE,] *or* 'happened that it might be filled out (or realized) that was spoken through the prophet,' in Isa. 62. 11; Zech. 9. 9.

5. TELL,] *lit.* 'say ye to the daughter of Zion (i.e. the dry *or* sunny place)..mounted on an ass, and a colt, a son of one under the yoke.'

6. COMMANDED,] *lit.* 'set before them.'

7. PUT,] *lit.* 'put up upon them..their garments, and they set him up upon them,' that is, upon the garments.

8. MULTITUDE,] *or* 'and most of the crowd strawed their own garments..were cutting branches..were strawing.'

9. MULTITUDES,] *lit.* 'crowds that were leading forward, and that were following.. Hosannah (*lit.* save us !) to the Son of David ! spoken well of is He who is Coming in the name of the Lord; Hosannah in the highest (places)!'

10. MOVED,] *or* 'shaken.'

11. MULTITUDE,] *lit.* 'crowds..who is from Nazareth.'

12. SOLD,] *lit.* 'turning over and attending the market in the temple, and the tables of those with small coin (for exchange) he turned thoroughly over.'

13. IT IS,] *lit.* 'it has been written, My houes a house for pouring out before (God) shall be called, but ye made it a cave of robbers.'

14. CAME,] *lit.* 'came forward..attended *or* cherished.'

15. CHILDREL,] *lit.* 'lads *or* boys..much displeased.'

16. HAVE YE NEVER,] *lit.* 'did ye not know fully at any time (the meaning of Ps. 8. 2), that, Out of..thou didst perfect praise fully.'

17. LEFT,] *lit.* 'left them fully, and went forth without the city into Bethany (i.e. 'house of affliction,') and made a court there,' for the night.

18. RETURNED,] *lit.* 'came up over.'

19. A FIG-TREE,] *lit.* 'one fig-tree upon the way, he came upon it,..and says to it, May no more fruit be out of thee to the age ! and at the thing (*or* matter) the fig-tree dried up.'

20. SOON,] *lit.* 'how did the fig-tree at the thing dry up !'

21. VERILY,] *lit.* 'Amen..If ye may have stedfastness, and may not be judged asunder (in your minds), not only this of the fig-tree shall ye do, but also if ye may say to this hill, Be thou lifted up, and be thou cast into the sea, it shall happen.'

22. WHATSOEVER,] *lit.* 'as many things as ye may ask for yourselves in the pouring forth before (God) remaining stedfast (to me), ye shall receive.' There is no reference whatever to what is called '*believing* prayer,' but to the 'prayers of *believers*.'

23. ELDERS,] *lit.* 'presbyters of the people (i.e. civil magistrates) come forward..in (the exercise of) what authority.'

24. THING,] *or* 'word, which if ye may say to me, I also will say to you, in what authority.'

25. FROM,] *lit.* 'out of heaven, or out of men.'

REASONED,] *lit.* 'were speaking diversely by themselves..if we may say, Out of heaven ..remain fully stedfast to him?'

26. SHALL,] *lit.* 'may say, Out of men, we fear the crowd.'

27. CANNOT TELL,] *lit.* 'we have not known.'

28. SONS,] *lit.* 'children, and he came forward..Child, go away.'

29. I WILL NOT,] *lit.* 'I do not wish, but at last having been concerned about (it), he went away,' to work as desired.

30. CAME,] *lit.* 'came forward..went not away.'

31. WHETHER,] *or* 'who out of the two did the wish of the Father?..Amen..custom-house-officers and the harlots go before you into the reign of the (true) God.'

32. THE WAY,] *lit.* 'in a way of righteousness, and ye remained not fully stedfast to him ..was not concerned about it at last so as to remain stedfast to him.'

33. PARABLE,] *lit.* a 'thing laid alongside of' another for the purpose of comparison and contrast.

HOUSEHOLDER,] *lit.* 'certain man, a house-despot..and put round about it a hedge, and dug in it a vat, and built a house (for) a tower, and gave it out to husbandmen (*lit.* earth-workers), and went away from the people.'

34. TIME,] *or* 'season..drew nigh he sent away..to receive his (share of the) fruits.'

35. BEAT,] *lit.* 'leathered..killed fully.'

36. SENT,] *lit.* 'sent away (from himself).'

37. SENT,] *lit.* 'sent away (from himself) toward them..they will be turned in (tc obedience) by my son.'

38. AMONG,] *lit.* 'in themselves..the heir (*lit.* one to whon a thing is 'assigned by lot'), come, let us kill him utterly, and let us hold thoroughly his inheritance,' *lit.* the thing 'assigned to him by lot.'

39. CAUGHT,] *lit.* 'having taken him..they killed him utterly.'

40. COMETH,] *lit.* 'may come.'

41. WICKED,] *lit.* 'Evil ones ! he will evilly destroy..will give out.'

42. READ,] *lit.* 'did ye not at any time know fully *or* again in the Writings; a stone which the builders of the house thought little of (*lit.* away from), this became for head of a corner; from (the) Lord hath this been.'

43. THEREFORE,] *lit.* 'because of this, I lay (it) down to you, thatthe reign of the heavens shall be lifted up from you, and given to a nation making its fruits.'

44. WHOSOEVER,] *lit.* 'he who is falling upon this stone shall be utterly broken..it may fall, it will scatter him' to the winds.

45. PERCEIVED,] *lit.* 'knew..speaks about them.'

46. WHEN,] *lit.* 'seeking (or desiring) to seize him..crowds, since as a prophet they held him.'

Chapter XXII. may be divided into five parts; v. 1—14 simile of a wedding-garment; v. 15—22 duty of tribute; v. 23—33 Sadducees and the Up-rising; v. 34—40 sum of the law and the prophets; v. 41—46 David's Son and Lord.

1. BY,] *lit.* 'in parables.'
2. KINGDOM,] *lit.* 'reign of the heavens was likened to a man, a king, who made marriage-feasts to his son.'
3. WERE BIDDEN,] *lit.* 'having been called (beforehand) to the marriage-feasts, and they did not wish to come.'
4. TELL,] *lit.* 'say to those having been called, My best meal I prepared, my oxen and the fatlings have been slaughtered, and all things are prepared, come ye to the marriage-feasts.'
MADE LIGHT,] *lit.* 'being careless, went away, the one to his own field.'
6. TOOK,] *or* 'seized..injured (*or* dishonoured), and slew them.'
7. WROTH,] *or* 'angry, and having sent his soldiers..set on fire their city,' i.e. Jerusalem.
8. WEDDING,] *lit.* 'marriage-feast, indeed.'
9. GO,] *lit.* 'go ye on upon the various ways of the way, and as many as ye may find, call ye to the marriage-feasts.'
10. HIGHWAYS,] *lit.* 'ways, and brought together..evil and good, and the wedding-feast-apartment was filled with those lying down' to meals, according to an ancient custom.
11. TO SEE,] *or* 'view those reclining (at food), not clothed with clothing of a marriage-feast.'
12. FRIEND,] *or* 'comrade..clothing of a marriage feast..silenced.'
13. SERVANTS,] *lit.* 'deacons..lift him up ..the outer darkness (of the street)..gnashing of the teeth,' with rage and disappointment at the expulsion from the festivities.
14. MANY,] as many as the servants met.
CHOSEN,] *lit.* 'choice, select, excellent,' as in 26. 16; he. (the representative of a class) proving himself unworthy of the invitation.
15. WENT,] *lit.* 'went on..and took united counsel..ensnare him by (in *or* with) a word.'
16. SENT OUT,] *lit.* 'away..Herodians (a political party in the state), saying, Teacher, we have known that thou art true..lookest not to the face of men,' so as to shew partiality.
17. TELL,] *lit.* 'say to us, therefore, How does it appear to thee? is it lawful to give a census (*or* poll-tax) to Caesar?'
18. PERCEIVED,] *lit.* 'knew their evil..try ye me, ye judges under' a pretence.
19. SHEW,] *lit.* 'shew openly to me the lawful money of the census (*or* poll-tax), and they brought forward to him a denary,' worth about 7½d.
20. SUPERSCRIPTION,] *lit.* 'writing-over (it).'
21. RENDER,] *lit.* 'give back *or* away.'
22. LEFT,] *lit.* 'let him go, and went away.'
23. THE SAME DAY,] *lit.* 'in that day came forward to him Sadducees, who are saying (that there is) not to be a standing up (of the dead), and they asked at him.'
24. MASTER,] *lit.* 'teacher..if any one may die away..marry openly (*or* over and above) his wife.'
25. BRETHREN,] *lit.* 'brothers..was ended (*or* finished), and having no seed, let go his wife..to his brother.'
26. SEVENTH,] *lit.* 'seven' brothers were gone over.
27. DIED,] *lit.* 'died away.'
28. RESURRECTION,] *lit.* 'standing up of the dead.
29. DO ERR,] *or* 'go astray..the Writings.
30. RESURRECTION,] *lit.* 'standing up (of the dead)..nor are married out, but are as messengers of the (true) God in heaven.'
31. AS TOUCHING,] *lit.* 'concerning the standing up of the dead, did ye not know again (*or* fully) that which was spoken to you by (*lit.* under) God, laying (it) down.'
32. I AM] still (not *was* merely) the 'God of Abraham,..God is not a God of dead men but of living ones.' Comp. Ex. 3. 3, where though the verb is wanting in the Hebrew, the present tense is imperatively required by the genius and idiom of the language. See particularly my 'Illustrations of the Hebrew Tenses.'
33. MULTITUDE,] *lit.* 'crowds..were greatly struck at his teaching.'
34. HAD PUT TO SILENCE,] *or* 'silenced,' *lit.* muzzled; as in v. 12.
GATHERED,] *or* 'brought together at the same place.'
35. TEMPTING,] *or* 'trying, testing, proving.'
36. MASTER,] *lit.* 'teacher..a great command.'
37. WITH,] *lit.* 'in all..in all..in all thy.'
38. THE,] *lit.* 'a first and a great command.
39. THE,] *lit.* 'a second.'
40. ON,] *lit.* 'in these two..are suspended.'
42. OF CHRIST,] *lit.* 'of the Christ.'
43. IN SPIRIT,] *or* 'by (the) Spirit.'
44. THE LORD,] In Hebrew 'Jehovah;' as in Ps. 110. 1.
SIT,] *or* 'be thou seated..I may set.'
45. SON,] seeing in the east a father never gives his son an appellation equal to or higher than his own, as it reverses the order of nature.
46. ASK,] *lit.* 'question him any more.'

Chapter XXIII. may be divided into three parts; v. 1—12 warning against lip-service, formalism and pride; v. 13—36 woes to the scribes and pharisees; v. 37, 38 lament over Jerusalem.
1. MULTITUDE,] *lit.* 'crowds.'
2. SIT,] *lit.* 'did set (themselves) down upon the seat of Moses,' as lawgiver in Israel.
3. WHATSOEVER,] *lit.* 'as many things as they may say to you to keep, keep and do, but according to their works do not do.'
4. BURDENS,] heavy (*or* weighty) and hardly bearable, and put over upon the shoulders of the men (under their control), but with their (own) fingers they do not wish to move them.'
5. SEEN,] *or* 'viewed.'
PHYLACTERIES,] *lit.* 'preservatives,' i.e. pieces of parchment containing passages of SS. and tied with ribbon round the forehead; a misapprehension of Nu. 15. 38; De. 6. 8; 22. 12; Prov. 3. 3, and used as a charm.
ENLARGE,] *or* 'make great the fringes

lit. that which trails on the ground.

6. UPPERMOST ROOMS,] *lit.* 'foremost places for reclining in the suppers, and the foremost seats.'

7. GREETINGS,] *or* 'the salutations in the market (or public) places..by men, Rabbi, Rabbi,' *lit.* my great one!

8. BE NOT YE,] *lit.* 'but ye—ye may not be called Rabbi, for one is your leader, the Christ.'

9. CALL,] *lit.* 'and ye may not call (any one) your father upon the earth, for one is your Father who is in the heavens.'

10. NEITHER] 'may ye be called leaders, for one is your leader, the Christ.' These verses have no reference whatever to *civil* or *worldly* titles, but to the appellation given to men *in the church;* the titles 'Reverend, Right Reverend, Father in God, and Doctor of Divinity,' seem direct violations of them, as these are given solely because of the *church-standing* of those who receive them. 'Bishop, presbyter, deacon, evangelist,' &c., do not come under the censure, as they are names of *offices* or *duties,* not of honour or courtesy.

11. GREATEST,] *lit.* 'great shall be your deacon.'

13. SCRIBES,] *or* 'writers..for (*or* that).. reign of the heavens.'

14. EAT UP,] *lit.* 'eat down (*or* fully)..for an appearance ye are pouring forth before (God) long-prayers, because of this ye shall receive more abundant judgment.'

15. COMPASS,] *lit.* 'go round the sea and the dry-land, to make one proselyte, (*lit.* one who 'comes forward,') and when it may happen, ye make him a son of Gehenna twofold more than yourselves.'

16. GUIDES,] *lit.* those 'bringing on the way.'

SHALL,] *lit.* 'may swear by (*lit.* in) the habitation (of God)..may swear by (*lit.* in) the gold of the habitation—is obliged.'

17. FOOLS,] *or* 'rebellious,' as in 5. 22, &c.

TEMPLE,] *lit.* 'habitation which is setting-apart the gold.'

18. SHALL,] *lit.* 'may swear by (*lit.* in) the place of sacrifice,..may swear by (*lit.* in) the gift that is upon it,—is obliged.'

20. SHALL,] *lit.* 'swore by (*lit.* in) the place of sacrifice, sweareth by (in) it, and by (in) all things on it.

21. SHALL,] *lit.* 'swore by (*lit.* in) the habitation, sweareth by (in) it, and by (in) him who is inhabiting it continually.'

22. SHALL,] *lit.* 'swore by (*lit.* in) the heavens, sweareth by (in) the throne of the (true) God, and by (in) him who is sitting down upon it.'

23. FOR,] *lit.* 'that ye tithe thoroughly the sweet-scented flower, and the dill, and the cumin, and let alone the weightier matters of the law, the judgment, and the kindness, and the stedfastness; these ye are bound to do, those not to let alone.'

24. GUIDES,] *lit.* 'bringers on the way.. who are straining out thoroughly the gnat, but the camel are drinking down.'

25. FOR,] *or* 'that, ye cleanse thoroughly the outside of the drinking-cup and of the plate, but within they are full of plunder and incontinence,' or as some MSS. read 'injustice.'

26. THAT WHICH,] *lit.* 'the inside of the drinking cup and of the plate, that..may become clean.'

27. FOR,] *or* 'that ye are nearly like to.'

BEAUTIFUL,] *lit.* 'that which may be seen.'

28. RIGHTEOUS,] *or* 'just, right.'

INIQUITY,] *lit.* 'lawlessness.'

29. BECAUSE,] *or* 'that ye build as houses the tombs..adorn the..just.'

31. WHEREFORE,] *lit.* 'so that,..ye are sons.'

32. FILL YE UP,] *or* 'ye fill up.'

33. SERPENTS,] *lit.* 'observing ones.'

GENERATION,] *or* 'brood, offspring, progeny..may ye flee from the judgment of the Gehenna?'

34. WHEREFORE,] *lit.* 'because of this, behold, I send away to you..and of them ye shall utterly kill,..cause to flee from city to city.'

35. SHED,] *lit.* 'poured out..the habitation (of God) and the place of sacrifice.'

36. VERILY,] *lit.* 'Amen (i.e. stedfast), I lay (it) down to you,..this generation;' within 40 years.

37. KILLEST,] *lit.* 'art killing thoroughly ..sent away to thee, how often did I wish to bring thy children fully together, even as (*lit.* in the manner that) a bird brings fully together her own young ones under the wings, and ye did not wish,' to be brought together.

38. LEFT,] *lit.* 'let alone to you—a desert.'

39. SHALL,] *lit.* 'may not see me from this time, till that ye may say, Blessed (*lit.* well-spoken of) is He who is coming,' an application of Messiah.

Chapter XXIV. may be divided into two parts; v. 1—41 signs of Christ's coming to destroy Jerusalem; v. 42—51 duty of watchfulness in reference to it.

1. CAME,] *lit.* 'came forward to shew to him fully the buildings of the temple.'

2. SHALL,] *lit.* 'may not be let alone.'

THROWN,] *lit.* 'loosed down.'

3. AS HE SAT,] *lit.* 'he sitting down upon the hill of the olives the disciples came forward, saying, Say to us,..sign of thy presence (*lit.* being 'along-side,') and of the full-end of the (Jewish) age?' not 'of the world,' as in the C. V.

4. TAKE HEED,] *lit.* 'see that no one may lead you astray.'

5. IN,] *lit.* 'upon my name, saying, I am the Christ, and many shall they lead astray.'

6. SHALL HEAR,] *lit.* 'ye are about to hear of wars..that ye cry not out, for it behoveth all things to happen,' that I am telling you of.

7. AGAINST,] *lit.* 'nation upon nation, and kingdom upon kingdom, and there shall be famines, and pestilences, and shakings, in divers places,' of the land of Palestine.

8. THE,] *lit.* 'a beginning.'

9. DELIVER,] *lit.* 'give you over to tribulation, and shall kill you utterly..by all the nations (of Israel) because of my name.'

10. OFFENDED,] *lit.* 'stumbled, and shall give one another over' to persecuting Jews.
11. DECEIVE,] *lit.* 'lead astray many.'
12. INIQUITY,] *lit.* 'of the filling up of the unlawlessness the dear-love of the many (i.e. multitude) shall become cold,' *lit.* be blown upon.
13. ENDURE,] *lit.* 'remain under (it),' till the end of the trial, or of the Jewish dispensation, as in Luke 21. 18, 19.
24. GOSPEL,] *or* 'good-news of the reign (of Christ) shall be proclaimed (as by a herald) in all the inhabited world, (which in Acts 11. 28; 17. 6; 24. 5; Luke 21. 26 means simply Palestine or the Roman empire), for a testimony to all the nations (see Rom. 1. 8), and then shall be the end' of the temple.
15. SHALL,] *lit.* 'may see the abomination of the desolation, which was spoken of through Daniel the prophet, standing in the (or *a*) holy place, he who is knowing (it) again *or* fully, let him mind,' i.e. attend to it.
16. INTO,] *lit.* 'upon the hills.'
17. HOUSE-TOP,] *lit.* 'building;' as in 10. 27.
18. RETURN BACK,] *or* 'turn round over it again..to lift up his raiment.'
19. WITH CHILD,] *lit.* 'having in the womb, and to those giving the breast in those days.'
20. PRAY,] *lit.* 'pour forth before (God), that your flight may not become (that) of winter (with the elements adverse to them), neither in a sabbath,' rousing thereby Jewish superstition and bigotry.
21. SINCE,] *lit.* 'from the beginning of the world (i.e. Jewish economy) till now, nor ever may happen.'
22. SHOULD BE,] *lit.* 'were cut off *or* shortened.'
NO FLESH,] *lit.* 'all flesh.'
SAKE,] *lit.* 'because of the elect,' *or* select, choice, excellent ones, i.e. the Christians.
23. SHALL,] *lit.* 'may say, Behold, here (is) the Christ,..may ye not believe (it).'
24. SHOW,] *lit.* 'give great signs and fearful things, so as to lead astray, if possible, also the elect,' (i.e. Christians,) as well as the Jews.
25. HAVE TOLD,] *lit.* 'said (it) to you before' *or* publicly.
26. SHALL,] *lit.* 'may say..may ye not go forth..secret (or hidden) chambers, may ye not believe it.'
27. EAST,] *lit.* 'uprisings (of the sun) and appeareth unto (its) places of going down, so shall be the presence of the Son of the Man.'
28. CARCASE,] *lit.* 'fallen thing may be;' that is, the Jewish people.
29. IMMEDIATELY,] *or* 'straightway with (not *after*)..from the heaven..heavens shall be moved like the sea.'
30. THE SON,] of 'the Man in the heavens, —and then shall all tribes of the land smite (the breast), and they shall see the Son of the Man coming upon the clouds of the heavens, with power and much glory,' to vindicate his word, and save his people.
31. SEND,] *lit.* 'send away his messengers, with a trumpet's great voice, and they shall bring fully together his elect (*or* select ones) from the four winds, from (the) extremities of (the) heavens unto their extremities.'
32. NOW,] *lit.* 'but from the fig-tree learn ye the simile..may become tender (*lit.* 'touchy'), and may put forth the leaves, ye know (*or* know ye) that the reaping is nigh.'
33. SHALL,] *lit.* 'may see..know (*or* ye know) that it is nigh,—upon the doors.'
34. SHALL,] *lit.* 'may not go by..may happen.'
35. HEAVEN,] *lit.* 'the heaven and the earth.'
36. KNOWETH,] *lit.* 'no one hath known, not even the messengers of the heavens,' nor 'the Son,' being, as such, a servant, see Mark 13. 32.
37. COMING,] *or* 'presence,' *lit.* 'being long-side.'
38. FLOOD,] *lit.* 'washing down . . and marrying out.'
40. TWO,] i.e. 'two men..be taken away (by the Romans,) and the one shall be let alone,' none touching him.
41. AT,] *lit.* 'in (with) the mill, one shall be taken away, and one shall be let alone.
42. WATCH,] *lit.* 'be awake..ye have not known.'
43. KNOW,] *or* 'ye know this, that if the house-despot had known in which watch (of the night) the thief cometh, he would have been awake,..to be broken through.'
44. THEREFORE,] *lit.* 'because of this become ye also ready,' or prepared.
45. A FAITHFUL,] *lit.* 'the stedfast and mindful servant, whom his lord did set down over his service, to give to them the nourishment in season.'
46. BLESSED,] *lit.* 'happy' is that servant.
47. HIS GOODS,] *lit.* 'over all the things he has under him he setteth him down,' as steward.
48. SHALL,] *lit.* 'may say..delayeth to come.'
49. SHALL,] *lit.* 'may begin to beat.'
50. LOOKETH,] *lit.* 'thinketh not of him.. that he knoweth not of.'
51. CUT HIM ASUNDER,] rather 'cut him off fully (from being in his service), and shall set his part (or portion) with the hypocrites (i.e. those judging or acting under pretences); there shall be the weeping and the gnashing of the teeth,' as in 8. 12; 25. 30.

Chapter XXV. may be divided into three parts; v. 1—13 simile of the ten virgins; v. 13—30 of the talents; v. 31—46 of a day of judgment.
1. THEN,] that is, when the things mentioned in the preceding chapter are taking place among the unbelieving Jews in Palestine, the rule of the reign of the heavens shall be exercised on the believing ones in a manner similar to the way in which ten virgins were treated by the bridegroom they professed to honour.
TEN,] i.e. a perfect number.
VIRGINS,] male or female, *lit.* those 'set *or* put beyond' reach.
LAMPS,] *or* torches, as customary at night.
BRIDEGROOM,] *lit.* one having a 'new appearance.'

2. FIVE,] that is, the half, but the proportion is not to be taken strictly, in interpreting the simile.

WISE,] *lit.* 'mindful (*or* thoughtful).. foolish,' or rebellious, as in v. 3, 8; 5. 22, &c.

3. THEIR,] *lit.* 'their own lamps..with themselves.'

5. TARRIED,] *lit.* 'made (i.e. used) time, they all nodded and were sleeping fast.'

6. CRY MADE,] *lit.* a 'cry came.'

7. TRIMMED,] *or* 'adorned.'

8. ARE GONE OUT,] *lit.* 'are going out.'

9. SAYING,] 'Lest at any time there may not be sufficient to us and you, go ye on rather to those turning over (*or* using it), and make market for yourselves.'

10. WENT,] *lit.* 'went away to make market ..to the marriage feasts.'

11. AFTERWARD,] *lit.* 'at last come also.. Sir, Sir, open up to us.'

12. I KNOW,] *lit.* 'I have not known you.'

13. WATCH,] *lit.* 'be awake;' as in 24. 42.

KNOW,] *lit.* 'have not known.'

14. FOR,] the 'Son of the Man is as a man, going from (his own) people, who called his own servants, and gave over to them the things he had under him.'

15. SEVERAL ABILITY,] *lit.* 'his own power ..went away from (his own) people.'

16. TRADED,] *lit.* 'worked *or* wrought in (with, by) them, and made (i.e. gained) other five talents.'

17. TWO,] *lit.* 'the two.'

18. ONE,] *lit.* 'the one..hid away *or* thoroughly.'

19. AFTER A LONG TIME,] *lit.* 'with much time..and lifteth up with them a word,' i.e. reckoning.

20. FIVE,] *lit.* 'the five talents came forward and brought forward other five..thou didst give over unto me..I did gain upon them.'

21. WELL DONE,] *lit.* 'well! good and stedfast servant, thou wast stedfast,..I will set thee down over.'

22. TWO,] *lit.* 'the two..came forward.. thou didst give over..I did gain upon them.'

23. WELL DONE,] *lit.* 'well! good and stedfast servant, thou was stedfast..I will set thee down over.'

24. HAD,] *lit.* 'who has received..came forward.'

HARD,] *lit.* 'dried-up man, reaping where thou didst not sow, and bringing together where thou didst not scatter fully.'

25. I WENT,] *lit.* 'I went away.'

26. WICKED,] *lit.* 'evil..thou knowest;' this language does not admit the correctness of the charge, but, takes the servant *on his own ground*, and proceeds to show his folly in not acting according to his *belief*.

27. TO HAVE PUT,] *lit.* 'to cast my money (*lit.* silver) to the tables (of the bankers), and having come I myself had taken care of my own with fruit,' or increase.

28. TAKE,] *lit.* 'take *or* lift up therefore.'

29. THAT HATH,] The one who hid his talent might be said to have none, as it produced no fruit.

ABUNDANCE,] *lit.* 'over-abundance.'

30. UNPROFITABLE,] *or* 'useless servant into the outer darkness..and the gnashing of the teeth.'

31. OF MAN,] *lit.* 'Son of the Man may come..a throne of his glory.'

32. ALL NATIONS,] *lit.* 'all the nations (or peoples of Israel, as in Acts 4. 25, 26, 27,) and he shall mark-them-out-fully one from another, even as the shepherd marketh-out-fully the sheep from the goats.'

34. BLESSED,] *lit.* 'well-spoken of by my Father, receive by lot the reign prepared for you from the foundation (*lit.* laying-down) of the world,' *lit.* order or arrangement of things, whether moral or physical.

35. MEAT,] *lit.* 'to eat..made me drink.. ye led me with (yourselves).'

36. NAKED,] *or* 'exposed, and ye cast around me; infirm, and ye looked over *or* after me; in watch (or ward) I was, and ye came unto me.'

37. FED,] *or* 'nourished..caused to drink?

38. TOOK IN,] *or* 'led with (ourselves); or exposed, and cast (anything) around thee?'

39. SICK,] *or* 'infirm, or in guard (or ward).'

41. DEPART,] *lit.* 'go on from me, ye execrated ones! into the fire, the age-during one, which was prepared *or* made ready for the Devil (*lit.* thruster through), and his messengers,' i.e. those men who do his bidding.

42. MEAT,] *lit.* 'not to eat..did not make me drink.'

43. TOOK IN,] *or* 'led with (yourselves); exposed, and ye put not around me; infirm, and in ward, and ye looked not over me.'

44. NAKED,] *or* 'exposed, or infirm, or in ward, and did not act-as-deacons to thee?'

46. PUNISHMENT,] or 'restraint (mutilation, pruning) age-during, but the righteous (just or right ones) to life age-during.'

Chapter XXVI. may be divided into twelve parts; v. 1, 2 coming of the passover; v. 3—5 plot of the chief priests; v. 6—13 Jesus anointed by a woman; v. 14—16 Judas plots against him; v. 17—25 Jesus reveals the betrayer; v. 26—29 institutes the Lord's supper; v. 30—35 foretells Peter's denial; v. 36—46 Jesus in Gethsemane; v. 47—50 is betrayed and seized; v. 51—58 Jesus heals, reasons, and is forsaken; v. 59—67 Jesus before the Chief Priest; v. 68—75 Peter denies him.

1. HAD FINISHED,] *lit.* 'ended all these words.'

2. YE KNOW,] *lit.* 'ye have known that with two days the passover happeneth, and the Son of the Man is given over to be crucified.'

3. ASSEMBLED,] *lit.* 'were brought together the head-priests, and the writers, and the elders (*lit.* presbyters) of the people, into the court of the head-priest.'

4. CONSULTED,] *lit.* 'took counsel together ..seize..kill (him) thoroughly.'

5. ON,] *lit.* 'in (i.e. during) the feast..lest there happen a bawling among (in *or* by) the people.'

7. THERE CAME,] *lit.* 'came forward..of

oil very precious (*or* greatly prized), and poured it down thoroughly (*or* utterly) upon his head, as he is lying back.'

8. INDIGNATION,] *lit.* 'were much displeased..for what is this loss?'

9. OINTMENT,] *or* 'oil was able to have been sold (*lit.* carried over) for much, and to be given to the poor.'

10. UNDERSTOOD,] *lit.* 'having known.. why hold ye forth trouble (*lit.* labour *or* strokes) to the woman; for a good work she wrought in reference to me.'

11. YOU,] *lit.* 'with yourselves.'

12. POURED,] *lit.* 'cast this oil.'

15. WILL,] *lit.* 'do ye wish to give me.. and I will give him over to you? and they set to him (the sum of) thirty silverlings.'

16. THAT TIME,] *lit.* 'then he was seeking (*or* desiring) a good time that he might give him over.'

17. UNLEAVENED BREAD,] or 'loaves, the disciples came forward..where dost thou wish.'

18. GO,] *lit.* 'go away..to such an one.. the Teacher saith, My time is nigh, I make the passover near thee.'

19. HAD APPOINTED,] *lit.* 'arranged together for them.'

20. SAT,] *lit.* 'lay back.'

21. BETRAY,] *lit.* 'give me over.'

22. SORROWFUL,] or 'grieved, and began each.'

23. DIPPETH,] *lit.* 'dipped..give me over.'

24. GOETH,] *lit.* 'goeth away (*or* under) as it has been written..is given over.'

25. BETRAYED,] *lit.* 'gave him over.. Rabbi.'

26. BREAD,] *lit.* 'the loaf, and having spoken well (of God,) *or* given thanks, he brake, and was giving.'

THIS IS,] i.e. this *represents* my body. So the substantive verb is used in v. 28; 1 Cor. 10. 4; Gal. 4. 24; Ge. 40. 12; 41. 26; Da. 7. 23.

27. THE CUP.] Some MSS. read 'a cup.'

28. TESTAMENT,] *or* 'covenant (*lit.* 'fully appointed' thing) which for many is being poured forth with a view to a letting go of sins,' or 'missings' of the mark.

29. WILL,] *lit.* 'may not drink..produce of the vine..I may drink it with you new (i.e. 'in a new manner') in the reign of my Father,' i.e. when he has raised me from the dead.

30. SUNG,] *lit.* 'hymned a hymn, (perhaps Ps. 113—118)..hill of the olives.'

31. OFFENDED,] *lit.* 'stumbled in (by) me in this night, for it has been written,.. thoroughly scattered.' This is not a prophecy, but an application to Christ, in a proverbial manner, of the necessary result of the death of a shepherd, viz. the dispersion of the flock; so Christ's seizure caused his to flee away. The shepherd in Zec. 13. 7 was '*evil*,' not 'good.'

32. AFTER,] *or* 'with my being raised, I will lead you forward into the (circuits of) Galil.'

33. THOUGH,] *lit.* 'if even all shall be stumbled in thee, I at no time will be stumbled.'

34. THAT THIS NIGHT,] *lit.* 'that in this night, before (the time of) cock-crowing, thrice shalt thou deny (*or* curse) me utterly.'

35. SAID,] *lit.* 'saith unto him, Even if it may be necessary for me to die utterly with thee, I will not deny (*or* curse) thee utterly.'

36. PLACE,] or 'space, named Gethsemane, (i.e. 'press of fatness,')..I go away and pour forth before (God) yonder.'

37. TOOK,] *lit.* 'took along with him.'

38. EXCEEDING SORROWFUL,] *or* 'sorrowful about it..and be wakeful with me.'

39. FARTHER,] or 'forward..poured forth before (God)..not as I wish, but as thou.'

40. UNTO,] *lit.* 'towards..fast asleep..so! ye had not strength to be wakeful with me one hour?'

41. WATCH,] *lit.* 'be wakeful, and pour forth before (God), that ye may not enter into trial; the spirit, indeed, is forward, but the flesh infirm.'

42. THE,] *lit.* 'a second time..thy will (*or* wish) happen,' or come to pass.

43. ASLEEP,] *lit.* 'sleeping fast.. were weighed down.'

44. LEFT,] *lit.* 'let them alone,..a third time..the same word.'

45. TO,] *lit.* 'towards..sleep fast henceforth, and rest thoroughly,..has come nigh, ..is given over.'

46. RISE,] *or* 'awake!..he has come nigh who is giving me over.'

47. MULTITUDE,] *lit.* 'crowd.. and sticks.. presbyters of the people.'

48. BETRAYED,] *lit.* 'he who is giving him over,.. I shall show love,.. seize him.'

49. CAME,] *lit.* 'came forward.. Rejoice! Rabbi, and shewed him much love,' probably by kissing him.

50. FRIEND,] *lit.* 'comrade, upon what (design) art thou present?..came they forward, and cast their hand over upon Jesus, and seized him.'

51. DREW,] *lit.* 'drew out.. the servant.. and took away his ear.'

52. SAID,] *lit.* 'saith.. turn away thy sword .. with (by) a sword.'

53. PRAY,] *lit.* 'call upon *or* near.. station near me.. of messengers.'

54. THE SCRIPTURES,] *or* 'writings be filled out, that thus it behoveth to happen?'

55. HOUR,] *lit.* 'in that hour.. crowds, As against a robber ye came forth with swords and sticks to take me at once! I was sitting .. seized me not.'

56. WAS DONE,] *or* 'happened,' *or* came to pass.

FORSOOK,] *lit.* 'let him go.'

57. HAD LAID HOLD,] *lit.* 'seized.'

ASSEMBLED,] *lit.* 'brought together.'

58. FOLLOWED,] *lit.* 'was following.. priest's court.. in within.. the under servants.'

59. ELDERS,] *lit.* 'the presbyters, and the whole sanhedrim, were seeking false-witness (*or* testimony) against Jesus, so as to put him to death.'

60. CAME,] *lit.* 'came forward.. came forward.'

61. FELLOW,] *lit.* 'this one said, I am able to loose down the habitation of God, and through three days to build-it-up-as-a-house.'

63. HELD HIS PEACE,] *lit.* 'was silent.'
ADJURE,] *lit.* 'adjure thee openly.. that thou mayest say to us, if thou art the Christ, the Son of the (true) God.' See 16. 16, &c.
64. HEREAFTER,] *or* 'henceforth (*lit.* from now) ye shall behold the Son of the Man, sitting at the right hand of the power (of God,) and coming upon the clouds of the heavens;' as in Acts 7. 35; Ps. 110. 1, &c.
65. RENT,] *lit.* 'rent thoroughly.. saying, that he spake injuriously (against God),.. now ye heard his injurious-speech.'
66. GUILTY,] *lit.* 'he is held-in by death.'
67. SPIT,] *lit.* 'spit fully into his face, and smote-with-the-fist, and others slapped with the palm of the hand.'
68. PROPHECY,] *or* 'say publicly to us.'
69. SAT,] *lit.* 'was sitting in the court, and there came forward to him a certain little girl,' *or* maid-servant.
70. DENIED.] See note on 10. 33, &c.
I KNOW,] *lit.* 'I have not known;' so in v. 72, 74.
71. PORCH,] *or* 'gateway.. and says to those there, This one also.'
73. CAME,] *lit.* 'came forward.. truly.. for even thy speaking maketh thee manifest.'
74. CURSE,] *lit.* 'anathematize thoroughly.'
IMMEDIATELY,] *lit.* 'straightway a cock crew.'
75. WORD,] *lit.* 'saying.. that before (the time of) cock-crowing.. went out without.'

Chapter XXVII. may be divided into seven parts; v. 1, 2 Jesus delivered to Pilate; v. 3—10 conduct of Judas and the priests; v. 11—26 Jesus before Pilate; v. 27—49 Jesus crucified; 50—56 the saints, centurion, and the women; v. 57—61 Jesus' burial; v. 62—66 sealing of the sepulchre.
1. TOOK COUNSEL,] *lit.* 'took counsel together against Jesus, so as to put him to death.'
2. DELIVERED,] *lit.* 'gave him over.. leader.'
3. BETRAYED,] *lit.* 'gave him up.. condemned (*lit.* judged down), was concerned afterwards (*or* at it), and turned back the thirty silverlings,..and the presbyters.'
4. HAVE SINNED,] *lit.* 'did sin, giving over innocent blood.. thou shalt see!'
5. PIECES OF SILVER,] *lit.* 'silverlings in the habitation (of God), and withdrew, and went away and thoroughly strangled himself.'
6. SILVER PIECES,] *lit.* 'silverlings.. to cast them into the place of Korbans (i.e. things 'brought near' to God), since it is a price of blood.'
7. TOOK COUNSEL,] *lit.* 'took counsel together, and bought out of them the field of the potter, for a burying-place to the strangers.'
8. THE FIELD,] *lit.* 'Field of Blood.'
9. FULFILLED,] *or* 'filled out, *or* realized.. through Jeremiah (*or* Zechariah 12. 13).. thirty silverlings, the price of him who has been priced,..did price.'
10. APPOINTED,] *lit.* 'arranged with me.'
11. GOVERNOR,] *lit.* 'leader.'
12. ACCUSED,] *lit.* 'publicly spoken against by.'

13. SAID,] *lit.* 'saith.'
14. A WORD,] *lit.* 'one saying *or* thing.'
15. THAT FEAST] *lit.* 'every feast the Leader had been accustomed to loose entirely one to the crowd a prisoner, whom they wished.'
16. NOTABLE,] *lit.* 'very noted.'
BARABBAS,] i.e. 'son of the father.'
17. GATHERED,] *or* 'come together..do ye wish that I loose thoroughly to you?'
18. KNEW,] *lit.* 'had known that through envy they had given him over.'
19. WAS SET DOWN,] *lit.* 'is sitting on the high place (of judgment), his wife sent away unto him, saying, Nothing is to thee and to that just (right *or* righteous) man; for I suffered.'
20. MULTITUDE,] *lit.* 'crowds that they might ask for themselves Barabbas.'
21. GOVERNOR,] *lit.* 'leader..do ye wish.'
23. GOVERNOR,] *lit.* 'leader..were crying out.'
24. HE COULD PREVAIL,] *lit.* 'that it profiteth nothing..a tumult happens,..washed thoroughly.. over-against the crowd.. ye shall see.'
25. BLOOD BE,] or rather, 'his blood is upon us.'
26. RELEASED,] *or* 'loosed entirely..he gave him over, that he might be crucified.'
27. GOVERNOR,] *lit.* 'leader took along with them Jesus into the Praetorium, brought together against him all the band.'
28. STRIPPED,] *lit.* 'unclothed him, and put around him a crimson cloak,' *lit.* a thing that 'warms' one.
29. OF,] *lit.* 'out of thorns *or* briers.'
IN,] *lit.* 'on his right' arm or shoulder.
MOCKED,] *lit.* 'were treating him as a child.'
HAIL,] *or* 'Rejoice, O King of the Jews.'
30. SPIT UPON,] *or* 'at him..were smiting on his head.'
31. AFTER,] *lit.* 'when they (had) treated him as a child, they unclothed him of the cloak, and clothed him in his own garments.'
32. COMPELLED,] *lit.* 'impressed in order that.'
34. WOULD,] *lit.* 'did not wish to drink.'
35. DIVIDED,] *lit.* 'parted thoroughly.. casting a lot, that it might be fulfilled, (*or* exemplified, as in Luke 22. 16) that was spoken by (*lit.* under) the prophet (David, Ps. 22. 18): They parted thoroughly.'
36. WATCHED,] *lit.* 'were watching him.'
37. ACCUSATION,] *lit.* 'cause' of death.
THIS IS, &c.] Mark omits 'this is,' he and Matthew referring probably to the *Hebrew* inscription; Luke omits the name 'Jesus,' following the *Greek*, while John may have copied the *Latin*, 'Jesus the Nazarene, the king of the Jews.'
38. WERE,] *lit.* 'there are then two robbers.'
39. THAT PASSED BY,] *lit.* 'those going along were speaking injuriously of him.'
40. DESTROYEST,] *lit.* 'looser down of the habitation (of God), and in three days the builder up (of it) as a house, save thyself, if son thou art of the (true) God.'
41. MOCKING,] *lit.* 'treating (him) as a child.'

42. IF HE BE THE,] *lit.* 'If king of Israel.'
43. IN,] *lit.* 'upon the (true) God..if he wishes it, for he said that (i.e. thus): Son of God I am.'
44. THIEVES,] *lit.* 'robbers..were reproaching him.'
45. THERE WAS,] *lit.* 'happened *or* came.'
46. CRIED,] *lit.* 'cried out with a great voice..why didst thou leave me utterly?'
48. PUT,] *lit.* 'put it round.'
49. LET BE,] *or* 'leave alone..Elias comes.'
50. LOUD,] *lit.* 'great voice..let away the spirit.'
51. TEMPLE,] *lit.* 'habitation..from above to below..shake, and the rocks were rent.'
52. GRAVES,] *or* 'tombs were opened up.. the (lately) fallen-asleep saints were raised.'
53. GRAVES,] *or* 'tombs after (or with) his up-rising..and were fully manifest to many,' who knew them when alive.
54. EARTHQUAKE,] *lit.* 'shaking and the things that happened..Truly this was God's Son,' that is, as Luke has it, 'Really this man was a righteous *or* just one;' see 23. 47.
55. MINISTERING,] *lit.* 'acting-as-deacons to him.'
56. MARY MAGDALENE,] *lit.* 'Mary the Magdalene,' a native of Magdala; see 15. 29.
MARY,] undoubtedly the mother of *Jesus* himself, who was also 'mother of James and Joses;' see Mat. 13. 55, &c.
MOTHER,] whose name was Salome.
57. OF,] *lit.* 'from Arimathea..was discipled (*or* taught in reference) to Jesus.'
58. WENT,] *lit.* 'went forward..asked for himself..to be given away.'
59. WRAPPED,] *or* 'enveloped it in clean linen.'
60. HEWN OUT,] *or* 'cut out of stone in the rocky part, and rolled forward.'
61. AND THERE WAS,] *lit.* 'and there were there Mary the Magdalene.'
62. THE NEXT DAY,] *lit.* 'on the morrow,' that is after the preparation.
63. REMEMBER,] *lit.* 'we have remembered.'
I WILL RISE AGAIN,] *lit.* 'I will rise.'
64. THAT IT BE MADE SURE,] *lit.* 'to be unthrown down (*or* open) till the third day.. may steal..may say, He was raised..the last deceit.
65. YE HAVE,] *or* 'have ye..go away, let it be unthrown down as ye have known (best).'
66. AND SETTING,] *lit.* 'with *or* after the watch.'

Chapter XXVIII. may be divided into four parts; v. 1—8 first announcement of the rising of Jesus; v. 9, 10 Jesus himself appears; v. 11—15 conduct of the watch and the chief priests; v. 16—20 Jesus appears to the 11 disciples in Galilee, and gives them a charge.

1. END,] *lit.* 'eve of the week (*lit.* sabbaths), at the shining-forth of the first of the week (*lit.* sabbaths), came Mary the Magdalene.. to view the sepulchre.'
2. THERE WAS,] *lit.* 'a great shaking happened, for a messenger of the Lord having come down out of heaven, having come forward, rolled away..and was sitting.'
3. COUNTENANCE,] *lit.* 'sight *or* appearance..his clothing.'
4. DEAD,] *lit.* 'as if dead.'
5. I KNOW,] *lit.* 'I have known.'
6. HE IS RISEN,] *lit.* 'he was raised.'
LAY,] *lit.* 'was lying.'
7. HE IS RISEN,] *lit.* 'he was raised.'
GOETH BEFORE,] *or* 'leadeth you forward.'
8. TO BRING,] *lit.* 'to tell (it) fully to his disciples.'
9. MET,] *lit.* 'was over-against them, saying, Rejoice! and they coming forward.'
10. SAID,] *lit.* 'saith..go away, tell fully.. in order that they might go away.'
11. GOING,] *lit.* 'going on, behold certain ..things that happened.'
12. ASSEMBLED,] *lit.* 'brought together with the presbyters, took counsel together, they gave sufficient silver.'
14. COME,] *lit.* 'may be heard by (*or* before) the leader..and keep you free from care.'
15. MONEY,] *lit.* 'silver..this word was spoken everywhere by Jews till this day.'
16. A,] *lit.* 'the mount,' but six MS. omit.
17. WORSHIPPED,] *lit.* 'kissed forward to him (the hand), but some wavered,' or were divided in mind.
18. CAME,] *lit.* 'came forward..all authority was given to me in heaven and upon earth.'
19. GO,] *lit.* 'having gone on (therefore), disciple ye all the nations, (by) baptizing them, with a regard to the name (or character) of the Father, and of the Son, and of the Holy Spirit,' and then by
20. TEACHING] them to keep all things, as many as I did command you, and behold, I am with you all the days, till the full end of the age,' when he 'may give over the reign to God, even the Father,..and then the Son also himself shall be subject to Him who did subject to him the all things, that God may be THE ALL IN ALL.' 1 Cor. 15. 24

MARK

THE WRITER of this Gospel is *generally* thought to be the same with the 'John whose surname was Mark,' (Acts 12. 12, 25), son of a certain woman called Mary, and cousin of Barnabas (Col. 4. 10), supposed to be the nameless 'young man' of Mark 14. 51, 52, and afterwards a convert of Peter (1 Pet. 5. 13), but this seems inconsistent with 2 Tim. 4. 11, where Paul speaks of him as having been and still likely to be useful to *him* as a deacon or ministering servant. Probably there were two of the same name. The style of this Evangelist is altogether that of an eye and ear-witness, and not a mere 'interpreter of Peter,' as most of the ancients have it. This gospel was probably written about A.D. 50, about ten years after that of Matthew, of which it seems practically an abridgement, but done with the view of bringing out, from personal observation, some peculiar traits of the character of Jesus —especially that of his being the diligent and unwearied '*servant* of God.'

Mark only mentions *three* special topics that are not found in the other gospels, viz., the parable of the sower (4. 26—29), the healing of a blind man (8. 22—26), and the salting with fire (9. 49, 50).

He only supplies *seven* passages which have nothing corresponding to them in Matthew, viz., 1. 21—28; 4. 21—25; 9. 38—41; 12. 41—44; 16. 12, 13; 16. 14—18; 16. 19, 20; all of which however are found in Luke.

The following chronological Harmony of Mark and Matthew is at once interesting and instructive.

Mark	1. 1—8,	see Mat.	3. 1—12, L. J.
,,	1. 9—11,	,,	3. 13—17, L. J.
,,	1. 12, 13,	,,	4. 1—11, L.
,,	1. 14; 6. 17,	,,	4. 12; 14. 3, L. J.
,,	1. 14. 15,	,,	4. 12, L. J.
,,	1. 16—20,	,,	4. 13—22. L.
,,	1. 21—28,	found only	Luke 4. 31—37.
,,	1. 29—34,	see Mat.	8. 14—17, L.
,,	1. 35—39,	,,	4. 23—25, L.
,,	1. 40—45,	,,	8. 1—4, L.
,,	4. 35—41,	,,	8. 18—27, L.
,,	5. 1—20,	,,	8. 28—34, L.
,,	5. 21—43,	,,	9. 18—26, L.
,,	2. 1—12,	,,	9. 1—8, L.
,,	2. 13—17,	,,	9. 9—13, L.
,,	2. 18—22,	,,	9. 14—17, L.
,,	2. 23—28,	,,	12. 1—8, L.
,,	3. 1—12,	,,	12. 9—21, L.
,,	3. 13—19,	,,	10 2—4, L.
,,	4. 1—20,	,,	13. 1—23, L.
,,	4. 21—25,	found only	Luke 8. 16—18.
,,	4. 26—29,	not found in any other Gospel.	
,,	4. 30—32,	see Mat.	13. 31, 32, L.
,,	4. 33, 34,	,,	13. 34, 35.
,,	3. 31—35,	,,	12. 46—50, L.
,,	6. 1—6,	,,	13. 53—58.
,,	6. 6,	,,	9. 35—8; 11. 1.
,,	6. 7—13,	,,	10. L.
,,	6. 14—16,	,,	14. 1, 2, L.
,,	6. 17—29,	,,	14. 3—12.
Mark	6. 30—44,	see Mat.	14. 13—21, L. J.
,,	6. 45—52,	,,	14. 22—33, J.
,,	6. 53—56,	,,	14. 34—36.
,,	7. 1—23,	,,	15. 1—20.
,,	7. 24—30,	,,	15. 21—28.
,,	7. 31—37,	,,	15. 29—31.
,,	8. 1—9,	,,	15. 32—30.
,,	8. 10—13,	,,	16. 1—4.
,,	8. 14—21,	,,	16. 5—12.
,,	8. 22—26,	not found in any other Gospel.	
,,	8. 27—29,	see Mat.	16. 13—19, L. J.
,,	8. 30—9. 1,	,,	16. 20—28, L.
,,	9. 2—10,	,,	17. 1—9, L.
,,	9. 11—13,	,,	17. 10—13.
,,	9. 14—29,	,,	17. 14—21, L.
,,	9. 30—32,	,,	17. 22, 23, L.
,,	9. 33—37,	,,	18. 1—5, L.
,,	9. 38—41,	found only	Luke 9. 49, 50.
,,	9. 42—48,	see Mat.	18. 6—9, L.
,,	9. 49, 50,	not found in any other Gospel.	
.,	3. 20—30,	see Mat.	12. 22—37, L.
,,	4. 30—32,	,	13. 31, 32, L.
,,	10. 1—12,	,,	19. 1—12.
,,	10. 13—16,	,,	19. 13—15, L.
,,	10. 17—27,	,,	19. 16—26, L.
,,	10. 28—31,	,,	19. 27—30, L.
,,	10. 32—34,	,,	20. 17—19, L.
,,	10. 35—45,	,,	20. 20—28, L.
,,	10. 46—52,	,,	20. 29—34, L.
,,	14. 3—9,	,,	26. 6—13, L. J.
,,	11. 1—10,	,,	21. 1—11, L. J.
,,	11. 15—18,	,,	21. 12—16, L. J.
,,	11. 11-14; 19-23,	,,	21. 17—22.
,,	11. 24—26,	,,	6. 14, 15.
,,	11. 27—33,	,,	21. 23—27, L.
,,	12. 1—12,	,,	21. 33—46, L.
,,	12. 13—17,	,,	22. 15—22, L.
,,	12. 18—27,	,,	22. 23—33, L.
,,	12. 28—34,	,,	22. 34—40.
,,	12. 35—37,	,,	22. 41—46, L.
,,	12. 38—40,	,,	23. 1—39, L.
,,	12. 41—44,	found only	Luke 21. 1—4.
,,	13. 1—37,	see Mat.	24. 1—51, L.
,,	14. 1, 2,	,,	26. 1—5, L.
,,	14. 10, 11,	,,	26. 14—16, L.
,,	14. 12—25,	,,	26. 17—29, L. J.
,	14. 26—31,	,,	26. 30—35, L. J.
,,	14. 32—42,	,,	26. 36—46, L. J.
,,	14. 43—52,	,,	26. 47—56, L. J.
,,	14. 53, 54, 66-72,	,,	26. 57, 58, 69-75, L. J.
,,	14. 55—65,	,,	26. 59—68, L.
,,	15. 1—5,	,,	27. 1, 2, 11-14, L. J.
,,	15. 6—15,	,,	27. 15—26, L. J.
,,	15. 16—20,	,,	27. 27—31, L. J.
,,	15. 21—28,	,,	27. 32—38, L. J.
,,	15. 29—32,	,,	27. 39—44, L.
..	15. 37,	,,	27. 50, L. J.
,,	15. 33—38,	,,	27. 45—53, L.
,,	15. 39—41,	,,	27. 54—56, L.
,,	15. 42—47,	,,	27. 57—61, L. J.
,,	16. 1—11,	,,	28. 1—10, L. J.
,,	16. 12, 13,	found only	Luke 24. 13—35.
,,	16. 14—18,	,,	,, 36. 49 John 20. 19—29.
,,	16. 19, 20,	,,	24. 50—53

LUKE

THE GOSPEL OF LUKE was probably written about A.D. 60, by one whom all antiquity attests to have been 'the beloved physician' and companion of Paul, referred to in Col. 4. 14; 2 Tim. 4. 11; Philemon 24. He was probably a Gentile (Col. 4. 11—14), and may have been one of the 70 disciples; he writes to a Gentile, and for Gentiles, and, in the purest Greek of the New Testament, views the Saviour as THE SON OF MAN, 'the glad-tidings of great joy that shall be to all people.' He is quoted by Justin Martyr, A.D. 140.

References to the Old Testament are found in 1. 17; 2. 23, 24; 3. 4, 5, 6; 4. 4, 8, 10, 11, 12, 18; 7. 27; 8. 10; 10. 27; 18. 20; 19. 46; 20. 17, 28, 42, 43; 22. 37; 23. 46, &c.

Incidents not found in any other Gospel are mentioned in 1. 1—80; 2. 8—38, 40—52; 4. 16—30; 7. 11—17, 36—50; 8. 1—3; 9. 52—56; 10. 1—42; 12. 32—59; 13. 1—17, 22—33; 14. 1—14; 15. 16. 17. 11—37; 18. 1—14; 19. 1—10; 22. 24—30; 23. 4—11.

The work may be divided into seven parts, viz:—

I. History of the birth and early history of John and Jesus, ch. i. ii.

II. Ministry of John and commencement of Jesus' work, ch iii—iv 13.

III. Christ in Galilee till the Call of Levi, ch. iv. 14—v. 39.

IV. Choosing of 12 Apostles, till their return from first Mission, ch. vi. 1—ix. 17.

V. Foretelling of his own death till his entrance into Jerusalem, ch. ix. 18—xix. 28.

VI. Entry into Jerusalem till his burial, ch. xix, 29—xxiii. 56.

VII. His resurrection and ascension, ch. xxiv. 1—53.

Chapter I. may be divided into seven parts; v. 1—4 preface; v. 5—25 Gabriel's message to Zechariah and its realization; v. 26—38 his message to Mary the Virgin; v. 39—45 her visit to Elizabeth; v. 46—56 Mary's song; v. 57—66 birth, and naming of John; v. 67—80 Zechariah's song.

1. FORASMUCH AS,] *lit.* 'since truly many took in hand to set up (*or* thoroughly) a declaration (*lit.* leading through) of the things fully borne through among (*or* by) us.'

2. DELIVERED,] *lit.* 'gave over to us, who from the beginning became themselves beholders, and under-rowers, of the Word (i.e. Christ), it seemed proper also to me, having followed along with the first (*lit.* from above) all things accurately, in thorough order (*or* succession) to write to thee, most powerful Theophilus.'

4. THAT] 'thou mightest know fully concerning the un-thrown-downness of the words (*or* things) in which thou wast instructed,' *lit.* 'sounded thoroughly.'

5. COURSE,] *lit.* 'open days of Abia.'

6. RIGHTEOUS,] *or* 'just;' relatively so, like Noah, &c.

ORDINANCES,] *lit.* 'righteous acts . . spotless.

7. WELL STRICKEN,] *lit.* 'gone forward or advanced.'

8. CAME TO PASS,] *or* 'happened.'

9. TEMPLE,] *lit.* 'habitation.'

10. MULTITUDE,] *lit.* 'fulness..pouring forth before (God)..of the perfume.'

13. PRAYER,] *lit.* 'supplication is hearkened to.'

14. GLADNESS,] *lit.* 'leaping..over his birth.'

15. SHALL,] *lit.* 'may drink..sweet drink, and of the Holy Spirit he shall be full.'

16. CHILDREN,] *lit.* 'sons..shall he turn over upon.'

17. GO,] *lit.* 'go forward before him in (*or* with the) spirit and power of Elijah, to turn over (the) hearts of fathers upon (i.e. in addition to the hearts of) children, and the unstedfast in the thoughtfulness of (the) just, to make ready to the Lord a people fully prepared.'

18. WHEREBY,] *lit.* 'according to what.. is gone forward in her days?'

19. GABRIEL,] i.e. 'man (*or* power) of God;' see Dan. 8. 16.

STAND IN,] *lit.* 'stand near before the (true) God, and I was sent away to speak unto thee, and to tell as good-news these things to thee.'

20. DUMB,] *lit.* 'silent..shall happen.. didst not remain stedfast to my words.'

21. WAITED,] *lit.* 'was waiting..wondering during his occupying time in the habitation (of God).'

22. PERCEIVED,] *lit.* 'knew fully (*or* by it) that,..habitation, and he was nodding fully to them, and remained entirely dumb.'

23. AS SOON AS,] *lit.* 'as..his public works were fulfilled.'

24. AFTER,] *or* 'with these days his wife Elizabeth received (seed) fully, and hid herself for it five months.'

25. DEALT WITH,] *lit.* 'done to me.'

AMONG,] *lit.* 'in (*or* by) men.'

26. SIXTH MONTH,] after John's conception, was 'the messenger Gabriel sent away by (*lit.* under) God.'

27. VIRGIN,] *lit.* 'one put beyond' reach.

ESPOUSED,] *or* 'betrothed.'

28. HAIL,] *or* 'Rejoice, favoured one.. well spoken of art thou among (*or* by) women.'

29. TROUBLED,] *lit.* 'greatly troubled at (*lit.* upon) his word, and was reasoning of what kind this salutation (*lit.* drawing very near) might be.'

30. MARY,] *lit.* 'Miriam;' as in v. 34, 38.

WITH,] *or* 'near *or* along-side of God.'

31. CONCEIVE,] *lit.* 'receive fully in (the womb.'

32. THE SON,] *lit.* 'Son of the Highest.'

FATHER,] that is ancestor; as in Mat. 1. 1

33. FOR EVER,] *lit.* 'to the ages.'
NO END,] till he has accomplished the designs of the mediatorial kingdom, when he was to cease to reign, as the Christ, the Son, the Servant; see 1 Cor. 15. 28.
34. I KNOW NOT,] as in Ge. 4. 1, 17, &c.
35. THE HOLY GHOST,] *lit.* 'holy spirit *or* influence (as in Mat. 1. 18) shall come over upon thee, and power of the Highest shall settle down over thee, because of which also the holy begotten thing shall be called Son of God.' The supernatural birth of the Divine Saviour—the Second Man, the Lord from heaven—was necessary for his re-occupying, as it were, the position lost by the first Man, as the head of humanity before God.
36. COUSIN,] *or* 'kinswoman,' *lit.* one of the same race or parentage.
CONCEIVED,] *lit.* 'received fully (in her womb).'
37. WITH *or* 'along-side of God.'
38. HANDMAID,] *lit.* 'servant..let it happen ..thy saying.'
39. AROSE,] *lit.* 'stood up..went on to the hill-country with speed,' to Hebron.
40. SALUTED,] *lit.* 'drew together Elizabeth.'
41. BABE,] *lit.* 'nourished-life.'
FILLED,] *or* 'full of holy spirit' from God
42. SPAKE OUT,] *lit.* 'sounded forth with a great voice, Well-spoken of hast thou been among (*lit.* in, by) women, and well-spoken of has been the fruit of thy womb;' as in 11. 27. This birth of Messiah had long been an object of intense longing among the daughters of Israel.
43. THAT,] i.e. 'so that..might come.'
44. SOUNDED,] *lit.* 'happened *or* came to.'
FOR JOY,] *lit.* 'in gladness *or* exultation.'
45. BLESSED,] *lit.* 'happy..that there shall be a completion to the things spoken to her.'
46. MY SOUL,] *lit.* 'breathing' powers.
47. HATH REJOICED,] *lit.* 'was leaping-for-joy upon (the) God my saviour.'
48. FOR,] *lit.* 'because he looked over upon the lowliness of his servant; for behold, from henceforth (*lit.* now) shall all the generations (of men) call me happy,' not 'blessed,' as in C.V.
49. HATH DONE,] *lit.* 'did to me great things.'
50. MERCY,] *lit.* 'kindness,' extended to the *unfortunate,* not 'mercy' to the *guilty.*
FROM,] *lit.* 'to generations of generations.'
51. HATH SHEWED,] *lit.* 'he made strength by (in) his arm; he scattered thoroughly those appearing high in (the) thorough-mind of their heart.'
52. HATH PUT,] *lit.* 'he lifted down mighty ones from thrones, and exalted lowly ones.'
53. HATH FILLED,] *lit.* 'he filled fully.'
54. HATH HELPED,] *lit.* 'received again.'
SERVANT,] *lit.* 'boy *or* lad,..remembering kindness.'
55. FOR EVER,] *lit.* 'to the age.'
57. FULL TIME,] *lit.* 'and to Elizabeth the time of her bringing forth was filled out, and she bare a son.'
58. COUSINS,] *lit.* 'kindred,' as in v. 61, &c.
HAD SHEWED,] *lit.* 'was making his kindness great with her, and they were rejoicing with her.'
59. ON,] *lit.* 'in the eighth day..circumcise (*lit.* cut around) the boy *or* lad, and they were calling him after (*lit.* 'upon') the name of his father, Zechariah.'
61. OF,] *lit.* 'in *or* among thy kindred.'
62. MADE SIGNS,] *lit.* 'were nodding (*or* waving)..what he would wish him to be called.'
63. WRITING TABLE,] *or* 'tablet.'
64. OPENED,] *lit.* 'opened again along with the matter, also his tongue, and he was speaking, eulogizing (i.e. speaking well of) God.'
65. DWELT ROUND,] *lit.* dwelling around them.'
SAYINGS,] *or* 'things were spoken fully of in all the hill-country Judea.'
66. HEARD,] *lit.* 'are hearing..put (them) in their heart, saying, What, then, shall this boy (*or* lad) be?'
67. FILLED,] *lit.* 'full of holy spirit, and prophesied (*or* spake openly,) saying.'
68. BLESSED,] *lit.* 'Well-spoken of (is) the Lord, the God of Israel, that he looked upon, and made a loosing to his people.'
69. HATH RAISED UP,] *lit.* 'and raised a horn..his servant (*lit.* lad, boy) David.'
70. BY,] *lit.* 'through the mouth of his holy ones, of his prophets from (the) age,' i.e. from of old.
71. THAT WE,] *lit.* 'salvation out of (the hand of) our enemies, and out of the hand of all of those hating us.'
72. PERFORM,] *lit.* 'to do kindness with our fathers, and to be mindful of his holy covenant' (*lit.* a thing 'set thoroughly up.')
73. THE,] *lit.* 'an oath.'
74. WOULD GRANT,] *lit.* 'to give to us. drawn[..fearlessly to tremble to him.'
76. CHILD,] *lit.* 'lad (*or* boy)..a prophet.. go on forward before.'
77. BY,] *lit.* 'in the letting go of their sins.'
78. THE TENDER MERCY,] *lit.* 'bowels of kindness of our God, in which the rising out of the high places looked upon us.'
79. TO GIVE LIGHT,] *or* 'shine over to those sitting in darkness and death-shade, to direct fully our feet into a way of peace.'
80. CHILD,] *lit.* 'lad (*or* boy) grew (in body) and was strengthened in spirit,..shewing forth (*or* thoroughly) toward the Israel' of God.

Chapter II. may be divided into seven parts; v. 1—7 cause of Jesus being born in Beth-Lehem; v. 8—14 revealed to shepherds: v. 15—20 their joy at it; v. 21—24 his circumcision and presentation at the temple; v. 25—35 Simeon's thanksgiving and prophecy; v. 36—39 Anna's thanks and work; v. 40—52 Jesus with the doctors in the temple.
1. IN THOSE DAYS,] when John was in the deserts, 'there came forth a decree (*lit.* dogma) from Caesar Augustus, (that) all the inhabited (land of Israel, as in 4. 5; 21. 26; Mat. 24. 14; Acts 11. 28, &c., is) to be fully written,' i.e. described, as to its soil, population, &c.

2. THIS TAXING,] *lit.* 'the full-writing itself first happened (i.e. took place, *or* was completed) when Cyrenius was Leader of Syria.'

3. WENT,] *lit.* 'were going on to be fully-written.'

4. LINEAGE,] *or* 'family, *or* paternal descent.'

5. TAXED,] *lit.* 'fully written..betrothed wife, being pregnant.'

6. SO,] *lit.* 'and it happened, in their being there, the days of her bearing were filled out.'

7. LAID,] *lit.* 'laid him up *or* back in the manger (*or* feeding-place) because there was not to them a place in the guest-chamber,' *lit.* place of 'loosing down' their baggage or clothes.

8. COUNTRY,] *lit.* 'space *or* quarter .. watching a watch of the night over their flock.'

9 THE,] *lit.* 'a messenger of the Lord stood over them, and a glory of the Lord shone around them, and they feared a great fear.'

10. I BRING,] *lit.* 'I tell to you good-news (of) great joy, which shall be to all the people.'

11. FOR,] *or* 'because there was born.'

12. SHALL BE,] *lit.* 'is the sign..a babe..a (or the) manger.'

13. SUDDENLY,] *or* 'unexpectedly there came..a fulness of a.'

14. GLORY TO.] The substantive verb must be understood; it is not a prayer, but the statement of a fact: 'Glory (is) to God in the highest (heavens), and on the land (is) peace, among men (is) good-thought *or* pleasure,' as the result of them both.

15. WERE GONE AWAY,] *lit.* 'went away.. into the heaven, the men, the shepherds also said to one another, We may go through truly unto.. has happened,.. Lord made known to us.'

16. WITH HASTE,] *lit.* 'hasting (*or* speeding on), and they found out both Miriam..the manger.'

17. MADE KNOWN ABROAD,] or 'made (it) thoroughly known about the saying that was spoken to them concerning this boy *or* lad.'

18. THAT HEARD,] *lit.* 'those hearing wondered concerning the things spoken by the shepherds to them.'

19. KEPT,] *lit.* 'was keeping together these sayings, and casting them together in her heart.'

20. FOR,] *lit.* 'upon all that they heard and saw, as it was spoken to them.'

21. OF,] *lit.* 'by the messenger before his being received fully in the womb.'

22. PURIFICATION,] *or* 'cleansing..filled out (Lev. 14. 2—6), they brought him up to ..station him along-side of the Lord.'

23. IT IS,] *lit.* 'it has been written..that every..opening fully a womb.'

24. OFFER,] *lit.* 'give a sacrifice (*lit.* a thing 'rushed upon,') according to that said.'

25. DEVOUT,] *lit.* 'taking well hold of (God),..and a holy spirit was upon him.'

26. REVEALED,] *lit.* 'divinely told to him by (*lit.* under) the Holy Spirit, not to see death, before he might see the Christ of the Lord.'

27. BY,] *lit.* 'in the spirit.. in the boy (*or* lad) Jesus.'

28. TOOK UP,] *or* 'received.. spake well of God.'

29. LETTEST THOU,] *lit.* 'dost thou loose away (*or* fully) thy servant in peace, O Despot (*lit.* one who 'binds the feet,' as in Acts 4. 24; 2 Pet. 2. 1; Jude 4; Rev. 6. 10; 1 Tim. 6. 1, 2; 2 Tim. 2. 21; Titus 2. 9; 1 Pet. 2. 18.) according to thy saying.'

30. FOR,] *or* 'because my eyes saw.'

31. BEFORE,] *lit.* 'according to the face of all the peoples.'

32. TO LIGHTEN,] *lit.* 'for an uncovering of nations.'

33. MARVELLED,] *or* 'were wondering over the things spoken concerning him.'

34. BLESSED,] *lit.* 'spake well to them.. laid for the fall and the standing up.'

35. SWORD,] *lit.* a thing 'turning-round.'

PIERCE,] *lit.* 'go through.'

THOUGHTS,] *lit.* 'reasonings.'

REVEALED,] *lit.* 'uncovered.'

36. PROPHETESS,] like Miriam, Deborah, Huldah, the four daughters of Philip, &c. and 1 Cor. 14. 3.

GREAT AGE,] *lit.* 'advanced in many days.'

37. WIDOW,] *lit.* 'deprived.'

DEPARTED,] *lit.* 'did not stand away from the temple, with fasts and supplications, trembling greatly, night and day.'

38. COMING IN,] *lit.* 'standing by that hour, was speaking the same thing over-against the Lord, and was speaking concerning him to all those receiving beforehand a loosing in Jerusalem.'

39. HAD PERFORMED,] *lit.* 'they ended.. they turned away into Galilee.'

40. CHILD,] *lit.* 'boy *or* lad increased (in stature), and was strengthened in spirit, full of wisdom.'

41. WENT,] *lit.* 'were going.'

42. HE WAS,] *or* 'he became..according to.'

43. FULFILLED,] *lit.* 'ended..the lad Jesus.

44. COMPANY,] *or* 'journeying party.'

SOUGHT,] *lit.* 'were seeking.'

46. SITTING,] *lit.* 'sitting down in the midst of the teachers.'

47. ASTONISHED,] *lit.* 'standing out.'

48. AMAZED,] *lit.* 'exceedingly struck.. Child, why didst thou thus to us?..were seeking thee.'

49. WIST,] *lit.* 'did ye not know that in the (things) of my Father it behoveth me to be?

50. UNDERSTOOD,] *lit.* 'bring together.'

51. SUBJECT,] *lit.* 'set under them..was keeping thoroughly.'

52. INCREASED,] *lit.* 'was striking forward in wisdom and station (*or* age, *lit.* greatness).'

Chapter III. may be divided into six parts; v. 1—6 John's baptism; v. 7—15 his warnings; v. 16—18 his testimony to Christ; v. 19, 20 his imprisonment; v. 21, 22 baptism of Jesus; v. 23—38 his birth-roll through (his mother's father) Heli.

1. FIFTEENTH YEAR,] viz. A.D. 30.
REIGN,] *lit.* 'leadership of .. leader of Judea.'
HEROD,] son of Herod the First.
TETRARCH,] *or* chief of a fourth part.
2. HIGH-PRIESTS,] the one being called the 'prince,' and the other the 'father' of the sanhedrim.
THE,] *lit.* 'a word (*or* matter, a burden, a thing 'lifted up') of God came upon John.'
3. COUNTRY,] *or* 'space around the Jordan, proclaiming-as-a-herald a baptism of a new mind with a view to a letting go of sins.'
4. IT IS,] *lit.* 'it has been written in a scroll.'
CRYING,] *lit.* 'lowing' as an ox.
PATHS,] *lit.* 'trodden ones.'
5. VALLEY,] *lit.* 'cleft place *or* gulf.'
HILL,] *lit.* 'ascent..shall become straightness.'
7. SAID,] *lit.* 'laid he it out to the crowds ..by (*lit. under*) him, Progeny (or offspring, brood) of vipers, who shewed to you secretly to flee from the anger that is about to be' upon the Jewish nation.
8. BRING FORTH,] *lit.* 'make, therefore, fruits worthy of the new mind (in v. 3),.. within (*lit.* in or among) yourselves, we have a father (even) Abraham,' whose merits are great before God.
9. AND NOW,] *or* 'already..not making good fruit is cut out (of the garden) and into fire is cast.'
10. PEOPLE,] *lit.* 'crowds asked at (or 'lifted up' questions upon) him.'
11. IMPART,] *lit.* 'give beyond,' i.e. out.
12. PUBLICANS,] *lit.* 'custom-house officers ..teacher.'
13. EXACT,] *or* 'do nothing more than that fully set to you.'
14. THE SOLDIERS,] *lit.* 'those warring asked at (*lit.* 'lifted up' questions upon) him, saying, And we—what shall we do?..ye may shake *or* move no one greatly, neither may ye be false accusers, .your wages,' *or* allowance, victuals.
15. WERE IN EXPECTATION,] *lit.* 'are looking *or* thinking towards John, and all are reasoning in their hearts concerning John, lest this may be the Christ,' i.e. the promised Messiah.
16. ANSWERED,] *lit.* 'John himself answered.'
ONE,] *lit.* 'but he cometh who is mightier.'
WORTH,] *lit.* 'sufficient *or* presentable.'
SHOES,] *or* 'sandals,' *lit.* 'things bound under.'
WITH,] in *or* 'by a holy spirit and fire.
17. GATHER,] *lit.* 'bring together..storehouse.'
CHAFF,] *lit.* an 'insecure' thing.
BURN,] *lit.* 'burn down with fire unquenched.'
18. EXHORTATION,] *or* 'calling upon' them.
PREACHED,] *lit.* 'proclaimed-as-good-news.'
19. REPROVED,] *or* 'convicted by him concerning..which Herod did.'
20. YET,] *lit.* 'also..and shut down.'
21. PRAYING,] *lit.* 'pouring forth towards (God), the heaven was opened thoroughly.'

22. GHOST,] *lit.* 'the Holy Spirit came down in (or with) a bodily appearance, as if a dove, upon him,..Thou art my Son—the dearly-beloved one! in thee I thought well (of all things);' as in Mat. 3. 17.
23. BEGAN,] *lit.* 'was as if thirty years (of age, in his) beginning (his ministry), being, as reckoned by law, son of Joseph, the (step-son) of Heli.' Comp. Mat. 1. 15.
24. SON.] The word '*son*' in genealogical lists, often means simply a '*descendant*,' either by birth or by law.
MATTHAT..LEVI.] These names are omitted by many ancient fathers, and were probably taken from v. 29.
31. MAINAN.] Omitted in Alexandrian MS.
36. CAINAN.] Not found in Ge. 10. 24; 11. 12; 1 Ch. 1. 18.

Chapter IV. may be divided into seven parts; v. 1—13 Jesus tempted; v. 14, 15 Jesus in Galilee; v. 16—27 Jesus in Nazareth teaching; v. 28—30 he is rejected there; v. 31—37 he teaches and cures a demoniac in Capernaum; v. 38—41 cures Peter's mother-in-law, and many others; v. 42—44 Jesus entreated to stay, but goes on.
1. THE,] *or* 'a holy spirit' or influence from God.
RETURNED,] *lit.* 'turned round under (it) from the Jordan, and was led in (*or* by) the Spirit into the desert.'
2. TEMPTED,] *lit.* 'tried *or* tested by (*lit.* under) the Devil,' *lit.* 'thruster through.'
ENDED,] *lit.* 'thoroughly ended, at last he hungered.'
3. THE SON,] *lit.* 'if Son thou art of the (true) God, speak to this stone in order that it may become bread.'
4. IT IS,] *lit.* 'it has been written, that. not upon bread alone (*or* only) shall the man live, but upon every saying of God.' De. 8. 3.
5. TAKING,] *lit.* 'leading him up.'
WORLD,] *lit.* 'inhabited place,' i.e. Palestine.
6. POWER,] *or* 'authority, *lit.* 'out-coming or out-being.'
FOR,] *or* 'that has been given over to me (by men), and to whomsoever I wish, I give it.'
7. WILT,] *lit.* 'mayest kiss forward (the hand) to me.'
8. GET THEE,] *lit.* 'get under behind me.'
SATAN,] *lit.* 'adversary;' see Mat 4. 10.
IT IS,] *lit.* 'it has been written, Thou shalt kiss (the hand) towards the Lord thy God, and to him alone shalt thou tremble greatly.' De. 6. 13; 10. 20.
9. BROUGHT,] *or* 'led..the little wing of the temple..If Son thou art of the (true) God.'
10. IT IS,] *lit.* 'it has been written, that His messengers he shall cause to rise fully for thee, to guard thee thoroughly.'
11. AND IN,] *lit.* 'and that upon (their) hands they shall lift thee, lest at any time thou mayest strike forward towards a stone thy foot.'
12. IT IS,] *lit.* 'it has been said, that, Thou shalt not try-beyond-measure the Lord thy God.' De. 6. 16.

13. ENDED,] *lit.* 'fully ended all (i.e. every) trial, he stood off from him for a season.'
14. RETURNED,] *lit.* 'turned round secretly in the power of the Spirit into the Galil,.. the surrounding space *or* place.'
15. TAUGHT,] *lit.* 'was teaching..by (*lit.* under) all' men, things, or circumstances.
16. ON,] *lit.* 'in (during) the day of the sabbaths..to read,' *lit.* 'know again *or* know fully' the word of God.
17. DELIVERED,] *lit.* 'given on to him a scroll of Isaias the prophet, and having folded back the scroll.'
18. HATH,] *lit.* 'did anoint (i.e. inaugurate) me, to tell fully good-things to poor ones, he hath sent me away to heal for myself the utterly-broken in the heart, to proclaim-as-a-herald to captives a letting go, and to blind ones a looking-up again, to send away bruised ones in (by *or* with) a letting go.'
19. PREACH,] *lit.* 'proclaim-as-a-herald an acceptable year of the Lord.'
20. CLOSED,] *lit.* 'folded the scroll, and gave (it) back to the under servant..were straining greatly towards him.'
21. THIS DAY,] *lit.* 'that, to-day has this writing been filled out (or realized) in your ears,' i.e. hearing.
22. BARE,] *lit.* 'were bearing testimony (i.e. acting as 'dividers' between truth and error) to him, and were wondering over the words of the grace which are passing forth out of his mouth, and they said, Is not this the son of Joseph?'
23. SURELY,] *lit.* 'always say (*or* lift up) to me this simile (*or* parallel), Healer, cherish (or attend) thyself, as many things as we heard happened in the Capernaum (i.e. village or covering of Nahum), do also here in thy father's place.'
24. VERILY,] *lit.* 'Amen..no one prophet is acceptable in his father's place.'
25. OF,] *lit.* 'over a truth, many widows (*or* bereaved ones)..shut fully for three..so that a great famine happened over all the land' of Israel.
27. IN THE TIME,] *lit.* 'upon Elisha.. cleansed.'
28. WHEN THEY HEARD,] *lit.* 'hearing.'
30. PASSING,] *lit.* 'going thoroughly through the midst of them, passed on.'
31. CAME DOWN,] *or* 'came thoroughly' to take up his abode; comp. Mat. 4. 13; apparently he never went back to Nazareth.
TAUGHT,] *lit.* 'was teaching,' i.e. 'giving *or* dividing' the word of truth.
32. ASTONISHED,] *lit.* 'greatly struck over his teaching, because..in (or with) authority.'
33. DEVIL,] *lit.* 'demon;' one of a class of beings whose bodies were anciently supposed to have been left unburied or unhonoured at death, and thus left, as it were, houseless, and reckoned accordingly 'unclean,' i.e. 'not lifted *or* taken down' to their place of rest.
LOUD,] *lit.* 'great voice.'
34. LET US ALONE,] *lit.* 'away! what to us and to thee (in common)? Jesus! Nazarene! thou art come to loose us away (*or* utterly); I have known thee who thou art,—the Holy (i.e. un-earthly) one of the (true) God.'

35. REBUKED,] *lit.* 'put a weight upon him,' Be silenced (*lit.* muzzled), and come forth out of him.'
36. WERE,] *lit.* 'and amazement came up on all, and they were speaking fully with one another, What is this word? because in authority and power he lays (it) upon the unclean spirits.'
37. FAME,] *lit.* 'and there was passing forth a noise concerning it (or him) to every place of the surrounding space' or country.
38. TAKEN,] *lit.* 'held fast..asked him about her.'
39. REBUKED,] *lit.* 'put a weight upon the fever, and it let her go, and along with the matter having stood up she was acting-as-a-deacon to them.'
40. SETTING,] *lit.* 'going in, all as many as had infirm ones with manifold unsoundnesses..cherished (*or* attended) them.'
41. DEVILS,] *lit.* 'demons..the Christ.. laying a weight upon them..him to be the Christ.'
42. PEOPLE.] *lit.* 'crowds were seeking after him,..were holding him back,' *lit.* down.
43. I MUST,] *lit.* 'to the other cities it behoveth me to tell fully good things also, because for this I have been sent away.'
44. PREACHED,] *lit.* 'was calling-as-a-herald.'

Chapter V. may be divided into five parts; v. 1—11 miraculous draught of fishes; v. 12—16 cleansing of a leper; v. 17—26 cure of a palsy; v. 27—32 call of Levi and his entertainment; v. 33—39 fasting and its season.
2. SHIPS,] *or* 'boats..mariners went away from them, and washed thoroughly the nets.'
3. SHIPS,] *or* 'boats..asked him to bring (it) back over from the land..was teaching the crowds.'
4. HAD LEFT,] *lit.* 'ceased speaking himself..bring (it) back over into the deep, and loose your nets for a catch (of fish).'
5. MASTER,] *lit.* 'one who stands over' anything.
TOILED,] *or* 'laboured..but upon thy saying I will loose the net.'
6. BRAKE,] *lit.* 'was being rent.'
7. BECKONED,] *lit.* 'beckoned down to those having (share) with them..and take along with them..so as to be sinking them.'
8. FELL DOWN,] *lit.* 'fell forward to the knees of Jesus.'
9. ASTONISHED,] *lit.* 'astonishment held him round about..taken together,' *or* at once.
10. PARTNERS,] *lit.* 'in common..from this time thou shalt catch men alive.'
11. BROUGHT,] *lit.* 'brought down their boats, they let go all, and followed him.'
12. CERTAIN,] *lit.* 'in one of the cities.. mayest wish.'
13. I WILL,] *or* 'I wish (it); be thou cleansed.'
14. CHARGED,] *lit.* 'told him fully at the same time,..bring forward..Moses set forth.'
15. WENT,] *lit.* 'was the word going abroad concerning him, and many crowds were coming together to hear, and to be

cherished (*or* attended) by him because of their infirmities.'

16. WITHDREW,] *lit.* 'was giving space, secretly in the deserts, and pouring forth before (God).'

17. CERTAIN,] *lit.* 'in one of the days.. teachers of law..village of Galilee..and there was a power of the Lord to heal them.'

18. BROUGHT,] *lit.* 'bearing upon a couch a man who was paralytic, and they were seeking.'

19. BY,] *lit.* 'through what..crowd, they went up upon the building.'

20. ARE,] *lit.* 'have been let go to thee.'

21. BLASPHEMIES,] *lit.* 'injurious words.'

FORGIVE,] *lit.* 'let go sins.'

PERCEIVED,] *lit.* 'knew fully their reasonings.'

23. EASIER,] *lit.* 'which is more laborious, ..have been let go to thee..Rise and be walking about?'

24. POWER,] *lit.* 'authority upon the earth to let sins go,..thy little couch, and pass on to thy house.'

25. IMMEDIATELY,] *lit.* 'along with the matter..he was lying.'

26. AMAZED,] *lit.* 'they all received an extasy (of joy),..we saw paradoxes (*lit.* things 'beyond an opinion') to-day.'

27. SAW,] *lit.* 'viewed for himself a custom-house-officer,..sitting over the custom-house ..Be following me.'

28. LEFT,] *lit.* 'left all at once,' or fully.

29. FEAST,] *lit.* 'reception..crowd of custom-house-officers..who were reclining with them.'

30. MURMURED,] *lit.* 'were murmuring at.'

31. PHYSICIAN,] *lit.* 'a healer, but those having ills.'

32. THE,] *lit.* 'righteous ones..to a new mind.'

33. MAKE,] *lit.* 'and supplications are made.'

34. CAN,] *or* 'ye are not able to make the sons.'

35. THE,] *lit.* 'but days..and whenever he may be lifted away from them.'

36. SPAKE,] *lit.* 'laid out also a parable (*or* parallel)..that no one casts over a patch of a new garment upon an old garment..and the patch that was from the new.'

37. BOTTLES,] made of skin in the east.

AND BE SPILLED,] *lit.* 'and itself be poured forth, and the bottles will be lost entirely.'

38. MUST,] *lit.* 'is to be put..kept together.'

39. DESIRETH,] *lit.* 'wisheth..is more useful.'

Chapter VI. may be divided into eight parts; v. 1—5 work of necessity on sabbath; v. 6—11 cure of a withered hand; v. 12—16 call of 12 apostles; v. 17—19 cure of many diseases; v. 20—26 blessings and woes: v. 27 —38 exhortations to kindness; v. 39—45 parable of the blind and the hypocrite; v. 46—49 the rocky and the sandy foundation.

1. ON,] *lit.* 'in a sabbath, a second-first, he is passing over through the sown places... were plucking..were eating.'

2. ON,] *lit.* 'in the sabbaths.'

3. READ,] *lit.* 'did ye not know fully even this.'

SHEW-BREAD,] *lit.* 'the loaves of the presence.'

5. THAT,] *or* 'because the son of the man is lord also of the sabbath;' therefore the disciples had a right to satisfy their hunger on it. Compare Mat. 12. 8; Mark 2. 28.

6. THERE WAS,] *lit.* 'there was there a man.'

WITHERED,] *or* 'dried up.'

7. WATCHED,] *lit.* 'were watching alongside of him, if he will cherish *or* attend (him) ..a public charge against him.'

8. KNEW,] *lit.* 'he himself had known their reasonings,..stand in.. and stood.'

9. ONE THING,] *lit.* 'a certain thing..or to loose entirely?'

10. WAS RESTORED,] *lit.* 'stood thoroughly forth.'

11. MADNESS,] *lit.* 'senselessness, and were speaking thoroughly to one another.'

12. TO A,] *lit.* 'to the mount to pour forth before (God), and he was passing all night in (the place of) the prayer of God.'

13. WAS,] *or* 'became day, he called forward..he laid out for himself.'

14. SIMON,] i.e. 'hearing;' Peter a 'rock;' Andrew, 'manly;' James, 'one who takes by the heel;' John, 'Jah is gracious;' Philip, a 'lover of horses;' Bartholomew, 'son of Tolmai.'

15. MATTHEW,] i.e. 'gift of Jah:' Thomas, a 'twin;' Alphaeus, 'chief;' Zelotes, a 'zealot.'

16. JUDAS,] i.e. 'praise, confession;' Iscariot, 'man of Carioth *or* of the city.'

WAS,] *lit.* 'became (the) giver over' to death.

17. IN,] *lit.* 'upon a level place, and a crowd of..the people.. from their unsoundnesses.'

18. VEXED,] *lit.* 'crowded by' *lit.* under.

19. MULTITUDE,] *lit.* 'and all the crowd was seeking to touch him, because power was going forth from him.'

20. BLESSED,] *lit.* 'happy the poor because.'

21. BLESSED,] *lit.* 'happy those hungering now.'

FILLED,] *or* 'fed, satisfied..shall be glad.'

22. SEPARATE,] *lit.* 'mark out fully' as with a border.

23. REJOICE,] *lit.* 'may ye rejoice and leap, .. for according to these things were their fathers doing.'

24. HAVE RECEIVED,] *or* 'hold off.'

25. FULL,] *lit.* 'filled in.. are glad now.'

26. SPEAK WELL OF YOU,] *or* 'speak you well.'

SO,] *lit.* 'according to these things were their fathers doing.'

27. LOVE,] *or* 'love-dearly.'

28. BLESS,] *or* 'speak well of those cursing you utterly, and pour forth before (God) for those accusing you falsely.'

29. OFFER,] *lit.* 'hold near also the other, and from him taking away the mantle, also the coat thou mayest not withhold.'

30. GIVE,] *lit.* 'be giving..be not asking back.'

31. WOULD,] *or* 'ye wish.'

32. FOR,] *lit.* 'and if..what grace..for the sinners.'

33. SINNERS,] *lit.* 'the sinners.'

34. LEND,] *or* 'give along side of whom ye hope to receive back, what grace..for the sinners..to receive back the same things.'

35. CHILDREN,] *lit.* 'sons.. kind (*or* helpful) over.'

36. BE,] *lit.* 'become ye pitiful..is pitiful.'

37. SHALL,] *lit.* 'may not be judged.'

CONDEMN,] *lit.* 'throw not down, and ye may not be thrown down; let go, and ye shall be let go.'

38. PRESSED DOWN,] as by 'the feet.'

METE,] *or* 'measure.'

39. PARABLE,] *or* 'parallel' saying.

CAN,] *lit.* 'is a blind man able to bring a blind man on the way.. into a deep place?'

40. THE,] *lit.* 'a learner is not above his teacher..perfected shall be as his teacher.'

41. MOTE,] *lit.* 'dry thing..mindest not fully.'

42. LET ME,] *lit.* 'let alone, I cast forth.'

SEE,] *lit.* 'behold thoroughly to cast forth.'

43. BRINGETH,] *lit.* 'is not making.'

44. EVERY,] *or* 'each tree.. thorns (*or* briers) they do not bring together..gather (*or* eat) a cluster-of-grapes.'

45. A,] *lit.* 'the good man..beareth forth ..beareth forth.. the overabundance.'

47. WHOSOEVER,] *lit.* 'every one who is coming..mywords..I will shew you secretly.'

48. BUILT,] *lit.* 'is building..digged and deepened, and laid a foundation upon the rock, and an overflow having come, the stream broke forward to that house, and had not strength to shake it,.. upon the rock.'

49. RUIN,] *or* 'breach of that house became great.'

Chapter VII. may be divided into six parts; v. 1—10 cure of a centurion's servant; v. 11—16 raising of widow's son; v. 17—23 Jesus' answer to John's enquiry; v. 24—28 he bears testimony to John; v. 29—35 character of that generation; v. 36—50 washing of Jesus' feet and its reward.

1. WHEN,] *or* 'after that he ended (*lit.* filled out) all his sayings in the ears.'

2. DEAR,] *lit.* 'very precious *or* weighty.'

WAS SICK,] *lit.* 'having ills, was about to die.'

3. SENT,] *lit.* 'sent away to him elders (*lit.* presbyters)..asking..save thoroughly.'

4. CAME,] *lit.* 'came near.. were calling upon him hastily, saying, that, he is worthy to whom thou shalt do this.'

5. HATH BUILT,] *lit.* 'he built us the synagogue,' from which they had come.

6. WENT,] *lit.* 'passed on..be not troubled.'

ROOF,] *lit.* 'covering.'

7. SAY,] *or* 'speak with a word, and my boy.'

8. SET.] *or* 'setting myself under authority,' i.e. showing myself obedient.

ME,] *lit.* 'under myself..to this one, Pass on, and he passes on; and to another, Be coming.'

9. PEOPLE,] *lit.* 'crowd.'

10. RETURNING,] *lit.* 'turning round secretly.'

SICK,] *lit.* 'infirm.'

11. THE DAY AFTER,] *lit.* 'in the succeeding (day), he was passing on..were passing on with him and a great crowd.'

12. ONLY,] *lit.* 'only-begotten son..she bereaved.. a great crowd.'

13. HE HAD COMPASSION,] *lit.* 'his bowels were moved over her.'

14. CAME,] *lit.* 'came forward..Be raised.

15. DELIVERED,] *lit.* 'gave.'

16. THERE CAME,] *lit.* 'and all received a fear.. has been raised among us, and that God looked over his people.'

17. RUMOUR,] *lit.* 'word.. space round about.'

18. SHEWED,] *lit.* 'told fully.'

19. CALLING,] *lit.* 'calling near a certain two.. he that is coming, *or* 'the Coming one,' a title of the Messiah.

20. COME,] *lit.* 'come near..John the Baptist sent us away unto thee.'

21. CURED,] *lit.* 'cherished many from (*or* because of) unsoundnesses, and scourges, and evil spirits, and to many blind he granted sight *or* seeing.'

22. GO,] *lit.* 'having passed on, tell ye fully to John what ye saw and heard, that blind ones behold again, lame ones walk about, lepers are cleansed (*or* lifted down thoroughly), deaf ones do hear, dead ones are raised, poor ones are told good-news fully.'

23. BLESSED,] *lit.* 'happy is he, who may not be stumbled by (*or* in) me.'

24. PEOPLES,] *lit.* 'crowds.. have ye yourselves gone forth into the desert to view? a reed shaken by a wind.'

25. WENT,] *lit.* 'have ye yourselves gone forth.. arrayed.. those in glorious raiment and luxury living, are in (houses of) the kings.'

26. WENT,] *lit.* 'have ye yourselves gone forth.'

27. IT IS,] *lit.* 'it has been written, Behold I send away my messenger (*or* angel)..make fully ready.'

28. KINGDOM,] *or* 'reign of the (true) God,' during the Christian dispensation.

29. PUBLICANS,] *or* 'custom-house officers.'

30. LAWYERS,] *lit.* 'and the lawyers put away the (revealed) counsel of God in reference to themselves, not being baptized by (*lit.* under) him.'

32. CHILDREN,] *or* 'boys, (lads), sitting in a public place, and sounding forth to one another, and saying, We piped to you, and ye did not dance; we mourned to you, and ye did not weep.'

33. A DEVIL,] *lit.* a 'demon.'

34. IS COME,] *lit.* 'came.. wine-drinker.'

35. WISDOM,] *lit.* 'the wisdom (of God) was justified from all her children.'

36. ONE,] *lit.* 'a certain one..was asking.. might eat.. he reclined.'

37. KNEW,] *or* 'knew fully that he reclineth.. of aromatic ointment.'

38. WASH,] *lit.* 'wet..with the tears, and was wiping with the hairs of her head, and was kissing (*lit.* befriending) his feet greatly, and was smearing (*lit.* fattening) with the aromatic ointment.'

39. HAD BIDDEN,] *lit.* 'who called..that she.'

40. MASTER,] *lit.* 'teacher.'

41. CREDITOR,] *lit.* 'giver had two owing necessary things..denaries.'

42. PAY,] *lit.* 'give back, he was gracious to both.'

43. SUPPOSE,] *lit.* 'apprehend secretly.. he was more gracious,.. Rightly didst thou judge.'

44. FOR,] *or* 'upon my feet, but she did wet my feet with the tears.'

45. A KISS,] *lit.* 'friendship (i.e. a mark of friendship or love)..did not leave off thoroughly befriending-thoroughly my feet.'

46. ANOINT,] *or* 'smear (*lit.* fatten).. but she smeared my feet with aromatic ointment.'

47. ARE,] *lit.* 'have been forgiven;' so in v. 48.

49. SAT AT MEAT,] *lit.* 'reclined.'

WITHIN,] *or* 'among themselves.. letteth go.'

50. HATH,] *lit.* 'did save thee; pass on.'

Chapter VIII. may be divided into seven parts; v. 1—3 work and companions of Jesus; v. 4—8 parable of the sower; v. 9—18 its meaning; v. 19—21 his true brethren; v. 22—25 he calms the sea; v. 26—39 cure of a demoniac and its consequences; v. 40—56 cure of an issue of blood and raising of Jairus' daughter.

1. AFTERWARD,] *lit.* 'in the succeeding (season) that he was making a way through ..proclaiming (as a herald), and telling fully as a good thing the reign of God.'

2. HEALED,] *lit.* 'cherished (*or* attended) from (or because of) evil spirits and infirmities.'

MAGDALENE,] *lit.* 'the Magdalene (i.e. the one from Magdala),..seven demons.'

3. JOANNA,] i.e. 'grace of Jah;' Chuza, i.e. 'seeing;' steward, *lit.* 'one upon whom things are turned over;' Susannah, i.e. 'a lily;' who 'were acting-as-deacons to him.'

4. MUCH PEOPLE,] *or* 'a great crowd were come together, and were passing over to him .. through parables' *or* parallel sayings.

5. A,] *lit.* 'the sower.. along the way,.. flying things of the heaven did eat it up.'

6. SOME,] *lit.* 'other fell upon the rocky-place,..because of its not having moisture,' *lit.* anything coming.

7. SOME,] *lit.* 'other fell in the midst of the thorns (*or* briers),.. and choked it utterly.'

8. ON,] *lit.* 'into the good land.. made fruit.. saying, he was sounding, He,' &c.

9. ASKED,] *lit.* 'were asking..this parallel (saying).'

10. IT IS,] *lit.* 'it has been given to know the secrets of the reign of the (true) God, but to the rest in similes, so that beholding they may not behold, and hearing they may not send (their heart) with (it).'

12. BY,] *lit.* 'along the road.. lifteth up.. from their heart, that they might not be saved, having believed,' *or* remained stedfast.

13. ROCK,] *or* 'rocky place.. they may hear,.. with leaping.. believe (*or* remain stedfast), and in a time of trial stand off.'

14. AMONG,] *lit.* 'to the thorns (*or* briers) .. under partings (of mind), and wealth, and sweetnesses of the (present) life, passing on, are entirely choked, and bare not to the end.'

15. ON,] *lit.* 'in the good land.. upright and good.. hold it thoroughly, and bear fruit in endurance,' or permanently.

16. CANDLE,] *or* 'lamp, hideth it with a vessel,.. a couch, but setteth it up upon a lamp-stand.. pass in may behold.'

17. BE MADE,] *lit.* 'become manifest (*or* shining), nor secreted away.. and may come manifestly.'

18. TAKE HEED,] *lit.* 'behold ye.. may have.. may not have.. lifted up.. thinketh to have.'

19. CAME,] *lit.* 'came near.. were not able to meet with him because of the crowd.'

20. TOLD,] *lit.* 'told him fully again.. wishing.'

21. ON,] *lit.* 'in one of the days.. a boat.. we may go through.. and they were led,' *or* brought up *or* back.

23. FELL ASLEEP,] *lit.* 'slept fast.. into the lake, and they were filling fast, and were in peril.'

24. CAME,] *lit.* 'came near.. roused him up thoroughly, saying, Master (*lit.* stander over), we are lost..laid a weight upon the wind and the washing of the waters,..and it became a calm (*lit.* smile).'

25. WHAT,] *lit.* 'who then is this, because he chargeth openly,..they hearken secretly to him.'

26. ARRIVED,] *lit.* 'sailed down to the place of.'

27. TO LAND,] *lit.* 'upon the land there met him secretly..demons.. was wearing ... in (*or* among) the tombs,' or places of 'remembrance.'

28. FELL DOWN,] *or* 'fell forward to him ..a great voice said, What to me and to thee (in common), Jesus! Son of God the Most High, I beseech of thee, mayest thou not try (*or* test) me!'

29. HAD,] *lit.* 'for he said again openly to the unclean spirit to come forth from the man, for many times it had seized him fast, and he was being bound with chains and fetters—guarded, and rending thoroughly the bands, and was being driven under the demon into the desert.'

30. DEVILS,] *lit.* 'demons.'

31. THEY BESOUGHT,] *lit.* 'he was calling on him, in order that he might not lay upon them to go away into the abyss,' *lit.* very deep (*or* bottomless) place.

32. HERD,] *or* 'drove..in the hill, and they were calling upon him, in order that he might turn over upon them to go into these; and he turned (it) over upon them.'

33. HERD,] *or* 'drove..the steep place.. utterly choked.'

34. WAS DONE,] *or* 'happened.. went away and told (it) again fully to (the inhabitants of) the city,' &c.

35. WAS DONE,] *or* 'has happened,..demons had gone forth..and sound-minded.'

36. TOLD,] *lit.* 'told again fully how the demoniac was saved.'

37. COUNTRY,] *lit.* 'place round about.. asked him..were held fast..the boat, and turned round again.'

38. DEVILS,] *lit.* 'demons had gone forth, was beseeching of him..loosed him from (himself), saying.'

39. SHEW,] *lit.* 'be shewing thoroughly.. God did..went away, proclaiming (as-a-herald).'

40. PEOPLE,] *lit.* 'crowd received him fully, for they were all thinking forward to him.'

41. JAIRUS,] i.e. 'he gives light.'

RULER,] *or* 'chief..near the feet..was calling upon him to.'

42. ONLY,] *lit.* 'only begotten..went away, the crowds were pressing him together.'

43. SPENT,] *lit.* 'utterly spent.'

44. CAME,] *lit.* 'came forward from behind ..fringe..and along with the act stood the flowing of her blood.'

45. DENIED,] *lit.* 'denied with an oath *or* utterly..the crowds hold thee fast, and press greatly.'

46. PERCEIVE,] *lit.* 'knew power having gone forth from me.'

47. DECLARED,] *lit.* 'told fully..through what.'

48. BE OF GOOD COMFORT,] *lit.* 'be courageous; thy stedfastness saved thee; be passing on into (*or* with a view to) peace.'

49. ONE,] *lit.* 'a certain one along-side of the chief of the synagogue,..saying that (*or* thus), Thy daughter died, trouble not the Teacher.'

50. BELIEVE,] *or* 'remain stedfast, and she shall be saved.'

51. NO MAN,] *lit.* 'no one.'

52. WEPT,] *lit.* 'were weeping and beating themselves for her..she did not die.'

53. LAUGHED,] *lit.* 'were laughing at him.'

54. TOOK,] *lit.* 'laid hold of her hand.'

MAID,] *or* 'O maid!'

55. CAME AGAIN,] *lit.* 'turned round again, and she stood up along with the action (*or* word), and he arranged thoroughly to give her to eat.'

56. WERE ASTONISHED,] *lit.* 'stood out' with amazement.

CHARGED,] *lit.* 'told them at the same time *or* farther.'

Chapter IX. may be divided into eleven parts; v. 1—6 commission to the twelve disciples; v. 7—9 Herod's desire to see Jesus; v. 10—17 feeding of 5000 men; v. 18—27 Peter's confession and Jesus' warning; v. 28—36 his transfiguration; v. 37—42 cure of a demoniac; v. 43—45 Jesus to be delivered up; v. 46—48 which is the greatest; v. 49—50 true toleration; v. 51—56 rebuke of James and John; v. 57—62 the forward and the backward disciple.

1. DEVILS,] *lit.* 'the demons, and to cherish (*or* attend) unsoundness.'

2. SENT,] *lit.* 'sent them away to proclaim (as-heralds) the reign of the (true) God, and to heal the infirm.'

3. TAKE,] *lit.* 'lift up nothing for the way neither staves (*or* rods), nor bag, nor bread, nor silver.'

4. YE ENTER,] *lit.* 'ye may enter into, there remain, and thence be ye coming forth.'

5. WHOSOEVER,] *lit.* 'as many as may not receive you, ye, coming forth from that city.'

6. DEPARTED,] *lit.* 'went forth and went through every village, telling fully the good things, and cherishing (or attending) everywhere.'

7. WAS DONE,] *or* 'happened, came to pass under him..by certain, that John has been raised out of the dead.'

8. OF SOME,] *lit.* 'by certain, that Elijah was manifested, and of others, that a prophet—one of the first (*or* chief) ones stood up.'

9. HAVE BEHEADED,] *lit.* 'I did behead ..was seeking.'

10 WERE RETURNED,] *lit.* 'turned round secretly (*or* in a little), brought thoroughly to him as many things as they did, and having taken them along with (himself), he made a little space by themselves into a desert place of a city called Bethsaida,' i.e. house of fishing *or* hunting, N.E. of the Lake.

11. PEOPLE,] *lit.* 'crowds..was speaking.'

12. WEAR AWAY,] *or* 'decline, then came forward..Let the crowd loose (*or* go), that having gone away into the surrounding villages and the field, they may loose themselves down, and may find corn (*or* food) for themselves.'

13. WE SHOULD GO,] *lit.* 'having passed on we may attend the public place for food.'

14. ABOUT,] *or* 'as it were..lie down.'

16. HEAVEN,] *lit.* 'to the heaven.'

BLESSED,] *lit.* 'spoke well..brake down, and was giving..to set near the crowd.'

17. OF FRAGMENTS,] *lit.* 'what was over and above to them of broken pieces twelve wicker baskets.'

18. AS,] *lit.* 'in his being much alone pouring forth before (God), the disciples were with him, and he asked at them, saying, Whom do the crowds say me to be?'

19. SOME,] *lit.* 'and others, Elijah; and others, that a prophet, a certain one of the first (*or* chief) has stood up.'

20. YE,] *lit.* 'but ye—whom do ye say me to be?'

21. STRAITLY CHARGED,] *lit.* 'having laid a weight upon them, told them over again to say this to no one.'

22. SAYING,] 'that *or* because it behoveth the Son of the Man to suffer many things, and to be tried utterly by the elders (*Gr.* presbyters), and chief-priests, and writers, and to be killed utterly, and the third day to be raised.'

23. SAID,] *or* 'laid (it) out to all, If any one doth wish to come after me, let him disown himself fully, and lift up his cross daily.'

24. WILL,] *lit.* 'may wish to save his soul, shall lose it thoroughly,..may lose his soul because of me.'

25. ADVANTAGED,] *or* 'profited, having gained the whole world (*lit.* cosmos), but having losed himself or suffered damage?'

26. SHALL,] *or* 'may be ashamed..when he may come.'

27. I TELL,] *lit.* 'truly I lay it down (*or*

out) to you, there are certain of those standing here, who shall not themselves taste of death till they may see the reign of God,' i.e. manifestations of its power and glory, as at the transfiguration, the day of Pentecost, the destruction of Jerusalem, &c.

28. SAYINGS,] *lit.* 'words, as if (it were) eight days, having taken along with (him) Peter and James and John, he went up into the hill to pour-forth-for-himself before (God).'

29. AS,] *lit.* 'in his pouring forth before (God), the appearance of his face became another thing, and his garment white, sparkling.'

30. TALKED,] *lit.* 'were speaking.'

31. APPEARED,] *or* 'were seen, and laid out (*or* down) his out-going, which he was about to fill out in Jerusalem.'

32. HEAVY,] *or* 'burdened.. thoroughly awake.'

33. DEPARTED,] *lit.* 'made a thorough space.'

TABERNACLES,] *lit.* 'places for settling down..says.'

34. THUS,] *lit.* 'these things..settled down upon them.'

35. BELOVED,] *or* 'dearly beloved.'

HEAR,] *or* 'ye hear him!'

36. WAS PAST,] *or* 'was,' simply.

KEPT CLOSE,] *lit.* 'were silent, and told again fully to no one..have seen.'

37. MUCH,] *or* 'a great crowd met with him.'

38. OF,] *lit.* 'from the crowd..Teacher,.. look over upon my son, because he is my only-begotten one.'

39. SUDDENLY,] *or* 'unexpectedly..teareth him with foaming, and bruiseth him also.'

40. TO CAST,] *lit.* 'in order that they might cast it forth, and they were not able.'

41. FAITHLESS,] *or* 'unstedfast and thoroughly turned round; till when..and hold you up? bring forward.'

42. COMING,] *lit.* 'coming forward, the demon rent and tore him sore, but Jesus laid a weight upon..lad, and gave him away to his father.'

43. AMAZED,] *lit.* 'struck exceedingly over the greatness of God..are wondering.'

44. LET,] *lit.* 'be ye setting these words to your ears, for the Son of the Man is about to be given over into hands of men.'

45. UNDERSTOOD,] *lit.* 'were not knowing this saying, and it was hid at the same time from them, that they might not themselves perceive (*or* hear) it, and they were afraid to ask him concerning that saying.'

46. AROSE,] *lit.* 'entered..may be great?'

47. PERCEIVING,] *lit.* 'having seen the reasoning..took up a lad (*or* boy), and set him along-side of himself.'

48. SHALL,] *lit.* 'may receive this lad upon my name (*or* character),..may receive me.. sent me forth..lesser.'

49. MASTER,] *lit.* 'over-stander.'

ONE,] *lit.* 'a certain one casting forth the demons upon thy name.'

51. WHEN,] *lit.* 'in the days of his being received up being filled out, that he fixed his face to pass on to Jerusalem.'

52. SENT,] *lit.* 'sent forth.. village of Samaritans.'

53. WAS,] *lit.* 'was passing on to.'

54. WILT THOU,] *lit.* 'dost thou wish..from the heaven, and loose them thoroughly.'

55. TURNED,] *or* 'turned round, and laid a weight upon them,..ye have not known.'

56. IS NOT,] *lit.* 'did not come to loose away men's souls, but to save; and they passed on.' Many MSS. and versions, omit the first part of this verse, as founded on John 3. 17; 12. 47.

57. GOEST,] *lit.* 'mayest go away.'

58. FOXES,] *lit.* 'the foxes (i.e. deceivers of sight) have holes (i.e. places without light), and the flying things of the heaven nests (i.e. places of settling down).'

59. FOLLOW,] *lit.* 'be following me..turn over upon me to go away first and to bury.'

60. LET,] *or* 'let the dead alone to bury their own dead, but thou having gone away declare thoroughly the reign of the (true) God.'

61. LET,] *lit.* 'turn over upon me first to set myself forth to those in my house.'

62. PUT,] *lit.* 'put forth his hand upon a plough, and beholding backward, is well-set in reference to the reign of the (true) God.'

Chapter X. may be divided into seven parts; v. 1—16 Jesus sends forth 70 disciples; v. 17—20 their return and his congratulation; v. 21—22 He rejoices and praises God; v. 23—24 and the disciples; v. 25—29 shows how to inherit life; v. 30—37 and who is our neighbour; v. 38—42 also the good part.

1. APPOINTED,] *lit.* 'shewed fully,' as in Acts 1. 24.

SENT,] *lit.* 'sent them forth..he was himself about to go.'

2. SAID,] *lit.* 'laid he out *or* down to them.

GREAT,] *or* 'much, *or* abundant, but the workers are few, supplicate therefore..may cast forth workers.'

3. GO YOUR WAYS,] *lit.* 'go away.'

4. PURSE,] *or* 'bag, nor scrip, nor sandals, and ye may draw no one in the way' to embrace them.

5 YE ENTER,] *lit.* 'ye may enter.'

6. BE,] *lit.* 'may be..rest fully.'

7. THINGS,] *lit.* 'the things long-side of them.'

LABOURER,] *lit.* 'worker.'

GO NOT,] *lit.* 'go not afterwards out of house into house.'

8. YE ENTER,] *lit.* 'ye may enter..the things.'

9. HEAL,] *lit.* 'cherish *or* attend those infirm in it..reign of God has come nigh upon you.'

10. YE ENTER,] *lit.* 'may enter..having gone forth to its broad places.'

11. CLEAVETH,] *lit.* 'hath cleaved..wipe off entirely to you, but know ye this.'

12. TOLERABLE,] *lit.* 'bearable.'

13. BEEN DONE,] *lit.* 'happened..which happened..long ago had a new mind.'

15. ART,] *lit.* 'wast exalted to the heaven, unto Hades (i.e. the unseen world) shall be brought down,' i.e. shall be annihilated, as is now the case.

16. HEARETH,] *lit.* 'is hearing..is putting you away, putteth me away..sent me forth.'
17. DEVILS,] *lit.* 'demons are being put under us in thy name.'
18. I BEHELD,] *lit.* 'I was beholding the Adversary as lightning out of the heaven having fallen.'
19. POWER,] *lit.* 'the authority..and upon all..may wrong you.'
20. SUBJECT,] *lit.* 'put under you..that your names were written in the heavens.'
21 IN,] *lit.* 'in *or* with the spirit, I speak out the same thing to thee..didst hide away..from wise and understanding ones, and didst uncover them to babes; yes, Father, that thus it became a good thought before thee.'
22. ALL THINGS,] *or* 'every one was given over to me by (*lit.* under) my Father, and no one knows..my counsel to uncover him.'
23. PRIVATELY,] *lit.* 'by themselves, Happy the eyes that are beholding what ye behold.'
24. HAVE DESIRED,] *lit.* 'did wish to see what ye behold, and did not see,..did not hear.'
25. TEMPTED,] *lit.* 'tried him greatly,.. Teacher..obtain by lot life age-during?'
26. IS,] *lit.* 'has been written.'
27. WITH,] *lit.* 'out of..out of..out of.. out of all thy full mind.'
28. RIGHT,] *or* 'rightly.'
29. WILLING,] *or* 'wishing.'
30. ANSWERING,] *lit.* 'having taken (it) up.'
FELL,] *lit.* 'fell over among robbers.'
WOUNDED,] *lit.* 'put strokes upon him.. leaving (him) almost half dead.'
31. BY CHANCE,] *or* 'coincidence..was going down..in that way..went along over-against (him),' contrary to Ex. 23. 4, 5.
32. WHEN,] *lit.* 'having been down (that) place.'
33. AS HE JOURNEYED,] *or* 'making (his) way.'
34. WENT,] *lit.* 'came forward and bound fast..pouring out over (them)..to an inn (*lit.* place for 'receiving all'), and was careful about him.'
35. TOOK OUT,] *lit.* 'cast forth two denaries ..**host** (*lit.* 'receiver of all,')..Be careful about him,..spend for (him),..may come back upon (thee), I will give back to thee.'
36. THINKEST THOU,] *or* 'doth it seem to thee, became neighbour of him who fell over among the robbers?'
37. SHEWED,] *lit.* 'did the kindness with him..Be passing on.'
38. MARTHA,] i.e. 'bitterness *or* lady.'
RECEIVED,] *lit.* 'received him secretly *or* a little.'
39. SAT,] *lit.* 'having seated herself alongside, near the feet of Jesus, was hearing.'
40. CUMBERED,] *lit.* 'drawn away about much service (*lit.* deaconship), and having stood by (him) said..left me utterly to act-as-a-deacon; say (it) therefore to her that she may help along with me.'
41. CAREFUL,] *lit.* 'parted (in mind) and.'
42. ONE THING,] *lit.* 'of one thing there is a need..did choose for herself the good part.'

Chapter XI. may be divided into six parts; v. 1—13 Jesus teaches to pray; v. 14—26 cures a dumb demoniac, and refutes his enemies; v. 27—28 who are happy; v. 29—36 a sign sought and given; v. 37—44 reproof of the Pharisees; v. 45—54 reproof of the lawyers.
1. PRAYING,] *lit.* 'pouring forth before (God)..a certain one.'
2. YE PRAY,] *lit.* 'ye may pray..in the heavens; let thy name be set apart; let thy reign come; let thy wish (*or* will) happen.. upon the earth.'
3. GIVE,] *lit.* 'our appointed (*or* necessary) bread be giving to us daily.'
4. FORGIVE,] *lit.* 'let go to us our sins (*or* 'missings' of the mark), for also (*or* even) we ourselves let go..mayest thou not (lead *or*) bring us to a temptation (*or* trial), but draw us from the evil.'
5. SAY,] *lit.* 'and may say..hand to me.'
6. FOR,] *lit.* 'since..came near to me out of his way.'
7. HE,] *or* 'that one..may say,..already the door has been closed, and the children with me are in the bed.'
8. THOUGH,] *lit.* 'even if he will not..because of his being a friend,..as is necessary.'
9. OPENED,] *lit.* 'opened up to you.'
10. ASKETH,] *lit.* 'is asking..is seeking.. is knocking..opened up.'
11. A SON,] *lit.* 'the son..a loaf..the father, will he give over to him a stone.. give over.'
12. SHALL,] *lit.* 'may ask..give over to him.'
13. KNOW,] *lit.* 'have known..shall the Father who is from heaven give a holy spirit,'—the fruit of *the* Holy Spirit.
14. DEVIL,] *lit.* 'demon, and it was dumb (*or* deaf),..demon..the crowds wondered.'
15. THROUGH,] *lit.* 'in (*or* by) Beelzeboul (i.e. lord of dung), chief (*or* first) of the demons.'
16. TEMPTING,] *or* 'trying (*or* testing) were seeking from him a sign out of heaven.'
17. THOUGHTS,] *lit.* 'full minds..greatly parted in itself is desolated, and house upon house falleth.'
18. IF,] *lit.* 'and if the Adversary also in himself be greatly parted..the demons in (by, with) Beelzeboul.'
19. BY,] *lit.* 'in (with) Beelzeboul cast forth the demons, by (in, with) whom.. because of this.'
20. WITH,] *lit.* 'in (by) the finger of God cast forth the demons, then come suddenly upon you did the reign of the (true) God.'
21. A,] *lit.* 'the strong one fully armed, may guard his own court.'
22. A,] *lit.* 'the stronger..may vanquish him, his whole-armour he lifteth up, on which he had trusted, and his spoils he giveth away.'
23. GATHERETH,] *lit.* 'is bringing together.'
24. IS GONE,] *lit.* 'may go forth from the man, he goeth much through waterless places, seeking rest again,..I turn round secretly to.'
25. GARNISHED,] *lit.* 'arranged *or* adorned.
26. TAKETH,] *lit.* 'taketh along with (him

self).. more evil,.. make a full-house there, and the last (troubles) of that man.'

27. COMPANY,] *lit.* 'crowd.. Happy the womb that carried thee,.. didst suck.'

28. BLESSED,] *lit.* 'happy those hearing the word of God and keeping it.'

29. PEOPLE,] *lit.* 'crowds were closed upon (each other).. they seek for a sign.'

30. WAS,] *lit.* 'became.'

31. THE,] *lit.* 'a queen of a south country ..shall judge them down,..out of the ends ..something fuller than Solomon.'

32. THE,] *lit.* 'men..stand up..judge it down, because they had a new mind at the proclamation of.. something fuller than Jonah.'

33. CANDLE,] *lit.* 'lamp..the bushel, but on the lamp-stand,..behold the brightness.'

34. LIGHT,] *lit.* 'lamp..may be not double ..body is lightened.'

35. TAKE HEED,] *lit.* 'look about *or* consider.'

36. FULL OF LIGHT,] *lit.* 'lightened,.. darkened,..lightened, as when the lamp by the brightness may give thee light.'

37. BESOUGHT,] *lit.* 'asked that he might lunch (*lit.* make the 'best' meal) with him, and having gone in, he reclined,' *lit.* fell back.

38. WASHED,] *lit.* 'was not first baptized *or* did not first baptize himself (by having water poured upon his hands and feet) before the lunch.'

39. WICKEDNESS,] *lit.* 'evil.'

40. FOOLS,] *lit.* 'thoughtless *or* unthinking.'

41. BUT,] rather 'the things within give ye (as) alms,' or kindness.

42. TITHE,] *lit.* 'tithe fully the sweet-smelling flower, and the rue, and every dug-herb, and ye pass by the judgment and the love of the (true) God; these it behoveth (you) to do, and those not to let alone.'

43. UPPERMOST,] *lit.* 'first *or* foremost..the drawings-near (of men to salute them) in the public places.'

44. GRAVES,] *lit.* 'the unseen tombs (*lit.* remembered things)..walk about upon them (them) have not known.'

45. ONE,] *lit.* 'a certain one..says to him, Teacher! these things saying, us also thou dishonourest.'

46. LADE,] *lit.* 'burden the men with burdens hardly bearable, and yourselves with one of your fingers do not touch forward to the burdens.'

47. KILLED,] *lit.* 'killed them utterly.'

48. TRULY,] 'ye testify, and are together well-pleased with the works,..killed them utterly, and ye—ye build.'

49. THEREFORE,] *lit.* 'because of this also the wisdom of God said, (perhaps Christ himself is here meant, compare Mat. 23. 34; 1 Cor. 1. 24): I will send forth to them..kill utterly and cause to flee.'

50. WAS SHED,] *lit.* 'is being poured forth from the foundation (*lit.* laying down) of the world (*lit.* arrangement or order, whether moral or physical), may be sought out from this generation.'

51. PERISHED,] *lit.* 'was lost between the place of sacrifice and the house; yes, I lay (it) down to you, It shall be sought out from this generation.'

52. TAKEN AWAY,] *lit.* 'lifted up the key of the knowledge.'

53. TO URGE,] *lit.* 'to hold in fearfully, and to cause him to speak about many things.'

54. ACCUSE,] *or* 'make it public against him.'

Chapter XII. may be divided into eight parts; v. 1—3 Jesus warns against hypocrisy; v. 4—12 against timidity; v. 13—21 against covetousness; v. 22—34 against anxiety; v. 35—40 exhorts to watchfulness; v. 41—48 to stedfastness; v. 49—53 result of his coming; v. 54—59 duty of discerning times.

1. GATHERED,] *lit.* 'brought fully together the myriads of the crowd so as to tread down one another.. first, Hold yourselves off from the leaven.'

2. COVERED,] *lit.* 'fully covered *or* concealed.. be uncovered.'

3. HAVE SPOKEN,] *lit.* 'did speak in the darkness..spake to the ear in the inner chambers.'

4. BE NOT,] *lit.* 'ye may not be afraid because of those killing utterly the body.'

5. FOREWARN,] *lit.* 'show secretly to you whom ye may fear: ye may fear him who after the killing utterly, has authority to cast fully into the Gehenna; yes, I lay (it) down to you, this one ye may fear.'

6. SPARROWS,] *lit.* 'young sparrows sold for two assars, and one of them is not at all hid before the (true) God.'

7. THE VERY,] *lit.* 'the hairs.. have been all numbered.. than many little-sparrows ye are borne through.'

8. WHOSOEVER,] *lit.* 'every one who may say the same thing with (*lit.* in) me before ..with (in) him shall the Son of the Man speak the same thing before the messengers of God.'

9. DENIETH,] *lit.* 'has denied me with an oath.'

10. SPEAK,] *lit.* 'lift up an (injurious) word in reference to the son of man (i.e. a human being?) it shall be let go to him, but to him who in reference to the Holy Spirit did speak injuriously, it shall not be let go.'

11. BRING,] *lit.* 'may carry you forward before the synagogues, and the chiefs, and the authorities, be not parted (in your mind) how or what ye may speak back, or what ye may say.'

13. ONE,] *lit.* 'a certain one out of the crowd, Teacher, Say to my brother, to divide with me the portion assigned by lot.'

14. MADE,] *lit.* 'set me down.'

15. TAKE HEED,] *lit.* 'see and be guarding yourselves from (*or* because of) the having-more-than-enough.'

16. PARABLE,] *lit.* 'thing cast along-side' of another for comparison or contrast.

GROUND,] *lit.* 'space (*or* place)..bare well.

17. THOUGHT,] *lit.* 'was reasoning in himself..I shall bring together.'

18. PULL,] *lit.* 'take down my store-houses, ..will I bring together all my productions.'

19. TAKE THINE EASE,] *lit.* 'be resting fully, eat, drink, be easy minded.'

20. FOOL,] *lit.* 'thoughtless!..they shall ask from thee..prepared *or* made ready.'
21. LAYETH UP,] *lit.* 'is treasuring up.'
22. THEREFORE,] *lit.* 'because of this..be not parted (in your mind) as to your life (*or* soul), what ye may eat,..may put on.'
23. LIFE,] *or* 'soul is more than the nourishment,.. the clothing.'
24. CONSIDER,] *lit.* 'mind thoroughly the ravens (*or* crows, *lit.* croakers), that..nourisheth them.. borne through than the flying creatures.'
25. WITH TAKING THOUGHT,] *lit.* 'parting (his mind), is able to put forward upon his age one cubit;' see Mat. 6. 27.
26. TO DO,] *lit.* 'for the least, why concerning the rest are ye parted (in mind).'
27. CONSIDER,] *lit.* 'mind thoroughly the lilies, how do they grow? they labour not,' *or* are not fatigued.
28. CLOTHE,] *or* 'envelope the herbage.. an oven.'
29. SHALL,] *lit.* 'may eat.. may drink, neither be ye lifted up after (them).'
30. KNOWETH,] *lit.* 'hath known.'
31. KINGDOM,] *or* 'reign of the (true) God.'
ADDED,] *lit.* 'put forward to you.'
32. FEAR,] *lit.* 'be not afraid, the little little-flock, because your Father was well-pleased.'
33. PROVIDE,] *lit.* 'make to yourselves.. orrupt thoroughly.
35. LIGHTS,] *lit.* 'lamps.'
36. THEIR LORD,] *lit.* 'their own lord, when he shall loose himself away out of the marriage-feasts,..straightway open up to him.
37. BLESSED,] *lit.* 'happy.. roused up,.. gird himself about, and cause them to recline (at meat), and having come along-side will-act-as-deacon to them.'
38. SHALL,] *or* 'may come.. may come.. may find (it) so, happy.'
39. GOODMAN,] *lit.* 'house-despot..cometh, ..roused himself up.'
42. THAT,] *lit.* 'the stedfast and thoughtful.. set down over his service, to give in due season the measure of sifted-corn.'
43. BLESSED,] *lit.* 'happy.'
44. OF,] *lit.* 'truly I lay (it) down to you, that over all his goods he will set him down.'
45. BUT AND IF,] *lit.* 'but if that servant may say.. taketh time to come, and may begin to beat the young men and the young women.'
46. AT,] *lit.* 'in an hour of which he knoweth not, and will cut him off, and will set his portion with the unstedfast.'
47. WILL,] *or* 'wish of his own lord, and not having made ready, nor having done according to his wish.'
48. IS,] *lit.* 'was given, much shall be sought from him, and on whom they put much, more abundantly they will ask of him.'
49. I AM,] *lit.* 'I came to cast fire into the land, and what wish I (to do), if already it was fully-lighted?'
50. TO BE BAPTIZED WITH,] *or* 'to baptize myself with..held together till it may be ended.'
51. SUPPOSE,] *lit.* 'think ye that I came along-side (of you) to give peace in the land? no, I lay (it) down to you, but rather a thorough-parting.'
52. DIVIDED,] *lit.* 'thoroughly-parted.'
53. THE,] *lit.* 'a father shall be thoroughly-parted with (*lit.* upon) a son, and a son with (upon) a father, a mother with (upon) a daughter, and a daughter with (upon) a mother, a mother-in-law with (upon) her daughter-in-law, and a daughter-in-law with (upon) her mother-in-law.'
54. PEOPLE,] *lit.* 'crowds..may see the cloud rising up from..shower (*lit.* flowing together) cometh, and it happens so.'
55. THE,] *lit.* 'a south wind is blowing ye say, that there will be heat and it happeneth.'
56. SKY,] *lit.* 'earth and of the heaven ye are able to test.'
57. RIGHT,] *or* 'just, righteous.'
58. WHEN,] *lit.* 'for as thou goest away with thy opponent to (*lit.* upon) the chief, in the way give labour to be let away from him, lest at any time he may draw thee down before the judge, and the judge give thee over to the officer (*lit.* doer), and the officer may cast thee into guard *or* ward.'
59. SHALT,] *lit.* 'mayest not go forth.. mayest give back.'

Chapter XIII. may be divided into six parts; v. 1—5 Jesus warns against judging others; v. 6—9 against fruitlessness; v. 10—17 against hypocrisy in the case of an infirm woman; v. 18—21 simile of leaven; v. 22—30 warning against vain curiosity and mere profession; v. 31—35 fearlessness and sympathy of Jesus.
1. TOLD,] *lit.* 'told him fully.. Pilate mingled.'
2. WERE,] *lit.* 'became sinners beyond.. have suffered.'
3. REPENT,] *lit.* 'may have a new mind.. be lost;' so in v. 5.
4. SLEW,] *lit.* 'killed them utterly.'
WERE SINNERS,] *lit.* 'became debtors beyond.. settle down.'
6. THEREON,] *lit.* 'came seeking fruit in it.'
7. DRESSER,] *lit.* 'worker..in this fig-tree; cut it out, why also the land doth it make unworkable?'
8. LORD,] *lit.* 'sir,..may dig about it, and cast dung.'
9. IF,] *lit.* 'if indeed it may make fruit; but if not so, at the delay thou shalt cut it out.'
10. ON,] *lit.* 'in (during) the sabbaths.'
11. COULD,] *lit.* 'was not able to bend back perfectly.'
12. CALLED,] *lit.* 'called (her) forward, thou hast been loosed.'
13. IMMEDIATELY,] *lit.* 'along with the act she was made straight again.'
14. RULER,] *lit.* 'first or chief..much displeased, because Jesus cherished (*or* attended)..the crowd,..to be working.. coming to be cherished.'
15. HYPOCRITE,] *lit.* 'judge under' a pretence.
STALL,] *lit.* 'feeding *or* eating place..to give (it) drink.'

16. WOMAN,] *lit.* 'this one.. whom the Adversary bound.'

17. ADVERSARIES,] *lit.* 'those set over-against him were being greatly ashamed, and all the crowd were rejoicing over.. happening under him.'

18. KINGDOM,] *lit.* 'reign of the (true) God.'

19. HIS,] *lit.* 'his own garden.'

WAXED,] *lit.* 'came into.. flying creatures of the heaven settled down.'

20. KINGDOM,] *lit.* 'reign of the (true) God.'

21. HID,] *lit.* 'hid fully.. of corn.'

22. WENT,] *lit.* 'was passing fully through cities.. making a passage to Jerusalem.'

23. ONE,] *lit.* 'a certain one.'

FEW,] *lit.* 'are those being saved few?' the question has no relation whatever to the number of those *finally* saved, but simply to those who were believing in Jesus at that time.

24. STRIVE,] *lit.* 'agonize (i.e. be as energetic as *wrestlers* are) to go in through the ..shall seek (*or* desire, in a general way), to go in, and shall not have strength (of mind necessary to make the attempt).'

25. WHEN ONCE,] *lit.* 'from the time that the house-despot may have risen, and have closed thoroughly the door, and ye may begin..Sir! Sir! open up to us..I have not known.'

26. SHALL,] *lit.* 'may begin to say, We did eat before thee and drank, and in our broad places thou didst teach.'

27. I KNOW NOT,] *lit.* 'I have not known.. stand off from me, all ye workers of the unrighteousness *or* injustice.'

28. THERE,] *lit.* 'there shall be there the weeping and the gnashing of the teeth, when ye may see..reign of the (true) God, and ye cast forth without.'

29. THE EAST,] *lit.* 'from east (places) and west (places), and from north and south, and shall recline in the reign of the heavens.'

30. FIRST.. LAST,] in receiving their reward.

31. THE SAME,] *lit.* 'in that day came forward certain Pharisees..Go forth, and be passing on from hence, because Herod wishes to kill thee utterly.'

32. GO YE,] *lit.* 'having passed on, say ye to that fox, Behold, I cast forth demons, and complete openly cures..I am being completed *or* ended.'

33. I MUST,] *lit.* 'it behoveth me to be passing on..the coming day, because it is not (a thing) to be received.'

34. KILLEST,] *lit.* 'is killing utterly..sent forth..did I wish to bring thy children openly together, in the manner (that) a bird her own brood under (her) wings, and ye did not wish.'

35. IS LEFT,] *lit.* 'is being left..may not see me till it may come that ye may see, Well-spoken of is He who is Coming in the name of the Lord.'

Chapter XIV. may be divided into six parts: v. 1—6 cure of a dropsical man on the sabbath; v. 7—11 warning against pride; v. 12—14 against seeking recompense: v. 15—25 who shall eat bread in the kingdom of the heavens; v. 26—33 warning against want of forethought; v. 34, 35 uselessness of unseasoned salt.

1. CHIEF,] *lit.* 'chiefs of the Pharisees.. were keeping watch over him.'

3. LAWFUL,] *lit.* 'is it out of measure.'

4. HELD THEIR PEACE,] *lit.* 'were silent, and having laid hold upon (him), he healed him, and loosed him' from his burden.

5. PIT,] *or* 'well..draw it up.'

7. PUT FORTH,] *lit.* 'laid out *or* down a simile (or parallel saying) unto those called, having upon (his heart) how they were laying out to themselves the foremost couches.'

8. BIDDEN,] *lit.* 'mayest be called by (*lit.* under) any one to marriage-feasts, thou mayest not recline in the foremost couch.. called by (*lit.* under) him.'

9. SAY,] *lit.* 'shall say..mayest begin.. to hold down (or fast) hindmost place.'

10. ART,] *lit.* 'mayest be called, having passed on lay thyself down in the hindmost place, that when he that called thee may come..Go up forward higher.. glory before those reclining along with thee.'

11. ABASED,] *or* 'humbled.'

12. SAID,] *or* 'laid he forth to him who called him.. mayest make a dinner (*lit* 'best' meal) or supper (*lit.* a thing 'necessary for labour'), be not inviting thy friends, nor thy brethren, nor thy kindred, nor rich neighbours..call thee in return, and a recompense may come to thee.'

13. MAKEST,] *lit.* 'mayest make a reception, be calling poor, maimed, lame, blind.'

14. BLESSED,] *lit.* 'happy because they have nothing to give to thee in return, for it shall be given back to thee in the standing up of the just.'

15. ONE,] *lit.* 'a certain one of those reclining with (him)..Happy..reign of the (true) God.'

16. BADE,] *lit.* 'called.'

17. SENT,] *lit.* 'sent forth his servant at the hour of the supper to say to those having been called, Be coming.'

18. WITH ONE CONSENT,] *lit.* 'from one thing (or another) to ask themselves off..I bought a field, and I need to go forth and see it, I pray thee, have me asked off.'

19. I HAVE BOUGHT,] *lit.* 'I bought..pass on to try them.'

20. I HAVE MARRIED,] *lit.* 'I married.'

21. CAME,] *lit.* 'came near, and told fully to his lord these things, then the house-despot..broad-places and alleys..poor and maimed, and lame, and blind, lead in hither.'

22. IT IS,] *lit.* 'it has been done, as thou didst arrange for, and yet there is space.'

23. COMPEL,] *or* 'constrain' by persuasion, of course, not by force.

25. WENT,] *lit.* 'were many crowds passing on with him.'

26. COME,] *lit.* 'cometh unto me, and hateth not his own father, and mother, and wife, and children, and brothers, and sisters, yea, even also his own soul.'

27. BEAR,] *or* 'carry.'

28. INTENDING,] *or* 'wishing.'

29. HAPLY,] *lit.* 'lest he having laid a foundation, and not having strength to end

(it) thoroughly, all viewing (it) may begin to treat him as a child.'

30. WAS NOT ABLE,] or 'had not strength to end (it) thoroughly.'

31. GOING,] *lit.* 'passing on to cast himself with another king into war (*lit.* a 'loosing *or* destruction of many') doth not, having sat down, first consult if he be able with (*lit.* in) ten thousand to stand against him who with twenty thousand is coming upon him?'

32. OR ELSE,] *lit.* 'and if not so,..sendeth forth an embassy (*lit.* seniority, i.e. seniors, elders,) and asketh the things for peace.'

33. FORSAKETH,] *lit.* 'setteth himself away from all his own goods.'

34. SALT,] *lit.* 'the salt..may have become insipid, in (by, with) what shall it be seasoned?'

35. FIT,] *lit.* 'well-set.'

Chapter XV. may be divided into four parts; v. 1, 2 Jesus receives sinners, which he vindicates by similes; v. 3—7 of a lost sheep; v. 8—10 of a lost piece of money; v. 11—32 of a lost son.

1. DREW NEAR,] *lit.* 'were drawing nigh.. custom-house-officers and the sinners,' (*lit.* those 'missing' the mark).

2. AND SCRIBES,] *lit.* 'and the writers were greatly murmuring, saying, that this one receiveth also sinners.'

3. PARABLE,] *or* simile, 'parallel' saying.

4. LEAVE,] *lit.* 'leave at once..pass on after (*lit.* upon) till he may find it.'

5. HIS,] *lit.* 'his own shoulders.'

6. HOME,] *lit.* 'to the house..I found.'

7. IN HEAVEN,] *lit.* 'in the heaven upon one sinner having a new mind,..have no need of a new mind.'

8. PIECES OF SILVER] *lit.* 'drachmas (worth 7½d. each), if she may lose one drachm doth not light a lamp,..very carefully, till that she may find it?'

9. I HAVE,] *lit.* 'I found the drachm that I lost.'

10. THERE IS,] *lit.* 'there cometh joy before the messengers of the (true) God upon one sinner having a new mind.'

11. FALLETH,] *lit.* 'falleth upon *or* over.'

12. DIVIDED,] *lit.* 'lifted up thoroughly.'

13. GATHERED,] *lit.* 'bringing all together, went from his (own) people into a far off place, and there thoroughly scattered his substance, living unsavingly.'

14. AROSE,] *lit.* 'happened..through that land, and himself began to be behind.'

15. JOINED HIMSELF,] *lit.* 'was glued..that place.'

16. WOULD FAIN,] *lit.* 'very desirous to fill ..were eating..was giving to him.'

17. BREAD,] *lit.* 'a superabundance of loaves, and I with famine am perishing,' *or* fully lost.

18. I WILL ARISE,] *lit.* 'having stood up, I will pass on myself unto my father..I did sin to the heaven.'

20. HIS,] *lit.* 'his own father, and he holding yet far off..his bowels were moved..fell over upon his neck, and befriended him greatly.'

21. I HAVE,] *lit.* 'I did sin to the heaven.'

22 BEST,] *lit.* 'first *or* foremost, and clothe him with (it), and give a ring for his hand, and sandals for his feet.'

23. BRING HITHER,] *or* 'bring in..sacrifice (it),..let us have good minds.'

24. IS ALIVE,] *lit.* 'did live again..and was found.. to have a good mind.'

25. IN THE,] *lit.* 'in a field.. symphony and leaping.'

26. CALLED,] *lit.* 'called forward one of the lads *or* boys, he was inquiring what these things might be.'

27. IS COME,] *or* 'arrived..did sacrifice.. he received him back sound,' or healthy.

28. WOULD NOT,] *lit.* 'did not wish to go in,.. was calling upon him.'

29. TRANSGRESSED,] *or* 'went beyond.. I might have a good mind.'

30. DEVOURED,] *lit.* 'eaten thoroughly.. didst sacrifice to him.'

31. THAT,] *lit.* 'mine are thine.'

32. IT WAS MEET,] *lit.* 'but to have a good-mind, and to leap with joy was needful,.. did live again,.. was found.' This parable represents the sinner as working out his own salvation unaided, while the two preceding represent him as doing nothing to help himself.

Chapter XVI. may be divided into four parts; v. 1—8 simile of an unjust steward; v. 9—13 difficulty of serving two masters; v. 14—18 reproof of the Pharisees; v. 19—31 simile of the rich man and Lazarus.

1. STEWARD,] *lit.* 'house-distributor.. accused (*lit.* cast *or* thrust through) to him as thoroughly scattering.'

2. HOW,] *lit.* 'what is this I hear about thee? give forth the reckoning (*lit.* word) of thy house-distribution.'

3. TAKETH,] *lit.* 'lifteth..to dig I have no strength, to ask openly I am ashamed.'

4. AM RESOLVED,] *lit.* 'have known what I shall do; that, when I may be away from.'

5. CALLED,] *lit.* 'called forward..his own lord's.'

6. MEASURES,] *lit.* 'baths.. Receive thy writing.'

7. THEN,] *lit.* 'afterwards.'

MEASURES,] *lit.* 'cors..says to him, Receive thy writing.'

8. THE LORD,] i.e. his master, not Jesus.

COMMENDED,] *or* 'praised openly.. did wisely (*lit.* mindfully), because the sons of this age are more mindful than the sons of the light, with respect to their own generation.'

9. OF,] *lit.* 'out of the mammon of the injustice, that, when ye may fail,..age-during tabernacles,' or places of 'settling down.'

10. FAITHFUL,] *lit.* 'stedfast in few things is stedfast also in many.'

11. BEEN,] *lit.* 'become stedfast in the unjust mammon,—the true who will entrust to you?'

12. BEEN,] *lit.* 'become stedfast in the things of others.'

13. SERVANT,] *lit.* 'domestic is able to serve..hold over-against one, and think down upon the other.'

MAMMON,] the Syriac god of riches.
14. COVETOUS,] *lit.* 'lovers of silver, were hearing.. were sneering greatly at him.'
15. MEN,] *lit.* 'the men, but the (true) God ..is highest.'
16. WERE,] rather 'are,' i.e. exist, rule.
KINGDOM,] *lit.* 'reign of the (true) God is told-fully-as-good-news, and every one is pressed towards it,' by moral suasion.
17. PASS,] *lit.* 'go away..tittle (*lit.* 'horn' of the letters)..to fall,' unfulfilled.
18. PUTTETH,] *lit.* 'is loosing away..the loosed away.'
19. FARED,] *lit.* 'well-minded every day, brilliantly,' in his own conceit.
20. BEGGAR,] *lit.* 'poor man.'
LAZARUS,] i.e. 'not helped, helpless.'
WAS,] *lit.* 'had been cast at his porch, covered with ulcers.'
21. DESIRING,] *lit.* 'very desirous..from the little scraps that are falling..had licked away his ulcers.'
22. BEGGAR,] *lit.* 'poor man died, and was borne away by the messengers (of God).'
23. HELL,] *lit.* 'in the Hades (i.e. unseen world, or state of departed spirits)..in trials, ..from afar.'
24. HAVE MERCY,] *or* 'be kind to me..cool a little my tongue, because I am consumed in this flame.'
25. SON,] *lit.* 'child..didst receive fully.. the evil things..is called near, and thou art consumed.'
26. BESIDE,] *lit.* 'upon *or* above..great chasm has been fixed, so that those wishing to go through..they pass through.'
27. PRAY,] *lit.* 'ask..mayest send.'
28. BRETHREN,] *or* 'brothers, that he may thoroughly witness (*lit.* divide *or* decide) to them..place of the trial.'
30. WENT,] *lit.* 'may pass on..they will have a new mind.'
31. ROSE,] *lit.* 'may stand up.'

Chapter XVII. may be divided into four parts; v. 1—4 duty of forbearance and forgiveness; v. 5—10 power of faith; v. 11—19 cleansing of ten lepers; v. 20—37 signs of the coming of God's reign.
1. IMPOSSIBLE.] The Greek word (*anendekton*) here used is not found again in N.T. The initial prefix *an* is generally supposed to be equal to the simple negative particle *a*, but it may be equal to *ana*, in which case the meaning is directly the reverse of the C.V. viz. 'it is fully possible for the stumbling-blocks not to come.'
2. IT WERE,] *lit* 'it is more profitable to him if a millstone, a weighty one (*lit.* one that might be driven by an 'ass,') is put round about his neck, and he has been cast into the sea, than that he may stumble one of these little ones.'
3. TAKE HEED,] *lit.* 'hold off to yourselves ..may sin in reference to thee, put a weight upon him; and if he may have a new mind, let (it) go to him.'
4. TRESPASS,] *lit.* 'may sin in reference to thee seven times in the day, and seven times in the day turn round upon thee, saying, I have a new mind, thou shalt let (it) go to him.'
5. INCREASE,] *lit.* 'set (put *or* place) beside us stedfastness.'
6. FAITH,] *lit.* 'stedfastness (in God).. would have said..uprooted..it would have secretly hearkened to you.'
7. BY AND BY,] *lit.* 'straightway,..Having come near lay thyself down.'
8. GIRD,] *lit.* 'gird thyself about, and act-as-deacon to me, till I eat and drink.'
9. DOTH,] *lit.* 'hath he favour..the things set fully in order to him? I think not.'
10. LIKEWISE,] *lit.* 'so also ye, when ye may have done all the things set fully in order to you, say ye, that, We are unnecessary servants; because *or* that, we have done that which we owed to do.'
11. PASSED,] *lit.* 'went thoroughly through.'
13. VOICES,] *lit.* 'voices..master (*lit.* one 'standing over,') pity us.'
14. SHEW,] *lit.* 'shew yourselves fully.'
15. HEALED,] *or* 'cured, turned round behind..great voice.'
16. AT,] *lit.* 'along-side of his feet, rejoicing greatly.'
17. TEN,] *lit.* 'were not the ten cleansed?'
18. ARE,] *lit.* 'were not found to turn round behind..alien.'
19. GO THY WAY,] *lit.* 'pass on; thy stedfastness has saved thee.'
20. DEMANDED,] *lit.* 'asked openly by the Pharisees, when the reign of the (true) God cometh..the reign of the (true) God cometh not with observableness.'
21. WITHIN,] *or* 'in the midst of you.'
22. THE DAYS,] *lit.* 'days..greatly desire ..not behold it.'
23. SEE,] *lit.* 'lo..lo..may ye not go away, nor pursue.'
24. LIGHTENETH,] *lit.* 'is lightening.'
25. REJECTED,] *lit.* 'thought little of by.'
26. WAS,] *lit.* 'happened.'
27. DID EAT,] *lit.* 'were eating, drinking, marrying, and marrying out (their daughters)..flood (*lit.* 'down-washing,') came, and loosed them all away.'
28. WAS,] *lit.* 'happened..were eating, drinking, buying (*lit.* attending public places), and selling (*lit.* 'turning over'), planting, building.'
29. BRIMSTONE,] *or* sulphur, *lit.* 'divinity;' so in Rev. 14. 10; 19. 20; 20. 10; 21. 8.
30. EVEN THUS,] *lit.* 'according to these things shall be the day the Son of the Man is revealed,' *lit.* uncovered.
31. HOUSE-TOP,] *lit.* 'built place..vessels .. lift it up,.. turn round to the things behind.'
32. REMEMBER,] *or* 'ye remember.'
33. SHALL,] *lit.* 'may seek to save his soul ..may lose his soul shall quicken it,' *or* give it life.
34. IN,] *lit.* 'upon one couch.. taken away, and the other let away.' So in v. 35, 36.
35. TOGETHER,] *lit.* 'at the same' place.
37. GATHERED,] *or* 'brought together.'

Chapter XVIII. may be divided into seven parts; v. 1—8 simile of an importunate widow; v. 9—15 of a Pharisee and a custom-house-officer; v. 16—17 Jesus receives little children; v. 18—27 cure of a rich chief; v.

28—30 rewards of the reign of God; v. 31—34 Jesus foretells his death and upraising; v. 35—43 cure of a blind man.

1. SPAKE,] *or* 'laid out *or* down also.. that it is necessary always to pour forth before (God), and not to faint,' *lit.* retire greatly.

2. A CITY,] *lit.* 'in a certain city a certain judge, who is not fearing God, nor turning round fully to man.'

3. WIDOW,] *lit.* 'bereaved one.. was coming .. Give me full justice from my opponent.'

4. WOULD,] *lit.* 'did not wish for a time, but after these things.. Even if I.. turn round fully to man.'

5. TROUBLETH,] *lit.* 'holdeth forth to me labour, I will give her full justice,..plague me,' *lit.* strike me under the eye.

7. AVENGE,] *lit.* 'do the full justice of his select ones who are crying,' *lit.* bellowing.

8. AVENGE,] *lit.* 'do their full justice in haste find the stedfastness (of the widow seeking right) upon the land of Israel?'

9. IN,] *lit.* 'upon themselves that they are just, and are thinking nothing of the rest.'

10. PRAY,] *lit.* 'pour forth before (God).'

PUBLICAN,] *or* 'custom-house-officer.'

11. WITH,] *lit.* 'towards himself.'

PRAYED,] *lit.* 'was pouring forth before (God) these things towards himself, O God ..as the rest of the men, rapacious.'

12. WEEK,] *lit.* 'sabbath.'

GIVE TITHES,] *lit.* 'I thoroughly tithe all, as many things as I acquire.'

13. WOULD NOT,] *lit.* 'did not wish to lift up openly even the eyes to the heaven, but was smiting..O God, be propitious (*or* mild) to me, the sinner,' *lit.* one 'missing' the mark.

14. JUSTIFIED,] i.e. 'reckoned just' by God.

ABASED,] *lit.* 'humbled.'

15. BROUGHT,] *lit.* 'were bringing near to him also (*or* even) the babes, that he may touch them, but the disciples having seen (it), laid a weight upon them.'

16. CALLED,] *lit.* 'calling them near, said, Suffer the little children to come to me, and hinder them not, for of such is the kingdom of the (true) God,' i.e. the gospel church.

17. SHALL,] *lit.* 'may receive..may not enter into it.'

18. RULER,] *lit.* 'chief asked at him, saying, Good Teacher,..life age-during?'

20. KNOWEST,] *lit.* 'hast known the commands (*lit.* full-doings): thou mayest not commit adultery; thou mayest do no murder; thou mayest not steal; thou mayest not bear false witness; be honouring.'

21. HAVE I KEPT,] *lit.* 'did I keep.'

22. LACKEST,] *lit.* 'one thing is left to thee (to do),..give (it) thoroughly to poor ones, ..be following me.'

23. WAS,] *lit.* 'became very..exceeding rich.'

24. WAS,] *lit.* 'became..have the goods.'

25. GO,] *lit.* 'go in through.'

26. CAN BE,] *lit.* 'is able to be saved?'

28. HAVE,] *lit.* 'we let go all.'

29. VERILY,] *or* 'Amen,' i.e. stedfast!

NO MAN,] *lit.* 'no one who let go..brothers ..because of the reign of the (true) God.'

30 SHALL,] *lit.* 'may not fully receive many-fold in this season, and in the coming age life age-during.'

31. TOOK,] *lit.* 'took along-side of (him) the..have been written through the prophets shall be completed to the Son of the Man.'

32. DELIVERED,] *lit.* 'given over to the nations, and shall be treated as a child, and insulted, and spitted on.'

33. DEATH,] *lit.* 'death thoroughly..stand up.'

34. UNDERSTOOD,] *lit.* 'sent (their heart) with none..was lying hid.'

35. COME NIGH,] *or* 'in his being nigh to Jericho,' in his way to Bethphage (see 19. 29); Matthew (20. 29) says, 'passed out from Jericho.'

SAT,] *lit.* 'was sitting by the way, asking earnestly.'

36. THE MULTITUDE,] *lit.* 'a crowd passing by, he was enquiring what this may be.'

37. TOLD,] *lit.* 'told him fully that Jesus the Nazarene cometh along.'

38. CRIED,] *lit.* 'bellowed..pity me.'

39. REBUKED,] *lit.* 'laid a weight upon him, that he might be silent, but he called ..pity me.'

41. WILT THOU,] *lit.* 'dost thou wish.. I may behold again.'

42. RECEIVE,] *lit.* 'behold again; thy stedfastness hath saved thee.'

43. IMMEDIATELY,] *lit.* 'along with the word he beheld again, and was following him.'

Chapter XIX. may be divided into six parts; v. 1—10 Jesus and Zacchaeus; v. 11—27 simile of the talents; v. 28—36 Jesus and the ass' colt; v. 37—40 praises of the disciples and rebuke of the Pharisees; v. 41—44 he bewails Jerusalem; v. 45—48 purging of the temple and its results.

1. PASSED,] *lit.* 'was passing.'

2. NAMED,] *lit.* 'by name called Zacchaeus (i.e. purity of Jah), and he was a chief-custom-house officer.'

3. SOUGHT,] *lit.* 'was seeking..who he is, and was not able from the crowd.. in stature.'

4. RAN,] *lit.* 'ran forward before, and went up upon a sycamore, that he might see him, because he was about to come through that way.'

5. WHEN,] *or* 'as he came upon the place ..to-day in thy house it behoveth me to remain.'

6. RECEIVED,] *lit.* 'received him under (his roof), rejoicing.'

7. MURMURED,] *lit.* 'were murmuring greatly, saying, that, with sinful men he went in to loose himself down,' i.e. rest from fatigue and cares.

8. GOODS,] *or* 'substance.. I took.. I give back.'

9. THIS,] *lit.* 'that, to-day salvation came .. a son,' by faith as well as by birth.

10. IS COME,] *lit.* 'came.'

11. ADDED,] *lit.* 'put forward.. is about along with it to be fully manifest.'

12. NOBLEMAN,] *lit.* 'man of good birth.. turn round again.'
13. HIS,] *lit.* 'his own ten servants..ten mnas..Do business.'
14. HATED,] *lit.* 'were hating him, and sent forth an embassy (of elders)..we do not wish.'
15. RETURNED,] *lit.* 'come again upon (them),..to whom he gave the silver..done fully in business.'
16. CAME,] *lit.* 'came near..thy mna produced besides ten mnas.'
17. VERY LITTLE,] *lit.* 'in a little.'
18. POUND,] *lit.* 'mna made five mnas.'
19. BE,] *lit.* 'become.'
20. POUND,] *lit.* 'mna, which I had lying away.'
21. BECAUSE,] *or* 'that..liftest up.'
22. WICKED,] *lit.* 'evil servant.'
23. MONEY,] *lit.* 'silver upon the table (of the bank),..used it with produce.'
24. TAKE,] *lit.* 'lift up from him the mna, and give to him having the ten mnas.'
26. HATH,] *or* 'holds,' i.e. uses.
HATH NOT,] *or* 'holds not,' i.e. does not use.
27. WOULD NOT,] *lit.* 'did not wish me to reign..slay thoroughly.'
28. WHEN,] *lit.* 'and having said these things, he passed on before.'
29. WHEN,] *lit.* 'as he was nigh..sent away.'
30. GO,] *lit.* 'go away..colt bound.'
31. ANY MAN,] *lit.* 'any one..that, the lord,' *or* master.
32. SENT,] *lit.* 'sent away went away..he said.'
33. OWNERS,] *lit.* 'lords, masters.'
35. CAST,] *lit.* 'cast over their own.'
36. WENT,] *lit.* 'passed on, they were strewing-by-degrees their garments.'
37. OLIVES,] *lit.* 'of the olives..leaping for joy to praise God with a great voice.'
38. BLESSED,] *lit.* 'well-spoken-of is He the coming King..the highest' places *or* persons.
39. SOME,] *lit.* 'certain..from the crowd.. Teacher, set a weight upon.'
40. SHOULD,] *lit.* 'shall be silent..will cry out.'
42. SAYING,] that, If thou didst know.. were lying hid.'
43. FOR,] *or* 'because days..and..cast around thee..press around thee on every side.'
44. LAY,] *lit.* 'lay thee low..let alone a stone upon a stone,..inspection.'
45. SOLD,] *lit.* 'turned over..made (it) a public place.'
46. IT IS,] *lit.* 'it has been written..of pouring forth before (God)..ye made a den of robbers.'
47. TAUGHT,] *lit.* 'was teaching daily.. writers were seeking.'
48. COULD,] *lit.* 'did not find..shall do.. were hanging on him greatly, hearing him.'

Chapter XX. may be divided into six parts; v. 1—8 Jesus silences the Jews; v. 9—18 simile of wicked husbandmen; v. 19—26 question about tribute; v. 27—38 about the rising of the dead; v. 39—44 David's son and lord; v. 45—47 warning against the writers.

1. ON,] *lit.* 'in, during..telling fully good-news..writers stood over him with the presbyters,' i.e. elders.
2. TELL,] *lit.* 'say to us, in what authority.'
3. THING,] *or* 'word, and say ye to me.'
4. FROM,] *lit.* 'out of..out of.'
5. REASONED,] *lit.* 'spoke together with themselves, saying, that, If we may say, Out of heaven; he will say, Wherefore then, did ye not remain stedfast to him?'
6. BUT,] if ye may say, Out of men, all the people will stone us down,' or thoroughly.
7. COULD,] *lit.* 'knew not where it was.'
8. BY,] *lit.* 'in what authority.' They had permitted John to teach and baptize without hindrance, and Jesus here claims a similar right.
9. PARABLE,] *or* 'parallel' saying.
LET IT FORTH,] *lit.* 'give it out to husbandmen (*lit.* 'earth-workers'), and went away from the people many times.'
10. AT,] *lit.* 'in a season he sent away a servant to the earth-workers, that they may give to him from..flogged him.'
11. ADDED,] *lit.* 'put forth..dishonoured him.'
12. AGAIN,] *lit.* 'put forth to sent.'
13. IT MAY BE,] *or* 'doubtless they will be turned fully round.'
14. HUSBANDMEN,] *lit.* 'earth-workers.. they were speaking much among themselves ..kill him utterly..may become ours.'
15. CAST,] *lit.* 'cast him forth outside of the vineyard, and killed (him) utterly.'
16. GOD FORBID,] *lit.* 'let it not be!'
17. BEHOLD,] *lit.* 'looked earnestly to them ..has been written, A stone which those building thought little of, it became for a head of a corner.'
18. WHOSOEVER,] *lit.* 'every one who is falling..utterly broken..may fall, it will shatter him much.'
19. THE SAME,] *lit.* 'in that hour desired to lay over upon him (their) hands..they knew that he said this simile about them.'
20. WATCHED,] *lit.* 'watched over (him),.. lyers in wait,..to give him over to the rule and authority of the leader,' i.e. Pilate.
21. MASTER,] *lit.* 'teacher, we have known ..receivest thou a face (of any one),..upon truth.'
22. TRIBUTE,] *lit.* 'a burden.'
23. PERCEIVED,] *lit.* 'perceived fully their whole work,..tempt,' *or* try.
24. SHEW,] *lit.* 'shew openly to me a denary.'
25. RENDER,] *lit.* 'give back.'
26. COULD NOT,] *lit.* 'had no strength..his saying..and were silent.'
27. CAME,] *lit.* 'came forward..speak against there being any rising up.'
28. MASTER,] *lit.* 'teacher..may die.. may die childless, in order that his brother may take the wife, and may cause seed to stand up.'
29. BRETHREN,] *lit.* 'brothers..childless.
30. HER TO WIFE,] *lit.* 'took the wife.'
31. LEFT,] *lit.* 'left no children at all.'
33. RESURRECTION,] *lit.* 'standing up, of

which of them does she become wife .. (as) wife.'

34. CHILDREN,] *lit.* 'sons of this age marry and are married out.'

35. THEY WHICH,] *lit.* 'those fully worthy to obtain that age and the standing-up out of (the) dead, neither marry nor are married out.'

36. EQUAL,] *or* 'angel *or* messenger-like, and are sons of God, being sons of the up-standing.'

37. AT,] *lit.* 'upon' narrating the circumstance of the Bush burning.

WHEN,] *lit.* 'as he calls.'

38. FOR,] *lit.* 'and .. of dead men, but of living.'

39. MASTER,] *lit.* 'teacher, thou didst say well.'

40. AND] 'no more durst they question him anything.'

41. CHRIST,] *lit.* 'the Christ.'

42. IN THEE,] *lit.* 'in a scroll of Psalms .. Be sitting.'

43. MAKE,] *lit.* 'set *or* put.'

45. THEN] 'all the people hearing he said.'

46. BEWARE,] *lit.* 'hold off from the writers, who wish to walk about in long robes, and love salutations (*lit.* drawings near) in the public places, and the foremost seats in the synagogues, and the foremost couches in the suppers.'

47. WHICH,] *lit.* 'who eat up (*lit.* down) the houses of the bereaved ones, and for an appearance pour forth before (God) long (speeches), these shall receive more abundant judgment.'

Chapter XXI. may be divided into four parts; v. 1—4 the widow's mite; v. 5—28 tokens of Jerusalem's destruction; v. 29—36 its time and manner; v. 37, 38 Jesus and the people.

1. TREASURY,] *lit.* 'treasure-hold.' Mark 12. 41.

2. POOR,] *or* 'working *or* labouring widow cast there two lepton,' the smallest coin, worth one half-farthing each.

3. OF A,] *lit.* 'truly I..widow cast in.'

4. HAVE,] *lit.* 'did of their over-abundance cast in..penury cast in.'

5. OF,] *or* 'concerning..it has been adorned with..devoted things.'

6. BEHOLD,] *or* 'view, days shall come in which a stone upon a stone shall not be let alone, which shall not be loosed down thoroughly.'

7. MASTER,] *lit.* 'teacher, when, then, shall these things be? and what is the sign when these things may be about to happen?'

8. TAKE HEED,] *lit.* 'see, may ye not be led astray..upon my name, saying, that, I am (He), and the season has come nigh; may ye not then pass on after them.'

9. SHALL,] *lit.* 'may hear of.. great-up-standings, may ye not be terrified..is not straightway.'

10. RISE,] *lit.* 'be raised upon nation.. upon kingdom.'

11. EARTHQUAKES,] *lit.* 'shakings..great fearful things and signs.'

12. LAY,] *lit.* 'lay over upon you.. may cause (you) to flee, giving you over to synagogues and wards, being led before (*lit.* upon) kings and leaders.'

13. TURN,] *lit.* 'come back to you for testimony.'

14. SETTLE,] *lit.* 'place it therefore for yourselves to your hearts not to be careful beforehand to speak back.'

15. ADVERSARIES,] *lit.* 'those set-against you..to speak-against *or* stand-against.'

16. BETRAYED,] *lit.* 'given over . brothers, and kindred,..shall they put to death.'

18. OF,] *lit.* 'out of your head be lost.'

19. PATIENCE,] *or* 'endurance acquire your souls,' *or* lives.

20. SHALL,] *lit.* 'may see..by (*lit.* under) encampments.'

21. COUNTRIES,] or districts around.

22. THESE BE,] *lit.* 'these are days of full-justice.. have been written.'

23. THEM,] *lit.* 'those having in the womb .. great necessity upon the land, and anger in (or among) this people.'

24. EDGE,] *lit.* 'mouth of a sword.. all the nations.. trodden down under nations till the seasons of nations may be filled out.'

25. IN THEE,] *lit.* 'in sun, and moon, and stars, and upon the land (of Israel) a holding-together of nations in passageless ways, .. sounding.'

26. HEARTS,] *lit.* 'souls.. thinking about the things coming upon the (Jewish) world, .. of the heavens.'

27. OF MAN,] *lit.* 'of the Man coming in a cloud with power and much glory.'

28. LOOK UP,] *lit.* 'bend backward.. your full-release (from Jewish superstition and bigotry) draweth nigh.'

29. PARABLE,] *lit.* a thing 'laid along-side of another for comparison or contrast.

30. SHOOT,] *lit.* 'cast forth..the summer.'

31. YE SEE,] *lit.* 'ye may see..ye know.'

32. VERILY,] *lit.* 'amen! I lay (it) down to you, that this generation may not go away, till all may have happened.'

33. HEAVEN,] *lit.* 'the heaven and the earth may go away,..may not go away.'

34. TAKE HEED,] *lit.* 'hold off for yourselves..may be burdened by (in, with) a moving of the head,..cares (*lit.* partings, distractions) of living,..may stand over (*or* fully) upon you.'

35. COME,] *lit.* 'come over (*or* fully) upon all those sitting on the face of all the land.'

36. WATCH,] *lit.* 'be ye sleepless therefore, in every season beseeching that ye may be full worthy to escape all these things that are about to happen.'

37. ABODE.] *lit.* 'was lodging at the mount.'

38. CAME,] *lit.* 'were early at him.'

Chapter XXII. may be divided into ten parts; v. 1—6 Judas agrees to deliver up Jesus; v. 7—13 preparation for the passover; v. 14—23 institution of the supper; v. 24—30 who is great; v. 31—34 Jesus and Simon Peter; v. 35—38 the two swords; v. 39—46 Jesus praying and warning; v. 47—54 Jesus delivered up, but heals the cut ear, and remostrates: v. 55—62 Peter denies him thrice; v. 63—71 Jesus abused and condemned.

1. BREAD,] *lit.* 'of the unleavened things.' THE,] *or* simply, 'Passover.'

2. SCRIBES,] *lit.* 'the scribes were seeking how to take him up (*or* away), for they were afraid of the people.'

3. SATAN,] *lit.* 'the Adversary into Judas, who is also called Iskariot,' i.e. 'man of Karioth *or* of the city.'

4. WENT,] *lit.* 'went away, and spake with the chief priests and the leaders of the force, how he might give him over to them.'

5. WERE GLAD,] *or* 'rejoiced, and covenanted (*lit.* put-together) to give him silver.'

6. PROMISED,] *lit.* 'spake out the same thing, and was seeking a good season to give him over to them, apart from the crowd,' *or* from tumult.

7. BREAD,] *lit.* 'of the unleavened things, in which it behoveth to sacrifice the passover.'

8. SENT,] *lit.* 'sent away..Passing on, make ready for us.'

9. WILT,] *lit.* 'dost thou wish (that) we may make ready?'

10. MEET,] *lit.* 'be fully-over-against you, bearing an earthen-pitcher..passeth into.'

11. SAY,] *lit.* 'lift up (the voice) to the house-despot, The Teacher..I may eat.'

12. HE,] *lit.* 'that one..furnished,' *lit.* strewn.

13. HAD SAID,] *lit.* 'as he has said.'

14. SAT,] *lit.* 'fell down.'

15. DESIRE,] *lit.* 'with full mind I was fully minded.'

16. BE,] *lit.* 'may be filled out (*or* realized) in the reign of the (true) God,' i.e. after his uprising.

17. TOOK,] *lit.* 'received the cup, and gave thanks (*lit.* rejoiced greatly),..part (it) thoroughly.'

18. WILL,] *lit.* 'may not drink from the produce..may come.'

19. BREAD,] *or* 'a loaf, and rejoiced greatly,..this is (i.e. represents) my body, which is being given for you; this do with a view to my full-remembrance.'

20. SUPPER,] *lit.* 'after the supping..new covenant (*lit.* 'a thing thoroughly set) in (with, by) my blood, which for you is being poured forth.'

21. BETRAYETH,] *lit.* 'is giving me up.'

22. TRULY,] *lit.* 'indeed..passeth on according to what has been determined (*lit.* bounded *or* bordered)..through whom he is given over.'

23. ENQUIRE,] *lit.* 'seek together by themselves who, then, out of them, it might be who is about to do this.'

24. WAS,] *lit.* 'happened also a friendly-contention..seems to be greater.'

25. GENTILES,] *lit.* 'nations lord (it) over them, and those having authority over them are called good-workers.'

26. GREATEST,] *lit.* 'great..let him become ..is leading as he who is acting-as-deacon.'

27. SITTETH,] *lit.* 'reclining, or he who is acting-as-deacon?..in the midst of you as he who is acting-as-deacon.'

28. CONTINUED,] *lit.* 'remained thoroughly with me in my trials.'

29. APPOINT,] *lit.* 'set thoroughly to you (as my Father set thoroughly to me a kingdom) that ye may eat and drink at, (*lit.* upon) my table, and may sit upon thrones. judging the twelve tribes of the Israel' of God, i.e. by means of their inspired writings.

31. SATAN,] *lit.* 'the Adversary asked you greatly for himself, and to shake you as the wheat.'

32. PRAYED,] *lit.* 'supplicated, that thy stedfastness may not fail greatly, and thou, when thou hast turned round fully.'

33. TO GO,] *or* 'to pass on.'

34. THIS DAY,] *or* 'to-day shall not sound ..mayest thrice deny with an oath.'

35. I SENT,] *lit.* 'sent you away without.. sandals.'

36. TAKE,] *lit.* 'lift (it) up.'

37. IS,] *lit.* 'has been written it behoveth yet to be ended in me, And with lawless ones he was reckoned,' *or* spoken of.

37. WENT,] *lit.* 'passed on, according to custom.'

40. AT,] *lit.* 'upon the place..trial.'

41. KNEELED DOWN,] *lit.* 'set the knees, and was pouring forth before (God).'

42. WILLING,] *lit.* 'be counselling to carry along this cup from me—; but let not my wish, but thine, come to pass'

43. ANGEL,] *lit.* 'messenger.'

44. BEING,] *or* 'having come into an agony, he pouring forth before (God) more extensively, and his sweat became, as if clots of blood coming down upon the earth.'

45. ROSE,] *lit.* 'stood up from the pouring forth before (God),..from the grief.'

46. SLEEP,] *lit.* 'sleep ye fast, having stood up pour ye forth before (God) that ye may not enter into trial.'

47. MULTITUDE,] *lit.* 'crowd,..to shew him (a token of) friendship.'

40. WITH A KISS,] *or* 'friendship..givest thou over.'

49. WOULD FOLLOW,] *lit.* 'shall be.'

50. ONE,] *lit.* 'a certain one..took off.'

51. HIM,] *or* 'it,' i.e. the ear; it is uncertain whether Jesus addressed the crowd or the disciples, more probably the former.

52. CAPTAINS,] *lit.* 'leaders of the force of the temple, and presbyters, those coming long-side of him. Have ye come forth as upon a robber..sticks.'

53. DARKNESS,] *lit.* 'of the darkness.'

54. TOOK,] *lit.* 'took they him along with themselves.. was following from him afar.'

55. HALL,] *or* 'court, and having sat down together Peter was sitting down in the midst of them.'

56. MAID,] *lit.* 'little maid.. sitting down towards the light, and strained (her eyes) at him.'

57. DENIED,] *lit.* 'denied him with an execration..I have not known him.'

59. ABOUT,] *lit.* 'and one hour, as it were, having intervened (*lit.* stood between), a certain other was very strenuous, saying.. he also is a Galilean.'

60. KNOW,] *lit.* 'I have not known..and along with the word, the cock sounded.'

61. TURNED,] *lit.* 'turned round..remembered secretly..he said.. that, Before cock

crowing thou mayest deny me utterly with an execration thrice.'

63. HELD,] *lit.* 'were holding Jesus fast, were treating him as a child.'

64. BLINDFOLDED,] *lit.* 'covered him round.'

STRUCK,] *lit.* 'were striking his face, and asking at him, Say openly, who is he who chastised thee?'

65. BLASPHEMOUSLY,] *lit.* 'speaking injuriously, they spake in reference to him.'

66. AS SOON,] *lit.* 'as it became day, the presbytery of the people, chief-priests also, and writers, came together, and they led him up to their own sanhedrim.'

67. TELL,] *lit.* 'say to us..I may say to you, ye may not believe.'

68. ASK,] *lit.* 'enquire, ye may not answer.'

69. HEREAFTER,] *lit.* 'from now there shall be the Son of the Man sitting.'

70. YE SAY,] *lit.* 'Ye—ye say that (*or* because) I am.'

71. HAVE HEARD,] *lit.* 'did hear.'

Chapter XXIII. may be divided into six parts; v. 1—7 Jesus before Pilate; v. 8—11 before Herod; v. 12—25 condemned by Pilate and given up; v. 26—32 Jesus on the way to Calvary; v. 33—49 his crucifixion and death; v. 50—56 his burial.

1. OF THEM,] i.e. of the sanhedrim-members.

UNTO,] *lit.* 'upon,' i.e. before Pilate.

2. ACCUSE,] *lit.* 'make (it) public against him..this one turning the nation thoroughly-round,..burdens to Caesar.'

3. ASKED] at, *lit.* 'upon him.'

4. PEOPLE,] *lit.* 'crowds..no cause (of punishment).'

5. MORE FIERCE,] *lit.* 'stronger upon (it), saying, He shakes up the people.'

6. ASKED,] *lit.* 'asked about (it)..man is.'

7. AS SOON AS,] *lit.* 'having fully known that he is out of the authority of Herod, he sent him back to Herod,..in Jerusalem in these days.'

8. DESIROUS,] *lit.* 'wishing exceedingly to see him, because of (his) hearing many things about him, and was hoping to see some sign happening by (*lit.* under) him.'

9. QUESTIONED,] *lit.* 'asked at him.'

10. SCRIBES,] *lit.* 'and the writers stood (before Herod), and very extensively made (it) public against him,' that he claimed to be the Son of God—the Christ.

11. MEN OF WAR,] *or* 'warriors thought nothing of him, and treated him entirely as a child, casting around him a shining robe.'

12. THE SAME,] *lit.* 'and in that day both Herod and Pilate become friends with one another, for they were before in enmity among themselves.'

13. RULERS,] *or* 'chiefs.'

14. HAVE BROUGHT,] *lit.* 'ye brought forward..turning round the people utterly.. having judged thoroughly..I found no cause (of punishment)..ye make (it) public against him.'

15. SENT,] *lit.* 'sent you back..done by him.'

16. RELEASE,] *lit.* 'loose him fully.'

17. FOR,] *lit.* 'and it was necessary for him to loose fully to them one every feast.'

18. ALL AT ONCE,] *lit.* 'all the multitude.'

AWAY,] *lit.* 'lift up this one!'

19. SEDITION,] *lit.* 'rising happening.'

20. WILLING,] *or* 'wishing to loose Jesus entirely.'

21. CRIED,] *lit.* 'were calling about (him).'

22. THE,] *lit.* 'a third time,..what evil did he? I found.'

23. WERE INSTANT,] *lit.* 'were lying upon (him) with great voices, asking him to be crucified.'

24. GIVE SENTENCE,] *lit.* 'judged fully their request to be done.'

25. SEDITION,] *lit.* 'rising..into the prison, whom they were asking for themselves, and Jesus he gave over to their wish.'

26. ONE,] *lit.* 'a certain one..from a field, ..after Jesus;' one at each end.

27. FOLLOWED,] *lit.* 'was following a great multitude of the people,..were beating themselves and lamenting him.'

28. TURNING,] *lit.* 'turning round..over me, but over yourselves, and over.'

29. THE DAYS,] *lit.* 'days come.. Happy the barren..bare not,..suckled not.'

30. HILLS,] *or* 'ascents.'

31. THE GREEN,] *lit.* 'a green tree, what may happen.'

32. MALEFACTORS,] *lit.* 'evil workers..put to death,' *lit.* lifted up.

33. WERE COME,] *lit.* 'came fully upon the place..Place of a Skull..evil workers, one ..and one.'

34. FORGIVE,] *lit.* 'let go (this crime) to them, for they have not known..and they parting thoroughly his garments, cast a lot.'

35. STOOD,] *lit.* 'were standing, viewing.. the chiefs..were sneering exceedingly..be the Christ, the select one of God.'

36. SOLDIERS,] *lit.* 'warriors also were treating him entirely as a child, coming forward and bringing forward to him vinegar.'

38. OF GREEK,] *lit.* 'Hellenistic, and Romaic, and Hebraic,'

39. MALEFACTORS,] *lit.* 'evil-workers.. was speaking injuriously of (*or* to) him,.. the Christ.'

40. REBUKED,] *lit.* 'laid a weight upon him ..fear even God, that (*or* because) thou art in the same judgment?'

41. RECEIVE,] *lit.* 'receive back things worthy of what we did, but this one did nothing out of place.'

42. COMEST,] *lit.* 'mayest come in thy reign.'

43. VERILY,] *lit.* 'amen..in the paradise.'

44. ABOUT,] *lit.* 'as if (it were) the sixth hour, and darkness happened over all the land (of Judea).'

45. TEMPLE,] *lit.* 'habitation' of God.'

46. LOUD,] *lit.* 'great..I put over my spirit, and these things having said, he expired,' *lit.* breathed out.

47. WAS DONE,] *or* 'happened.. truly this man was just.'

48. PEOPLE,] *lit.* 'crowds..upon that sight ..which happened, beating their own breasts turned away round.

49. FOLLOWED,] *lit.* 'followed with him.'

50. COUNSELLOR,] *lit.* 'being a counsellor.'
51. CONSENTED,] *lit.* 'was not putting down (his vote) with their counsel and deed, from Arimathaea, .. was expecting the reign of God.'
52. WENT,] *lit.* 'went forward .. asked for himself.'
53. WHEREIN,] *lit.* 'where no one was yet laid.'
54. THAT DAY,] *or* 'the day was a preparation, and sabbath shone on.'
55. FROM,] *lit.* 'out of Galilee followed fully, viewed for themselves the tomb.'
56. RETURNED,] *lit.* 'turned round secretly .. aromatics and ointment.'
RESTED,] *or* 'were quiet.'

Chapter XXIV. may be divided into six parts; v. 1—7 the women are informed of Jesus' rising; v. 8—12 Peter visits the tomb; v. 13—32 Jesus appears to two disciples; v. 23—44 and to the eleven; v. 45—49 he explains to them the Writings; v. 50—53 he blesses them and is borne up to heaven.

1. WEEK,] *lit.* 'sabbaths, at early dawn, they came upon the tomb bearing the aromatics they made ready.'
2. ROLLED,] *lit.* 'having been rolled.'
4. MUCH PERPLEXED,] *lit.* 'thoroughly passageless.'
SHINING,] *or* 'sparkling.'
5. WERE AFRAID,] *lit.* 'they having become afraid, and inclined (their) face to the earth .. with the dead?'
6. IS RISEN,] *lit.* 'was raised.'
7. SAYING] that it behoveth the Son of the Man to be given over into the hands of sinful men, .. to stand up.'
8. WORDS,] *or* 'sayings.'
9. RETURNED,] *lit.* 'turned round away from .. told fully again .. rest,' or remnant.
10. MARY,] *lit.* 'the Magdalene Mary .. Mary of James, and the rest (*or* remnant of the women) with them, which spake.'
11. WORDS,] *lit.* 'sayings appeared before them, as if idle-talk, and they were not believing them.'
12. UNTO,] *lit.* 'upon .. having bent over, he beholds the linen clothes lying alone, and went away to his own (company) wondering at what has happened.'
13. WENT,] *lit.* 'were passing on during that day .. was off from.'
14. TALKED,] *lit.* 'were speaking together with one another concerning all these things that have come together.'
16. COMMUNED,] *lit.* 'spake together, and sought together .. passed on with them.'
16. HOLDEN,] *lit.* 'held fast (so as) not to know him fully.'
17. COMMUNICATIONS,] *lit.* 'what are these things that ye cast over-against one to another, as ye walk round about, and are sad of countenance?'
18. CLEOPAS,] i.e. Alphaeus.
ART THOU,] *lit.* 'alone dost thou dwell beyond Jerusalem, and didst thou not know the things that happened in it in these days?'
19. WHAT THINGS,] *or* 'of what kind?'
CONCERNING,] *lit.* 'the things concerning .. who became a man, a prophet, powerful in work and word.'
20. AND HOW,] *lit.* 'how also our chief-priests and chiefs gave him over to a judgment of death.'
21. TRUSTED,] *lit.* 'were hoping that it is he who is about to redeem (*lit.* 'loose for himself,') the Israel (of God), but truly with all these things this third day is passing today since these things happened.'
22. YEA,] *lit.* 'also certain women of ours made us stand out, coming early upon the tomb.'
23. VISION,] *or* 'apparition of messengers who say he is living.'
24. WENT,] *lit.* 'went away .. found (it) so, even as also the women said.'
25. FOOLS,] *lit.* 'mindless (*or* thoughtless), and burdened in heart to be stedfast upon all the things that the prophets spake.'
26. OUGHT NOT,] *lit.* 'was it not behoving the Christ to suffer.'
27. BEGINNING,] *lit.* 'having begun from Moses and from all the prophets, he was thoroughly interpreting (*lit.* lifting up) to them.'
28. WENT,] *lit.* 'were passing on, and he was making forward to pass on further.'
29. CONSTRAINED,] *lit.* 'pressed upon him for themselves, saying, Remain .. day declined .. to remain.'
30. AS HE SAT,] *lit.* 'in his reclining back with them, having taken the loaf, he spake well (of God), and having broken (it) he was giving (it) over to them.'
31. OPENED,] *lit.* 'thoroughly opened, and they knew him fully, and he became unseen by them.'
32. DID NOT,] *lit.* 'was not our heart burning in us, as he was speaking to us in the way, and as he was opening thoroughly to us the Writings?'
33. RETURNED,] *lit.* 'turned round away .. thronged together.'
34. SAYING,] that, The Lord was truly raised, and was seen by Simon.'
35. TOLD,] *lit.* 'were bringing out the things .. he became known to them in the breaking of the loaf.'
36. AS,] *lit.* 'they speaking these things.'
37. WERE,] *lit.* 'they became amazed .. were thinking themselves to see (*or* view) a spirit.'
38. THOUGHTS,] *or* 'reasonings rise up.'
39. IT IS I MYSELF,] *or* 'I am he; touch.'
40. THUS,] *lit.* 'this spoken, he shewed fully to them.'
41. BELIEVED NOT,] *lit.* 'are unstedfast from the joy .. food.'
42. GAVE,] *lit.* 'gave over to him part of a boiled fish, and from a honey-comb.'
44. THAT,] *or* 'because it behoveth all things to be filled out, that have been written.'
45. OPENED,] *lit.* 'opened he fully their mind, to send (their hearts) with the Writings.'
46. THUS,] *lit.* 'that, thus it has been written, and thus it was behoving the Christ to suffer, and to stand up out of (the) dead.
47. REPENTANCE,] *lit.* 'a new mind and a letting go of sins be proclaimed-as-by-a-

herald upon his name to all the nations, having begun from Jerusalem.'

48. YE,] *lit.* 'ye, ye are (*or* be ye) witnesses of these things.'

49. SEND,] *lit.* 'send forth the promised-thing (i.e. the Holy Spirit).. sit ye down in the city.. till ye be clothed upon with power out of (the) high place.'

50. AS FAR AS,] *lit.* 'without even to Bethany, and having lifted up above them his hands he spake well of (*or* to) them.

51. BLESSED,] *lit.* 'spake well of (*or* to) them, he stood apart from them, and was borne up to the heaven.'

52. WORSHIPPED,] *lit.* 'having kissed forward (the hand) to him, turned round away to.'

53. CONTINUALLY,] *lit.* through all (time) in the temple, praising and speaking well of God'

GOSPEL QUOTATIONS FROM THE OLD TESTAMENT.

Mat.	1. 23.	see	Isa. 7. 14.
,,	2. 6.	,,	Mic. 5. 2.
,,	2. 15.	,,	Hos. 11. 1.
,,	2. 18.	,,	Jer. 31. 15.
,,	3. 3.	,,	Isa. 40. 3.
,,	4. 4.	,,	De. 8. 3.
,,	4. 6.	,,	Ps. 91. 11.
,,	4. 7.	,,	De. 6. 16.
,,	4. 10	,,	De. 6. 13.
,,	4. 15	,,	Isa. 8. 23; 9. 1.
,,	5. 21.	,,	Ex. 20. 13.
,,	5. 27.	,,	Ex. 20. 14.
,,	5. 31.	,,	De. 24. 1.
,,	5. 33.	,,	Le. 19. 12; De. 23. 23.
,,	5. 38.	,,	Ex. 21. 24.
,,	5. 43.	,,	Lev. 19. 18
,,	8. 17.	,,	Isa. 53. 4.
,,	9. 13.	,,	Hos. 6. 6.
,,	11. 10.	,,	Mal. 3. 1.
,,	12. 7.	,,	Hos. 6. 6.
,,	12. 18.	,,	Isa. 42. 1.
,,	13. 14.	,,	Isa. 6. 9.
,,	13. 35.	,,	Ps. 78. 2.
,,	15. 4.	,,	Ex. 20. 12; 21. 17.
,,	15. 8.	,,	Isa. 29. 13.
,,	17. 11.	,,	Mal. 3. 1; 4. 5.
,,	19. 4.	,,	Ge. 1. 27.
,,	19. 5.	,,	Ge. 2. 24.
,,	19. 7	,,	De. 24. 1.
,,	19. 18.	,,	Ex. 20. 12; Lev. 19. 18.
,,	21. 5.	,,	Zech. 9. 9.
,,	21. 9.	,,	Ps. 118. 25.
,,	21. 13.	,,	Isa. 56. 7, Jer. 7. 11.
,,	21. 16.	,,	Ps. 8. 2.
,,	21. 42.	,,	Ps. 118. 22.
,,	22. 24.	,,	De. 25. 5.
,,	22. 32.	,,	Ex. 3. 6.
,,	22. 37.	,,	De 6. 5.
,,	22. 39.	,,	Lev. 19. 18.
,,	22. 44.	,,	Ps. 110. 1.
,,	23. 35.	,,	Ge. 4. 8; 2 Ch. 24. 21.
,,	23. 39.	,,	Ps. 118. 26.
,,	24. 15.	,,	Da. 9. 27.
,,	24. 29.	,,	Isa. 13. 10.
,,	24. 37.	,,	Ge. 6. 11.
,,	26. 31.	,,	Zec. 13. 7.
,,	26. 52.	,,	Ge. 9. 6 (?)
,,	26. 64.	,,	Da. 7. 13.
,,	27. 9.	,,	Zec. 11. 13.
,,	27. 35.	,,	Ps. 22. 18.
,,	27. 43.	,,	Ps. 22. 8.
,,	27. 46.	,,	Ps. 22. 1.
Mark	1. 2.	,,	Mal. 3. 1.
,,	1. 3.	,,	Isa. 40. 3.
,,	1. 44	..	Lev. 14. 2.
Mark	2. 25.	see	1 Sam. 21. 6.
,,	4. 12.	,,	Isa. 6. 10.
,,	7. 6.	,,	Isa. 29. 13.
,,	7. 10.	,,	Ex. 20. 12; 21. 17.
,,	9. 44.	,,	Isa. 66. 24.
,,	10. 4.	,,	De. 24. 1.
,,	10. 7.	,,	Ge. 2. 24.
,,	10. 19.	,,	Ex. 20. 12—17.
,,	11. 17.	,,	Isa. 56. 7; Jer. 7. 11.
,,	12. 10.	,,	Ps. 118. 22.
,,	12. 19.	,,	De. 25. 5.
,,	12. 26.	,,	Ex. 3. 6.
,,	12. 29.	,,	De. 6. 4.
,,	12. 31.	,,	Lev. 19. 18.
,,	12. 36.	,,	Ps. 110. 1.
,,	13. 14.	,,	Dan. 9. 27.
,,	13. 24.	,,	Isa. 13. 10.
,,	14. 27.	,,	Zech. 13. 7.
,,	14. 62.	,,	Da. 7. 13.
,,	15. 28.	,,	Isa. 53. 12.
,,	15. 34.	,,	Ps. 22. 1.
Luke	1. 17.	,,	Mal. 4. 4, 5.
,,	2. 23.	,,	Ex. 13. 2.
,,	2. 24.	,,	Lev. 12. 8.
,,	3.4-6.	,,	Isa. 40. 3—5.
,,	4. 4.	,,	De. 8. 3.
,,	4. 8.	,,	De. 6. 13.
,,	4.10,11.	,,	Ps. 91. 11, 12.
,,	4. 12.	,,	De. 6. 4.
,,	4. 18.	,,	Isa. 61. 1, 2.
,,	7. 27.	,,	Mal. 3. 1.
,,	8. 10.	,,	Isa. 6. 9.
,,	10. 27.	,,	De. 6. 5; Lev. 19. 18.
,,	18. 20.	,,	Ex. 20. 12.
,,	19. 46.	,,	Isa. 56. 7; Jer. 8. 11.
,,	20. 17.	,,	Ps. 118. 22, 23.
,,	20. 28.	,,	De. 25. 5.
,,	20.42-3.	,,	Ps. 110. 1.
,,	22. 37.	,,	Isa. 53. 12.
,,	23. 46.	,,	Ps. 31. 7.
John	1. 23.	,,	Isa. 40. 3.
,,	2. 17.	,,	Ps. 69. 9.
,,	6. 31.	,,	Ps. 78. 24, 25.
,,	6. 45.	,,	Ps. 54. 13.
,,	7. 42.	,,	Ps. 132. 11; Mic. 5. 2.
,,	10. 34.	,,	Ps. 82. 6.
,,	12. 15.	,,	Zec. 9. 9.
,,	12. 38.	,,	Isa. 53. 1.
,,	12. 40.	,,	Isa. 6. 9, 10.
,,	13. 18.	,,	Ps. 49. 1.
,,	15. 25.	,,	Ps. 35. 19; 69. 4
,,	19 24.	,,	Ps. 22. 18.
,,	19. 28.	,,	Ps. 69. 21.
,,	19. 36.	,,	Ex. 12. 46; Ps. 34. 20.
,,	19. 37.	,,	Ps. 22. 16, 17; Zec. 12 16

JOHN

THE GOSPEL OF JOHN was most probably written at Ephesus, A.D. 68, and, judging from the comparative purity of its Greek, *after* the composition of the 'Revelation' in Patmos.

He was the younger of the two sons (surnamed Boanerges), of Zebedee and Salome, residing at Beth-Saida, by the sea of Galilee; he was directed to Jesus by John (1. 36), called a first time (Mat. 4. 21, 22), a second time (Luke 5. 1—11), and a third time (Mat. 10. 2.) This gospel is quoted by Ignatius (A.D. 100), Diognetus (A.D. 120), Justin Martyr (A.D. 140), Tatian (A.D. 170), &c. Marcion, Cerdon, the Montanists, &c., admitted it to be the work of the Apostle, but alleged it was interpolated, or that he was mistaken. It is chiefly occupied with viewing Jesus Christ, the Saviour, as 'THE SON OF GOD, THE REVEALER OF THE FATHER.'

It may be divided into three parts: the Prologue, the History, the Conclusion.

I The PROLOGUE, ch. 1. 1—18.

II. The HISTORY, ch. 1. 19—20. 29.

1). Jesus' first journey, 1. 19—2. 12.

2). His second, 2. 13—4. 54.

3). His third, 5. 1—47.

4). His fourth, 6. 1—71.

5). His fifth, 7. 1—10. 21.

6.) His sixth, 10. 22—42.

7). His seventh, 11. 1—54.

8). His eighth, 11. 55—12. 50.

9). Preparation for his Passion, 13. 1-17. 26.

10). Circumstances of his Death, 18. 1—19. 42.

11). His Up-Rising and its proofs, 20. 1—29.

III. The CONCLUSION, ch. 20. 30—21. 25.

The following passages are peculiar to John, viz. ch. 1. 1—14, 35—51; 2. 1—3. 36; 4. 1—42, 46—54; 5. 1—47; 6. 4, 16—65; 7. 11—11. 57; 12. 20—50; 14. 1—17. 26; 19. 31—37; 20. 30, 31; 21. 1—25. He alone mentions Peter as the person who cut off the ear of the chief-priest's servant, as Peter was then probably dead.

Chapter I. may be divided into six parts; v. 1—5 Pre-existence and all-creative energy of the Word; v. 6—14 His object in coming into the world in the flesh; v. 15—18 His revelation of the Father; v. 19—36 John's testimony to the Jews and his disciples; v. 37—42 John, Andrew, and Peter, brought to Jesus; v. 43—51 also Philip and Nathanael.

1. IN THE BEGINNING,] when (or before) God created man upon the earth; comp. Ge. 1. 1.

WAS,] that is, 'existed,' not 'came,' merely.

THE WORD,] which (according to v. 14), became incarnate in the person of Jesus the Christ; as 'words' are the usual medium by which men explain their plans to others, so it is applied to Jesus as the revealer of the Father; the title is very common in the Chaldee Targums of the Old Testament, which, though not committed to writing till A.D. 250, had been in use *five* hundred years earlier.

AND THE WORD WAS WITH,] *lit.* 'towards the (true) God,' i.e. he existed, and was manifesting or developing himself in or with a reference to the great God.

AND THE WORD WAS GOD,] more *lit.* 'and a God (i.e. a Divine Being) was the Word,' that is, he was existing and recognized as such.

2. THE SAME,] *lit.* 'this one was (i.e. existed) in the beginning towards (in *or* with a reference to) the (true) God,' as his Manifester.

3. ALL THINGS WERE MADE,] *lit.* 'happened through (*or* by means of) him, and apart from him happened not even one thing which has happened.'

4. OF MEN,] *lit.* 'of the men,' the human race.

5. COMPREHENDED,] *lit.* 'receive it fully.

6. THERE WAS,] *lit.* 'there came a man having been sent forth from God.'

7. THE SAME,] *lit.* 'this one came for testimony, that he might bear-testimony about the Light.'

8. HE,] *lit.* 'That one was not the Light, but (came) that he might bear-testimony about the Light.'

9. THAT,] *lit.* 'he was the true Light, who lighteneth (i.e. designs to lighten) every man, (by) coming into the world,'—*Gr.* cosmos, i.e. order, arrangement, whether physical or moral.

10. WAS MADE,] *lit.* 'happened (*or* came) through him.'

11. HIS OWN,] *lit.* 'his own things, and his own people did not receive him along-side of (them).'

12. POWER,] *lit.* 'authority (*or* licence) to become children of God, to those remaining stedfast in reference to his name,' that is, character.

13. BORN,] *lit.* 'begotten, not out of bloods (a Heb. idiom), not even out of a wish of flesh, not even out of a wish of man, but out of God.'

14. WAS MADE,] *lit.* 'become flesh, and settled among us and we viewed his glory—glory as of an only-begotten along-side of a father..full of grace and truth.'

15. BARE,] *lit.* 'bears testimony concerning him, and has cried..I said..coming after me has come before me.'

16. HAVE,] *lit.* 'did..grace over-against grace.'

17. BY,] *lit.* 'through Moses, the grace and the truth came through.'

18. IN,] *or* 'on..that one led (him) out.'

19. RECORD,] *lit.* 'testimony..sent forth..

out of Jerusalem, that they might ask him.'

20. CONFESSED,] *lit.* 'spake the same thing (as he had done before), and..spake the same thing, that, I am not.'

21. THAT,] *lit.* 'the prophet;' see De. 18. 15, 18.

22. OF,] *lit.* 'concerning thyself.'

23. THE,] *lit.* 'a voice of one calling,' *lit.* lowing.

24. SENT,] *lit.* 'sent forth.'

25. THAT,] *lit.* 'the Christ nor even Elijah, nor even the prophet,' spoken of by Moses.

26. WITH,] *lit.* 'in (*or* by) water..has stood ..have not known.'

27. HE,] *or* 'this one..has come before me, of whom I am not (so) worthy that I may loose.'

28. WERE DONE,] *lit.* 'happened in Bethany (so the best MSS.), beyond the Jordan.'

29. UNTO,] *or* 'towards..who is lifting up the sin of the world.'

30. IS HE,] *lit.* 'this one it is concerning.. who has come before me.'

31. KNEW,] *lit.* 'had not known him, but that he might be manifested to Israel, because of this came I in (*or* with, by) the water baptizing.'

32. RECORD,] *or* 'testimony, saying, that, I have viewed the Spirit coming down as (if) a dove out of heaven.'

33. KNEW,] *lit.* 'had not known him..in (with, by) water, that one said..mayest see ..this one it is who is baptizing in (with, by) a holy spirit,' or influence from *the* Spirit.

34. SAW,] *lit.* 'have seen and borne testimony.'

35. STOOD,] *lit.* 'was standing.'

36. AS HE WALKED,] *lit.* 'walking about.'

37. TURNED,] *lit.* 'turned round, and viewing..Teacher, where remainest thou?'

39. COME,] *lit.* 'be coming..he remains, and remained along-side of him that day, and.'

40. HEARD,] *lit.* 'heard from John.'

42. BROUGHT,] *or* 'led him towards Jesus ..is interpreted, A stone;' *Gr.* Petros.

43. FOLLOWING,] *or* 'next day;' as in v. 29, 35.

WOULD,] *lit.* 'wished to go forth..be following me.'

44. OF,] *lit.* 'from Beth-saida, out of the city.'

45. OF,] *lit.* 'from Nazareth.'

46. CAN,] *lit.* 'out of Nazareth is any good thing able to be?..be coming and see.' Nathanael was perhaps Bartholemew.

47. TO,] *lit.* 'towards him, and saith concerning him, Behold truly an Israelite, in whom guile is not;' unlike Jacob, Ge. 25. 27.

49. SON..KING.] Two synonymous phrases, taken from Ps. 2. 6, 7.

50. UNDER,] *lit.* 'underneath..a greater thing.'

51. VERILY,] *lit.* 'Amen, Amen,' i.e. 'Stedfast! Stedfast! I lay (it) down to you, from this time (*lit.* now) ye shall see the heaven opened up, and the messengers of the (true) God going up and coming down upon the Son of the Man;' i.e. they would see from that time the daily intercourse established between God and men through the medium of Christ, the representative man, and the communication of every spiritual blessing. Compare Ge. 28. 12, 13.

Chapter II. may be divided into three parts; v. 1—11 Jesus turns water into wine; v. 12—22 cleanses the temple; v. 23, 24 believed on by many.

1. WAS,] *or* 'happened..marriage-feast.. Cana;' there was another Cana in Ephraim.

2. WANTED,] *lit.* 'wine having been lacking.'

4. HAVE I TO DO WITH THEE,] *lit.* 'what to me and to thee (in common).'

WOMAN,] as in 19. 26; 20. 13, &c.

HOUR] of shewing my glory to men.

5. SERVANTS,] *lit.* 'deacons;' as in v. 9.

SAITH,] *lit.* 'may say.'

6. FIRKINS,] *lit.* 'measures,' of about nine gallons each.

7. WATER-POTS,] *or* 'jugs..to the top.'

8. GOVERNOR,] *lit.* 'chief-of-the-threefold-couch.'

9. HAD TASTED,] *lit.* 'as he tasted the water become wine, and had not known whence it is, but the deacons who have drawn the water had known..calls.'

10. AT THE BEGINNING,] *lit.* 'placeth first the good wine, and when (men) may have drunk-sufficiently, then the inferior.'

11. MIRACLES,] *lit.* 'of the signs.'

12. BRETHREN,] *or* 'brothers.'

13. AT HAND,] *lit.* 'nigh.'

14. TEMPLE,] its outer court, no doubt.

15. SMALL CORDS,] *lit.* 'rushes..both the sheep and the oxen,..small-changers' coins, and fully over-turned.' Mat. 21. 12 records a second cleansing.

16. DOVES,] *lit.* 'the doves, Lift up..of passing in (for trade).'

17. WAS,] *lit.* 'is written..did eat me up, *lit.* down, i.e. fully.

19. DESTROY,] *lit.* 'loose down this habitation (of God);' the imperative form here is simply predictive or permissive, as in 13. 27; Eph. 4. 26, &c.

20. TEMPLE,] *lit.* 'habitation..raise it.'

22. RISEN,] *lit.* 'was raised out of the dead ..he said this..the Writing..Jesus said.'

23. AT,] *lit.* 'in (during) the passover, in (during) the feast..in reference to his name (*or* character) viewing his signs that he was doing.'

24. DID NOT,] *lit.* 'was not trusting himself to them, because of his knowing all,' things *or* persons.

25. AND] 'because he had no need that any may bear testimony concerning man, for he himself was knowing what was in man.'

Chapter III. may be divided into four parts; v. 1—12 Jesus and Nicodemus; v. 13 —21 object of His mission; v. 22—30 John's testimony to Jesus; v. 31—36 the evangelist's testimony.

1. THERE WAS,] *lit.* 'but (*or* now) there was.'

NICODEMUS,] i.e. 'innocent blood.'

PHARISEES,] i.e. 'separated' ones.

RULER,] *lit.* 'chief.'

2. THE SAME,] *lit.* 'this one.'
RABBI,] *lit.* in *Heb.* 'my great one!'
WE KNOW,] *lit.* 'we have known,' i.e. the Pharisees generally.
ART,] *lit.* 'hast come from God—a teacher, for no one is able to do these signs..if God may not be with him.'
3. AGAIN,] *lit.* 'if any one may not be born (*or* begotten) from above, he is not able to see (i.e. enjoy) the reign of God,' or the gospel dispensation.
4. OLD,] *lit.* 'seeing the earth,' bending with years and cares.
CAN HE,] *or* 'he is not able to enter a second time.'
5. EXCEPT,] *lit.* 'if any one may not be born of water and spirit, i.e. spiritual water or water, (i.e. seed of the Spirit), he is not able to enter (really and truly) into the reign of God,' but only nominally. There is no reference here to water baptism, as that was not yet instituted.
6. FLESH..SPIRIT.] Like produces like.
7. MARVEL,] *lit.* 'may ye not wonder..It behoves you to be born from above.'
8. WIND,] *lit.* 'Spirit breatheth where He wishes, and thou hearest His voice, but thou hast not known whence He cometh, and whither He goeth away; so (*or* thus) is every one who has been born of the Spirit.'
9. BE,] *lit.* 'happen?'
10. ART THOU,] *or* 'Thou art the teacher of the Israel (of God), and these things thou dost not know!'
11. WE,] *lit.* 'that, we (the language of authority) speak what we have known, and testify what we have seen, and..testimony.'
12. HAVE,] *lit.* 'did tell you of the things (done) upon the earth, and ye do not believe, how, if I might you the things (done) above the heavens, will ye believe?'
13. NO MAN,] *lit.* 'no one went up to the heaven, except..out of the heaven, the Son of the Man who is in the heaven.' The difficulties connected with this verse are best solved by supposing v. 13—21 to be the language of the evangelist, rather than that of Jesus, the record of whose conversation with Nicodemus appears to end with the emphatic question of v. 12, though others suggest that it ends with v. 15.
14. MUST,] *lit.* 'it behoveth.'
15. WHOSOEVER,] *lit.* 'every one who is believing on (*or* remaining stedfast to) him may not be loosed-away, but may have life age-during.'
16. WORLD,] i.e. its inhabitants.
17. SENT,] *lit.* 'sent not forth..that he might judge (i.e. pronounce judgment on) the world.
18. BELIEVETH,] *lit.* 'is remaining-stedfast to him is not judged, but he who is not remaining-stedfast is already judged, because he has not remained-stedfast to the name (*or* character, i.e. person) of the only-begotten Son of God.'
19. CONDEMNATION,] *lit.* 'judgment, that the Light came to the world, and the men (of the world) loved the darkness rather than the Light, for their works were evil.'
20. DOETH EVIL,] *lit.* 'is practising foulness..toward..that his works may not be convicted.'
21. DOETH,] *lit.* 'is doing the truth cometh toward the Light that his works may be manifested, that in (with, by) God they are having been wrought.'
22. TARRIED,] *lit.* 'spent-thoroughly (the time), and was baptizing,' by the instrumentality of his disciples, see 4. 2.
23. ENON,] i.e. 'fountains.'
SALIM,] i.e. 'peace;' in Isaachar west of Jordan, 8 miles from Scythopolis.
MUCH WATER,] *lit.* 'many waters,' i.e. springs or fountains, to drink from, and refresh themselves.
CAME,] *lit.* 'came along-side of (him), and were being baptized.'
24. PRISON,] *lit.* 'the prison,' watch or guard.
25. AROSE,] *lit.* 'happened..inquiry from the disciples of John with (some) Jews.' Many MS. read 'a Jew.'
26. TO,] *lit.* 'towards John..the Jordan, to whom thou hast borne testimony,..all,' i.e. many.
27. FROM,] *lit.* 'out of the heaven.'
28. I AM SENT,] *lit.* 'I am having been sent forth.'
29. HATH,] *lit.* 'is having..is bridegroom, who has stood and is hearing him, rejoiceth with joy..has been filled out,' *or* realized.
30. BUT I,] *lit.* 'but me to become less.' John's language appears to close here, while the rest is that of the evangelist.
31. COMETH,] *lit.* 'is coming from above is above all; he who is out of the earth is out of the earth. and speaketh out of the earth, he who is coming out of the heaven is above all.'
32. THAT,] *lit.* 'this..no one.'
33. HATH,] *lit.* 'is receiving..did seal.'
34. SENT,] *lit.* 'sent forth..sayings of God ..out of a measure,' but without limit.
35. HATH GIVEN,] *lit.* 'gave every (thing *or* person) into his hand.'
36. BELIEVETH,] *lit.* 'is remaining-stedfast to the Son has life age-during, but he who is un-stedfast (to) the Son.'

Chapter IV. may be divided into three parts; v. 1—29 Jesus and the woman of Samaria; v. 30—42 Jesus, his disciples, and the Samaritans; v. 43—54 Jesus received by the Galileans, and cures a courtier's son.
1. HOW,] *lit.* 'that..heard..makes and baptizes.'
2. BAPTIZED,] *lit.* 'was not baptizing.'
3. LEFT,] *lit.* 'let Judea go.'
4. HE MUST NEED,] *lit.* 'it was behoving him to go thoroughly through Samaria.'
5. PARCEL OF GROUND,] *lit.* 'place *or* space.'
6. WELL,] *or* 'fountain, spring.'
WITH,] *lit.* 'out of the way-passage, was sitting..about.' *lit.* as if (it were).
7. OF,] *lit.* 'out of Samaria.'
8. TO BUY,] *lit.* 'in order that they might attend the public place for sustenance.'
9. WOMAN OF SAMARIA,] *lit.* 'the Samaritan woman..asketh to drink from me, being a Samaritan woman, for Jews have no dealings with Samaritans.'

10. KNEWEST,] *lit.* 'hadst known..is saying to thee..asked him.'
11. TO DRAW WITH,] *lit.* 'not even a drawing vessel..pit..the living water.'
12. CHILDREN,] *lit.* 'sons, and his cattle,' or household.
13. WHOSOEVER DRINKETH,] *lit.* 'every one who is drinking out of this water.'
14. DRINKETH,] *lit.* 'may drink out of the water..may not thirst to the age..shall become in him a fountain of water..life age-during.'
15. I THIRST,] *lit.* 'I may not thirst.'
16. GO,] *lit.* 'go away *or* secretly.'
17. HAST,] *lit.* 'didst well say, that, I have not a husband.'
18. IN THAT,] *lit.* 'this.'
20. WORSHIPPED,] *lit.* 'kissed forward (the hand)..where it behoveth to kiss forward (the hand).'
21. BELIEVE ME,] 'that, there cometh an hour, when not even in this hill, not even in Jerusalem, shall ye kiss forward (the hand) to the Father.'
22. WORSHIP,] *lit.* 'kiss forward (the hand) to what ye have not known, we..to what we have known, because the salvation (promised to the fathers) is out of the Jews.'
23. THE HOUR,] *lit.* 'there cometh an hour.'
24. GOD,] *lit.* 'a spirit is the (true) God.'
25. KNOW,] *lit.* 'have known..when he may come, he will tell us all things fully.'
26. SPEAK,] *lit.* 'am speaking.'
27. TALKED,] *lit.* 'was speaking with a woman.'
28. WATER-POT,] *or* 'jug, and went away to the city.'
29. ALL THINGS,] *lit.* 'all, as many things as I did; is this the Christ?'
30. CAME,] *lit.* 'were coming towards him.'
31. PRAYED,] *lit.* 'were asking..Rabbi.'
32. MEAT,] *or* 'sustenance..have not known.'
34. MEAT,] *or* 'sustenance is, that I may do the will (or wish)..and may end (*or* finish) his work.'
35. HARVEST,] *lit.* 'and the reaping cometh..and view the places (*or* spaces), that (*or* because)..towards (the) reaping.'
36. REAPETH,] *lit.* 'is reaping receiveth a wage, and bringeth together fruit with a view to life-age-during.. is sowing.. is reaping.'
37. HEREIN,] *lit.* 'in this (case) the word is the true one: that (*or* because) one is the sower, and another the reaper.'
38. SENT,] *lit.* 'sent you forth.. have not laboured.. have entered into their labour.'
39. OF,] *lit.* 'out of that city.. because of the word of the woman testifying, that, He said to me all things, as many as I did.'
40. BESOUGHT,] *lit.* 'were asking him to remain along with them.'
41. HIS OWN WORD,] *lit.* 'his word.'
42. AND SAID,] *lit.* 'they said also.. that, no more because of thy speaking do we believe.'
43. TWO,] *lit.* 'the two days he went forth from thence, and went away to the Galil.'
44. HATH,] *lit.* 'shall not have honour in his own father's place.'
45. WAS COME,] *lit.* 'came.. in Jerusalem in (during) the feast.'
46. SO,] *lit.* 'therefore.. to the Cana of the Galil.. nobleman (*lit.* king's-man) whose son was infirm in Capernaum.'
47. WAS,] *lit.* 'is come.. went away towards him, and asked him, in order that he might come down.. he was about to die utterly.'
48. WONDERS,] *lit.* 'fearful things.. ye may not believe.'
49. CHILD,] *lit.* 'little boy.'
50. GO THY WAY,] *lit.* 'be passing on.. Jesus said.. was going on.'
51. TOLD,] *lit.* 'told (him) fully, saying, that, Thy boy liveth.'
52. ENQUIRED,] *lit.* 'he enquired for himself *or* he himself enquired, from them the hour in which he became better.. fever let him alone.'
53. SO,] *lit.* 'therefore *or* then.'
54. THIS,] *lit.* 'this, again, a second sign, did Jesus, having come.'

Chapter V. may be divided into seven parts; v. 1—9 Jesus cures an infirm man; v. 10—13 who is challenged by the Jews; v. 14 warned by Jesus; v. 15—16 whom the Jews seek to kill; v. 17—30 Jesus asserts his authority; v. 31—35 appeals to the testimony of John; 36—47 to that of his own works, his Father, and the Writings.

1. FEAST,] either that of the Passover, or of Purim, or of Tabernacles, or of Pentecost.
2. AT,] *lit.* 'in Jerusalem by (*lit.* upon) the sheep-(gate) a swimming-bath, which is surnamed in Hebrew Beth-Esda (i.e. house of kindness) having five porches' *lit.* standing-places.
3. LAY,] *lit.* 'were lying down.. of the infirm, blind, lame, withered.'
WAITING.] This clause, and the whole of the 4th verse, is of doubtful authority, being wanting in the oldest MSS.
4. ANGEL,] *or* 'messenger each season was going down in the swimming-bath, and was troubling.. became whole of whatsoever unsoundness he was held down by.'
5. WHICH HAD AN INFIRMITY,] *or* 'having been in (his) infirmity.
6. LIE,] *lit.* 'lying down.. Dost thou wish to become whole?'
7. IMPOTENT,] *lit.* 'infirm.. man, that, whenever the water may be troubled he may cast me into the swimming-bath..goes down.'
8. RISE,] *or* 'raise thyself, lift up thy couch (*or* mattress), and be walking about.'
9. IMMEDIATELY,] *lit.* 'straightway the man became whole, and took up his mattress, and was walking about, and there was a sabbath on that day.'
10. WAS,] *lit.* 'has been cherished, It is a sabbath,.. lift up thy mattress.'
11. TAKE,] *lit.* 'lift up thy mattress, and be walking about.'
12. WHAT,] *lit.* 'who is the man who is saying to thee, Lift up thy mattress, and be walking about?'
13. WIST NOT,] *lit.* 'had not known who he is, for Jesus moved away, a crowd being in the place.'

14. AFTERWARDS,] *lit.* 'after these things . . thou hast become whole . . that a worse thing may not happen to thee.'
15. TOLD,] *lit.* 'told fully . . it is Jesus who made him whole.'
16. THEREFORE,] *lit.* 'because of this . . pursue Jesus, and were seeking to put him utterly to death . . was doing in a sabbath.'
17. HITHERTO,] *lit.* 'till now.'
18. THEREFORE,] *lit.* 'because of this, then, were the Jews seeking the more to kill him utterly, because not only was he loosing (down) the sabbath, but also called God his own Father, making himself equal (*or* like) to God.'
19. OF,] *lit.* 'from himself, if he may not behold any thing the Father is doing, for what things He may do, these also the Son likewise (*or* in like manner) doeth.'
20. LOVETH,] *or* 'befriendeth (*or* is friend to) the Son.'
21. QUICKENETH,] *lit.* 'maketh alive . . so also the Son maketh alive whom he wisheth.'
22. JUDGETH,] *lit.* 'doth not even judge any one, but hath given all the judgment.'
23. SHOULD,] *lit.* 'may honour the Son, according as . . he who is not honouring . . who sent him.'
24. HE,] *lit.* 'that, he who is hearing . . is remaining-stedfast to him . . life age-during, and does not come to judgment, but has gone-beyond out of the death to the life.'
25. THE HOUR,] *lit.* 'there cometh an hour.'
26. HATH HE GIVEN,] *lit.* 'did he give also.'
27. HATH GIVEN,] *lit.* 'gave . . also to do judgment, because he is (a) Son of man.'
28. THE HOUR,] *lit.* 'there cometh an hour.'
29. COME,] *lit.* 'pass . . did the good things to an up-standing of life, and those who practised the foul things to an up-standing of judgment.'
30. I CAN,] *lit.* 'I am not able to do anything from myself . . own wish, but the wish of the Father who sent me.'
31. OF,] *lit.* 'concerning . . true,' i.e. legal.
32. BEARETH,] *lit.* 'is bearing testimony concerning one, and I have known . . concerning me.'
33. SENT,] *lit.* 'have sent away . . has borne testimony.'
34. TESTIMONY,] *lit.* 'the testmony . . may be.'
35. A,] *lit.* 'the burning and shining lamp, and ye, ye wished to rejoice for an hour in his light.'
36. GREATER,] *lit.* 'the testimony greater than John . . gave me, that I might finish . . concerning me . . sent me forth.'
37. HATH SENT,] *lit.* 'did send . . concerning me . . his appearance.'
38. HATH SENT,] *lit.* 'did send forth.'
39. SEARCH,] *or* 'ye search the Writings, because ye, ye think to have (i.e. find) life age-during in them . . are bearing-testimony concerning me.'
40. WILL,] *lit.* 'do not wish.'
41. I RECEIVE NOT,] i.e. I do not need it.
42. I KNOW,] *lit.* 'have known you . . in (*or* among) yourselves.'
43. I AM,] *lit.* 'I have come . . may come.'
44. HONOUR,] *lit.* 'glory from one another receiving, and the glory which is from the only God ye seek not.'
45. ACCUSE,] *lit.* 'make (it) public against you; there is who is making (it) public against you—Moses—in reference to whom ye have hoped.'
46. HAD,] *lit.* 'if ye were believing . . been believing me . . concerning me.'
47. WORDS,] *or* 'sayings.'

Chapter VI. may be divided into five parts; v. 1—15 Feeding of the five thousand men; v. 16—21 Jesus walks on the sea; v. 22—40 reproves the people for worldly desires; v. 41—51 the living bread; v. 52—71 some of the disciples stumbled.

1. WENT,] *lit.* 'went away beyond the sea.'
2. MULTITUDE,] *or* 'crowd was following him, because they were seeing his signs that he was doing on the infirm.'
3. A,] *lit.* 'the mount, and there he was sitting.'
4. A,] *lit.* 'the feast.'
5. COMPANY,] *lit.* 'crowd . . buy loaves.'
6. TO PROVE,] *lit.* 'trying *or* testing him, for he himself had known what he is about to do.'
7. PENNYWORTH,] *lit.* 'denaries-worth of loaves.'
9. LAD,] *lit.* 'one little lad . . little fishes, but these, what are they to so many?'
10. SIT DOWN,] *lit.* 'fall back . . the men, therefore, fell back, in number as if (it were) five thousand.'
11. HAD GIVEN THANKS,] *lit.* 'having rejoiced greatly, he gave thoroughly . . those reclining . . little fishes, as much as they wished.'
12. FILLED,] *lit.* 'filled fully, he says . . Bring together the superabundant broken-pieces.'
13. GATHERED,] *lit.* 'brought . . hand-baskets with broken pieces out of the five loaves of the barley which were superabundant to those having eaten.'
14. THOSE,] *lit.* 'the men . . sign Jesus did, said, that, this is truly the prophet that is coming to the world.' De. 18. 15.
15. PERCEIVED,] *lit.* 'knew that they are about to come and to seize him, that they may make him king, he withdrew again to the mount.'
16. WAS,] *lit.* 'came . . upon the sea.'
17. ENTERED,] *lit.* 'went in to the boat, and were going beyond the sea to Capernaum, and darkness had already come, and Jesus had not come to them.'
18. AND,] *lit.* 'the sea also—a great wind blowing—was being thoroughly raised.'
19. ROWED,] *or* 'pushed forward . . walking about . . coming nigh to the boat.'
20. IT IS I,] *or* 'I am he.'
21. WILLINGLY,] *lit.* 'they were wishing to take him into the boat, and straightway the boat came upon the land whither they were going.'
22. PEOPLE,] *lit.* 'crowd that was standing beyond the sea . . little boat . . disciples entered . . little boat . . disciples went away alone.
23. BOATS,] *lit.* 'little boats . . eat the bread.'

24. PEOPLE,] *lit.* 'crowd..is not there, they also went into the boats..seeking Jesus.'
25. ON,] *lit.* 'beyond the sea..hast thou come.'
26. THE MIRACLES,] *lit.* 'signs.'
27. LABOUR,] *lit.* 'work not the perishing food, but the abiding food with a view to life age-during,..for this one (*or* thing) did the Father seal—even God.'
28. SHALL,] *lit.* 'may we do that we may work the works of God?' i.e. those he would have us to do.
29. THAT,] i.e. 'even that, ye may remain stedfast to him whom he sent forth.'
30. SHEWEST,] *lit.* 'doest.'
31. MANNA,] *lit* 'the manna..has been written, Bread out of the heaven.'
22. THAT,] *lit.* 'the bread out of the heaven.'
33. COMETH,] *lit.* 'is coming down out of the heaven, and giving.'
35. OF LIFE,] *lit.* 'of the life; he who is coming unto me may not hunger, and he who is remaining stedfast to me may not thirst at any time.'
37. ALL,] *or* 'every thing that the Father giveth to me (to do) will come (*or* happen) to me, and he who is coming to me I may in no wise cast out without.'
38. CAME,] *lit.* 'have come down out of the heaven, not that I may do my (own) wish, but the wish of.'
39. WILL,] *or* 'wish..that every thing that he has given me I may not lose of it, but may cause it to stand up in the last day.'
40. WILL,] *or* 'wish..is viewing the Son, and remaining stedfast to him, may have life age-during, and I—I will cause him to stand up (at) the last day.'
41. MURMURED,] *lit.* 'were murmuring about him,..out of the heaven.'
42. WE KNOW,] *lit.* 'we have known..how, then, doth this one say, that, Out of the heaven I have come down?'
43. MURMUR,] *lit.* 'be not murmuring with one another.'
44. NO MAN,] *lit.* 'no one is able to come to me, if the Father who sent me may not draw him,' through a knowledge of the revealed truth as it is in Jesus regarding God's love and man's helplessness.
45. IT IS,] *lit.* 'it has been written in (*or* by) the prophets: And they shall be all taught-of-God,' i.e. be disciples of God, so that they shall be without excuse, if they continue disobedient, in the possession of a knowledge of His Revealed Wish for their salvation.
MAN,] *lit.* 'every one, therefore, who is hearing (*or* hearkening) along-side of the Father, and hath learned (aright) cometh to me.'
46. ANY MAN,] *lit.* 'any one ..who is along-side of the Father.'
48. THAT,] *lit.* 'the bread of the life.'
49. MANNA,] *lit.* 'the manna..and they died.'
50. COMETH,] *lit.* 'is coming down out of the heaven, in order that any one may eat.'

51. FROM,] *lit.* 'out of the heaven, if any one may eat..bread also.'
52. STROVE,] *lit.* 'were striving with one another, saying, How is this one able to give.'
53. EXCEPT,] *lit.* 'if ye may not eat..may not drink..in yourselves.'
54. EATETH,] *lit.* 'is eating..is drinking.'
55. MEAT,] *lit.* 'truly is food.. truly is drink.'
56. EATETH,] *lit.* 'is eating..is drinking.'
DWELLETH,] *lit.* 'remaineth.'
57. SENT,] *lit.* 'did send me forth..through (*or* because of) the Father..is eating..through (*or* because of) me.'
58. THAT,] *lit.* 'the bread..out of the heaven,..the manna, and died, he who is eating this bread.'
59. THE,] *lit.* 'in a synagogue, teaching in.'
60. THIS,] *lit.* 'this word is hard.'
61. MURMURED,] *lit.* 'are murmuring about this..stumble you?'
62. WHAT,] *lit.* 'if then ye may view the Son of the Man going up where he was at first?'
63. QUICKENETH,] *lit.* 'is making alive.. the sayings that.'
64. SOME,] *lit.* 'certain..had known from the beginning (that) there are certain who believe not, and who he is who is giving him over.'
65. THEREFORE,] *lit.* 'because of this I have said to you, that no one is able to come to me, if it may not have been given to him from my Father.'
66. TIME,] *or* 'circumstance..went away to the back, and were walking-about.'
67. WILL,] *lit.* 'do ye also wish to go away secretly?'
68. GO,] *lit.* 'go away? sayings of life age-during thou hast.'
69. BELIEVE,] *lit.* 'have believed and have known that thou art the Christ;' see on 1. 29; 11. 27; Mat. 16. 6, &c.
70. HAVE,] *lit.* 'did not I choose you for myself—the twelve,— and out of you one is a devil,' *lit.* thruster through.
71. IT WAS,] *lit.* 'was about to give him over.'

Chapter VII. may be divided into six parts; v. 1—9 Jesus and his brothers; v. 10—13 Jews' opinions of him; v. 14—24 Jesus vindicates his sabbath-works; v. 25—31 many Jerusalemites believe in him; v. 32—44 Jesus before the officers; v. 45—53 who are reproved by the Pharisees, but defended by Nicodemus.
1. WALKED,] *lit.* 'was walking about..was not wishing to walk about..were seeking to kill him utterly.'
2. TABERNACLES,] *lit.* 'fixing of tents was nigh.'
3. BRETHREN,] *or* 'brothers..remove..go away..thy works.'
4. FOR,] *lit.* 'for no one doeth anything in secret, and himself seeketh to be in public.. manifest thyself.'
5. NEITHER,] *lit.* 'not even were his brothers.'
6. SAID,] *lit.* 'says..not yet present.'

8. IS NOT,] *lit.* 'has not yet been filled out.'
9. WORDS,] *or* 'things ..he remained in.'
10. OPENLY,] *or* 'manifestly.'
11. SOUGHT,] *lit.* 'were seeking him during.'
IS HE,] *or* 'is that one?'
12. PEOPLE,] *lit.* 'crowds..said that..he leadeth-astray the crowd.'
13. NO MAN,] *lit.* 'no one was speaking with full-speech.'
14. TAUGHT,] *lit.* 'was teaching.'
15. MARVELLED,] *lit.* 'were wondering, saying, How has this one known letters?'
16. DOCTRINE,] *lit.* 'teaching.'
17. ANY MAN,] *lit.* 'any one may wish to do his wish, he shall know concerning the teaching..from myself.'
18. SPEAKETH,] *lit.* 'from himself is speaking..is seeking.'
19. KEEPETH,] *lit.* 'doeth the law; why do ye seek to kill me utterly?'
20. PEOPLE,] *lit.* 'crowd..a demon, who seeketh to kill thee utterly?'
21. HAVE DONE,] *lit.* 'I did.'
22. THEREFORE,] *lit.* 'because of this..the circumcision..ye during sabbath.'
23. ON,] *lit.* 'during sabbath.. may not be loosed (down), are ye galled at me that I made a man all whole during sabbath.'
24. TO THE,] *lit.* 'to appearance (or face) ..the righteous judgment.'
25. SOME,] *lit.* 'certain out of the Jerusalemites.'
SEEK,] *lit.* 'are seeking to kill utterly.'
26. DO,] *lit.* 'did the chiefs truly know at any time that this is truly the Christ?'
27. KNOW,] *lit.* 'have known this one,.. but the Christ, when he may come, no one.'
28. AS HE TAUGHT,] *lit.* 'teaching and saying, Ye have both known me, and have known..I have not come from myself.. ye have not known.'
29. KNOW,] *lit.* 'have known..did send me forth.'
30. SOUGHT,] *lit.* 'were seeking to seize him, and no one put the hand upon him, ..had not yet come.'
31. PEOPLE,] *lit.* 'out of the crowd..said that, The Christ, when he may come,..more signs.. this one did?'
32. MURMURED,] *lit.* 'are murmuring these things..sent forth under-servants that they might seize him.'
33. WHILE,] *lit.* 'time..I go away.'
34. CANNOT,] *lit.* 'are not able to come.'
35. AMONG,] *lit.* 'to themselves, Where is this one about to pass on,..to the thoroughly-scattered-part of the Hellenes is he about to pass on, and to teach the Hellenes?'
36. MANNER,] *lit.* 'what word is this?
37. IN,] *lit.* 'and in..the great one..Jesus had stood..any one do thirst.'
38. BELIEVETH,] *lit.* 'is remaining-stedfast to me, according as the Writing said,' i.e. described, with love and patience. The next clause is not a quotation from the Writings, but a promise of blessing from Christ, that his disciples shall be a fountain of blessings like himself, as explained in the next verse. See also Isa. 55. 1; 58. 11.
39. OF,] *lit.* 'concerning the influence (of the Spirit)..were about to receive, for there was not yet a holy influence.'
40. PEOPLE,] *lit.* 'out of the crowd..this word, said, This is truly the prophet,' spoken of in De. 18. 15, 18.
41. SOME,] *lit.* 'others said, Doth the Christ.'
42. HATH,] *lit.* 'did not the Writing say, that the Christ.. and from the village.'
43. SO,] *lit.* 'there happened therefore a schism in the crowd.'
44. SOME,] *lit.* 'certain of them were wishing to seize him, but no one.'
45. OFFICERS,] *lit.* 'under-servants .. wherefore did ye not bring him?'
46. OFFICERS,] *lit.* 'under-servants..Never so spake a man as this man!'
47. DECEIVED,] *lit.* 'led astray?'
48. HAVE,] *lit.* 'did any one of the chiefs ..believe?'
49. PEOPLE,] *lit.* 'crowd that is not knowing the law is very-thoroughly-cursed.'
50. CAME TO JESUS,] *lit.* 'came to him.'
51. ANY MAN,] *lit.* 'the man (i.e. Jesus), if it may not hear from him first, and may know.'
52. OF,] *lit.* 'out of Galilee..that a prophet out of Galilee hath not risen;' Jonah and Nahum were both from Galilee, and Isa. 9. 1, 2, speaks of a great light there.
53. EVERY,] *lit.* 'each passed on to.'

Chapter VIII. may be divided into six parts; v. 1—11 Jesus and the woman taken in adultery; v. 12—19 Jesus the light of the world; v. 20—29 he warns the Jews; v. 30 —36 freedom of the Gospel; v. 37—44 the father of the wicked; v. 45—59 Jesus before Abraham.

1. WENT,] *lit.* 'passed on to the mount of the olives.'
2. EARLY,] *lit.* 'and at dawn he came over again..was teaching them.'
3. PHARISEES,] *lit.* 'the Pharisees bring.. fully taken.'
4. MASTER,] *lit.* 'teacher..fully taken in the very act, committing adultery.'
5. COMMANDED,] *lit.* 'caused to exist fully to us (that) such (are) to be stoned; thou, therefore, what sayest thou?'
6. THIS,] *lit.* 'and this they said, trying him, that they might have (something) to make public against him..bent down,— with the finger wrote on the earth.'
7. SO,] *lit.* 'and as they remained openly asking him, he bent back and said .The sinless one of you, let him first cast the stone upon her.'
8. STOOPED,] *or* 'bent.. on the earth.'
9. BY,] *lit.* 'under the conscience,' *lit.* a knowing with (one's self.)
ELDEST,] *lit.* 'presbyters.. left thoroughly alone.'
10. LIFTED UP HIMSELF,] *lit.* 'bent back ..O woman, where are those making (it) public against thee? did no one judge thee thoroughly?'
11. SHE,] *lit.* 'and she said, No one, sir.'
CONDEMN,] *lit.* 'judge down *or* thoroughly.'
GO,] *lit.* 'be passing on.'

12. FOLLOWETH,] *lit.* 'is following.. walk about in the darkness.. of the life.'
13. RECORD,] *or* 'testimony concerning thyself.'
14. OF,] *lit.* 'concerning.. I have known whence I come, and whither I go away, but ye have not known whence I come, and whither I go away.'
15. AFTER,] *lit.* 'according to.'
17. IT IS,] *lit.* 'it has been written.'
18. ONE,] *lit.* 'I am he who is bearing witness concerning myself, also the Father.'
19. KNOW,] *lit.* 'have known.. would have known.'
20. WORDS,] *or* 'sayings.. treasure-ward, teaching.. seized him.. had not yet come.'
21. GO MY WAY,] *lit.* 'go away.. your sin, whether I go away.'
22. GO,] *lit.* 'I go away.'
24. BELIEVE,] *lit.* 'may not believe that I am (he, whom the prophets spake of).' The doctrine that 'Jesus is the Christ,' is the basis of Christianity. Mark 13. 6; Acts 13.25.
25. SAITH,] *lit.* 'said to them, What I even spake of to you (at) the beginning' of the present discourse, or of his ministry; *or* 'the chief thing (that I am is) what also I spake of to you,' viz. the light of the world.
26. OF,] *lit.* 'concerning you.. which I heard from him.'
27. UNDERSTOOD,] *lit.* 'knew.'
28. HAVE LIFTED,] *lit.* 'ye may lift up.. from myself.. Father taught me.'
29. HATH,] *lit.* 'did not leave me.'
31. CONTINUE,] *lit.* 'may remain.. truly.'
33. WERE,] *lit.* 'have never been servants to any one;' forgetting that even then they were subject to Rome.
BE MADE,] *lit.* 'become.'
34. WHOSOEVER,] *lit.* 'that every one who is doing the sin is servant of the sin.'
36. SHALL,] *lit.* 'may make you free, ye shall be really free.'
37. I KNOW,] *lit.* 'I have known.. no place (of entrance).'
38. WITH,] *lit.* 'near my.. near your.'
39. WERE,] *lit.* 'ye had been *or* may be.. ye were doing.'
40. KILL,] *lit.* 'kill me utterly.. I heard from God.'
41. WE BE,] *lit.* 'we out of whoredom have not been born.'
42. JESUS SAID,] *lit.* 'Jesus therefore said ..ye were loving me, for I came forth out of God, and I am come, for neither have I come from myself, but he sent me forth.'
43. WHY,] *lit.* 'wherefore do ye not know my speech, because ye are not able (i.e. not willing) to hear my word.' Compare v. 21, 22; 5. 19, 30, 44; 6. 44, 65; 7. 7, 34, &c.
44. LUSTS,] *lit.* 'full-mind of your father ye wish to do. That one was a man-killer.. has not stood.. when he (*or* one) may speak the lie, out of his own he speaketh, because a liar he is, also his (*or* its) father.'
45. I TELL YOU,] *lit.* 'I say;' as in v. 46.
46. WHICH,] *or* 'who of you convicteth me concerning sin.'
47. OF,] *lit.* 'out of God heareth God's sayings, because of this ye do not hear, because out of God ye are not.'
48. DEVIL,] *lit.* 'demon.'
49. DEVIL,] *lit.* 'demon.'
50. SEEKETH,] *lit.* 'is seeking and judging.
51. A MAN,] *lit.* 'if any one may keep my word, death he may not view.'
52. KNOW,] *lit.* 'have known that thou hast a demon; Abraham died, also the prophets, and thou sayest, If any one may keep my word he shall not taste for himself of death.'
53. IS DEAD,] *lit.* 'who died, the prophets also died.'
54. HONOUR,] *lit.* 'glorify myself, my glory ..is glorifying me.'
55. KNOW,] *lit.* 'have known him, and if I say that I have not known him.. I have known him, and keep his word.'
56. TO SEE,] *lit.* 'in order that he might see,' my day.
57. ART,] *lit.* 'thou hast not yet 50 years.'
58. WAS,] *lit.* 'before Abraham's coming I am *He*,' that is, the promised Messiah. The simple phrase 'I am,' is used by Jesus 15 times, and in every case (but the present) it is rendered in the Common Version 'I am *He*,' *or* 'it is I;' see Mat. 14. 27; Mark 6. 50; 14. 62; Luke 21. 8; 22. 70; 24. 39; John 4. 26; 6. 20; 8. 24, 28; 13. 19; 18. 5, 6, 8.
59. TOOK,] *lit.* 'lifted up stones, that they might cast (them) upon him, and Jesus was hid (i.e. hid himself, the *passive* form being often used for the *reflexive*), and went forth out of the temple, going thoroughly through the midst of them, and so he led (his disciples) along.'

Chapter IX. may be divided into five parts; v. 1—7 Jesus cures a blind man; v. 8—12 the blind man and his neighbours; v. 13—34 the blind man and the Pharisees; v. 35—38 the blind man and Jesus; v. 39—41 Jesus and the Pharisees.
1. PASSED BY,] *lit.* 'and he leading (the disciples) along, saw a man blind from birth.'
2. MASTER,] *lit.* 'Rabbi,.. so that he might be born blind?'
3. SHOULD,] *lit.* 'might be manifested in him.'
4. MUST,] *lit.* 'It behoveth me to be working.. a night cometh, when no one is able to work.'
6. THUS,] *lit.* 'these things.. earth.. openly-smeared the clay upon the eyes of the blind man.'
7. GO,] *lit.* 'go away, wash (thine eyes) at the swimming-bath of Siloam, (which is, being interpreted, Sent forth); he went away.'
8. NEIGHBOURS,] *lit.* 'countrymen.. is sitting and asking earnestly?'
9. SOME,] *lit.* 'others said, that, this is he; and others, that, he is like to him; he himself said, I am (he).'
10. OPENED,] *lit.* 'opened up.'
11. HE,] *lit.* 'that one answered.. openly smeared.. go away to the swimming-bath .. I looked up,' *or* beheld thoroughly.
12. HE,] *lit.* 'that one; he says, I have not known.'
13. BROUGHT,] *lit.* 'bring.. once was blind.'

14. THE,] *lit.* 'a sabbath . . opened fully.'
15. ASKED,] *lit.* 'were asking . . how he looked up? . . he openly put clay.'
16. SOME,] *lit.* 'certain . . from God . . sabbath . . signs . . schism.'
17. THAT,] in that, *or* as to his opening.
18. HAD BEEN,] *lit.* 'was blind and looked up . . who looked up.'
19. WAS,] *lit.* 'that he was born blind.'
20. KNOW,] *lit.* 'have known.'
21. BY WHAT MEANS,] *lit.* 'how . . have not known . . opened up . . have not known, he has age.'
22. WORDS,] *or* 'things . . were fearing . . been put together (i.e. united) that if any one may assent (to him) that he was Christ, he may become a non-synagogite.'
23. THEREFORE,] *lit.* 'because of this . . that, he has age.'
24. AGAIN,] *lit.* 'a second time . . Give glory to God, we have known.'
25. HE,] *lit.* 'that one . . if he be a sinner, I have not known; one thing I have known, that, (once) being blind, now I see.'
26. OPENED,] *lit.* 'opened he up.'
27. I HAVE TOLD,] *lit.* 'I said to you . . do ye wish to hear (it) again? do ye also wish to become his disciples?'
28. HIS,] *lit.* 'a disciple of that one.'
29. KNOW,] *lit.* 'have known . . but this one, we have not known whence he is.'
30. KNOW,] *lit.* 'have not known . . opened up.'
31. KNOW,] *lit.* 'have known . . any one may be God-reverencing, and may do his wish.'
32. SINCE,] *lit.* 'from the age it was not heard that any one opened up.'
33. MAN,] *lit.* 'this one were not from God, he were not able to do anything.'
34. CAST,] *lit.* 'cast him forth without.'
35. BELIEVE,] *lit.* 'remain stedfast to the Son.'
37. TALKETH,] *lit.* 'is speaking.'
38. WORSHIPPED,] *lit.* 'kissed forward (the hand) to him.'
39. FOR,] *lit.* 'with a view to judgment I came to this world, that those not beholding may behold, and (that) those beholding (i.e. thinking that they do so) may become blind.'
41. SHOULD,] *lit.* 'were not having sin.'

Chapter X. may be divided into three parts; v. 1—21 simile of the good shepherd; v. 22—38 unity of the Father and the Son; v. 39—42 Jesus beyond Jordan.
1. VERILY.] *Gr.* Amen, Amen, i.e. 'stedfast, stedfast,' *or* 'very stedfast' is the word now to be said.
SAY,] *lit.* 'lay (it) out *or* down,' to you.
ENTERETH,] *lit.* 'is not coming in through the door to the fold (*or* court) of the sheep, but is going up from elsewhere.'
2. ENTERETH,] *lit.* 'is coming in through the door.'
3. PORTER,] *lit.* 'door-keeper openeth up.'
4. PUTTETH,] *lit.* 'may put forth . . he passeth on . . they have known.'
5. STRANGER,] *lit.* 'another . . they have not known the voice of others.'

6. PARABLE,] *or* 'proverb said . . knew not . . he was speaking.'
8. THAT EVER,] *lit.* 'as many as came before' him, in regard to *place* not *time.*
9. BY,] *lit.* 'through me if any one may come in.'
10. FOR,] *lit.* 'that he may steal, and slaughter, and loose away utterly; I came . . more abundantly,' i.e. enjoy it more.
11. GIVETH,] *lit.* 'setteth (*or* putteth) his soul over the sheep,' in order to defend and help them.
12. NOT THE,] *lit.* 'and not being shepherd . . leaveth alone . . seizeth.'
13. CARETH,] *lit.* 'and there is no care to him about the flock.'
14. MY SHEEP,] *lit.* 'my own . . by my own.'
15. EVEN SO,] *lit.* 'I also know . . my soul I put (*or* set) over the sheep.'
16. FOLD,] *or* 'court; them also it behoveth me to lead, and they shall become one flock, and one shepherd.'
17. THEREFORE,] *lit.* 'because of this the Father loveth me, because I set my soul (in danger), that again I may receive it.'
18. TAKETH,] *lit.* 'no one lifteth it up from me, but I set it from myself; I have authority to set it, and I have authority again to receive it. This command I received from my Father.'
19. DIVISION,] *lit.* 'schism, then, again, came among the Jews, because of these words.'
20. DEVIL,] *lit.* 'demon, and is possessed.'
21. WORDS,] *lit.* 'sayings of one demonized; is a demon able blind men's eyes to open up?'
22. IT WAS,] *lit.* and the festival-days-for the-renewing (of the temple by Judas Maccabæus) happened in Jerusalem, and it was winter,' *lit.* the 'pouring' or rainy season.
23. WALKED,] *lit.* 'was walking about in the temple, in the porch (*lit.* standing-place) of Solomon,' called after him.
24. CAME ROUND ABOUT,] *or* 'encircled him . . till when dost thou lift up our soul,' as it were between heaven and earth, in uncertainty.
28. PERISH,] *lit.* 'they may not lose themselves—to the age.'
29. GAVE,] *lit.* 'has given.'
30. I AND THE FATHER.] What presumption it would be in a *created* being to put himself before GOD, as is done here' I and the King!'
ONE.] The Particle *en* being of the neuter gender, can hardly signify 'one being, i.e. one God,' but rather 'one in will, purpose, counsel, might, &c.' So Calvin, &c. Compare 17. 11, 21, 22, 23, &c.
31. TO,] *lit.* 'that they might stone him.'
32. HAVE,] *lit.* 'did I shew you.'
33. BLASPHEMY,] *lit.* 'injurious-speaking . . makest thyself a god,' not 'God,' as in C.V., otherwise the definite article would not have been omitted, as it is here, and in the next two verses,—'gods . . gods,' where the title is applied to magistrates, and others, because in a certain sense they are God's representatives. Compare also Acts 28. 6; 2 Cor. 2. 4.
34. WRITTEN,] *lit.* 'a written thing in your

Law (Ps. 82. 6), I said, gods ye are,' in your own and others' estimation, because of their office or character.

35. CALLED,] *lit.* 'if it (i.e. the law) said that those are gods to whom the word of the (true) God came (either by dreams or by prophets), and the Writing is not able to be loosed' or explained away.

36. HATH,] *lit.* 'did set-apart and send forth to the world, that thou speakest injuriously, because I said, Son I am of the (true) God?'

38. BELIEVE,] *lit.* 'ye may believe.'

39. SOUGHT,] *lit.* 'were seeking..seize him, and he went forth out of their hand.'

40. JORDAN,] *lit.* 'the Jordan..was at first baptizing..remained.'

41. RESORTED,] *lit.* 'came..that John indeed, did no sign, but everything—as many as John said concerning this one—was true'

Chapter XI. may be divided into nine parts; v. 1—3 sickness of Lazarus; v. 4—17 Jesus on his sleep and death; v. 18—27 Jesus and Martha; v. 28—32 Jesus and Mary; v. 33—38 Jesus and the Jews; v. 39—44 He raises Lazarus; v. 45—46 many believe; v. 47—53 many reject him; v. 54—57 Jesus and the Jews.

1. SICK,] *lit.* 'infirm, Lazarus (i.e. helpless), from Bethany, out of the village of.'

2. ANOINTED,] *lit.* 'fattened *or* smeared (afterwards).. thoroughly-wiped.. was infirm.'

3. HIS,] *lit.* 'the sisters sent away..thou art-friend-to is infirm.'

4. SICKNESS,] *lit.* 'infirmity..through it.'

5. LOVED,] *lit.* 'was loving.'

6. HAD,] *lit.* 'he heard..infirm, he remained..in the place.'

7. LET,] *or* 'we may go.'

8. MASTER,] *lit.* 'Rabbi, now were the Jews seeking to..goest thou away?'

9. MAN,] *lit.* 'any one may walk about.. he striketh not forward (his foot against a stone).' See Mat. 4. 1.

10. A MAN,] *lit.* 'any one may walk about ..he striketh forward (his foot against a stone), because the light is not in him,' *or* 'in it.'

11. SLEEPETH,] *lit.* 'hath lain-down-to-rest, but I pass on that I may bring him out of sleep.'

12. SLEEP,] *lit.* 'has lain-down-to-rest, he will be saved,'—from his danger.

13. SPAKE,] *lit.* 'had spoken concerning.. he speaketh of the lying-down-to-rest of sleep.'

14. PLAINLY,] *lit.* 'speaking-all-out, Lazarus has died.'

15. SAKES,] *lit.* 'because of you.. we may go.'

16. THOMAS,] *Heb.* 'twin,' like *Gr.* Didymus.

17. THAT,] *lit.* 'him being four days already in the tomb.'

18. FIFTEEN FURLONGS,] or two miles.

19. CAME,] *lit.* 'had come..that they might discourse along-side of them concerning their brother.'

20. WAS COMING,] *lit.* 'cometh, met him secretly, but Mary kept sitting in the house.'

22. KNOW,] *lit.* 'have known, that, as many things as thou mayest ask God.'

23. RISE AGAIN,] *lit.* 'stand up.'

24. KNOW,] *lit.* 'have known that he shall stand up in the standing-up in the last day.'

25. RESURRECTION,] *lit.* 'standing-up (i.e. its author)..is believing..he may die, shall live.'

26. WHOSOEVER,] *lit.* 'every one who is living and believing.. may not die.'

27. BELIEVE,] *lit.* 'have believed..who is coming to.' See 1. 49, &c.

28. SO,] *lit.* 'these things said, she went away..The Teacher is present, and calleth thee.'

29. CAME,] *lit.* 'cometh.'

30. WAS,] *lit.* 'had not yet come to the village, but was in the place where Martha met him secretly.'

31. COMFORTED,] *lit.* 'discoursed alongside of her.. stood up..that she goeth away.. that she may weep there.'

32. WAS COME,] *lit.* 'came.. fell at.'

33. GROANED,] *lit.* 'he himself was indignant in the spirit, and troubled himself;' the *middle* voice being probably used for the *passive*, and often *vice versa*.

34. LAID,] *or* 'put him, they say to him, Sir, be coming and see.'

35. WEPT,] *lit.* 'Jesus shed-tears.'

36. LOVED,] *lit.* 'was a friend to him.'

37. SOME,] *lit.* 'certain.. Was not this one —who opened up the eyes of the blind man —able to act (*lit.* do) that even this one might not have died?'

38. GROANING,] *or* 'being indignant in himself.. was lying above upon it.'

39. SAID,] *lit.* 'says, Lift ye up the stone ..already it smelleth, for it is four days.'

40. WOULDST,] *lit.* 'mayest believe, thou shalt see.'

41. TOOK AWAY,] *lit.* 'lifted up..the eyes upwards.. didst hear me.'

42. KNEW,] *lit.* 'had known.. crowd standing round.. didst send me forth.'

43. THUS,] *lit.* 'these things..great voice.'

44. WAS DEAD,] *lit.* 'he who died, being bound feet and hands with death bands.. was bound round about.. and suffer him to go away.'

45. HAD SEEN,] *lit.* 'and beheld.'

46. SOME,] *lit.* 'certain.. went away.. Jesus did.'

47. GATHERED,] *lit.* 'led together..council (*or* convocation).. what may we do.. many signs.'

48. TAKE AWAY,] *lit.* 'lift up.'

49. ONE,] *lit.* 'a certain one.. being chief-priest of that year.. ye have not known anything.'

50. CONSIDER,] *or* 'reason that it bears thoroughly to us that one man may die.. be not lost.'

51. OF,] *lit.* 'from himself, but being chief-priest of that year he spake beforehand (*or* openly) that (*or* because) Jesus was about to die for the nation.'

52. THAT,] *lit.* 'the nation only, but that also the children of God who have been thoroughly-scattered he may lead together into one.'

53. FOR,] *lit.* 'that they might kill him utterly.'

54. WALKED,] *lit.* 'was no more walking.. went away thence to the place nigh the wilderness.. there he spent all (the time) with his disciples.'

55. WENT OUT,] *lit.* 'went up to Jerusalem out of the place before the passover, that they might purify themselves.'

56. SOUGHT,] *lit.* 'were they seeking Jesus, and spake with one another.. may not come.'

57. MAN,] *lit.* 'any one may know where he is, he may.. seize him.'

Chapter XII. may be divided into four parts; v. 1—8 Jesus anointed by Mary; v. 9—19 enters Jerusalem in triumph; v. 20—36 rejoices over the Greeks, and warns the Jews; v. 37—50 Jewish unbelief, timidity, and danger.

1. HAD BEEN DEAD,] *lit.* 'who died.'

2. THERE,] *lit.* 'there, then, they made.. was-acting-as-a-deacon,.. lying-back-along-with him.'

3. SPIKENARD,] *lit.* 'genuine spikenard, much prized, anointed (*lit.* fattened, smeared) .. thoroughly wiped.. from the fragrance.'

4. SHOULD,] *lit.* 'who is about to give him over.'

5. SOLD,] *lit.* 'made to pass over (to the merchant) for three hundred denaries, and given to poor ones.'

6. HE CARED,] *lit.* 'there was care to him .. bag (*lit.* place of keeping the tongues, i.e. reeds of wind instruments), and the things cast (into it) he was bearing' *or* carrying off.

7. AGAINST,] *lit.* 'with a view to the day of my embalming,' *or* burying.

8. YOU,] *lit.* 'yourselves.'

9. MUCH PEOPLE,] *lit.* 'a great crowd.. he is there,.. not because of Jesus only,.. he raised out of the dead.'

10. PUT,] *lit.* 'utterly kill Lazarus also.

11. BY REASON OF,] *or* 'because of.'

12. MUCH PEOPLE,] *lit.* 'a great crowd that had come.. Jesus cometh.'

13. BRANCHES,] *lit.* 'the branches of the palms.. Hosannah! well-spoken of is He who is coming in the name of the Lord, the King of Israel.'

15. AS,] *lit.* 'according as it is having been written, Be not afraid.' Zech. 9. 9.

16. UNDERSTOOD,] *lit.* 'knew not.. at first .. were having been written, and these things they did to him.'

17. PEOPLE,] *lit.* 'crowd then, that is with him, was bearing-witness that he called Lazarus out of the tomb, and raised him out of the dead.'

18. PEOPLE,] *lit.* 'crowd.. this sign.

19. PERCEIVE,] *lit.* 'see ye that ye profit nothing?.. went away after him.'

20. AMONG,] *lit.* 'of those coming up, that they might kiss forward (the hand to God) in the feast.'

21. THE SAME,] *lit.* 'these then came forward to Philip, who is from Bethsaida of Galilee, and asked him, saying, Sir, we wish to see Jesus.'

23. IS,] *lit.* 'has come.. may be glorified.'

24. A CORN,] *lit.* 'the grain of the wheat falling to the earth may die.. it may die, it beareth much fruit.'

25. LOVETH,] *lit.* 'is the friend of his soul, shall lose it utterly,.. is hating.. guard it to life age-during.'

26. MAN,] *lit.* 'if any one may act-as-deacon to me,.. my deacon.. any one may act-as-deacon to me.'

27. IS,] *lit.* 'has my soul been troubled.. out of this hour.'

28. FROM,] *lit.* 'out of the heaven.. I both glorified.'

29. PEOPLE,] *lit.* 'crowd.. stood and heard, said that thunder happened.. a messenger has spoken to him.'

30. FOR,] *lit.* 'because of you.'

31. THE,] *lit.* 'a judgment.. the chief.. cast out without.'

32. BE,] *lit.* 'if I may be lifted up from (*lit.* out of) the earth, will draw all (men *or* things) to myself;' the natural result will be so, he intends and wishes it to be so, but it does not follow that the 'drawing' is always effectual, as the Universalists pretend. Compare similar idiom in 1. 9; 3. 17.

33. SHOULD,] *lit.* 'he was about to die.'

34. PEOPLE,] *lit.* 'crowd.. we heard.. that the Christ remaineth to the age.'

35. WHILE,] *lit.* 'time.. walk about.. may take you fully, and he who is walking about in the darkness has not known whither he goes away.'

36. LIGHT,] *lit.* 'the light.. that sons of light ye may become.'

DEPARTED,] *lit.* 'having gone away he was hid from them.'

37. MIRACLES,] *lit.* 'signs.. they were not believing on him.'

38. SAYING,] *lit.* 'word.. who remained stedfast to that which we heard?.. was it uncovered?'

39. THEREFORE,] *lit.* 'because of this they were not able to remain stedfast, because (*or* so that) Isaiah.'

40. HE HATH BLINDED,] *or* 'it (i.e. the people of Israel) has blinded.. may not see .. and turn round upon (me), and I may heal them.'

41. HIS GLORY,] most naturally Christ's, not the Father's, as Socinians maintain.

42. AMONG,] *lit.* 'out of the chiefs.. they were not speaking the same thing, that they might not become non-synagogites.'

43. PRAISE,] *lit.* 'glory.. glory.'

44. BELIEVETH,] *lit.* 'is believing.. on me (only).'

45. SEETH,] *lit.* 'is seeing.'

46. AM,] *lit.* 'have come.. that every one who is believing in me may not remain in the darkness.'

47. MAN,] *lit.* 'any one may hear my sayings, and may not believe.. that I might judge.. but that I might save the world.'

48. REJECTETH,] *lit.* 'is putting me away, and is not receiving my sayings.. hath that which is judging him, the word that I spake, that shall judge.'

49. FOR,] *or* 'because I did not speak out of myself.. I may say, and what I may speak.'

50. KNOW,] *lit.* 'have known.. the things I.. has said.'

Chapter XIII. may be divided into four parts; v. 1—11 Jesus washes the apostles' feet; v. 12—20 his reasons for doing it; v. 21—30 uncovering of Judas; v. 31—38 Jesus glorified, a new command, prophesy about Peter.

1. WAS,] *lit.* 'has come, that he may go on ..who are in the world,.. end' of his being with them.

2. BEING ENDED,] *lit.* 'having come.. already cast (it) into.. that he may give him over.'

3. HAD,] *lit.* 'has given all (*or* every person *or* thing) to him, into (his) hands,.. he came forth from God, and goeth away to God.'

4. FROM,] *lit.* 'out of the supper, and placeth (his) garments.. girded himself thoroughly.'

5. POURETH,] *lit.* 'putteth *or* casteth water into the washing-vessel,..to wipe (them) thoroughly.. was being thoroughly girded.'

6. PETER,] *lit.* 'that one says to him.'

7. KNOWEST,] *lit.* 'hast not known.. thou thyself shalt know after these things.'

8. SHALT,] *lit.* 'mayest.. I may not wash thee.'

10. IS WASHED,] *lit.* 'has been bathed.. is altogether clean.'

11. KNEW,] *lit.* 'had known him who is giving him over.'

12. HAD,] *lit.* 'he washed.. and took.. having fallen back again.'

13. MASTER,] *lit.* 'the teacher and the lord.'

14. LORD,] *lit.* 'the lord and the teacher, washed.'

15. EXAMPLE,] *lit.* 'private-example I gave to you, that even as I did to you, ye also may do.'

16. THE,] *lit.* 'a servant.. an apostle.'

17. KNOW,] *lit.* 'have known..ye may do.'

18. KNOW,] *lit.* 'have known whom I (myself) chose for myself.. the Writing may be filled out (*or* exemplified), He who is eating the loaf with me lifted up openly his heel against me.'

19. NOW,] *lit.* 'from now (i.e. this time) I say to you before (its) happening, that when it may happen, ye may believe that I am' the promised Messiah, as in 8. 58, &c.

20. RECEIVETH,] *lit.* 'is receiving.. is receiving.'

21. THUS,] *lit.* 'these things..shall give me over.'

22. LOOKED,] *lit.* 'were looking to one another, doubting (*lit.* without-a-passage) concerning whom he speaks.'

23. LEANING,] *lit.* 'lying back in the bosom of Jesus.. was loving.'

24. BECKONED,] *lit.* 'beckons (*or* nods) to this one himself to enquire who he may be concerning whom he speaks.'

25. HE,] *lit.* 'and that one falling over upon.'

26. ANSWERED,] *lit.* 'answers, It is that one to whom I shall give over the morsel.. the morsel, he gives (it).'

27. SOP,] *lit.* 'morsel, then the Adversary went in to that one, Jesus therefore says to him, That which thou doest, do quickly,' a permission, of course, not a command.

28. MAN,] *lit.* 'and no one of those lying back.'

29. SOME,] *lit.* 'certain were thinking, since.. Jesus says.. for the feast.. may give.'

30. HE,] *lit.* 'that one.. the morsel, straightway went forth.'

31. WAS GONE,] *lit.* 'went forth Jesus says, Now was the Son of the Man glorified, and God was glorified in (*or* by) him.'

32. BE,] *lit.* 'if God was glorified in (by) him.'

33. WHITHER,] *lit.* 'that, whither I go away..also to you I say (it) now.'

34. HAVE,] *lit.* 'I loved you.'

35. BY,] *lit.* 'in this.. ye may have love in one another.'

36. SAID,] *lit.* 'says..goest thou away.. go away.. at last.'

37. SAID,] *lit.* 'says..I will place my soul over (*or* for) thee.'

38. LAY,] *lit.* 'place thy soul over (*or* for) me? a cock shall not sound (i.e. before the time of cock-crowing) till thou mayest deny me with an oath thrice.'

Chapter XIV. may be divided into six parts; v. 1—4 Jesus encourages the disciples; v. 5—11 answers Thomas and Philip; v. 12—14 promises to help and hear them; v. 15—21 promises the Comforter; v. 22—24 answers Judas; v. 25—31 and promises knowledge, peace, and joy.

1. TROUBLED,] *or* 'harassed.'

YE BELIEVE,] *or* 'remain ye stedfast to the (true) God, also to me remain ye stedfast.'

2. I GO,] *lit.* 'I pass on to make ready a place to you;' so in v. 3.

3. WILL,] *lit.* 'I come again, and will receive you over to myself.'

4. GO,] *lit.* 'I go away ye have known..ye have known.'

5. KNOW,] *lit.* 'have not known.. goest away.'

6. THE,] *lit.* 'and the truth..no one cometh ..but through me.'

7. SHOULD,] *lit.* 'would.. and from now ye have known him.'

9. HAVE I BEEN,] *lit.* 'am I so long.'

10. WORDS,] *or* 'sayings..from myself..is remaining in me.'

11. FOR,] *lit.* 'because of the works themselves.'

12. BELIEVETH,] *lit.* 'is believing.. I pass on.'

13. SHALL,] *lit.* 'may ask;' so in v. 14.

14. I WILL DO IT.] Jesus here represents himself as the Hearer and Answerer of Prayer, and who accordingly must be at once *omnipresent, omniscient,* and *omnipotent.* Such a passage as this proves the Divinity of Christ a hundred-fold more convincingly than any mere appellations (such as GOD, LORD, WORD, SON, SAVIOUR, &c.) can possibly do.

16. PRAY,] *lit.* 'ask.. Comforter,' *lit.* 'one

who calls along-side of' another, i.e. helper, advocate.

17. EVEN,] *lit.* 'the Spirit of the Truth, because it sees it not, neither knoweth it, but ye know it, because it remaineth along-side of you.'

18. COMFORTLESS,] *lit.* 'orphans; I come to you.'

19. ALSO,] *lit.* 'and ye shall live.'

20. AT,] *lit.* 'in that day.'

21. HAS,] *lit.* 'is having.. that one it is who is loving me; and he who is loving me .. by (*lit.* under) my Father.'

22. ISCARIOT,] *lit.* 'not the Iscariot,' i.e. 'not the man of Karioth *or* of the city.'

HOW IS IT,] *lit.* 'what has happened that to us thou art about to manifest.'

23. A MAN,] *lit.* 'if any one may love me .. my word.. alongside of him.'

24. LOVETH,] *lit.* 'is loving.. my words .. mine (only).'

25. BEING,] *lit.* 'remaining long-side of you.'

26. COMFORTER.] See on v. 16.

GHOST,] *lit.* 'the Holy Spirit.'

WHOM,] *lit.* 'which,' preserving the neuter gender of the original Greek.

IN MY NAME.] Here again, the Divine glory of Jesus appears: The Father sends the Spirit 'IN THE NAME OF CHRIST,'—a mere creature, according to Socinians.

HE,] *lit.* 'it shall teach you all' things needful for their work.

WHATSOEVER,] *lit.* 'which I said to you.'

27. LEAVE,] *or* 'send forth to you.'

28. HAVE,] *lit.* 'ye heard that I.. if ye were loving me ye would have rejoiced that I said, I pass on to the Father, because my Father is greater than I,'—as he who sends is greater than he who is sent; but what presumption (on the Socinian hypothesis) for a mere man to speak thus of himself and the Almighty! as if it were a wonderful fact to admit that GOD is greater than MAN!

29. IT COME TO PASS,] *lit.* 'before (its) happening, that when it may happen, ye may believe.'

30. HEREAFTER,] *lit.* 'I will no more speak many things with you, for the chief.'

31. ARISE,] *lit.* 'be roused up; we may go hence.'

Chapter XV. may be divided into two parts; v. 1—11 Jesus compares himself and his disciples to a vine and its branches; v. 12—27 exhorts to love and warns of hatred.

1. VINE.] Compare Ps. 80. 8—11; Isa. 5. 1—7; Jer. 2. 21, &c.

HUSBANDMAN,] *lit.* 'earth-worker.'

2. BEARETH,] *lit.* 'is not bearing fruit he lifteth up, and every one bearing the fruit he lifteth down (*or* thoroughly) that it may bear more fruit.'

3. NOW,] *lit.* 'already ye are clean (*lit.* lifted down *or* thoroughly) because of (*or* through) the word.'

4. ABIDE,] *or* 'remain,' no compulsion.

OF,] *lit.* 'from itself, if it may not remain ..ye may remain.'

5. ABIDETH,] *lit.* 'is remaining..he beareth much fruit, because apart from me.'

6. A MAN,] *lit.* 'if any one may not remain in me, he was (*or* he cast himself, the *passive* being used for the *reflexive*) cast without as the branch, and was withered (*or* withered himself), and they bring them together, ..and are set-on-fire.'

7. ABIDE,] *lit.* 'may abide.. my sayings may abide.. ye may wish, and it shall happen to you.'

8. IS,] *lit.* 'was my Father glorified, that ye may bear much fruit, and shall become my disciples.'

9. HATH,] *lit.* 'did love me, and I loved you.'

10. KEEP,] *lit.* 'may keep.'

12. HAVE,] *lit.* 'did love you.'

13. MAN,] *lit.* 'no one.. any one may set his soul over his friend (to protect him).'

14. DO,] *lit.* 'may do as many things as.'

15. HENCEFORTH,] *lit.* 'no more do I..has not known..I heard from (*or* along-side of) my Father I made known.'

16. HAVE,] *lit.* 'did not choose me, but I chose you, and set (put, *or* place) you, that ye might go away and might bear fruit, and your fruit might remain, that whatsoever ye may ask the Father.'

17. COMMAND,] *lit.* 'raise up to you.'

18. HATE,] *lit.* 'doth hate you, ye know (*or* know ye).'

19. WOULD,] *lit.* 'were loving its own.. I chose you.'

20. THE,] *lit.* 'a servant..they pursued me ..pursue you.. they kept my word.'

21. FOR,] *lit.* 'because of my name, because they have not known.'

22. HAD,] *lit.* 'did not come, and did not speak..pretext.'

23. HATETH,] *lit.* 'is hating.'

24. HAD,] *lit.* 'did not do among them what no other one hath done.'

25. IS,] *lit.* 'has been written..that, They hated me without a cause,' *lit.* gratuitously, freely. Ps. 35. 19; 69. 4.

26. COMFORTER,] *lit.* 'one calling along-side of' another.

IS,] *lit.* 'may come,..the Spirit of the truth, who passeth-forth from the Father.'

27. HAVE BEEN,] *lit.* 'ye are.'

Chapter XVI. may be divided into five parts; v. 1—4 Jesus warns against persecution; v. 5—11 comforts sorrow by the promise of the Comforter; v. 12—16 describes his work; v. 17—24 promises joy by his return; v. 25—33 professes and is confessed to have come forth from God.

1. SHOULD,] *lit.* 'may not be stumbled.'

2. PUT YOU OUT,] *lit.* 'make you non-synagogites, but there cometh an hour, that every one who has killed you utterly may think to bear-forward service (*lit.* much trembling) to God.'

3. HAVE,] *lit.* 'did not know.'

4. TIME,] *lit.* 'hour may come..from the beginning.'

5. GO MY WAY,] *lit.* 'go away.'

6. SORROW,] *lit.* 'the sorrow.'

7. EXPEDIENT,] *lit.* 'it bears-together to you..if I pass on.'

8. REPROVE,] *lit.* 'convince *or* convict the

world concerning sin, and concerning righteousness, and concerning judgment.'

9. OF,] *lit.* 'concerning sin, indeed.'

10. GO,] *lit.* 'go away.'

11. PRINCE,] *lit.* 'chief *or* first one.'

IS,] *lit.* 'has been judged.'

13. TRUTH,] *lit.* 'of the truth may come he will lead you on the way to all the truth ..from himself, but as many things as he may hear.. tell you fully the coming things.'

14. RECEIVE,] *or* 'take.. tell it fully to you.'

15. THAT,] *lit.* 'as many as the Father.. because of this..receive..tell it fully.'

16. GO,] *lit.* 'go away.'

17. AMONG THEMSELVES,] *lit.* 'to one another.'

NOT SEE,] *lit.* 'not view..I go away.'

18. A,] *lit.* 'the little while, we have not known what he says.'

19. DESIROUS,] *lit.* 'were wishing ..do ye seek with one another..not view me.'

20. BE TURNED,] *lit.* 'happen (*or* come to) joy.'

21. A,] *lit.* 'the woman when she may bear a child..came..may bear the little child,.. the tribulation, because of the joy that a man (i.e. a human being) was born.'

22. TAKETH,] *lit.* 'lifteth up.'

23. ASK,] *or* 'question me nothing.'

WHATSOEVER,] *lit.* 'that, as many things as ye may ask (in prayer).'

25. PROVERBS,] *or* 'similes, but there cometh an hour..shall tell you fully with full-speech concerning the Father.'

26. PRAY,] *lit.* 'question the Father about you.'

27. LOVETH,] *lit.* 'is your friend, because ye have been my friends..I came forth from God.'

28. AM,] *lit.* 'have come to..let go the world, and pass on to.'

29. SAID,] *lit.* 'say..with full-speech thou talkest.'

30. ARE WE SURE,] *lit.* 'have we known that thou hast known all,..any one do question thee in this.'

31. THE,] *lit.* 'there cometh an hour, yea, now it hath come, that ye may be scattered, each to his own things, and may leave me alone.'

32. BE OF GOOD CHEER,] *lit.* 'be courageous.'

Chapter XVII. may be divided into two parts; v. 1—19 Jesus asks for his twelve apostles; v. 20—26 and for all who shall believe on him hereafter.

1. WORDS,] *or* 'these things..to the heaven ..has come.'

2. HAST GIVEN,] *lit.* 'didst give authority (*or* privilege) over all flesh, that to all (the mass) whom thou hast given to him, he may give to them life age-during.'

3. LIFE.] *lit.* 'the life age-during...thou didst send forth.'

4. I HAVE,] *lit.* 'I did glorify..I finished.. hast given.'

5. WITH,] *lit.* 'along-side of thyself..along-side of thee.'

6. I HAVE,] *lit.* 'I manifested..hast given ..hast given.'

7. WHATSOEVER,] *lit.* 'as many as..from thee.'

8. WORDS,] *lit.* 'sayings that thou hast given me, and themselves received, and have known truly that from thee I came forth, and they believed that thou didst send me forth.'

9. PRAY,] *lit.* 'ask..do I ask, but.'

10. ALL MINE,] *lit.* 'all my things are thine, and thy things are mine, and I have been glorified in them.'

11. THESE,] the twelve disciples.

THROUGH,] *lit.* 'in thy name those whom.'

ONE,] in will, not in person; see 10. 30, &c.

12. KEPT,] *lit.* 'was keeping..hast given me I guarded, and not one of them was loosed-away, except the son of the loosing-away (i.e. the loosed-away son) that the Writing may be filled out,' i.e. realized, exemplified.

13. IN THEMSELVES,] *or* 'among them.'

14. HATH,] *lit.* 'did hate.'

15. PRAY,] *lit.* 'ask not that thou mayest lift them up.. mayest keep them out of the evil.'

17. SANCTIFY,] *lit.* 'set-them-apart in (*or* by) thy truth.'

18. HAST,] *lit.* 'didst send me forth to.. I also sent them forth.'

19. THEIR SAKES,] *lit.* 'and for them I—I set-myself-apart,..set apart in (*or* by) truth.'

20. PRAY,] *lit.* 'ask..shall be believing.'

21. THEY ALL,] *lit.* 'that all may be one (as in v. 11.)..didst send me forth.'

22. GAVEST,] *lit.* 'hast given.'

23. IN ONE,] *or* 'with a view to (being) one ..didst send me forth, and didst love them, as thou didst love me.'

24. WILL,] *lit.* 'I wish.. may view.. didst give me, because thou didst love me from the laying-down of the world,' in *Gr. kosmos*, order or arrangement of things, whether physical or moral.

25. WORLD,] *lit.* 'world also did not know thee, but I knew thee.. didst send me forth.'

26. HAVE DECLARED,] *lit.* 'made known ..and will make (it) known..didst love me.'

Chapter XVIII. may be divided into five parts; v. 1—14 Jesus delivered up and led to Annas; v. 15—18 Peter's first denial; v. 19—24 Jesus before Annas; v. 25—27 Peter's second denial; v. 28—40 Jesus before Pilate.

1. WORDS,] *or* 'things.. winter-brook of Kedron.'

2. BETRAYED,] *lit.* 'gave him over had known.. many times came together there with.'

3. A,] *lit.* 'the band, and under-servants.. torches and lamps and weapons.'

4. SHOULD,] *lit.* 'are coming.'

5. OF NAZARETH,] *lit.* 'Jesus the Nazarene ..gave him over, was standing.'

I AM,] *lit.* 'that, I am he, they went away backward.'

7. OF NAZARETH,] *lit.* 'Jesus the Nazarene.'

8. HAVE TOLD,] *lit.* 'I said,.. these go away.'

9. SAYING,] *lit.* 'word..that, those whom thou hast given to me I lost none.'
10. CUT OFF,] *lit.* 'cut off thoroughly.'
11. PUT UP,] *or* 'cast..may I not.'
12. CAPTAIN,] *lit.* 'chief of a thousand.'
OFFICERS,] *lit.* 'under-rowers,' as in v. 3.
13. HIGH,] *lit.* 'chief-priest of that year.'
14. GAVE,] *or* 'took counsel together with.'
SHOULD DIE,] *lit.* 'for one man to perish for the people.'
15. FOLLOWED,] *lit.* 'was following Jesus, also the other disciple,' whom most suppose to have been John, but who may have been Judas.
PALACE,] *lit.* 'hall *or* court of the chief priest;' King James' predilection for bishops no doubt converted the simple court-yard of the high-priest into a 'palace!'
16. STOOD,] *lit.* 'was standing..the other disciple..portress.'
17. DAMSEL,] *lit.* 'little damsel, the portress.'
18. OFFICERS,] *lit.* 'under-rowers were standing..were warming themselves.. was standing and warming himself.'
19. DOCTRINE,] *lit.* 'teaching.'
20. OPENLY,] *lit.* 'with full-speech.. always come together..I spake nothing.'
21. HAVE SAID,] *lit.* 'I spake..these have known.'
22. THUS,] *lit.* 'these things.'
OFFICERS,] *lit.* 'under-rowers..gave Jesus a slap,' with his palm *or* his rod.
23. HAVE,] *lit.* 'if I spake well.'
24. HAD,] *lit.* 'sent him away.'
25. STOOD,] *lit.* 'was standing and warming.'
26. THE,] *lit.* 'a cock sounded.'
28. HALL OF JUDGMENT.] *Gr.* praitorion, *Lat.* praetorium.
SHOULD,] *lit.* 'might be defiled.'
29. ACCUSATION,] *lit.* 'public fault bear ye.'
30. HE,] *lit.* 'if this one were not an evildoer, we had not given him over to thee.'
31. PUT,] *lit.* 'kill any one utterly.'
32. SAYING,] *lit.* 'word.. by what death he was about to die utterly.'
33. JUDGMENT HALL,] *lit.* 'praetorium.'
34. OF,] *lit.* 'from thyself.. concerning me.'
35. HAVE,] *lit.* 'did give thee over.. what didst thou?'
36. WOULD,] *lit.* 'had my underlings striven (*or* agonized) that I might not be given over to the Jews.'
37. ART THOU,] *lit.* 'then thou art not a king?.. for this I have been born, and for this have I come to.. that I may.'
38. NO FAULT,] *lit.* 'no cause (of punishment).'
39. CUSTOM,] *lit.* 'a united-custom that I shall loose fully to you one in (during) the passover; do ye wish, therefore.'

Chapter XIX. may be divided into five parts; v. 1—18 Jesus scourged, crowned, condemned; v. 19—24 his title and his garments; v. 25—30 he remembers his mother, and gives up his spirit; v. 31—37 his body pierced but not broken; v. 38—42 his burial.
1. SCOURGED,] probably with rods or wands.
2. PUT ON,] *lit.* 'cast around him.
3. HAIL,] *or* 'rejoice, O king of the Jews, and were giving to him slaps,' with their rods *or* hands.
4. WENT FORTH,] *lit.* 'went forth without.'
FAULT,] *lit.* 'cause (of punishment).'
5. FORTH,] *lit.* 'forth without, bearing the thorny crown, and the purple garment.'
6. OFFICERS,] *lit.* 'underlings..cause (of punishment).'
7. BY,] *lit.* 'according to..die fully.'
8. SAYING,] *lit.* 'word.'
9. JUDGMENT-HALL,] *lit.* 'praetorium.'
10. KNOWEST,] *lit.* 'hast thou not known that I have authority (*or* privilege)..loose thee fully.'
11. COULDEST HAVE,] *lit.* 'hadst no authority,..because of this he who is giving me over to thee has greater sin.'
12. AND,] *lit.* 'from that (circumstance) Pilate was seeking to loose him fully..were crying out, saying, If this one thou mayest loose fully..every one who is making himself a king.'
13. SAYING,] *lit.* 'word..upon the tribunal in a place named A strawing of stone, and in Hebrew A high place.'
14. ABOUT,] *lit.* 'and as if (the) ninth hour.'
15. AWAY,] *lit.* 'lift (him) up, lift (him) up!'
16. DELIVERED,] *lit.* 'gave he him over to them that he might be crucified, and they took Jesus along-side (of themselves), and led him away.'
17. IN THE,] *lit.* 'in Hebrew,' i.e. Aramaean.
19. WRITING,] *lit.* 'and it was written, Jesus the Nazarene.'
20. READ,] *lit.* 'knew again *or* recognized ..Hebraistic, Hellenistic, Romaic.'
23. HAD,] *lit.* 'they crucified..to each soldier..was seamless.'
24. AMONG,] *lit.* 'to one another..the Writing..They parted thoroughly my garments to themselves, and upon..cast a lot.'
25. MAGDALENE,] *lit.* 'Mary the Magdalene.'
26. LOVED,] *lit.* 'was loving.'
27. HIS OWN HOME,] *or* 'his own friends.'
28. WERE,] *lit.* 'have been ended, that the Writing might be ended.'
29. PUT,] *lit.* 'put it round upon hyssop, and brought it forward to his mouth.'
30. HAD,] *lit.* 'Jesus received..It has been ended..gave over the spirit'—to God.
31. BECAUSE,] *lit.* 'since..might not remain during the sabbath..a great day, asked Pilate.'
34. PIERCED,] *or* 'pricked.'
35. SAW,] *lit.* 'has seen, has borne testimony, and his testimony..has known.'
36. WERE DONE,] *or* 'happened, that the Writing might..broken utterly.'
37. SCRIPTURE,] *or* 'Writing.. pierced through.'
38. THIS,] *lit.* 'these things..from Arimathea..but concealed through the fear of the Jews, asked Pilate that he might lift up the body of Jesus, and Pilate turned (it) over upon (him)..lifted up.'

39. BROUGHT,] *lit.* 'bare..as if (it were) a hundred lbs. (weight).'

40. TOOK,] *or* 'received.. bound.. aromatics, even as it is a custom to the Jews to entomb.'

41. MAN,] *lit.* 'no one.'

42. NIGH,] not 'nigh at hand.'

Chapter XX. may be divided into five parts; v. 1—9 Jesus' tomb found empty; v. 10—18 Jesus and two messengers appear to Mary the Magdalene; v. 19—23 He appears to the disciples; v. 24—29 also to them and Thomas; v. 30, 31 object in recording Jesus' signs.

1. FIRST,] *lit.* 'one;' a common idiom, in Greek and Hebrew.

WEEK,] *lit.* 'sabbaths,' as in v. 19; Mat. 28. 1; Mark 16. 2, 9; Luke 24. 1; but from Luke 18. 12; Acts 20. 7; 1 Cor. 16. 2, the Greek word appears to be not really a plural, but a transcription of the Hebrew word 'sabbaton,' occurring in Ex. 16. 23; 31. 15; 35. 2; Lev. 16. 31; 23. 24. See my 'Biblical Tracts for Every Day in the Year.'

TAKEN AWAY,] *lit.* 'having been lifted up out of the sepulchre.'

2. LOVED,] *lit.* 'was befriending.. They lifted up the Lord out of the sepulchre, and we have not known where they laid him.'

3. THAT,] *lit.* 'the other..were coming.'

4. RAN,] *lit.* 'the two were running..ran forward more quickly than Peter.'

5. STOOPING-DOWN,] *lit.* 'having bent along, sees.'

6. SEETH,] *lit.* 'vieweth..lying.'

7. ABOUT,] *lit.* 'upon..but apart, having been folded up into one place.'

8. THEN,] *lit.* 'then, therefore,..the other ..believed,' what Mary had told them.

9. SCRIPTURE,] *lit.* 'writing, that it behoveth him to stand up out of (the) dead.'

10. OWN HOME,] *or* 'their own friends.'

11. STOOD,] *lit.* 'was standing..was weeping, she bent along into.'

12. SEETH,] *lit.* 'vieweth two messengers ..one.. and one.. been laid.'

13. THEY,] *lit.* 'these.. they lifted up.. I have not known where they laid him.'

14. THUS,] *lit.* 'these things .views Jesus standing, and had not known that it is Jesus.'

15. SUPPOSING,] *lit.* 'thinking that it is the gardener..if thou didst bear him off.. didst lay.. lift him up.'

16. MASTER,] *lit.* 'teacher.'

17. TOUCH,] *lit.* 'be not touching me, for I have not yet gone up.. be passing on.'

18. MAGDALENE,] *lit.* 'the Magdalene cometh telling again fully to the.. has seen ..he spake.'

19. THEN,] *lit.* 'it being then evening, that day, the first (one) of the week (sabbaths), and the doors having been closed where the disciples were brought together, through the fear of the Jews.. Jesus came,' but how he entered is not recorded.

20. SO,] *lit.* 'this.'

21. MY,] *lit.* 'even as the Father hath sent me forth, I also send you.'

22. BREATHED,] *lit.* 'breathed fully, and says to them, Receive a holy spirit (*or* influence).'

23. WHOSOEVER,] *lit.* 'if of any ye may let go (i.e. declare forgiven) the sins.. if of any ye may strengthen (i.e. declare strong), they have been strengthened.'

25. SHALL,] *lit.* 'may see.. the mark (*lit.* type).. put my hand to.'

26. CAME,] *lit.* 'cometh Jesus.'

27. REACH,] *lit.* 'bear hither.. bear hither .. put in to my side, and be not becoming unstedfast, but stedfast.'

28. MY GOD,] worthy of all adoration.

29. BLESSED,] *lit.* 'happy.'

30. DISCIPLES,] after his up rising as well as before his death.

ARE,] *or* 'have not been written.'

31. ARE,] *lit.* 'have been written.'

CHRIST.. SON,] as in 6. 69; 11. 27; Mat. 26. 63; Luke 4. 41, &c.

THROUGH,] *lit.* 'in (or by) his name.'

Chaper XXI. may be divided into four parts; v. 1—14 Jesus manifests himself a third time to his disciples; v. 15—19 draws out Peter's love, and foretells his death; v. 20—24 Peter's enquiry about John; v. 25 the conclusion.

1. SHEWED,] *lit.* 'manifested himself.. on the sea.. manifested himself thus.'

2. CALLED,] *lit.* 'who is named..from Cana.'

3. I GO.] *lit.* 'I go away to fish,' (*lit.* to be a salt-man).

A SHIP,] *lit.* 'the boat (they commonly used), and during that night.'

4. THE,] *lit.* 'when morning..at the beach ..had not known that it is Jesus.'

5. CHILDREN,] *or* 'Lads, what food have ye.'

6. SIDE,] *lit.* 'parts of the boat..and no more..from the multitude of the fishes.'

8. LOVED,] *lit.* 'was loving..it is the Lord, girded thoroughly on the outer garment, for he was naked,' i.e. comparatively so, as in 1 Sa. 19. 24; 2 Sa. 6. 20; Isa. 20. 2, 3; Acts 19. 16, &c.

8. A LITTLE,] *lit.* 'the little boat from the land, but as (it were) two hundred cubits off, dragging the net of the fishes.'

9. WERE COME,] *lit.* 'they came away to the land, they behold a fire of coals laid, and a little fish laid upon (it), and a loaf.'

10. OF,] *lit.* 'from.'

11. TO LAND,] *lit.* 'upon the land..though ..rent.'

12. DINE,] *or* 'breakfast;' *lit.* take the 'best' meal.

DURST,] *lit.* 'was daring to ask him openly ..it is the Lord.'

13. BREAD,] *lit.* 'the loaf..the little fish.'

14. THE,] *lit.* 'a third time (recorded by John).. was manifested..raised out of (the) dead.'

15. HAD DINED,] *lit.* 'dined *or* breakfasted..these (other disciples).'

KNOWEST,] *lit.* 'hast known that I am thy friend..little lambs.'

16. THE,] *lit.* 'a second time..hast known that I am thy friend,.. tend my sheep.'

17. LOVEST,] *lit.* 'befriendest thou me?..

befriendest thou me?.. hast know all, thou knowest that I am thy friend.'

18. YOUNG,] *lit.* 'younger, thou wast girding thyself, and wast walking about where thou didst wish..mayest be old (*lit.* seeing the earth)..dost not wish.'

19. SHOULD,] *lit.* 'shall glorify..Be following me.'

20. TURNING,] *lit.* 'turning round upon (him) beholds..was loving..fell back.. during the supper..who is he that is giving thee over?'

21. WHAT,] *lit.* 'and this one—what (of him)?'

22. WILL,] *lit.* 'wish him to remain..thou, be thou following me.'

23. SAYING,] *lit.* 'word forth to..does not die utterly.'

TILL I COME,] to destroy Judaism and Jerusalem.

24. TESTIFIETH,] *lit.* 'is testifying concerning.'

KNOW,] *lit.* 'we have known;' this clause was most probably a marginal note at first; but see the use of the plural in Rom. 7. 14; 1 Thes. 2. 18, &c.

25. WHICH,] *lit.* 'as many as Jesus did, which, if they might be written each one, not even the world itself I think to have space (for) the books that are written.'

QUESTIONS ADAPTED TO ANY CHAPTER IN THE GOSPELS.

1. What are the principal topics of this Chapter?
2. Are these topics mentioned elsewhere?
3. What Various Readings are in the Original Text?
4. State the chief Interpolations in MSS., Versions, &c.?
5. Give the chief Omissions, Transpositions?
6. Point out the more prominent Mistranslations of King James' Version, in reference to the:—
   1) *Meaning* of Words and Particles.
   2) The *Voices* of the Verb, Active, Passive, or Reflexive.
   3) Its *Moods*, whether Indicative, Subjunctive, Potential, Imperative, Infinitive or Optative.
   4) Its *Tenses*, whether Present, Imperfect, Past, Perfect, Pluperfect or Future.
   5) The use or abuse of parenthesis, capital letters, punctuation, italics, &c.
7. What peculiar Idioms—Hebrew, Greek?
8. What peculiar words or phrases?
9. What does it teach about the Being, Character, Works, and Ways of God? and of Christ? and of the Holy Spirit?
10. What does it teach about the Origin, Nature, Character, Works, Doings, or Destiny of Man?
11. What duty to God, or Man, or Ourselves?
12. What error, fault, or defect to be avoided?
13. What should we specially strive after?
14. What invitations, promises, or threatenings?
15. What Eastern, Jewish, or ancient custom civil or sacred, is mentioned?
16. What Persons, Places, Sects?
17. What reference to the Old Testament, the Oral Law, or the Law of Nature?
18. What prediction, past or future?
19. What reference to the Animal kingdom?
20. What reference to the Vegetable kingdom?
21. What reference to the Mineral kingdom?
22. What false notions have been founded on it?
23. What graces, gifts, and offices of Jesus are here?
24. What miracles, or parables?
25. What illustrations of the character of the Writer is here given? his defects, excellencies, excesses?
26. When or where did the chief events occur?
27. What types, symbols, or imagery are used?
28. What questions, answerable or unanswerable?
29. What apparent contradictions?
30. What rite or custom is now abrogated?
31. What references to Heaven and its inhabitants?
32. What to Hades and its inhabitants?
33. What to the Powers of Evil?
34. What reference to death and judgment?
35. What to trials, afflictions, persecutions?
36. What to privileges and responsibilities?
37. What to dangers and temptations?
38. What to encouragement and joy?
39. To what are believers compared?
40. To what are unbelievers compared?
41. What is the main lesson of the whole?

DEEDS OF THE APOSTLES

THIS account of the 'DEEDS OF (some of) THE APOSTLES,' is professedly a continuation of the 'GOSPEL' according to LUKE, and by the same writer. Its genuineness and authenticity are unquestionable; it is quoted by the Church of Lyons (A.D. 177), by Irenaeus, (A.D. 167), Clement of Alexandria (A.D. 192), and Tertullian (A.D. 192). It was rejected by the Marcionites in the 3d, and by the Manichaeans in the 4th, century. It comprises a period of thirty years, being written about A.D. 63, when Paul was a prisoner in Rome, see 28. 30. The Various Readings of the Greek MSS. are more numerous in this than in any other of the New Testament Books.

It may be divided as follows:—

I. From the Ascension of Jesus till the Conversion of Saul, ch. 1. 1—8. 40.

II. From the Conversion of Saul till his return to Antioch, ch. 9. 1—12. 25

III. Paul's First Journey, ch. 13. 1—15. 35.

IV. His Second Journey, ch. 15. 36—18. 22.

V. His Third Journey, ch. 18. 23—26. 32.

VI. His Voyage to Rome, ch. 27. 1—28. 31.

The following are the chief allusions to the Old Testament found in this book; De. 18. 15—18; 2 Sa. 7. 12, 13; 2 Ch. 36. 16; Ps. 2. 1; 16. 8, 10; 41. 9; 109. 8; 110. 1; Isa. 6. 9; 29. 14; 55. 5; Joel 2. 28, 29; Amos 5. 25; 9. 11, 12, &c.

Chapter I. may be divided into six parts; v. 1—5 Luke's introduction, and Jesus' promise; v. 6—8 the apostles' question and Jesus' answer; v. 9—11 Jesus taken up and two messengers appear; v. 12—14 a prayer meeting; v. 15—22 Peter's proposal to supply the place of Judas; v. 23—26 Matthias chosen by lot.

1. FORMER,] *lit.* 'first account, indeed, I myself made concerning all (i.e. many) things, O Theophilus, that Jesus began both to do and to teach.'

2. TAKEN,] *or* 'received up, having given commandment through a holy influence to the apostles whom he himself laid out.'

3. TO,] *lit.* 'along-side of whom also he stationed himself alive after his suffering, in (*or* by) many tokens, through forty days being visible to them, and speaking the things concerning.'

4. ASSEMBLED,] *or* 'eating together,' *lit.* taking salt with (them); salt being a token of friendship and amity; as in Ezra 4. 14, &c.

COMMANDED,] *lit.* 'told them over again not to . . but to remain for the openly-spoken-of-thing of the Father, which ye heard of me.'

5. THE,] *lit.* a 'holy spirit,' or influence.

6. ASKED,] *lit.* 'were asking him, . . Dost thou during this time cause the kingdom to stand thoroughly back to Israel?'

7. FOR YOU,] *lit.* 'yours to know times or seasons which the Father put (*or* set) in (*or* by) his own authority,' *or* privilege.

8. AFTER,] *lit.* 'at the open-coming of the Holy Spirit upon you, . . end of the land,' *or* earth.

9. TAKEN,] *or* 'lifted up . . received him (away) from (before) their eyes.'

10. LOOKED,] *lit.* 'were straining (their eyes) to the heaven, in his passing on . . stood along-side of them.'

11. OF GALILEE,] *lit.* 'men! Galileans! why stand ye looking intently to the heaven? this Jesus, who was received up from you to the heaven . . ye saw him passing on to the heaven.'

12. RETURNED,] *lit.* 'turned round away . . called of Olives, which is nigh Jerusalem, being a sabbath's journey,' i.e. half-a-mile.

13. WERE COME,] *lit.* 'they came in, they went up to the upper room (where they used to meet), where they were continually remaining, both . . Simon the Zealot.'

14. CONTINUED,] *lit.* 'were strong with the same mind, as to the pouring forth before (God), and the supplication, with women, . . brothers,' *or* brethren.

15. NUMBER,] *lit.* 'crowd also of names at the same (place) was about.'

16. AND,] *lit.* 'men, brethren (i.e. brother-men), it behoved this Writing to be filled-out, which the Holy Spirit said before-hand (*or* openly) through the mouth of David, concerning Judas, who became leader of the way to those who took Jesus with (them).'

17. NUMBERED,] *lit.* 'fully numbered . . and obtained the lot of this deaconship.'

18. NOW,] *lit.* 'this one, indeed, then, himself acquired (i.e. was the cause of the ground being purchased by the chief-priests) a space (of ground) out of the reward of the injustice, and moving forward he burst in the midst, and all his bowels were shed forth.'

19. WAS,] *lit.* 'became . . inhabiting Jerusalem, so that that space is called in their proper dialect Akeldama, that is, Space of Blood.' This verse is a parenthesis by Luke.

20. IT IS,] *lit.* 'it has been written (Ps. 69. 25) . . open-court become . . his oversight let another receive.'

21. WHEREFORE,] *lit.* 'therefore of the men who went with us during all the time in which.'

22. TAKEN,] *or* 'received up, it behoveth one to become . . his up-standing.'

23. APPOINTED,] *lit.* 'set.'

BARSABAS,] i.e. 'son of hope.'

SURNAMED,] *lit.* 'called also.'

JUSTUS,] i.e. 'just.'

MATTHIAS,] i.e. 'gift of God,' like Nathanael.

24. PRAYED,] *lit.* 'poured forth before (God).'

WHICH,] *lit.* 'heart-knower of all.'

SHEW,] *lit.* 'shew-fully which one of these two thou didst lay out for thyself.'

25. THAT,] *lit.* 'to receive the lot of this deaconship and apostleship (out of which Judas went over) to pass on to his own place,' and witness for Christ; the reference is not to Judas, but to him who might succeed him.

26. GAVE FORTH,] *lit.* 'gave .. thoroughly voted one with the eleven apostles.' The propriety of this whole election has been much canvassed. Against it there is urged, 1)-that Christ gave them no injunction or indication that they were to fill up the place of Judas; 2) that Paul (if any) really was destined to fill up the number of the twelve; 3) that they should have waited for the outpouring of the Spirit, as commanded; 4) that they practically confessed their error, by refraining from filling up the places of any of the other apostles, as they died out; 5) that Scripture nowhere acknowledges the apostleship of Matthias, while the labours of Paul are held up in peculiar fulness.

On the other hand, it has been said with propriety, that if the apostles were mistaken in this election, it is difficult, if not impossible, to regard their *conduct* (at least, if not their *teaching*) in other church arrangements as necessarily of binding obligation (except it be supposed that after the Day of Pentecost only did they begin their course as inspired teachers); to which it has been answered, that when it is remembered that Peter's *conduct* was blameworthy in at least one case (Gal. 2. 11, 12), Paul's also perhaps (Acts 21. 4, 12, 20—26), that of James, Peter and others in attempting to retain Jewish distinctions of things strangled and blood (Acts 15. 29), it is not improbable but that the hasty zeal of Peter may have hurried on an election that was unwarranted in the circumstances. But the whole subject requires more thorough investigation than it has yet received.

Chapter II. may be divided into seven parts; v. 1—4 descent of the Spirit; v. 5—11 amazement of the hearers; v. 12—21 Joel's prophecy fulfilled; v. 22—29 fulfilment of David's prophecy; v. 30—36 Jesus at the right hand of God; v. 37—42 conversion, baptism, and communion of 3000; v. 43—47 great signs and mutual joy.

1. OF,] *lit.* 'of the Pentecost,' i.e. 50 days after the passover; see Lev. 23. 15.

ACCORD,] *or* 'mind, at the same place.'

ALL] the apostles, with the 120 others.

2. SUDDENLY,] *lit.* 'un(for)seen..out of the heaven, as of a bearing-on violent wind (spirit, or breath).'

3. CLOVEN,] *lit.* 'thoroughly-parted tongues, as if of fire, it (i.e. the tongue) sat also upon each one of them.'

4. FILLED,] *or* 'full of holy spirit, and began to speak with other tongues, even as the Spirit (of God) was giving to them to sound forth.'

5. DEVOUT,] *lit.* 'well-received,' i.e. by God.

OUT OF,] *or* 'from every (i.e. many a) nation under the heaven.'

6. WHEN,] *lit.* 'the voice (*or* noise) of this having come (abroad).. was confounded (*lit.* poured together), because they were each one in his proper dialect hearing their speaking.'

7. WERE ALL AMAZED,] *lit.* 'all stood-out, and wondered.. who are speaking.'

8. EVERY MAN,] *lit.* 'each one in our proper dialect.'

9. JUDEA.] Some conjecture 'Idumea.'

10. ABOUT,] *lit.* 'down by Cyrene.'

PROSELYTES,] *lit.* 'comers to'—Judaism.

11. SPEAK,] *lit.* 'their speaking (*or* speakers) in our own tongues the great things of God.'

12. WERE AMAZED,] *lit.* 'all stood-out and were doubting (*lit.* passing on differently), .. What would this wish to be?'

13. THESE,] *lit.* 'that, they are full of sweet wine.'

14. LIFT,] *lit.* 'lifted up.. sounded forth to them, Men, Jews,.. give ear (to) my sayings.'

15. SUPPOSE,] *lit.* 'take it up.'

16. BY,] *lit.* 'through.'

17. SHALL COME TO PASS,] *lit.* 'shall be.. forth from my.' See Joel 2. 28.

18. SERVANTS,] *lit.* 'men-servants.. women-servants.'

19. SHOW,] *lit.* 'give terrible things in the heaven above, and signs upon the land beneath.'

20. TURNED,] *lit.* 'turned round with (it) to darkness..before the coming of the great and very manifest day of the Lord, when he' will abolish the Old, and bring in the New, Covenant.

21. SHALL COME TO PASS,] *lit.* 'shall be, every one whoever shall call upon the name,' i.e. invoke his help in prayer.

22. MEN OF,] *lit.* 'Men, Israelites.. Jesus the Nazarene, a man shewn-forth to you from God by powers, and terrible things, and signs.. through him, even as yourselves also have known.'

23. HIM,] *lit.* 'this one being given forth (to the world) by the marked-out counsel and foreknowledge of God (revealed in the Scriptures).. through lawless hands, ye crucified (*lit.* fixed forward) and lifted up.'

24. HATH,] *lit.* 'did make to stand up.. of the death..for him to be held fast under it.'

25. CONCERNING,] *lit.* 'in reference to him.'

FORESAW,] *or* 'saw openly the Lord before me through all (time), because..I may not.'

26. THEREFORE,] *lit.* 'because of this was my heart well-minded..settle down on hope.'

27. LEAVE,] *lit.* 'leave utterly my soul to Hades (the unseen world of spirits), nor give (up) thy kind one to see (i.e. experience) full-corruption.'

28. HAST,] *lit.* 'didst make known to me ways of life, thou shall fill me with a good-mind after (or with) thy face.'

29. AND,] *lit.* 'men, brethren, it is lawful to speak with full-speech to you concerning ..he both ended (his life) and was entombed, .. among us.'

30. HAD,] *lit.* 'sware.. out of the fruit.. to cause the Christ to stand up, to sit.'

31. SEEING,] *lit.* 'he having seen (it) before *or* openly, spake concerning the up-standing of the Christ,.. left utterly to Hades,.. full-corruption.'

32. HATH,] *lit.* 'did God cause to stand up.'

33. OF,] *lit.* 'from the Father the promised thing.. he was pouring forth.'

34. IS NOT,] *lit* 'did not go up to the.. Be sitting.'

35. MAKE,] *lit.* 'set *or* place.'

36. ASSUREDLY,] *lit.* 'un-thrown-down,' *or* incontrovertibly.

HATH,] *lit.* 'did make this Jesus.'

37. PRICKED,] *lit.* 'pricked down to the heart.. Men! brethren!'

38. REPENT,] *lit.* 'have another mind, and let each of you be baptized upon the name of Jesus Christ, with a view to a letting go of sins.'

39. SHALL,] *lit.* 'may (himself) call forward for himself.'

40. DID,] *lit.* 'was he both testifying-fully and calling along-side (of them), saying, Be saved from this perverse generation.'

41. GLADLY,] *or* 'sweetly received of his word were baptized, and there were set forward (*or* besides) on that day souls, as if (it were) three thousand.'

42. CONTINUED STEDFASTLY,] *lit.* 'were strong-towards the teaching of the apostles, and the communion, and the breaking of the bread (*lit.* loaf), and the pouring forth before (God).'

43. UPON,] *or* 'to.. terrible things.. were happening through the apostles.'

44. TOGETHER,] *lit.* 'upon the same (thing *or* place).'

45. SOLD,] *lit.* 'were selling (i.e. 'causing to pass over' to others) the acquisitions and the goods, and were parting them thoroughly to all, even as any one had need.'

46. ACCORD,] *lit.* 'mind.. at every house, were receiving with (others) nourishment in gladness and simplicity of heart.'

47. WITH,] *or* 'towards all the people,' doing them good as they had opportunity.

48. ADDED,] *lit.* 'was putting forward those who are being saved (i.e. believers) every day to the assembly.'

Chapter III. may be divided into two parts; v. 1—11 cure of a lame man; v. 12—26 Peter's address to the Jews.

1. WENT,] *lit.* 'were going up (according to their usual custom) at the same (time) to the temple, at the hour of the (evening) pouring forth before (God), the ninth (hour, i.e. 3 p.m.).'

2. CARRIED,] *lit.* 'was being carried, whom they were putting every day towards the door of the temple.. to ask kindness from those passing on into the temple.'

3. ASKED,] *lit.* 'was requesting to receive kindness.'

4. FASTENING,] *lit.* 'straining (his eyes) at him with John, said, Look to us.'

5. GAVE HEED,] *lit.* 'was holding on to them, thinking forward to receive something from them.'

6. RISE,] *lit.* 'raise thyself up and be walking about.'

7. TOOK,] *lit.* 'seized.. and along with the word.. were strengthened.'

8. LEAPING UP,] *or* 'leaping forth stood, and was walking about,.. walking about.'

9. WALKING,] *lit.* 'walking about.'

10. KNEW,] *lit.* 'were knowing also about him that this was he who was sitting for the kindness.. and ecstasy (*lit.* a standing-out) at what has come together to him.'

11. IN,] *lit.* 'to the porch.'

12. MEN OF,] *lit.* 'Men, Israelites, why wonder.. why strain ye (your eyes) at us.. or good-worship we have made him to walk about.'

13. HATH,] *lit.* 'did glorify his Son (*or* servant, lad) Jesus, whom ye gave over.. against the face of Pilate, he having judged to loose him utterly.'

14. HOLY,] *lit.* 'holy and just one, and asked a man, a murderer, to be given as a favour to you.'

15. KILLED,] *lit.* 'killed utterly the chief-leader of the life, whom God raised out of (the) dead.'

16. AND,] *lit.* 'and upon the faith of his name, this one, whom ye view and have known, his name made strong, and the faith that is through him did give to him this perfect lot.'

17. WOT,] *lit.* 'have known that in (*lit.* down) ignorance.. your chiefs.'

18. BEFORE HAD SHEWED,] *lit.* 'told thoroughly before (*or* in public, openly) through the mouth of all (i.e. many of) his prophets that the Christ.'

19. REPENT,] *lit.* 'have another mind, therefore, and turn round upon (him), with a view to your sins be fully besmeared,—so that seasons of refreshing may come from the face of the Lord.'

20. SHALL,] *lit.* 'may send forth him who has been proclaimed before (*or* openly) to you—Jesus Christ,' in *spirit*, not in person, in *power*, not in name, merely. Comp. v. 26; 1 Pet. 3. 19; Eph. 2. 17, &c.

21. WHOM,] *lit.* 'behoveth heaven indeed, to receive to itself till times of the standing-thoroughly-back of all (things *or* persons), of which God spake through.. from (the) ages.'

22. TRULY,] *lit.* 'indeed.. that, A prophet.. out of your brethren as (he did) me.. through all things, as many as he may speak to you.'

23. COME TO PASS,] *lit.* 'shall be.. may not hear.. shall be utterly destroyed (*or* lost) out of the people.'

24. THAT FOLLOW AFTER,] *lit.* 'holding through,' i.e. succeeding.

HAVE,] *lit.* 'as spake, told-thoroughly-beforehand.'

25. THE,] *lit.* 'ye are sons of the prophets and of the covenant (*lit.* thoroughly-set thing) which God set-thoroughly to our fathers.. families (*or* fathers' houses) of the land be well spoken of *or* to,' by God and man.

26. SON,] *or* 'servant, lad,' as in v. 13.

SENT,] *lit.* 'sent him forth (in the preaching of the Gospel) to speak well of (*or* to) you, in the turning fully round of each one from your evils.'

Chapter IV. may be divided into five parts; v. 1—4 the apostles seized, many believe; v. 5—12 the apostles interrogated; v. 13—22 and threatened; v. 23—30 their prayer to God; v. 31—37 out-pouring of the Spirit, and brotherly love abounding.

1. SPAKE,] *lit.* 'are speaking..leader of the force..stood over them.'

2. GRIEVED,] *lit.* 'thoroughly wearied because of their teaching the people, and telling-thoroughly in Jesus the upstanding that is out of (the) dead.'

3. HOLD,] *lit.* 'keeping till the morrow.'

4. WAS,] *lit.* 'became as if (it were).'

5. RULERS,] *lit.* 'foremost-men, and presbyters.'

6. HIGH,] *or* 'foremost priest.. foremost priest.'

GATHERED,] *lit.* 'brought together to.'

7. ASKED,] *lit.* 'were enquiring, In what . in what name, did ye this?'

8. FILLED,] *lit.* 'full of holy spirit..Ye foremost-ones..and presbyters.'

9. EXAMINED,] *lit.* 'judged thoroughly about the good-work of the infirm man, in whom he has been saved.'

10. BY,] *lit.* 'in the name..out of (the) dead, in him has this one stood along-side before you whole.'

11. SET AT NOUGHT,] *lit.* 'thought nothing of..which became for head of a corner.'

12. SALVATION,] *lit.* 'the safety..under the heaven.. in which it behoveth us to be saved.'

13. WHEN,] *lit.* 'viewing the full-speech.. taking (it) up thoroughly that they are men unlettered and private, they were wondering,theyweretakingfull-knowledgealsothat.'

14. WAS,] *lit.* 'has been cherished.. they had nothing to say against (it).'

15. GO,] *lit.* 'go away outside of the sanhedrim, they cast fully (their thoughts) to one another.'

16. NOTABLE,] *lit.* 'known sign has happened through them.'

17. SPREAD,] *lit.* 'may be distributed no more to the people, with threatening we may ourselves threaten them, to speak no more upon this name to any man.'

18. COMMANDED,] *lit.* 'told them fully through the whole (of their lives) not to utter nor to teach upon the name of Jesus.'

19. RIGHT,] *or* 'just, righteous.'

20. HAVE,] *lit.* 'we saw and heard.'

21. THEY MIGHT,] *lit.* 'how to punish them themselves..were glorifying God upon what has happened.'

22. MIRACLE,] *lit.* 'sign of the healing had happened.'

23. LET GO,] *lit.* 'loosed away (*or* thoroughly)..own (friends), and told fully as many things to them as the foremost-priests and the presbyters said.'

24. ACCORD,] *lit.* 'mind..Despot, thou art the God who made the heaven, and the land, and the sea, and all that are in them.'

25. BY,] *lit.* 'through..David said, Why did nations snort, and peoples regard vain things?'

26. EARTH,] *or* 'land stood along-side, and the foremost men were brought together at the same time (*or* place).'

27. FOR,] *lit.* 'for brought together upon a truth were both Herod and Pontius Pilate, with nations and peoples of Israel, upon thy holy Son (*or* servant) Jesus, whom thou didst anoint (28) to do as many things as thy hand and thy counsel marked out openly (*or* beforehand, in the Scriptures) to happen.'

29. BEHOLD,] *lit.* 'look over upon their threats, and give to thy servants with all full-speech to speak thy word.'

30. BY,] *lit.* 'in the stretching forth of thy hand for healing, and signs and fearful things to happen, through the name of thy holy servant Jesus.'

31. PRAYED,] *lit.* 'supplicated, the place in which they were brought together was shaken, and they were all full of holy spirit, and were speaking the word of God with full-speech.'

33. GAVE,] *lit.* 'were the apostles giving away the testimony of the up-standing.'

34. LACKED,] *lit.* 'had lack..fields or houses selling (them) were bearing the weight of the things sold (*lit.* 'caused to pass over).'

35. LAID,] *lit.* 'and were putting alongside . of, and there was thoroughly given to each, according as any one had need.'

36. WHO,] *or* 'who was called also Barnabas (from among the apostles), which is, having been interpreted,Son of Exhortation,' *lit.* 'calling long-side of' another. Comp. 14. 4, 14; Rom. 16. 7, &c.

COUNTRY,] *lit.* 'of Cyprus by birth.'

37. LAND,] *lit.* 'a field..money (*lit.* matter), and put it.'

Chapter V. may be divided into five parts; v. 1—11 Ananias and Sapphira; v. 12—16 many signs and conversions; v. 17—21 imprisonment and deliverance of the apostles; v. 22—32 their appearance before the sanhedrim; v. 33—42 delivered by the counsel of Gamaliel.

1. ANANIAS,] i.e. 'grace of Jah.'

SAPPHIRA,] i.e. 'fair, beautiful.'

2. KEPT BACK,] *lit.* 'set apart for themselves from the weight (of money), his wife also having fully known..and put (it).'

3. HATH,] *lit.* 'did the Adversary fill thy heart to lie for thyself to the Holy Spirit, and to set-apart for thyself from the weight? remaining, did it not remain to thee? and passing over (to others), it was in thine own authority; why (is it) that thou didst thyself put this matter in thy heart? thou didst not lie for thyself to men (only), but to God (also),'—whose servants the apostles were. By 'God' we are not to understand the Holy Spirit only, but the united THREE.

5. FELL DOWN,] *lit.* 'having fallen breathed out (the spirit).'

6. YOUNG,] *lit.* 'younger men (*or* 'new' converts) having stood up, bound him together, and having borne (him) forth, entombed him.'

7. WAS,] *lit.* 'came to pass, (after) about three hours' interval, his wife also, not being conscious of what has happened, came in.'

8. SOLD,] *lit.* 'gave away the space (of ground).'

9. HOW,] *lit.* 'why (is it) that it was sounded-together to you to try the Spirit of the Lord..who entombed.'

10. FELL,] *lit.* 'fell she along with the word, near his feet, and breathed out (the spirit).'

11. CHURCH,] *lit.* 'assembly, and upon all who heard these things.'

12. BY,] *lit.* 'through..came many signs and terrible things among..one mind in Solomon's Porch,' which, being open to all comers, was a convenient place of meeting for such a large assembly as the apostles could now convene.

13. DURST,] *lit.* 'was no one daring to be joined..were magnifying them.'

14. ADDED,] *or* 'and the more were believers adding themselves (*lit.* putting themselves forward) to the Lord, a multitude both of men and women.' Verse 14 only should be read parenthetically.

15. INSOMUCH,] *lit.* 'so as to bear forth the infirm into all the broad-places, and to put (them) upon couches and mattresses, that, at the coming of Peter, even (his) shadow might over-shadow some one of them.'

16. THERE CAME,] *lit.* 'and there were coming-together also the multitude of the surrounding cities to Jerusalem, bearing (the) infirm, and those crowded by (*lit.* under) unclean spirits, who were all healed.'

17. ROSE,] *lit.* 'stood up, and all those with him, being the sect (*Gr.* heresy, i.e. an opinion 'lifted up,' whether right or wrong) of the Sadducees, and were full of zeal.'

18. THE,] *lit.* 'a common watch-house.'

19. THE,] *lit.* 'a messenger..through the night opened up the doors of the guard-house.'

20. GO,] *lit.* 'pass on..saying of this life,' i.e. of Christianity.

21. EARLY,] *lit.* 'under the dawn, and were teaching..came along..sanhedrim.. senate (*lit.* very aged ones) of the sons of Israel, and sent away to the prison.'

22. OFFICERS,] *lit.* 'under-servants came along..the guard-house, they turned round again, and told fully.'

23. SAYING] that,..closed in all un-thrown-down-ness, and the guard.. we opened up ..no one.'

24. HIGH-PRIEST,] *lit.* 'the priest, and the leader of the force of.. these words, they were doubting (*lit.* 'passing on differently' in judgment) concerning them, to what this would come.'

25. CAME,] *lit.* 'came along a certain one and told them fully, saying, that, behold.. the guard-house.'

26. WENT,] *lit.* 'went away the leader of the force with the under-servants, and led them,..were fearing.. that they might not be stoned.'

27. BROUGHT,] *or* 'led..in the sanhedrim, ..enquired at them.'

28. STRAITLY,] *lit.* 'telling did we not tell you thoroughly not to teach upon this name ..your teaching, and counsel to bring over upon us.'

29. WE OUGHT,] *lit.* 'it behoveth (us) to be persuaded by God more than by men.'

30. SLEW,] *lit.* 'handled thoroughly, and suspended upon wood.'

31. HATH,] *lit.* 'did.. a foremost-leader and saviour..another mind..a letting go of sins.'

32. THINGS,] *lit.* 'sayings..God gave to those being persuaded by him.'

33. CUT,] *lit.* 'cut through,..were taking counsel to take them away (*or* lift them up).'

34. ONE,] *lit.* 'a certain one in the Sanhedrim.'

GAMALIEL,] i.e. 'weaned of God;' said to be Hillel's grandson.

DOCTOR,] *lit.* 'a law-teacher, honoured by all the people, and he commanded the apostles to make some little space without.'

35. MEN OF,] *lit.* 'men, Israelites, hold off from yourselves, about these men, what ye are about to do.'

36. ROSE,] *or* 'stood up Theudas;' there were probably two rebels of the name.

BOASTING,] *lit.* 'saying him to be some one ..as if (it were) four hundred, were joined together, who was taken away (*or* lifted up), and all, as many as were persuaded by him, were thoroughly loosed, and came to nought.'

37. MAN,] *lit.* 'this one stood up Judas the Galilean, in the days of the enrolling, and caused much people to stand forth after him, that one also was lost, and all, as many as were persuaded by him were thoroughly scattered.'

38. REFRAIN,] *lit.* 'stand off from these men, and suffer them,..may be out of men, it will be loosed down.'

39. BE,] *lit.* 'is out of God, ye are not able to loose it down, lest at any time ye may be found fighting-with-God.'

40. AGREED,] *lit.* 'were persuaded..called forward..told them farther not to speak upon the name.'

41. DEPARTED,] *lit.* 'were passing on from the face of the sanhedrim,..were thought full worthy to be dishonoured.'

42. DAILY.] *lit.* 'every day.. were not ceasing, teaching and telling-fully-as-good-news Jesus the Christ.'

Chapter VI. may be divided into two parts; v. 1—6 election of seven almoners; v. 7—15 Stephen, one of them, accused before the sanhedrim.

1. NUMBER,] *lit.* 'when the disciples are multiplying there happened.. Hellenists towards..that their bereaved ones were being overlooked in the every-day deaconship.'

2. CALLED,] *lit.* 'called forward.. not pleasing..leave at all..to act as deacons at tables.'

3. LOOK YE OUT,] *lit.* 'look ye yourselves out thoroughly (as 'overseers or bishops').'

AMONG,] *lit.* 'out of yourselves seven men witnessed to (*or* testified of), full of holy spirit and wisdom, whom we may set down over this necessity,' not 'business,' as in C.V.; from 11. 30 it would appear that the duty here proposed was shortly afterwards transferred to the 'elders.' The 'seven' are never called 'Deacons,' as the word in the N. T. is everywhere indefinitely applied to any and every kind of servant, civil and sacred, public and private, whether man or woman, preacher or magistrate, angel or devil, believer or unbeliever. See my 'Biblical Tracts for Every Day in the Year.'

4. GIVE OURSELVES CONTINUALLY,] *lit.* 'strengthen ourselves towards the pouring forth before (God), and the deaconship of the word.'

5. SAYING,] *lit.* 'word..chose (*or* laid out for themselves) Stephen (i.e. a crown),..and holy spirit, and Philip (i.e. lover of horses), and Prochorus (i.e. forward in the chorus), and Nicanor (i.e. victorious man), and Timon (i.e. honouring), and Permenas (i.e. permanent), and Nicolas (i.e. a victorious people), a proselyte (*lit.* one who 'comes to' any thing) of Antioch.'

6. LAID,] *lit.* 'put (i.e. gave) over to them the hands,' a common eastern form of entreating a blessing on them, conferring miraculous gifts, and shewing their approval, as in 9. 12, 17; 13. 3, &c.

7. COMPANY,] *lit.* 'crowd were obedient (*lit.* hearkening-under) to the faith.'

8. DID,] *lit.* 'was doing..and signs.'

9. AROSE,] *lit.* 'stood up..from Cilicia.. seeking-together (questions) with Stephen.'

10. WERE NOT ABLE,] *or* 'had no strength to stand over-against the wisdom and the spirit with which he was speaking.'

11. SUBORNED,] *lit.* 'cast forth secretly.. that..injurious sayings in reference to Moses and God.'

12. STIRRED UP,] *lit.* 'moved together.. presbyters..stood over (him), and seized him at once, and led him to the sanhedrim.'

13. WHICH SAID,] *lit.* 'saying..speaking injurious sayings.'

14. SAY,] *lit.* 'saying, that this Jesus the Nazarene shall loose-down this place (i.e. the temple), and shall alter the customs which Moses gave over to us.'

15. THAT SAT,] *lit.* 'those sitting in the sanhedrim, straining (their eyes) at him, saw his face as if (it were) the face of a messenger' from God.

Chapter VII. may be divided into six parts; v. 1—7 Stephen's narrative of the calling of Abraham and promised inheritance; v. 8—16 of the covenant of circumcision and the descent into Egypt; v. 17—34 of the sufferings in Egypt and the call of Moses; v. 35—43 of signs in Egypt and the wilderness, with the idolatry of the people; v. 44—53 of the tabernacle, the temple, their continual resistance of the Spirit, and murder of the Son; v. 54—60 the Jews' fury and Stephen's death.

1. HIGH,] *lit.* 'first *or* chief-priest..Have then these things such (a bearing *or* application).'

2. HEARKEN,] *or* 'hear ye, The God of the glory.'

3. COUNTRY,] *lit.* 'land, and out of.. to a land.'

4. DWELT,] *lit.* 'settled down..after the dying of his father (*query* brother?) he gave (him) another house in this land.'

5. INHERITANCE,] *lit.* 'distribution by lot, not even a footstep, and promised (*lit.* told it over again) to him to give it for a possession' (*lit.* a thing to be 'held down.')

6. ON THIS WISE,] *lit.* 'thus, that his seed shall be sojourning in another land, and they shall cause it to serve, and do (it) evil four hundred years,' strictly speakly 430, as in Ex. 12. 40, 41.

7. BE IN BONDAGE,] *lit.* 'serve..after these things..serve (*lit.* tremble greatly to) me.'

8. THE,] *or* 'a covenant,' *lit.* a thorough-set thing.'

9. ENVY,] *lit.* 'zeal, gave away Joseph to.'

10. DELIVERED,] *lit.* 'himself lifted him up out..set him down leader.'

11. DEARTH,] *or* 'failure.. were not finding.'

13. WAS,] *lit.* 'become fully known..became manifest.'

14. SENT,] *lit.* 'sent away Joseph, and called near.'

15. DIED,] *lit.* 'ended (his life).'

16. CARRIED,] *or* 'put over to Sychem, and were put in the tomb which Abraham (*query* Jacob?) bought for himself for a weight of silver from the sons of Emmor of Sychem.'

17. WHEN,] *lit.* 'according as the..was drawing nigh, of which God sware.'

18. AROSE,] *lit.* 'stood up, who had not known Joseph,' i.e. approved of his doings.

19. SUBTILLY,] *lit.* 'very wisely, and used our fathers evily, to make their babes outcasts, with a view to suffer them not to live.'

20. TIME,] *lit.* 'season..fair (*or* polished) to (or by) God.'

21. WHEN,] *lit.* 'and he (being) an outcast, ..and nourished him herself to herself for a son.'

22. LEARNED,] *lit.* 'taught in..powerful in words and in works.'

23. HE WAS,] *lit.* 'there was filled out to him a time of 40 years, it went up upon his heart himself to inspect his brethren the sons of Israel.'

24. ONE,] *lit.* 'a certain one unjustly used, himself helped, and did (*lit.* made) full-justice to the oppressed.'

25. FOR,] *lit.* 'and he was supposing his brethren to send along with it (this) that God through his hand doth give to them safety; but they did not send (this thought) along with (it).'

26. NEXT,] *lit.* 'coming day—they fighting —he appeared to them, and urged them fully to peace, saying, Men, brethren are ye! wherefore use ye one another unjustly?'

27. DID,] *lit.* 'is using..unjustly..who set thee down a chief?'

28. WILT,] *lit.* 'dost thou wish to end me in the manner thou didst end.'

29. AT,] *lit.* 'in this word, and became a sojourner in the land of Midian.'

30. EXPIRED,] *lit.* 'fulfilled..the flame of fire of a bush.'

31. SIGHT,] *or* 'vision,' as in 9. 10, 12; 10. 3, 17, 19, &c.

DREW NEAR,] *lit.* 'went forward to consider it thoroughly, a voice.'

32. TREMBLED,] *lit.* 'became very tremulous, and was not daring to consider (it) thoroughly.'

33. PUT OFF,] *lit.* 'loose the sandal of thy feet..in which thou hast stood.'

34. I HAVE SEEN,] *lit.* 'seeing I saw (i.e. I fully saw) the evil (*or* misery) of.. and I heard.. and came down to lift them up out of (it).. send thee away.'

35. REFUSED,] *lit.* 'they themselves disowned.. set thee down chief and judge? that one God sent forth a chief and deliverer (*lit.* looser away), in (by) the hand of a messenger.'

36. HE,] *lit.* 'this one (i.e. Moses).. done terrible things.'

37. CHILDREN,] *lit.* 'sons.. as (he raised up) me.'

38. WAS,] *lit.* 'came in the assembly.. living words.'

39. WOULD,] *lit.* 'did not wish to become obedient,.. turned round to Egypt.'

40. TO GO,] *lit.* 'who shall pass on before us.. led us forth.. we have not known what has happened to him.'

41. OFFERED,] *lit.* 'led up a.. and were rejoicing (*lit.* having a good mind).'

42. TURNED,] *or* 'turned round, and gave them over to serve (*lit.* tremble much) to the host of the heaven, even as it has been written in the scroll.. did ye bring forward to me.'

43. TABERNACLE,] *lit.* 'settling-place of the Moloch (*lit.* king),.. the figures (*lit.* types) which..to kiss forward to them (the hand), and I-will-make-you-another-house beyond Babylon.'

44. WITNESS,] *lit.* 'of the witness was among our fathers in the wilderness, even as he set thoroughly in order who is speaking to Moses, to make it according to the type.'

45. THAT CAME AFTER,] *lit.* 'having thoroughly received, brought in with Jesus (i.e. Joshua, as in Heb. 4. 8), in the possession (*lit.* thing held down) of the nations..from the face.'

46. DESIRED,] *lit.* 'asked for himself to find a-place-of-settling-down to the.'

48. TEMPLES,] *lit.* 'habitations.'

49. HEAVEN,] *lit.* 'the heaven..the earth ..or which is a place of any thorough-resting.'

50. HATH,] *lit.* 'did..make all these?'

51. ASSIST,] *lit.* 'fall against.'

52. HAVE,] *lit.* 'did..pursue? and they killed fully those who told-thoroughly-beforehand concerning the.. of whom ye givers-up and murderers have become.'

53. HAVE,] *lit.* 'who received the Law with a view to (*or* for, as) thorough-arrangements of messengers, and did not guard (it).'

54. CUT,] *lit.* 'cut through to their heart, and were gnashing the teeth against him.,

55. THE,] *lit.* 'of holy spirit, straining (his eyes) to the heaven.'

56. OPENED,] *lit.* 'opened up.'

57. LOUD,] *lit.* 'great voice, and held-together..with one mind.'

58. CAST,] *lit.* 'cast (him) forth outside of the city, and were casting stones, and the witnesses put away for themselves their.. called Saul.'

59. STONED,] *lit.* 'were stoning..calling upon and saying, Lord Jesus (*or* Lord of Jesus), receive for thyself my spirit.'

60. KNEELED,] *lit.* 'and having set the knees he cried with a great voice, Lord, mayest thou not set to them this sin! and having said this he was laid down.'

Chapter VIII. may be divided into four parts; v. 1—4 burial of Stephen, havoc of Saul, increase of the Word; v. 5—13 Philip in Samaria, and Simon; v. 14—25 Peter and John visit Samaria and Simon's offer; v. 26 —40 Philip and an Ethiopian Eunuch.

1. CONSENTING,] *lit.* 'thinking well with (them) of his lifting up, and there happened in (*or* during) that day a great pursuit upon the assembly that (is) in Jerusalem, and all (i.e. very many) were thoroughly dispersed, down the regions.'

2. DEVOUT,] *lit.* 'and men well-received (by God and men) laid Stephen together, and made for themselves a great beating (of the breast) over him.'

3. AS FOR,] *lit.* 'but Saul was ravaging the assembly, passing on into the several houses, dragging both men and women he was giving them over into guard.'

4. SCATTERED,] *or* 'thoroughly dispersed, went throughout (*or* differently) telling-as-good-news the word.'

5. THE,] *lit.* 'to a city..was proclaiming to them the Christ.'

6. PEOPLE,] *lit.* 'crowds with one mind held forward to the things said by Philip, in their hearing and beholding the signs that he was doing.'

7. FOR,] *lit.* 'for out of many of those having unclean spirits, crying (*lit.* lowing) with a great voice, they were coming forth, and many paralytic and lame were cherished,' *or* attended.

8. WAS,] *lit.* 'there came *or* happened.'

9. CALLED,] *lit.* 'Simon by name, who was before-hand (*or* openly) in the city a Magian, and startling (*lit.* causing to stand out) the nation of Samaria, saying himself to be a certain great one.'

10. GAVE HEED,] *lit.* 'were holding forward, from little to great, saying, This one.'

11. HAD REGARD,] *lit.* 'were holding forward, because of his having for a long time with the Magian arts startled them.'

12. PREACHING,] *lit.* 'telling fully as good news the things about the..were being baptized.'

13. CONTINUED,] *lit.* 'he was strengthening (himself) towards Philip, and was himself startled, beholding both great signs and powers happening.'

14. AT,] *lit.* 'in Jerusalem..has received ..sent away towards them Peter and John.

15. PRAYED,] *lit.* 'themselves poured forth before (God) concerning them, that they might receive holy spirit.'

16. HE,] *lit.* 'it was having fallen..but only they were having been baptized with a view (*or* regard, relation) to the name (i.e. character) of the Lord Jesus.'

17. LAID,] *lit.* 'they were putting.. received holy spirit.'

18. LAYING,] *or* 'putting on..is given, he brought forward to them things.'

19. POWER,] *lit.* 'authority (*or* privilege) ..I may put the hands, he may receive holy spirit.'

20. MONEY,] *lit.* 'silver with thee—may it be to destruction (*or* full-loss), because the gift of God thou didst suppose to possess through (such) things.'

21. MATTER,] *lit.* 'word.. straight before God.'

22. REPENT,] *lit.* 'have another mind, therefore, because of this thy evil, and supplicate God,..upper-mind of thy heart may be let go to thee.'

23. IN,] *lit.* 'for a gall of bitterness (i.e. bitter gall) and a full-bond of unrighteousness (to the church).'

24. PRAY,] *lit.* 'supplicate ye—ye—to.. may come.'

25. TESTIFIED,] *lit.* 'thoroughly testified and spoken..turned round away to Jerusalem, and told-the-good-news-fully in.'

26. THE,] *lit.* 'a messenger of..Stand up, and be passing on, through the middle of the day, upon the road that is going down.'

27. AROSE,] *lit.* 'stood up and passed on, and lo, a man, an Ethiopian, a eunuch of power, of Candace, the queen of the Ethiopians, who was over all her treasure, who had himself come to Jerusalem, kissing forward (the hand to God).'

28. RETURNING,] *lit.* 'was turning round again, and is sitting upon his chariot (*lit.* anything filled-up), and was reading (*lit.* knowing again) the prophet Isaiah.'

29. GO NEAR,] *lit.* 'go forward and be joined (*lit.* glued) to.'

30. THITHER,] *lit.* 'forward..knowest thou then.'

31. MAN,] *lit.* 'some one may lead me on the way?..called Philip near to come up.'

32. PLACE,] *or* 'passage of the Writing that he was reading was this: As a sheep to slaughter he was led, and as a lamb before his shearer dumb, so he opens not his mouth.' See Isa. 53. 7, 8.

33. TAKEN AWAY,] *or* 'lifted up, and (the men of) his generation who shall describe thoroughly? because his life is lifted up from the earth.'

34. PRAY,] *lit.* 'beseech of thee, concerning whom..concerning himself, or concerning some other one?'

35. AT,] *lit.* 'from that Writing, and toldfully to him as good news—Jesus.'

36. WENT,] *lit.* 'were passing on down the way they came upon a certain water,' probably a little spring by the way side.

37. This verse is wanting in the oldest MSS., Versions, and Fathers, hence it is cancelled by Mill, Wetstein, Matthaei, Griesbach, Bloomfield, Tischendorff, &c.

38. INTO,] *lit.* 'to the water.'

39. OUT OF,] i.e. 'from,' as very often.

THE,] *or* 'a spirit of the Lord seized Philip, and the eunuch..for he was passing on.'

40. AT,] *or* 'towards Azotus (the ancient Ashdod), and coming through (it) he was telling-fully all the cities the good-news,' till his coming to Caesarea, between Dora and Joppa.

Chapter IX. may be divided into four parts; v. 1—9 Saul struck blind near Damascus; v. 10—16 Ananias sent to him; v. 17—22 who heals and baptizes him, when he begins to preach; v. 23—31 he escapes from the Jews to Jerusalem and Tarsus, while the assemblies have rest.

1. AND SAUL,] after the events noticed in 8. 3, with which this chapter is connected.

BREATHING OUT,] *lit.* 'breathing earnestly of lifting of and of murder in reference to the disciples of the Lord, went forward to the foremost-priest.'

2. DESIRED,] *lit.* 'asked for himself from him epistles..he might find any being of the Way (revealed by Jesus), both men and women, he might lead them.'

3. AS,] *lit.* 'and in the passing on he happened to be nigh to Damascus, and unexpectedly..from the heaven.'

4. TO,] *lit.* 'upon the earth..pursuest.'

5. PERSECUTEST,] *lit.* 'pursuest.' The last clause of this verse and the next verse up to the word 'Arise,' is cancelled by the best critics, as wanting in the best MSS., Versions, and Fathers, and copied from 22. 10; 26. 14.

6. ARISE,] *lit.* 'but stand up..it behoveth thee to do.'

7. JOURNEYED,] *lit.* 'are going on the way had stood (i.e. remained) breathless, hearing indeed the voice, but seeing no one.'

8. AROSE,] *lit.* 'was raised..he was beholding no one..led (him).'

9. WITHOUT SIGHT,] *lit.* 'not beholding.'

10. AT,] *lit.* 'in Damascus.'

11. ARISE,] *lit.* 'having stood up be passing on upon the street (*or* alley), and seek in the house of Judas, a Tarsian, Saul by name, for lo, he poureth forth before (God).'

12. HATH,] *lit.* 'and saw in vision.. putting a hand upon him, that he might behold again *or* look up.'

13. HAVE,] *lit.* 'I myself have heard from many concerning this man, how many evils he did to thy holy ones in Jerusalem.'

14. CHIEF,] *or* 'foremost priests.. those calling.'

15. GO THY WAY,] *lit.* 'be passing on, because a vessel (*or* instrument) of choice is he to me, to bear (*or* carry) my name before nations..sons of Israel.

16. I WILL,] *lit.* 'I—I will show him secretly how many things it behoveth him to suffer.'

17. WENT HIS WAY,] *lit.* 'went away.. Saul! brother!.. thou wast coming, has sent me forth,.. behold again (*or* look up),

and mightest be full of holy spirit.'

18. IMMEDIATELY,] *lit.* 'straightway there fell away.. as if (it were) scales, and beheld again along with the word, and having stood up he was baptized.'

19. MEAT,] *or* 'nourishment he was much strengthened,.. some days.'

20. PREACHED,] *lit.* 'was proclaiming (Jesus *or*) the Christ, that (*or* because) he is the Son of the (true) God.'

21. AMAZED,] *lit.* 'startled.. laid waste in Jerusalem those calling upon.. and had come.. lead them bound before.'

22. INCREASED,] *lit.* 'was the more fully strengthened, and was confusing the.. bringing up together (*or* fully) that this is the Christ.'

23. TOOK COUNSEL,] *lit.* 'consulted together to (lift him up *or*) take him off.'

24. LAYING-WAIT,] *lit.* 'their counsel against him was known to Saul; they (i.e. men) were also watching along-side of the gates both day and night that they might take him off.'

25. LET,] *lit.* 'sent (him) down through (a window in) the wall in a corn-basket.'

26. COME,] *lit.* 'come along (from his second visit to Arabia three years afterwards) .. tried to be joined (*lit.* glued) to the disciples, and they were all fearing him, not believing that he is a disciple.'

27. TOOK,] *lit.* 'took it upon (him) and led him to the apostles (Peter and James).. declared thoroughly how he saw.. he spake ..he himself was speaking all (things) in Damascus.'

28. COMING,] *lit.* 'passing in and passing out in Jerusalem,' for fifteen days, Gal. 1. 18.

29. BOLDLY,] *or* 'all things.. he was both speaking and seeking together to the Hellenists, but they were openly taking in hand to take him off.'

30. KNEW,] *or* 'knew fully, they led him down.. sent him away forth.'

31. THEN,] *or* 'therefore had the assemblies, (*or* 'assembly' as in best MSS. and Versions) peace..were built up (not merely *edified*) and passing on in.. the exhortation (*lit.* calling-along-side) of the Holy Spirit.'

32. PASSED,] *lit.* 'came thoroughly through all (quarters), he came-down also.'

33. ENEAS,] i.e. 'praise-worthy.'

HAD KEPT,] *lit.* 'is lying-down upon a couch eight years, who was paralyzed.'

34. CHRIST,] *lit.* 'Jesus the Christ, himself healeth thee; stand up and spread (it) thyself; and straightway he stood up.'

35. SARON,] *or* 'Sharon,' between Joppa and Cesarea.

TURNED,] *lit.* 'turned round upon the Lord,'—for help and protection.

36. DISCIPLE,] *lit.* 'female-disciple.'

TABITHA,] i.e. a 'hind or gazelle.'

ALMS-DEEDS,] *lit.* 'kind acts which she was doing.'

37. SICK,] *lit.* 'infirm and died away (*or* fully),..bathed, they put her.'

38. WAS THERE,] *lit.* 'is in it, they sent away to him two men, calling (him) near, not to delay to come through unto them,'—to restore her to life.

39. AROSE,] *lit.* 'stood up..come near they led him up to..the bereaved ones stood near him..showing openly coats..as many as Dorcas was making.'

40. ALL FORTH,] *lit.* 'all out without, and set (his) knees, and poured forth before (God) for himself, and turned round upon .. stand up, and she opened up.'

41. LIFT,] *lit.* 'set her up.. the bereaved ones, he set her along-side (of them) alive.'

42. WAS,] *lit.* 'became.. believed upon.'

Chapter X. may be divided into six parts; v. 1—8 a messenger appears to Cornelius; v. 9—16 Peter's vision; v. 17—22 he receives Cornelius' messengers; v. 23—33 and Cornelius' explanations; v. 34—43 proclaims Jesus to him and his friends; v. 44—48 who are baptized with the Holy Spirit and water.

1. THE BAND,] *or* 'a cohort, called Italian.'

2. DEVOUT,] *or* 'pious, and fearing.'

GAVE,] *lit.* 'who is doing many kind acts to the people, and is beseeching God through every (season of prayer).'

3. EVIDENTLY,] *or* 'manifestly, as if (it were).'

4. LOOKED,] *lit.* 'strained (his eyes) at him, he became..Lord (*or* Sir)?..Thy pourings forth before (God), and thy kind acts came up.'

5. CALL,] *lit.* 'send after Simon, who is surnamed (*or* called also) Peter.'

6. LODGES,] *lit.* 'this one is lodged along-side of a certain one.. along-side of the sea.'

The next clause is wanting in the oldest MSS., Versions, and Fathers, and is taken from 9. 6; 11. 14; 22. 10.

7. ANGEL,] *lit.* 'messenger who is speaking..his domestics.. strengthening themselves towards him.'

8. WHEN,] *lit.* 'and having himself brought forth all (these) things to them, he sent them away.'

9. THEY,] *lit.* 'these are passing on the way..house-top (*or* building) to pour forth before (God) for himself.'

10. WOULD,] *lit.* 'wished to taste (something, as in 20. 11), and these making ready at the same time, there fell over upon him an ecstasy,'—as in 11. 5; 22. 17, &c.

11. SAW,] *lit.* 'views the heaven opened up,..as a great linen sheet bound.. upon the earth.'

12. MANNER,] *lit.* 'all the four-footed beasts of the earth, and the wild beasts, and the creeping-things, and the flying-things of the heaven.'

13. RISE,] *lit.* 'having stood up, Peter, sacrifice (as in Mat. 22. 4) and eat.'

14. NOT SO,] *or* 'by no means, Lord, because at no time did I eat anything common or unclean,'—by the law of Moses.

15. THE,] *lit.* 'a second time, What God cleansed (i.e. declared clean) make not thou common,' i.e. reckon it not so.

16. WAS DONE,] *or* 'happened.. to the heaven.'

17. DOUBTED,] *lit.* 'was passing over (the matter) thoroughly within himself what the

vision which he saw might be, ..sent away from, ..asked thoroughly for.'

18. ASKED,] *lit.* 'were enquiring if Simon who is also called Peter is lodged hither.'

19. THOUGHT,] *or* 'thought-fully about.'

20. ARISE,] *lit.* 'but having stood up, go down, and be passing on with them, judging nothing differently, because I have sent them forth.'

21. WHICH WERE SENT UNTO HIM FROM CORNELIUS.] These words are wanting in the best MSS., Versions, and Fathers.

COME,] *or* 'present.'

22. THE,] *lit.* 'a centurion, a just man and fearing God, testified to by all the nation of the Jews, was divinely warned by a holy angel, to send after thee to his house, and to hear sayings from thee.'

23. AWAY,] *lit.* 'went forth with them, and certain of the..went with him,'—six in number, see 11. 12.

24. AFTER,] *lit.* 'and on the morrow they ..was expecting them, and called together his kindred and intimate (*lit.* necessary) friends.'

25. AT,] *lit.* 'upon *or* over his feet, and kissed forward (the hand).'

26. TOOK HIM UP,] *lit.* 'raised him;' this the pretended successors of Peter have rarely done. Comp. 2 Thes. 2. 4.

27. AS HE TALKED,] *lit.* 'close-together with him he went in, and finds many come together.'

28. KNOW,] *lit.* 'ye—ye know well, how mis-placed it is for a man, a Jew, to be joined, or to come-towards one of another tribe, but God shewed me to call no man.'

29. AS SOON AS,] *lit.* 'having been sent after, I enquire, therefore, for what word ye sent after me?'

30. PRAYED,] *lit.* 'pouring forth before (God)..white clothing.'

31. IS HEARD,] *lit.* 'was hearkened to, and thy kind acts were remembered.'

32. CALL HITHER,] *lit.* 'call after Simon, who is also called Peter, ..cometh near.'

33. IMMEDIATELY,] *lit.* 'from that (hour) ..thou didst well that thou hast come near ..have been set forth to thee by God.'

34. OF,] *lit.* 'upon a truth I receive (it) fully, that God is not a receiver of faces,' *or* appearances, i.e. persons.

35. FEARETH,] *lit.* 'is fearing..working.. is receivable by him.'

36. SENT,] *lit.* 'sent forth to the sons..telling-again-as-good-news peace through Jesus Christ.'

37. THAT,] *lit.* 'the saying ye have known, which came through.'

38. OF,] *lit.* 'who is from Nazareth, with holy spirit and power, who went throughout (the land) doing good, ..all those pressed down by the Devil.'

39. LAND,] *or* 'space, region..they lifted up, hanging upon wood.'

40. HIM,] *lit.* 'this one..gave him to become fully-manifest.'

41. CHOSEN BEFORE,] *lit.* 'having the hand extended forward (*or* publicly) by the (true) God, ..his standing up out of the dead.'

42. COMMANDED,] *lit.* 'told us again also to proclaim to the people, and to testify thoroughly, that this is he who is having been marked out by God judge of living and dead.'

43. WHOSOEVER,] *lit.* 'every one who is remaining-stedfast to him (is) to receive a letting-go of sins.'

44. SPAKE,] *lit.* 'is speaking these sayings, the Holy Spirit fell also upon those hearing the word.'

45. ASTONISHED,] *or* 'startled,' *lit.* stood out.

GENTILES,] *lit.* 'nations, also has been poured out.'

46. HEARD,] *lit.* 'were hearing them speaking with tongues, and magnifying God.'

47. CAN,] *lit.* 'the water (of baptism) is any one able to forbid (being brought hither)..who received the Holy Spirit.'

48. COMMANDED,] *lit.* 'set them forward to be baptized..asked they him to remain over certain days.'

Chapter XI. may be divided into three parts; v. 1—18 Peter vindicates the baptism of Cornelius; v. 19—26 spread of the Gospel among Jews and Hellenes, Barnabas' mission, and his work with Saul in Antioch; v. 27—29 prophesy of a dearth, and charity of the disciples.

1. WERE,] *lit.* 'are throughout Judea..the nations also received.'

2. CONTENDED,] *lit.* 'were judging diversely with him.'

3. SAYING,] that, To men having a foreskin thou wentest in.'

4. REHEARSED,] *lit.* 'having begun, was setting (it) forth for himself to them in full-succession, saying.'

5. PRAYING,] *lit.* 'pouring forth before (God).'

TRANCE,] *or* 'ecstasy;' as in 10. 9, &c.

DESCEND,] *lit.* 'coming down, as a great linen sheet, with four corners, sent down out of the heaven, and it came unto me.'

6. UPON,] *lit.* 'in regard to which having strained (my eyes) I was thinking much.. the wild..the creeping..the flying things of the heaven.'

7. ARISE,] *lit.* 'having stood up, Peter, sacrifice and eat.'

8. HATH,] *lit.* 'did..enter.'

9. AGAIN,] *lit.* 'a second time out of the heaven..did cleanse (*or* declare clean) be not thou making (*or* declaring, regarding as) common.'

10. WAS DONE,] *or* 'happened thrice over.'

11. IMMEDIATELY,] *lit.* 'from that (hour) ..men stood openly before the house wherein I was, sent away from Caesarea to me.'

12. BADE,] *lit.* 'said to me to go with them, judging nothing diversely..went with me.'

13. SHEWED,] *lit.* 'told us thoroughly how he saw the messenger in his house standing and saying to him, Send away..send after Simon, who is also called Peter.'

14. TELL,] *lit.* 'spake to thee sayings, in (*or* by) which thou mayest be saved, thou and all thy house.'

15. FELL,] *lit.* 'fell over *or* also upon them, even as also upon us in the beginning.'

16. WORD,] *or* 'saying..with (in, by) holy spirit.'

17. FORASMUCH,] *lit.* 'if then God..and I, how was I able to hinder God?'

18. HELD THEIR PEACE,] *lit.* 'were silent ..did..nations give the new-mind with a view to (their obtaining) life; see 13. 48, &c.

19. SCATTERED ABROAD,] *lit.* 'thoroughly dispersed from the tribulation that happened about Stephen, went through unto Phenice.. speaking the word to none except Jews only.'

20. SOME,] *lit.* 'certain..who coming to Antioch, were speaking to the Hellenists (or Hellenes), telling-again-as-good-news the Lord Jesus.'

21. TURNED,] *lit.* 'turned round over on the Lord.'

22. THEN,] *lit.* 'and the word about them was heard (i.e. reported, the *passive* being used for the *active*, as often elsewhere) in the ears of the assembly that is in Jerusalem,..to go through unto Antioch.'

23. CAME,] *lit.* 'came near and saw..was calling upon all, with the purpose (*lit.* setting forth) of the heart to remain beside the Lord.'

24. OF THE,] *lit.* 'of holy spirit and stedfastness, and a great crowd was set towards the Lord,' that they might be saved.

25. DEPARTED,] *lit.* 'went forth.. to seek Saul again;' see 9. 30.

26. ASSEMBLED THEMSELVES,] *lit.* 'were brought together in (*or* with) the assembly, and taught a great crowd.'

CALLED,] *lit.* 'divinely-called;' the original verb occurs also in Mat. 2. 12, 22; Luke 2. 26; Acts 10. 22; 11. 26; Rom. 7. 3; Heb. 8. 5; 11. 7; 12. 25; see also Rom. 11. 4; 1 Pet. 4. 16; Acts 26. 28.

27. CAME,] *lit.* 'came down.'

28. AGABUS,] i.e. 'beloved.'

BY,] *lit.* 'through the Spirit (that) a great famine (*lit.* failure) to be about to be over all the inhabited land (of Palestine), which also happened about (the time of) Claudius Caesar,' A.D. 47; see Josephus' Antiquities, xx. 2. 6.

29. EVERY MAN,] *lit.* 'according as any one was prospering (*lit.* passing on well), marked out, each of them, (so much) for deaconship to send to the brethren dwelling in Judea.'

30. SENT,] *lit.* 'sent it away to the presbyters through the hands of Barnabas and Saul.' The general community of goods, as well as the 'seven' men chosen to administer it, having ere this passed away, it was sent to the presbyters, the colleagues of the apostles, as in 15. 2, &c.

Chapter XII. may be divided into four parts; v. 1—4 Herod slays James and imprisons Peter; v. 5—17 the assembly praying Peter is delivered: v. 18—23 Herod punishes the guards, and is himself eaten by worms; v. 24, 25 increase of the word and safe return of Saul and Barnabas.

1. ABOUT,] *lit.* 'through that season' of famine.

HEROD THE KING,] so called only by courtesy; he was grandson of Herod the Great.

STRETCHED FORTH,] *lit.* 'cast (his) hands upon certain of those of the assembly, to do evil (to them).'

2. KILLED,] *lit.* 'lifted up *or* took away;' fulfilling Mat. 20. 23. Bloomfield suggests that he 'beheaded' him.

3. IT PLEASED,] *lit.* 'it is pleasing..he set himself besides to take at once also Peter.'

BREAD,] *or* 'unleavened food,' as in De. 16. 3.

4. AND,] *lit.* 'whom also having seized, he put in guard, having given him over to four quaternions of soldiers to guard him, counselling after the passover to bring him up (*or* again) to the people.'

5. IN,] *lit.* 'in the guard-house, but pouring forth before (God) was being strenuously made by the assembly to God for him.'

6. WOULD,] *lit.* 'was about to bring him forth, that night..and guards before the door were keeping the guard-house.'

7. THE,] *lit.* 'an angel of the Lord stood over (him), and a light shone in the buildings..Stand up in haste.'

8. FOLLOW,] *lit.* 'be following me.'

9. FOLLOWED,] *lit.* 'was following him, and had not known that it is true which is done through the messenger, but was thinking to see a vision.'

10. WHEN,] *lit.* 'and having gone through a first guard and a second,..that is carrying (one on) to the city, which opened up to them of its own accord, and having gone forth, they went forward one street (*or* alley), and straightway the messenger stood off from him.'

11. I KNOW,] *lit.* 'I have known truly, that the Lord sent forth his messenger, and himself lifted me out of the hand of Herod.'

12. AND WHEN,] *lit.* 'and having-known (it) fully he came upon the house of Mary ..crowded together and pouring forth before (God).'

13. CAME,] *lit.* 'come near to hearken secretly.'

RHODA,] i.e. a 'rose-bud.'

14. KNEW,] *lit.* 'known fully..from the gladness.. told fully of the standing of Peter.'

15. CONSTANTLY,] *or* 'was strongly affirming it to be so..his messenger,' i.e. his guardian angel, or rather his disembodied spirit, which had became an angel, i.e. was now employed by God to execute his will, as angel is not the name of nature, but of office.

16. CONTINUED,] *lit.* 'remained still..were startled.'

17. BECKONING,] *lit.* 'shaking the hand a little to them they were silent, and he himself brought out thoroughly to them how the Lord brought him out from the guard-house..Tell ye fully.. passed on to.'

18. AS SOON AS,] *lit.* 'day having come.'

19. EXAMINED,] *lit.* 'again judged the guard,..to be led away' to punishment.

perhaps scourging or imprisonment, not necessarily to death, as in C.V.

ABODE,] *lit.* 'rubbed *or* wore away (the time).'

20. HIGHLY DISPLEASED,] *lit.* 'had a mind to war with the Tyrians and Sidonians, but with one mind they were coming near towards him, and having persuaded Blastus, who is over the bed-chamber of the king, they were asking peace.'

21. ARRAYED,] *lit.* 'having arrayed himself in a kingly robe, and having sat down upon the tribunal, was publicly addressing the populace.'

22. PEOPLE,] *or* 'populace were shouting out, God's voice and not man's!'

23. IMMEDIATELY,] *lit.* 'along with the word a messenger..and having himself become eaten of worms, he breathed out (the soul), *or* became very cold.'

25. RETURNED,] *lit.* 'turned round shortly out of Jerusalem, having filled out the deaconship, taking also along with them John, who is also called Mark.'

Chapter XIII. may be divided into three parts; v. 1—12 call of Barnabas and Saul, with punishment of Elymas; v. 13—41 Paul's address at Antioch of Pisidia; v. 42—52 opposition of the Jews and reception of the Gentiles.

1. IN,] *or* 'throughout the assembly that is in Antioch..Niger (i.e. black)..and Manaen (i.e. comforter) Herod the tetrarch's foster-brother, and Saul (i.e. asked).'

2. MINISTERED,] *lit.* 'did public work to the Lord..the Holy Spirit said, 'Mark ye out thoroughly to me both Barnabas and Saul with a view to the work to which I myself have called them (for myself).'

3. SENT AWAY,] *lit.* 'loosed (them) fully,' from their other engagements.

4. DEPARTED,] *lit.* 'went down to Seleucia, .sailed away to Cyprus.

5. WHEN,] *lit.* 'having been in Salamis, they told again fully the word..John (as) an under-servant.'

6. SORCERER,] *lit.* 'magian.'

BAR-JESUS,] i.e. 'Son of Jesus.'

7. DEPUTY,] *or* 'proconsul Sergius Paulus, a man prudent,' *lit.* one 'sending or bringing things together.'

CALLED FOR,] *or* 'called near..sought also to hear.'

8. ELYMAS,] i.e. 'magian..being interpreted, was setting him over-against them seeking to turn thoroughly round the proconsul from the faith.'

9. WHO ALSO,] *lit.* 'even Paul, full of holy spirit, and having strained (his eyes) at him.'

10. SUBTILTY,] *or* 'guile and of all light-work (i.e. sleight of hand), son of a devil,' *lit.* 'thruster through,' one who insidiously attacks any one; as 'a son of God' is a godly man, so 'a son of a devil' is an ungodly one.

CEASE,] *lit.* 'cease for thyself, turning thoroughly round the straightforward ways of the Lord'

11 IMMEDIATELY,] *lit.* 'along with word there fell over upon him.. and going about, he was seeking those leading by the hand.'

12. DEPUTY,] *or* 'proconsul, having seen what has happened, believed, being exceedingly struck about the teaching of the Lord.'

13. NOW WHEN,] *lit.* 'and those around Paul being led up from Paphos, they came to Perga of Pamphylia, but John having parted entirely from them, turned round secretly (*or* shortly) to Jerusalem.' See 15. 38.

14. DEPARTED,] *lit.* 'went through from Perga, they came near to Antioch of Pisidia ..sat down,'—probably in the seat of the elders.

15. RULERS,] *lit.* 'foremost ones of the synagogue sent away to them, saying, Men, brethren, if there is among you a word of exhortation,' *lit.* 'calling near.' If the Synagogue be the model for the Church, why is *this* custom neglected?

16. BECKONING,] *lit.* 'waving down (the people) with the hand, said, Men, Israelites! and those fearing God, hearken!'

17. CHOSE OUT,] *lit.* 'laid out our fathers for himself,..in the sojourning in the land ..led them forth out of it.'

18. SUFFERED,] *or* 'bare he them with nourishment in the wilderness.'

19. HAD DESTROYED,] *lit.* 'lifted down (*or* lifted away thoroughly), he distributed thoroughly by lot their land to them.'

20. THAT,] *lit.* 'these things.. about 450 years,'—according to the Septuagint and Josephus.

21. AFTERWARD,] *lit.* 'and from that (time) they asked for themselves a king.. Saul, son of Kish, a man out of the tribe of Benjamin, forty years.'

22. HAD REMOVED,] *lit.* 'set him aside (*or* beyond), he raised to them David for king, to whom also testifying he said, I found..man according to my heart, who shall do all my wish.'

23. MAN'S,] *lit.* 'this one's seed did God ..raise.'

24. WHEN,] *lit.* 'John having proclaimed publicly before the presence of his entrance a baptism of a new mind.'

25. FULFILLED,] *lit.* 'was fulfilling the race (set before him) he said, Whom do ye secretly think me to be?'

26. AND,] *lit.* 'Men, brethren, sons of the race of..was the word.. sent forth.'

27. AT,] *lit.* 'in Jerusalem, and their foremost ones, not knowing this One, and the voices of the prophets which are being read through every sabbath they fulfilled, having judged (him).'

28. DESIRED,] *lit.* 'they asked Pilate for themselves his being lifted up.'

29. HAD FULFILLED,] *lit.* 'they ended all the things written about him, they lifted him down from the wood, and put (him) into a tomb.'

30. FROM,] *lit.* 'out of the dead.'

31. MANY,] *lit.* 'over many days.

32. DECLARE,] *lit.* 'and we—we tell you good news—the full-message made to the

33. GOD,] *lit.* 'that this has God filled thoroughly out to us their children, having set up Jesus, as also in the second (*or* first) Psalm it has been written, My Son thou art, I to-day have begotten thee,' i.e. brought thee forth as My Anointed King.

34. AS,] *lit.* 'and that he set him up out of (the) dead, no more about to turn over shortly to thorough corruption, as he said, that, I will give to you the stedfast kindnesses (promised to) David.'

35. PSALM,] *or* 'place, Thou wilt not give thy kind one to see thorough corruption.'

36. SERVED,] as an 'under-servant.'

WILL,] *lit.* 'counsel of God, lay down to sleep, and was put forward unto his fathers, and saw thorough corruption.'

38. AND,] *lit.* 'Men! brethren!..is told fully to you a letting go of sins.'

39. BY HIM,] *lit.* 'and from all things, in which ye were not able in the law of Moses to be declared just, in this one every one who is believing is declared just.'

40. BEWARE,] *lit.* 'see, therefore, it may not come over upon you that has been said in the prophets.'

41. BEHOLD,] *or* 'See, ye despisers (*lit.* 'thinkers down upon'), and.. disappear,.. may not believe, if any one may lead it forth to you.'

42. THE JEWS,] *lit.* 'and (they) having gone forth out of the synagogue of the Jews, the nations were calling upon (them) for these sayings to be spoken to them on the next (*or* intermediate) sabbath.'

43. CONGREGATION,] *lit.* 'synagogue having been let go,..devout proselytes..to remain openly in the grace of God.'

44. NEXT,] *lit.* 'coming sabbath almost all the city was brought together.'

45. MULTITUDE,] *lit.* 'crowds, were filled with zeal,.. speaking against and calling injuriously.'

46. WAXED BOLD,] *lit.* 'spake fully for themselves..but since ye push it away, and judge yourselves not worthy of the age-during life, lo, we are turned,' i.e. we turn ourselves, the *passive* being used for the *reflexive* as also in v. 48.

47. TO BE,] *lit.* 'for a light of nations.'

48. GLORIFIED,] *lit.* 'were glorifying.'

WERE ORDAINED,] *or* 'set themselves in array with a view to eternal life.' The original verb may be regarded either as a *passive* or a *reflexive*, and the meaning is equally Scriptural, for while God is often in the Bible represented as doing *all*, and the sinner as doing *nothing*, (e.g. in the parables of the 'lost sheep' and the 'lost piece of silver,') the sinner is also represented as doing *all* and God as doing *nothing* but receiving him (e.g. in the parable of the 'prodigal son'). The other passages in which the original word occurs are 1 Cor. 16. 15 'they set themselves;' Luke 7. 8 'setting myself under authority;' Rom. 13. 1 'setting themselves in array under God;' Acts 28. 23 'they set him a day;' Acts 22. 10 'which have been arranged for thee to do.' Mat. 28. 16 'which Jesus himself arranged for them.' Acts 15. 2 'they arranged for Paul and Barnabas to go up.' The whole phrase has its exact counterpart in v. 46 'ye judge yourselves unworthy of the age-during life,'—'they set themselves in array with a view to life age-during.'

49. PUBLISHED,] *lit.* 'borne thoroughly through all.'

50. HONOURABLE,] *lit.* 'well-conditioned ..foremost men.. openly raised a pursuit on Paul.'

51. THEY,] *lit.* 'they themselves shook off.'

52. WITH,] *lit.* 'and holy spirit.'

Chapter XIV. may be divided into four parts; v. 1—7 stir in Iconium; v. 8—18 and in Lystra; v. 19—23 persecution and consolidation; v. 24—28 return to Antioch and labours there.

1. GREEK,] *lit.* 'Hellenes.'

2. UNBELIEVING,] *or* 'unstedfast openly raised up and made evil the souls of the nations.'

3. ABODE,] *lit.* 'rubbed they thoroughly (i.e. spent or occupied) speaking fully about the Lord, who is testifying..giving signs.. to happen through their hands.'

4. DIVIDED,] *lit.* 'rent (*or* torn by schism) and some were with..and some were with.'

5. THERE WAS,] *or* 'there happened an excitement both of the nations and of the Jews, with their foremost men, to insult and to stone them.'

6. WARE,] *lit.* 'and having fully-known, they fled down to the cities of Lycaonia, Lystra, and Derbe.'

7. PREACHED,] *lit.* 'were telling the good news.'

8. SAT,] *lit.* 'was sitting..in Lystra, powerless in the feet.. being lame..walked about.'

9. THE SAME,] *lit.* 'this one was hearing Paul speaking, who having strained (his eyes) at him, and seen that he has faith to be saved (from his infirmity).'

10. LOUD,] *lit.* 'great..Stand up on thy feet upright, and he was springing up and walking about.'

11. PEOPLE,] *lit.* 'crowds.. Paul did.. voice, saying in Lycaonistic, The gods having become like men, came down to us.'

12. CALLED,] *lit.* 'were calling.. Jupiter (*or* Zeus)..Mercurius (*or* Hermes), since he was the leader of the discourse.'

13. JUPITER.] *Gr.* 'Zeus.. garlands (*or* crowns).. and wished to sacrifice with the crowds.'

14. RENT,] *lit.* 'rent thoroughly their garments, and leaped in among (*or* out into) the crowd.'

15. SIRS,] *lit.* 'men!.. to you, and tell you good news, to turn round over from these vanities upon the living God, who made the heaven, and the land, and the sea, and all the things in them.'

16. TIMES PAST,] *lit.* 'in the past generations suffered all the nations to pass on in their own ways,' except the Jews.

17. WITHOUT WITNESS,] *lit.* 'unwitnessed, doing good, from heaven giving us rains and fruit-bearing seasons, filling-full of

hearts with nourishment and a good-mind (*or* thought).'

18. WITH,] *lit.* 'and these things saying, scarcely did they cause the crowds to cease from sacrificing to them.'

19. THITHER,] *lit.* 'came upon (them) Jews ..the crowds..were drawing (him) outside of the..him to have died.'

20. HOWBEIT,] *lit.* 'and the disciples having surrounded him, having stood up, he went into the city, and on the morrow he went forth.'

21. WHEN,] *lit.* 'and having told that city good-news, and made many disciples, he turned round a little to.'

22. CONFIRMING,] *or* 'strengthening fully ..calling along-side (of them) to remain in the faith, and that it behoveth us through.. reign of the (true) God.'

23. ORDAINED,] *or* appointed those who had been chosen by the 'extending of the hand'—the primitive mode of voting.

ELDERS,] i.e. 'presbyters (for ruling and teaching) in every (*lit.* down the) assembly, ..they put them near to the Lord, in whom they had believed.,

25. PREACHED,] *lit.* 'spoken.'

26. SAILED,] *lit.* 'sailed away..they were given over to the grace.'

27. COME,] *lit.* 'come along-side (of them) and brought the assembly together, they told again as many things as God did with them, and that he opened up to the nations a door of faith.'

28. ABODE,] *lit.* 'rubbed through (i.e. used, spent, occupied) not a little time.'

Chapter XV. may be divided into five parts; v. 1—5 dispute regarding circumcision and appeal to Jerusalem; v. 6—21 opinions of Peter and James; v. 22—29 decision of the assembly; v. 30—34 its reception in Antioch and the work there; v. 35—41 missionary labours and contention.

1. TAUGHT,] *lit.* 'were teaching the brethren, that, If ye may not be circumcised with the rite of Moses, ye are not able to be saved.'

2. WHEN,] *lit.* 'there having been, therefore, a standing-up and thorough searching not a little by Paul and Barnabas with them, they arranged for..to go up.'

3. BROUGHT,] *lit.* 'being sent forward (*or* openly) by the assembly, they were going through..leading thoroughly forth (in their conversation) the open-turning round of the nations, and were making great joy.'

4. COME,] *lit.* 'come along-side (of them) to..received fully by the assembly, and the apostles, and the presbyters, and they told again as many things as God did with them.'

5. THERE ROSE UP,] *lit.* 'but (that) there stood up suddenly (in Antioch) certain of the believers from the sect (*lit.* heresy) of the Pharisees, saying that it behoveth to circumcise them, and to tell (them) at the same time to keep the law of Moses.'

6. ELDERS,] *lit.* 'and the presbyters were brought together to see about this word (*or* doctrine).'

7. DISPUTING,] *or* 'thorough searching, (*or* searching together), Peter having stood up, said to them, Men! brethren! ye—ye know also that from former days (i.e. thirteen years before) God himself chose among us through my mouth for the nations to hear the word of the good-news, and to believe.'

8. GOD,] *lit.* 'and the heart-knowing God.'

9. PUT NO DIFFERENCE,] *lit.* 'and judged nothing differently between us and them, by the faith having purified,' *or* lifted down.

10. TEMPT,] *or* 'try ye God, to put a yoke over upon.. had strength to bear.'

11. WE SHALL BE SAVED,] *lit.* 'to be saved, in the same manner as also these.'

12. KEPT SILENT,] *or* 'were silent, and were hearkening to..bringing forth as many things as signs and fearful things as God did among the nations through them.'

13. HAD HELD,] *lit.* 'were silent,.. Men! brethren!'

14. HATH,] *lit.* 'Simeon brought out how God at first looked over to receive out of (the) nations a people upon his name.'

15. AGREE,] *lit.* 'sound-together.. has been written,' in Amos 9. 11, 12.

16. THIS,] *lit.* 'after these things will I turn round again, and will build up again the tabernacle', *lit.* place of settling-down.

RUINS,] *lit.* 'things dug down.'

SET IT UP,] *lit.* 'make it straight again.'

17. SEEK,] *lit.* 'seeks out the Lord.. has been called over.. is doing.'

18. BEGINNING,] *lit.* 'from the ages.'

19. SENTENCE,] *lit.* 'wherefore I judge, not to crowd-in (things) upon those who from the nations turn-round over upon God.'

20. WRITE,] *lit.* 'to send over to them to hold off from the pollutions of the idols, even the whoredom, and the strangled thing, and the blood.'

As there is not the slightest indication in the narrative that this prohibition was designed to be either of a local or of a temporary character, the eating of blood and of strangled things can only be forbidden *as parts of the pollutions of the idol worship*, and not otherwise, or it will be impossible to hold the teaching (much less the example) of the Apostles as of perpetual obligation, unless indeed we suppose that the whole Christian church has been chargeable with a systematic violation of apostolic doctrine in this case, which is not likely to be the case.

21. OLD TIME,] *lit.* 'of former generations.. those proclaiming him as heralds.. through every sabbath.'

22. PLEASED,] *lit.* 'then it appeared good to the apostles and the presbyters, with the whole assembly, choice men out of themselves to send to Antioch.. Judas, called also Barsabas, and Silas, leading men.'

23. AND,] *lit.* 'having written through their hands thus: The Apostles, and the Presbyters, and the Brethren, to the brethren of (the) nations throughout Antioch, and Syria, and Cilicia: Rejoice.'

24. FORASMUCH AS,] *lit.* 'since we heard that certain out of us having gone forth troubled you with words, perverting your souls, saying, to be circumcised and to keep

the law, with whom we sent nothing through.'

25. SEEMED,] *or* 'appeared good to us, coming with one mind, choice men to send to you.'

26. HAZARDED,] *lit.* 'given over their souls for.'

27. SENT,] *lit.* 'sent away.. and they by word are telling forth the same things.'

28. HOLY SPIRIT,] speaking in the Scriptures, as quoted by James.

AND TO US,] the whole assembly of apostles, presbyters, and brethren.

GREATER,] *or* 'more weight than these very necessary things.'

29. THAT YE ABSTAIN,] *lit.* 'to hold yourselves off from idol-sacrifices, and blood, and a strangled thing, and whoredom; out of which keeping yourselves thoroughly, ye shall do well. Be strengthened!'

30. SO,] *lit.* 'they, then, indeed, having been loosed away, went to Antioch, and having brought together the multitude, they gave over the epistle,' *lit.* thing sent openly.

31. FOR,] *lit.* 'upon the exhortation.'

32. PROPHETS,] i.e. public preachers.

WITH,] *lit.* 'through much discourse.. and strengthened (them) further.'

33. AFTER,] *lit.* 'and having made (i.e. used the) time, they were loosed away with peace.'

34. PLEASED,] *lit.* 'appeared good to Silas.'

35. CONTINUED,] *lit.* 'rubbed thoroughly ..and telling as good-news the word.'

36. SOME,] *or* 'certain..Having turned round upon (them), we may look over our brethren in every city in which we have told fully the word.'

37. DETERMINED,] *lit.* 'took counsel for himself to take along with (them) John, called Mark.'

38. THOUGHT NOT GOOD,] *lit.* 'was thinking (it) right not to take him along with them, who stood off from them from Pamphylia.'

39. AND,] *lit.* 'there happened, therefore, a paroxysm (*or* over-sharpness), so as to part them from one another; and Barnabas having taken along (with him) **Mark**, to sail off to Cyprus.'

40. CHOSE,] *lit.* 'having also laid out for himself Silas, went forth, having been given over to the grace of God by the brethren.'

41 WENT,] *lit.* 'was going through.. strengthening fully the assemblies.'

Chapter XVI. may be divided into five parts; v. 1—3 Timothy circumcised; v. 4—12 journeys from Lystra to Philippi; v. 13—15 conversion of Lydia; v. 16—24 a spirit of Python cast out, and Paul and Silas imprisoned; v. 25—34 conversion of the jailor; v. 35—40 deliverance from prison.

1. CAME,] *lit.* 'went down to Derbe.'

TIMOTHEUS,] i.e. 'honouring God.'

WHICH WAS,] *lit.* 'a believing Jewess, but of a Greek father.'

2. WHICH,] *lit.* 'who was testified to by.. in Lystra.'

3. WOULD,] *lit.* 'did Paul wish to go.. those places.' This circumcising of Timothy has been much canvassed, as apparently a questionable compliance with Jewish rites, which the apostle himself afterwards refused to do with Titus (Gal. 2. 3), and most emphatically condemns in Gal. 5. 2. 'Behold I Paul say to you, that if ye be circumcised Christ shall profit you nothing.'

4. WENT,] *lit.* 'were passing through the cities, they were giving over to them the dogmas to keep that have been judged by the apostles and the presbyters who are in Jerusalem.'

5. CHURCHES,] *lit.* 'assemblies..and were abounding in number every day.'

6. PREACH,] *lit.* 'speak the word in Asia,' i.e. proconsular Asia, of which Ephesus was the capital. The personality of the Holy Spirit seems here very distinctly indicated.

7. COME TO,] *lit.* 'having come down by Mysia, they were trying to pass on down by Bithynia, and the Spirit did not suffer them.' Some MSS., Versions, and Critics read 'the spirit of Jesus,' but most evidently it is the same 'Spirit' spoken of in the immediately preceding verse.

8. PASSING BY,] *or* 'going along Mysia.'

9. IN,] *lit.* 'through the night..a certain man, a Macedonian, calling upon him and saying, Having come through to Macedonia, help us.'

10. AFTER,] *lit.* 'and when he saw the vision, straightway we (Paul, Silas, Luke, and Timothy) sought to go forth to Macedonia, gathering fully that the Lord has called us forward ourselves to tell them good-news.'

11. LOOSING,] *lit.* 'having been led up from Troas, we ran straight to Samothracia, and on the morrow to Neopolis.'

12. THE CHIEF,] *lit.* 'a foremost city of that part..abiding (*lit.* rubbing thoroughly, i.e. spending, occupying) certain days.'

13. SABBATH,] *lit.* 'sabbath-day..alongside of a river, where there was thought to be a proseuche (i.e. a place of pouring forth before God), and having sat down we were speaking to the women who came together.'

14. WHICH,] *lit.* 'reverencing God, was hearing.. opened thoroughly to hold towards the things spoken by Paul.'

15. BESOUGHT,] *lit.* 'called upon us.. remain; and she herself forced us along.'

16. CAME TO PASS,] *lit.* 'and there happened to meet us, in our passing on to a proseuche a certain little maid having a spirit of Python, who brought to her masters much work, being mad,' and therefore reckoned to be inspired.

17. THE SAME,] *lit.* 'this one having followed after Paul and us cried, saying, These men are servants..who tell us thoroughly a way of salvation.'

18. DID SHE,] *lit.* 'she was doing over many days; and Paul being wearied out, and having turned round upon the spirit said, I tell thee fully in the name.'

19. GAINS,] *or* 'work was gone away, they themselves took Paul and Silas openly..the public place before the foremost men.'

20. BROUGHT,] *lit.* 'brought them forward to the leaders of the force.'

21. TEACH,] *lit.* 'tell-down customs (*or* rites), which it is not lawful for us to receive fully, nor to do.'

22. MULTITUDE,] *lit.* 'crowd stood together against them, and the leaders of the force rent off their clothes round about, and were commanding to beat (them) with rods.'

23. LAID,] *or* 'put many strokes upon them ..telling the prison-guard aside.'

24. CHARGE,] *or* 'side-tale cast them into the inner ward, and himself made their feet safe to the wood.'

25. AT,] *lit.* 'down the midnight pouring forth before (God) were praising God in hymns, and the prisoners were hearkening to them.'

26. SUDDENLY,] *or* 'unexpectedly there happened a great shaking,..prison-hold was shaken like the sea, and along with it all..and the bands of all were loosed,' *lit.* sent back.

27. AWAKING,] *lit.* 'becoming awakened out of sleep..drew a sword, and was about to take himself away, supposing the prisoners to have fled out.'

28. LOUD,] *lit.* 'great voice, saying, Mayest thou not do to thyself any evil.'

29. CALLED,] *lit.* 'asked lights.. and becoming very fearful, fell forward to Paul and Silas.'

30. BROUGHT,] *lit.* 'having led them forth without, said, Sirs, what ought I to do, that I may be saved?' If the jailor feared merely *temporal* danger, the apostles, knowing there was no risk of that, took advantage of his question to direct him to his *spiritual* danger, but as the Apostles had been preaching, for several days at least, in the city, he may have had opportunities of knowing their religious character.

31. HOUSE,] *or* 'household.'

33. TOOK,] *lit.* 'took them along-side (of himself) in that hour of the night, he bathed (them) because of the stripes,..all his along with the word.'

34. BROUGHT,] *lit.* 'led them up (out of the dungeon) into his house he put a table near (them), and was glad, with all the household, he having believed in God;' nothing is said of their believing.

35. WHEN,] *lit.* 'and day having come the leaders of the force sent away the rod-bearers, saying, Loose these men thoroughly.'

36. TOLD,] *lit.* 'told again fully these words to Paul, that, the leaders of the force have sent forth, that ye may be thoroughly loosed, now therefore, going forth, pass ye on in peace.'

37. THEM,] i.e. the rod-bearers.

OPENLY,] *or* 'publicly uncondemned,' *lit.* unjudged-down.'

ROMANS,] *lit.* 'being men, Romans.'

HAVE CAST,] *lit.* 'and cast..cast us forth privately! why no! but having come themselves, let him lead us forth.'

38. SERJEANTS,] *lit.* 'rod-bearers told again these sayings to the leaders of the force ..they are Romans.'

39. BESOUGHT,] *or* 'called upon them, and led them forth, asking them to go out of the city.'

40. COMFORTED,] *or* 'exhorted them and went forth.'

Chapter XVII. may be divided into six parts; v. 1—4 progress of the good-news in Thessalonica; v. 5—9 uproar of the Jews there; v. 10—14 progress in Berea and uproar; v. 15—21 Paul disputes with some philosophers in Athens; v. 22—31 his address on Areopagus; v. 32—34 progress and rejection.

1. PASSED,] *lit.* 'and having made way through..was the synagogue,' some particular one, not mentioned elsewhere; but many MSS. Versions, Fathers, and Critics omit the article entirely.

2. MANNER,] *lit.* 'according to custom.. and upon three sabbaths was speaking thoroughly to them from the Writings.'

3. OPENING,] *lit.* 'opening up thoroughly and putting along-side (of them) that The Christ it was behoving to suffer and to stand up out of (the) dead, and that this is The Christ, (even) Jesus, whom I tell fully of to you.'

4. CONSORTED,] *lit.* 'cast in their lot with ..worshipping Hellens..foremost women.'

5. MOVED WITH ENVY,] *lit.* 'being zealous, took also to (them) of the loungers certain evil men, and made a crowd, and were disturbing the city, and having stood against (*or* before) the house of Jason, were seeking to lead them to the public.'

6. UNTO,] *lit.* 'upon (*or* before) the city chiefs, crying,' *lit.* lowing.

TURNED,] *lit.* 'set up the inhabited (world) are also here present.'

7. RECEIVED,] *lit.* 'received secretly, and these all do in opposition to the dogmas of Caesar.'

8. PEOPLE,] *lit.* 'crowd and the city-chiefs.'

9. SECURITY,] *lit.* 'the sufficiency from Jason and the rest, they loosed them entirely.'

10. IMMEDIATELY,] *lit.* 'straightway sent forth..through the night..coming along-side, went away into.'

11. MORE NOBLE,] *lit.* 'of better birth,' in a spiritual, not a worldly, point of view.

READINESS,] *lit.* 'forwardness of mind, and judged-thoroughly the Writings every day.'

12. HONOURABLE,] *lit.* 'well-conditioned Greek women.'

13. OF,] *lit.* 'from Thessalonica knew that also in Berea the word of God was fully-told,..and moved the crowds like the sea.'

14. IMMEDIATELY,] *lit.* 'straightway..sent away out Paul to pass on as upon the sea ..remained behind there.'

15. CONDUCTED,] *lit.* 'set down Paul led him unto Athens..that they should come quickly to him, they went forth.'

16. WAITED,] *or* 'expected them..sharpened in him, viewing the city full-of-idols.'

17. DISPUTED,] *lit.* 'was he reasoning.. the worshippers, and in the public place

daily (*lit.* 'down every day') with those happening to be near.'

18. EPICUREANS,] who held that the Creator took no interest in the affairs of his creatures.

STOICS,] a kind of fatalists.

ENCOUNTERED,] *lit.* 'were casting together (words) at him, and certain said, What does this seed-gatherer wish to say? and others, He seems to be a thorough-announcer of strange demons,' i.e. the shades of the mighty dead reverenced by the populace as demi-gods.

PREACHED,] *lit.* 'was telling fully as good news Jesus and the up-standing.'

19. TOOK,] *lit.* 'took hold upon him, and led him upon the Areo-Pagus (i.e. Mars' hill), saying, Are we able to know what this new teaching is, that is spoken by thee?'

20. BRINGEST,] *or* 'bearest..we take counsel, therefore, to know, what these things wish to be.'

21. WHICH WERE THERE,] *lit.* 'strangers sojourning (*lit.* upon the people) had a good-opportunity for no other thing than to tell something, or to hear some other newer thing.'

22. MARS' HILL,] *Gr.* 'Areo-Pagus, and said, Men! Athenians'

THAT IN ALL,] *lit.* 'through all things how much ye are given to demon-worship,' having every possible kind of idolatry.

23. PASSED BY,] *lit.* 'came through and viewed again the objects of your worship, I found also a high-place in which it was written above: To an Unknown God! Whom therefore, not knowing—ye worship, this One I announce fully to you.'

24. SEEING,] *lit.* 'he being Lord of..in habitations'

25. WORSHIPPED,] *lit.* 'warmed, (cherished, attended)..needing anything further, he giving to all..the all things.'

26. HATH,] *lit.* 'he made out of one blood every nation of men..and marked out prearranged (*or* fully arranged) seasons, and the boundary marks of their dwelling.'

27. THAT,] *lit.* 'to seek the Lord.'

28. HAVE OUR BEING,] *lit.* 'and are; as also certain of the makers (of verse) among you have said, For of Him also we are offspring.' See Aratus, Phaen. 5; Cleanthes' Hymn on Jupiter, v. 5; Pindar, Nem. Od. 6; Apollonius, Epist. 44.

29. FORASMUCH,] *lit.* 'being then, offspring of God..to suppose..to a graving of art and inner mind of man.'

30. AND,] *lit.* 'therefore indeed the times of the ignorance God having overlooked, doth now tell fully to all men everywhere to have another mind.'

31. HAS,] *lit.* 'did set a day in which he is about to judge the inhabited world in justice by (*lit.* in) a man whom he marked out, having held assurance near to all, having caused him to stand up out of (the) dead.'

32. RESURRECTION,] *lit.* 'upstanding.. some indeed, were mocking'

33. SO,] *lit.* 'and so Paul went forth out of their midst.'

34. HOWBEIT,] *lit.* 'but certain men, having been attached (*lit.* glued, i.e. having glued themselves) to him believed.'

Chapter XVIII. may be divided into six parts; v. 1—6 Paul reasoning with the Jews at Corinth; v. 7—11 his success and vision; v. 12—17 Gallio's indifference; v. 18—22 Paul leaves Corinth and returns to Antioch; v. 23 Paul's travels in Galatia and Phrygia; v. 24—28 Apollos labours in Ephesus.

1. DEPARTED,] *lit.* 'having been parted, the *passive* being used as often elsewhere for the *middle* voice.

2. BORN,] *lit.* 'a native of Pontus, as to race.'

LATELY,] *lit.* 'fresh *or* newly come from Italy (because of Claudius having thoroughly arranged (for) all the Jews to be parted out of Rome), and came forward to them.'

3. HE WAS,] *lit.* 'of (his) being of the same art, he remained along-side of them, and was working, for they were tent-makers as to art.'

4. REASONED,] *lit.* 'was reasoning.. through every sabbath, and was persuading both Jews and Hellenes.'

5. COME,] *lit.* 'come down..was held together in the spirit testifying thoroughly to the Jews Jesus Christ.'

6. OPPOSED,] *lit.* 'set *or* arranged themselves over-against, and spake injuriously, shaking off for himself (his) garments, he said to them, Your blood (is) upon your head, I (am) clean; from this time I pass on to the nations.'

7. DEPARTED,] *lit.* 'went over..was bordering with.'

8. CHIEF-RULER,] *or* 'foremost synagogite ..were believing and were being baptized.'

9. SPAKE,] *lit.* 'said..through a vision.. but be speaking, and thou mayest not be silent.'

10. HURT,] *lit.* 'to do thee evil.'

11. CONTINUED,] *lit.* 'sat,' i.e. dwelt or abode.

12. THE DEPUTY,] *lit.* 'and Gallio being proconsul..made a full stand against Paul with one mind, and led him before the tribunal.'

13. FELLOW,] *lit.* 'that this one.'

14. WHEN,] *lit.* 'and Paul being about.. If indeed, then, it were any act of injustice or evil roguery (*lit.* easy-work, cheating), according to reason I would uphold you.'

15. WORDS,] *lit.* 'word,' (i.e. doctrine)..and of the law that is among you, see ye these: for I counsel not to be judge of these.'

16. JUDGMENT SEAT,] *or* 'tribunal.'

17. GREEKS,] *lit.* 'Hellenes took hold upon Sosthenes, the foremost synagogite, and were beating (him) before the tribunal, and not even for these things was Gallio caring.'

18. AFTER THIS,] *lit.* 'Paul remained still yet many days, and having himself arranged thoroughly with the brethren, sailed forth to Syria..for he was having a vow,' *or* prayer, *lit.* a pouring forth.

19. CAME,] *lit.* 'came thoroughly..left them entirely there..reasoned fully.'

20. DESIRED,] *lit.* 'asked (him) to remain much longer time alongside of them, he assented not,' *lit.* did not nod to it.

21. BADE THEM FAREWELL,] *lit.* 'set himself from them, saying, It behoveth me by all means to make the coming feast at Jerusalem, but I will bend back again to you, God wishing (it); and he was brought up from Ephesus.'

22. LANDED,] *lit.* 'come down to.. embraced the assembly.'

23. SPENT,] *lit.* 'made or used.'

WENT OVER,] *lit.* 'came through in full succession the region of..strengthening fully all.'

24. BORN,] *lit.* 'an Alexandrian as to birth, a man of words (*or* doctrines), being powerful in the Writings, came through to Ephesus.'

25. MAN,] *lit.* 'this one was instructed in (*lit.* 'sounded down through)..in spirit, was speaking and teaching accurately the things concerning the Lord, knowing fully.'

26. BOLDLY,] *or* 'openly..took him near, and they themselves put forth to him the way of God more accurately.'

27. DISPOSED,] *lit.* 'counselled to go through to Achaia, the brethren themselves turning round publicly, wrote to the disciples to receive him fully, who, having come along cast much together to those who have believed, through the grace,' given to him of eloquence and learning.

28. MIGHTY,] *lit.* 'was very strenuously thoroughly-convicting the Jews publicly, showing fully through the Writings Jesus to be the Christ.'

Chapter XIX. may be divided into five parts; v. 1—7 Paul in Ephesus and some of John's disciples; v. 8—12 he preaches, cures and casts out demons; v. 13—20 which certain Jews tried and were punished, so that the Gospel prospered more; v. 21—23 Paul sends to Macedonia; v. 24—41 great uproar in Ephesus.

1. AT,] *lit.* 'in Corinth gone through the upper parts.'

2. HAVE,] *lit.* 'having believed, did ye receive holy spirit;' the *influences* of the Spirit, not the *person*, is meant here.

WE HAVE,] *lit.* 'but we did not even hear if there is any holy spirit.'

4. THE,] *lit.* 'with a baptism of a new mind..that is, on Jesus the Christ.'

5. IN,] *lit.* 'with a view to the name.'

6. LAID,] *lit.* 'upon..the holy spirit..they were speaking..were prophesying.'

7. ABOUT,] *lit.* 'as if (it were).'

8. SPAKE,] *lit.* 'was speaking openly for three months, reasoning thoroughly.'

9. DIVERS,] *lit.* 'certain were being hardened and not believing, speaking evil of the way..he stood off from them and marked off the disciples, reasoning every day in the school (*or* place of ease) of a certain Tyrannus.'

10. CONTINUED,] *lit.* 'happened during two years, so that all,' i.e. most, very many.

11. WROUGHT,] *lit.* 'was doing mighty things—not ordinary—through the hands of Paul.'

12. BROUGHT,] *lit.* 'borne over upon the infirm handkerchiefs (for removing sweat), or aprons (*lit.* half girdles), and the unsoundnesses.'

13. VAGABOND,] *lit.* 'those going round about.'

EXORCISTS,] *lit.* those 'swearing out' demons.

TOOK UPON THEM,] *or* 'took in hand to name over those having the evil spirits..Paul proclaims.'

14. WERE,] *lit.* 'were certain, seven sons of Sceva, a Jew, a foremost priest, who are doing this.'

15. PAUL I KNOW,] *lit.* 'Paul I know fully; but ye—who are ye?'

16. OVERCAME,] *lit.* 'had full-lordship over them, and was strong against them.'

17. WAS,] *lit.* 'became known to all, both Jews and Hellenes, dwelling..was being magnified.'

18. CAME,] *lit.* 'were coming, confessing (*lit.* saying out the same thing) and telling again their deeds,' *or* acts, practices.

19. USED,] *lit.* 'practised the round-about works, brought the books together, and were burning fully before all, and they counted together the price of them, and found (it) five myriads of silverlings.'

20. GREW,] *lit.* 'was..growing and becoming strong.'

21. ENDED,] *lit.* 'filled out, Paul set himself in the spirit, having gone through..to pass on to Jerusalem, saying, that, after my being there, it behoves me also to see Rome.

22. SENT,] *lit.* 'and having sent forth to Macedonia two of those acting-as-deacons to him,..he himself held on a time in Asia.'

23. THE SAME,] *lit.* 'and there happened during that season not a little stir (*or* trouble) about the way,' i.e. Christianity.

24. SILVERSMITH,] *lit.* 'worker in silver, making silver habitations of Artemis, was holding forth to the artificers not a little work.'

25. CALLED,] *lit.* 'crowded together, also those working about such things, and said, Men! ye know fully that out of this work is our prosperity.'

26. TURNED AWAY,] *lit.* 'set away a great crowd,..through hands.'

27. SO,] *lit.* 'and not only is this department endangered to us by coming into a full-rejection, but..be reckoned for nothing, and also her greatness is about to be brought down, whom all Asia and the inhabited world worshippeth.'

28. WERE FILLED,] *lit.* 'became full of wrath and were crying..the Artemis of the Ephesians.'

29. FILLED,] *or* 'full of confusion (*lit.* pouring together), and having seized at once Gaius..with one mind.'

30. WOULD,] *lit.* 'consulted to go in..were not suffering him.'

31. CHIEF OF ASIA,] *lit.* 'Asiarchs,' certain presidents of religious rites, chosen yearly.

DESIRING,] *lit.* 'were calling upon him not to give himself to the theatre.'

32. CRIED,] *lit.* 'were crying..assembly (*Gr.* ekklesia) was..the most knew not for what they themselves had come together.'

33. DREW,] *lit.* 'put forward Alexander

out of the crowd..the Jews thrusting him forward,..having waved-down (his) hand wished to apologize (*lit.* make a speech from himself) to the populace.'

34. KNEW,] *lit.* 'knew fully that he is a Jew, one voice came out of all, for about two hours.'

35. TOWN-CLERK,] *lit.* 'scribe,' or writer.

HAD APPEASED,] *lit.* 'sent down (the noise of) the people, he said, Men! Athenians!..is a worshipper (*or* devotee, *lit.* a sweeper of the habitation) of.'

36. CANNOT BE,] *lit.* 'are not spoken against..to be sent down..precipitately.'

37. HAVE,] *lit.* 'ye brought these men, who are neither robbing temples nor speaking injuriously of your goddess.'

38. CRAFTSMEN,] *or* 'artificers..a word with any, public courts are brought on, and there are pro-consuls; let them be calling in one another.'

39. INQUIRE,] *lit.* 'seek also about any other things, in the lawful assembly (*Gr.* ecclesia) it shall be loosed openly.'

40. CALLED IN QUESTION,] *lit.* 'called in (to court) for the standing of to-day,..we shall be able to give forth an account of this concourse,' *lit.* 'turning round together.'

41. THUS,] *lit.* 'these things he loosed-fully the assembly,' *lit.* ecclesia.

Chapter XX. may be divided into four parts; v. 1—6 Paul's journeys from Ephesus to Troas; v. 7—12 where he restores Eutychus to life; v. 13—16 he proceeds to Miletus; v. 17—28 where he addresses the elders of Ephesus.

1. DEPARTED,] *lit.* 'went forth to pass on to.'

2. GONE OVER,] *lit.* 'gone through those parts, and called upon them with many words.'

3. ABODE,] *lit.* 'made (i.e. used, occupied) three months, a counsel by the Jews, having come against him, he being about to be brought up to Syria, there came (to him) a resolution (*lit.* judgment) to turn round a little through Macedonia.'

4. ACCOMPANIED,] *lit.* 'were pressing together with him unto Asia..and of Thessalonians..and Asiatics.'

5. TARRIED,] *lit.* 'were remaining for us in.'

6. AWAY,] *lit.* 'sailed forth..of the unleavened things..we spent (*lit.* rubbed thoroughly) seven days.'

7. UPON,] *lit.* 'in the one (day) of the sabbaths;' see on Mat. 28. 1.

WHEN,] *lit.* 'the disciples having been brought together to break bread,' as in 2. 42. There is no doubt whatever but that in the earliest ages of the church the Lord's Supper was observed every Lord's Day, as it might (perhaps *ought* to) be with profit, yet the *passive* form of the verb here would seem to indicate that the custom was not habitual at Troas.

PREACHED,] *lit.* 'was reasoning with them, about to go forth on..and was extending the word till mid-night.'

8. LIGHTS,] *lit.* 'lamps *or* torches..brought together.'

9. SAT,] *lit.* 'is sitting upon the little door (*or* window)..being borne down by a deep sleep, and Paul reasoning very much, he was borne down from the sleep, and fell from the third floor (*lit.* covering *or* roof), and was lifted up dead.'

10. EMBRACING,] *lit.* 'taking (him) wholly round, said, Be not disturbed, for his soul is in him.'

11. WHEN,] *lit.* 'and having came up, and broken bread, and tasted (wine), and..till dawn, so he went forth.'

12. BROUGHT,] *or* 'led (up) the lad alive.'

13. TO SHIP,] *lit.* 'upon the ship, and were brought up to Assos, there about to take up Paul, for so it was arranged throughout (by himself), he being himself about to go on foot,' *or* by land, as in Mat. 14. 13; Mark 6. 33.

14. MET,] *lit.* 'took (counsel) with us, taking him up we went to.' .

15. SAILED,] *lit.* 'sailed away..came down the coming (day)..we cast (anchor) near to Samos, and remained in Trogyllium.'

16. HAD DETERMINED,] *lit.* 'judged (proper) to sail near Ephesus, that there might not be to him a wasting of time in Asia,..in Jerusalem the day of the Pentecost.'

17. CALLED,] *lit.* 'called to himself the presbyters of the assembly;' as each congregation had originally a plurality of these it is not certain whether those now called were connected with one congregation or with more than one; in the former case they would be now called (among presbyterians) a *kirk-session*, and in the latter a *presbytery;* among Episcopalians a *synod*.

18. COME,] *lit.* 'come along..ye—ye know well, from the first day in which I came over to Asia, how I was with you the whole time.'

19. TEMPTATIONS,] *lit.* 'trials, that came together to me in the counsels of the Jews against me.'

20. KEPT BACK,] *lit.* 'I myself put nothing under of the things that are profitable (*lit.* bearing together), not to tell again to you, and to teach you publicly, and in houses.'

21. TESTIFYING,] *lit.* 'testifying thoroughly ..the new mind in reference to God, and the faith in reference to Jesus Christ our Lord.'

22. GO,] *lit.* 'pass on..to Jerusalem.'

23. WITNESSETH,] *lit.* 'doth thoroughly testify..tribulations remain for me.' (See 21. 4, 11.)

24. MOVE ME,] *lit.* 'but of none of these do I make account, nor do I hold my life precious to myself, so as to end my race (*or* course) with joy, and the deaconship which I received from the Lord Jesus, to testify thoroughly the good news of the grace of God.'

25. I KNOW,] *lit.* 'I have known..I went through proclaiming the reign.'

26. TAKE YOU TO RECORD,] *lit.* 'I testify to you this very day that I am clear from the blood of all,' i.e. of any one of them.

27. SHUNNED,] *lit.* 'for I kept nothing under so as not to tell fully to you the whole (of the revealed) counsel of God.'

28. TAKE HEED,] *lit.* 'hold forward, therefore, to yourselves, and to all the flock, in which the Holy Spirit himself set you overseers (*lit.* episcopous, i.e. bishops), to feed the assembly of God.' Many MSS. for 'God' read 'Lord;' some 'Lord and God;' others 'Lord God,' &c. That 'elder' and 'bishop' in the Scriptures are applied interchangeably to the same persons there cannot reasonably be the slightest doubt.

HATH PURCHASED,] *lit.* 'he made for himself (1 Tim. 3. 13) through his own blood.'

29. I KNOW,] *lit.* 'I have known this.. going away shall grievous (*lit.* heavy, weighty) wolves come in to you.'

30. ARISE,] *lit.* 'set themselves up, speaking perverted things (*lit.* things turned thoroughly round), to draw away the disciples.'

31. WATCH,] *lit.* 'be ye wakeful, remembering that (during) three years, night and day, I myself ceased not with tears putting each one of you in mind (of these things).'

32. COMMEND,] *lit.* 'put (*or* place) you over to God..build up fully,..inheritance (*lit.* any thing 'distributed by lot'), among all those sanctified,' *lit.* not of the earth.

33. COVETED,] *lit.* 'I set (my) mind upon no one's.'

34. HAVE MINISTERED,] *lit.* 'acted as under rowers.'

35. HAVE SHEWED,] *lit.* 'I showed you all things fully, that so labouring (even to fatigue) it behoveth (us) to take hold over-against the infirm, and to be mindful of . that (*or* because) he himself said, It is more happy to give than to receive.'

36. THUS,] *lit.* 'these things..having set his knees, with them all he himself poured forth before (God).'

37. SORE,] *lit.* 'and there happened a great weeping of all, and falling over upon the neck of Paul they were befriending him greatly.'

38. SPAKE,] *lit.* 'had said that they are about to see..were sending him forward to the ship.'

Chapter XXI. may be divided into five parts; v. 1—3 Paul's journey from Miletus to Tyre; v. 4—6 his reception there; v. 7—16 from Tyre to Jerusalem; v. 17—26 Paul's compliance with Jewish customs; v. 27—40 its evil consequences.

1. AND,] *lit.* 'and when it came for us to be led up, having been drawn away from them, running direct, we came to Koos, and the next day to Rhodes.'

2. SAILING OVER,] *lit.* 'passing through to Phenicia, we went upon (it), and were brought up.'

3. DISCOVERED,] *lit.* 'and we having been again shown Cyprus, and having left it down on the left,..were brought down to Tyre,.. was unburdening her fulness.'

4. FINDING,] *lit.* 'found again the disciples, we remained on there seven days,' probably till next Lord's Day.

THAT HE SHOULD,] *lit.* 'not to go up to Jerusalem.' It is not easy to see why Paul should have refused to hear the voice of the 'Spirit' on this occasion (as also in v. 11; 22. 19), as from 19. 21 the proposed visit rose from himself, rather than from the 'Spirit;' probably he thought that if the Spirit really wished him to desist, the communication should (or would) have been made to himself, rather than to others.

5. ACCOMPLISHED,] *lit.* 'we came to complete the days fully, we went forth, and passed on, they all sending us forward.. unto the outside of the city, and having bent the knee upon the beach, we poured forth before (God).'

6. WHEN,] *lit.* 'and having embraced one another, we went up to the ship, and these turned away to their own (friends).'

7. AND WHEN,] *lit.* 'and we, having thoroughly finished the sailing from Troas came down to.'

8. NEXT,] *lit.* 'and on the morrow we (those about Paul) went forth and came to.'

EVANGELIST,] *lit.* 'teller again of good;' as in Eph. 4. 11; 2 Tim. 4. 5.

SEVEN] brethren, mentioned in 6. 5; 8. 26, 40.

9. THE SAME,] *lit.* 'and to this one were four virgin daughters prophesying.' It is difficult to say whether this means that they foretold future events, or simply that they proclaimed the praises of God (as in Ex. 15. 20; 1 Chron. 25. 1); most probably the latter, in which case they may have formed a *public band* in the congregation for leading the psalmody, and were accordingly required (in 1 Cor. 11. 5) only to keep their heads covered as an (eastern) mark of modesty (see Gen. 20. 16). Some females (1 Cor. 14. 34) had ventured to 'speak' in the assembly, i.e. to interrupt the speaker by asking questions, which they could easily have got solved at home, this Paul forbids; as however he does not now appear to have forbidden these four virgins from exercising their gifts and graces, probably he thought that special graces demanded special privileges.

10. TARRIED,] *lit.* 'remained on..Agabus.' (11. 38).

11. TOOK,] *lit.* 'lifted up,..in Jerusalem.. whose is this girdle, and shall give him over into the hands of nations.'

22. OF,] *lit.* 'in the place, called upon him.'

13. MEAN,] *lit.* 'what do ye—weeping and breaking-together my heart? for I have readiness ..die fully.'

14. WHEN,] *lit.* 'and he not being persuaded, we were quiet, saying, Let the wish of the Lord happen!'

15. TOOK UP OUR CARRIAGES,] i.e. our 'bundles or luggage.' Carriage in modern English means the *vehicle* that conveys anything, formerly it meant *the thing carried.* Or translate thus: 'we having been preparing ourselves fully went up to Jerusalem.'

16. WENT,] *lit.* 'went together with us also of the disciples from Caesarea bringing (us) to a certain Cyprian,..might sojourn.'

17. RECEIVED,] *lit.* 'themselves received us gladly.'

18. WENT,] *lit.* 'was going in with us to James (15. 13), and all the presbyters came along.'

19. DECLARED,] *lit.* 'was bringing forth, one by one, each of the things God did among the nations through his deaconship.'

20. GLORIFIED,] *lit.* 'were glorifying.. myriads of Jews there are who have believed.'

21. ARE,] *lit.* 'were sounded-fully concerning thee,..Jews throughout the nations a standing-away from Moses, saying not to circumcise..to walk about according to the customs.'

22. THE,] *lit.* 'a multitude it behoveth by all means to come together,.. thou hast come.'

23. THEM,] *lit.* on 'themselves.'

24. THEM TAKE,] *lit.* 'having taken these along, be purified with them, and spend (something) upon them, that they may shave for themselves the head,..the things of which they have been sounded-fully concerning thee..art observing the law.'

25. AS TOUCHING,] *lit.* 'but concerning those of the nations who have believed, we sent openly, having judged them to keep no such thing, except to guard themselves as to the thing sacrificed to idols, even the blood, and strangled thing, and whoredom.' (See 15. 20—29.)

26. TOOK,] *lit.* 'having taken the men along (with himself), on the coming day having been purified with them, was going in to the temple, telling fully the filling-out of the days of the purification, till the offering (*lit.* thing borne forward) was borne forward for each one of them.'

27. ALMOST,] *lit.* 'about to be fully ended, the Jews from Asia,..were pouring the crowd together.'

28. OF ISRAEL,] *lit.* 'men! Israelites! be helping!.. is teaching all.. hath made common.'

29. AN,] *lit.* 'the Ephesian, whom they were supposing that Paul brought.'

30. ALL,] *or* 'the whole city was moved, and there came a running together of the people, and having laid hold upon Paul, they were drawing him outside of the temple, and straightway the doors were closed.'

31. AS THEY,] *lit.* 'they seeking to kill him utterly, a rumour went up to the chiliarch (i.e. chief of 1000 men) of the cohort, that all Jerusalem has been poured together,'—into a mass.

32. IMMEDIATELY,] *lit.* 'from that (moment) having taken along (with him)..ran down upon them..ceased beating Paul.'

33. TOOK,] *lit.* 'took hold on him himself, ..two chains (*lit.* unloosable things), and was inquiring who he may be, and what it is he has been doing.'

34. CRIED,] *lit.* 'were crying (*or* lowing).. among the crowd,..led into the encampment.'

35. STAIRS,] *lit.* 'ascents (or steps) it came also (for) him to be carried by the soldiers, because of..the crowd.'

36. FOLLOWED,] *lit.* 'was following.'

37. WAS,] *lit.* 'is about to be led into the encampment, he says to the chiliarch, Is it lawful for me to say something to thee? and he said, Dost thou know Hellenistic?'

38. ART NOT,] *or* 'thou art not, then, the Egyptian, who before these days having stood up, led forth also into..murderers.' *Gr.* sicarii, men who used the *sica*, a short sword or dagger.

39. MEAN,] *lit.* 'undistinguished.'

SUFFER,] *lit.* 'turn over upon me to speak.'

40. WHEN,] *lit.* 'and having turned (it) over upon him, Paul having stood upon the steps, having waved down with the hand to the people, and much silence having come, he sounded forth in the Hebrew dialect (of that period), saying.'

Chapter XXII. may be divided into three parts; v. 1—21 Paul's defence; v. 22—24 Jewish uproar and military cruelty; v. 25—30 Paul asserts his privileges and is brought before the Sanhedrim.

1. DEFENCE.] *Gr.* 'apology.'

2. SPAKE,] *lit.* 'was sounding forth to them in the Hebrew dialect, they held greater quietness near (him).' This passage shows that while the vernacular Aramaean still held its ground among the lower classes, it was more naturally expected that every public address should be in Greek, which was then almost universally spoken throughout the Roman empire, and hence more suitable than the Hebrew for recording the New Testament Oracles.

3. BORN,] *lit.* 'having been born in Tarsus of Cilicia, but having been fully-nourished in..according to (the) accuracy of the law of the fathers, being zealous of God.'

4. PERSECUTED,] *or* 'pursued, caused to flee.'

THIS WAY] of thinking, i.e. Christianity.

THE DEATH,] *lit.* 'unto death.'

DELIVERING,] *lit.* 'giving over.'

5. HIGH,] *or* 'foremost priest doth (i.e. is able to) testify to me, and all the presbytery;' as in Luke 22. 66; 1 Tim. 4. 14.

LETTERS,] *lit.* things 'sent upon *or* about' a person or thing.

WENT,] *lit.* 'was going on to Damascus, about to bring..that they might be seen punished.'

6. CAME TO PASS,] *or* 'and it happened to me, in my passing on and being nigh to Damascus, about mid-day, unforseen a great light to shine around me out of the heaven.'

7. PERSECUTEST,] *or* 'pursuest.'

8. OF NAZARETH,] *lit.* 'Jesus the Nazarene, whom thou—thou dost pursue.'

9. SAW,] *lit.* 'saw for themselves, and became much afraid, but they heard (i.e. understood) not the voice of Him who is speaking to me.'

10. ARISE,] *lit.* 'having stood up, be passing on to..which have been set for thee to do.'

11. I COULD NOT,] *lit.* 'I was not seeing from..hand by those with me.'

12. ONE,] *lit.* 'a certain one, Ananias

a man very worshipful according to the law, witnessed to by all the Jews dwelling (there).'

13. STOOD,] *lit.* 'stood over (me)..Saul, brother, look up .to him.'

14. HATH CHOSEN,] *lit.* 'did openly choose thee for himself by his own hand, to know his wish *or* will, and to see the just One, and to hear a voice out of his mouth.'

15. HIS WITNESS,] *lit.* 'a witness to him towards all men.'

16. WHY TARRIEST THOU,] *or* 'what art thou about (to do)? having stood up, baptize (i.e. receive baptism for) thyself, and wash thyself from thy sins, having called for thyself upon the name of the Lord.'

17. IT CAME TO PASS,] *lit.* 'and it happened to me, on my having turned round shortly to Jerusalem, and my pouring forth before (God) in the temple, my coming into an ecstasy.'

18. SAW,] *lit.* 'and my seeing him speaking to me, Haste, and go forth with speed out of Jerusalem, because they will not receive from thee the testimony concerning me.'

19. KNOW,] *lit.* 'they know about (it), that I had been imprisoning and beating throughout the synogogues, those believing on thee.'

20. MARTYR,] *or* 'witness Stephen was being poured forth, I also had been standing, and thinking well along with (them) of his being taken away, and guarding the garments of those taking him away.'

21. DEPART,] *lit.* 'be passing on..because I will send thee away far out to nations.'

22. AUDIENCE,] *lit.* 'and they were hearing him unto this word, and they lifted up openly their voice, saying, Take away such a one from the earth! for it is not fit for him to live.'

23. CAST OFF,] *or* 'cast down,' that they might be ready for action.

24. CHIEF CAPTAIN,] *Gr.* 'chiliarch..led into the encampment, saying. By scourges let him be examined again, that he might know fully for what cause they were sounding so against him.'

25. BOUND,] *lit.* 'stretched forth to him the thongs (*or* straps)..was standing by,.. a man, a Roman, and not-judged-down.'

26. WENT,] *lit.* 'went forward and told (it) fully to the chiliarch, saying, See what thou art about to do.'

27. CHIEF CAPTAIN,] *lit.* 'chiliarch having come forward said.'

28. OBTAINED,] *lit.* 'I myself acquired this citizenship..but I have been even born (a citizen).'

29. DEPARTED,] *lit.* 'stood off from him who are about to examine him again, and the chiliarch also was afraid, having known about (him) that he is a Roman;' see 16. 38.

30. BECAUSE,] *lit.* 'taking counsel to know the certainty wherefore he is publicly spoken against by the Jews..all their sanhedrim to come, and having led Paul down he set him before them.'

Chapter XXIII. may be divided into five parts; v. 1—9 Paul before the Sanhedrim, v. 10, 11 he is rescued and encouraged; v. 12—15 plot to slay him; v. 16—21 revealed to him and reported to the chiliarch; v. 22 —35 who sends him to Felix with a letter.

1. EARNESTLY BEHOLDING,] *lit.* 'having strained (his eyes) towards the sanhedrim, said, Men, brethren, I have been a citizen with all good conscience towards God unto this day.'

2. HIGH,] *or* 'foremost priest set openly those standing near.'

3. SHALL,] *lit.* 'is about to smite thee, (by an assassin, according to Josephus) O whitened wall! (see Mat. 23. 27)..judging me according to the law, and..against law.'

4. BY,] *or* 'stood near..revile *or* pierce with cutting words.'

5. WIST,] *lit.* 'I had not known, brethren, that he is foremost priest, for it has been written (in Ex. 22. 28), Of the foremost one of thy people thou shalt not speak (*lit.* 'lift up' the voice) evilly.'

6. PERCEIVED,] *lit.* 'known..part is of (the) Sadducees, and the other of (the) Pharisees,.. sanhedrim, Men, brethren.. concerning (the) hope and up-standing of (the) dead I am judged.'

7. SO,] *lit.* 'this said, there happened a standing (up) of..divided,' *lit.* rent or became schismatic.

8. THE,] *lit.* 'for Sadducees indeed say (that) an upstanding is not to be, neither messenger nor spirit, but Pharisees confess (*lit.* say the same thing) them both.' (Luke 20. 37.)

9. AROSE,] *or* 'came, happened..and were striving (*lit.* fighting) thoroughly,..a messenger (22. 27) spake to him, we may not fight with God.' (See 5. 39.)

10. AROSE,] *lit.* 'happened much standing (up), the chiliarch having been afraid lest Paul might be drawn asunder by them.. and to snatch him out of their midst, and to lead him into the encampment.

11. GOOD CHEER,] *lit.* 'be courageous,.. didst testify fully the things concerning me (i.e. Jesus) to Jerusalem, so doth it behove thee also to testify to Rome.' (See 19. 21.)

12. WAS,] *lit.* 'became day..Jews having made a turning-round together, laid themselves up (on the altar, i.e. devoted themselves), saying neither to eat nor to drink till they might kill Paul utterly.' (1 Sam. 14. 24; 2 Sam. 3. 35.)

13. HAD,] *lit.* 'have made this mutual oath.'

14. CAME,] *lit.* 'came forward..and the presbyters said, With a laying up (upon the altar) we have laid ourselves up, to taste nothing till we may kill Paul utterly.'

15. COUNCIL,] *lit.* 'sanhedrim, manifest ye inwardly (i.e. secretly) to the chiliarch..lead him down.. as being about to know thoroughly more accurately the things concerning him, and we, before his coming nigh, are ready to take him away.'

16. THEIR LYING IN WAIT,] *lit.* 'the inner seat;' as in 25. 3.

WENT,] *lit.* 'went along.. encampment and told (it) fully to Paul.'

17. CALLED,] *lit.* 'called forward.. Lead away this youth to the chiliarch.'

18. SO,] *lit.* 'he, then, indeed, having taken him along, led (him) to the chiliarch,.. having called me forward, asked (me) to lead this youth to thee.'

19. ASIDE,] *lit.* 'went back by themselves and was inquiring, What is it that.'

20. SAID,] *lit.* 'said, that, the Jews set themselves together to ask..mayest lead down.. to the sanhedrim, as about to inquire something concerning him more accurately.'

21. BUT,] *lit.* 'mayest thou therefore not trust to them..who placed themselves up (on the altar) neither to eat nor drink till they may take him away..the promise.'

22. SO,] *lit.* 'the chiliarch, then, indeed, let the youth away, having told him aside to speak out to no one, that thou didst secretly manifest these things to me.'

23. CALLED,] *lit.* 'called forward a certain two of the centurions..that they may pass on to Caesarea.'

AND SPEARMEN,] *or* 'even two-hundred right-hand men,' *lit.* those taking the right hand; it seems absurd to suppose 470 men, —nearly the half of the whole band—to have been sent with one prisoner.

THIRD HOUR,] i.e. nine o'clock, p.m.

24. PROVIDE,] *lit.* 'to set along-side also beasts (of burden), that having set Paul upon (one), they may save (him) thoroughly for Felix the Leader.'

25. AND,] *lit.* 'having written an epistle, which had this type (i.e. form of expression) about it.'

26. EXCELLENT,] *lit.* 'powerful,' expressive of position, not of character.

GOVERNOR,] *lit.* 'leader.'

GREETING,] *lit.* 'to leap for joy;' the infinitive being used for the imperative, as in Hebrew.

27. TAKEN,] *lit.* 'wholly taken by the Jews, and being about to be taken away by them, having stood over (them) with the soldiery I myself lifted him out (of the crowd), having learned that he is a Roman.'

28. WHEN,] *lit.* 'and taking counsel to know the cause for which they were calling him in (to judgment), I led him down to their sanhedrim.'

29. PERCEIVED,] *lit.* 'found called in (to judgment) concerning questions of their law, but having no calling in worthy of death or of bonds.'

30. TOLD,] *or* 'shewn to me of a contrary-counsel to be about to be by the Jews in reference to the man, from that (moment) I sent (him) to thee, having told at the same time also to those making (it) public against him, to say before thee the things regarding him. Be strengthened!' (A Hebraistic form of salutation.)

31. AS,] *lit.* 'according to that set thoroughly in array to them, having taken up Paul (on horseback), led (him) throughout the night towards Antipatris,' built by Herod the Great in honour of his father Antipater, forty miles from Jerusalem, on the way to Caesarea.

32. LEFT,] *lit.* 'suffered the horsemen to pass on with him, (for the remaining 25 miles), and they (themselves) turned round shortly to the encampment.'

33. WHEN,] *lit.* 'having come into Caesarea, and given up the epistle to the Leader, set also Paul alongside of him.'

34. PROVINCE,] *or* 'government he is, and having ascertained for himself that (he is) from Cilicia.'

35. HEAR,] *lit.* 'hear thoroughly of thee, when those making (it) public against thee may themselves come along..watched (*or* guarded) in the praetorium of Herod.'

Chapter XXIV. may be divided into three parts; v. 1—9 Paul accused by Tertullus; v. 10—21 He defends himself; v. 22—27 Felix defers sentence, trembles at Paul's preaching, and leaves him bound.

1. HIGH,] *or* 'foremost priest..presbyters ..speaker (*lit.* rhetorician) Tertullus (a Roman advocate perhaps), who made fully manifest to the Leader the things against Paul.'

2. ACCUSE,] *lit.* 'make public against (him the charges), saying, We having much peace (by the suppression of insurrections) because of thee, and very upright things happening to this nation through thy forethought (*or* public mind).'

3. ACCEPT,] *or* 'receive (it) from (thee), always and everywhere, most powerful Felix, with all thankfulness,' *lit.* 'good leaping for joy.'

4. NOTWITHSTANDING,] *lit.* 'and that I may not further weary thee much, I call upon thee to hear us concisely (*lit.* cutting-together) in thy clemency,' *lit.* 'yieldingness.'

5. A PESTILENT FELLOW,] *lit.* 'a pestilence ..habitable world, and one who stands first among the sect (*lit.* heresy, i.e. opinion, 'lifted' up) of the Nazarenes.'

6. HATH,] *lit.* 'who also tried to profane ..we took hold of, and wished to judge.'

7. CHIEF,] *lit.* 'but Lysias the chiliarch having come along, with much violence, led.'

8. ACCUSERS,] *lit.* 'those making (it) public against him to come before thee, (*or* alongside of) whom thou thyself having judged again mayest be able to know fully concerning all the things which we make public against him.'

9. ASSENTED,] *lit.* 'put themselves together (*or* with him), affirming these things to be so.'

10. GOVERNOR,] *or* 'leader,' for six or seven years.

FORASMUCH,] *lit.* 'having known fully of thy being for many years judge to this nation I do the more willingly speak fully of (*or* apologize for) the things about myself.'

11. BECAUSE,] *lit.* 'thou being able to know that it is not more than twelve days since I went up about to kiss forward (the hand) in Jerusalem.'

12. DISPUTING,] *or* 'reasoning..nor making an insurrection of the crowd, nor in the synagogues, nor throughout the city.'

13. NEITHER,] *lit.* 'nor are they able to

stand along-side of me concerning the things which they now make public against me.'

14. CONFESS,] *lit.* 'say the same thing.'

AFTER,] *lit.* 'down *or* according to a way which they call a sect (as in v. 5), so I go very tremblingly to the fathers' God.. written throughout the Law and in the prophets.'

15. ALLOW,] *or* 'receive fully—(for) an up-standing to be about to be of (the) dead, both of just and unjust.'

16. VOID OF OFFENCE,] *lit.* 'not striking towards' any one; see 23. 1.

17. CAME,] *lit.* 'came along, being about to do kind acts to my nation, and offerings,' *lit.* 'things borne forward (to God).' See Rom. 15. 25.

18. WHEREUPON,] *lit.* 'in which..sanctified..crowd..tumult.'

19. WHO OUGHT,] *lit.* 'whom it behoveth (*or* was behoving) to be present before thee, and to make it public against (me) if they would have anything against me.'

21. EVIL DOING,] *lit.* 'injustice *or* unrighteousness in me in my standing before the sanhedrim.'

22. TOUCHING,] *lit.* 'that, concerning (the) upstanding of (the) dead I am judged by you to-day.'

MORE PERFECTLY,] *lit.* 'having known more accurately the things concerning the way (i.e. Christianity), he himself cast them back, saying..may come down I will know thoroughly the things concerning you.'

23. COMMANDED,] *lit.* 'himself thoroughly arranged with the centurion to keep Paul, to (let him) have also relaxation, and to forbid none of his own (friends) to serve (*lit.* act as under-rower), or to come to him.'

24. CAME,] *lit.* 'came along..he himself sent after Paul,.. faith in reference to Christ.'

25. OF,] *lit.* 'concerning..temperance (*lit.* inward power), and the judgment that is about to be, Felix became inwardly afraid ..Be passing on for the present, and having got time afterwards.'

26. MONEY,] *or* 'necessary things shall be given him by Paul..him oftener, and was conversing with him.'

27. AFTER,] *lit.* 'but two years having been filled out, Felix received a successor Porcius Festus, and Felix wishing to put down a favour (*or* grace, *lit.* thing causing leaping for joy) to the Jews, left Paul fully bound,' hoping to mollify their opposition to himself. Jos. Ant. xx. 8. 10.

Chapter XXV. may be divided into three parts; v. 1—12 the Jews accusing Paul to Festus, he appeals to Caesar; v. 13—22 which Festus relates to Agrippa; v. 23—27 who desires to hear Paul himself, and Paul is brought forth.

1. NOW,] *lit.* 'Festus, therefore, having come up upon the province,' *or* prefecture, as in 23. 34.

2. CHIEF,] *lit.* 'first men..and were calling upon him.'

3. DESIRED,] *lit.* 'asked favour *or* grace,' *lit.* a cause of joy)

LAYING WAIT,] *lit.* 'making an ambush to take him away through the way.'

4. SHOULD BE,] *lit.* 'is to be kept in Caesarea, and himself to be about speedily to pass on hence.'

5. SAID,] *lit* 'says..and if there be any thing in this man, let them make (it) public against him.'

6. TARRIED,] *lit.* 'rubbed thoroughly,' i.e. spent.

MORE,] *or* 'not more than eight or ten days..tribunal.'

7. COME,] *lit.* 'come along..bare many and heavy causes (of complaint)..they had no power to show forth.'

8. ANSWERED,] *lit.* 'apologized.. neither in reference to the law of the Jews nor in reference to the temple, nor in reference to Caesar, did I sin anything.'

9. WILLING,] *lit.* 'wishing to put down for himself a favour (*or* grace) to the Jews ..Dost thou wish..concerning these.'

10. AT,] *or* 'before (*lit.* upon) Caesar's tribunal I am standing, where it behoveth me to be judged, to the Jews I did nothing unjust, as thou also very well knowest fully.'

11. I BE,] *lit.* 'for if, indeed, I am unjust, and have done (*or* practised) any thing worthy of death, I deprecate not to die fully.. which these make public against me, no one is able to make me a cause of rejoicing to them, (that is, by giving me up to their wishes), I call upon Caesar!' (i.e. Nero).

12. APPEALED,] *lit.* 'called upon Caesar for thyself? to Caesar thou shalt pass on.

13. AFTER,] *lit.* 'and certain days having fully come Agrippa (son of H. A. xiii.) the king and Bernice (grand-daughter of Salome), came down to Caesarea, about to embrace Festus.'

14. HAD BEEN,] *lit.* 'they spent (rubbed through) many days there, Festus himself put forth the things against Paul to the king, saying.'

15. DESIRING,] *lit.* 'asking justice upon him.'

16. IT IS,] *lit.* 'that it is not a custom of Romans to make a favour of any man to utter-loss, before that he whom anything is made public against, may have those making it public against (him) face to face, and may receive also a place of apology concerning the thing for which he is called in.'

17. COME,] *lit.* 'come together hither, I myself making no delay (*lit.* casting back), on the next (day) having sat upon the tribunal I commanded.'

18. AGAINST,] *lit.* 'concerning whom.. they were bringing no cause (of complaint) of the things I was thinking about.'

19. SUPERSTITION,] *lit.* 'demon-worship;' see Acts 17. 22.

DEAD,] *lit.* 'and of a certain Jesus deceased.'

20. BECAUSE,] *lit.* 'and I doubtful (*lit.* passage-less) in regard to the question concerning this, said, If he would counsel to pass on to Jerusalem, and there be judged concerning these things.'

21. HAD APPEALED,] *lit.* 'openly called

for himself to be kept for the full-knowledge of Sebastus,' i.e. Augustus.

22. I WOULD,] *lit.* 'I was counselling also myself to hear the man.'

23. POMP,] *lit.* 'show,..the audience-chamber, with the chiliarch, and the prominent.'

24. HAVE DEALT,] *lit.* 'have been in to me ..crying openly.'

25. FOUND,] *lit.* 'but I, having taken down that..and that he also had called for himself upon Sebastus, I judged to send him.'

26. MY LORD,] *lit.* 'to the lord' of the empire, i.e. Augustus.

EXAMINATION,] *lit.* 'a re-judging having happened.'

27. UNREASONABLE,] *or* 'irrational, sending a prisoner, and not to signify (*or* notify) the causes (of complaint) against him.'

Chapter XXVI. may be divided into two parts; v. 1—23 Paul's defence of himself; v. 24—32 its effects upon Festus and Agrippa.

1. THOU ART,] *lit.* 'it is turned over upon thee to speak for thyself.'

ANSWERED,] *lit.* 'was making an apology.'

2. THINK,] *lit.* 'I have thought myself happy, king Agrippa, being about to make an apology before thee to-day concerning all things of which I am called in (to court) by the Jews.'

3. ESPECIALLY,] *lit.* 'especially (because of) thy being acquainted with all the customs.'

PATIENTLY,] *lit.* 'with length of mind.'

4. MY YOUTH,] *lit.* 'from youth, which happened from the beginning (to be) among my own nation in Jerusalem.'

5. KNEW,] *lit.* 'knowing me openly from the above (period), if they may wish to testify, that, according to the most exact sect (*lit.* heresy, an opinion 'lifted up,' whether right or wrong), of our religion (*lit.* bawling, making a noise,) I lived a Pharisee.'

6. STAND,] *lit.* 'have stood, being judged about (the) hope.'

7. TWELVE TRIBES,] as in James 1. 1; the two tribes who returned from Babylon having gradually gathered to themselves all of the other ten tribes who feared God, were recognized as the true representatives of Israel, while those remaining among the heathen became themselves heathens, or mixed with their Jewish brethren in other lands.

INSTANTLY,] *lit.* 'with intensity night and day trembling much (towards God), hope to come down (*or* fully)..because of which hope, king Agrippa, I am called in by the Jews.'

8. SHOULD,] *lit.* 'is it judged incredible with you—if God doth raise (the) dead.'

10. SHUT UP,] *lit.* 'shut down..the authority..taken away I carried a vote against (them).'

11. PUNISHED,] *lit.* 'and punishing often through all the synagogues I was necessitating them to speak injuriously..at them, I was pursuing (*or* 'causing to flee') even unto the cities without (the land of Judea).

12. WHEREUPON,] *lit.* 'in which things also passing on to Damascus, commission (*lit.* a thing 'turned over upon' any one).'

13. IN,] *lit.* 'down *or* through..shining of ..shining around and those passing on with me.'

14. FALLEN,] *lit.* 'fallen down..Hebrew dialect (of that age): Saul, Saul, why me dost thou pursue?'

15. PERSECUTEST,] *or* 'pursuest.'

16. RISE,] *lit.* 'stand up..for I (have) appeared to thee with a view to this, to hand thee forward an under-servant and witness both of the things thou sawest, and of the things (in which) I shall appear to thee.'

17. DELIVERING,] *lit.* 'lifting thee up out of the people and (out) of the nations, to whom now I send thee away.'

18. TURN,] *lit.* 'turn (them) over from darkness..authority of the Adversary upon God, for their receiving forgiveness (*lit.* a sending away) of sins, and a lot among those sanctified (*lit.* set apart *or* declared not of the earth), by faith that is toward me.'

19. WAS,] *or* 'became..sight.'

20. SHEWED,] *lit.* 'I was telling forth first to those in Damascus, and (in) Jerusalem, and to all the region of Judea, and to the nations, to change (their) minds and turn over upon God, doing works worthy of the change-of-mind.'

21. CAUGHT,] *lit.* 'took me together (*or* at once), and were trying to handle me roughly.'

22. OBTAINED,] *or* 'had help (*or* an over-helmet) from God, I have stood unto..say as being about to happen.'

23. THAT,] *lit.* 'whether the Christ (must) suffer, whether first by an upstanding of (the) dead he is about to tell light fully to the people (of Israel), and to the nations.'

24. THUS,] *lit.* 'these things..great voice ..thou art mad; the many letters do turn thee round into madness.'

25. SAID,] *lit.* 'says..most powerful Festus, but utter forth sayings of truth and a sound-mind.'

26. KNOWETH,] *lit.* 'knoweth fully concerning these things..speak freely (*or* with all open speech),..has not been done.'

27. KNOW,] *lit.* 'I have known.'

28. ALMOST,] *lit.* 'in a little thou dost persuade me to become a Christian;' this is clearly the language of hardened contempt not of sincere conviction.

29. I WOULD,] *lit.* 'I would have wished to God, both in a little (time) and in much (degree, that) not only thou, but also all those hearing me to-day, to become altogether.'

30. THUS,] *lit.* 'these things..stood up, and the Leader, Bernice also and those sitting together with them.'

31. GONE ASIDE,] *lit.* 'and having withdrawn they were speaking to one another saying that.'

32. MIGHT,] *lit.* 'was able to have been wholly loosed, if he had not called for himself upon Caesar.'

Chapter XXVII. may be divided into five parts; v. 1—8 Paul sails to the Fair Havens; v. 9—16 and from thence to Clauda; v. 17—29 ship driven about; v. 30—38 sailors try to escape, prevented, and all encouraged by Paul; v. 39—44 ship broken up, but all lives saved.

1. DETERMINED,] *lit.* 'our (Luke and Paul) sailing to Italy was decided, they were giving over Paul to a centurion, Julius by name, of the cohort of Sebastus,' i.e. Augustus.

2. ADRAMYTTIUM,] on the N.E. coast of the Agean sea.

WE LAUNCHED,] *lit.* 'being about to sail to the place along (proconsular) Asia, we were brought up, there being with us Aristarchus, a Macedonian of Thessalonica.' (See 19. 20; 20. 4; Col. 4. 14; Phil. 24.)

3. TOUCHED,] *lit.* 'were brought down to Sidon (70 miles north of Caesarea), and Julius behaving humanely to Paul, turned over upon (him) as he passed on to the friends (of Christ, 11. 19; 21. 4) to receive much care.'

4. HAD LAUNCHED,] *lit.* 'were brought up ..because of the winds being contrary.'

5. SAILED OVER,] *lit.* 'sailed through the sea over against Cilicia (Paul's native shores) ..we came down to Myra of Lycia.'

6. SHIP OF,] *lit.* 'an Alexandrian ship (of burden bearing corn),..caused us to go up into it.'

7. MANY,] *lit.* 'during many days, and scarcely coming.. not suffering us (to go) forward, we sailed.'

8. HARDLY,] *or* 'scarcely lying near it, we came to a certain place called Fair Havens (a little east of cape Matala,) nigh to which was a city, Lasea.'

9. SPENT,] *lit.* 'come through (since leaving Caesarea), and the sailing being already much retarded, because of the fast (of the day of atonement) having already come along (at the end of September), Paul was admonishing (*or* speaking much).'

10. SIRS,] *lit.* 'men,..the sailing is about to be..burden and of the ship.. our souls.'

11. BELIEVED,] *lit.* 'was believing.'

MASTER,] *or* 'pilot and the shipowner.'

12. COMMODIOUS,] *lit.* 'not well set.'

MORE PART,] *or* 'most gave counsel to go up from thence.'

PHENICE,] *or* Phenix, now called *Sphacia*, or Lutro.

LIETH,] *lit.* 'is looking.'

13. THE,] *lit.* 'a south wind blew somewhat.'

LOOSING,] *lit.* 'lifting up (the anchor).'

SAILED,] *lit.* 'lay along very near to.'

14. AROSE,] *lit.* 'beat..Euroclydon,' i.e. Eastern Wave, blowing E. N. E.

15. CAUGHT,] *lit.* 'wholly seized..against the wind, giving her up, we were borne on.'

16. ISLAND,] *lit.* 'little isle called Clauda (now Gonzo) we had scarcely strength to become masters of the boat,' *lit.* 'skiff.'

17. USED,] *lit.* 'were using..might fall off towards the Syrtis,' now called the Gulf of Sidra, on the coast of Africa, south west of Crete.

STRAKE SAIL,] *lit.* 'let down the mast (*lit.* instrument), and so were borne on.'

18. LIGHTENED,] *lit.* 'were making a clearance,' *lit.* casting out.

TACKLING,] *lit.* 'instrument *or* furniture.'

20. IN,] *lit.* 'during many days appeared, (opened *or* shone over us), and not a little tempest *or* wintry weather..of our being saved was wholly taken away.'

21. SIRS,] *lit.* 'O men, it behoved (you), indeed, trusting to me as to a chief, not to be brought up from Crete,..and damage.'

22. EXHORT,] *lit.* 'praise,' as in v. 9.

GOOD-CHEER,] *lit.* 'good-mind.'

LOSS,] *lit.* 'casting away.'

23. STOOD BY,] *lit.* 'stood along-side of me ..a messenger (16. 9; 23. 11)..I serve,' *lit.* to whom I tremble much, *or* go very tremblingly.

24. MUST,] *lit.* 'it behoveth thee to stand alongside of Caesar..has granted.'

25. GOOD CHEER,] *lit.* 'good mind, men!.. has been spoken to me.'

26. MUST,] *lit.* 'it behoves us to fall out (of our way) into a certain isle.'

27. WAS COME,] *or* 'came, we being borne up and down in the Adrian (sea), through the middle of the night, the sailors were thinking secretly to go towards a certain region.'

28. SOUNDED,] *lit.* 'cast (the lead) they found twenty fathoms,' of six feet each, *lit.* length of the limbs *or* human frame.

GONE,] *lit.* 'stood a little separate.'

29. SHOULD,] *lit.* 'might fall on rough places..and were wishing (*or* praying) day to come.'

30. SHIPMEN,] *or* 'sailors are seeking..the skiff into..in pretence as being about to extend,' or carry out.

31. ABIDE,] *or* 'remain..ye are not able to be saved.'

32. CUT OFF,] *or* 'cut away the ropes,' *lit.* bull rushes, being made of such.

33. WHILE,] *lit.* 'till the day was about to come Paul was calling (them) all to take further nourishment, saying, Fourteen days to-day, looking forward, ye continue (*lit.* end thoroughly) fasting, having taken nothing to yourselves.'

34. PRAY,] *lit.* 'call upon you to take nourishment to yourselves..your salvation,' *or* safety.

35. THUS,] *lit.* 'these things..a loaf.'

36. WERE,] *lit.* 'became..good mind..took to themselves nourishment.'

38. ENOUGH,] *lit.* 'abundance of nourishment, they were lightening.'

39. WAS,] *lit.* 'when day came they were not knowing (anything) about the land, but were minding fully a certain bay having a beach, into which they took counsel, to drive forth the ship, if possible,' *or* if they were able.

40. TAKEN UP,] *lit.* 'lifted up round about ..they were giving (the ship) to the sea, at the same time..they were holding down (*or* through) to the beach.'

41. FALLING,] *lit.* 'falling around into a place—an isthmus—they drove the ship up ..broken,' *lit.* loosed or loosening.

42. WAS,] *lit.* 'and there came a counsel of the soldiers, in order that they might

utterly kill the prisoners, lest any one swimming out may flee abroad.'

43. WILLING,] *lit.* 'taking counsel to save Paul thoroughly, hindered them from the counsel, . . those able to swim, having cast themselves forth first, to go out upon the land.'

44. BROKEN,] *lit.* 'on certain of the things of the ship . . were all thoroughly saved upon the land.'

Chapter XXVIII. may be divided into five parts; v. 1—6 Paul saved from a viper; v. 7—10 and cures many diseases; v. 11—15 proceeds to Rome; v. 16—24 calls the Jews and reasons with them; v. 25—31 reproves them and turns to the Gentiles.

1. ESCAPED,] *lit.* 'and having been thoroughly saved, then they knew also that the island is called Melita,' now Malta, between Sicily and Africa.

2. BARBAROUS,] *lit.* 'barbarians,' i.e. 'rustics, clowns;' they were Phenician colonists. SHEWED,] *lit.* 'were holding along to us no ordinary philanthropy, for having set fire to a pile of wood, they received us all to themselves, because of the present (*or* imminent) rain.'

3. GATHERED,] *lit.* 'turned round together a quantity of faggots, and laid over upon the fire . . fastened thoroughly.'

4. HANG,] *lit.* 'suspended *or* suspending itself from his hand, they said to one another, Certainly . . escaped (*lit.* been thoroughly saved out of) the sea, the justice (of God) did not suffer to live.'

6. HOWBEIT,] *lit.* 'but they were thinking of him being about to be inflamed, or to fall down . . nothing unseasonable . . a god.' See 14. 13, 19; Mark 16. 18.

7. POSSESSION,] *lit.* 'regions *or* lands of the Foremost man (an official title) . . received us up.'

8. LAY SICK,] *lit.* 'was laid down, held together by feverish heats and dysentery . . poured forth before (God).'

9. DISEASES,] *lit.* 'infirmities . . were coming forward.'

10. WHEN,] *lit.* 'and we being brought up, they laid upon us the things (requisite) for the need.'

11. DEPARTED,] *lit.* 'were brought up in a ship (which had wintered in the isle) of Alexandria, (see 27. 6) with the sign along (it) of Dioskouroi,' i.e. 'twins of Jupiter,' the titular gods of mariners.

12. LANDED,] *lit.* 'been brought down to Syracuse, (80 miles north of Malta,) we remained over three days.'

13. FETCHED A COMPASS,] *lit.* 'came round and came down to Rhegium (now Reggio) . . a south wind having come over (it), we came . . to Puteoli,' now Pozzuolli.

14. DESIRED,] *lit.* 'called upon (by Julius perhaps) to remain over upon them.'

15. OF US,] *lit.* 'the things about us, they came forth to meet us unto Appii Forum (i.e. 'market-place of Appias,' forty-one miles from Rome) and Trion Tabernon (i.e. 'three taverns,' about thirty miles from Rome).'

16. DELIVERED,] *lit.* 'gave over . . chief of the encampment (supposed to have been Burrus Aframus) but to Paul it was turned over to remain by himself with the soldiers guarding him.'

17. CHIEF,] *lit.* 'foremost men . . Men, brethren, . . done nothing . . of the fathers, I was given over.'

18. EXAMINED,] *lit.* 'judged me again (*or* thoroughly) counselled to.'

19. CONSTRAINED,] *lit.* 'necessitated to call for myself upon Caesar, not as having anything to make public against my nation.'

20. HAVE,] *lit.* 'did I call you near to see.' HOPE OF ISRAEL,] i.e. the promised Messiah; see 26. 6, 7.
BOUND,] *lit.* 'laid around.'

21. ANY,] *lit.* 'any one . . came along told . . any evil about thee.'

22. DESIRE,] *lit.* 'think it fitting to hear from thee . . sect (*Gr.* heresy) it is known to us.

23. APPOINTED,] *lit.* arranged . . set forth and testified thoroughly the reign of God, persuading them of the things about Jesus, both from.'

24. BELIEVED,] *lit.* 'were believing . . were not believing.'

25. AGREED NOT,] *lit.* 'sounded not together with one another, they were let go, Paul having said one saying (*or* thing), that;' see Mat. 13. 13—15.

26. GO,] *lit.* 'pass on . . with hearing ye shall hear, and ye shall not bring (your minds) with it, and beholding ye shall behold, and shall not see.'

27. IS WAXED GROSS,] *lit.* 'was made fat, *or* made itself fat, and with the ears they heard heavily, and their eyes they shut down, lest at any time they may see with the eyes, and hear with the ears, and with the heart bring (things) together, and turn round upon (me), and I may heal them.'

28. IS,] *lit.* 'was sent away to the nations;' see 13. 46; 18. 6.

29. WORDS,] *or* 'things . . much seeking together among themselves.

30. DWELT,] *lit.* 'remained an entire two years . . received openly all those passing in to him.'

31. PREACHING,] *lit.* 'crying *or* proclaiming as a herald the reign of the (true) God, and teaching the things concerning the Lord Jesus Christ, with all full-speech unhindered.'

PAUL'S LETTER TO THE ROMANS

THAT this Letter is the composition of the Apostle Paul has never been seriously questioned by any one, and needs not be here discussed. It was written A.D. 58, in Corinth, when Paul was about to visit Jerusalem with an offering for the poor saints, see Rom. 15. 23—28 compared with Acts 20. 2, 3; 24. 17, also 16. 21, 23 with Acts 20. 4; 1 Cor. 1. 14; and it was sent to Rome by Phebe (16. 1) a deaconess of Cenchrae, the eastern port of Corinth.

The strangers of Rome (Acts 2. 10) who heard the apostles on the day of Pentecost were undoubtedly the founders of the church of Christ in their native city; there is no good proof that Peter was ever at Rome, certainly not at least when Paul wrote to the church there, or he would most assuredly have given in it some indication (however slight) of his presence among the many Christian salutations he sends to it. A majority of the Christians at Rome at that date were of Jewish origin, hence the apostle's frequent references to the Mosaic Law (unlike the Letter to the almost wholly Gentile Church of Ephesus), but still there were in it many Gentiles; see 1. 13—15; 15. 15, 16).

This Letter is placed first of all the Apostolic Letters because of its being longer than any of the others, of its thorough exhibition of Christian faith and practice, and of the pre-eminence of the church at Rome over all others. It was written, not in Latin, but in Greek, like all the other New Testament books, and for the same good reason, viz. that Greek was universally known. It may be divided into *two* great divisions, ch. i—xi chiefly *doctrinal*, and ch. xii—xvi chiefly *practical;* or into five parts, ch. i—v treating on *Justification;* ch. vi—viii on *Sanctification;* ch. ix—xi on *Calling and Rejection;* ch. xii—xv. 13 on *Christian Practice;* ch. xv. 14—xvi. 27 the *conclusion.*

Chapter I. may be divided into four parts; v. 1—7 Paul's salutation; v. 8—12 thanksgiving and prayers; v. 13—18 desire to see them and proclaim the Gospel righteousness of God; v. 19—32 inexcusable vileness of the heathen.

1. PAUL,] i.e. the 'little' one; see on Acts 13. 9.

A SERVANT,] *lit.* 'bondsman,' one who is 'bound' to do anything.

JESUS CHRIST,] i.e. the 'anointed saviour.'

CALLED TO BE,] *lit.* 'a called apostle;' not self-sent; see Acts 9. 5; 23. 14; 1 Cor. 9. 1.

SEPARATED,] *lit.* 'thoroughly marked out.'

GOSPEL,] *lit.* 'good-news of God.'

2. PROMISED,] *lit.* 'which he himself told beforehand (*or* publicly) through his prophets in holy (i.e. 'not of the earth,') writings.'

3. CONCERNING,] *or* 'in behalf of his Son, who is come out of David's seed, according to (his) flesh,' i.e. his human nature.

4. DECLARED,] *lit.* 'who is marked out Son of God in power (i.e. powerfully), according to (his) spirit of holiness, by (*lit.* out of) an up-standing from the dead,—Jesus Christ our Lord.'

5. BY,] *lit.* 'through whom we received grace (*lit.* that which causes 'leaping for joy,') and apostleship, with a view to an obedience of faith (i.e. a stedfast obedience, *lit.* a hearkening submissively) in *or* among all the nations.'

6. THE CALLED,] *lit.* 'called (ones) of Jesus Christ.'

7. BELOVED,] *lit.* 'to the beloved of God, to the called holy ones.'

PEACE,] *lit.* 'that which brings into unity.'

OUR FATHER,] *lit.* 'Father of us, and of our Lord Jesus Christ.'

8. THANK,] *lit.* 'leap much with joy before God..that the faith *or* stedfastness of you is.'

9. WHOM,] *lit.* 'to *or* with whom I go very tremblingly in my spirit..make remembrance.'

10. MAKING REQUEST,] *or* 'beseeching *or* wanting.'

11. IMPART,] *lit.* 'gave over to you some spiritual grace..be confirmed.'

12. COMFORTED,] *or* 'exhorted together among you.'

13. PURPOSED,] *or* 'set myself forward *or* publicly..was hindered..the other nations.'

14. GREEKS.] *lit.* 'Hellenes..to wise *or* skilful ones, and to thoughtless ones.'

15. I AM READY,] *lit.* 'the forward mind is in me myself to tell the good-news.'

16. OF CHRIST,] *lit.* 'of the Christ, for it is a power..to all those believing *or* remaining stedfast; to the Jew foremost, and to Hellen.'

17. THE,] *lit.* 'is a righteousness of God uncovered out of *or* by faith..has been written, But the just (righteous *or* right one) out of *or* by faith (*or* stedfastness) shall live.' See Hab. 2. 4.

18. THE,] *lit.* 'for wrath of God is uncovered..upon all *or* every irreverence and unrighteousness *or* injustice of men, who are holding down the truth in *or* by unrighteousness *or* injustice.'

19. MAY BE,] *lit.* 'is known..apparent among them..did make it apparent to them.'

20. CREATION,] *lit.* 'building *or* formation ..perpetual power and godhead, with a view to their being without apology.'

21. THANKFUL,] *lit.* 'did leap much for joy..their reasonings, and their unintelligent heart became dark.'

22. PROFESSING,] *or* 'affirming..skilful.'

23. CHANGED,] *or* 'exchanged .into the likeness of an image of.'

24. GAVE THEM UP,] *or* 'over to uncleanness, in *or* with the full-minds of their hearts, for their own bodies to be dishonoured among themselves.'

25. CHANGED,] *lit.* 'exchanged..with the lying thing (i.e. idol), and reverenced and went very tremblingly to *or* with the creature (*or* created thing), more than to *or* with the creator *or* builder, who is well-spoken-of to the ages.'

26. UP,] *or* 'over to an affection of dishonour..females exchanged.'

27. MEN,] *lit.* 'males..the female, burned exceedingly in their lust, (*lit.* extending of the arms) to one another; males with males working thoroughly the shameful thing.'

28. LIKE,] *lit.* 'think *or* approve of having God in full-knowledge..an unthinking *or* disapproved mind..not fit.'

29. UNRIGHTEOUSNESS,] *or* 'injustice, whoredom, evil, covetousness, badness, full of envy, murder, strife, guile, bad customs, whisperers.'

30. BACKBITERS,] *lit.* 'speakers-down,' i.e. detractors.

31. UNDERSTANDING,] *lit.* 'not sending things together,..unpoured forth, unkind.'

32. JUDGMENT,] *lit.* 'just judgment..those practising..but also are well-pleased along with those practising (them).'

Chapter II. may be divided into five parts; v. 1, 2 every one self-condemned; v. 3—10 God's forbearance and judgments on all; v. 11—16 who are judged righteously; v. 17—24 Jewish boasting and condemnation; v. 25—29 circumcision of heart better than that of letter only.

1. INEXCUSABLE,] *lit.* 'without apology.. art judging..the other..art judging dost practise.'

2. ARE SURE,] *lit.* 'have known..upon those practising.'

3. THINKEST,] *or* 'reckonest..art judging those practising such things, and art doing the same..shall flee out of.'

4. DESPISEST,] *lit.* 'thinkest thou down upon..his benignity..benignity of.. to another mind.'

5. AFTER,] *lit.* 'according to.. anger in a day of anger, and of uncovering of.'

6. WILL,] *or* 'shall give back to each according to his works.'

7. BY,] *lit.* 'through.. are seeking glory .. incorruptibility.'

9. TRIBULATION,] *lit.* 'trouble and straitness.. that is working thoroughly that which is bad, both of Jew.. of Hellen.'

10. WORKETH,] *lit.* 'that is working that which is good.'

11. RESPECT,] *lit.* 'lifting up of faces.'

12. HAVE,] *lit.* 'as sinned' (i.e. missed the mark).. also be fully loosed away.. as sinned.. judged through law.'

13. BEFORE,] *lit.* 'alongside of God.. declared just.'

14. THE,] *lit.* 'where nations.. not a law, may do by.. a law.'

15. SHEW,] *lit.* 'shew inwardly .. thoughts *or* reasonings between one another either making it public against them or apologizing.'

16. THE,] *lit.* 'in a day when God shall *or* does judge.. through Jesus Christ.'

17. CALLED,] *or* 'surnamed.. restest back upon.. in God.'

18. MORE EXCELLENT,] *lit.* 'bearing on differently, being instructed in the law.'

19. GUIDE,] *lit.* 'one bringing on the way.'

20. THE,] *lit.* 'of thoughtless ones.. of the knowledge.'

21. TEACHEST,] *lit.* 'art teaching another ..criest as a herald not to steal.'

22. SAYEST,] *lit.* 'art saying not to commit .. art abhorring the idols, dost thou rob temples.'

23. OF,] *lit.* 'in the law, through the transgression.'

24. BLASPHEMED,] *lit.* 'injuriously spoken of.. has been written.'

25. CIRCUMCISION,] *lit.* 'a cutting-round.' KEEP,] *lit.* 'mayest practise law.. a transgressor of law..has become uncircumcision,' *lit.* a foreskin.

27. FULFIL,] *lit.* 'finish (*or* complete).. who through.. art a transgressor of law.'

28. HE,] *lit.* 'for the (true) Jew is not in the appearance (only), neither the (true) circumcision in the appearance, in flesh.'

29. HE,] *lit.* 'but the (true) Jew is in the secret.. in spirit not letter, whose public praise is.'

Chapter III. may be divided into five parts; v. 1, 2 the Jew's privileges; v. 3—8 which are not made entirely useless; v. 9—18 Jew and Gentile alike wicked; v. 19, 20 by works of law none are declared just; v. 21—31 but by faith or stedfastness.

1. ADVANTAGE,] *or* 'superiority.'

2. CHIEFLY,] *lit.* 'for foremost, indeed,.. the little words of God,' i.e. short revelations at different times and divers manners.

3. BELIEVE,] *or* 'were faithless *or* unstedfast? shall their faithlessness make the faithfulness of God at all useless?'

4. GOD FORBID,] *lit.* 'let it not be (*or* happen), but let God be true..has been written, so that..thy words .judged *or* judging for thyself.'

5. COMMEND,] *lit.* 'stands together with. who is bearing on the anger?'

6. GOD FORBID,] *lit.* 'let it not be (*or* happen)!..shall *or* does God'

7. HATH,] *lit.* 'did more abound in *or* by ..judged sinful?'

8. SLANDEROUSLY,] *or* 'injuriously spoken of..do the bad things, that the good ones may come, whose judgment (of condemnation) is inwardly just.'

9. BETTER,] *or* 'do we hold ourselves forward? not at all, for we ourselves made a former charge of both Jews and Gentiles being all.'

10. IS,] *lit.* 'has been written,..not even one.'

11. UNDERSTANDETH,] *lit.* 'is sending *or* bringing things together .earnestly seeking

12. GONE OUT,] 'declined greatly.'

13. OPEN,] *or* 'opened-up sepulchre.. were using guile.'
14. CURSING,] *or* 'execration.'
15. SWIFT,] *or* 'sharp to pour forth blood.'
16. DESTRUCTION,] *lit.* 'a full-crushing and hard endurance are.'
17. THE,] *or* 'a way of peace they knew not.'
18. BEFORE,] *lit.* 'over-against their eyes.'
19. WE KNEW,] *lit.* 'we have known, that, as many thiugs as.. come under judgment to God.'
20. BY THE,] *lit.* 'out of works of law.. through law is a full knowledge of sin.'
21. WITHOUT,] *lit.* 'apart from law has been manifested *or* apparent, being testified to.'
22. BY,] *lit.* 'through the faith of.. those believing.'
23. HAVE,] *lit.* 'did sin, and are behind of.'
24. REDEMPTION,] *lit.* 'a thorough loosing.'
25. SET FORTH,] *or* 'set publicly a place of propitiation.. with a view to an inward shewing of his righteousness, because of the passing over of the sins formerly *or* publicly done, in the holding back of God.'
26. TO DECLARE,] *lit.* 'towards an inward shewing at the present time of his rightousness,..of him who is of the faith of Jesus.'
27. BOASTING,] *lit.* 'the boasting then? It was shut out! Through what law? of the works?'
28. CONCLUDE,] *or* 'reckon a man to be.. apart from works of law.'
30. BY,] *lit.* 'out of faith.. through the faith.'
31. THERE,] *or* 'therefore make law useless through the faith? let it not happen! we set up law!'

Chapter IV. may be divided into three parts; v. 1—17 justification by faith apart from works of law; v. 18—22 account of Abraham's faith; v. 23—25 application to us.
1. THEN,] *lit.* 'what, therefore, shall we say Abraham cur father to have found, according to flesh?'
2. BY,] *lit.* 'out of works, he has a cause of boasting.'
3. BELIEVED,] *or* 'remained stedfast to God, and it was reckoned to him with a view to righteousness.'
4. WORKETH,] *lit.* 'is working is the hire.'
5. WORKETH,] *lit.* 'is not working, but believing.. the irreverent.. reckoned with a view to righteousness.'
6. DESCRIBETH,] *lit.* 'speaketh of the happiness of.. reckons.. apart from works.'
7. BLESSED,] *lit.* 'happy they whose lawless acts are sent away.'
8. BLESSED,] *lit.* 'happy.. reckon sin.'
9. BLESSEDNESS,] *or* 'happiness.. that the faith.. with a view to righteousness.'
11. ALL,] *lit.* 'all those believing, through uncircumcision'
12. THE,] *lit.* 'and father of circumcision .. step *or* tread in the steps *or* tracks of the faith.. in the circumcision.'
13. HEIR,] *lit.* one to whom a 'distribution by lot' is made.
THE,] *lit.* 'through law.'

14. HEIRS,] *or* 'if the heirs are out of *or* by law, the faith has been made vain, and the promise useless.'
15. WRATH,] *or* 'anger against (all).'
16. BY,] *or* 'according to grace.'
17. IT IS,] *lit.* 'it has been written, I have set thee father..who is making the dead alive, and calling the things.'
18. AGAINST,] *or* 'beyond hope..that said.
19. WEAK,] *or* 'infirm in the faith, he thought not little of his body already become dead, being about.'
20. STAGGERED,] *lit.* 'judged not diversely in the faithlessness, but became powerful in the faith.'
21. PERSUADED,] *or* 'borne on..has promised he is able also to do.'
22. FOR,] *lit.* 'with a view to righteousness.'
24. SHALL,] *lit.* 'it is about to be reckoned, to those believing on him.'
25. DELIVERED,] *lit.* 'given over because of our fallings (from duty), and was raised up because of our being declared just.'

Chapter V. may be divided into two parts; v. 1—10 results of justification; v. 11—21 parallel between Adam and Christ.
1. BEING,] *lit.* 'having been declared righteous by (*lit.* out of) faith, we have (*or* may we) peace toward God.'
2. BY,] *lit.* 'through whom also we have (had) the introduction (*or* leading near) by the faith with a view to this grace in which we have stood, and we boast upon hope.'
3. GLORY,] *lit.* 'boast in the troubles also, having known that the trouble worketh out endurance.'
4. PATIENCE,] *lit.* 'and the endurance, approval, and the approval, hope.'
5. HOPE,] *lit.* 'and the hope bringeth not shame down upon (us) .has been poured forth.. through holy spirit that was given to us.'
6. WITHOUT STRENGTH,] *lit.* 'infirm. through time Christ fully died in behalf of irreverent ones.'
8. COMMENDETH,] *lit.* 'sets with (this) his own love..in our behalf.'
9. BY,] *lit.* 'in his blood..the wrath.'
10. RECONCILED,] *lit.* 'thoroughly changed to..having been thoroughly changed . in his life.'
11. JOY,] *lit.* 'are boasting in God.. through whom we now received the thorough-change.'
12. BY,] *lit.* 'through one man the sin.. and the death through the sin, and so the death came through to all men, because that all sinned.'
13. IMPUTED,] *or* 'reckoned.'
14. DEATH,] *lit.* 'the death..who did not sin upon the..is a type of him who is about to be.'
15. OFFENCE,] *or* 'trespass (*lit.* falling off) so also the grace, for if in (*or* by) the falling away of the one the many died fully,..in (*or* by) grace, by the one.. did abound to the many.'
16. BY,] *lit.* 'through .judgment of the one is to..the grace..fallings off to.'

17. BY,] *lit.* 'in the falling-off of the one the death reigned through the one, . . those receiving the abundance of the grace . . of the righteousness . . through the one.'

18. BY,] *lit.* 'through one falling-off (it is) to all . . through one righteous act (it is) to all.'

19. BY,] *lit.* 'through the hearkening amiss of the one man the many were set down sinners, so also through the submissive hearkening of the one shall the many be declared righteous.'

20. THE,] *lit.* 'but law came in along-side that the falling-off might abound, . . the sin . . the grace.'

21. SIN,] *lit.* 'the sin . . the death . . the grace . . the eternal life through.'

Chapter VI. may be divided into two parts; v. 1—11 believers baptized, buried, planted, crucified, dead, and raised with Jesus; v. 12—23 and are no longer under sin and law, but under holiness and grace.

1. SHALL,] *or* 'do we say? . . remain over the sin, that the grace.'

2. GOD FORBID,] *lit.* 'let it not happen! . . who died in *or* by the sin.'

3. INTO,] *lit.* 'with a view to.'

4. ARE,] *lit.* 'were entombed with him, through the baptism, with a view to the death . . through the glory . . walk about.'

5. BEEN,] *lit.* 'have become planted.'

6. IS,] *lit.* 'was crucified . . of the sin might be made useless . . not be in bondage to the sin.'

7. IS DEAD,] *lit.* 'died has been declared righteous from *or* by the sin.'

8. BE DEAD,] *lit.* 'if we died.'

9. KNOWING,] *lit.* 'having known . . death is no longer his lord.'

10. IN THAT HE,] *or* 'for he who died, died to the sin at once, but he who liveth, liveth to God.'

11. SIN,] *lit.* 'to the sin . . in Jesus Christ.'

12. SIN,] *lit.* 'the sin . . dying body, with a view to (your) hearkening submissively to it in its over-desires.'

13. YIELD,] *lit.* 'set near . . weapons of . . to the sin, but set yourselves near to God . . weapons of.'

14. SHALL,] *lit.* 'is no longer your lord . . under law.'

15. THE LAW,] *lit.* 'under law . . let it not be!'

16. KNOW,] *lit.* 'have ye not known . . set yourselves near (as)bondmen with a view to a submissive hearkening, bondsmen ye are to whom ye hearken submissively . . or of a submissive hearkening.'

17. THANKED,] *lit.* 'but grace (is) to God, because . . ye hearkened submissively . . to the type of teaching to which ye were given over,' *or* gave yourselves over.

18. SIN,] *lit.* 'from the sin, ye became bondsmen to the righteousness.'

19. AFTER,] *lit.* 'in the . . ye set your members near (as) bondsmen to the uncleanness, and to the lawlessness with a view to the lawlessness . . set near . . bondsmen to the righteousness, with a view to holiness.'

20. THE,] *lit.* 'were bondsmen of the sin . . as to the righteousness.'

21. IN,] *or* 'upon *or* over.'

22. SERVANTS,] *lit.* 'bondsmen.'

23. SIN,] *lit.* 'of the sin . . grace of God . . in Jesus.'

Chapter VII. may be divided into four parts; v. 1—6 the dead are freed from the law; v. 7—12 apart from which sin is dead; v. 13—20 the law is good, but sin is working; v. 21—25 the war in the members, and the deliverer.

1. KNOW,] *lit.* 'those knowing law, that the law is lord of the man as long time as he liveth.'

2. HATH,] *lit.* 'is under a husband has been bound by law to the living husband but if the husband die, she has been made thoroughly free from.'

3. IF,] *lit.* 'the husband being alive, if she become another man's she shall be divinely-called an adulteress, but if the husband die . . the law, so as not to be an adulteress, becoming another man's.'

4. WHEREFORE,] *or* 'so that . . were put to death . . through the body of Christ, with a view to your becoming another's . . was raised . . bear fruit.'

5. MOTIONS,] *or* 'passions of the sins, the things through the law, were working themselves inwardly . . bear fruit to the death.'

6. ARE,] *lit.* 'were thoroughly freed . . we being dead to that in which we were held down, for our being bondsmen . . of spirit . . of letter.'

7. SHALL,] *or* 'do we say? . . let it not happen! but I did not know the sin except through law, . . the over-desire, if the law (had) not said, Thou shalt not over-desire (any thing).'

8. SIN,] *lit.* 'but the sin, having received an impulse through the precept, worked thoroughly for itself every (kind of) over-desire, for apart from law, sin (is) dead.'

9. WITHOUT,] *lit.* 'apart from law then . . the sin.'

10. I FOUND,] *lit.* 'was found by me.'

11. SIN,] *lit.* 'for the sin, having received an impulse through . . greatly deceived me, and through it slew me utterly.'

12. WHEREFORE,] *or* 'so that the law indeed.'

13. WAS,] *lit.* 'has . . become death . . let it not happen! but the sin, thoroughly working death to me through . . that the sin through the precept might become very exceeding sinful.'

14. KNOW,] *lit.* 'have known . . am fleshly, caused to pass over under the sin.'

15. DO,] *lit.* 'work thoroughly, I do not know *or* acknowledge . . I wish, that I practise not.'

16. WOULD,] *or* 'wish not, I say with the law.'

17. DO IT,] *lit.* 'work thoroughly, but the sin dwelling in me.'

18. KNOW,] *lit.* 'have known . . to wish is lying near me, but to thoroughly work.'

19. THE,] *lit.* 'that good which I wish . .

that evil which I wish not, that I practise.'

20. WOULD,] *lit.* 'wish..that work (it) thoroughly, but the sin dwelling.

21. A,] *lit.* 'the law..wish to do good, that the evil is lying near me.'

22. DELIGHT,] *or* 'am pleased.'

23. BRINGING,] *lit.* 'taking me (as) by a spear to the law of the sin.'

24. WRETCHED,] *lit.* 'a misery-burdened man (am) I! who shall free.'

25. SERVE,] *lit.* 'am a bondsman to the.. to a law of sin.'

Chapter VIII. may be divided into six parts; v. 1—4 believers free from condemnation; v. 5—14 are spiritually-minded; v. 15—17 have the spirit of sons; v. 18—25 are not disheartened; v. 26, 27 have the aid of the spirit; v. 28—39 have all things.

1. CONDEMNATION,] *or* 'counter-judgment ..walk not about according to flesh, but according to spirit.'

2. LIFE,] *lit.* 'of the life.. did free me.. of the sin, and of the death.'

3. WEAK,] *or* 'infirm.. of flesh, of sin, and because of sin, condemned the sin.'

4. IN,] *or* 'among *or* by us, who walk not about according to flesh, but according to spirit.'

5. AFTER,] *lit.* 'according to flesh.. to spirit.'

6. TO BE,] *lit.* 'for the minding of the flesh ..but the minding of the spirit.'

7. CARNAL MIND,] *lit.* 'the minding of the flesh.. not arranged (*or* does not arrange itself) under.'

9. THE,] *lit.* 'in flesh, but in spirit.'

11. CHRIST,] *lit.* 'the Christ.. dying bodies, because of his indwelling Spirit in you.'

12. THEREFORE,] *or* 'so then,.. according to flesh.'

13. AFTER,] *lit.* 'according to flesh ye are about to die utterly.. in spirit do put to death.'

14. THE,] 'are sons of God.'

15. HAVE,] *lit.* 'did not receive a spirit of ..ye received a spirit of sonship.. O Father!'

16. THAT,] *or* 'because we are children.'

17. WITH,] *lit.* 'of Christ.'

18. THE,] *lit.* 'this present season are not worthy beside the glory about to be uncovered in reference to us.'

19. CREATURE,] *or* 'creation.. uncovering of.'

20. CREATURE,] *or* 'creation was set under the vanity, not yieldingly.. who set (it) under—upon hope, that the creation also shall.. of the corruption with a view to the freedom of the glory of the sons of God.'

22. KNOWN,] *lit.* 'have known.. groaneth together and travaileth together till now.'

23. THE,] *lit.* 'waiting for sonship—the full loosing of our bodies.'

24. BY,] *or* 'in the hope.'

25. WITH,] *or* 'through endurance.'

26. HELPS,] *lit.* 'takes hold over against along with (us) on our..have not known.. may pour forth before (God) as it behoves us.. itself is inwardly on our behalf (with) groanings unuttered *or* unspoken.'

27. SEARCHES,] *lit.* 'is searching.. has himself known.. because(*or* that) it is inwardly on behalf of holy ones according to God.'

28. KNOW,] *lit.* 'have known that every thing works together.. those loving God.. are called according to a purpose *or* setting forth.'

29. FOREKNEW,] i.e. 'knew (recognized, *or* approved) beforehand (*or* publicly, openly, see 11. 2; 1 Pet. 1. 20; Acts 26. 5), he also did mark-out beforehand (*or* publicly), conformed to the image of his Son, with a view to his being first-born among many brethren.'

30. MOREOVER,] *lit.* 'and whom he marked-out beforehand (*or* publicly), these he also called; and whom he called, these he also declared just, and whom he declared just, these he also glorified.'

31. SHALL,] *or* 'do we say.'

32. SPARED,] *lit.* 'spared not to himself even his.. graciously give us the all things.'

33. LAY,] *lit.* 'who shall call (anything in to court) against the elect (i.e. select, excellent, or approved ones) of God.'

34. CONDEMNETH,] *lit.* 'is judging-down .. was raised.. also is inwardly on our behalf.'

35. CHRIST,] *lit.* 'the Christ? trouble, or distress, or pursuit, or hunger, or nakedness, or danger, or sword.'

36. IT IS,] *lit.* 'it has been written, that, put to death all the day, we were reckoned as sheep of slaughter,'

37. WE ARE,] *lit.* 'we more than conquer.'

38. PERSUADED,] *or* 'confident.. things standing in, nor things about to be.'

39. CREATURE,] *or* 'created thing.'

Chapter IX. may be divided into four parts; v. 1—5 Paul's love and sorrow for the Jews; v. 6—13 their fall consistent with God's former dealings; v. 14—24 also with his justice and mercy; v. 25—33 and with prophecy.

1. THE,] *lit.* 'truth I say..in *or* with a holy spirit.'

2. HEAVINESS,] *or* 'grief and unceasing pain.'

3. COULD,] *lit.* 'for I was pouring forth—I myself—to be an anathema (i.e. something 'laid up' on the altar) from *or* because of the Christ, (i.e. the Messiah), in behalf of.. according to flesh.'

4. TO WHOM,] *lit.* 'whose is the sonship,.. covenants (*lit.* things thoroughly set), and the law-setting, and the much trembling.'

5. CHRIST,] *lit.* 'is the Christ, who is over all God, well-spoken of to the ages.'

6. NOT,] *lit.* 'but not such as that.. hath fallen through, for all are not (the true) Israel who are of (the natural) Israel.'

7. THE,] *lit.* 'are (part of the) seed of Abraham, are all (true) children, but 'In Isaac (alone) shall a seed be called to thee.'

8. THEY,] *lit.* 'the children of the flesh are not (necessarily) children of God, but the children of the promise it (i.e. the Scripture) reckons for seed.'

9. TIME,] *or* 'season.. there shall be to Sarah.'

10. BY,] *lit.* 'out of one.'

11. PURPOSE,] *lit.* 'thing set forth.'
STAND,] *lit.* 'remain..who is calling.'
12. ELDER,] *lit.* 'greater (in age) shall be in bondage to the lesser.'
13. IS,] *lit* 'has been written, Jacob I loved, and Esau I hated,' i.e. loved less; a very common Scripture idiom; see Ge. 39. 21; De. 21. 15; Mat. 6. 24; 10. 37, &c. This was manifested by giving Esau a less fertile territory, Mal. 1. 3.
14. SHALL,] *or* 'do we say..let it not be!'
15. MERCY,] *lit.* 'kindness on whom I have kindness,' i.e. I will do great kindness and compassion.
16. WILLETH,] *lit.* 'is wishing (i.e. Abraham and Isaac), nor of him who is running (i.e. Esau), but of God, who is doing kindness.'
17. EVEN,] *lit.* 'with a view to this thing itself I raised thee up,' from the bed of sickness on which he was cast by the plague of the boils, before which even the magicians of Egypt could not stand; see Ex. 9. 11, 16; or it may be rendered 'I have suffered thee to stand,' i.e. to remain or continue in life, or health, or obstinacy.
SHEW,] *lit.* 'shew inwardly my power in thee;' Ex. 9. 16 reads 'shew thee my power.'
NAME,] i.e. renown or character.
DECLARED,] *lit.* 'thoroughly told in all the land,' of Egypt, or of the earth
18. THEREFORE,] *lit.* 'so then, he has kindness on whom he wishes, and on whom he wishes he puts hardship,' to test their obedience, or punish their sins.
19. FIND FAULT,] *or* 'blame? for who has stood against his counsel,' or plan of advancing one nation above another.
20. NAY BUT,] *or* 'indeed, then, O man, thou—who art thou that art judging over-against God? shall the thing fashioned say to its fashioner, Why me hast thou made thus?' *or* Why hast thou done thus with me?
21. POWER,] *lit.* 'authority (*or* privilege) over the clay, out of his lump to make that which indeed is a vessel to honour, and that (also) which is to dishonour,' *or* less honour, *lit.* without honour.
22. WHAT,] *lit.* 'and if God, wishing to shew inwardly for himself the anger (against sin), and to make known his power, bare in much long-suffering vessels of anger become thoroughly fit for destruction,' *lit.* a loosing-away.
23. RICHES,] *or* 'wealth of his glory upon vessels of kindness, which he made ready beforehand (*or* openly) for glory.'
24. HATH,] *lit.* 'did call.'
25. THEM,] *or* 'that..which is not.'
26. THE,] *lit.* 'called sons of a living God.'
27. CONCERNING,] *or* 'in behalf of Israel, If the number of the sons of Israel may be ..the full-remnant (only) shall be saved.'
28. WILL,] *lit.* 'is ending at once and cutting-short (the) reckoning in righteousness, because a reckoning cut short will the Lord make upon the land.'
29. SAID BEFORE,] *or* 'said publicly, If the Lord of Hosts had not left behind among us a seed, we would have been.. would have been made.'
30. SHALL,] *or* 'do we say then? that nations that are not pursuing righteousness received righteousness fully, but righteousness.'
31. WHICH,] *lit.* 'pursuing a law of righteousness did not obtain to a law.'
32. BY,] *lit.* 'out of faith, but as (it were) out of works of law.'
33. IS,] *lit.* 'it has been written..and no one who is remaining-stedfast upon it shall be at all ashamed.'

Chapter X. may be divided into four parts; v. 1—3 Paul's desire for, and testimony of, the Jews; v. 4—13 his description of the righteousness of the law and of faith; v. 14, 15 desirableness of preaching the gospel; v. 16—21 Jewish unbelief foretold.
1. DESIRE,] *or* 'good thought and supplication..is, with a view to salvation.'
2. KNOWLEDGE,] *lit.* 'full-knowledge.'
3. BEING IGNORANT,] '*lit.* not knowing *or* not recognizing *or* not approving.'
GOING ABOUT,] *lit.* 'seeking to set up.. were not arranged (*or* did not arrange themselves) under the.'
4. THE,] *lit.* 'is an end of law..is believing.'
5. DESCRIBETH,] *lit.* 'writeth.. has done .. in them.'
6. SAY,] *lit.* 'thou mayest not say.. to the heaven.'
7. DEEP,] *Gr.* 'abyss,' i.e. very deep place.
8. WORD,] *or* 'matter.. the matter of the faith that we proclaim.'
9. SHALT,] *or* 'mayest say the same thing with thy.. and mayest believe with thy heart that God raised him out of (the) dead thou mayest be saved.'
10. MAN,] *lit.* 'it is believed with a view to righteousness, and with (the) mouth the same thing is said with a view to salvation.'
11. WHOSOEVER,] *lit.* 'no one who is believing upon him shall be at all ashamed.'
12. THE,] *lit.* between Jew and Hellen.. Lord of all..thou calling upon him.'
14. IN,] *or* 'upon whom they did not believe?..believe where they did not hear? ..apart from a crier?'
15. PREACH,] *or* 'cry.. it has been written, How timely (*or* seasonable) the feet of those proclaiming peace as good news, of those proclaiming as good news the good things.'
16. HAVE,] *lit.* 'did not all hearken submissively to.. who believed that which we heard?'
17. FAITH,] *lit.* 'the faith (is) from hearing, and the hearing (is) through a saying of God.'
18. HAVE,] *lit.* 'did they not hear? therefore indeed,.. the land, and their sayings.. habitable world.'
19. PROVOKE,] *lit.* 'I will make you very zealous by (*or* about what is) not a people, by (*or* about) an unintelligent nation I will greatly anger you.'
20. BOLD,] *or* 'daring,.. found by those not seeking me, I became manifest to those not asking about me.'

21. LONG,] *lit.* 'all the day I stretched.. unbelieving and gainsaying people.'

Chapter XI. may be divided into five parts: v. 1—10 a remnant saved by grace, others are hardened; v. 11—16 future results; v. 17—24 no ground of boasting; v. 25—32 all Israel shall be saved; v. 33—36 thanksgiving.

1. HAS,] *lit.* 'did God push away from himself his people? let it not happen!..out of seed of Abraham, of tribe of Benjamin.'

2. HATH,] *lit.* 'did not push away from himself his people whom he foreknew (i.e. knew, recognized *or* approved of publicly *or* beforehand); have ye not known what the Writing says in (the case of) Elijah? how he is inwardly towards God against Israel.'

3. HAVE,] *lit.* 'they utterly killed..altars (*lit.* places of sacrifice), and I was left behind alone.'

4. ANSWER OF GOD,] *lit.* 'divine word?' 'I left behind to..who bowed not a knee to Baal.'

5. AT,] *lit.* 'in the present season also there has been.'

6. OF,] *lit.* 'out of works, otherwise the grace becomes no.. out of work.. the work.'

7. HATH,] *lit.* 'did not come upon..came upon (it), and the rest became callous,' *or* made themselves hard.

8. IS,] *lit.* 'has been written, God gave (i.e. permitted to come) to them a spirit of deep sleep, eyes not beholding, and ears not hearkening.'

9. BE MADE,] *lit.* 'become for a snare, and for a trap (*lit.* hunting), and for a stumbling-block,' *lit.* anything causing lameness.

10. THAT THEY,] *lit.* 'not beholding, and do thou bend together.'

11. HAVE,] *lit.* 'did they stumble that they might fall? let it not be! but by their falling away the salvation (is preached) to the nations, to make them very zealous.'

12. THE FALL,] *lit.* 'their falling-away (is) the wealth of the world, and there inferiority the wealth of nations.'

13. GENTILES,] *lit.* 'to the nations..an apostle of nations I glorify my deaconship.'

14. MAY,] *lit.* 'shall make mine own flesh very zealous.'

15. THE,] *lit.* 'for if their casting-away (of the gospel offer) is a thorough-change of the world, what their receiving (of it), but (an indication of) life from the dead.'

17. SOME,] *lit.* 'certain..were broken off ..field-olive..becamest a partaker..and of the fatness.'

18. BOAST,] *lit.* 'dost boast.'

20. WELL,] *or* 'right (*or* good)! by unstedfastness.. hast stood.. but be fearing.'

21. SPARED,] *lit.* 'spared not for himself ..perhaps he will not spare for himself even thee.'

22. GOODNESS,] *or* 'benignity and cutting-away of God, on those indeed who fell, a cutting away, but upon thee benignity, if thou mayest remain on in the benignity.'

23. ABIDE,] *lit.* 'may not remain on in the unbelief

24. OLIVE-TREE,] *lit.* 'natural field-olive.

25. WOULD NOT,] *lit.* 'do not wish you to be ignorant, brethren, as to this secret, that ye may not be wise among yourselves, that callousness in part has happened.. of the nations may come in,' when the true seed of Abraham shall be complete.

26. ALL ISRAEL,] the true wrestlers with God, out of every nation.

IT IS,] *lit.* 'it has been written,.. the Rescuer, and he shall thoroughly turn round irreverence.'

27. COVENANT,] *lit.* 'thoroughly set thing.' TAKE AWAY,] *or* 'lift up from (them) their sins.'

29. GIFTS,] *or* 'graces and the calling are unrepented of.'

30. IN TIMES,] *lit.* 'also once did not..but did now find kindness by.'

31. HAVE,] *lit.* 'so also were these unbelieving by the kindness (done) to you that these also may find kindness.'

32. HATH,] *lit.* 'did shut up together the whole to unbelief, that with the whole he might deal kindly.'

33. OF THE RICHES,] *or* 'of wealth and wisdom and knowledge..untraceable his ways.'

34. HAS,] *lit.* 'did know..who became his fellow-counsellor.'

35. HAS,] *lit.* 'did first give.'

36. ALL,] *lit.* 'the all things! to him (is) the glory to the ages! Amen.'

Chapter XII. may be divided into three parts; v. 1—5 call to dedication, holiness, and lowliness; v. 6—17 mutual love and duty; v. 18—21 love of enemies.

1. BESEECH,] *lit.* 'call upon you, through the compassions of God, to set forth your bodies a sacrifice—living, holy, well-pleasing to God—your rational service.'

2. WORLD,] *lit.* 'age. with a view to your proving what is the wish of God, which (is at once) good, and well-pleasing, and complete.'

3. GIVEN,] *lit.* 'that was given..about (himself) beyond what it behoves him to think, but to think with a view to thinking soundly, as God did divide to each a measure.'

4. ALL,] *lit.* 'all the members.. same work.'

5. BEING,] *lit.* 'so we, the many..the member.'

6. GIFTS,] *or* 'graces..was given..proportion (*lit.* analogy) of the faith.'

7. MINISTRY,] *lit.* 'deaconship—In the deaconship; or he who is teaching—In the teaching.'

8. EXHORTETH,] *lit.* 'is calling upon (others)—In the calling upon (others); he who is giving anything over—In simplicity *or* singleness; he who is setting himself forward—In diligence; he who is doing kindness—In cheerfulness.'

9. LOVE,] *lit.* 'the love, unhypocritical; shuddering from the evil; glued to the good thing.'

10. BE KINDLY,] *lit.* 'with natural affection loving one another in the brotherly

love; in the honour, leading one another forward.'

11. BUSINESS,] *lit.* 'in the diligence; fervent in the spirit, in bondage to the Lord.'

12. HOPE,] *lit.* 'the hope; remaining submissive in the trouble; strong towards (God) in the pouring forth (of desires).'

13. DISTRIBUTING,] *lit.* 'having communion with the..of the holy ones; pursuing the friendship of strangers.'

14. BLESS,] *lit.* 'speak well to those pursuing you; speak well, and curse not at all.'

15. REJOICE,] *lit.* 'to rejoice with rejoicing ones, and to weep with weeping ones.'

16. BE,] *lit.* 'minding the same thing in reference to one another, not minding the high things, but being led along with the body; became not prudent among yourselves.'

17. PROVIDE,] *lit.* 'minding beforehand right things for yourselves before all men.'

18. AS MUCH,] *lit.* 'the thing required of you is, being at peace with.'

19. DEARLY BELOVED,] *or* simply 'beloved.'

WRATH,] *lit.* 'to the wrath (of God), for it has been written.'

20. HUNGER,] *lit.* 'hungers..thirsts, cause him to drink..burning coals of fire.'

21. OF,] *lit.* 'by the evil *or* wickedness,.. the wickedness by the good.'

Chapter XIII. may be divided into two parts; v. 1—7 exhortation to civil obedience; v. 8—14 and to love and holiness.'

1. SUBJECT,] *or* 'arranging itself under higher authorities, for there is no authority but from God, and the authorities existing are arranging themselves under God.'

2. RESISTETH,] *lit.* 'is arranging himself against the authority, has stood against the arrangement of God, and those standing against (it) shall receive to them a judgment.'

3. RULERS,] *lit.* 'the foremost ones are not (the) fear of the good works, but of the bad ones; and dost thou wish not to fear the authority, be doing..from it.'

4. THE,] *lit.* 'a deacon of God to thee with a view to that which is good; but if thou mayest do that which is bad, be fearing,.. a deacon of God, an avenger in anger on him who in practising that which is bad.'

5. WHEREFORE,] *lit.* 'because of which it is necessary to subject yourselves, not only because of the anger, but also because of the conscience.'

6. TRIBUTE,] *lit.* 'burdens..God's public-workers, strengthening themselves for.'

7. THEIR DUES,] *lit.* 'the things owing (to them); the burden..the burden..the custom ..the custom..the fear..the fear..the honour..the honour.'

8. LOVETH,] *lit.* 'is loving the other has fulfilled law.'

9. KILL,] *lit.* 'murder..over-desire (anything),..it is summed up in this word, in this.'

10. LOVE,] *lit.* 'the love worketh nothing bad to the neighbour, therefore the love is fulness of law.'

11. KNOWING,] *lit.* 'having known the season, that (it is the) hour already for us to be aroused out of sleep.'

12. IS FAR SPENT,] *lit.* 'struck forward, and the day came nigh, let us put away for ourselves the works of the darkness, and let us put on for ourselves the weapons of the light.'

13. HONESTLY,] *lit.* 'let us walk about becomingly, as in day-time, not in revellings and drunkennesses, not in embracings and impurities, not in contention and zeal.'

14. PUT,] *lit.* 'put ye on for yourselves..no forethought for (*lit.* of) the flesh, with a view to (its) over-desires.'

Chapter XIV. may be divided into four parts; v. 1—9 of eating herbs and observing days; v. 10—13 Christ the only judge; v. 14, 15 nothing unclean, walking in love; v. 16—23 serving the Christ, building up one another.

1. WEAK,] *or* 'infirm..receive to (yourselves), not to a thorough-judging of reasoning.'

2. FOR,] *lit.* 'one indeed believes..but he who is infirm eats (only) herbs.'

3. EATETH,] *lit.* 'is eating think nothing of him who is not eating,..is not eating..is eating, for God received him to (himself).'

4. WHO,] *lit.* 'thou, who art thou that art judging another's domestic,..be made to stand.'

5. ESTEEMS,] *lit.* 'judges between day and day, and one judges every day..be fully borne through *or* on.'

6. REGARDETH,] *lit.* 'mindeth..is not minding..is eating.. leaps greatly with joy before God,..is not eating..and leaps much for joy before God.'

7. DIETH,] *lit.* 'dies utterly.'

8. DIE,] *lit.* 'die fully..die fully..die fully.'

9. ROSE,] *lit.* 'stood up, and lived again,.. of dead.'

10. BUT WHY,] *lit.* 'and those, why or thou, why dost thou think nothing of thy ..stand for ourselves near the tribunal of the Christ.'

11. IS,] *lit.* 'has been written..shall speak the same thing to God.'

12. EVERY ONE,] *or* 'each of us shall give a reckoning about himself.'

13. THAT NO,] *lit.* 'not to put the stumbling-block as offence before the brother.'

14. KNOW,] *lit.* 'I have known..in the Lord..common through itself..is reckoning ..common, to that one (it is) common.'

15. WITH THY,] *lit.* 'because of food, thou dost no more walk about according to love; be not loosing-away (from the faith) him in behalf of whom Christ died fully.'

16. YOUR GOOD,] *lit.* 'that which is good of you be injuriously spoken of.'

17. KINGDOM,] *or* 'reign..eating and drink ing..in holy spirit.'

18. SERVETH,] *lit.* 'in bondage to the Christ is well-pleasing to God, and approved by man.'

19. FOLLOW,] *lit.* 'pursue the things of the peace, and the things of building up one another.'

20. MEAT,] *lit.* 'for the sake of food be not loosing down..but evil (is) to the man who is eating through a stumbling block.'
21. GOOD,] *or* 'right..or becometh infirm.'
22. HAST,] *or* 'thou hast faith!..is not judging himself..approves of.'
23. DOUBTETH,] *lit.* 'is judging diversely is judged down.'

Chapter XV. may be divided into seven parts; v. 1—4 exhortation to bear the infirmities of the weak; v. 5—7 to maintain unanimity; v. 8—13 Christ the saviour of Jew and Gentile; v. 14—16 Paul's confidence in the Roman believers; v.17—21 his labours in Asia; v. 22—29 his intention to visit Rome; v. 30—33 his call on their prayers.
1. WE THEN,] *lit.* 'and we owe (it to God), we who are powerful, to bear..powerless.'
2. EDIFICATION,] *lit.* up-building.'
3. CHRIST,] *lit* 'the Christ..has been written.'
4. AFORETIME,] *or* 'written publicly.'
LEARNING,] *or* 'teaching..the endurance and the exhortation..have the hope.'
5. PATIENCE,] *lit.* 'the endurance and of the exhortation give to you to mind the same thing with one another.'
6. AND ONE,] *lit.* 'by one mouth glorify the God and Father of.'
7. RECEIVE,] *lit.* 'receive to yourselves..to himself.'
8. THAT.] *lit* 'to have become a deacon of circumcison..promises of the fathers.'
9. THAT,] *lit.* 'to glorify..the kindness, as it has been written..speak out the same thing to the many nations, and in thy name I will sing-psalms,' i.e. pruned, chastened compositions accompanied by instrumental music.
10. HE,] *or* 'it (i.e. the Writing) says, Have a good mind, ye nations.'
11. LAUD,] *lit.* 'praise him greatly, all ye people.'
12. A,] *lit.* 'the root..who is setting himself up to rule nations; upon him shall nations hope.'
13. HOPE,] *lit.* 'of the hope..in the believing..in the hope, in power of a holy spirit.'
15. HAVE WRITTEN,] *lit.* 'I wrote more daringly to you in part..mind again,..was given to me by God.'
16. THE,] *lit.* 'a public worker of..working as a priest the good-news..may become acceptable, having been in (with, by) a holy spirit.'
17. WHEREOF,] *lit.* 'a boasting in Jesus.'
18. HATH,] *lit.* 'did not work through me, with a view to the submissive hearkening of nations, by word and work.'
19. THROUGH,] *lit.* 'in (the) power of signs..in the power of..I have made full the.'
20. YEA,] *lit.* 'and so loving the honour of evangelizing for myself, not where..that I might not build.'
21. IS,] *lit.* 'has been written..heard for themselves.'
22. HINDERED,] *lit.* 'was inwardly struck many (times) to come to you.'

23. PLACE,] *or* 'a place in these regions, and having an over-desire for (*lit.* from) many.'
24. WHENSOEVER,] *or* 'as soon as I pass on to..I trust to see you for myself, and to be sent forward thither by you, if I be partly filled by you first.'
25. I GO,] *lit.* 'pass on to Jerusalem, a deacon to the holy ones.'
26. IT PLEASED,] *lit.* 'for Macedonia and Achaia thought proper themselves to make a common contribution for the poor of the holy ones who are in Jerusalem.'
27. IT HATH,] *lit.* 'for they thought proper..had a common fellowship in their spiritual things..to work publicly to them in their fleshly things.'
28. PERFORMED,] *or* 'ended this fully..will go from (this) through you.'
29. AM SURE,] *lit.* 'have known..fulness of the good-word.'
30. BESEECH,] *or* 'call upon you,..through our..and through..to agonize yourselves with me in the pouring forth before (God) in my behalf.'
31. DELIVERED,] *lit* 'freed from those unbelieving..my deaconship..may become very acceptable to the holy ones.'
32. WITH,] *or* 'in joy through God's will, and may myself be refreshed together with you.'
33. PEACE,] *lit.* 'of the peace.'

Chapter XVI. may be divided into four parts; v. 1—16 various salutations; v. 17—20 cautions against divisions and stumbling blocks; v. 21—24 salutation of Paul's companions; v. 25—27 ascription of glory to God.
1. COMMEND,] *lit.* 'present with (these)..a deaconess of the assembly that is in Cenchrea,'—the eastern port of Corinth, see Acts 18. 18. Nothing is more certain in ecclesiastical history then that there were a class of females who ministered to, and laboured among, the early Christian assemblies (doubtless specially among their own sex); that they were *formally* appointed as to an office, however, there is no proof in the New Testament, though they were so in the second and succeeding centuries; the fact is, that the *deaconship* was not an office at all, but a duty, binding on every member of the church, both male and female; in the vast majority of cases when the word 'deacon' occurs it is commonly translated '*minister*,' and applied to a spiritual, mental, intellectual, service, rather than to an outward, bodily, temporal one; see Rom. 15. 8; 1 Cor. 3. 5; 2 Cor. 3. 6; 6. 4; 11. 15, 23; Gal. 2. 17; Eph. 3. 7; 6. 21; Col. 1. 7, 23, 25; 4. 7; 1 Thes. 3. 2; 1 Tim. 4. 6; Heb. 1. 14, &c.
2. RECEIVE,] *lit.* 'may receive her to yourselves..the Lord, worthily of the holy ones, and stand along-side of her in whatever matter ye may have need of you, for she also became a leader (*lit.* one standing in the front rank) of many, and of myself,'—encouraging them by word and deed to persevere.
3. SALUTE,] *lit.* 'embrace (*lit.* draw near) Priscilla and Aquila, my fellow-workers in Christ Jesus.'

4. HAVE,] *lit.* 'who in behalf of my soul put their own necks under (danger).'
5. LIKEWISE,] *lit.* 'and—the assembly at their house; embrace my beloved Epenetus,' i.e. 'praise worthy.'
6. SALUTE,] *lit.* 'embrace Miriam, who toiled much for us.'
7. SALUTE,] *lit.* 'embrace Andronicus,' i.e. the 'victorious man.'
OF NOTE,] *lit.* 'much noted among *or* by the apostles, who have even came before me in Christ,'—in some spiritual graces.
8. SALUTE,] *lit.* 'embrace Amplias,' i.e. 'ample.'
9. SALUTE,] *lit.* 'embrace Urbane (i.e. polite), our fellow-worker in Christ.'
STACHYS,] i.e. 'an ear of corn.'
10. SALUTE,] *lit.* 'embrace Apelles, the approved *or* accepted in Christ.'
ARISTOBULUS,] *lit.* 'best counsellor.'
11. SALUTE,] *lit.* 'embrace Herodian (i.e. little hero), my kinsman *or* kinswoman.'
12. TRYPHENA,] i.e. luxurious, Tryphena (i.e. luxurious), who are toiling in the Lord.
PERSIS,] i.e. persian, 'who toiled much.'
13. RUFUS,] i.e. red, 'the elect *or* select one in the Lord.'
14. ASYNCRITUS,] i.e. not to be judged together.
PHLEGON,] i.e. 'burning.'
HERMAS,] i.e. 'Mercury, the speaker.'
PATROBAS,] i.e. 'following a father.'
15. PHILOLOGUS,] i.e. 'lover of words.'
NEREUS,] i.e. 'humble.'
SAINTS,] *or* 'holy ones.'
16. WITH,] *or* 'in a holy friendship.'
17. BESEECH,] *lit.* 'call upon you..to mark those making the divisions and the stumbling-blocks, contrary to the teaching..turn away from them.'
18. SERVE NOT,] *lit.* 'are not in bondage to..through the kind words and good words utterly deceive the hearts of the badless.'
19. OBEDIENCE,] *lit.* 'submissive hearkening came from itself to all.. I wish you to be wise..unhurt *or* unmixed *or* unhorned.'
20. PEACE,] *lit.* 'the peace shall trample also the Adversary..with speed.'
21. TIMOTHEUS,] i.e. one honouring God.
JASON,] i.e. a healer.
SOSIPATER,] i.e. saving a father.
22. TERTIUS,] i.e. third.
23. GAIUS,] in Latin, Caius.
ERASTUS,] i.e. beloved *or* best.
STEWARD,] *lit.* 'house-distributor.'
CITY] of Corinth.
QUARTUS,] i.e. fourth, 'the brother.'
25. IS OF POWER,] *or* 'is able, has power to confirm you..uncovering of the secret in the times of the ages kept silent.'
26. SCRIPTURES,] *lit.* 'through prophetic writings, according to an arrangement of the age-during God,.. submissive hearkening of faith.'
27. TO GOD,] *lit.* 'to the only wise God, through Jesus Christ, to him (is) the glory, to the ages of the ages. Amen!'

PAUL'S LETTER TO THE CORINTHIANS (THE FIRST)

CORINTH was the capital city of Achaia in Greece, famous for its commerce and luxury, where Paul laboured for nearly two years (A.D. 52—3), gathering many Jews and Gentiles chiefly of the humbler class into the church of Christ (Acts 18. 1—17), and was succeeded by Apollos (ch. 18. 27, 28; 19. 1). Clement of Rome (A.D. 100), Polycarp (A.D. 108), and Irenaeus (A.D. 167), Ignatius (A.D. 101), Clement of Alex. (A.D. 192), quote the present Epistle as being the work of Paul, and indeed, no one has ever ventured to doubt it. From ch. 5. 9 it would appear that he had written to the Corinthians an earlier letter which is now lost; but the present was written from Ephesus (ch. 16. 8) about Easter or Pentecost A.D. 57, and sent by the hands of Stephanus, Fortunatus, and Achaicus. It may be divided into three parts, viz:—

I. DISCUSSION BY WAY OF REPROOF, ch. i—vi.
1. Introduction, &c. 1. 1—9.
2. Reproof of Dissention and schism, 1. 10—4. 21.
3. Reproof of Incestuous Person, 5. 11-13.
4. Reproof of Covetous and Litigious spirit, 6. 1—11.
5. Reproof of Fornication, 6. 12—20.

II. DISCUSSION BY WAY OF DIRECTION, ch. 7. 1—15. 58.
1. On Marriage and Celibacy, 7. 1—40.
2. On Things offered to Idols, 8. 1—13.
3. Digression on Paul's conduct, 9. 1—27.
4. Digression on Corinthians' conduct, 10. 1—22.
5. On Public Worship, 11. 1—16.
6. On the Lord's Supper, 11. 17—34.
7. On Spiritual Gifts, 12. 1—14. 40.
8. On the Resurrection, 15. 1—58.

III. THE CONCLUSION, ch. 16. 1—24.
1. Various particulars, v. 1—12.
2. Admonitions and Salutations, v. 13—24.

Chapter I. may be divided into four parts; v. 1—3 Paul's salutation; v. 4—8 his thanksgiving; v. 9—21 his call to unity, and reproof of party spirit; v. 22—31 the true way of preaching the gospel.

1. PAUL,] i.e. the 'little' one, so called either from his stature, or his humility.

TO BE,] *lit.* 'a called apostle (as in Rom. 1. 1) of Jesus Christ, (the 'anointed saviour,') through the will (*or* wish) of God, and Sosthenes (i.e. 'sound strength,' Acts 18. 17), the brother.'

2. CHURCH,] *lit.* 'assembly.. in Corinth, .. hallowed.. called saints, with all those calling.'

3. GRACE,] *lit.* 'that which causes leaping with joy.'

PEACE,] *lit.* 'that which brings into unity.'

FROM,] *or* 'the (Father of) our Lord Jesus Christ;' as in Rom. 1. 7, &c.

4. THANK,] *lit.* 'make a great leaping with joy before my God always concerning you over the grace of God that was given to you in Christ Jesus.'

5. THAT,] *or* 'because.. were enriched in him, in every matter and all knowledge.'

6. EVEN,] *lit.* 'according as.. of the Christ .. in (*or* among) you.'

7. CAME BEHIND,] *lit.* 'were last in no gift *or* grace, waiting *or* looking for the uncovering of our Lord Jesus Christ.'

8. BLAMELESS,] *lit.* 'un-called-in (to court).'

9. FAITHFUL,] *or* 'stedfast, through whom ye were called with a view to (the) fellowship,' *or* communion.

10. BESEECH,] *lit.* 'call upon you,.. through the.. ye may all.. may be no rents (*Gr.* schisms).. ye may be thoroughly perfected in.. judgment,' *or* opinion.

11. HATH,] *lit.* 'was manifested.. concerning you,.. Chloe (i.e. 'fresh grass,').. strifes.'

12. EVERY,] *or* 'each one.'

13. IS,] *lit.* 'has the Christ been parted?.. with a view to the name.'

14. THANK,] as in v. 4 above.

CRISPUS.. GAIUS,] as in Acts 18. 8; Rom. 16. 23.

15. LEST,] *lit.* 'that no one may say that I baptized with a view to my own name.'

16. BESIDES,] *lit.* 'further, I have not known,' i.e. I do not recollect; the 'all truth,' and 'all things' which the Spirit was to bring to the knowledge and memory of the apostles was of a *spiritual,* not of an arithmetical character.

17. NOT.. BUT.] A Hebrew mode of expressing the preference of one thing above another; comp. Prov. 8. 10, &c.

NOT TO BAPTIZE,] which was in the early church done by underlings, John 4. 2; Acts 10. 48. Tertullian, (A.D. 192), expressly claims it as a 'right' of laymen, and even so late as A.D. 396, Jerome and Augustine lay it down as indisputable that baptism is valid though 'given by any one whatsoever to whomsoever it may.' See an exhaustive and elaborate volume, entitled 'Whose are the Fathers,' by John Harrison, a learned scholar and minister of the Church of England in Sheffield, published in London in 1867.

WITH,] *lit.* 'in wisdom of discourse, that the cross of the Christ may not be made empty *or* vain.'

18. PREACHING,] *lit.* 'word, (matter, *or* discourse) of the cross is to those who are loosed away foolishness, but to those who are being saved—to us—it is a power of God.'

19. IS,] *lit.* 'has been written,.. and will displace.'

20. THE WISE,] *lit.* 'a wise one? where a

scribe? where a joint-searcher of this age did not God make.'

21. AFTER THAT,] *lit.* 'since in.. through wisdom.'

22. FOR,] *lit.* 'since even Jews ask.. and Hellenes seek wisdom.'

23. PREACH,] *lit.* 'cry *or* proclaim as heralds.. to Jews indeed a.. to Hellenes.'

25. WEAKNESS,] *lit.* 'infirmity.'

26. NOBLE,] *lit.* 'well-born.'

27. HATH,] *lit.* 'laid out for himself.. that he might thoroughly shame.. did lay out for himself the infirm things.. that he might thoroughly shame.'

28. BASE,] *lit.* 'and the base-born things .. are thought nothing of, did God lay out for himself.. that he might make useless the things that are.'

29. SHOULD,] *lit.* 'may boast.'

30. OF HIM,] *lit.* 'out of him.. who from God became to us wisdom..holiness, and a full-loosing away.'

31. IS,] *lit.* 'has been written, He who is boasting, let him boast in the Lord.'

Chapter II. may be divided into three parts; v. 1—5 Paul's ministry; v. 6—11 the hidden wisdom of God; v. 12—16 the natural and the spiritual man.

1. WITH,] *lit.* 'through a superiority of discourse or of wisdom, telling thoroughly to you.'

2. DETERMINED,] *lit.* 'judged not to have known.'

3. WAS,] *lit.* 'came to you in infirmity.'

4. SPEECH,] *lit.* 'word.. in persuasive words of human wisdom, but in the shewing-forth of spirit and power.'

5. SHOULD,] *lit.* 'might not be in.'

6. PERFECT,] *or* 'complete, finished *or* ended.'

THE,] *lit.* 'not wisdom of this age, nor of the chiefs of this age, who are being made useless.'

7. HIDDEN,] *lit.* 'which has been fully hidden,. which God marked out beforehand (*or* publicly) before the ages, with a view to our glory.'

8. PRINCES,] *lit.* 'chiefs of this age has known.. Lord of the glory.'

9. IS,] *lit.* 'has been written, What eye saw not, and ear heard not, and upon the heart of man came not up, these God made ready for those loving him.'

10. BUT,] *or* 'and God uncovered (them) to us through.'

11. WHAT MAN,] *lit.* 'who of men has known for himself the things of the man,.. spirit of the man..hath no man known for himself.'

12. HAVE,] *lit.* 'we received.. out of God..were granted to us by (*lit.* under) God.'

13. THE WORDS,] *lit.* 'not in words taught by human wisdom, but in those taught by holy spirit, judging spiritual (men) with (*or* in) spiritual things.'

14. THE NATURAL,] *lit.* 'but an animal (*or* sensual) man.. spiritually judged-thoroughly.'

15. JUDGETH,] *lit.* 'judgeth all.. indeed thoroughly, but he himself is judged-thoroughly by no one.'

16. HAS,] *lit.* 'who knew..who shall bring it together.'

Chapter III. may be divided into five parts; v. 1—4 condition of the Corinthians; v. 5—7 dissuasives from division; v. 8—17 persuasives to concord; v. 18—20 caution to teachers; v. 21—23 admonition to all.

1. COULD NOT,] *lit.* 'was not able to speak ..fleshly,.. babes (*lit.* non-speakers).'

2. HAVE,] *lit.* 'I caused you to drink milk.'

3. CARNAL,] *lit.* 'fleshly.. zeal, and contention, and double-standings,.. fleshly and walk about according to (the way of an unregenerate) man.'

4. ONE,] *lit.* 'any one may say, I indeed am of Paul.'

5. MINISTERS,] *lit.* 'deacons, through..to each.'

6. HAVE,] *lit.* 'I planted, Apollos gave drink, but God was giving increase.'

7. PLANTETH,] *lit.* 'is planting.. is giving drink.. is giving increase.'

8. PLANTETH,] *lit.* 'is planting.. is giving drink..our toil.'

9. LABOURERS,] *lit.* 'workers-together of God,' i.e. both are in his service.

10. IS,] *lit.* 'was given to me, as a wise chief-artizan (*Gr.* architect), I laid a foundation.. each one see how he.'

11. CAN,] *lit.* 'is no one able to lay beside that laid, which is Jesus the Christ.'

12. MAN,] *lit.* 'any one builds.'

13. EVERY,] *lit.* 'of each the work shall become apparent, for the day shall make it evident, because in (*or* with, by) fire it is uncovered,and the fire shall try, (test, prove) the work of each of what kind it is.'

14. ABIDE,] *lit.* 'remains which he built.'

15. BURNED,] *lit.* 'burned down..through fire.'

16. KNOW,] *lit.* 'have ye not known that ye are a habitation of God.'

17. DEFILE,] *or* 'corrupt, *or* lays waste the habitation of God..for a habitation.'

18. DECEIVE,] *or* 'lead himself at all astray; if any one..in this age..he may become wise.'

19. WITH,] '*lit.* 'along-side *or* near God, for it has been written, He is grasping the wise in their own cleverness,' *lit.* every (kind) of work.

20. THOUGHT,] *or* 'reasonings (*lit.* dialogues) of the wise that they are vain *or* empty.'

21. GLORY,] *lit.* 'boast..all things *or* men.

22. PRESENT,] *lit.* 'standing in, whether about to be.'

Chapter IV. may be divided into five parts; v. 1, 2 how we ought to think of the under-rowers of Christ; v. 3—5 not to judge hastily; v. 6, 7 against partiality and pride, v.8—13 doings and sufferings of the apostles; v. 14—21 Paul's relation to the Corinthians.

1. ACCOUNT,] *or* 'reckon us, as under-rowers of Christ, and house-distributors of the secrets of God.'

2. MOREOVER,] *lit.* 'and as to the rest, it

is sought in the house-distributors, that any one be found faithful,' *or* stedfast.

3. WITH,] *lit.* 'but to me it is for a very little thing that I may be thoroughly-judged by you, or by man's day.'

4. KNOW,] *lit.* 'have known nothing fully by myself, but I have not been declared just *or* right in (*or* by) this, but he who is judging me thoroughly.'

5. TIME,] *or* 'season..of the darkness.. make apparent..shall come the praise to each from God.'

6. HAVE,] *lit.* 'I transferred to..because of you, that.. has been written . in behalf of the one against the other.'

7. MAKETH,] *lit.* 'for who judgeth thee thoroughly *or* diversely?..thou boast as not receiving?'

8. NOW,] *or* 'already ye have been satiated, already ye were rich, ye did reign apart from us, and I wished also ye did reign.'

9. HATH,] *lit.* 'God shewed off..as fully dead, because we became a theatrical-exhibition to the world, both to angels and to men.'

10. FOR,] *or* 'because of Christ,..wise *or* mindful in Christ; we (are) infirm,.. honourable (*lit.* in glory) but we (are) dishonoured,' *or* unhonoured.

11. HAVE NO,] *lit.* 'and stand not still.'

12. LABOUR,] *lit.* 'toil..bless (*lit.* speak well), being pursued (*or* caused to flee), we hold up.'

13. DEFAMED,] *lit.* 'blasphemed (i.e. injuriously-spoken of), we entreat *or* exhort, (*lit.* call alongside of any one), we became as filth of the world, (the) offscouring of all till now.'

14. TO SHAME,] *lit.* as 'turning you in (to yourselves from men), but as my beloved children I set (your) mind' right.

15. TEN THOUSAND,] *lit.* 'a myriad of child-conductors .I begat you.'

16. BESEECH,] *lit.* 'call alongside of you, become ye imitators of me.'

17. FOR,] *lit.* 'because of this I sent.. beloved child and stedfast in the Lord, who shall remind you again..assembly.'

18. SOME,] *or* 'certain were puffed up.'

19. WILL,] *or* 'may wish..the word of those puffed up.'

20. KINGDOM,] *or* 'reign.'

21. WILL,] *or* 'what do ye wish?.. with (*lit.* in) a rod, or with (*lit.* in) love, and with a spirit of meekness?'

Chapter V. may be divided into four parts; v. 1, 2 the evil report; v. 3—5 expulsion of the offender; v. 6—8 of the old leaven; v. 9—13 of the expulsion of other offenders.

1. REPORTED,] *lit.* 'whoredom is universally heard of among you, and such whoredom as is not even named among the nations, as that a certain one has the wife of the father.'

2. ARE,] *or* 'have been puffed up, and did not.. who did this work...out of your midst.'

3. VERILY,] *or* 'indeed,as being away as to the body, but being alongside as to the spirit, I judged already, as being alongside, him who so wrought against (us) this thing.'

4. GATHERED,] *lit.* 'brought together.'

5. DELIVER,] *lit.* 'give over such an one to the Adversary,' by henceforth treating him as a 'heathen man,' who has returned to his old master and his old service.

FOR,] *lit.* 'with a view to a loss (*or* loosing-away) of the flesh.'

6. GLORYING,] *lit.* 'boasting..have ye not known.'

7. PURGE,] *lit.* 'cleanse out.. was sacrificed.'

8. THEREFORE,] *lit.* 'so that we may feast ..with leaven of malice and evil, but with unleavened things of clear-judgment and truth.'

9. AN.] *lit.* 'in the epistle (now lost), not to be mixed up with whoremongers.'

10. YET,] *lit.* 'yea not at all with the whoremongers of this world, or with the covetous, or extortioners, or idolaters, seeing ye ought, in truth, to go out of the world.'

11. HAVE,] *lit.* 'I wrote to you, not to be mixed up with (them), if any one, being named Brother, may be.'

13. PUT,] *or* 'take away the evil.'

Chapter VI. may be divided into two parts; v. 1—11 against lawsuits, and unrighteousness; v. 12—20 against whoredom.

1. AGAINST,] *lit.* 'with *or* towards the other, to be judged before (*lit.* upon) the unrighteous..the holy ones,'

2. DO,] *lit.* 'have ye not known that the holy ones judge the world (daily)? and if the world is judged among you, are ye unworthy of the smaller *or* lesser judgment-seats?'

3. KNOW,] *lit.* 'have ye not known that we shall judge messengers (i.e. teachers)? why not then things of life.'

4. HAVE,] *lit.* 'may have judgment-seats (for) things of life, cause those to sit who are nothing thought of in the assembly.'

5. SHAME,] *lit.* 'in-turning, so there is not one wise one among you—not even one—who shall be able to judge-thoroughly in the midst of.'

6. GOETH TO LAW,] *lit.* 'is judged..before unstedfast ones.'

7. FAULT,] *or* 'lack among you that ye have judgments with yourselves.. suffer injustice?'

8. WRONG,] *or* 'injustice.'

9. KNOW,] *lit.* 'have ye not known.'

DECEIVED,] *or* 'led astray; neither whoremongers.. sodomites.'

10. REVILERS,] *or* 'railers.'

11. ARE WASHED,] *lit.* 'washed yourselves, but ye were hallowed, but ye were declared righteous.. by (*lit.* in) the Spirit.'

12. ALL,] *or* 'every thing (in the way of food) is lawful (*lit.* goes out) to me, but every thing does not bear together, every thing is lawful to me, but I—I will not be under authority of any.'

13. MEATS,] *lit.* 'the meats.. the meats.. shall make useless..for the whoredom.'

14. HATH,] *lit.* 'did both raise the Lord and will raise us fully through his power.'

15. KNOW,] *lit.* 'have ye not known . . are members . . of the Christ . . make (them) members of a whore? let it not happen!'

16. KNOW,] *lit.* 'have ye not known that he who is glued (*or* is gluing himself) to the whore . . for the two, saith he, shall be with a view to one flesh.'

17. JOINED,] *lit.* 'glued *or* is gluing himself.'

18. FORNICATION,] *lit.* 'flee the whoredom.'

SIN,] *or* 'missing' of the mark.

DOES,] *lit.* 'may do . . is committing whoredom, sins in reference to his own body.'

19. KNOW,] *lit.* 'have ye not known . . a habitation of the Holy Spirit (that is) among you, which ye have from God.'

20. ARE BOUGHT,] *lit.* 'were made public *or* gathered into a market-place.'

Chapter VII. may be divided into five parts; v. 1—7 of the married state, and married persons; v. 8, 9 of unmarried and widowed; v. 10—24 divorce and separation; v. 25—38 of single unmarried persons; v. 39, 40 second marriages lawful.

1. TO TOUCH,] *lit.* 'touch for himself.'

2. TO AVOID,] *lit.* 'because of the whoredoms, let each have . . and let each have.'

3. BENEVOLENCE,] *lit.* 'good mind *or* thought.'

4. POWER,] *or* 'authority . . authority.'

5. WITH,] *lit.* 'out of, *or* from consent for a season, that ye may be free to the fasting and the pouring-forth before (God), and be coming together again to the same, that the Adversary may not tempt you because of your want of strength.'

6. BY,] *lit.* 'according to concurrence (*lit.* joint-opinion), not according to a higher arrangement.'

7. WOULD,] *lit.* 'I wish all men to be even as I myself, but each has his proper grace from God, one indeed thus, and one thus.'

8. WIDOWS,] *lit.* 'bereaved may remain even as I.'

9. CANNOT CONTAIN,] *lit.* 'have not strength in (yourselves) . . to be on fire.'

10. COMMAND,] *lit.* 'tell further . . be separated (*or* separate herself) from the husband.'

11. DEPART,] *lit.* 'may be separated (*or* may separate herself) changed thoroughly *or* back to the husband, and let not a husband send away a wife.'

12. ANY,] *lit.* 'if any one—a brother—has an unbelieving wife, and she is well-pleased to keep house with him, let him not send her away.'

13. THE,] *lit.* 'and a woman *or* wife who has an unbelieving husband, and he is well-pleased to keep house with her, let her not send him away.'

14. BY,] *lit.* 'in the wife . . in the husband, otherwise your children are unclean, but now they are holy or hallowed ones.'

15. DEPART,] *or* 'is separated (*or* separates herself), let him be separated (*or* separate himself); the brother or the sister is not in bondage in (*or* with) such cases (*or* persons) . . in peace.'

16. KNOWEST,] *lit.* 'hast thou known . . the husband? or what hast thou known . . the wife.'

17. BUT AS,] *lit.* 'if not (so), as God divided to each, as the Lord has called each, so let him walk about; and so *or* thus I myself thoroughly arrange in all the assemblies.'

18. IS,] *lit.* 'was any one called having been circumcised? let him not draw (it) over; was any one called in uncircumcision? let him not become circumcised.'

19. CIRCUMCISION,] *lit.* 'the circumcision is nothing, and the uncircumcision is nothing, but a keeping of God's precepts.'

20. EVERY,] *lit.* 'each remain.'

21. ART,] *lit.* 'was thou called? let it not be a care to thee; but if thou art also able to become free.'

22. IS,] *lit.* 'was called . . freedman . . was called.'

23. ARE,] *lit.* 'were brought . . become not bondsmen of men.'

24. EVERY,] *lit.* 'each . . was called . . remain near God.'

25. VIRGINS,] *lit.* 'the virgins (whether male or female) . . full arrangement of the Lord, but I gave an opinion, as . . kindness from (*lit.* under) the Lord to be stedfast.'

26. SUPPOSE,] *or* 'make it a law, . . because of the present *or* standing in necessity . . man to be thus.'

27. ART,] *lit.* 'hast thou been bound . . hast thou been loosed.'

28. HAST,] *lit.* 'didst not sin, and if the virgin marry she did not sin . . but I am sparing you.'

29. SAY,] *or* 'affirm, the season henceforth is having been contracted (*lit.* sent together), that both those having wives may be as those not having.'

30. THEY,] *lit.* 'those weeping, as not weeping, and those rejoicing as not rejoicing, and those buying, as not buying.'

31. THEY,] *lit.* 'and those using the world, as not using (it) amiss, . . going along.'

32. WOULD,] *lit.* 'wish you to be without care (*lit.* partings) . . shall please.'

33. IS,] *or* 'has married . . shall please the wife.'

34. THERE IS,] *lit.* 'the wife and the virgin has been divided . . that has married . . shall please the husband.'

35. PROFIT,] *lit.* a 'bearing together.'

SNARE,] *or* 'noise . . for the seemliness and devotedness to the Lord undistractedly.'

36. ANY MAN,] *lit.* 'any one thinketh (it) to be unseemly to his virgin (daughter), if she may be beyond the bloom of age, and it ought so to be, let him do what he wishes. he sins not, let them give (her) in marriage.

37. STANDETH,] *lit.* 'has stood settled in (his) heart, . . authority . . has determined (*lit.* judged) this in . . to keep his own virgin (daughter), does well.'

38. SO THEN,] *lit.* 'so that he who is giving out in marriage . . is not giving out.'

39. THE,] *lit.* a 'wife has been bound by law as long time as her husband may live

but if her husband sleep (in death) she is free to..she wishes.'

40. ABIDE,] *lit.* 'remain, according to my own judgment.'

Chapter VIII. may be divided into three parts; v. 1—3 knowledge not so good as love; v. 4—7 an idol is nothing, but all have not this knowledge; v. 8—13 victuals are nothing compared to Christian love.

1. KNOW,] *lit.* 'have known . . the knowledge (alone)..the love buildeth up.'

2. ANY MAN,] *lit.* 'any one thinks to know anything, he has known..it behoves (him) to know.'

3. ANY MAN,] *lit.* 'any one loves God, he has been known by him.'

4. KNOW,] *lit.* 'have known.'

5. THROUGH,] *lit.* 'even if there are those.'

6. ALL,] *lit.* 'the all things, and we with a view to him,..through whom are the all things, and we through him.'

7. EVERY MAN,] *lit.* 'in all the knowledge (just mentioned), but certain with the conscience..being infirm.'

8. MEAT,] *or* 'victuals do not set us alongside of God.. may eat..may not eat, are we behind,'

9. TAKE HEED,] *lit.* 'see, behold..authority of yours may become.. to the infirm.'

10. SIT AT MEAT,] *lit.* 'lying down in an idol-temple..is infirm be built up, with a view to eating the idol-sacrifices.'

11. THROUGH,] *lit.* 'upon *or* over thy.. infirm brother be lost, because of whom Christ died.'

12. WHEN,] *lit.* 'thus sinning in reference to the brethren, and striking their infirm conscience, ye sin in reference to Christ.'

13. MEAT,] *or* 'victuals cause my brother to stumble, I may not eat flesh to the age, that I may not cause my brother to stumble.'

Chapter IX. may be divided into four parts; v. 1—6 Paul asserts his right as an apostle; v. 7—14 the worker is worthy of his hire; v. 15—23 his own disinterested conduct; v. 24—27 the Christian life compared to a race.

1. APOSTLE,] *lit.* one 'sent forth.'

2. ANSWER,] *lit.* 'apology to those judging me thoroughly is this.'

4. POWER,] *lit.* 'authority.'

5. POWER,] *lit.* 'authority to lead about a sister-wife, as also the apostles and the brothers of the Lord, and Cephas,' i.e. Peter, a rock *or* stone.

6. POWER,] *lit.* 'authority not to work?'

7. GOETH A WARFARE,] *or* 'serveth as a soldier..feedeth,' *lit.* shepherdeth *or* tendeth.

8. AS,] *lit.* 'according to man.. these also.'

9. IS,] *lit.* 'has been written..an ox treading out..of the oxen.'

10. FOR,] *lit.* 'because of us? because of us it was written, that he who is plowing ought to plow in (*lit.* on) hope, and he who is treading (ought) to have with (him) of his hope in (*lit.* on) hope.'

11. HAVE,] *lit.* 'did sow to you the spiritual things.'

12. POWER,] *lit.* 'authority.. we did not use this authority, but bear all, that we might not give any hindrance (*lit.* a striking in) to.'

13. DO,] *lit.* 'have ye not known that those working the things of the temple do eat of the temple? and those waiting at the altar are partakers with the altar.'

14. EVEN SO,] *lit.* 'so also did the Lord thoroughly-arrange to those telling fully the good news—of the good news to live.'

15. HAVE,] *lit.* 'but I used for myself none.. nor did I write.. it might so happen in my case,..any one might make my boasting vain,' *or* empty.

16. THOUGH,] *lit.* 'if I..there is no cause of boasting to me.'

17. DO,] *or* 'practise this yieldingly..unyieldingly, with a stewardship I have been intrusted.'

18. MAKE,] *lit.* 'set the good-news of the Christ freely, (*or* inexpensively), with a view to my not abusing (*lit.* using down) my power in the good-news.'

19. THOUGH,] *lit.* 'for being free..did I make myself bondsman to all.'

20. THE JEWS,] *lit.* 'gain Jews; to those under law as under law..those under law.'

21. WITHOUT LAW,] *lit.* 'lawless as lawless, not being lawless to God, but in law to Christ..gain lawless ones.'

22. AM MADE,] *lit.* 'I have become the all (things) to all (men).'

23. FOR,] *lit.* 'because of the good-news that I might become for myself a fellow-partaker of it.'

24. DO,] *lit.* 'have ye not known, that those running in a race (*Gr.* stadium).. may receive (the prize) down.'

25. MAN,] *lit.* 'every one who is agonizing, is inwardly powerful in all things,..that they may receive a.'

26. FIGHT,] *lit.* 'use the fists..beating air.'

27. I KEEP UNDER,] *lit.* 'strike under the eye,' i.e. bruise *or* buffet.

SUBJECTION,] *lit.* 'lead (it) into bondage ..cried (as a herald) to others, I myself may become disapproved,' *or* unaccepted, unthought of. i.e. despised.

Chapter X. may be divided into four parts; v. 1—4 Israelitish blessings typical of Christian ones; v. 5—13 their punishments also a warning to us; v. 14—22 against idolatry and self-pleasing; v. 23—33 regarding idol-sacrifices.

1. WOULD,] *lit.* 'I do not wish you to be ignorant that all our fathers.'

2. WERE,] *lit.* 'and did all baptize themselves with a view to Moses (as their leader) in the cloud (which dropt as it were upon them), and in the sea (by going down into its depths);' thus affording the true compound view of the mode of baptism.

3. MEAT,] *i.e.* food, even the promises of God.

4. DRANK,] *lit.* 'were drinking from a spiritual Rock following them, and the

rock was the Christ,' i.e. the promised Messiah and Saviour.

5. WITH MANY,] *lit.* 'with (*or* in) the most of them..strewn down in the desert.'

6. WERE,] *lit.* 'became types of us, with a view to our not over-desiring evil things, as these over-desired (them).'

7. BE,] *lit.* 'become ye idolators, as certain of them (became), as it has been written.. stood up to play,' *lit.* act as children.

8. FORNICATION,] *or* 'whoredom, as certain of them committed whoredom, and there fell.'

9. TEMPT,] *or* 'try beyond measure the Christ, as certain of them also tried, and perished by the serpents.'

10. SOME,] *lit.* 'certain..perished by the destroyer.'

11. HAPPENED,] *lit.* 'were coming together to these (for) types, and they were written for the setting of our mind, over-against whom the ends of the ages came down.'

12. WHEREFORE,] *lit.* 'so that let him who is thinking to stand see that he fall not.'

13. SUCH AS IS COMMON,] *lit.* 'except human..faithful *or* stedfast..tried..trial also the outlet,..bear up under it.'

14. DEARLY,] *lit.* 'my beloved, flee from the idolatry.'

15. WISE,] *lit.* 'prudent, *or* full of mind.'

I SAY,] *or* 'affirm.'

16. BLESSING,] *lit.* 'of the blessing (*lit.* good-speech) which we bless (*lit.* speak well of), is it not a (token of the) communion (*or* fellowship) of the blood of the Christ? the loaf..of the Christ.'

17. BEING,] *lit.* 'the many.. the one loaf.'

18. AFTER,] *lit.* 'according to flesh..those eating these sacrifices in the communion of the altar.'

19. SAY,] *or* 'affirm? that an idol is anything? or that an idol-sacrifice is anything?'

20. GENTILES,] *lit.* 'nations..to demons (i.e. shades of departed men),..I do not wish you to come into the communion (*or* fellowship) of the demons.'

21. DEVILS,] *Gr.* 'demons; ye are not able to partake..of demons.'

22. PROVOKE,] *lit.* 'shall we make the Lord very zealous?'

23. ALL THINGS,] i.e. in the way of food.

EXPEDIENT,] *lit.* 'do not bear *or* carry together.'

EDIFY,] *lit.* 'do not build up.'

24. EVERY,] *lit.* 'each the (good) of the other.'

25. WHATSOEVER,] *lit.* 'every thing that is sold in a meat-market eat, judging nothing again, because of the conscience.'

26. FULNESS.] See Ps. 24. 1; 50. 12.

27. THEM,] *lit.* 'any one of the unbelieving call you, and ye wish to pass on, every thing that is set near you eat, judging nothing again, because of the conscience.'

28. OFFERED,] *lit.* 'an idol-sacrifice.'

29. LIBERTY,] *lit.* 'freedom.'

30. BY,] *lit.* 'with grace partake, why am I injuriously-spoken of?'

31. WHATSOEVER,] *lit.* 'do anything.'

32. GIVE,] *lit.* 'become offenceless, both to Jews and Hellenes, and to the assembly of God.'

33. PROFIT,] *lit.* a thing 'bearing together.'

MANY,] *lit.* 'of the many.'

Chapter XI. may be divided into three parts; v. 1—16 directions as to prayer and praise in the public assembly; v. 17—22 as to divisions therein; v. 23—34 as to the Lord's Supper.

1. BE,] *lit.* 'become ye mindful of me,' in my teaching and conduct.

2. REMEMBER,] *lit.* 'are mindful of me in all (i.e. most) things, and as I gave over to you, do hold-thoroughly the things given over.'

3. WOULD,] *lit.* 'I wish you to know..is the Christ.'

4. PRAYING,] *lit.* 'pouring forth before (God) or prophesying (i.e. speaking publicly) having (any thing) upon the head, shameth his head thoroughly.'

5. PRAYING..PROPHESYING.] As in v. 4.

DISHONOURETH,] *lit.* 'shameth thoroughly her own head, for it is one and the same thing with (her) being shaven.'

6. THE,] *lit.* 'a woman is not thoroughly covered..be thoroughly covered.'

7. COVER,] *lit.* 'cover thoroughly, being *or* having an image and glory of God, but a woman (is the) glory of a man.'

8. THE,] *lit.* 'for a man is not out of a woman, but a woman out of a man.'

9. THE,] *lit.* 'a man was not created (*or* built) because of the woman, but a woman because of the man.'

10. POWER,] *lit.* 'authority,' i.e. a token or sign of it, such as a veil.

ANGELS,] *lit.* 'messengers,' i.e. ministers.

11. THE,] *lit.* 'a man apart from a woman, nor a woman apart from a man.'

12. OF,] *lit.* 'out of, (from) the man, so also the man (is) through the woman, but the all things (are) out of God.'

13. JUDGE,] *lit.* 'judge ye these things among yourselves; is it proper for a woman to pour forth before (God) not thoroughly covered?'

14. NATURE,] *lit.* 'the nature,' as regulated by use and custom, peculiar to each country and age.

HAVE,] *lit.* 'has (long) hair..dishonour.'

15. IS,] *lit.* 'has been given for the sake of a covering,' *lit.* a thing 'cast around.'

16. SEEM,] *lit.* 'if any one thinketh to be a lover-of-contention..such united custom.'

17. NOW,] *lit.* 'but this I am telling also I praise not, that *or* because.'

18. CHURCH,] *lit.* 'assembly, I hear of rents (*Gr.* schisms) being among you.'

19. HERESIES,] *lit.* things 'lifted up,' opinions, sects.

APPROVED,] *or* 'accepted may become apparent among you.'

20. INTO ONE PLACE,] *or* 'at one time.'

21. EATING,] *lit.* 'in the eating each his own supper taketh publicly, and one indeed eateth, and one drinketh.'

22. DESPISE,] *lit.* 'think ye down upon

the assembly of God, and thoroughly shame those not having (houses *or* food)?'

23. HAVE,] *lit.* 'for I received from the Lord (Jesus) that which also I gave over to you,..in the night in which he was given over took a loaf.'

24. THIS IS,] i.e. 'this represents,' a very common idiom in all languages, and more especially in Greek and Hebrew. See again in next verse.

BROKEN,] *lit.* 'is being broken in behalf of you, this do ye with a view to my remembrance.'

25. WHEN,] *lit.* 'after the supping, saying, This—the cup—is (i.e. represents) the New Covenant (*lit.* a thing thoroughly set) in my blood.'

26. SHEW,] *lit.* 'tell thoroughly.'

27. WHEREFORE,] *lit.* 'so that whosoever may eat this bread, *or* may drink the cup of the Lord unworthily (*lit.* unled on), shall be guilty (*lit.* held in) of the body.'

28. EXAMINE,] *lit.* 'prove.'

29. EATETH,] *lit.* 'is eating and drinking unworthily,' (*lit.* 'unled on' by the Spirit).

DAMNATION,] *lit.* 'judgment,' of condemnation for the abuse of privileges, resulting in decreasing spiritual vigour, comfort, and perhaps even temporal afflictions.

DISCERNING,] *lit.* 'judging-thoroughly (the symbols of) the body of the Lord,' from an ordinary meal.

30. WEAK,] *or* 'infirm.. are asleep,' spiritually.

31. WOULD,] *lit.* 'were judging ourselves thoroughly, we would not.'

32. SHOULD,] *lit.* 'may not be judged-down.'

33. WHEREFORE,] *lit.* 'so that.. receive one another fully.'

34. MAN,] *lit.* 'any one hungers..to judgment; and the things left behind whenever I come I will set thoroughly in order.'

Chapter XII. may be divided into three parts; v. 1—11 working of the Spirit and diversity of spiritual gifts; v. 12—21 unity and diversity of Christians; v. 22—31 their mutual sympathies and gifts.

1. SPIRITUAL,] *lit.* 'the spiritual things (*or* persons)..I do not wish you to be ignorant.'

2. KNOW,] *lit.* 'have known..voiceless idols..led away.'

3. GIVE,] *lit.* 'I make known to you.. in (the) Spirit..anathema (*lit.* a thing 'lifted up' upon the altar), and no one is able to say Jesus (is) Lord, except in holy spirit.'

4. GIFTS,] *or* 'graces.'

5. DIFFERENCES,] *or* 'diversities of deaconships.'

6. OPERATIONS,] *lit.* 'workings..is working the all things in every man.'

7. MANIFESTATION,] *or* 'appearance..has been given.. for to bear together.'

8. BY,] *lit.* 'through the Spirit a word of wisdom, and to another a word of knowledge, according to the same Spirit.'

9. FAITH,] *or* 'stedfastness in the same Spirit, and to another gifts (*or* graces) of healings in the same Spirit.'

10. MIRACLES,] *lit.* 'powers..judging of spirits; and to another races of tongues, and to another interpretation of tongues.'

11. WORKETH,] *lit.* 'worketh inwardly the one and the same Spirit, dividing to each his own as it counsels.'

12. THAT,] *lit.* 'the one body.. is the Christ.'

13. BY,] *lit.* 'in (*or* with) one spirit were we all baptized with a view to one body, whether Jews or Hellenes, whether bondsmen or freedmen, and were all..with a view to one spirit.'

15. SHALL,] *lit.* 'may say..a hand.. it is not, because of this, not of the body.'

16. SHALL,] *lit.* 'may say.. an eye.. it is not, because of this, not of the body.'

17. HATH,] *lit.* 'did God set.. each one . as he wished.'

19. THEY,] *lit.* 'the whole were one member.'

20. THE,] *lit.* 'an eye is not able to say.'

21. THOSE,] *lit.* 'the members of the body seeming to be more infirm.'

22. UPON,] *lit.* 'around these we put more ..seemly.. seemliness.'

24. COMELY,] *or* 'seemly..but God tempered (*or* mixed) the body together.'

25. SCHISM,] i.e. rent, division.

CARE,] *or* 'anxiety.'

26. SUFFER,] *lit.* 'suffers . is glorified.'

27. THE,] *lit.* 'a body of Christ (i.e. Christians?) and members of a part.'

28. CHURCH,] *or* 'assembly; first, apostles (*lit.* those 'sent forth'), second, prophets (*lit.* those 'speaking before' *or* openly), third, teachers, after that powers (*or* abilities), then graces of healings, helps (*lit.* 'taking hold over-against'), governings,' *lit.* 'steerings' as of a ship.

DIVERSITIES,] *lit.* 'kinds,' as in v. 10.

29. WORKERS OF MIRACLES,] *lit.* 'powers.'

30. GIFTS,] *lit.* 'all graces of healings.'

31. COVET EARNESTLY,] *lit.* 'be zealous of the best graces..far more excellent way.'

Chapter XIII. may be divided into three parts; v. 1—3 love the best grace; v. 4—8 its praise, workings, and perpetuity; v. 9—13 our present state imperfect, and the sum of all.

1. MEN,] *lit.* 'the men ..the angels..I have become..brass (*or* copper).'

2. UNDERSTAND,] *lit.* 'see all the mysteries (*or* secrets), and all the knowledge,..all the faith, so as to remove (*or* overturn) mountains.'

3. BESTOW,] *lit.* 'may make all my goods morsels..may give over my body that it may be burned.'

4. CHARITY,] *lit.* 'the love..is not jealous; the love is not vaunting.'

5. BEHAVE,] *lit.* 'act unseemly; seeketh not her own things; is not soon sharpened; reckoneth not that which is bad.'

6. REJOICETH,] *lit.* 'leapeth not for joy over the unrighteousness; but leapeth for joy along with the truth.'

7. BEARETH,] *or* 'covereth.'

8. CHARITY,] *lit.* 'the love at no time

falleth off . . shall become useless . . it shall become useless.'

9. IN,] *lit.* 'of a part.'

10. IS,] *lit.* 'may come. of a part shall become useless.'

11. CHILD,] *or* 'babe I was speaking . . I was thinking . . reckoning (*or* reasoning) . . I have become . . I have made useless the things of the babe.'

12. GLASS,] *or* 'looking-glass in an enigma . . know of a part . . I know fully . . am fully known.'

13. ABIDETH,] *or* 'remaineth . . love . . is the love.'

Chapter XIV. may be divided into two parts; v. 1—19 commendation of prophesying; v. 20—40 directions regarding the use of tongues.

1. FOLLOW,] *lit.* 'pursue the love; and be zealous for the spiritual things, and (the) rather that ye may prophesy,' i.e. speak publicly the praises of God.

2. SPEAKETH,] *lit.* 'is speaking a language . . no one hearkens, but in (*or* with) spirit he speaketh secrets.'

3. PROPHESIETH,] *lit.* 'is prophesying . . upbuilding.'

4. EDIFIETH,] *lit.* 'buildeth up himself . . an assembly.'

5. WOULD,] *lit.* 'wish you all to speak with tongues, and the more, that ye may prophesy . . except (one) interpret thoroughly . . up-building.'

6. BY,] *lit.* 'in uncovering (of hidden things), or in . . or in . . or in teaching.'

7. AND,] *lit.* 'yet the soul-less things giving voice . . may give . . with the sounds, how shall what is piped or harped become known?'

8. THE,] *lit.* 'a trumpet . . with a view to battle.'

9. UTTER,] *lit.* 'give through the tongue significant speech . . shall be speaking to air.'

10. WITHOUT,] *lit.* 'voiceless.'

11. MEANING,] *lit.* 'power . . with (*lit.* in) me.'

12. GIFTS,] *lit.* 'of spirits . . abound to the upbuilding of the assembly.'

13. IN,] *or* 'with a language pour forth before (God), that (one) may interpret thoroughly.'

14. UNDERSTANDING,] *or* 'mind.'

15. UNDERSTANDING,] *lit.* 'mind . . sing-psalms . . sing-psalms with the mind also.'

16. ELSE,] *lit.* 'since, if thou mayest speak well . . is filling up . . unlearned (*or* common people) say the Amen upon . . he has not known.'

17. EDIFIED,] *lit.* 'built up.'

18. SPEAK,] *lit.* 'I am speaking.'

19. THE,] *lit.* 'in an assembly I wish to speak . . through my mind, that I may sound-down (upon) others also, than a myriad of words.'

20. BE,] *lit.* 'become not boys as to the mind, but be ye babes as to the evil, . . become ye perfect.'

21. IS,] *lit.* 'it has been written, that, In other tongues (*or* languages) and in other lips . . not hearken to me.'

22. WHEREFORE,] *lit.* 'so that the tongues . . but the prophesy.'

23. BE,] *lit.* 'may come together . . all may speak . there may come in common people or unbelieving ones.'

24. PROPHESY,] *lit.* 'may prophesy . . may come in any one, unbelieving or common person, he is convicted under (*or* by) all, he is judged again under (by) all.'

25. ARE MADE,] *lit.* 'become apparent *or* manifest . . will kiss forward the hand to God, telling forth again that God is really among you.'

26. HOW,] *lit.* 'what . . each of you has a psalm (of their own composition), has a teaching (founded on the same), has a tongue (*or* language), has an uncovering (of hidden truth), has an interpretation (or explanation).' From this and other passages it is clear that the upbuilding of the church was not confined then, as now, to one, or at most two, of the congregation, but was the privilege of all the members, and though such a practice is liable to abuse (James 3. 1), it is possible that its entire disuse now has led to still greater evils obvious to all,—'quenching the Spirit.' But, no doubt, the whole of these things—being merely incidental, and not essential—are left to the prudence and discretion of the various Christian Assemblies themselves. 'Let all things be for upbuilding.'

27. SPEAK,] *lit.* 'speaks in (*or* with) . . enterpret thoroughly.'

28. BE,] *lit.* 'may not be a thorough-interpreter (present) . . in an assembly.'

29. OTHER,] *lit.* 'others judge thoroughly.'

30. REVEALED,] *lit.* 'may be uncovered . . first be silent.'

31. MAY,] *lit.* 'ye are all able to prophesy . . be exhorted.'

32. THE,] *lit.* 'spirits (*or* spiritual gifts) of prophets are arranged (*or* arrange themselves) under prophets.'

33. CONFUSION,] *lit.* 'unsettledness . . all the assemblies.'

34. WOMEN,] *or* 'wives (not 'virgins,' see Acts. 21. 9) be silent, for it has not been turned over upon them to speak (*or* talk, i.e. ask questions perhaps), but to arrange themselves under (their husband), as also the law saith.' The 'law' here can hardly be the Old Testament, for no such injunction has been pointed out, hence perhaps the apostle refers to some oral or traditional custom having the force of a law.

35. WILL,] *lit.* 'wish to learn anything, let them ask at their own husbands in the house.'

37. MAN,] *lit.* 'if any one thinketh (*or* seemeth) to be a prophet or spiritual, let him know fully . . are commands,' *or* precepts.

38. MAN,] *lit.* 'if any one is ignorant.'

39. WHEREFORE,] *lit.* 'so that, brethren, be zealous to prophesy, and hinder not.'

40. DECENTLY,] *lit.* 'becomingly, and according to arrangement,' *or* order.

Chapter XV. may be divided into six parts; v. 1—4 sum of the good-news; v. 5

—11 proof of Christ's up-rising; v. 12—19 consequences of denying it; v. 20—34 a general up-rising maintained; v. 35—49 its manner illustrated; v. 50—58 destruction of Death and Hades.

1. DECLARE,] *lit.* 'make known to you the good-news which I told as-good-news to you..ye received alongside..ye have stood.'

2. BY,] *lit.* 'through which also ye are being saved, (in what speech I told good-news to you, if ye hold it fast), except ye believed in vain.'

3. DELIVERED,] *lit.* 'gave over to you, among the first things, that which also I received alongside, that Christ died fully in behalf of our sins.'

4. BURIED,] *or* 'entombed,..has risen the.'

5. WAS SEEN,] *lit.* 'appeared to Cephas.'

6. UNTO,] *lit.* 'till now, but certain fell asleep.'

7. WAS SEEN,] *lit.* 'appeared to Jacob,' i.e. James.

8. WAS SEEN,] *lit.* 'appeared to me also, as to the abortion.'

9. PERSECUTED,] *lit.* 'caused to flee.'

10. WAS BESTOWED,] *lit.* 'is towards me came not in vain, but I toiled..is with me.'

11. PREACH,] *lit.* 'cry *or* proclaim (as heralds).'

12. BE,] *lit.* 'is proclaimed that he has risen out of (the) dead, how say certain among you that there is not an up-standing of (the) dead?'

13. BE,] *lit.* 'is not an up-standing of (the) dead, neither has Christ risen.'

14. BE,] *lit.* 'has not risen..our proclamation void..also void.'

15. HAVE TESTIFIED,] *lit.* 'did witness according to God, that he raised the Christ... if then (the) dead rise not.'

16. THEN,] *lit.* 'neither has Christ risen.'

17. BE,] *lit.* 'has not risen.'

18. WHICH ARE,] *lit.* 'who have fallen asleep in Christ did perish,' *or* were lost.

19. HAVE HOPE,] *lit.* 'we are hoping..most to be pitied.'

20. IS,] *lit.* 'has Christ risen out of (the) dead, a first fruit of those sleeping he became.'

21. BY,] *lit.* 'through man (is) the death, through man also (is) an upstanding of (the) dead.'

22. EVERY,] *or* 'each one..a first-fruit..in his presence.'

23. COMETH,] *or* 'is the end, when he may give over the reign to the God and Father, when he may make useless all principality.'

25. HE MUST,] *lit.* 'it behoves him to be king, till he may have put all the enemies.'

26. THAT SHALL,] *lit.* 'is made useless—Death.'

27. HATH PUT,] *lit.* 'he put all under his feet, and when one may say that all has been put under..put the all things under him.'

28. ALL,] *lit.* 'the all things may be put..be put under him who put all..the all things in every one.'

29. FOR THE DEAD,] i.e. in behalf of him who was dead, even Christ. The plural form (in the Greek) is used by way of *emphasis* for the singular, as in Mat. 2. 20; 8. 11; 9. 8; 24. 27; 27. 44, &c. Or perhaps it may mean, 'in behalf of (the resurrection of) the dead.'

30. STAND,] *lit.* 'are we in peril.'

31. I PROTEST,] *lit.* 'by your (*or* our) boasting.'

32. AFTER THE MANNER,] *lit.* 'according to man I fought wild beasts in Ephesus? what is the profit to me if (the) dead rise not? we may eat and drink, for to-morrow we die fully.'

33. DECEIVED,] *or* 'led astray; bad (*or* evil) crowdings corrupt kind customs.'

34. AWAKE,] *lit.* 'righteously drink not greatly; and do not miss the mark, for certain have an ignorance of God; to turn you in I say (it).'

35. SOME,] *lit.* 'a certain one..do the dead rise?'

36. FOOL,] *lit.* 'mindless *or* thoughtless one! thou—what thou sowest is not made alive.'

37. SHALL BE,] *lit.* 'shall come, but naked grain..of a certain one of the others.'

38. HATH PLEASED,] *lit.* 'as he wished, and to each of the seeds its own body.'

39. BEASTS,] *or* 'cattle,' *lit.* possessions

BIRDS,] *lit.* 'flying things.'

40. CELESTIAL,] *lit.* 'bodies upon the heavens, and bodies upon the earth.'

41. ONE,] *lit.* 'for star from star bears diversely in glory.'

42. RESURRECTION,] *lit.* 'upstanding.'

43. DISHONOUR,] *or* 'want of honour..infirmity.'

44. NATURAL,] *lit.* 'physical..physical.'

45. IS,] *lit.* 'has been written..became a living soul (i.e. physical creature), the last Adam (became) a life giving spirit.'

46. NATURAL,] *or* 'physical.'

47. OF,] *lit.* 'out of the land, earthy..out of heaven.'

49. HAVE BORNE,] *lit.* 'bare.'

50. SAY,] *or* 'affirm..are not able to inherit.. doth the corruption inherit the incorruption.'

51. SHEW,] *lit.* 'say *or* tell to you a secret .. all be asleep.'

CHANGED,] *lit.* 'become another thing.'

52. MOMENT,] *lit.* 'an 'indivisible' point of time.

AT,] *lit.* 'in (i.e. during *or* with) the last trumpet (for it shall sound).'

53. MUST,] *lit.* 'it behoveth..this dying (body) to put on undyingness.'

54. SHALL,] *lit.* 'may have put on..this dying (body) may have put on undyingness then shall happen the word that has been written, The Death was swallowed up—to unyieldingness.'

55. GRAVE,] *Gr.* Hades, i.e. the 'unseen' world.

56. DEATH,] *lit.* 'of the death (is) the sin, and the power of the sin (is) the law.'

57. THANKS,] *lit.* that which 'causes leaping with joy.'

GIVETH,] *lit.* 'is giving to us the unyieldingness.'

58. THEREFORE,] *lit.* 'so that . . become steady (*lit.* seated, founded), . . knowing that your toil is not vain.'

Chapter XVI. may be divided into five parts: v. 1—4 on the collection for the poor saints; v. 5—9 Paul's plans regarding himself v. 10—12 and regarding Timotheus and Apollos; v. 13—18 exhortations, entreaties, and rejoicings; v. 19—24 various salutations.

1. COLLECTION,] *lit.* thing 'laid out, that (is) with a view to the holy *or* sanctified ones, as I thoroughly arranged.'

2. UPON,] *lit.* 'through one of (the) sabbaths, let each of you put by himself, treasuring up whatever he may have prospered in, that there may be no collections (*or* 'layings out,') when I come.'

3. COME,] *lit.* 'I may come along, whomsoever ye may approve, through letters, these will I send to bear away your favour (*or* grace) to Jerusalem.'

4. MEET,] *lit.* 'worthy (*or* leading on) for me to pass on also, they shall pass on with me.'

5. SHALL,] *lit.* 'I go through . . I come through.'

6. ABIDE,] *lit.* 'remain alongside, or even winter along with you . . may send me forward whithersoever I pass on.'

7. WILL,] *lit.* 'wish not to see you in the passing by, but I hope to remain on a certain time with you, if the Lord turn (it) over upon (me).'

8. TARRY,] *lit.* 'remain on in Ephesus till the pentecost.'

9. EFFECTUAL,] *lit.* 'inworking, has been opened, and withstanders (are) many.'

10. BE,] *lit.* 'become fearless towards you.'

11. LET,] *lit.* 'no one, then, may think nothing of him, but send him forward.'

12. TOUCHING,] *or* 'concerning . . I called much upon him, that he might come . . and there was not at all a wish that he may come now, but . . he may have a convenient season.'

13. WATCH,] *lit.* 'be wakeful, stand in the faith, be men, be strengthened *or* strengthen yourselves.'

14. WITH,] *lit.* 'in love.'

15. BESEECH,] *lit.* 'I call upon you, brethren, ye yourselves have known the household of Stephanus (i.e. a crown), that it is a first-fruit . . and (that) they set themselves with a view to deaconship to the holy ones.'

16. SUBMIT,] *lit.* 'arrange yourselves under such, and every one who is helping with (us) and toiling.'

17. GLAD,] *lit.* 'I leap with joy over the presence of Stephanus, Fortunatus, (i.e. fortunate), and Achaicus (i.e. a native of Achaia), . . these filled up.'

18. HAVE,] *lit.* 'did refresh . . know fully.'

19. SALUTE,] *lit.* 'draw you near.'

ASIA,] that is, Proconsular Asia.'

AQUILA,] i.e. an eagle.

PRISCILLA,] i.e. a little ancient one.

20. GREET,] *lit.* 'draw you near.'

KISS,] *lit.* 'in a hallowed friendship.'

21. SALUTATION,] *lit.* 'drawing near.'

22. MAN,] *lit.* 'any one befriends not the Lord Jesus Christ, let him be anathema,' i.e. a thing 'laid up' on the altar of God.

MARAN-ATHA.] A sentence in the Syriac language of Paul's day, signifying 'The (*or* Our) Lord has come!'

23. OUR,] *lit.* 'of the Lord Jesus Christ (is).

24. BE,] *or* 'is with you.'

PAUL'S LETTER TO THE CORINTHIANS
(THE SECOND)

THIS LETTER was probably written from Macedonia, shortly after the First, and was sent to Corinth by the hands of Titus (and Luke?). Paul's former Letter had produced good effects, but still the Judaizing party persisted in opposing his apostolic authority. Being informed of this by Titus (and also by Timotheus?) Paul resolved to vindicate his character and position, which he does with great boldness and success. The whole may be divided into four sections:—

I. ACCOUNT OF HIS SPIRITUAL LABOURS AND LOVE, ch. i—vii.
1. He thanks God for their general state, ch. 1. 1—14.
2. Alludes to his proposed visit to them, v. 15—24.
3. Alludes to points in his previous Letter, 2. 1—11.
4. Returns to his own plans, v. 12—17.
5. Pleads his own Apostolic dignity, 3. 1—18.
6. Dwells upon his own labours, 4. 1—18.
7. Dwells upon his own hopes, 5. 1—21.
8. Dwells upon his own sufferings, 6. 1—18.

II. DIRECTIONS ABOUT THE COLLECTIONS, ch. viii. ix.
1. From the example of Macedonia, ch. 8. 1—6.
2. From their own spiritual progress, v. 7, 8.
3. From the example of Christ, v. 9—17.
4. Present mission of Titus, v. 18—24.
5. Why they were sent, ch. 9. 1—5.
6. Reasons for liberality, v. 6—11.
7. Benefits of liberality, v. 12—15.

III. REPROOFS AND WARNINGS, ch. x—xii.
1. Vindicates and asserts his authority, ch. 10. 1—11.
2. Contrasts himself with opponents, v. 12—18.
3. His godly jealousy and equality, 11. 1—6.
4. His disinterestedness and forbearance, v. 7—15.
5. His grounds of boasting, v. 16—21.
6. Descent, labours, and sufferings, v. 22—33.
7. His wonderful revelations, 12. 1—10.
8. His office, and affection to them, v. 11—21.

IV. THE CONCLUSION, ch. xiii.
1. He threatens to use severity, v. 1—4.
2. Admonishes and assures, v. 5—11.
3. Various Salutations, v. 12—14.

This Letter is quoted or referred to, both as being the writing of Paul, and as being canonical, by Irenaeus (A.D. 178), Athenagorus (A.D. 178), Clement of Alexandria (A.D. 194), Tertullian (A.D. 200).

Chapter I. may be divided into five parts; v 1, 2 salutation; v. 3—11 thanksgiving; v. 12—16 boasting and confidence; v. 17—22 stedfastness of the apostles and of God; v. 23, 24 reasons for not coming.

1. PAUL,] i.e. the 'little' one.

APOSTLE,] *lit.* 'one 'sent forth.'

JESUS CHRIST,] i.e. an 'anointed saviour.'

BY,] *lit.* 'through (the) wish of God.'

TIMOTHEUS,] i.e. one 'honouring God.'

OUR,] *lit.* 'the brother (in the Lord), to the assembly of the (true) God that is in Corinth.'

2. GRACE,] *lit.* what 'causes leaping for joy.'

PEACE,] *lit.* that which 'brings into unity.'

FROM,] *lit.* 'and (the Father of) the Lord Jesus Christ.'

3. BE,] *or* 'blessed (i.e. well-spoken of) is the God and Father of..of the mercies, and God of every comfort,' *or* exhortation.

4. COMFORTETH,] *lit.* 'is comforting (*or* exhorting) us over all..with a view to our being able to comfort (*or* exhort) those in any tribulation, through the comfort (*or* exhortation)..by God.'

5. CHRIST,] *lit.* 'of (i.e. for) the Christ abound toward us..through Christ.'

6. EFFECTUAL,] *lit.* 'inwrought.'

7. OF,] *lit.* 'in behalf of you.'

8. WOULD,] *lit.* 'did not wish you to be ignorant, concerning our tribulation which happened to us, that we were exceedingly burdened beyond (our) power, to our despairing (*lit.* not finding a passage) even of life.'

9. HAD,] *lit.* 'we ourselves have had the judgment of the death in ourselves, that we may not be trusting on ourselves, but on God who is raising.'

10. DELIVERED,] *lit.* 'freed us out of..free; in reference to whom we have hoped that he will even yet free.'

11. HELPING,] *lit.* 'working together in our behalf by the supplication, that the grace (done) toward us from many persons may be thankfully acknowledged through many.'

12. REJOICING,] *lit.* 'boasting..sincerity of God, not in..but in the..we turned (ourselves) round in.'

13. THERE,] *lit.* 'but what ye either recognize or even know fully, and I hope.. know fully.'

14. HAVE,] *lit.* 'did know us fully in part ..your boasting.'

15. MINDED,] *lit.* 'counselling.. second grace.'

16. PASS,] *lit.* 'go through by you..by you to be sent forward.'

17. WHEN,] *lit.* 'this then counselling, did I then use the lightness?..I counsel, did I counsel according to flesh, that alongside of me there might be the No, No! and the Yes, Yes?'

18. TRUE,] *lit.* 'faithful, that our..became not.'

19. BY,] *lit.* 'through us, through me,.. became not..became yea.'

20. ALL,] *lit.* 'as many as (are) promises ..the Yes,..the Amen..through us.'

21. STABLISHETH,] *lit.* 'is confirming.. with a view to Christ, and anointed.'

22. HATH,] *lit.* 'who also sealed us for himself, and gave the pledge.'

23. CALL,] *lit.* 'call upon God (for) a witness upon..that sparing you.'

24. FOR,] *lit.* 'not that we are lords of your faith, but are fellow-workers..ye have stood.'

Chapter II. may be divided into three parts; v. 1—4 reasons for writing; v. 5—11 regarding the incestuous person; v. 12—18 mental trouble but spiritual triumphs.

1. DETERMINED,] *lit.* 'judged this to myself, not to come again to you in sorrow.'

2. GLAD,] *lit.* 'giving me a good mind.. from me.'

3. LEST,] *lit.* 'that having come, I may not have..from whom it was behoving me ..over you all.'

4. AFFLICTION,] *lit.* 'tribulation and pressure (*lit.* holding-together)..through many ..might be sorry.'

5. HAVE,] *lit.* 'has caused sorrow, he has not caused me sorrow..not over-burden you all.'

6. MAN,] *lit.* 'such a one is this heavy weight which (is) by the multitude,' *or* most part.

7. CONTRARIWISE,] *lit.* 'on the contrary it is rather for you to be gracious yourselves and to comfort,.. may be ..over-abundant sorrow.'

8. BESEECH,] *or* 'call upon you to confirm.'

9. END,] *lit.* 'with a view to this also..are hearkening submissively in reference to all things.'

10. FORGIVE,] *or* 'are gracious in anything ..I also have been gracious in anything, to whom I have been gracious, (it is) because of you.'

11. LEST,] *lit.* 'that we may not be held more (firmly) by the Adversary.. his thoughts.'

12. PREACH,] *lit.* 'for the gospel of the Christ..having been opened in the Lord.'

13. HAD,] *lit.* 'I have had no relaxation.. but setting myself from them, I went forth to Macedonia.'

14. CAUSETH,] *or* 'leadeth us in triumph (*or* triumphantly) in the Christ, and maketh apparent the fragrance of his knowledge through us.'

15. SWEET SAVOUR,] *or* 'sweet smell.'

IN,] *or* 'among them those being saved, and among those being lost,' *or* loosing themselves away.

16. THE ONE,] *lit.* 'to these indeed, a fragrance of death to death, and to these, a fragrance of life to life.'

17. MANY,] *lit.* 'as the many, making merchandize of.. over-against God.'

Chapter III. may be divided into three parts; v. 1—6 living letters of Christ; v. 7—11 glory of the ministration of the Spirit; v. 12—18 the liberty of the Spirit.

1. COMMEND,] *lit.* 'set (with others *or*) together.. as certain.'

2. WRITTEN,] *lit.* 'written inwardly.. and known again by all men.'

3. MANIFESTLY,] *lit.* 'made apparent that ye are a letter of Christ deaconized by us, written inwardly, not with ink, but with (the) Spirit of the living God, not in tablets of stone, but in the fleshly tablets of (the) heart.'

4. CHRIST,] *lit.* 'through the Christ.'

5. OF,] *lit.* 'from ourselves to reason anything as from ourselves.'

6. HATH,] *lit.* 'who also made us able (to be) deacons of a new covenant (*lit.* thoroughly set thing), not of (the) letter, but of (the) spirit.. maketh alive.'

7. MINISTRATION,] *lit.* 'deaconship of the death, in letters struck in stones, came in glory, to the sons of Israel not being able to strain (their eyes) to the face of Moses, because of the glory of his face—which (deaconship) was being made useless.'

8. MINISTRATION,] *lit.* 'deaconship.. in glory.'

9. MINISTRATION,] *lit.* 'deaconship of the judging-down (is) glory..deaconship of the righteousness abound in glory.'

10. WAS,] *lit.* 'has been glorified has not been glorified..over-excelling glory.'

11. DONE,] *lit.* 'being made useless (is) through glory,..is remaining (is) in glory.'

12. SEEING,] *lit.* 'having then such a hope, we use much full-speech.'

13. NOT,] *lit.* 'and (are) not as Moses, who was putting a vail upon his own face, for the sons of Israel not to strain (their eyes) to the end of that which is being made useless.'

14. BLINDED,] *or* 'became hard *or* callous, for till to-day the same vail remaineth not-unveiled upon the reading of the Old Covenant, because *or* that it (i.e. the Old Covenant) is being made useless in Christ.'

15. EVEN,] *lit.* 'but till to-day..a vail lies upon their heart.'

16. SHALL,] *lit.* 'may turn over to the Lord, the vail is lifted up round about.

17. THAT,] *lit.* 'the Spirit..liberty,' *lit.* looseness.

18. OPEN,] *lit.* 'unvailed face, seeing for ourselves as in a mirror the..are being transformed..from the Lord's spirit.'

Chapter IV. may be divided into five parts; v. 1—5 manner of preaching the gospel; v. 6 ground for doing so; v. 7—12 life in death; v. 13—15 confidence in truth and in God; v. 16—18 result of all.

1. THEREFORE,] *lit.* 'because of this, having this deaconship, as we received kindness we act not badly.'

2. HAVE,] *lit.* 'did renounce,' *lit.* 'speak away for ourselves.'

DISHONESTY,] *lit.* 'of the shame, not walking about in every (kind of) work, or guile fully using the word of God, but by the manifestation of the truth setting ourselves together to every conscience of men.'

3. BE HID,] *lit.* 'is vailed, it is vailed among those loosing themselves away.'

4. IN,] *or* 'among whom the god of this age blinded the minds *or* thoughts of those unbelieving *or* unstedfast, with a view to the light of the gospel of the glory of the Christ not shining to them, who is an image of God.'

5. PREACH,] *or* 'proclaim (as heralds).. your bondsmen, because of Jesus.'

6. COMMANDED,] *lit.* 'said light..darkness shone in our hearts, for the enlightening of.'

7. EARTHEN,] *lit.* 'sun-burnt clay *or* shelly.' EXCELLENCY,] *or* 'super-excellence.'

8. TROUBLED,] *lit.* 'in every thing (we are) in tribulation, but not straitened, passageless, but not wholly passageless.'

9. PERSECUTED,] *lit.* 'caused to flee, but not wholly left inwardly... loosing ourselves.'

10. MADE MANIFEST,] *or* 'become apparent.'

11. LIVE,] *lit.* 'are living are given over to death because of Jesus,..become apparent in our dying flesh.'

12. DEATH,] *lit.* 'the death worketh inwardly in us, but the life in you.'

13. FAITH,] *lit.* 'of the faith, according to that which has been written..I spake.'

14. BY,] *lit.* 'through Jesus..set us alongside (of himself) with you.'

15. ALL,] *lit.* 'the all things (are) because of you, that the multiplied grace, through (*or* because of) the thanksgiving (*lit.* good leaping for joy) of the many, might abound to.'

16. FOR,] *lit.* 'wherefore we act not badly ..man is being thoroughly corrupted,' *or* marred.

17. OUR LIGHT,] *lit.* 'for the momentary light matter of our tribulation worketh fully to us more and more exceedingly an age-during weight of glory.'

18. WHILE,] *lit.* 'we not viewing the things beheld, but the things not beheld, for the things beheld (are) for a season, but the things not beheld (are) age-during.'

Chapter V. may be divided into three parts; v. 1—8 the earthly and the heavenly house; v. 9—15 Paul's conduct in the ministry; v. 16—21 his idea of the gospel.

1. WE KNOW,] *lit.* 'we have known.' EARTHLY,] *lit.* 'upon earth..be loosed down.'

2. EARNESTLY DESIRING,] *lit.* 'being very desirous to clothe ourselves with our house.'

3. BEING CLOTHED,] *lit.* 'having clothed ourselves.'

4. NOT FOR,] *lit.* 'upon which we do not wish to unclothe ourselves, but to be ourselves clothed over, that the mortality..by the life.'

5. HATH WROUGHT,] *lit.* 'himself wrought us thoroughly with a view to this same thing ..also gave the pledge.'

6. WE ARE,] *lit.* 'have always courage.. being at home in .. away from home.'

7. WALK,] *lit.* 'walk about through faith, not through sight.'

8. ARE CONFIDENT,] *lit.* 'have courage, and are well-pleased rather to be from home, from the body, and to be at home towards the Lord.'

9. LABOUR,] *lit.* 'are loving the honour, whether at home or from home, of being well-pleasing to him.'

10. WE MUST,] *lit.* 'it behoveth us all to be manifested (*or* manifest ourselves) before the tribunal of the Christ, that every one may himself receive the things (done) through the body, according to what he practised.'

11. TERROR,] *or* 'fear..persuade (i.e. try to do so) men, and have been..I hope also to have been.'

12. COMMEND,] *lit.* 'set-together..are giving an impulse to you of boasting..have (something) for those boasting.'

13. BE BESIDE OURSELVES,] *lit.* 'we set ourselves forth (it is) to God, whether we be of sound mind (it is) to you.'

14. CHRIST,] *lit.* 'the Christ holdeth us together, having judged thus, that if one died fully in behalf of all, then they all died,' in his dying.

15. THAT,] *lit.* 'and in behalf of all he died, that the living might no longer live to themselves, but to him who died and rose in their behalf.'

16. KNOW,] *lit.* 'have we known no one according to flesh.. according to flesh.'

17. ANY MAN,] *lit.* 'any one (is) in Christ, —a new creature *or* building; the old things went along, behold, the all things have become new.'

18. ALL,] *lit.* 'the all things.. who changed us thoroughly to himself through Jesus Christ, and gave to us the deaconship of the thorough-change.'

19. TO WIT,] *lit.* 'how that God.. changing thoroughly a world to himself, not reckoning their falling-aside to them, and put in us the word of the thorough-change.'

20. FOR,] *lit.* 'in behalf of Christ, as though God were calling upon (men) through us, we beseech, in behalf of Christ, Be ye thoroughly-changed to God.'

21. HATH,] *lit.* 'he made him a sin (offering) in our behalf.. become God's righteous ones (*lit.* righteousness) in him.'

Chapter VI. may be divided into four parts; v. 1, 2 exhortation not to delay; v. 3—10 behaviour of the apostles; v. 11—13 prayer for enlargement; v. 14—18 on being unequally yoked.

1. AS,] *lit.* 'and we also, working together, call upon you not to receive the grace of God in vain;' compare Heb. 6. 4; 12. 15, &c.

2. HAVE,] *lit.* 'I heard thee fully in an acceptable season, and in a day of salvation I helped thee; behold, now is a very acceptable season, behold, now is a day of salvation,' or safety, ease. Isa. 49. 8.

3. GIVING,] *lit.* 'we are giving no cause of stumbling in anything, that the deaconship may not be blemished.'

4. ALL,] *lit.* 'every thing setting ourselves

together as God's deacons, in much endurance, in tribulations, .. in straits.'

5. STRIPES,] *or* 'strokes, in watches, in uprisings, in toils, in sleeplessnesses, in fastings.'

6. BY,] *lit.* 'in chastity, in knowledge, in long-suffering, in benignity (*or* utility), in holy spirit, in love unhypocritical.'

7. BY,] *lit.* 'in (the) word of truth, in (the) power of God, through the armour (*or* weapons) of the righteousness of the right and of the left.'

8. BY,] *lit.* 'through glory and dishonour, through harsh speech and good speech; as leading astray and (yet) true.'

9. UNKNOWN,] *or* 'ignorant, and (yet) recognized *or* known about..put to death.'

10. SORROWFUL,] *or* 'grieving..leaping for joy.. having all things thoroughly.'

11. IS OPEN,] *lit.* 'has been open..has been widened *or* broadened.'

13. NOW FOR,] *lit.* 'but the same recompense (I pray for), as to children I say (it), Be ye widened *or* broadened.'

14. BE,] *lit.* 'become ye not yoked with others—unbelievers (*or* unstedfast)—for what holding-together has righteousness and lawlessness?'

15. CONCORD,] *lit.* 'sounding-together.'

PART.] *or* 'portion (is) to believer and unbeliever.'

16. AGREEMENT,] *lit.* 'setting-down together (is) to a habitation of God with idols? for ye are a habitation of a living God, as God himself said, that, I will dwell in (*or* among) them, and walk about among (them).'

17. OUT,] *lit.* 'come forth out of their midst, and be ye marked out,..and be not touching for yourselves an unclean thing, and I will receive you in.'

18. BE,] *lit.* 'will be to you for a Father, and ye shall be to me for sons and daughters.'

Chapter VII. may be divided into four parts; v. 1 general lesson; v. 2—8 brotherly sympathy; v. 9—11 double effects of sorrow; v. 12—16 congratulation and joy.'

1. PROMISES,] *lit.* 'things told over again.'

LET,] *or* 'may we cleanse..all pollution of flesh and spirit, completing holiness,' *lit.* not being of the earth.

2. RECEIVE,] *or* 'give us place; we did injustice to no one; we defrauded no one.'

3. SPEAK,] *lit.* 'I say it not for condemnation, for I said before *or* publicly.'

4. GREAT,] *lit.* 'much to me (is) full speech toward you, much to me (is) boasting in your behalf, I have been filled with the comfort (*or* exhortation), I over-abound with the joy over all our tribulation.'

5. HAD,] *lit.* 'has had no relaxation, but we are in tribulation in every thing.'

6. COMFORTETH,] *or* 'is exhorting the lowly, exhorted us in the presence of Titus.'

7. BY,] *lit.* 'in his presence..in the exhortation with which he was exhorted over you, telling again to us your over-desire.. your zeal in my behalf, as also to rejoice me more.'

8. THOUGH,] *lit.* 'because even if I made you sorry in (*or* by, with) the letter I am not concerned about (it) even if I was concerned about (it) that that letter made you sorry, if even for an hour.'

9. SORROWED,] *lit.* 'were made sorry with a view to a new mind.. according to God.. from us.'

10. GODLY,] *lit.* 'for the sorrow according to God worketh thoroughly a new mind with a view to salvation not to be concerned about,..worketh death thoroughly.'

11. SELF-SAME,] *lit.* 'this same thing—your being made sorry according to God—how much diligence it thoroughly-wrought to you, also apology (i.e. defence), also much displeasure, also fear, also over-desire, also zeal, also full-justice; in every thing ye set yourselves together to be pure in the matter.'

12. WHEREFORE,] *lit.* 'if then I also wrote .. that did unrighteously, .. suffered unrighteously, .. our diligence in behalf of you ..being made apparent to you.'

13. WERE,] *lit.* 'have been comforted (*or* exhorted) over your comfort (*or* exhortation), and more abundantly did we joy over the joy.. has been refreshed again from you all.'

14. OF YOU,] *lit.* 'in behalf of you, I was not at all put to shame..became truth.'

15. INWARD AFFECTION,] *lit.* 'bowels are more abundantly towards you, remembering fully the submissive hearkening of you all.'

16. THEREFORE,] *lit.* 'because in every-thing I have courage in you.'

Chapter VIII. may be divided into two parts; v. 1—15 exhortation to liberality; v. 16—24 to reception of Titus and others.

1. DO YOU TO WIT,] *lit.* 'make known to you the grace of God that has been given among the assemblies of Macedonia.'

2. HOW THAT,] *or* 'because in much testing of tribulation..their very deep.. the wealth of simplicity,' *or* singleness.

3. TO,] *lit.* 'according to (their) power, I testify,..choose of themselves.'

4. PRAYING,] *lit.* 'beseeching of us with much exhortation, our receiving the grace and the communion of the deaconship that (is) with a view to the saints.'

5. THIS,] *lit.* 'and not (only) as we hoped, but.. us through.'

6. INSOMUCH,] *lit.* 'with a view to our exhorting Titus, that even as he himself began before, so also he might fully end in reference to you.'

7. THEREFORE,] *lit.* 'but.. in word.. among us.. may abound.'

8. BY,] *lit.* 'according to a higher arrangement, but because of the diligence of others, and proving the genuineness of your love.'

9. YE KNOW,] *or* 'know ye.. that being rich, because of us.'

10. HEREIN,] *lit.* 'in this I give an opinion, for this bears together to you, who began before..to wish from past time.'

11. PERFORM,] *lit.* end fully.. is a for-

ward desire (*or* mind) to wish, so also the ending fully out of.'

12. THERE BE,] *lit.* 'if the forward mind is put forward, (it is) very acceptable according to that which any one may have.'

13. I MEAN,] *lit.* 'for (it is) not that to others (there may be) relaxation, and to you tribulation.'

14. BY,] *lit* 'but from equality, during the present season your abundance—for their lack..their lack.'

15. IS,] *lit.* 'has been written.. had no less.'

16. THANKS,] *lit.* 'grace (is) to God, who is giving the same diligence in the heart of Titus in behalf of you.'

17. ACCEPTED,] *or* 'received.. more diligent, chose of himself to go forth to you.'

18. HAVE,] *lit.* 'we sent along with..assemblies.'

19. CHOSEN,] *lit.* 'appointed (by the stretching out of the hand), by the assemblies our fellow-traveller, with this gracious gift that is administered-as-deacons by us, unto.. your forward mind.'

20. AVOIDING,] *lit.* 'sending out this for ourselves, that no one may blame.. that is administered-as-deacons by us.'

21. PROVIDING,] *lit.* 'thinking *or* minding beforehand right things.'

22. HAVE,] *lit.* 'we sent along with.. we oftentimes..by the much confidence which (is felt) in reference to you.'

23. FELLOW-HELPER,] *lit.* 'fellow-worker in regard to you..(they are) apostles of assemblies—glory of Christ.'

24. BEFORE,] *lit.* 'to..the shewing of.'

Chapter IX. may be divided into four parts; v. 1—5 Paul's confidence in their liberality; v. 6—9 its blessedness; v. 10, 11 prayer for them; v. 12—15 benefits of liberality.

1. MINISTERING,] *lit.* 'deaconship which is to.'

2. KNOW,] *lit.* 'I have known your forward mind which I boast of in your behalf to Macedonia, that Achaia has been fully ready from past time.. zeal stirred up the many.'

3. HAVE,] *lit.* 'but I sent. boasting in your behalf be vain (*or* empty) in this part ..be fully ready.'

4. THEY OF,] *lit.* 'if Macedonians come.. not fully prepared..may be put to shame in this foundation (*lit.* under-standing) of the boasting.'

5. THOUGHT,] *lit.* 'I myself thought it necessary to call upon the brethren, that they might go before to you, and might make thoroughly complete your formerly announced blessing, this so to be ready as a blessing, and not as extortion,' *lit.* a having more.

6. SOWETH,] *lit.* 'is sowing..is sowing over blessings..also over blessings.'

7. EVERY,] *lit.* 'each one according as he lifteth up beforehand in the heart; not out of sorrow or out of necessity.'

8. ALL,] *lit.* 'every grace.. in every thing.'

9. IS,] *lit.* 'has been written, He dispersed, he gave to the labourer.'

10. MINISTERETH,] *lit.* 'is fully furnishing seed to the sower and bread for food, furnish and supply your sown-seed.'

11. BOUNTIFULNESS,] *or* 'simplicity, which thoroughly worketh.'

12. ADMINISTRATION,] *lit.* 'deaconship of this public work is not only filling up again the lacks of the holy ones.. through many.'

13. WHILES,] *lit.* 'through the proof (*or* test) of this deaconship glorifying God, over your professed (*or* confessed) under-arrangement with a view to the gospel of the Christ, and the simplicity (*or* singleness) of the fellowship (*or* communion) in reference to them and to all.'

14. PRAYER,] *lit.* 'supplication in your behalf, desiring you fully, because of the exceeding (*lit.* over-casting) grace of God upon you.'

15. THANKS,] *lit.* 'grace.. over his unthoroughly-led out gift.'

Chapter X. may be divided into three parts; v. 1—6 Paul's entreaty and weapons; v. 7—11 asserts his right to speak; v. 12—18 contrasts himself with his opponents.

1. BESEECH,] *lit.* 'call upon you..of the Christ, who according to appearance indeed (am) lowly among you, but being away, have courage toward you.'

2. BE BOLD,] *or* 'have courage, being alongside, with the,..I reckon to be bold about certain reckoning us as walking about according to flesh.'

3. THOUGH,] *lit.* 'for walking about in flesh, we do not war according to flesh.'

4. WEAPONS,] *or* 'instruments.. fleshly but powerful to God for bringing.'

5. CASTING,] *lit.* 'bringing down reasonings, and every high thing lifted up against ..and taking by a spear every thought to the submissive-hearkening of the Christ.'

6. REVENGE,] *lit.* 'execute full-justice (on) every hearkening-amiss..your submissive-obedience may be fulfilled.'

7. LOOK,] *lit.* 'behold the things according to appearance? if any one has trusted.. reckon this again.

8. THOUGH,] *lit.* 'if I shall boast something more abundantly concerning.. gave us for building up.. your casting down, I shall.'

9. SEEM,] *or* 'think as if to greatly-testify you through the Letters.'

10. SAY THEY,] *lit.* 'saith he (i.e. any one) ..and strong..(is) infirm, and the word (*or* doctrine), has been thought nothing of.'

11. THINK,] *or* 'reckon.. in the word through letters, being away, such also (we are) in the work, being alongside.'

12. DARE,] *lit.* 'are not bold (enough) to judge ourselves, among or with certain of those setting themselves together.. with themselves, and judging themselves with themselves, are not prudent.'

13. OF THINGS,] *lit.* 'in reference to the things un-measured,.. the canon (*or* reed, cane), which the God of measure divided to us—to reach over to you.

14. BEYOND,] *lit.* 'over much, as not

reaching over to you, for we came even unto you in the good-news of the Christ.'

15. OF,] *lit.* 'in reference to the things unmeasured, in other men's toils,..your faith being increased, to be enlarged in (*or* among) you, according to our canon, to abundance.'

16. PREACH,] *lit.* 'proclaim good-news to the places beyond you, not..canon in reference to the things made ready.'

17. GLORIETH,] *lit.* 'is boasting, let him boast.'

18. COMMENDETH,] *lit.* 'is setting himself together..setteth together.'

Chapter XI. may be divided into six parts; v. 1—4 Paul's jealousy; v. 5, 6 his equality with other apostles; v. 7—11 his disinterested conduct; v. 12—15 false apostles, v. 16—21 endurance of the Corinthians; v. 22—33 Paul's descent, labours, sufferings, and zeal.

1. WOULD,] *lit.* 'I would ye were bearing up with me a little in the thoughtlessness, but indeed ye do bear with me.'

2. JEALOUS,] *lit.* 'zealous for you with a zeal of God, for I myself prepared (*or* fitted) you for one husband, to set you alongside of the Christ.'

3. FEAR,] *or* 'am afraid..greatly deceived Eve in his all-work.. might be corrupted.. in the Christ.'

4. HE,] *lit.* 'if indeed he who is coming proclaimeth.. did not proclaim.. did not receive..did not accept, well do ye bear up.'

5. SUPPOSE,] *or* 'reckon myself to be nothing behind.'

6. THOUGH,] *lit.* 'and even if peculiar in the speech, yet not as to the knowledge, but in everything we were manifested among all in reference to you.'

7. HAVE,] *lit.* 'did I sin (in) humbling myself..I proclaimed as good news.'

8. ROBBED,] *or* 'plundered other assemblies, receiving wages, for your deaconship.'

9. WHEN,] *lit.* 'being alongside of you, and having been in lack, I was not at all torpid to any one, for my lack..coming..filled up besides, and in every thing I kept myself unburdensome.'

10. AS.] Omit 'as,' not in the Greek.

NO MAN,] *lit.* 'because this boasting shall not be stopped (*or* restrained) in reference to me in the regions (*lit.* inclines) of Achaia.'

11. KNOWETH,] *lit.* 'God has known.'

12. CUT OFF,] *lit.* 'cut off thoroughly the cause of excitement of those wishing a cause of excitement..they boast.'

13. DECEITFUL,] *or* 'guileful..into apostles.'

14. MARVEL,] *or* 'wonder, for the Adversary himself transforms himself into a messenger of light.'

15. MINISTERS,] *lit.* 'deacons also transform themselves as deacons of.'

16. MAN,] *lit.* 'may no one think me to be thoughtless; but if otherwise, even as a thoughtless one receive me, that I also may boast some little.'

17. AFTER,] *lit.* 'according to the Lord, but as in thoughtlessness, in this substance (*lit.* under-standing) of the boasting.'

18. GLORY,] *lit.* 'boast according to the flesh, I also will boast.'

19. SUFFER,] *lit.* 'bear up sweetly with the thoughtless, being (yourselves) thoughtful.'

20. SUFFER,] *or* 'bear up if any one make you a thorough bondsman, if any one devour (*lit.* eat you down), if any one taketh away, if any one raise himself up, if any one.'

21. CONCERNING,] *lit.* 'according to dishonour, as that we were infirm, but in whatsoever any one is bold (I speak in thoughtlessness).'

22. SO,] *lit.* 'I also.. I also..they seed of.. I also.'

23. MINISTERS,] *lit.* 'deacons of Christ? (I speak very thoughtlessly,) I more! in toils more frequent.'

24. OF,] *lit.* 'under *or* by Jews.'

25. SUFFERED,] *lit.* 'was I shipwrecked..I have passed in the deep.'

26. OFTEN,] *lit.* 'many times, perils of rivers..among kindred, perils from nations.'

27. WEARINESS,] *or* 'toil.. many times.. many times.'

28. BESIDE,] *lit.* 'apart from the things without, the crowding (*lit.* setting together) upon me which is daily, the care (*or* anxiety, *lit.* division) of all the assemblies,' which he had planted.

29. WEAK,] *lit.* 'infirm.. not infirm.. is scandalized (i.e. stumbled), and I am not set on fire?'

30. MUST,] *lit.* 'if it behoveth me to boast I will boast of the things of my infirmities.'

31. WHICH,] *lit.* 'who is being well-spoken of to the ages, has known.'

32. GOVERNOR,] *lit.* 'ethnarch of.. was watching..wishing to seize me.'

33. WINDOW,] *or* 'little door, in a wicker-basket..through the wall, and fled out of his hands.'

Chapter XII. may be divided into three parts; v. 1—13 Paul boasts in his revelations, and in his sufferings; v. 14—18 in his disinterestedness; v. 19—21 he expresses his fears for them.

1. IS EXPEDIENT,] *lit.* 'it does not doubtless bear together to me to boast, therefore I will come to sights and uncoverings of the Lord.'

2. KNEW,] *lit.* 'I have known..in a body, I have not known..I have not known; God has known.. snatched away unto a third heaven.'

3. KNEW,] *lit.* 'I have known ..in a body ..I have not known; God has known.'

4. HOW THAT,] *lit.* 'that he was snatched away to the paradise (of God), and heard unspoken things *or* words, which it is not possible *or* lawful to a man to speak.'

5. OF,] *lit.* 'over such a one will I boast, but over myself I will not boast, except in'

6. THOUGH,] *lit.* 'for if I wish to boast myself..be thoughtless, for I will speak truth, but I spare (it), lest any one may reckon in reference to me above.'

7. SHOULD,] *lit.* 'might be over-exalted by the over-abundance of the uncoverings, there was given (i.e. permitted to come) to me a thorn in the flesh, a messenger—an adversary—that it might buffet me, that I might not be over-exalted.'

8. FOR,] *lit.* 'over this thing I called upon the Lord (Jesus) thrice, that it might stand off from me.' Another instance of prayer to Christ.

9. HE SAID,] *lit.* 'he has said..infirmity. Most sweetly.. boast..of the Christ may over-shadow me.'

10. TAKE,] *lit.* 'I am well-pleased in.. reproaches (*or* damages).. persecutions (*or* being caused to flee)..am ailing.'

11. AM,] *lit.* 'I have become thoughtless, boasting (thus): ye necessitated me,.. set together by you..was I behind..even if I am nothing.'

12. AN,] *lit.* 'of the apostle were thoroughly wrought.. all endurance.. terrible and powerful things.'

13. OTHER,] *lit.* 'the other assemblies.. not at all torpid among you; be gracious to me with respect to this unrighteousness.'

14. THE,] *lit.* 'a third time I am ready (*lit.* have readiness) to come to you, and I will not be at all torpid among you..to treasure up.'

15. VERY GLADLY,] *lit.* 'most sweetly..be fully spent in behalf of your souls, even if, more abundantly loving you, less I am loved.'

16. BURDEN,] *or* 'weigh you down, but being an all-worker, with guile I took you.'

17. MAKE A GAIN,] *lit.* 'did I hold you for gain through any one of those whom I have sent to you.'

18. DESIRED,] *lit.* 'called upon (*i.e.* entreated) Titus, and sent with him the brother (formerly spoken of); did Titus hold you for gain? walked we not about.'

19. EXCUSE OURSELVES,] *lit.* 'are apologizing to you? we speak over-against the face of God in Christ, but the all things, beloved, (are) in behalf of your up-building.'

20. FEAR,] *or* 'am afraid, lest, at any time, having come, I may find you not such as I wish..ye wish not, lest at any time—strifes, zeals, rushings, strivings, speakings-against (others), whisperings, puffings-up, standings-against (powers).'

21. WHEN,] *lit.* 'having come again my God may humble me beside you, and I may bewail many of those who sinned before (*or* publicly), and had not another mind over *or* about the uncleaness, and whoredom, and lewdness which they practised.'

Chapter XIII. may be divided into three parts; v. 1—4 a warning and its cause; v. 5—10 exhortation and prayer; v. 11—13 encouragements and salutations.

1. THE,] *lit.* 'third time I..upon the mouth..every thing be settled.'

2. TOLD,] *lit.* 'have said before (*or* publicly), and say (it) before *or* publicly, as being alongside the second time, and being away now, I write to those who sinned before (*or* publicly), and to all the rest.'

3. CHRIST,] *lit.* 'of the speaking-Christ in me, who is not ailing (*or* infirm) in reference to you, but is powerful in you.'

4. THOUGH,] *lit.* 'for even if..from infirmity, yet..from the power.. are infirm in him..from the power.'

5. EXAMINE,] *lit.* 'try *or* test yourselves, if (i.e. since) ye are..know ye not fully.. if ye are not somewhat disapproved,' *or* unproved.

6. TRUST,] *lit.* 'hope..disapproved,' *or* unproved.

7. PRAY,] *lit.* 'pour forth toward God, for you not to do anything evil; not that we may appear approved, but that ye may do that which is right *or* good, and we may be as disapproved,' *or* unproved.

8. CAN,] *lit.* 'are not able.'

9. ARE GLAD,] *lit.* 'leap with joy..may be infirm (*or* ailing), and ye may be powerful ..we pour forth (before God)—your thorough preparation *or* fitness.'

10. ABSENT,] *or* 'being away, lest, being alongside, I behave cuttingly, according to the authority which the Lord gave to me with a view to building-up, and not to casting-down.'

11. FINALLY,] *or* 'as to the rest, brethren, leap with joy; be thoroughly prepared, be comforted *or* exhorted, be of the same mind, be at peace, and the God of the love and peace.'

12. GREET,] *lit.* 'draw one another near in a holy friendship.'

13. SAINTS,] *or* 'holy ones draw you near.'

14. GRACE,] *lit.* that which 'causes joy.'

COMMUNION,] *or* 'fellowship of the Holy Spirit (is) with you all.'

AMEN.] Omitted in the oldest MSS.

PAUL'S LETTER TO THE GALATIANS

THAT this Letter was written by the apostle Paul is (and has always been) universally acknowledged; it was quoted by Clement (of Rome), Hermas, Ignatius, and Polycarp, A.D. 100, and was declared authentic by Irenaeus, A.D. 178, Clement (of Alexandria), A.D. 194, Tertullian, A.D. 200, Caius (of Rome), A.D. 200, Origen, A.D. 230, and even by Marcion, A.D. 175. It was probably written at Ephesus (Acts 18. 23; 19. 1), or Corinth (Acts 20. 2, 3) about A.D. 57-8 after the Second Letter to the Thessalonians and before that to the Romans. Galatia (*or* Gallograecia) in Asia Minor was subdued by the Romans B.C. 189, became a Roman province A.D. 26, was visited by Paul, A.D. 50-1 (Acts 16. 6, 7), and again in A.D. 54-5 (Acts 18. 23). His great object in writing this Letter was to counteract the tendency to Judaize, i.e. to modify and restrain the liberty of the Gospel Dispensation by the observance of rites and customs derived from the Old Covenant, which had been totally abolished by the death of Christ. It may be divided as follows:—

I. The Introduction, ch. i. 1—5.
II. Paul's Personal Defence, ch. i. 6—ii. 21.
III. His Exposure of Judaism, ch. iii—iv. 7.
IV. His Reproof of the Galatians, ch. iv. 8—v. 9.
V. Instructions and Exhortations, ch. v. 10—vi. 10.
VI. The Conclusion, ch. vi. 11—18.

Chapter I. may be divided into four parts; v. 1—5 Paul's salutations; v. 6—10 his surprize at the change of the Galatians; v. 11—19 his own preaching; v. 20—23 his reception in Judea.

1. PAUL,] i.e. the 'little' one.

APOSTLE,] *lit.* one 'sent forth.'

OF,] *lit.* 'from men, nor through man, but through Jesus Christ, (the 'anointed saviour,')..out of (the) dead.'

2. CHURCHES,] *lit.* 'assemblies of the (Roman province of) Galatia (in Asia Minor).'

3. GRACE,] *lit.* 'that which causes leaping for joy.'

PEACE,] *lit.* 'that which brings into unity.'

4. SINS,] *lit.* 'missings' of the mark.

DELIVER,] *lit.* 'raise us out of this evil age (which) has set in.'

GOD AND,] *lit.* 'of our God and Father.'

5. BE,] *or* 'is the glory to the ages of the ages, Amen.'

6. MARVEL,] *or* 'wonder that ye are so hastily moved (*or* moved yourselves) away from..in (*or* by the) grace of Christ, to another good-news.'

7. BUT,] *lit.* 'except there are certain who are troubling you, and wishing to overturn the good-news of the Christ.'

8. THOUGH,] *lit.* 'but even if we, or a messenger out of heaven, may tell-as-good-news to you aside from what we told-as-good-news to you, let him be laid up (on the altar as a sacrifice to God).'

9. SAID,] *lit.* 'have said before (*or* publicly), even now I say again, If any one tell you good-news for himself different from what ye received from (us), let him be laid up' on the altar of God for a sacrifice.

10. SHOULD,] *lit.* 'would not have been Christ's bondsman.'

11. CERTIFY,] *lit.* 'make known to you.. by me is not according to man.'

12. OF,] *lit.* 'from man..through an uncovering.'

13. HAVE,] *lit.* 'ye heard of my behaviour (*lit.* 'turning up and down') once in the Judaism, that very exceedingly was I causing the assembly of God to flee, and laying (it) waste.'

14. PROFITED,] *lit.* 'I was striking forward in the Judaism, above many equals-in-age in my own race, being more abundantly zealous of the traditions (*lit.* 'things given over') of my fathers.'

15. IT PLEASED,] *lit.* 'God was well-pleased —who marked me out from..called through.'

16. REVEAL,] *lit.* 'uncover his Son in (*or* by) me, that I might tell-him-as-good news among the nations, straightway I set not (myself) again towards flesh.'

17. RETURNED,] *lit.* 'turned round again shortly.'

18. SEE,] *or* 'know..remained on.'

20. BEFORE,] *lit.* 'in the face of God.'

22. BY,] *lit.* 'as to face to the assemblies.'

23. HAD HEARD,] *lit.* 'were hearing only, That he who is persecuting us once is now telling-as-good-news for himself the faith which once he was laying waste; and they were glorifying God in me.'

Chapter II. may be divided into three parts; v. 1—10 Paul's behaviour and reception at Jerusalem; v. 11—16 his rebuke of Peter; v. 17—21 his consistency and views.

1. WITH,] *lit.* 'along with (me) also.'

2. BY,] *lit.* 'according to an uncovering (of God's will) and set up to them for myself the good-news..to those esteemed.. might run or did run in vain.'

3. GREEK,] *lit.* 'Hellen.'

4. FALSE,] *lit.* 'the false-brethren brought in alongside, who came in alongside to look-down our freedom..into thorough bondage.

5. GAVE PLACE,] *lit.* 'yielded..remain thoroughly toward you.'

6. SEEMED,] *lit.* 'were esteemed to be

something—of what kind they were once it makes no difference to me, God accepteth not the face of man, for those esteemed set up nothing towards me.'

7. WHEN,] *lit.* 'having seen that I have been entrusted with the good-news.'

8. EFFECTUALLY,] *lit.* 'inwardly with Peter with a view to the..wrought also inwardly with me with a view to the nations.'

9. SEEMED,] *lit.* 'were esteemed to be pillars (*or* columns), knew..fellowship,' *or* communion.

10. SHOULD,] *or* 'might be mindful of.. I hastened to do.'

11. WAS COME,] *or* 'came..I stood (*or* set myself) against him..so that it was thoroughly known.'

12. THAT,] *lit.* 'the coming of certain from James, he was eating..they came, he was withdrawing (*lit.* sending himself under), and marking himself out from (them).'

13. DISSEMBLED,] *lit.* 'also judged under along with him..led away along with them in the under-judgment,'

14. ACCORDING,] *lit.* 'towards..livest as a heathen, and not as a Jew..to Judaize?'

15. OF,] *lit.* 'out of the nations.'

16. JUSTIFIED,] *or* 'declared right out of works of law, except through (the) faith of Jesus Christ, even we believed in reference to Christ Jesus..declared right out of (the) faith..out of works of law, because out of works of law.'

17. BY,] *lit.* 'in Christ.. were found.. Christ a deacon of sin? let it not be!'

18. DESTROYED,] *lit.* 'loosed down..set myself with (Peter) a transgressor.'

19. THE,] *lit.* 'through law, did die to law.'

20. I AM,] *lit.* 'I have been crucified..and that which I now live in flesh I live in faith by the Son.. gave himself up in my behalf.'

21. FRUSTRATE,] *lit.* 'displace (*or* set aside)..is through law, then Christ died in vain.'

Chapter III. may be divided into seven parts; v. 1—5 an expostulation and enquiry; v. 6—9 Abraham declared just by faith; v. 10 the law leaves man under a curse; v. 11, 12 man declared just by faith; v. 13—18 Abraham's blessing confirmed by Christ; v. 19—22 origin and temporary character of the law; v. 23—29 design of the law and its abrogation.

1. FOOLISH,] *lit.* 'thoughtless (*or* mindless) Galatians, who did fascinate (i.e. cast an evil eye upon) you, not to be persuaded by the truth, before whose eyes Jesus Christ was described publicly (*or* beforehand) among you—crucified.'

2. WOULD,] *lit.* 'do I wish to learn from you..out of works of law, or out of (the) hearing of faith.'

3. FOOLISH,] *lit.* 'thoughtless..in spirit, do ye now end fully in flesh.'

4. HAVE,] *lit.* 'did ye suffer.'

5. MINISTERETH,] *lit.* 'is supplying..working powerful things among (*or* in) you, (is it) out of works of law, or out of a hearing of faith?'

6. BELIEVED,] *or* 'remained stedfast to God, and it was reckoned to him with a view to righteousness.'

7. KNOW YE,] *or* 'ye know..these are sons of Abraham.'

8. SCRIPTURE,] *lit.* 'Writing having foreseen that God justifies the nations out of faith told-good-news-beforehand (*or* publicly) to Abraham, that *or* because, In thee shall all the nations be well-spoken of,' *or* to.

9. BE,] *lit.* 'who are out of faith are well-spoken of with the stedfast Abraham.'

10. OF,] *lit.* 'out of works of law are under a thorough curse, for it has been written, Thoroughly cursed.. remains not.. have been written.'

11. MAN,] *lit.* 'no one is declared just in (*or* by) law alongside of God, (is) manifest, because The righteous one out of faith shall live.' Hab. 2. 4.

12. OF,] *lit.* 'out of faith..that did them.'

13. HATH,] *lit.* 'bought us out of the full-curse of the law, having become a full-curse in our behalf, for it has been written, Thoroughly-cursed..is hanging on wood,' *or* a tree.

14. BLESSING,] *lit.* 'good-word (spoken) to Abraham might happen to the nations in Christ Jesus..through the faith.'

15. AFTER,] *or* 'as a man, Even (the) confirmed covenant of a man no one sets aside or arranges differently about (it).'

16. MADE,] *lit.* 'spoken; it says not, And to the seeds, as about many, but as about one, And to thy seed, which is Christ,' the head and representative of Abraham's spiritual seed; see v. 28, 29.

17. THAT THE,] *lit.* 'a covenant confirmed beforehand *or* publicly by God with a view to Christ, the law that happened 430 years after does not make lordless, with a view to making the promise thoroughly useless.'

18. OF,] *lit.* 'out of law..out of promise, but God has graciously given..through promise.'

19. WHEREFORE,] *or* 'what..of the transgressions, (till the seed might come to which the promise was made,) having been thoroughly arranged through messengers in (the) hand of a mediator,' *or* middle-man.

20. NOW A,] *lit.* 'but the mediator is not of one, but God is one.' This clause is supposed to be a marginal gloss, by Michaelis, Newcome, Marsh, Boothroyd, &c.

21. GOD FORBID,] *lit.* 'let it not happen! for if a law were given which has power to make alive, truly the righteousness would have been out of law.'

22. SCRIPTURE,] *lit.* 'Writing shut up together the whole under sin, that the promise out of (the) faith.'

23. FAITH,] *lit.* 'the coming of the faith we were being kept under law, shut up together with a view to the faith about to be uncovered.'

24. WHEREFORE,] *lit.* 'so that the law has become our pedagogue (i.e. child-conductor) with a view to Christ,..declared just out of faith.'

25. AFTER,] *lit.* 'but the faith having come ..a child-conductor.'
26. THE,] *lit.* 'all sons of God through the faith in Christ Jesus.'
27. HAVE,] *lit.* 'were baptized with a view to Christ, did put on Christ.'
28. GREEK,] *lit.* 'Hellen..bondsman nor freeman..not male and female.'
29. BE,] *or* 'are Christ's, then of Abraham ye are seed, and according to promise (ye are) heirs.'

Chapter IV. may be divided into four parts; v. 1—7 the heir as a babe and as a son; v. 8—11 former and present state; v. 12—20 former and present treatment of Paul; v. 21—31 simile of the two Covenants.
1. CHILD,] *lit.* 'babe..a bondsman, being lord of all.'
2. TUTORS,] *or* 'guardians and stewards till the time set forth of the father.'
3. CHILDREN,] *lit.* 'babes..elements,' *or* first principles or steps.
4. WAS COME,] *lit.* 'came..come out of a woman, come under law.'
5. TO REDEEM,] *lit.* 'that he might buy those under law, that we might fully receive the sonship.'
6. HATH,] *lit.* 'God sent..O Father!'
7. WHEREFORE,] *lit.* 'so that..a bondsman ..also an heir.'
8. HOWBEIT,] *lit.* 'but then, indeed, not knowing God, ye were in bondage to those by nature not gods.'
9. AFTER,] *lit.* 'having known God, yea rather being known by (*lit.* under) God, how turn ye round again upon the infirm and poor elements (*or* rudiments, first steps), to which again ye wish anew to be in bondage?'
10. OBSERVE,] *lit.* 'keep alongside of days (i.e. sabbaths) and months (i.e. new moons), and seasons (i.e. stated Jewish festivals), and years,' i.e. sabbatical and jubilee.
11. AM AFRAID,] *lit.* 'I fear you, lest any how I toiled in vain in regard to you.'
12. BE,] *lit.* 'become..I also am as ye are; ye did me no unrighteousness.'
13. KNOW,] *lit.* 'and ye have known that through..I proclaimed good-news.'
14. TEMPTATION,] *or* 'trial that is in flesh (i.e. failure of sight?) ye did not think nothing of, nor spit out, but..messenger of God.'
15. WHERE,] *lit.* 'what then was your happiness? for I testify to you that,..dug out your eyes.'
16. AM I,] *lit.* 'so that have I become your enemy, being true to you?'
17. ZEALOUSLY,] *lit.* 'they are zealous for you, (but) not well; but they wish to shut us out, that ye might be zealous for them.'
18. ZEALOUSLY,] *lit.* 'zealous in good, at all time..in my being alongside of you.'
19. LITTLE,] *lit.* 'my children, with whom again I am pained, till Christ be formed in (*or* among) you.'
20. DESIRE,] *lit.* 'and I was wishing to be alongside of you now,..because I am passageless among you.'

21. TELL,] *lit.* 'say to me, ye who are wishing to be under law.'
22. IS,] *lit.* 'it has been written..sons, one out of the maid-servant, and one out of the free-woman.'
23. BONDWOMAN,] *lit.* 'maid-servant has been born according to flesh..through the promise.'
24. WHICH THINGS,] *lit.* 'there are things which are allegorized..one, indeed, from mount Sinai, bringing forth with a view to bondage.'
25. THIS,] *lit.* 'for Agar..steppeth along with the present Jerusalem.'
26. THE,] *lit.* 'is mother of us all.'
27. IS,] *lit.* 'it has been written, Be of a good mind..art not bearing..cry aloud, thou who art not pained, because many more are the children of the desolate than of her having the husband.'
28. AS ISAAC WAS,] *lit.* 'in the manner of Isaac, are children of promise.'
29. AFTER,] *lit.* 'according to flesh..according to spirit, so also now.'
30. NEVERTHELESS,] *lit.* 'but what says the Writing? Cast forth the maid-servant .. maid-servant may not have inheritance.'
31. THE,] *lit.* 'of a maid-servant.'

Chapter V. may be divided into six parts; v. 1—6 warning against circumcision; v. 7—12 against leavening the whole lump; v. 13—15 call to freedom and love; v. 16—18 to oppose the flesh; v. 19—21 works of the flesh; v. 22—26 and of the spirit.
1. IN,] *or* 'with the liberty wherewith Christ made you free,..held in again with a yoke of bondage.'
3. FOR,] *lit.* 'but I testify.'
4. CHRIST IS,] *lit.* 'ye were freed from the Christ, ye who are declared just in (by, with) law; ye fell from the grace.'
5. THROUGH,] *lit.* 'in spirit out of faith a hope of righteousness look greatly for.'
6. WHICH,] *lit.* 'faith working inwardly through love.'
7. HINDER,] *lit.* 'smite you in, not to trust for yourselves the truth.'
8. PERSUASION,] *or* 'trust (is) not of Him calling you.'
10. IN YOU,] *lit.* 'in reference to you in the Lord.. is troubling.. the judgment.. may be.'
11. DO I SUFFER,] *lit.* 'am I yet caused to flee? then has the stumbling-block of the cross been made useless.'
12. I WOULD,] *lit.* 'oh that they would even cut themselves off who are setting you up.'
13. HAVE BEEN,] *lit.* 'ye were called upon freedom, only the freedom (is) not with a view to a cause of excitement in the flesh, but through the love be in bondage to one another.'
15. DEVOUR,] *lit.* 'eat down one another, see that ye be not taken away by one another.'
16. THIS,] *lit.* 'but I say, Walk about in (the) spirit, and may ye not end (*or* finish, complete) an over-desire of flesh.'
17. LUSTETH,] *lit.* 'over-desireth.. laid

over-against one another, that ye may not do what things ye wish.'

18. OF,] *lit.* 'in (the) spirit, ye are not under law.'

19. MANIFEST,] *or* 'apparent; these are adultery, whoredom.'

20. WITCHCRAFT,] *lit.* 'pharmacy, enmity, strifes, zeals, desires, strivings, dissensions, opinions (*or* sects).'

21. MURDERS,] *or* 'homicides, drinkings .. of which I say to you beforehand (*or* publicly), according as I also said before, that they who are practising.'

22. JOY,] *lit.* 'leaping for joy..kindness.'

23. TEMPERANCE,] *lit.* 'inward power.'

24. CHRIST'S,] *lit.* 'the Christ's did.. passions and the over-desires.'

25. LIVE,] *lit.* 'if we may live in spirit, in spirit also we may step on.'

26. LET,] *lit.* 'may we not become vain-glorious, calling forward one another, being envious at one another.'

Chapter VI. may be divided into five parts; v. 1—5 on forbearance, mutual help, pride; v. 6—10 mutual fellowship, practical results, due reward; v. 11—13 motives of Judaizers; v. 14—16 and of Paul, with Christian blessings; v. 17, 18 emphatic conclusion and benediction.

1. MAN,] *lit.* 'man also be taken-before (*or* publicly) in a certain falling away.. be making thoroughly perfect such a one in a spirit of meekness, viewing thyself.. be tried,' *or* tested.

2. BURDENS,] *lit.* 'weighty things.'

FULFIL,] *or* 'fill up..of the Christ.'

3. A MAN,] *lit.* 'any one thinks.. deceiveth his own mind.'

4. EVERY MAN,] *lit.* 'each one..have the boasting in reference to himself alone, and not in reference to the other.'

5. BURDEN.] Different *Greek* word in v. 2.

6. TAUGHT,] *lit.* 'sounded-thoroughly in the word (*or* doctrine).. is sounding-thoroughly.'

7. DECEIVED,] *or* 'led astray.. mocked (*or* sneered at).. may sow.'

8. FOR,] *lit.* 'because he who is sowing with a view to his own flesh.. is sowing with a view to the spirit.. life age-during.'

9. BE WEARY,] *lit.* 'act badly in doing that which is good *or* right, for in (its) own season we shall reap, not being loosed out.'

10. OPPORTUNITY,] *lit.* 'season, may we work that which is good towards all, but especially to those of the household of the faith.'

11. LARGE,] *lit.* 'in how large letters I wrote to you.'

12. DESIRE,] *lit.* 'wish to have a good appearance in flesh.. they be persuaded with (*or* by) the cross of the Christ.'

13. KEEP,] *or* 'guard (watch) law, but wish you to be circumcised that they may boast.'

14. GOD FORBID,] *lit.* 'but to me, let it not be, to boast,' *or* 'make a (long) neck.'

BY,] *lit.* 'through which (the) world has been crucified.'

15. AVAILETH,] *or* 'is..new creation.'

16. WALK,] *or* 'step on by this canon (reed *or* rule), peace (is) on them, and kindness ..Israel of God,' i.e. the spiritual seed of Abraham.

17. MAN,] *lit.* 'no one hold toils near to me..scars.'

18. BE,] *or* 'is with your spirit. Amen.'

PAUL'S LETTER TO THE EPHESIANS

THIS LETTER was written when Paul was a prisoner (ch. 3. 1; 4. 1) in Rome, about A.D. 62, and is cited as his by Ignatius (A.D. 107), Polycarp (A.D. 108), Irenaeus (A.D. 178), Clement of Alexandria (A.D. 194), Tertullian (A.D. 200), Origen (A.D. 230). Even Marcion admitted that Paul was its author, but asserted that it was written to the Laodiceans, a worthless theory adopted also by Grotius, Mill, Wetstein, Vitringa, Venema, Benson, Paley, &c., but contrary to all the MSS. (except B.) Ancient Versions, &c.

Paul's first visit to Ephesus (A.D. 54), is related in Acts 18. 19—21, and his second in Acts 19. 1—41; want of time prevented him making a third visit, but he called the elders or bishops of Ephesus to meet him at Miletus (A.D. 57), as in Acts 20. 17—38, and exhorted them warmly. His converts in Ephesus were chiefly—if not entirely—Gentiles (2. 11, 19; 3. 1; 4. 17), hence he has few allusions to Judaistic errors and tendencies, and expatiates on the love of God the Father, the grace of Christ, and the fruits of the Spirit, as in his remarkably similar Epistle to the 'Colossians,' written also about the same time, and sent by the same bearer—Tychicus.

It may be divided into two great parts, chap. i.—iii. doctrinal statements, and ch. iv.—vi. practical duties.

Old Testament references are: De. 5. 16; Isa. 28. 9, 16; 46. 10, 11; 60. 1; Jer. 35. 18; Ezek. 18. 9; Zec. 9. 10.

Chapter I. may be divided into three parts; v. 1, 2 salutation; v. 3—14 praise to God for his spiritual blessings bestowed in and through Christ; v. 15—22 thanks and prayers for a spirit of wisdom.

1. PAUL,] *lit.* a 'little' one; see Acts 13. 9.

APOSTLE,] *lit.* one 'sent forth.'

JESUS CHRIST,] i.e. the 'anointed Saviour.'

BY,] *lit.* 'through God's will,' *or* wish.

SAINTS,] *lit.* those 'not of the earth.'

IN EPHESUS.] Codex B. omits these words. It was a city of Ionia, and capital of proconsular Asia, and famous for its temple of Diana.

FAITHFUL,] *or* 'stedfast' ones.

2. GRACE,] *lit.* that which 'causes leaping for joy,' and peace, that which 'brings into unity.'

OUR FATHER,] *lit.* 'Father of us, and (Father) of the Lord Jesus Christ,' as in Rom. 1. 7; 1 Cor. 1. 3; 2 Cor. 1. 2; Gal. 1. 3; Phil. 1. 2; Col. 1. 2; 1 Thess. 1. 2; 2 Thess. 1. 2.

3. BLESSED,] *lit.* 'well-spoken of is the God..who blessed us in every spiritual blessing in (*or* among) the heavenly things (*or* ones) in Christ.'

4. HATH,] *lit.* 'chose (*or* laid) us out for himself in him before (the) laying down of (the) arrangement, for our being holy (i.e. not of the earth) and unblemished over-against him in love,'

5. PREDESTINATED,] *lit.* 'having marked us out beforehand (*or* publicly) with a view to sonship through Jesus Christ to himself according to the good-thought of his will, *or* wish.

6. HATH,] *lit.* 'he made us gracious.'

7. REDEMPTION,] *lit.* 'the thorough-loosing.. letting-go of the fallings-aside.. wealth of.'

8. HATH,] *lit.* 'he abounded.. mindfulness.'

9. GOOD-PLEASURE,] *lit.* 'good-thought which he set forward in him,' i.e. Christ.

10. THAT,] *lit.* 'in reference to (the) dispensation of the fulness of the seasons to head again for himself the all things in the Christ, both the things in the heavens and the things upon the earth—in him,' i.e. Christ.

11. HAVE,] *lit.* 'we obtained inheritance (*or* lot), having been marked out beforehand (*or* publicly), according to a setting-forth of him who the all things is working inwardly according to the counsel of his will.'

12. THAT,] *lit.* 'with a view to our being to..who hoped beforehand (*or* publicly) in the Christ.'

13. AFTER,] *lit.* 'having heard the word of the truth, the good-news of your salvation..the Holy Spirit of the promise.'

14. THE,] *lit.* 'a pledge of our inheritance with a view to (the) thorough-loosing of the thing fully made.'

15. LOVE,] *lit.* 'the love which is to.'

16. CEASE,] *lit.* 'I cease not giving thanks in your behalf..upon my pourings forth before (God).'

17. GLORY,] *lit.* 'of the glory..a spirit and uncovering in his full knowledge.'

18. UNDERSTANDING,] *or* 'heart.'

THAT,] *lit.* 'with a view to your knowing ..wealth of the glory..in (*or* among) the saints.'

19. EXCEEDING,] *lit.* 'over-casting..who are believing..inworking of might of his strength.'

20. WROUGHT,] *lit.* 'inwrought in the Christ, having raised him out of the dead, and set (him) down in his own right hand in (*or* among) the heavenly things (persons *or* places).'

21. FOR,] *or* 'over above..authority.. lordship..this age, but also in the one about to be.'

22. HATH PUT,] *lit.* 'and arranged all things submissively under.'

23. FILLETH,] *lit.* 'is filling the all things in every thing.'

Chapter II. may be divided into five

parts; v. 1—3 past state of the Ephesians by nature; v. 4—10 their present state by the love of God; v. 11, 12 their former state; v. 13—18 their present condition in Christ; v. 19—22 their privileges.

1. AND YOU,] *or* 'even you,' he is filling *or* he made alive.

IN,] *or* 'with (*or* by) the fallings-aside and the sins.'

2. IN TIME PAST,] *lit.* 'in which ye then walked about according to the age of this world, according to the chief..is now working in among the sons of the disobedience,' *or* unbelief.

3. HAD,] *lit.* 'were turned round thoroughly then in the full-desires of our flesh, doing the wishes of the flesh and of the diverse-minds..nature children of anger even as the rest (of men).'

4. WHO,] *lit.* 'being rich *or* wealthy in kindness, because of his much love.'

5. EVEN WHEN,] *lit.* 'and we being dead in (with, by) the fallings aside, made us alive with the Christ—by *or* with grace ye are having been saved.'

6. HATH,] *lit.* 'and raised (us) together, and set (us) down together in (*or* among) the heavenly places (persons *or* things).'

7. TO COME,] *lit.* 'that are coming on he might shew inwardly the over-casting riches (*or* wealth)..upon us in Christ Jesus.'

8. GRACE,] *lit.* 'by (*or* with) the grace ye are having been saved through the faith, and this (salvation) is not of you—(but) the gift of God.'

9. SHOULD,] *or* 'might boast,' *or* make a (long) neck.

10. CREATED,] *or* 'built, (formed), in Christ Jesus upon good works, to which God prepared (us) beforehand (*or* publicly), that in them we might walk about.'

11. REMEMBER,] *lit.* 'be mindful, that ye (were) then the nations in flesh,..called Circumcision in flesh.'

12. AT,] *lit.* 'that during that season we were apart from Christ, having been estranged from..of the promise.. and atheists,' *or* godless.

13. SOMETIMES,] *lit.* 'then far off became nigh in the blood of the Christ.'

14. HATH,] *lit.* 'who made (them) both one, and dissolved (*lit.* loosed) the middle wall of the fence.'

15. ABOLISHED,] *lit.* 'made useless..of the precepts in ordinances (*or* decrees), that he might create (build *or* form) in himself the two into one new man, making peace.'

16. RECONCILE,] *lit.* 'thoroughly-change (them) both in one body to God through the cross, having thoroughly put to death the enmity in it.'

17. CAME,] *lit.* 'having come (in spirit, *not* in person, as in Acts 1. 11; 3. 20; 1 Pet. 3. 19) he told good-news—peace to you, to those (still) far off, and to those (already) nigh,' that is, believers.

18. FOR,] *lit.* 'because..the introduction in one spirit towards the Father.'

19. FOREIGNERS,] *or* 'sojourners, but fellow citizens of the holy ones, and a household of God.'

20. AND,] *lit.* 'being built up upon the foundation of the apostles and prophets,' of the New Testament Church, as in 4. 11, Acts 11. 27.

21. FITLY FRAMED,] *lit.* 'laid perfectly together increaseth to a holy habitation.'

22. FOR,] *or* 'into a dwelling-place of God in spirit.'

Chapter III. may be divided into two parts; v. 1—13 Paul called to be a deacon to the nations; v. 14—21 his prayer for the Ephesians.

1. PRISONER,] *lit.* 'bound one..in behalf of you the nations.'

2. HAVE,] *lit.* 'ye heard of..was given to me in reference to you.'

3. HOW THAT,] *lit.* 'that *or* because according to an uncovering He made known to me the secret (of the calling of the nations), according as I wrote before (*or* publicly) in few words,' *or* short space; see 1. 9, 10. 2. 11, &c.

4. WHEREBY,] *or* 'in regard to which, having read (it), ye are able to understand my intelligence in the secret of the Christ,' regarding the heathen, see v. 6.

5. AGES,] *or* 'generations..was now uncovered to his holy apostles and prophets (see 2. 20) in spirit.'

6. THAT,] *lit.* 'the nations to be fellow-heirs, and (the) same body, and fellow-partakers of his promise in the Christ, through the good news.'

7. WHEREOF,] *lit.* 'of which I became a deacon..according to the inner working of his power.'

8. WHO,] *lit.* 'to the less..was this..to tell as good-news among the nations the untraced riches *or* wealth of the Christ.'

9. MAKE ALL SEE,] *lit.* 'and to enlighten all (as to) what is the fellowship (*or* dispensation) of the secret which was fully hid from the (past) ages in God, who created (built *or* formed) the all things through Jesus Christ.'

10. TO THE INTENT,] *lit.* 'in order that now to the chiefs and the authorities in (*or* among) the heavenly places (persons *or* things) might be made known through the assembly the multifarious wisdom of God.'

11. ETERNAL,] *lit.* 'set-forward-thing of the ages, which he made in.'

12. BOLDNESS,] *lit.* 'the all-speech and the introduction in confidence through his faith.'

13. DESIRE,] *or* 'ask (you) not to be very ill in (*or* during) my tribulations in your behalf.'

14. BOW,] *or* 'bend.'

15. OF,] *lit.* 'out of (*or* from, by) whom (the) whole family (*or* every family) in (the) heavens and upon (the) earth is named.'

16. WOULD,] *lit.* 'may give to you..wealth of..with power through his Spirit, in reference to the inner man.'

17. THAT,] *or* 'for the Christ to dwell through the faith in your hearts, ye in love having been rooted and grounded.'

18. MAY BE,] *lit.* 'that ye may have great

strength to receive thoroughly with all the hallowed ones.'

19. CHRIST,] *lit.* 'of the Christ, which is over-casting the knowledge.'

WITH,] *lit.* 'to *or* with a view to, in reference to, up to.'

20. THINK,] *or* 'understand.. is working inwardly in us.'

21. BE,] *lit.* 'is the glory in the assembly in Christ Jesus to all the generations of the ages of the ages. Amen!'

Chapter IV. may be divided into four parts; v. 1—6 exhortation to work worthily; v. 7—16 gifts of Christ to the assembly; v. 17—24 the old and the new man; v. 25—32 sins to be avoided and duties to be done.

1. PRISONER,] *lit.* 'bound ones in (not *of*) the Lord, call upon you to walk about worthily of the calling with which ye were called.'

2. LOWLINESS,] *lit.* 'lowliness of mind, holding up one another in love.'

3. ENDEAVOURING,] *lit.* 'hasting to keep.. full bond of the peace.'

4. SPIRIT,] not 'Spirit,' as in C.V.

ARE,] *lit.* 'were called.'

7. EVERY,] *lit.* 'each one of us was given the grace..of the Christ.'

8. HE,] *or* 'it (i.e. Scripture) saith (in Ps. 68. 18) Having gone up to (the) height he led captivity captive,' *lit.* 'he took by a spear taking-by-a-spear.'

GAVE.] The Hebrew in Ps. 68. 18 more commonly signifies 'he received *or* took,' but in some few cases (e.g. Hos. 14. 2) it signifies 'gave;' so Chaldee, Syriac, Arabic and Septuagint Versions read here.

9. NOW THAT,] *lit.* 'but this—he went up —what is it, except that he also went down first,'—into the grave, Ps. 69. 3.

10. HEAVENS,] *lit.* 'all the heavens, that he might fill out the all things.'

11. HE GAVE,] *lit.* 'and he himself gave indeed, the apostles, and the prophets, and the tellers of good-news, and the pastors (who are) also teachers, toward the thorough-perfecting of the hallowed ones, with a view to a work of deaconship, with a view to an upbuilding of the body of Christ.'

13. COME,] *lit.* 'may all come thoroughly to..the full-knowledge..of the Christ.'

14. CHILDREN,] *lit.* 'babes, washed away and borne about by every wind of the teaching, in the craftiness (*or* dice-playing) of the men, in every (kind of) work, to the method of the going-astray.'

15. SPEAKING,] *lit.* 'but being true in love, may increase in reference to him (in) the all things..the Christ.'

16. FROM,] *lit.* 'out of (*or* by) whom the whole body, being perfectly laid together and caused to go up together, through every joint of the over-supply, according to (the) energy (*or* in-working), in measure of each single part, makes for itself the increase of the body with a view to the up-building of itself in love.'

17. THAT,] *or* 'for your no more walking about, even as the other nations walk about.'

18. HAVING,] *lit.* 'being darkened in the understanding.. because of the ignorance.. hardness of their heart.'

19. PAST FEELING,] *or* 'away from pain gave themselves over to the wantonness with a view to an in-working of every (kind of) uncleanness in greediness.'

20. HAVE,] *lit.* 'did not so learn the Christ.'

21. THAT,] *lit.* 'if so be ye heard him, and were taught in him, as truth is in Jesus.'

22. THAT,] *lit.* 'for your putting away the old man that is being corrupted according to the former behaviour, according to the over-desires of the deceit.'

23. BE,] *lit.* 'and to be renewed in.'

24. THAT,] *lit.* 'and to put on for yourselves the new man, which is created (*or* built, formed) according to God in righteousness, and kindness of the truth.'

25. LYING,] *lit.* 'the falsehood, speak ye truth each with his neighbour.'

26. ANGRY,] as Christ often was, with sin and evil, but 'sin not,' i.e. do not 'miss' the mark, by being over-angry; Ps. 4. 4.

GO DOWN,] *lit.* 'go in upon your greatest anger.'

28. THAT STOLE,] *lit.* 'who is stealing.. let him toil..to impart to him having need.'

29. COMMUNICATION,] *lit.* 'word pass forth ..to the upbuilding of the necessary thing, that it may give grace to those hearing.'

30. WHEREBY,] *lit.* 'in which ye were sealed with a view to a day of loosing-away.'

31. EVIL-SPEAKING.] *Gr.* blasphemy, i.e 'injurious-speaking, be taken away from you, with all evil,' *or* badness.

32. BE,] *lit.* 'become ye kind to each other, with bowels of compassion, gracious to one another, as also God in Christ was gracious to you.'

Chapter V. may be divided into five parts; v. 1—5 exhortations to imitate God and Christ, and to avoid sin; v. 6—14 once darkness now light; v. 15—21 walking as wise not as fools, to rejoice in the Lord; v. 22—24 exhortation to wives; v. 25—36 and to husbands, to imitate Christ.

1. BE,] *lit.* 'become, therefore, imitators of God, as children beloved.'

2. WALK,] *lit.* 'walk about..as the Christ also loved us and gave himself over in our behalf a thing-borne-forward and a sacrifice to God with a view to an odour of a sweet smell.'

3. FORNICATION,] *or* 'whoredom..greediness..be even named..as is proper to hallowed ones.'

4. NEITHER,] *lit.* 'and..or jesting (*or* well-turned sayings), the things not fit (*or* 'coming up' to the mark), but rather good-joy.'

5. KNOW,] *lit.* 'ye are knowing..greedy persons..of the Christ (who is) also God.'

6. MAN,] *lit.* 'let no one..anger of God upon the sons of the disobedience,' *or* unstedfastness, *or* unbelief, i.e. those remaining obstinate

7. BE,] *lit.* 'become not therefore holders-together-with them.'

8. SOMETIMES,] *lit.* 'then..walk about.'

10. ACCEPTABLE,] *lit.* 'well-pleasing.'

11. FELLOWSHIP,] *or* 'communion..of the darkness, but rather even convict.'

12. THOSE,] *lit.* 'the secret things being done by them.'

13. ALL,] *lit.* 'but the all things being convicted by the light are apparent, for everything that makes itself apparent is light.'

14. HE,] *or* 'it (i.e. Scripture) saith, Rouse thyself, O thorough sleeper, and stand up out of the dead, and the Christ shall shine upon thee.'

15. THAT,] *or* 'how ye walk about accurately, not as unwise.'

16. REDEEMING,] *lit.* 'buying up the season.'

17. THEREFORE,] *lit.* 'because of this become ye not thoughtless.'

18. EXCESS,] *or* 'want of safety..in spirit.'

19. YOURSELVES,] *or* 'one another (responsively) in psalms (i.e. compositions accompanied by musical instruments), and hymns (generally of praise), and spiritual songs, (*Gr.* 'odes,') making odes and psalms with your heart to the Lord,' i.e. Jesus. There is here an express divine warrant for New Testament Hymns, and it has no reference whatever to the Psalms of David, otherwise the definite article would have been found, 'in *the* psalms, and hymns, and spiritual songs.' So Eusebius, Bloomfield, Fausset, &c.

20. GIVING THANKS,] *lit.* 'leaping much for joy always over all things to the God (who is) also Father.'

21. SUBMITTING,] *lit.* 'being arranged (*or* arranging yourselves) under one another, in (the) fear of God,' or as many MSS. Versions, and Fathers have it—' of Christ.'

22. WIVES,] *or* 'the wives! be arranged (*or* arranging yourselves) under your own husbands.'

23. THE,] *lit.* 'is head..the Christ..is head..is saviour of the body,' i.e. the assembly, as in 1. 23.

24. THEREFORE,] *or* 'but, even as the assembly is arranged (*or* arranges itself) under the Christ, so also the wives to their own husbands in every thing'—lawful of course.

25. HUSBANDS,] *lit.* 'the husbands! love your own wives, even as the Christ loved the assembly, and gave himself up in its behalf.'

26. SANCTIFY,] *or* 'hallow it, having cleansed (it) in the bath of the water, in (with, by) a saying.'

27. PRESENT,] *lit.* 'set it alongside of himself—the assembly in glory..any of such things..might be.'

28. MEN,] *lit.* 'the husbands to love their own wives..he who is loving his own wife.'

29. MAN,] *lit.* 'no one..nourisheth it exceedingly.'

30. FOR,] *lit.* 'because.'

31. LEAVE,] *lit.* 'thoroughly leave..be glued..and the two shall be with a view to one flesh.'

32. MYSTERY,] *lit.* 'this secret is great.. in reference to Christ, and in reference to the assembly.'

33. NEVERTHELESS,] *or* 'but ye also, every one in particular, let each his own wife so love as himself, and the wife that she may fear (*or* reverence) the husband.'

Chapter VI. may be divided into five parts; v. 1—9 exhortations to children, fathers, servants, masters; v. 10—17 to stand fast, with the whole armour of God; v. 18—20 to pray for all saints and Paul; v. 21 he sends Tychicus; v. 23, 24 closing salutation and prayer.

1. CHILDREN,] *lit.* 'the children! hearken submissively to your parents..righteous.'

2. THE FIRST,] *lit.* 'a first *or* chief command,' as the Second also has a promise.

3. BE,] *lit.* 'become..shall be a long time upon the land.' Exod. 20. 12; De. 5. 16; Mat. 15. 4; Mark 7. 10.

4. YE,] *lit.* 'and ye, the fathers! provoke not your children greatly, but nourish them much in (the) instruction.'

5. SERVANTS,] *lit.* 'the servants! hearken submissively to the lords according to flesh ..to the Christ.'

6. WITH,] *lit.* 'according to eye-bondage ..as bondsmen of the Christ..out of the soul.'

7. GOOD-WILL,] *lit.* 'good-minds being bondsmen.'

8. KNOWING,] *lit.* 'having known..each one may do, this he shall bring for himself from the Lord.'

9. YE,] *lit.* 'the lords *or* masters..keeping back the threatening, having known that your (and) their Lord is in the heavens..reception of faces.'

10. FINALLY,] *lit.* 'as to the rest, be powerful..might of his strength.'

11. WHOLE ARMOUR,] *Gr.* 'panoply..for your being able to stand for the methods (*or* change of ways) of the Devil.'

12. FOR,] *lit.* 'because we have not the wrestling with blood and flesh, but with the chiefdoms, with the authorities, with the world-powers of the darkness of this age, with the spiritual things of the evil in (*or* among) the heavenly places (persons *or* things).'

13. TAKE,] *lit.* 'take up the panoply of God..to stand against..having wrought all things thoroughly.'

15. YOUR,] *lit.* 'and having the feet bound beneath in a preparation (*or* readiness) of the good-news of the peace.'

16. ABOVE,] *or* 'over (*or* upon) all, having taken up the shield (*lit.* door) of the faith, in (*or* with, by) which..of the evil.'

17. TAKE,] *lit.* 'receive for yourselves the helmet (*lit.* thing 'around the head,') of the salvation..a saying of God,' i.e. any one and every one.

18. PRAYING,] *lit.* 'pouring forth before (God) in every season, through every prayer and supplication in spirit, and in reference to this very thing being wakeful in all..the saints.'

24. THAT LOVE,] *lit.* 'all those loving..in uncorruptedness. Amen.'

PAUL'S LETTER TO THE PHILIPPIANS

PHILIPPI was the 'first city' of Macedonia visited by Paul (Acts 16. 6—12) in A.D. 50. Its original name was Datos, but Philip, father of Alexander, gave it his own name when he rebuilt and fortified it. Paul visited it a second, if not a third, time (Acts 20. 1—6), and was once and again helped by the liberality of the assembly he formed there (Phil. 2. 25; 4. 10, 14—18; 2 Cor. 11. 9), to which he addressed this Letter, which is quoted by Polycarp (A.D. 108), Irenaeus (A.D. 178), Clement of Alexandria (A.D. 194), Tertullian (A.D. 200), Marcion (A.D. 140), the Churches of Vienna and Lyons (A.D. 177), Cyprian (A.D. 248) Eusebius (A.D. 320), &c. It was written when Paul was a prisoner in Rome (1. 7, 13; 4. 22), probably in A.D. 63, and sent by the hands of Epaphroditus, who had been sent to him from Philippi with their gifts.

The object of the Letter is five-fold; *first*, to express thanks to God and love to them, with confidence in them and the Spirit (ch. i. 1—26); *second*, to exhort them to perseverance, love, humility, working with God, blamelessness (ch. i. 27—ii. 18); *third*, to encourage them and himself by, the presence of Timothy and Epaphroditus (v. 19—30); *fourth*, to avoid Judaizing, and press close to Christ (iii. 1—21); *fifth*, special and general exhortations, congratulations, salutations, (iv. 1—23).

Old Testament references are to Ps. 22. 6; 55. 22; Isa. 40. 23; 56. 10; Jer. 9. 23, 24; Da. 9. 26, &c.

Chapter I. may be divided into eight parts; v. 1, 2 salutation; v. 3—7 thanksgiving for them; v. 8—11 love to them; v. 12—14 encouraging news; v. 15—18 joy in proclamation of the gospel; v. 19—21 confidence in them and the Spirit; v. 22—26 a strait between two; v. 27—30 exhortation to persevere.

1. PAUL,] i.e. the 'little' one.

TIMOTHEUS,] i.e. the one 'honouring God.'

THE,] *lit.* 'bondsmen of..the hallowed ones (i.e. not of the earth)..are in Philippi, with overseers and deacons.'

BISHOPS,] *lit.* 'overseers,' of whom there was a plurality in every assembly, however small, in the early church; elsewhere called presbyters, i.e. elders, a more honourable title taken from the Jewish state and synagogue.

DEACONS.] All who in any way helped the assembly—not as filling an office, but as discharging a duty or service—whether male or female; such as readers, precentors, beadles, doorkeepers, distributors of alms, preachers, teachers, &c. In the great majority of cases the name in the New Testament is expressly applied to *spiritual* rather than to *secular* work, to which it is now most injuriously limited in most modern Churches. The Church of England fortunately still recognizes its spiritual application.

2. GRACE,] *lit.* 'what causes leaping for joy.'

PEACE,] *lit.* 'what brings into unity.'

FROM,] *lit.* 'and (the Father of) our Lord Jesus Christ.'

3. THANK,] *lit.* 'I-leap-much-for-joy-before my God upon all the remembrance of you.'

4. PRAYER,] *lit.* 'supplication..making the supplication with joy.'

5. FOR,] *lit.* 'upon (*or* over) your communion in reference to the good-news.'

6. HATH BEGUN,] *lit.* 'began inwardly in (*or* among) you a good work, will end (it) fully during (*or* before) the day of Jesus Christ.'

7. MEET,] *lit.* 'righteous.. concerning you all..all are partakers with me of the grace.'

8. RECORD,] *or* 'witness, how I have a desire for you all.'

9. PRAY,] *lit.* 'pour forth before (God) that..in full knowledge and in all perception.'

10. THAT,] *lit.* 'with a view to your approving the things that bear diversely.. pure and offenceless with a view to (the) day of Christ.'

11. FILLED,] *or* 'full of the.. through (Jesus) Christ, with a view to (the) glory and praise of God.'

12. WOULD,] *lit.* 'I counsel you to know, brethren, that the things concerning me have come rather with a view to an advancement of the good-news.'

13. ARE,] *lit.* 'became apparent in the whole prætorium, and all the rest.'

14. MANY,] *lit.* 'the greater part of..having confidence..fearlessly.'

15. SOME,] *lit.* 'certain, indeed, proclaim the Christ through..certain also through good-will,' *or* pleasure.

16. THE ONE,] *lit.* 'these, indeed, tell the Christ fully out of contention, not purely .. to bring tribulation also upon my bonds.'

17. OF,] *lit.* 'out of love, having seen (*or* known)..placed for (the) apology.'

18. WHAT THEN,] *or* 'for why?..told thoroughly of.'

19. KNOW,] *lit.* 'have known..shall come out for my safety..supplication..full supply.'

20. BOLDNESS,] *lit.* 'full speech..through life or through death.'

21. LIVE,] *lit.* 'the living in flesh this is to me a fruit of work..choose (*lit.* lift up) I know not,' *or* I cannot make known.

23. IN A STRAIT,] *or* 'pressed (*lit.* poured together) from the two, having the full-desire to be let away..much better.'

24. NEVERTHELESS,] *lit.* 'but to remain on ..on your account.'

25. KNOW,] *lit.* 'I have known that I shall remain and remain alongside with you all, with a view to your advancement and joy of the faith.'

26. REJOICING,] *lit.* 'boasting may abound ..in me, through my presence again with you.'

27. CONVERSATION,] *lit.* 'citizenship be worthy of the good news of the Christ..hear the things concerning you that ye stand in one spirit, with one soul, striving together (for) the faith of the good news.'

28. YOUR,] *lit.* 'by those set over against.. token (*or* inward sign) of a full loss..from God.'

29. IS GIVEN,] *lit.* 'was granted..in his behalf.'

30. CONFLICT,] *Gr.* 'agony,' i.e. wrestling or contest.

Chapter II. may be divided into six parts; v. 1—4 exhortation to love and humility; v. 5—11 Christ's humility and exaltation; v. 12, 13 work with God; v. 14—18 to be cheerful, blameless, life-giving; v. 19—24 character of Timotheus; v. 25—30 reasons for sending Epaphroditus.

1. CONSOLATION,] *or* 'exhortation.. communion of spirit.'

2. FULFIL,] *lit.* 'make full..that ye may mind the same thing..fellow-souled, minding the one thing,'—as in Luke 10. 42.

3. LET,] *lit.* 'nothing according to .. but with lowly-mindedness esteeming one another as being above yourselves.'

4. EVERY,] *lit.* 'each..but each also.'

5. LET,] *lit.* 'for let this be minded among you.'

6. BEING,] *lit.* 'beginning secretly in (the) form of God thought (it) not an act of robbery to be equal to God,' i.e. treated as His equal.

7. OF NO REPUTATION,] *lit.* 'made himself vain (*or* empty), having taken (*or* received) the form of a bondsman, having come (*or* happened) in the likeness of men.'

8. BEING,] *lit* 'having been found in habit (*Gr.* scheme)as a man, he made himself low, having become a submissive-hearkener unto death—death even of a cross.'

9. HATH,] *lit.* 'did highly exalt him, and granted to him.'

10. AT,] *lit.* 'in the name of Jesus every knee might bend, of those above the heavens, and upon the land, and under the earth, and every tongue might speak out the same thing, that.'

12. WHEREFORE,] *lit.* 'so that..ye always hearkened submissively..work out thoroughly.'

13. WORKETH,] *lit.* 'is inwardly working in (*or* among) you both to wish and to inwardly work in behalf of the well-pleasing thing.'

14. WITHOUT,] *lit.* 'apart from..diverse reasonings.'

15. BE,] *lit.* 'may become..unhorned (unmixed, unhurtful), children of God, unblemished in the midst of a generation, thorned and thoroughly turned-round, among whom ye appear as luminaries in the world.'

16. FORTH,] *or* 'holding to the word of life, with a view to my boasting..I did not run..nor toil.'

17. YEA,] *lit.* 'but even if I am poured forth upon..public work of.'

19. TRUST,] *or* 'hope..may have a good soul, having known the things concerning you.'

20. LIKE-MINDED,] *lit.* 'like-souled, who will sincerely care for the things about you.'

21. ALL,] *lit.* 'for they all seek their own things, not the things of.'

22. PROOF,] *or* 'test..child with a father, he was in bondage with me with a view to the good-news.'

23. PRESENTLY,] *or* 'immediately, as soon as I may see thoroughly the things concerning me.'

24. SHORTLY,] *or* 'speedily.'

25. SUPPOSED,] *or* 'thought *or* counted.'
EPAPHRODITUS,] *lit.* 'lovely.'
COMPANION,] *lit.* 'fellow-worker.. but your apostle, and a public-worker for my necessities.'

26. FOR,] *lit.* 'seeing he was desiring greatly (to see) you all, and weary (*or* fainting), because that ye heard that he was infirm *or* ailing.'

27. INDEED,] *lit.* 'for he was also infirm (*or* ailing)..God pitied him, and not him only, but also me, that I might.'

28. THE,] *lit.* 'more speedily..be without sorrow.'

29. RECEIVE,] *lit.* 'receive him to (yourselves) therefore..in honour.'

30. FOR,] *or* 'on account of the work of the Christ he drew nigh unto death, counselling for himself apart from (his) soul, that he might fill up your lack of the public work toward me.'

Chapter III. may be divided into five parts; v. 1—7 to avoid Judaizing; v. 8—11 gains and losses for Christ; v. 12—14 striving for the prize; v. 15—17 future revelations and present conduct; v. 18—21 a contrast, future hope.

1. FINALLY,] *or* 'as to the rest..tiresome ..is sure.'

2. BEWARE,] *lit.* 'see the dogs (i.e. the impure), see the evil-workers, see the cutting down,' i.e. the fleshly circumcisors.

3. WORSHIP,] *lit.* 'are trembling much towards God in spirit, and boasting..trust in flesh.'

4. MIGHT,] *lit.* 'I also am having cause of trust in flesh; if any other one thinketh *or* seemeth to have trust in flesh.'

5. STOCK,] *lit.* 'out of the race of..out of Hebrews, according to law.'

6. CONCERNING,] *lit.* 'according to zeal, causing the assembly to flee, according to righteousness that is in law becoming blameless.'

7. COUNTED,] *lit.* 'I have counted loss because of the Christ.'

8. BUT,] *lit.* 'to be loss, because of the.. because of whom I lost the all things,.. to be refuse.. gain Christ.'

9. OF,] *lit.* 'out of law, but that through faith of Christ, the righteousness out of God upon the faith.'

10. THAT,] *lit.* 'to know him..his upstanding..communion of..being conformed.'

11. BY ANY MEANS,] *lit.* 'if any how..upstanding out of the dead,' in its fullest extent and blessing; a spiritual resurrection is here meant (as in John 5. 25) as the apostle could not possibly doubt whether he should partake in the general up-rising.

12. AS THOUGH,] *lit.* 'not that I already received (it), or have been already perfected, but I pursue, even if I may receive (it) fully, that for which also I was received fully by Christ Jesus.

13. COUNT,] [illegible] reckon not myself to have received (it) fully, but one thing—forgetting fully indeed the things behind, and stretching forth to the things before.'

14. PRESS,] *lit.* 'according to the goal I pursue for.'

15. LET,] *lit.* 'as many, therefore, as (are) perfect, let us mind this, and if ye otherwise mind anything.'

16. NEVERTHELESS,] *lit.* 'but in reference to what we have come (to), by the same canon (*lit.* reed, cane) to step, the same thing to mind.'

17. BE,] *lit.* 'become imitators together of ..observe those walking about, according as ye have us (as) a type.'

18. WALK,] *lit.* 'walk about of whom I said to you many times, and now also say, wailing..of the Christ.'

19. DESTRUCTION,] *or* 'a full loss..are minding the things upon earth.'

20. CONVERSATION,] *lit.* 'citizenship (*or* 'behaviour as citizens') begins secretly among heavenly persons,' places *or* things.

21. CHANGE,] *or* 'transform the body of our lowliness (*or* humiliation) with a view to its becoming conformed to the body of his glory, according to the in-working of him who is able even to arrange the all things under himself.'

Chapter IV. may be divided into four parts; v. 1—9 special and general exhortations; v. 10—12 Paul's contentment; v. 13—20 their gifts and his prayer; v. 21—23 mutual salutations.

1. THEREFORE,] *or* 'so that, my brethren beloved and greatly desired..thus stand in the Lord, beloved.'

2. BESEECH,] *lit.* 'call upon,' *or* exhort.

EUODIA,] i.e. 'sweet odour.'

SYNTYCHE,] i.e. 'affable;' both female names; probably the deaconesses alluded to in the next verse.

THAT,] *lit.* 'to mind the same thing in the Lord.'

3. ENTREAT,] *lit.* 'ask..genuine yoke-fellow, be helping along with them who strove along with me in the good-news.'

CLEMENT,] i.e. 'clement, merciful.'

OTHER,] *lit.* 'the others my fellow-workers.

BOOK OF LIFE,] as in Luke 10. 20; Rev. 3. 5; 13. 8; 20. 12; 21. 27, and compare 3. 5.

5. MODERATION,] *lit.* 'much yieldingness ..is nigh.'

6. CAREFUL,] *lit.* 'divided (in mind)..by the pouring forth before (God), and the supplication, with much leaping for joy.'

7. PASSETH,] *or* 'is excelling all understanding (*or* every mind), shall guard your hearts and thoughts in Christ Jesus.'

8. FINALLY,] *lit.* 'as to the rest..as many things as (are) true, as many things as (are) right..pure..friendly..of good fame.. courage,' *or* pleasing thing.

9. HAVE,] *lit.* 'ye both learned, and received from, and heard, and saw in me, practise, and the God of the peace.'

10. THE LAST,] *lit.* 'at length your thoughtfulness in my behalf flourished again, for which also ye were thoughtful, but were without opportunity.'

11. IN RESPECT OF,] *lit.* 'through want..I learned, in (*or* among) whatever persons *or* places I am, to be satisfied with it.'

12. KNOW,] *lit.* 'have known to be humbled *or* made low, I have known also to abound; in every (place) and in all things I have been initiated both to be full and to be hungry.. to be in want.'

13. I CAN DO,] *lit.* 'I am strong *or* have strength (for) all things *or* every thing, in Christ's strengthening me inwardly.'

14. HAVE,] *lit.* 'ye did well having communicated with me in the tribulation.'

15. NOW,] *lit.* 'but ye have known for yourselves, even ye, O Philippians..I went forth from..assembly..in reference to (the) matter of.'

16. FOR,] *or* 'because (*or* that) also (*or* even)..both once and twice with a view to my need.'

17. DESIRE,] *or* 'seek after the gift, but I seek after the fruit that is becoming more, with a view to your account.'

18. HAVE,] *lit.* 'I have all fully..I am filled..from Epaphroditus.'

19. SUPPLY,] *lit.* 'fill up your every need ..in Christ Jesus.'

20. GOD,] *lit.* 'our God and Father (is) the glory to the ages of the ages. Amen.'

21. SALUTE,] *lit.* 'draw ye near every hallowed one.'

SALUTE,] *lit.* 'draw you near.'

22. SAINTS,] *lit.* 'hallowed ones draw you near, but especially those of Caesar's house.'

23. BE,] *or* 'is with you all. Amen.'

PAUL'S LETTER TO THE COLOSSIANS

THIS LETTER of Paul to the Colossians is quoted by Justin Martyr (A.D. 140), Theophilus of Antioch (A.D. 181), Irenaeus (A.D. 178), Clement of Alexandria (A.D. 194), Tertullian (A.D. 200), Origen (A.D. 230), &c. It was sent apparently from Rome about the same time as the Letter to the Ephesians, with which it agrees in very many places. Colosse (*or* Colasse) was a large city of Phrygia, and is now called Khonae; its Christian inhabitants were chiefly Gentiles (2. 13), gathered together perhaps by Epaphras, Timothy, Philemon, or Paul himself. The Greek style, both as to words and phrases, is peculiar. The writer's object is to counteract a tendency to Judaism—the greatest curse of the primitive church,—with a mixture of oriental theosophy, angel worship, and asceticism.

The following table shews the parallelism of the Letters to the Ephesians and Colossians; viz:—

Ephesians.	*Colossians.*
1. 1, 2.	1. 1, 2.
1. 6, 7.	1. 13.
1. 10.	1. 19, 20.
1. 15, 16.	1. 3, 4.
1. 17—21.	1. 9—15.
1. 22; 3. 10, 11.	1. 16—18.
1. 19; 2. 1—5.	2. 12, 13.
2. 1.	1. 21.
2. 13—16.	1. 20; 2. 14.
3. 1.	1. 24, 25.
3. 3, &c.	1. 26—29.
4. 2—4.	2. 12—15.
4. 16.	2. 19.
4. 22—25.	3. 9, 10.
4. 17—21.	1. 21; 2. 6; 3. 8—10.
4. 29.	4. 6.
4. 32.	3. 12, 13.
4. 31.	3. 8.
5. 5.	3. 5.
5. 6.	3. 6.
5. 7, 8.	3. 7, 8.
5. 15, 16.	4. 5.
5. 18—20.	3. 16, 17.
5. 21—23; 6. 1—9.	3. 18—25; 4. 1.
6. 18—20.	4. 2—4.
6. 21, 22.	4. 7—9.

This Letter contains references to De. 30. 6; Ecc. 10. 10; Ezek. 13. 3; John 1. 1; Rom. 8 38; 1 Cor. 8. 6; Heb. 1. 2, &c.

It may be divided into three parts; the *first*, (1. 1—2. 5) being chiefly doctrinal, and the *second* (2. 6—4. 6) chiefly practical, and the *third*, containing salutations.

Chapter I. may be divided into five parts; v. 1, 2 introductory salutation; v. 3—8 expression of gratitude; v. 9—14 and of desire for them; v. 15—23 dignity and work of Christ; v. 24—29 Paul's joy and work.

1. PAUL,] i.e. the 'little' one.'

APOSTLE,] *lit.* one 'sent forth.'

JESUS CHRIST,] i.e. an 'anointed saviour.

BY,] *lit.* 'through (the) wish of God.'

TIMOTHEUS,] i.e. one 'honouring God.'

OUR,] *lit.* 'the brother.'

2. SAINTS,] *lit.* 'hallowed and stedfast ones, brethren in Christ, who are in Colosse,' *or* Colasse, as in many ancient MSS.

GRACE,] *lit.* what 'causes leaping for joy.

PEACE,] *lit.* what 'brings into unity.'

AND THE,] *or* 'and (Father of the) Lord Jesus Christ.' But many ancient MSS., Versions, and Fathers omit the last clause entirely.

3. GIVE THANKS,] *or* 'leap much for joy in the God and Father of..always pouring forth before (God) concerning you.'

4. SINCE,] *lit.* 'having heard of.'

5. FOR,] i.e. 'because of, on account of.'

LAID UP,] *or* 'aside to you in the heavens, which ye heard before *or* publicly of in.'

6. COME,] *lit.* 'present *or* alongside in reference to you, as also in all the (Roman) world, and is bearing fruit (and increasing, as in many MSS. Versions, and Fathers), as also in you from the day ye heard it, and knew fully.'

7. OF,] *lit.* 'from Epaphras, our beloved fellow-bondsman, who is in your (*or* our) behalf a stedfast deacon of the Christ.'

8. DECLARED,] *or* 'manifested..in spirit.'

9. SINCE,] *lit.* 'from the day..cease pouring forth before (God) in your behalf, and asking that ye may be full of the full-knowledge of his wish in all wisdom.'

10. THAT,] *lit.* 'to your walking about worthily of the Lord in reference to all (desire of) pleasing, bearing fruit in every good work, and increasing with a view to the full-knowledge of God.'

11. STRENGTHENED,] *lit.* 'being made powerful, in every act of power, according to the strength *or* might of his glory, in reference to all endurance.'

12. GIVING THANKS,] *lit.* 'ye leaping much for joy in the Father, who made us sufficient with a view to the portion of the lot of the hallowed ones in the light.'

13. HATH,] *lit.* 'who freed us out of the authority of the darkness, and set with (them) with a view to the kingdom of the Son of his love.'

14. REDEMPTION,] *lit.* 'the full-loosing.. letting go of the sins.'

15. THE,] *lit.* 'an image of the unseen God, first-born (i.e. heir) of all creation,' *or* every creature, *or* created thing.

16. FOR,] *lit.* 'because in him were the all things created (built *or* formed), the things in the heavens, and the things upon the earth, the things seen and the things unseen, whether thrones, or lordships. authorities, the all things through him and with a view to him, have been created, built *or* formed.

17. HE,] *lit.* 'himself is..in him the all things stood together.'

18. HE,] *lit.* 'himself is..is a beginning, a first born out of the dead, that himself may become in *or* among all first.'

19. FOR,] *lit.* 'because all the fulness was well-pleased to dwell thoroughly.'

20. BY,] *lit.* 'through him to thoroughly change the all things in reference to him, through him, whether the things upon the earth, or the things in the heavens.'

21. THAT WERE,] *lit.* 'being once alienated and enemies with the full mind in the evil works, yet now did he thoroughly change.'

22. DEATH,] *lit.* 'the death, to set you alongside hallowed, and unblemished, and uncalled in (to court) over-against his face.'

23. IF,] *lit.* 'if (*or* since) indeed ye remain upon the faith founded and seated,..ye heard, which was proclaimed in all the creation which is under the heaven, of which I Paul became a deacon.'

24. WHO,] *lit.* 'I now..in your behalf, and fill up in return the things lacking of the tribulations of the Christ in my flesh in behalf of his body.'

25. AM I MADE,] *lit.* 'I became a deacon.. stewardship (*lit.* house-distribution) of God, which was given to me in reference to you, to make full the word of God.'

26. MYSTERY,] *or* secret, *lit.* a thing to be kept for the initiated.

HID,] *lit.* 'hid away (*or* fully) from the ages and from the generations, but was now made apparent.'

27. WOULD,] *lit.* 'wished *or* willed..in (*or* among) you, the hope of the glory.'

28. PREACH,] *lit.* 'tell thoroughly of, admonishing..may set every man alongside (of ourselves) perfect.'

29. WHEREUNTO,] *lit.* 'with a view to which I also toil, agonizing according to his energy (*or* inward-working) which is working-inwardly in me in power.'

Chapter II. may be divided into four parts; v. 1—5 Paul's desire and prayer; v. 6—8 exhortation and warning; v. 9—15 fulness of Christ and his people; v. 16—23 warning against Judaism and Gnosticism.

1. WOULD,] *lit.* 'wish you to know how great a conflict (*Gr.* agony) I have concerning you, and those in Laodicea..in flesh.'

2. MIGHT,] *or* 'may be comforted, growing up together in love, and in reference to all (the) wealth of the full-bearing of the understanding, with a view to the full-knowledge of the secret of the God and Father, and of the Christ.'

3. IN WHOM,] *or* 'in which..of the wisdom and of the knowledge.'

4. LEST,] *lit.* 'that no one may reason amiss (*or* alongside of you) with persuasive words.'

5. THOUGH,] *lit.* 'for even if I am away in the flesh..firmness of your faith in reference to Christ.'

6. HAVE,] *lit.* 'ye received..walk about.'

7 BUILT,] *lit.* 'being builded up.'

ESTABLISHED,] *or* 'confirmed..ye were taught..in much leaping for joy.'

8. BEWARE,] *lit.* 'behold *or* see that no one shall be leading you (as) prey through the love of wisdom (*Gr.* philosophy) and vain (*or* empty) deceit, according to the tradition (*lit.* 'thing given over') of the men, according to the steps (*or* steppings, rudiments, elements) of the world, and not according to Christ.'

9. FOR,] *lit.* 'because.'

10. COMPLETE,] *lit.* 'made full..authority.'

11. PUTTING,] *lit.* 'in the putting off of.. in the circumcision of the Christ.'

12. WITH,] *lit.* 'entombed together with him in the baptism, in which also ye were raised together through..inward working of God, who raised him out of the dead.'

13. YOUR SINS,] *lit.* 'in the fallings-aside ..did he make alive..all the fallings-aside.'

14. BLOTTING,] *lit.* 'having blotted..in the thoughts (*or* determinations, *Gr.* dogmas of the law) which was over-against us, and lifted it out of the midst, having nailed it to the cross.'

15. SPOILED,] *lit.* 'thoroughly stripped for himself the principalities and the authorities, he showed (them) off in full-speech, having led them in triumph in it (*or* himself).'

16. MEAT,] *lit.* 'eating or in drinking, or in respect of a feast (*or* festival-day), or of a new moon, or of sabbaths.' The observance of the 'first day of the week' cannot be justly included under the 'sabbaths' here referred to, as the primitive Christians, following the example of the New Testament Writers, scrupulously avoided calling it a 'sabbath,' preferring 'Sunday' as less objectionable, or better still, 'the Lord's Day.'

17. TO COME,] *lit.* 'things about to be..of the Christ.'

18. MAN,] *lit.* 'no one be defrauding you of the prize, being willing in humblemindedness and worship of the messengers, treading among what he..by the mind of his flesh.'

19. HOLDING,] *or* 'holding fast the head, out of which (*or* whom)..through the joints and mutual bands getting supply, and coming up together.'

20. WHEREFORE,] *lit.* 'if then ye died with the Christ from the steps (*or* steppings, rudiments or elements) of..ye dogmatized (*or* were under) dogmas,' i.e. thoughts, determinations, whether of Jews or Gentiles.

21. TOUCH,] *lit.* 'thou mayest not handle, nor even taste, nor even touch.'

22. TO PERISH,] *lit.* 'with a view to corruption with the full-use, according to the ..teachings of the men.'

23. SHEW,] *lit.* 'word *or* reckoning..lowliness of mind, and unsparingness of body, not in any honour, towards satiety of the flesh.'

Chapter III. may be divided into seven parts; v. 1—4 exhortations to seek and mind things above; v. 5—8 to avoid various sins; v. 9—11 to put on the image of Christ;

v. 12—15 to bear, forbear, be thankful; v. 16, 17 to praise Christ and glorify God; v. 18—21 address to wives; v. 22—25 to bondsmen.

1. YE BE,] *lit.* 'ye were raised with the Christ, seek the things above, where the Christ is sitting.'

2. SET,] *lit.* 'mind ye the things above, not the things.'

3. ARE DEAD,] *lit.* 'died fully..has been hid with the Christ in God.'

4. CHRIST,] *lit.* 'the Christ.. may appear (*or* be apparent)..also be apparent.'

5. MORTIFY,] *lit.* 'put to death.. whoredom..passion, bad over-desires, and the avarice.'

6. FOR,] *or* 'because of which things the anger..sons of the unbelief *or* untrustfulness.'

7. THE,] *lit.* 'in which ye also walked about once.'

8. ALSO,] *lit.* 'now put off—even ye—the whole anger, fury, badness, injurious speaking, shameful speech.'

9. LIE,] *lit.* 'be not lying to one another, having put thoroughly off..practises.'

10. IS RENEWED,] *lit.* 'is being renewed with a view to a full-knowledge.'

11. NEITHER,] *lit.* 'not Hellen and Jew, circumcision and uncircumcision.. bondsman, freedman, but the all and in all—Christ.'

12. THE,] *lit.* 'as elect (*or* select, choice) ones of God..lowliness of mind.'

13. FORBEARING,] *lit.* 'holding up..being gracious to each other, if any one may have anything blameable in reference to any, as even the Christ was gracious to you.'

14. ABOVE,] *or* 'over..the love, which is a full-band of the perfectness.'

15. RULE,] *or* 'preside (*or* decide)..in reference to which also ye were called..become ye leaping with joy.'

16. WORD,] *or* 'doctrine of the Christ (as revealed in N.T., not as under the shadows of the O.T.) dwell inwardly in you, richly in every (kind of) wisdom, teaching and admonishing yourselves in (*or* with) psalms (accompanied with musical instruments), and hymns and spiritual odes, in joy odeing in your heart to the Lord'—Jesus; as in Eph. 5. 19.

17. DO,] *lit.* 'may do in word or in work ..leaping much before the God and Father through him.'

18. WIVES,] *lit.* 'the wives! be arranged (*or* arranging yourselves) under your own husbands, as he has come up (to you) in the Lord.'

19. HUSBANDS,] *lit.* 'the husbands! love the wives.. towards them.'

20. CHILDREN,] *lit.* 'the children! hearken submissively to the parents through all things..in (*not* unto) the Lord.'

21. FATHERS,] *lit.* 'the fathers! vex (*or* irritate) not..be disheartened.'

22. SERVANTS,] *lit.* 'the bondsmen! hearken submissively through all things to the lords according to flesh, not in eye-bondage..simplicity.'

23. DO,] *lit.* 'may do, work ye from the soul.'

24. KNOWING,] *lit.* 'having known that from the Lord ye shall receive fully the recompense of the distribution by lot, for ye are in bondage to the Lord Christ.'

25. DOETH,] *lit.* 'is doing unrighteously shall bring to himself what he did unrighteously, and there is no acceptance of persons *or* faces.'

Chapter IV. may be divided into seven parts; v. 1 exhortations to masters; v. 2—6 to prayer, wise behaviour, and seasonable conversation; v. 7—9 intimation of the sending of Tychicus and Onesimus; v 10—15 various salutations; v. 16 this Letter to be publicly read; v. 17 charge to Archippus; v. 18 closing salutation and prayer.

1. MASTERS,] *lit.* 'the lords! hold ye forth to the bondsmen what is right and equitable, having known..a Lord in the heaven.'

2. CONTINUE,] *or* 'be strong towards the pouring forth before (God), being wakeful in it, in much leaping for joy.'

3. WITHAL,] *lit.* 'pouring forth before (God) together also concerning us, that God may open up (the) door of the word, to speak the secret of the Christ (regarding the nations), because of which I even have been bound.'

4. MANIFEST,] *or* 'apparent, as it behoves me.'

5. WALK,] *lit.* 'walk about..those without, the season buying off.'

6. WITH,] *lit.* 'in grace, having been made fit with salt, to know how it behoves you.'

7. STATE,] *lit.* 'all the things concerning me shall Tychicus—the beloved brother—and stedfast deacon and fellow bondsman in the Lord, make known to you.'

8. HAVE,] *lit.* 'I sent to you in reference to this very thing, that he may know the things concerning you.'

9. ONESIMUS,] i.e. 'useful.'

A,] *lit.* 'the stedfast.'

ALL THINGS,] *lit.* 'all the things here.'

10. ARISTARCHUS,] i.e. the 'best of chiefs.

PRISONER,] *lit.* 'one taken by a spear.'

SALUTETH,] *lit.* 'draweth you near.'

MARCUS.] Etymology uncertain.

SISTER'S SON,] *lit.* 'connection.'

BARNABAS,] i.e. 'son of exhortation.'

TOUCHING,] *lit.* 'concerning whom.'

COME,] *lit.* 'may come.'

11. JESUS,] i.e. 'saviour.'

JUSTUS,] i.e. 'just.'

UNTO,] *lit.* 'in reference to, *or* with a view to the reign of God, who became.'

12. EPAPHRAS,] i.e. 'lovely,' i.q. Epaphroditus.

SERVANT,] *lit.* 'bondsman..agonizing in your behalf in the pourings forth before (God)..and made full.'

13. A GREAT,] *lit.* 'much zeal in behalf of you and of those in Laodicea, and of those in Hierapolis,' both cities in Phrygia.

14. LUKE.] Etymology uncertain.

PHYSICIAN,] *or* 'healer, *or* curer.'

DEMAS,] i.e. a 'plebeian,' one of the people.

18. GRACE,] *lit.* 'the grace (is) with you. Amen.'

PAUL'S LETTER TO THE THESSALONIANS
(THE FIRST)

PAUL himself first preached the Gospel (A.D. 50), in Thessalonica, a sea-port and capital of Macedonia (Acts 17. 1—9), and formed there a church consisting chiefly, if not entirely, of Gentiles; being driven away by the Jews he went to Berea and then to Athens, whence he sent Timothy to Thessalonica, who on his return found Paul in Corinth, who on receiving his comparatively favourable report, wrote, in conjunction with Silvanus and Timotheus, this Letter—the first of all his writings that have been transmitted to us—about A.D. 52—to confirm their faith, to encourage them under persecution, and excite them to holiness.

It may be divided into two parts, the *first*, (ch. i. ii. iii.) exhorting to constancy and perseverance, the *second*, (ch. iv. v.) to progress and become perfect. Like the Second Letter it contains very few allusions to the Old Testament, owing to the Gentile origin of the Thessalonian assembly.

It is quoted or referred to by Irenaeus (A.D. 178), Clement of Alexandria (A.D. 194), Tertullian (A.D. 200), Caius (A.D. 212), Origen (A.D. 230). It is contained in the earliest Latin and Syriac Versions, the Canon of the Muratorian fragment, and in that of Marcion. Doubtful are the allusions to it in Clement of Rome, Polycarp, Ignatius, &c.

Chapter I. may be divided into three parts; v. 1 the writers' salutation; v. 2—6 their joy over the Thessalonians' full reception of the good-news; v. 7—10 with exemplary character, missionary zeal, and turning to God.

1. PAUL,] i.e. the 'little' one.
SILVANUS,] i.e. a 'forester.'
TIMOTHEUS,] i.e. one 'honouring God.'
CHURCH,] *lit.* 'assembly of Thessalonians.'
GRACE,] *lit.* what 'causes leaping for joy.'
PEACE,] *lit.* what 'brings into unity.'
AND,] *lit.* 'and (the Father of) our Lord Jesus Christ.'

2. GIVE THANKS,] *lit.* 'leap much for joy before God always concerning you all, ..upon (above, over, during) our pouring forth before (God), unceasingly.'

3. REMEMBERING,] *or* 'making mention of you—the work of the faith, and the toil of the love, and the endurance of the hope of our Lord Jesus Christ, before our God and Father.'

4. KNOWING,] *lit.* 'having known, brethren beloved by God, your election,' *or* select, choice state.

5. FOR,] *lit.* 'because our (declaration of the) gospel became not in reference to you ..in holy spirit, and in much full-bearing, as ye have known we became such among you on your account.'

6. FOLLOWERS,] *lit.* 'imitators..tribulation, with (the) joy of a holy spirit.'

7. SO THAT,] *lit.* 'so as to your becoming types to all those believing.'

8. SOUNDED OUT,] *lit.* 'has sounded forth ..faith which is toward God has gone forth for itself.'

9. SHEW,] *lit.* 'tell fully concerning us what sort of way in .turned round fully toward God from the idols, to be in bondage to.'

10. WAIT,] *lit.* 'remain on his Son out of *or* from the heavens, whom he raised out of (the) dead.—Jesus, who is freeing us from the anger that is coming.'

Chapter II. may be divided into four parts; v. 1—6 Paul's boldness and disinterestedness; v. 7—12 his gentleness, and faithfulness; v. 13—16 his thankfulness for their faith, and condemnation of the Jews; v. 17—20 his desire to see them and joy in them.

1. KNOW,] *lit.* 'have known our way in towards you, that it has not become vain.'

2. EVEN,] *lit.* 'but having both suffered before (*or* publicly) and been insulted—as ye have known—among (the) Philippians, we had full-speech in our God..in much agony,' *or* conflict.

3. EXHORTATION,] *lit.* 'calling along (is) not out of *or* from deceit.'

4. WERE,] *lit.* 'have been approved by God to be intrusted..giving pleasure to men, but to God who is approving our hearts.'

5. NEITHER,] *lit.* 'for at no time did we come in a word of flattery, as ye have known, nor in a pretence of (for) covetousness.'

6. SOUGHT,] *lit.* 'are we not seeking glory, neither from you nor from others, we being able to be in heaviness (upon you), as Christ's apostles.'

7. WERE,] *lit.* 'became gentle (*or* mild) in your midst, as a nursing-woman may cherish her own children.'

8. BEING AFFECTIONATELY DESIROUS,] *lit.* 'sending forth for ourselves our love of you, we are well-pleased to impart to you, not only the good-news of God, but also our own souls (*or* lives), because ye became beloved to us.'

9. LABOUR,] *lit.* 'toil (*or* weariness, fatigue) and travail, for night and day working, in order not to be a burden upon any of you, we proclaimed to you.'

10. HOLILY,] *lit.* 'kindly, and righteously, and blamelessly, we became to you who are believing.'

11. AS,] *lit.* 'even as ye have known, how we are calling upon you, and comforting, and testifying, to each one of you, as a father his own children.'

12. THAT,] *lit.* 'with a view to your walk-

ing worthily of the God who is calling you to his own reign and glory.'

13. THANK,] *lit.* 'leap much for joy before God unceasingly, because, having taken alongside (of yourselves) God's word of hearing from us, ye received, not a word of man, but as it is truly, a word of God, (who) also inwardly worketh for himself in (*or* among) you who are believing.'

14. FOLLOWERS,] *lit.* 'imitators..which are in Judea in..because ye also suffered the same (*or* like) things under your own fellow clansmen (*lit.* tribe-men) as even they under the Jews.'

15. KILLED,] *lit.* 'killed fully Jesus the Lord..and caused us to flee greatly, and are not pleasing to God.'

16. FORBIDDING,] *or* 'hindering..nations, that they may be saved, with a view to the filling up of their sins always, but the anger (of God) came upon them—with a view to the end.' In A.D. 48, at the passover, 30,000 are said to have been slain, and in A.D. 70 Jerusalem was destroyed.

17. BEING TAKEN,] *lit.* 'having become utter orphans from you for an hour's season, in face not in heart, did haste more abundantly to..in much over-desire.'

18. WOULD,] *lit.* 'wished to come.. both once and twice, but the Adversary struck us in.'

19. REJOICING,] *lit.* 'boasting?.. ye before ..in his presence?'

Chapter III. may be divided into three parts; v. 1—5 reasons for sending Timotheus; v. 6—10 comfort received from his good report; v. 11—13 prayers for mutual blessings.

1. WHEN,] *lit.* 'wherefore no longer forbearing,' *or* 'covering' his anxiety.'

LEFT,] *lit.* 'left behind in Athens alone.'

2. MINISTER,] *lit.* 'deacon..fellow-worker in the good-news of the Christ, with a view to confirm you.'

3. MAN,] *lit.* 'for no one to be moved *or* shaken in..have known that with a view to this we are laid,' *or* set.

4. VERILY,] *or* 'even..before (*or* publicly) that we are about to be in tribulation.. ye have known.'

5. WHEN,] *lit.* 'I no longer forbearing (*or* 'covering' his anxiety)..did tempt you, and our toil might become vain,' *or* empty.

6. BROUGHT,] *or* 'told good-news to us.'

7. AFFLICTION,] *lit.* 'tribulation and necessity, through.'

8. FOR,] *or* 'because..ye made stand in.'

9. THANKS,] *lit.* 'leaping for joy are we able to give back again to God concerning you, over all..because of you.'

10. PRAYING,] *lit.* 'very exceedingly beseeching to see..to perfect the lacking things of your faith.'

11. NOW,] *lit.* 'now our God and Father himself, and our Lord Jesus Christ, make our way thoroughly straight to you.' A direct prayer to Christ.

12. LOVE,] *lit.* 'in the love to one another, and to all, even as we also to you.'

13. TO THE END,] *or* 'with a view to confirm.. before our God and Father, in the presence of.'

Chapter IV. may be divided into three parts; v. 1—8 prayers for their progress and sanctification; v. 9—12 of the brotherly love and a becoming behaviour; v. 13—18 against sorrow for the dead in the Lord.

1. FURTHERMORE,] *lit.* 'as to the rest, therefore, we ask you brethren, and call upon (you) in the Lord Jesus, as ye received from us how it behoves you to walk about ..that ye may abound the more.'

2. KNOW,] *lit.* 'have known..through the.'

3. THE WILL,] *or* 'a wish..to hold yourselves off from the whoredom.'

4. EVERY,] *lit.* 'to know each of you to acquire *or* possess his own vessel,' 1 Cor. 7. 2.

5. LUST,] *lit.* 'a passion of over-desire.. have not known God.'

6. THAT,] *lit.* 'not to go beyond and have more in the matter than his brother..is an avenger concerning all these things..also said beforehand (*or* publicly) and thoroughly testified.'

7. HAS,] *lit.* 'did not call us upon..but in.'

8. DESPISETH,] *lit.* 'is putting away, doth not put away man (only) but God, who also gave.'

9. AS TOUCHING,] *lit.* 'but concerning the brotherly love ye have no need (for anyone) to write to you, for ye yourselves are God taught;' compare 'God-inspired,' in 2 Tim. 3. 16, and John 6. 45; James 1. 17, &c.

10. BESEECH,] *lit.* 'call upon you, brethren, to increase (the) more.'

11. STUDY,] *lit.* 'be ambitious to be quiet, and to practise your own (customs *or* trades).'

12. WALK,] *lit.* 'walk about becomingly.. of nothing, *or* of no one.'

13. I WOULD.] Many old MSS. and Versions read 'we do not wish..have fallen asleep.. may not sorrow, even as the rest.'

14. IF,] i.e. 'since *or* seeing we ..died fully and stood up again, so also those asleep through Jesus'

14. IF,] *lit.* 'in..who are left over to the presence.. go before those asleep.'

16. FOR,] *lit.* 'because..in a shout, in (the) voice of a chief-messenger, and in (the) trump of God.'

17. REMAIN,] *lit.* 'who are left over shall be snatched away in clouds to a meeting of the Lord in (the) air.. always be.'

18. WHEREFORE,] *or* 'so then comfort (*or* exhort, call upon) one another in these words,' *or* things.'

Chapter V. may be divided into five parts; v. 1—3 how the day of the Lord comes; v. 4—8 character of believers; v. 9—11 reasons for comfort; v. 12—22 various exhortations; v. 23—28 prayers and salutations.

1. OF,] *lit.* 'concerning.. need to be written to.'

2. KNOW,] *lit.* 'have known accurately.'

3. SAFETY,] *or* 'surety..unexpected to them ruin stands for itself over (them), even

as the pain to her having in the womb, and they shall not flee out.'

4. THAT,] *lit.* 'that the day may take you down.'

5. THE,] *lit.* 'for all ye are sons of light, and sons of day; we are not of night.'

6. LET,] *lit.* 'therefore, then, we may not sleep at all, as also the rest, but may we be wakeful and sober,' (*lit.* not drinking).

7. SLEEP,] *lit.* 'are sleeping, sleep by night, and those becoming (*or* made) drunk are drunk by night.'

8. WHO ARE,] *lit.* 'being of the day, may we be sober (*lit.* not drunk), putting on a breastplate of..and a helmet (*lit.* thing round the head), a hope of salvation.'

9. HATH APPOINTED,] *lit.* 'did not set us to anger, but to a thorough acquisition of salvation through our.'

10. DIED,] *lit.* 'died fully in our behalf.. we may wake, whether we may sleep thoroughly, we may live.'

11. COMFORT,] *or* 'exhort ye one another, and build ye up, one the other.'

12. BESEECH,] *lit.* 'ask.. those toiling.. standing before you in..and putting you in mind.'

13. ESTEEM,] *or* 'account, reckon them very abundantly in love because of their work..among (*or* in) yourselves.'

14. EXHORT,] *lit.* 'call upon you..be putting the disorderly in mind, be comforting the little-souled, be holding up over-against the not-strong.'

15. RENDER,] *lit.* 'give away badness in the place of badness to any one, but always pursue.. in reference to one another and to all.'

16. REJOICE,] *lit.* 'be always leaping for joy.'

17. PRAY,] *lit.* 'be pouring forth before (God) unceasingly.'

18. GIVE THANKS,] *lit.* 'be leaping much for joy..a wish of God in Christ Jesus in reference to you.'

19. QUENCH,] *lit.* 'be not quenching.'

20. DESPISE,] *lit.* 'be not thinking nothing of prophecy,' *or* prophesying.

21. PROVE,] *lit.* 'be testing every thing, be holding thoroughly the good,' *or* right.

22. ABSTAIN,] *lit.* 'be holding off from every appearance of evil,'—in others.

23. VERY GOD,] *lit.* 'and the God of the peace himself hallow you to the whole end, and may your whole-lot—the spirit, and the soul, and the body—be kept blamelessly in the presence of our Lord Jesus Christ.'

24. FAITHFUL,] i.e. 'stedfast is he who is calling.'

25. PRAY,] *lit.* 'be pouring forth before (God) concerning us.'

26. GREET,] *lit.* 'draw ye near all the brethren in hallowed friendship,'

27. CHARGE,] *lit.* 'I adjure..the Letter be read,' *or* known fully.

28. BE,] *or* 'is with you. Amen.'

PAUL'S LETTER TO THE THESSALONIANS
(THE SECOND)

THIS SECOND LETTER was written by Paul, Timotheus, and Silvanus, apparently a few months after the first, at Corinth, A.D. 53, in the 12th year of Claudius. It is quoted or referred to by Polycarp (A.D. 108), Justin Martyr (A.D. 140), Irenaeus (A.D. 178), Clement of Alexandria (A.D. 192), Tertullian (A.D. 192), &c.

It may be divided into three parts, corresponding to its three chapters.

I. Salutation (v. 1, 2); thanksgiving with encouragements (v. 3—10); prayers for progress (v. 11, 12).

II. Correction as to Christ's coming (v. 1—4); description of the apostacy (v. 5—12); thanks, exhortations and prayers (v. 13—17).

III. Request, and expression of confidence (v. 1—5); charge and example (v. 6—12); exhortation, prayer, and salutation (v. 13—18).

It contains references or parallels to Ex. 7. 11, 12; 8. 18; 9. 11; Mat. 16. 14; Acts 14. 22; 2 Pet. 1. 20, 21.

1. PAUL,] i.e. the 'little' one.

SILVANUS,] i.e. the 'forester.'

TIMOTHEUS,] i.e. one 'honouring God.'

CHURCH,] *lit.* 'assembly of Thessalonians.'

2. THE LORD,] *or* 'and (the Father of the) Lord Jesus Christ.'

3. ARE BOUND,] *lit.* 'we owe it (*or* ought) to leap much for joy before God, always concerning you,..is worthy (*lit.* 'leading on')..increaseth exceedingly, and the love of each one of you all in reference to one another.'

4. GLORY,] *lit.* 'boast..over your endurance in all your pursuits and tribulation which ye hold up under.'

5. MANIFEST,] *lit.* 'an inward signal (*or* shewing) of the..with a view to your being reckoned thoroughly worthy of the reign of God, in behalf of which.'

6. SEEING,] *or* 'since *or* if indeed..give back in return.'

7. REST,] *or* 'release (relaxation, i.e. a sending away)..in the uncovering of the Lord Jesus from heaven, with messengers of his power, in fire and flame, giving full justice to those not knowing God, and to those not hearkening submissively to.'

9. BE PUNISHED,] *lit.* 'shall honour (*or* pay) justice—ruin age-during—from the face..his strength.'

10. SHALL,] *lit.* 'may come to be inwardly glorified in (*or* among) his sanctified ones, and to be wondered at in (*or* among) all

those who are believing,' *or* who did believe.

11. WHEREFORE,] *lit.* 'with a view to which also we pour forth before (God) always concerning you,..may reckon.. the calling, and may fill out every good-thought of goodness, and a work of faith in power.'

12. AND THE,] *or* 'our God and Lord—Jesus Christ.' One person only is referred to.

Chapter II. may be divided into three parts; v. 1—4 correction as to Christ's coming; v. 5—12 description of the apostacy; v. 13—17 thanks, exhortations, and prayers.

1. BESEECH,] *lit.* 'ask..in behalf of the presence of the Lord Jesus Christ (which is always with his people), and our openly gathering together (as a church or synagogue-meeting) upon him,'—the reference is not to a *future* gathering, but to ordinary Lord's day meetings. Heb. 10. 25.

2. THAT,] *lit.* 'with a view to your not being hastily shaken (*or* tossed) from the mind (ye had), nor be tumultuous, neither through spirit (as if of prophecy), nor through word (of mouth), nor through letter, as through us, as that the day of (the vengence of) the Christ has set in (upon the land of Judah).' It took place about seventeen years later, in A.D. 70, but Claudius having just expelled the Jews from Rome, some of the Thessalonians thought that *the* day of Christ had actually arrived,and were neglecting their usual Christian meetings.

3. MAN,] *lit.* 'may no one lead you at all astray, in any way, because, if the apostacy (*or* 'falling away' of many from their first love, as foretold by Christ) may not come first, and the man of the sin, (i.e. the sinful man, who is) the son of the utter-loss, (i.e. the utterly-lost son, as in John 17. 12) who is laying himself over-against, and is lifting himself up above, all called a god or an object of reverence, so as himself in reference to the habitation of God as a god to sit down, showing himself off that he is a god.' The reference here probably is to *Nero*, perhaps the greatest monster of iniquity who ever lived; he claimed divine worship, and was saluted as 'the Eternal One!' His sitting in judgment (as God's vicegerent) on the Christians, whom he accused of setting Rome on fire, is doubtless what is meant by the reference to the 'habitation' of God (i.e. the Christian church, as in 1 Cor. 3. 16, 17; 2 Cor. 6. 16; 1 Tim. 3. 15; Rev. 3. 12). By the false translation '*in* the temple,' the common opinion has been that 'the man of sin' must be a Christian apostate!

5. WHEN I WAS,] *lit.* 'being yet with you, I said to you these things.'

6. KNOW,] *lit.* 'ye have known what is holding down (*or* fast) with a view to his (*or* its) being uncovered in his (*or* its) own season.'

7. MYSTERY,] *or* 'secret principle of the lawlessness already worketh in (*or* inwardly), only till he who (*or* that which) is holding down (*or* fast), may come out of the midst,'—i.e. the love of the truth, the fear of God, &c., may pass away.

8. THAT,] *lit.* 'the lawless one be uncovered, whom the Lord shall take away with the spirit of his mouth, and make thoroughly useless with the full-appearance of his presence—whose presence is against the in working of the Adversary in every (kind of) power and signs, and wonders—lying ones.'

10. AND WITH,] *lit.* 'and in every (kind of) deceitfulness of the unrighteousness, in (*or* among) those loosing themselves away, because they received not for themselves the love of the truth, with a view to their being saved.'

11. SEND,] i.e. in the course of his providence, 'an in-working of delusion, in reference to their believing the lying thing.'

12. DAMNED,] *lit.* 'may be judged..but thought well (of themselves) in the unrighteousness.'

13. ARE BOUND,] *lit.* 'owe it as a debt to ..concerning you..by the Lord, that God took you up from the beginning with a view to salvation in sanctification of spirit and belief of truth.'

14. WHEREUNTO,] *lit.* 'with a view to which he called you through our (proclamation of the) good-news, with a view to an acquisition of.'

16. WHICH,] *lit.* 'who loved us and gave age-during comfort (*or* exhortation) and a good hope in grace.'

Chapter III. may be divided into three parts; v. 1—5 a request, and an expression of confidence; v. 6—12 a charge and an example; v. 13—18 an exhortation, prayer, and salutation.

1. FINALLY,] *lit.* 'as to the thing left behind, pour ye forth before (God), brethren, concerning us.. may run and.. toward you.'

2. DELIVERED,] *lit.* 'freed *or* rescued from the placeless and evil men, for the faith is not of all.'

3. FAITHFUL,] *or* 'stedfast..confirm and guard you from the evil.'

4. CONFIDENCE,] for ourselves..about you ..we tell forth to you.'

5. DIRECT,] *lit.* 'make thoroughly straight ..with a view to *or* in reference to the.. endurance of the Christ.'

7. KNOW,] *lit.* 'have known how it behoveth (all) to imitate us, because (*or* that) we did not act disorderly.'

8. MAN'S,] *lit.* 'any one's bread as a gift but working in toil and travail..for our not being a burden upon any one of you.'

9. POWER,] *lit.* 'authority, but that we may give ourselves a type to you with a view to your imitating us.'

11. THAT,] *lit.* 'of certain walking about working nothing, but working about (everything).'

13. WEARY,] *lit.* 'beaten in doing well.'

14. MAN,] *lit.* 'any one hearken not submissively to..through the Letter, note (*lit.* sign) that one, and mix not up yourselves with him, that he may be turned in.'

17. SALUTATION,] *or* 'drawing near..a sign in every letter: thus I write.'

18. BE,] *or* 'is with you all. Amen.'

PAUL'S LETTER TO TIMOTHY
(THE FIRST)

TIMOTHEUS was the son of a Gentile father, and a Jewish mother, named Eunice, who, with her mother Lois, were believers in Christ, and residing apparently in Lystra, in Lycaonia. Paul having taught and chosen him for his fellow-evangelist, caused him to be circumcised, to propitiate the Jews. He afterwards sent him to Corinth, Philippi, Thessalonica, and left him at Ephesus to check error, and establish order. Paul is also supposed to have written the First Letter to him from Laodicea or Athens, about A.D. 64. It is quoted or referred to by Clement of Rome (A.D. 96), Polycarp (A.D. 108), Ignatius (A.D. 108), Hegisippus (A.D. 173), Athenagoras (A.D. 178), Justin Martyr (A.D. 140), Theophilus of Antioch (A.D. 181), Caius (A.D. 212), Irenaeus (A.D. 178), Clement of Alexandria (A.D. 194), Tertullian (A.D. 200), Eusebius (A.D. 320), &c.

The Gnostics in ancient times rejected both of the Letters to Timothy and also that to Titus; in modern days doubts have been held by Baur, De Wette, Eichhorn, Schleiermacher, &c.

The opinions chiefly combated in this Letter are those of the Judaizing Gnostics, as tending to godlessness, (see 1. 7, 8, 19; 4. 2; 6. 5, &c.) lawlessness, pomp, female ambition, word-striving, coveteousness, both among the flock and its leaders.

Chapter I. may be divided into five parts; v. 1, 2 address and salutation; v. 3, 4 design in leaving Timothy in Ephesus; v. 5—11 end of the charge and object of law; v. 12—17 thanksgiving for his own conversion, and object of Christ's coming; v. 18—20 charge to Timothy.

1. PAUL,] i.e. the 'little' one.

APOSTLE,] *lit.* one 'sent forth.'

JESUS CHRIST,] i.e. an 'anointed saviour.'

BY,] *lit.* 'according to an over-arrangement.'

2. TIMOTHY,] *Gr.* Timotheus, i.e. one 'honouring God.'

OWN,] *lit.* 'genuine (*or* born) child in faith.'

GRACE,] *lit.* what 'causes leaping for joy.'

MERCY,] *or* 'kindness.'

PEACE,] *lit.* what 'brings into unity.'

3. BESOUGHT,] *or* 'exhorted thee to remain on in Ephesus, I passing on to..tell along to certain not to teach any other thing.'

4. GIVE HEED,] *lit.* 'to hold toward fables (*Gr.* myths)..which hold along questions (*or* searchings) rather than the upbuilding (*or* stewardship, *lit.* house-distribution) of God.'

5. NOW,] *or* 'but..is love..conscience (*lit.* knowing-together),..unhypocritical.'

6. FROM,] *or* 'out of which certain, having stepped greatly, turned round thoroughly into vain discourse, wishing to be law-teachers, not keeping in mind either the things they say, nor concerning what they asseverate fully.'

7. DESIRING,] *lit.* 'wishing to be law-teachers, not minding either the things they say, nor concerning what they assert strongly.'

8. KNOW,] *lit.* 'we have known..if any one.'

9. KNOWING,] *lit.* 'this having known, that law is not laid down for a righteous man, but for lawless and disorderly ones, for irreverent and sinful ones, for unkind and impious, for strikers of fathers, and strikers of mothers, for manslayers.'

10. WHOREMONGERS,] *or* 'fornicators, for liers with males, for man-enslavers, for liars, for perjured ones, and if there is any other thing that lies over-against the sound (*or* healthy) teaching.'

11. GLORIOUS,] *lit.* 'good-news of the glory of the happy God, with which I was entrusted.'

12. THANK,] *or* 'I have cause of leaping before him who gave me power—Jesus Christ our Lord—that he reckoned me stedfast, having set me for himself with a view to deaconship.'

13. WHO,] *lit.* 'being formerly (*or* at first) an injurious-speaker, and causing to flee, and insulting, but I was kindly dealt with.'

14. WAS,] *or* 'exceedingly abounded.'

15. THIS IS,] *lit.* 'stedfast is the word, and worthy of all full-reception, that *or* because Jesus..am foremost.'

16. OBTAINED MERCY,] *lit.* 'was kindly dealt with, that in me foremost..shew inwardly for himself all the long-suffering, for an under-type of those about to believe on him with a view to life age-during.'

17. ETERNAL,] *lit.* 'king of the ages, uncorruptible, unseen, the only (wise) God, (is) honour and glory to the ages of the ages! Amen.'

18. CHARGE,] *or* 'message I put along to thee, child Timotheus! according to the leading-on prophecies (*or* public rumours) concerning thee.' The good character he bore from childhood probably induced Paul to fit him more thoroughly to be his own companion.

BY,] *lit.* 'among them (in Ephesus) mayest war the good warfare.'

19. SOME,] *or* 'certain having pushed away for themselves, concerning the faith made shipwreck.'

20. IS,] *lit.* 'are Hymenaeus (i.e. nuptial) and Alexander, whom I gave over to the Adversary,' i.e. as in 1 Cor. 5. 5, *declaring* them no long subjects of Christ, for their 'injurious' language and acts.

Chapter II. may be divided into two

parts; v. 1—8 exhortations to prayer for all men, with reasons; v. 9—15 exhortations to women.

1. EXHORT,] *lit.* 'call along, therefore, first of all, for supplications..to be made in behalf of all men.'

2. FOR,] *lit.* 'in behalf of kings, and of all who are in eminence, that we may thoroughly-lead (*or* spend) a tranquil and quiet life in all reverence and veneration.'

3. GOOD,] *or* 'right *or* honest and very acceptable in the face of God our Saviour.'

4. WILL,] *lit.* 'who wishes (i.e. desires, take counsel for) all men to be saved, and to come to a full-knowledge (*or* acknowledgement) of the truth.'

5. FOR,] *lit.* 'for God (is) one, one also (is the) middle-man between God and men—(the) man Christ Jesus.'

6. RANSOM,] *lit.* 'a corresponding (*or* equivalent) ransom in behalf of all,—the testimony (of which God gives) in its proper seasons,' i.e. when men accept the offer of the gospel.

7. WHEREUNTO,] *lit.* 'with a view to which I was set a herald (*lit.* crier) and an apostle—truth I say in Christ, I lie not—a teacher of nations in faith and truth.'

8. WILL,] *lit.* 'I counsel therefore the men to pour forth before (God) in every place, lifting up kind hands, apart from anger and reasoning,' *or* disputing.

9. THAT,] *lit.* 'the women to adorn themselves in a long seemly robe, with want of shew (*lit.* unseenness) and soundness of mind; not in plaits (of hair), or in gold, or in pearls, or in a high-priced garment.'

10. BECOMETH,] *or* 'is proper to women professing (*or* promising) for themselves a reverence of God—through good works.'

11. LET,] *lit.* 'a woman (*or* wife)—in quietness let her learn, in all under-arrangement.'

12. SUFFER,] *lit.* 'I turn (it) not over to a woman (*or* wife) to teach, neither to act for herself apart from a man (*or* husband), but to be in quietness.'

13. DECEIVED,] *or* 'led astray, but the wife having been deceived came into transgression.'

14. IN,] *lit.* 'through (*or* because of) the child-bearing,'—as it was foretold that the 'seed' of the woman should bruise the serpent's head, if 'they remain..love.. with soundness of mind.'

Chapter III. may be divided into three parts; v. 1—7 character of an overseer; v. 8—13 of deacons and deaconesses; v. 14—16 reasons for thus writing.

1. THIS,] *lit.* 'stedfast is the word!' Perhaps this clause should close the preceding chapter; compare 1. 15; 4. 9.

MAN,] *lit.* 'if any one stretches out for himself the arms for an oversight, he desires a right work.'

2. A,] *lit.* 'the overseer, therefore, it behoves to be unlaid-hold-upon, husband of one woman (only), not drinking, sober-minded, seemly (in behaviour), a friend of strangers, apt to teach,'—as in 2 Tim. 2. 24; Tit. 1. 9. This last qualification is strangely neglected by many churches.

3. GIVEN TO WINE,] *or* 'not (going) amiss in wine, not a smiter, not (seeking) shameful gain, very yielding, not a fighter, not loving silver.'

4. ONE,] *lit.* 'standing for himself before his own household well, having children in under-arrangement, with all veneration.'

5. A MAN,] *lit.* 'but if any one has not known (how) to stand before his own household, how shall he be careful about an assembly of God?'

6. NOVICE,] *lit.* one 'newly planted, lest having been puffed up, he may fall inwardly into a condemnation of the devil.'

7. MOREOVER,] *lit.* 'now *or* but it behoves him also to have a good testimony from those without, that he may not fall.'

8. MUST,] *lit.* 'Deacons likewise (it behoves to be) venerable, not double-tongued (*lit.* worded), not holding to much wine, not (seeking) shameful gain.'

9. MYSTERY,] *lit.* 'secret.'

10. PROVED,] *or* 'tested, tried, approved, afterwards let them deaconize (i.e. act as deacons), being un-called-in (to court).'

11. EVEN SO,] *lit.* 'women (i.e. deaconesses it behoves to be) venerable, not devils, (i.e. 'thrusters through,') not drinking, stedfast.'

12. LET,] *lit.* 'deacons! let them be husband of one wife (only), standing before their children and own households well.'

13. HAVE,] *lit.* 'who deaconized well acquire a good step (*or* good progress) to themselves, and much full-speech, in faith which is in Christ Jesus.'

14. SHORTLY,] *or* 'more speedily.'

15. TARRY LONG,] *or* 'delay *or* be slow.. how it behoveth (thee) to turn round up and down for thyself among (the) household of God, which is an assembly of (the) living God, a pillar and prop (*or* basement) of the truth.'

16. WITHOUT CONTROVERSY,] *lit.* 'confessedly *or* professedly great is the secret of the reverence:—God (*or* He who, i.e. the living God) was manifested in flesh, was declared just in spirit, appeared to messengers, was proclaimed among nations, was trusted to in (the) world, was taken up in glory!'

Chapter IV. may be divided into two parts; v. 1—5 coming corruptions; v. 6—16 exhortations to Timothy.

1. NOW,] *lit.* 'but the Spirit says verbally (*lit.* speakingly), that in (the) latter seasons certain shall stand off from the faith, holding towards erring spirits, and teachings of (i.e. about) demons.'

2. LIES,] *or* 'falsehood, having been seared (*or* seared themselves) in their own conscience.'

3. FORBIDDING,] *or* 'hindering..to hold off from meats which God created (*or* formed) for participation with much leaping for joy by those stedfast and acknowledging (*or* having full-knowledge of) the truth.'

4. FOR,] *or* 'because created thing..is cast away, being received.'

5. SANCTIFIED,] *or* 'hallowed through a word of God and intercession.'

6. IF THOU PUT,] *lit.* 'putting these things submissively to the brethren, thou shalt be a deacon of Jesus Christ, being nourished inwardly with the words of the faith, and of the right teaching, which thou hast gone alongside of.'

7. REFUSING,] *lit.* 'be asking thyself off from the profane and old wives' myths..towards reverence.'

8. BODILY,] *lit.* 'the bodily exercise is profitable for a little (thing *or* time), but the reverence is.. everything.. is about to be.'

9. THIS,] *lit.* 'stedfast is the word, and worthy of all full-reception.'

10. THEREFORE,] *lit.* 'for with a view to this we both toil and are reproached, because (*or* that) we hope on (the) living God, who is Saviour of all men, especially of believing (*or* stedfast) ones.' He is willing to save all, He is wishing to save all, He came to save all, He saves all from many miseries, in body and spirit, but those who remain 'stedfast' to Him in Christ he saves in a higher degree than others, and also finally.

11. COMMAND,] *lit.* 'be telling fully and teaching.'

12. MAN,] *lit.* 'no one think down upon thy youth, but become thou a type of the believing ones, in word, in behaviour (*lit.* turning round again), in love.' Many MSS. Versions, and Fathers, omit 'in spirit.'

13. GIVE ATTENTION,] *lit.* 'hold towards the reading, to the calling-upon, to the teaching.'

14. NEGLECT,] *lit.* 'be not careless of the grace (free-gift) in thee, which was given to thee, through prophecy (*or* public report), with a laying on of the hands of the eldership,' the usual mode of commending any one to God for help in the discharge of any duty committed to him; see 5. 22; Acts 6. 6; 8. 17, 18, 19; 13. 3; 19. 6; Heb. 6. 2, &c.

15. MEDITATE,] *lit.* 'be careful in these things; be in them; that thy advancement (*lit.* striking-forward) may be manifest in all things.'

16. TAKE HEED,] *lit.* 'hold on upon thyself, and upon the teaching, remain on in them; for doing this, thou shalt both save (i.e. be the instrument of saving) thyself and those hearing thee.'

Chapter V. may be divided into five parts; v. 1, 2 how to treat aged men and women; v. 3—16 widows; v. 17—21 elders; v. 22, 23 himself; v. 24, 25 sins and works all manifest.

1. REBUKE,] *lit.* 'strike not upon an aged man, but be calling upon him as a father; younger ones, as brethren.'

2. THE ELDER,] *lit.* 'elderesses *or* aged (women), as mothers; younger ones, as sisters, in all purity.'

3. WIDOWS,] *lit.* 'bereaved (women)! honour (i.e. support) those really widows;' see Mat. 15. 4, 6, &c.

4. WIDOW,] *or* 'bereaved one has children or offspring, let them learn first to be reverent in their own house, and to give back a recompence to the progenitors.'

5. WIDOW,] *lit.* 'truly is bereaved, and left alone, has hoped on God, and remains on in the supplications and the pourings forth before (God).'

6. LIVETH,] *or* 'is covered with ornaments of skin, living, has died.'

7. GIVE IN CHARGE,] *lit.* 'tell along-side.. be un-laid-hold-on.'

8. ANY,] *lit.* 'any one think not beforehand of his own, and especially of those of the household, he has denied *or* disowned for himself the faith, and is worse than an unbeliever.'

9. WIDOW,] *or* 'bereaved one be laid down (in the list of *female* elders and deacons) less than 60 years of age.'

10. WELL,] *lit.* 'testified of in good works, if she nourished children, if she received strangers, if she washed saints' feet, if she gave sufficiently to troubled ones, if she followed after.'

11. THE,] *lit.* 'but younger bereaved ones be asking off from, for when they may at all abandon the reins of the Christ, they wish to marry.'

12. DAMNATION,] *lit.* 'a judgment' of condemnation, 'because they did put away the first faith.'

13. WITHAL,] *or* 'at the same time..going about the houses..babblers also and workers about every thing, speaking the things they ought not.'

14. I WILL,] *lit.* 'I counsel, therefore, younger (female officials) to marry, to bear children, to-act-as-despot-in-the-house, to give nothing (as) a cause of excitement to the one lying over-against for the sake of reviling.'

15. SOME,] *or* 'certain were turned round (*or* turned themselves round) entirely behind *or* after the Adversary;' *or* 'were turned round entirely behind of (i.e. by) the Adversary.'

16. ANY MAN,] *lit.* 'any one, a male or female believer, has bereaved ones, let him give sufficiently to them, and let not the assembly be burdened, that it may give sufficiently to those really widows.'

17. ELDERS,] *lit.* 'the well-standing-forward elders of double (i.e. much) honour let them be reckoned worthy, especially those toiling-laboriously in word and teaching.' The extra honour or reward does not arise from the *nature* of the several spiritual duties, but from the *character* of the exertions put forth—a most just and suitable basis for discrimination.

18. SCRIPTURE,] *or* 'writing says (in De. 25. 4; 1 Cor. 9. 9), An ox treading (the corn) thou shalt not muzzle, and, The worker is worthy of his hire;' apparently a quotation from Luke 10. 7, (comp. Mat. 10. 10).

19. ELDER.] *Gr.* 'presbyter,' as in v. 17; but some translate 'elderly person.'

RECEIVE,] *lit.* 'be not receiving..except upon (the testimony of) two or three witnesses.'

20. THEM,] *lit.* 'those sinning (*or* missing

the mark) be convicting before all, that those left over may have fear.'

21. CHARGE,] *lit.* '**I testify thoroughly before the God and Lord of Jesus Christ, and of the choice** (*or* select, excellent) messengers (i.e. apostles and first preachers), that thou mayest guard these things, without pre-judging, doing nothing according to a prior-leaning.'

22. LAY,] *lit.* 'be putting hands hastily upon no one, neither be partaker (*or* have fellowship) with others in sins, be keeping thyself pure.'

23. DRINK,] *lit.* 'be no longer drinking water, but be using a little wine, because of thy stomach, and thy frequent want of strength.'

24. SOME,] *lit.* 'certain..openly manifest leading openly to a judgment, but certain also.'

25. BEFOREHAND,] *or* 'openly, and those having (it) otherwise are not able to be hid.'

Chapter VI. may be divided into six parts; v. 1, 2 advice to bondsmen; v. 3—10 warning against pride and covetousness; v. 11—13 exhortations to Timotheus; v. 14—16 with a solemn charge; v. 17—19 duty of the rich; v. 20, 21 concluding charge.

1. SERVANTS,] *lit.* 'bondsmen..a yoke be reckoning their own despots worthy of every honour..and the teaching (of his servants) may not be injuriously spoken of.'

2. THEY,] *lit.* 'but those having believing (*lit* stedfast, faithful) despots, let them not think down upon (them)..rather let them be in bondage, faithful (*or* stedfast, believing) and beloved, who are receivers on the other side, of the good-work. These things be teaching, and calling upon.'

3. MAN,] *lit.* 'any one teaches another thing, and comes not to wholesome (*or* healthy) words, to those of..teaching according to reverence.'

4. PROUD,] *lit.* 'has been puffed up, knowing about nothing, but unsound about questions and word-strivings, out of which comes injurious speakings, under-thoughts.'

5. PERVERSE DISPUTINGS,] *or* 'wastings (of time) of men thoroughly corrupt in mind, and having deprived themselves of the truth, supposing the reverence to be (a means of) gain; be standing off for thyself from such.'

6. GODLINESS,] *lit.* 'the reverence with self-sufficiency is a great (means of) gain.'

7. CERTAIN,] *lit.* 'manifest that we are not able to carry anything out.'

8. AND,] *or* 'but having full-nourishment and covering, with these we shall suffice ourselves (*or* be sufficed).'

9. WILL,] *lit.* 'those counselling to be wealthy..many thoughtless and trustful over-desires, which sink the men into full-ruin and full-loss.'

10 THE,] *lit.* 'is a root of all the evils, which certain stretching out the arms for themselves they strayed away from the faith ..many pains.'

11. FOLLOW AFTER,] *or* 'pursue..reverence ..endurance, meek-spiritedness.'

12. FIGHT,] *lit.* 'be agonizing the good agony of the faith, be taking hold upon the age-during life, with a view to which also thou wast called, and hast confessed (*lit.* spoken the same thing) the good confession in the presence of many witnesses.'

13. CHARGE,] *lit.* 'tell along to thee in the presence of God, who is making (*or* keeping) the all things alive, and of Christ Jesus,.. the good confession.'

14. THAT,] *or* 'for thy keeping the precept spotless, un-laid-hold-on, till the full-manifestation of.'

15. HIS TIMES,] *lit.* 'its proper seasons.. happy and only Potentate (*or* Power), the king of the kings.'

16. HAS,] *lit.* 'is having deathlessness, dwelling in light unapproached, whom no one of men saw, nor is able to see; to whom (is) honour, and strength age-during. Amen!'

17. CHARGE,] *lit.* 'tell along to the rich (*or* wealthy) in the present age, not to be high-minded, neither to hope on (the) manifestlessness of riches (*or* wealth)..who holds along to us..with a view to enjoyment.'

18. THAT,] *lit.* 'to do (*or* work) good (*or* well) to be rich (*or* wealthy)..to be pleasant sharers (of what they have), partakers (with others).'

19. LAYING,] *or* 'treasuring away to them a good (*or* right) foundation, with a view to that which is about to be, that they may lay hold upon the age-during life.'

20. TIMOTHY,] *or* 'Timotheus! guard the thing placed along-side (of thee), turning round from the profane, vain sounds, and setting over-against of the falsely-named knowledge.'

21. SOME,] *lit.* 'certain professing for themselves stepped aside. The grace (is) with thee. Amen.'

PAUL'S LETTER TO TIMOTHY

(THE SECOND)

THIS second Epistle to Timotheus is generally supposed to have been written from Rome about A.D. 66 or 67, some months before Paul's martyrdom under Nero. Timotheus was residing in Asia Minor, probably at Troas or Ephesus, and being perhaps constitutionally timid, Paul exhorts him to faithfulness, sound doctrine, and patience amid trials. The Second Letter is quoted as canonical by the same ancient authors as quote the First; it contains apparent references to Exod. 7. 11, 12; 8. 18: 9. 11; Mat. 16. 24; Acts 14. 22; 2 Pet. 1. 20, 21; and may be divided into three parts, viz :—

I. The Inscription and Salutation, i. 1—5.

II. An Exhortation to Timothy, ch. i. 6—iv. 8.

III. The Conclusion, and Salutations, ch. iv. 9—22.

Chapter I. may be divided into four parts; v. 1, 2 Paul's address and salutation; v. 3—5 his joy before God over Timotheus; v. 6—12 his exhortation to activity, boldness, endurance; v. 13—18 to sound words and remembrance of Onesiphorus.

1. BY,] *lit.* 'through the will (*or* wish).

2. TIMOTHY,] *Gr.* Timotheus, i.e. 'honouring God.'

DEARLY.] Omit this word as unnecessary.

SON,] *lit.* 'child.'

GRACE,] *lit.* what 'causes leaping for joy.'

MERCY,] *lit.* 'kindness.'

PEACE,] *lit.* what 'brings into unity.'

3. THANK,] *lit.* 'I have leaping for joy before God, to (*or* before) whom I go very tremblingly from (the) progenitors in a pure conscience, how unceasingly I have the remembrance concerning thee in my supplications.'

5. WHEN I CALL,] *lit.* 'receiving *or* taking a secret remembrance of the unhypocritical faith in thee, which inwardly dwelt first in the (grand) mamma Lois, and in thy mother Eunice,' i.e. easy victory.

6. WHEREEORE,] *lit.* 'because of which I remind thee to revive *or* rekindle the gracious-gift of God..through the putting on of my hands.' Comp. 1 Tim. 4. 14, for a similar but (most probably) different act, also 5. 22; Acts 6. 6; 8. 17; 13. 2; 19. 6, &c.

7. HATH,] *lit.* 'did not give to us a spirit.'

8. BE NOT,] *lit.* 'thou mayest not therefore be ashamed about..but suffer evil with the good-news.'

9. HAS,] *lit.* 'did save us and called (us) with a hallowed calling..to a proper setting forth and grace..from times of (the) ages.'

10. IS,] *lit.* 'was now manifested through the full-manifestation of..who made the death thoroughly idle, but enlightened life and uncorruptedness through the good-news.'

11. WHEREUNTO,] *lit.* 'with a view to which I was set a herald (*or* crier), and an apostle, and a teacher of nations.'

12. FOR,] *lit.* 'because of which I..but I am not ashamed about (them), for I have known in whom I have trusted, and I trust that he is able to guard my deposit (*lit.* thing 'laid alongside' of him), in reference to *or* with a view to that day.'

13. HOLD FAST,] *or* 'have an under-type of sound words, which (words) thou didst hear from (*or* alongside of) me.'

14. THAT,] *lit.* 'guard the good deposit through (the) holy spirit that is inwardly dwelling in us.'

15. KNOWEST,] *lit.* 'hast known that all those in (Proconsular) Asia were turned round away from me.'

PHYGELLUS,] i.e. a 'fugitive.'

HERMOGENES,] i.e. 'son of Hermes.'

16. MERCY,] *lit.* 'kindness.'

ONESIPHORUS,] i.e. 'bearing profit.'

FOR,] *lit.* 'because he many times.'

17. WHEN HE WAS,] *lit.* 'being in..me more speedily.'

18. GRANT,] *lit.* 'give to him to find kindness from..he acted as deacon in Ephesus, thou knowest better,'—having probably been an eye-witness.

Chapter II. may be divided into four parts; v. 1—7 exhortations to be strong, disentangled, considerate; v. 8—13 to remember Christ, Paul's endurance, and union with Christ; v. 14—19 to avoid word-striving, profane talking, and error; v. 20—26 become vessels of honour, avoid lusts and foolish questions, and be meek to opposers.

1. SON,] *lit.* 'child, be strong,' *or* strengthened.

2. HAST,] *lit.* 'didst hear from me through many witnesses, these be putting alongside for thyself to.'

3. ENDURE,] *lit.* 'suffer evil as a right warrior of Jesus Christ.'

4. MAN,] *lit.* 'no one warring is entangled in (*or* with) the businesses of the life, that he may be pleasing to him who collected the warriors.'

5. MAN,] *lit.* 'any one may strive (in the games)..strive (in the games) lawfully.'

6. HUSBANDMAN,] *lit.* 'the toiling earth-worker it behoveth first to partake of the fruits.'

7. CONSIDER,] *lit.* 'be considering what things I say; therefore may the Lord give to thee.'

8. REMEMBER,] *lit.* 'be remembering Jesus Christ having been raised out of (the) dead, out of (the) seed of David, according to my (proclamation of the) good-news.'

9. TROUBLE,] *lit.* 'evil unto bonds—as an evil-worker..has not been bound.'

10. ENDURE,] *lit.* 'remain under because of the elect, (*or* select ones, i.e. the visible

church), that they also may obtain salvation..with glory age-during.'

11. IT IS,] *lit.* 'stedfast is the word; therefore if we died with (him).'

12. SUFFER,] *lit.* 'remain under..deny (him) for ourselves, he also will deny us for himself.'

13. BELIEVE,] *or* 'be not stedfast, he remains stedfast.'

14. PUT,] *lit.* 'be reminding them somewhat, fully testifying .not to fight with words, useful for nothing, over a thorough overturn of those hearing.'

15. STUDY,] *lit.* 'be diligent to set thyself near to God approved, a worker unashamed rightly dividing (*lit.* cutting-straight) the word of the truth,' as a father 'cuts' the loaf of bread for his children.

16. SHUN,] *lit.* 'but the profane vain-voices (*or* sound) be setting away for thyself, for they will strike forward upon more irreverence.'

17. WORD,] *or* 'doctrine as a gangrene will have pasture, of whom is Hymenaeus (i.e. nuptial) and Pheletus (i.e. beloved).'

18. HAVE ERRED,] *lit.* 'did step aside, saying the up-standing to have happened already, and turn the faith of certain round again.'

19. THE,] *lit.* 'the firm foundation of God has stood. The Lord knew (i.e. will make known), those who are his;' comp. Nu. 16. 5, 26.

THAT,] *lit.* 'who is naming..stand away from unrighteousness.'

20. EARTH,] *lit.* 'earthen-ware..to less honour,' *or* want of honour.

21. A MAN,] *lit.* 'any one may cleanse himself thoroughly from (i.e. out of) these ..and very useful to the despot, having been prepared (*or* made ready) with a view to every (kind of) good work.'

22. ALSO,] *lit.* 'but flee the youthful over-desires, but pursue..love, peace with those calling upon.'

23. FOOLISH,] *lit.* 'but the foolish (*or* rebellious) and uninstructed questions be asking thyself off from, having known that they beget wars *or* fightings.'

24. SERVANT,] *lit.* 'a bondsman of the Lord it behoves not to fight *or* war, but to be gentle toward all..holding up under evil.'

25. OPPOSE,] *lit.* 'those setting themselves thoroughly on the other side, if at any time God may give to them a new-mind with a view to a full-knowledge of truth.'

26. AND THAT,] *lit.* 'and they may become sober again out of the Devil's snare, having been taken alive (Luke 5. 10) by him (i.e. the servant of the Lord), with a view to His (i.e. God's) will.'

Chapter III. may be divided into three parts; v. 1—9 prophetic description of evil men; v. 10—13 Paul's sufferings, and progress of evil; v. 14—17 exhortation to the knowledge of the Scriptures.

1. ALSO,] *lit.* 'but know this, that in (the) last days hurtful seasons shall set themselves in,' upon the church and world.

2. MEN,] *lit.* 'the men shall be lovers of themselves, lovers of money, boasters (*or* taking hold of all), over-shining, injurious-speakers, disobedient to parents, unthankful (*lit.* not leaping for joy), unkind.'

3. TRUCE-BREAKERS,] *or* 'implacable,' *lit.* 'not pouring out' libations.

FALSE ACCUSORS,] *lit.* 'devils,' i.e. 'thrusters-through.'

INCONTINENT,] *lit.* 'not-strong' in resisting evil.

FIERCE,] *lit.* 'not mild *or* ungentle.'

DESPISERS,] *lit.* 'not lovers of good.'

4. TRAITORS,] *lit.* 'givers-up, fallers-forward, puffed up.'

5. GODLINESS,] *lit.* 'reverence, but having denied for themselves its power, and be turning away from these.'

6. THIS SORT,] *lit.* 'out of these there are those going into the houses, and taking as by a spear the silly-women, having been heaped (*or* having heaped themselves) up with sins, having been led on by manifold over-desires.'

7. THE,] *lit.* 'to a full-knowledge of truth.'

8. NOW,] *or* 'but as Jannes (i.e. afflicted, heard) and Jambres stood against Moses, so also these stand against the truth, men thoroughly corrupted in the mind, unproved (*or* disapproved of).'

9. PROCEED,] *lit.* 'strike forward upon more.'

FOLLY,] *lit.* 'mindlessness, thoughtlessness.'

MANIFEST,] *lit.* 'very manifest..also became.'

10. FULLY KNOWN,] *lit.* 'followed alongside of me in the teaching, the leading on, the setting forth, the faith, the long suffering, the love, the remaining under (trials), the pursuits, the sufferings, such as happened to me in Antioch (of Pisidia), in Iconium, in Lystra, such pursuits I bore up under, and out of all the Lord freed me.'

12. THAT WILL LIVE,] *lit.* 'all (i.e. most) who wish reverently to live in Christ Jesus, shall be pursued, *or* caused to flee.'

13. SEDUCERS,] *lit.* 'groaners,' conjurors.'

WAX,] *lit.* 'strike forward upon the worst, leading astray and being led astray.'

14. CONTINUE,] *lit.* 'but thou, be thou remaining in which things thou didst learn and wast entrusted with, having known from whom thou didst learn.'

15. THAT,] *or* 'because from a babe thou hast known the Sacred Letters (of the Old Covenant), which are able to make thee wise in reference to (*or* with a view to) salvation, through faith, which (safety) is in Christ Jesus.'

16. ALL SCRIPTURE,] *or* 'every writing (of those referred to in v. 15) is God-breathed *or* God-blown;' (i.e. comes from Him), comp. 'God-taught,' as used of all Christians in 1 Thess. 4. 9; John 6. 45. Every good gift is from above, (Jas. 1. 17), and the Scripture Writers reverently and truly ascribe all such to his Spirit, the fitness of the 70 elders (Nu. 11. 16, 17), of Saul (1 Sa. 10. 6), of Solomon (1 K. 10. 24), of Samson (Jud. 13. 25), or Jephthah (Jud. 11. 29), of Othniel (Jud. 3.

10), of Gideon (Jud. 6. 34), of Bezaleel and Aholiab and every wise-hearted man (Ex. 31. 3, 6), of the plowman (Isa. 28. 26), &c. See Blakeley's 'Theology of Invention.' Not so natural is the rendering: 'Every God-breathed writing is also profitable;' or that other: 'Every writing (of man) is the effect of God's inspiration,' as in Job 32. 8.

DOCTRINE,] *lit.* 'teaching, for conviction, for full-rightening-again, for instruction which is in righteousness.'

17. PERFECT,] *lit.* 'fitted *or* prepared, thoroughly fitted *or* prepared toward every good work.'

Chapter IV. may be divided into four parts; v. 1—4 exhortations with public reasons; v. 5—8 exhortations with personal reasons; v. 9—18 Paul's associates and trials; v. 19—22 concluding salutations and exhortations.

1. CHARGE,] *lit.* 'testify thoroughly..who is about to judge living and dead, according to his full-manifestation, and his reign.'

2. PREACH,] *lit.* 'cry the word as a herald, convict, put a weight upon (them), call alongside in all longsuffering, and teaching.'

3. THE,] *lit.* 'for there shall be a season when they will not hold up whole (*or* healthy) teaching, but, according to their own over-desires, shall they heap up to themselves teachers, tickling the ear.'

4. THEIR EARS,] *lit.* 'the hearing from.. turned fully upon the myths.'

5. WATCH,] *lit.* 'but thou, be thou sober in all things, suffer evils, do work of an announcer of good-news, fulfil thy deaconship.'

6. NOW,] *or* 'already poured forth, and the season of my full-loosing has set upon (me).'

7. FOUGHT,] *or* 'agonized the good agony (as a wrestler), I have ended the course (set before me).'

8. HENCEFORTH,] *lit.* 'as to the rest (*or* thing left behind), there is laid away for me the crown of the righteousness, shall give away to me in that day..all who have loved his full-manifestation.'

9. DO,] *lit.* 'be diligent to come to me speedily.'

10. DEMAS,] i.e. a plebeian, one of the 'people.'

HATH,] *lit.* 'did leave me thoroughly, having loved the present age, and passed on to Thessalonica, Crescens (i.e. increasing) to Galatia, Titus (i.e. honourable) to Dalmatia.'

11. LUKE,] *Gr.* 'Lukas..having taken up Mark, lead (him) on with thyself, for he is very useful to me with a view to deaconship.

12. TYCHICUS,] i.e. 'fortunate.'

HAVE I SENT,] *lit.* 'did I send away.'

13. CLOKE,] *or* 'tunic (in *Latin* paenula), that I left in Troas alongside of Carpus, coming be carrying.'

14. ALEXANDER.] Comp. Acts 19. 33; 1 Tim. 1. 20.

COPPERSMITH.] Most Jewish Rabbis had trades.

DID,] *lit.* 'shewed me for himself many evils; may the Lord give back to him.'

15. WARE,] *lit.* 'guarded..stood against.'

16. AT,] *lit.* 'in my first apology no one came for himself along with (me), but all left me fully; may it not be reckoned to them.'

17. WITH,] *or* 'alongside of me, and strengthened me inwardly, that through me the (subject of my) preaching may be borne fully on..freed out of the mouth of a lion.'

18. DELIVER,] *lit.* 'free me..will save with a view to his..is the glory to the ages of the ages! Amen.'

19. SALUTE,] *or* 'embrace,' *lit.* draw near.

PRISCA,] i.e. 'ancient.' In Rom. 16. 3, 4 Priscilla.

AQUILA,] i.e. an 'eagle.' Acts 18. 2, 3.

ONESIPHORUS,] i.e. 'bearing (*or* bringing) profit.'

20. ERASTUS,] i.e. 'beloved.' Rom. 16. 23.

ABODE,] *lit.* 'remained in Corinth.'

TROPHEMUS,] i.e. 'feeder, nourisher.'

HAVE,] *lit.* 'did I leave in Miletus not-strong.'

21. DO,] *lit.* 'be diligent..Eubulus (i.e. good counsellor).'

PUDENS,] i.e. 'bashful;' a Roman knight, who afterwards married Claudia, a British Lady, surnamed Rufina, see Martial iv. 13; xi. 54, Tacitus, Agricola, 14; Annals, 3. 32.

LINUS.] Afterwards a bishop in Rome.

22. GRACE,] *lit.* 'the grace.'

PAUL'S LETTER TO TITUS

TITUS was a Gentile by birth (Gal. 2. 1, 3), an uncircumcised convert (1. 4) and beloved fellow-worker with Paul, who took him to the Jerusalem assembly (Acts 15. 2), and to Ephesus, and then sent him to Corinth (2 Cor. 7. 6—9; 8. 6; 12. 18), and called him to Troas in Macedon (2 Cor. 2. 12, 13; 7. 6), and thereafter sent him to Corinth (2 Cor. 6. 16, 17, 23), and to Crete (1. 5), where he received this Letter about A.D. 65—6, but others date it as early as A.D. 52.

This Letter is designed to oppose Judaism, false science, and wickedness, to state the qualifications and graces of presbyters and others, young and old, male and female. It is quoted or referred to by Clement of Rome (A.D. 108), Irenaeus (A.D. 178), Theophilus (A.D. 177), Clement of Alexandria (A.D. 194), Tertullian (A.D. 200), &c. It greatly resembles 1st Timothy in many phrases, comp. 1. 4, 5 with 1 Tim. 1. 1—3; 1. 14 with 1 Tim. 1. 4; 2. 7, 15 with 1 Tim. 4. 12; 1. 6—8 with 1 Tim. 3. 2—4.

Chapter I. may be divided into three parts; v. 1—4 address and salutation; v. 5—9 qualifications of presbyters; v. 10—16 character of Jewish teachers.

1. PAUL,] i.e. the 'little one.'

SERVANT,] *lit.* 'bondsman of God, but an apostle (i.e. one 'sent forth,') of Jesus Christ (i.e. the 'anointed saviour,') according to the faith of the elect (*or* select, excellent ones) of God, and the full-knowledge of truth which is according to reverence'

2. IN,] *lit.* 'on hope of life age-during, which the un-lying God promised for himself before (*or* from the) times of ages.'

3. HATH,] *lit.* 'did in (its) proper seasons his word in (the) preaching, which I was entrusted with, according to an over-arrangement of.'

4. TITUS,] i.e. 'honourable.'

OWN,] *lit.* 'genuine *or* born child according to the common faith.'

GRACE,] *lit.* what 'causes leaping for joy.'

MERCY,] *lit.* 'kindness.'

PEACE,] *lit.* what 'brings into unity.'

5. LEFT,] *lit.* 'left I thee down in Crete (i.e. Candia), that thou mightest make the things left over thoroughly right, and mightest set-down presbyters in every city, as I myself thoroughly arranged for thee.'

6. BE,] *lit.* 'if any one is un-called in (to court), husband of one wife, not in (i.e. under) an accusation of extravagance (*lit* un-saving-ness), or unruly,' *lit.* not arranged under.

7. A BISHOP,] *lit.* 'for it behoves the overseer (*Gr.* episcopos, i.e. presbyter of v. 5) to be un-called-in (to court), as God's house distributor, not self-pleased *or* pleasing, not soon angry, not given to wine, not a striker, not given to shameful gain; but a friend of strangers, a friend of good (men *or* things) with a sound-mind, just, kind, with in ward-strength.'

9. HOLDING FAST,] *lit.* 'holding over-against the stedfast word according to the teaching, that he may be able both to call upon in the wholesome *or* healthy teaching, and to convict those speaking in opposition.'

10. UNRULY,] *lit.* 'not-arranged-under, vain-speakers and mind-deceivers.'

11. WHOSE MOUTHS,] *lit.* 'whom it behoves to muzzle, who turn upside down whole houses..because of shameful gain.'

12. ONE,] *lit.* a 'certain one (i.e. Epimenides) out of themselves, a prophet (i.e. public speaker *or* poet) of their own, said, Cretans! always liars! bad beasts! idle bellies.'

13. WITNESS,] *or* 'testimony..be convicting them cuttingly, that they may be healthy.'

14. GIVING HEED,] *lit.* 'not holding-towards Jewish myths..turning round.'

15. THAT ARE,] *lit.* 'having been defiled and unstedfast..but of them both the mind and the conscience has been defiled.'

16. PROFESS,] *lit.* 'say the same thing *or* speak together.'

THAT,] *lit.* 'to have known God.'

IN,] *or* 'with the works they deny him for themselves..unstedfast *or* unconfiding, and ..disapproved.'

Chapter II. may be divided into four parts; v. 1—5 rules for aged men, also for women aged and young; v. 6—8 younger men; v. 9, 10 servants; v. 11—15 object of the saving grace of God.

1. THOU,] *lit.* 'but thou, be speaking what things are proper to wholesome teaching.'

2. THAT,] *lit.* 'aged (*or* elders, elderly) men to be not-drinking, reverent, sound-minded, healthy in the faith, the love, the endurance.'

3. AGED,] *or* 'elderly women *or* elderesses ..in staidness as is proper to priestesses, not devils (*lit.* 'thrusters through,') not having been in bondage to much wine, teachers of good (persons *or* things).'

4. TEACH,] *lit.* 'make the young women sound-minded, to be friends of (their) husbands, friends of (their) children.'

5. DISCREET,] *lit.* 'sound-minded, chaste, keepers of the house, good, arranging themselves under their own husbands..may not be injuriously spoken of.'

6. YOUNG,] *lit.* 'the younger men likewise be calling upon to be sound-minded.'

7. IN,] *lit.* 'concerning all things holding thyself along a type of good works, in the teaching through-uncorruptedness, reverence, incorruptibility.'

8. SOUND,] *or* 'healthy speech *or* discourse uncondemned, (*lit.* 'nothing known against it,) that he who is of the contrary part may

turn in, having nothing evil *or* worthless to say concerning you.'

9. SERVANTS,] *lit.* 'bondsmen to be arranged under their own despots, to be well-pleasing in all things, not speaking in opposition.'

10. PURLOINING,] *lit.* 'putting (anything) apart for themselves, but inwardly shewing all good stedfastness, that..teaching of our Saviour God.'

11. THAT BRINGETH SALVATION,] *lit.* 'for the saving grace of God to all men was manifested openly.'

12. TEACHING,] *or* 'instructing us, that denying for ourselves the irreverence and the worldly over-desires, we might live sound-mindedly, and justly, and reverently, in the present age.'

13. LOOKING FOR,] *lit.* 'receiving to (ourselves) the happy hope and full manifestation of the glory of our great God and Saviour Jesus Christ.'

14. FOR,] *lit.* 'in our behalf, that he might ransom (*or* loose us by a price) from all lawlessness, and might purify to himself a people pre-eminent,' *lit.* over-existence.

15. SPEAK,] *lit.* 'be speaking, and calling upon, and convicting, with all over-arrangement; let no one be thinking (himself) above thee.'

Chapter III. may be divided into three parts; v. 1—9 present duty, past state, and future hopes of Christians; v. 10, 11 to reject a sectarian man; v. 12—15 closing commands and salutations.

1. PUT THEM IN MIND,] *lit.* 'be reminding them to be arranged under (*or* to arrange themselves under) chiefs and authorities, to be chief in obedience.'

2. EVIL,] *or* 'injuriously (*lit.* blasphemously) of no one, to be unwarlike (*or* without fighting), very-yielding, shewing inwardly all.'

3. SOMETIMES,] *lit.* 'then thoughtless, untrusting, deceived (*or* deceiving ourselves), being in bondage to manifold over-desires and pleasures, leading (ourselves) thoroughly in badness, and envy.'

4. AFTER,] *lit.* 'when..the philanthopy of our Saviour God was openly manifested.'

5. BY,] *lit.* 'out of works in righteousness which we did for ourselves, but..kindness he saved us through (the) laver of a being born again (Mat. 19. 28), and (the) renewing of a holy spirit.'

6. SHED,] *lit.* 'poured on us richly.'

7. JUSTIFIED,] *or* 'declared just by..we may become heirs (according to *or* in hope) of life age-during.'

8. THIS IS,] *lit.* 'stedfast is the word, and I counsel thee concerning these things to make thoroughly firm, that they who have believed God may be mindful to set before themselves good-works. These things are the good (*or* right).'

9. AVOID,] *lit.* 'be setting away foolish (*or* rebellious) searchings..law fightings.'

10. HERETIC,] *lit.* a 'heretical man,' i.e. one given to 'lift up' opinions, sound *or* unsound, an unstable, unsettled individual who wishes to form 'sects.'

THE,] *lit.* 'after a first and second admonishing, be asking off from thyself,' i.e. avoid his company.

11. KNOWING,] *lit.* 'having known that he who is such has been greatly turned round, and sinneth (i.e. 'misseth' the mark), being self-condemned,' *lit.* judged down by himself.

12. ARTEMAS,] i.e. 'honest *or* sound.'

TYCHICUS,] i.e. 'fortunate.'

BE DILIGENT,] *lit.* 'hasten.'

NICOPOLIS,] i.e. 'city of victory,' in Thrace.

DETERMINED,] *or* 'decided, *lit.* judged.'

13. BRING,] *lit.* 'send forward Zenas (i.e. Jove's)..Apollos speedily..may be left to them (to do).'

14. MAINTAIN,] *lit.* 'set forward good works with a view to the necessary uses.'

15. SALUTE,] *lit.* 'draw thee near; draw near those loving us in faith; the grace (is) with you all. Amen.'

PAUL'S LETTER TO PHILEMON

PHILEMON lived at Colosse, and was a rich convert and fellow-labourer of Paul, who, when a prisoner in Rome, A.D. 61-2, wrote him this letter to induce him to receive back a run-away bondsman—Onesimus—whom Paul had met with and converted to the gospel. This letter was quoted or referred to by Tertullian (A.D. 192), Caius (A.D. 212), Origen (A.D. 230), Jerome (A.D. 392), Eusebius (A.D. 320), and perhaps Ignatius (A.D. 107).

THIS LETTER may be divided into six parts; v. 1—3 address and salutation; v. 4—7 thanksgiving for Philemon's state; v. 8—16 entreaty for Onesimus; v. 17—19 personal reasons for this; v. 20—22 expression of confidence and a request; v. 23—25 closing salutations.

1. PAUL,] i.e. the 'little' one.

PRISONER,] *lit.* 'bound one.'

JESUS CHRIST,] i.e. the 'anointed saviour.'

TIMOTHEUS,] i.e. the one 'honouring God.'

OUR,] *lit.* 'the brother,' in the faith.

PHILEMON,] i.e. 'loving, befriending.'

DEARLY.] Omit as unnecessary.

FELLOW-LABOURER,] *lit.* 'joint worker,' in building up the Colossians.

2. OUR,] *lit.* 'the beloved Apphia (a female), and Archippus (i.e. chief-horseman, Col. 4. 17),..church (*or* assembly) at thy house;' see Rom. 16. 15; 1 Cor. 16. 11.

3. GRACE,] *lit.* what 'causes leaping for joy.'

PEACE,] *lit.* what 'brings into unity.'

AND,] *or* 'and (Father of the) Lord Jesus Christ.'

4. THANK,] *lit.* 'leap much for joy before my God always..upon (*or* during) my pouring-forth before God.'

5. THY,] *lit.* 'of thee the love and the faith..and in reference to all the saints,' *lit.* those 'not of the earth.'

6. COMMUNICATION,] *or* 'communion, fellowship..become inworking in (the) full knowledge of..in reference to Christ Jesus.'

7. GREAT,] *lit.* 'much..exhortation upon thy..have been refreshed through thee.'

8. THOUGH,] *lit.* 'having in Christ much full-speech to arrange for thee what comes up.'

9. YET,] *lit.* 'because of the love I rather call upon (thee).'

10. BESEECH,] *lit.* 'call upon thee concerning my child, whom I begat in my bonds, Onesimus,' i.e. profitable.

11. WHICH,] *or* 'who was useless to thee once, but now very useful.'

12. HAVE,] *lit.* 'I sent back..receive to thyself.'

13. WOULD,] *lit.* 'counselled to hold fast for myself, that in thy behalf he might be a deacon to me.'

14. WITHOUT,] *lit.* 'apart from thy knowledge I wished to do nothing, that thy goodness might not be as of necessity, but as of willingness.'

15. DEPARTED,] *lit.* 'was separated for an hour, that age-duringly thou mightest have him entirely;' as in Ex. 21. 6.

16. NOT NOW,] 'no more as a bondsman.'

17. COUNT,] *lit.* 'hast communion *or* fellowship with me, receive him to thyself as myself.'

18. IF,] *lit.* 'but if he used thee unjustly.. be laying that to me.'

19. HAVE,] *lit.* 'wrote..that I may not say.'

20. JOY,] *lit.* 'profit.'

21. CONFIDENCE,] *lit.* 'having been confident of thy submissive hearkening..having known..above what I say.'

22. WITHAL,] *or* 'at the same time..I hope ..be granted to you.'

23. SALUTE,] *lit.* 'draw thee near doth Epaphras,' i.e. Epaphroditus, upon Venus, i.q. lovely.

FELLOW-PRISONER,] *lit.* one 'taken jointly by a spear.'

24. MARCUS,] i.e. 'far, distant.'

ARISTARCHUS,] i.e. 'best of chiefs.'

DEMAS,] i.e. a 'plebeian,' of the 'people.

LUKAS,] i.e. 'shining.'

FELLOW-LABOURERS,] *or* 'fellow-workers.'

25. GRACE,] *lit.* what 'causes leaping for joy.'

LETTER TO THE HEBREWS

THE PARTIES to whom this Epistle was originally addressed were undoubtedly the Jewish Christians in Palestine, who were exposed to peculiar inducements to apostatize to Judaism; and hence the elaborate exhibition of the superiority of Christ and Christianity to all preceding revelations of the Divine Will. It was probably written from Rome about A.D. 62-3, when the author was expecting shortly to be restored to them. He gives no name, but must have been well-known to those whom he addressed, and accordingly they (i.e. the Eastern Churches) have almost unanimously maintained that he was the apostle Paul, while the Western (or Roman) Church was divided in opinion, Tertullian ascribing it to Barnabas, others to Apollos, Luke, Silas, &c.

Ignatius (A.D. 108), Polycarp (A.D. 108), Clement of Rome (A.D. 108), Justin Martyr (A.D. 140), Clement of Alexandria (A.D. 194), Origen (A.D. 230), Dionysius (A.D. 247), Theognostus (A.D. 282), Methodius (A.D. 292), Pamphilus (A.D. 294), Archelaus (A.D. 300), Arnobius (A.D. 306) Lactantius (A.D. 306), &c., all considered Paul to be the author, though the *composition of the sentences*, and the *colourings of the style*, are by no means so Pauline, as are the *casts of thought*, and *modes of reasoning*.

The object of this Epistle is to shew the pre-eminent dignity of Christ and Christianity, to prevent Jewish believers from relapsing into Judaism, and to exhort them to stedfastness by the example of ancient worthies. It may be divided into two great parts:—

I. DOCTRINAL,—Superiority of Christ to Angels, Moses, Aaron, and the Levitical priesthood; ch. i. 1—10. 18

II. PRACTICAL,—Application of the Doctrine; ch. 10. 19—13. 25.

Chapter I. may be divided into two parts; v. 1—4 superiority of God's Son over his other Messengers; v. 5—14 reasons for this.

1. AT SUNDRY TIMES,] *lit.* 'in many (separate) parts and many (various) ways spake anciently to the fathers in (the person of) the prophets,' i.e. those announcing the will of God, whether it related to things past, present, or future.

2. HATH,] *lit.* 'spake during the last of these days to us in (the person of) a Son, whom he set (*or* placed) heir of all, through whom also he made the ages,' *or* dispensations, whether Adamic, Noachic, Abrahamic or Mosaic.

3. BRIGHTNESS,] *lit.* 'an off-shining of the glory, and an impress (*Gr.* character) of his under (*or* hidden) state, (*Gr.* hypostasis), bearing on the all things by the saying of his power, having through himself made a cleansing of our sins (*or* 'missings' of the mark), he sat down in the right-hand-place of the greatness in (*or* among) the highest,' persons, places, *or* things.

4. MADE,] *lit.* 'having become so much stronger (*or* nobler) than the (other) messengers (of God) as he has inherited (*or* received by lot) a thoroughly different name from them;' they being simply called 'prophets,' and he 'Son,' as in v. 1, 2.

5. ANGELS,] *lit.* 'messengers (whether men or unclothed spirits)..I to-day have begotten thee,' i.e. brought thee forth and declared thee my son; this may be referred to the first formation of the Covenant with Christ, to the promise to our first parents, to his birth, to his inauguration, and to his resurrection; see 5. 5; Ps. 2. 7; Acts 13. 33; Rom. 1. 4; Rev. 1. 5.

6. BE,] *or* 'become,' *lit.* 'be to him for a Father, and he will be to me for a Son,' i.e. a new and endearing relationship will be formed; see 2 Sam. 7. 14.

AGAIN,] *lit.* 'but when again he may lead in (i.e. mention) the First-born to the inhabited world, he says, And let all messengers of God kiss forward (the hand) to him;' see Ps. 97. 7; Rom. 8. 29; Col. 1. 18.

7. OF,] *lit.* 'and to the messengers he says, Who is making his messengers (as) winds, and his public workers (as) a flame of fire,' i.e. He uses the 'prophets' and others as He uses the mere elements of nature to accomplish his purposes, but the work of the 'Son was not so.

8. O GOD.] This is a clear instance where Christ is called 'God,' but as v. 9 speaks of God as his 'God,' we cannot lay stress upon it here as proving the supreme divinity of the Saviour, besides it may be justly rendered, 'God is thy throne—to the ages of the ages;' in either case it is applicable to the mediatorial throne only.

SCEPTRE,] *lit.* 'rod of straightforwardness is the rod.'

9. HAST,] *lit.* 'didst love..lawlessness.. did anoint..thy partners,' *lit.* those 'having along with' him.

10. IN,] *or* 'at..did found the earth..are works.'

11. PERISH,] *or* 'loose themselves away, but thou remainest thoroughly..become old as a garment (does).'

12. VESTURE,] *or* wrapper, *lit.* a thing 'cast around' one.

FOLD,] *or* 'roll..shall become another thing..not utterly fail.'

13. SIT,] *lit.* 'be sitting at (*lit.* out of) my ..I set (*or* place) thine enemies (as the) footstool of thy feet.'

14. MINISTERING,] *lit.* 'public-working spirits, sent forth with a view to deaconship, because (*or* on account) of those about to inherit salvation.'

Chapter II. may be divided into four parts; v. 1—4 a practical inference from the preceding chapter; v. 5—9 glory of man and Jesus; v. 10—13 reasons for Jesus being perfected through sufferings; v. 14—18 and for his incarnation.

1. THEREFORE,] *lit.* 'because of this it behoves (us) to hold more abundantly to the things heard, lest at any time we may flow by,' *or* beyond, aside.

2. BY,] *lit.* 'through messengers (e.g. Moses) became firm, and every transgression and mis-hearkening received an inwardly just giving back of hire.'

3. ESCAPE,] *lit.* 'flee forth, having been careless of so great salvation, which having received a beginning of being spoken through the Lord, was confirmed to us by those having heard (him *or* it).'

4. WITNESS,] *lit.* 'joint-testimony about (it)..terrible things and manifold powers, and distributions of holy spirit, according to his will,' *or* wish.

5. THE,] *lit.* 'for he did not arrange the (people of the) inhabited world that is coming, concerning which we speak, under messengers.'

6. ONE,] *lit.* 'but a certain one thoroughly testified somewhere, saying, What is man (i.e. the human race) that thou art mindful of him, or a son of man (i.e. a human being) that thou lookest-over upon him?'

7. A LITTLE,] *lit.* 'some little less than messengers.' In Ps. 8. 4 the Hebrew is, 'Thou hast caused him to lack a little of God,' i.e. of the God-head, or divine nature; being made in his image, he was his representative here below. The apostle quotes the Septuagint, which, though perfectly true, does not express *all* that the Psalmist does.

SET,] *lit.* 'set him down over.'

8. HAST,] *lit.* 'didst arrange-somewhat all under his feet, for in the arranging the all things under him, he sent nothing away to him not-arranged-under..the all things arranged under him.'

9. A LITTLE,] *lit.* 'some little less than messengers, (that by the grace of God he might taste of death in behalf of every one), because of the suffering of the death, crowned with glory and honour.'

10. BECAME,] *lit.* 'was proper for him, because of whom are the all things, and through whom are the all things, having led many sons to glory, to perfect (*lit.* end) the chief-leader.'

11. THAT,] *lit.* 'who is hallowing, (i.e. setting apart, *lit* making 'not of the earth,') and those who are being hallowed, are all out of one.'

12. DECLARE,] *lit.* 'tell forth..an assembly will I hymn (i.e. praise) thee.'

13. PUT,] *lit.* 'trust for myself upon him.. God gave to me.'

14. FORASMUCH,] *lit.* 'since then the children have partaken of flesh and blood, himself also held with (them) of these very nearly, (yet without sin), that through the death he might make thoroughly useless him having the power (*or* strength, might) of the death, that is, the Devil,' *lit.* 'thruster through.'

15. DELIVER,] *lit.* 'and might thoroughly change those, as many as in fear of death through all (their) life were held in of bondage.'

16. VERILY,] *or* 'for indeed *or* doubtless, it (i.e. the fear of death) takes not hold upon angels, but it takes hold upon (the) seed of Abraham.'

17. WHEREFORE,] *lit.* 'whence it was profitable (for him) through all things to become like the brethren, that he might become a kind and stedfast chief-priest, in the things relating to God, with a view to making mild (in the sight of God) the sins of the people.'

18. IN THAT,] *lit.* 'for wherein he..to hold those being tried.'

Chapter III. may be divided into two parts; v. 1—6 superiority of Christ to Moses; v. 7—19 and the greater sin of those who reject him.

1. WHEREFORE,] *or* 'whence..holders together of..consider thoroughly the apostle (i.e. one 'sent forth,') and chief-priest of our confession (*lit.* using the same words).'

2. WHO,] *lit.* 'being stedfast to him who made him (apostle and chief-priest), even as Moses, among all his household.'

3. MAN,] *lit.* 'for this one has been reckoned worthy..even as he who made it thoroughly ready has (the) greater honour of the house.'

4. BUILDED,] *lit.* 'made thoroughly ready by some one..made the all things thoroughly ready is God.'

5. VERILY,] *or* 'indeed (was) stedfast among all his household, as a nourisher (curer *or* healer,) with a view to a testimony of the things that shall be spoken.'

6. HIS OWN,] *lit.* 'his (i.e. God's) house hold, whose household we are, if we may hold thoroughly the free-speech and the (matter of) boasting.'

7. GHOST,] *lit.* 'spirit..may hear.'

8. HARDEN,] *lit.* 'may ye not dry up..in the great bitterness, according to the day of the trial.'

9. WHEN,] *or* 'where your fathers tried me.'

10. GRIEVED,] *or* 'very vexed..go astray with the heart, and these did not know'

11. SO,] *lit.* 'as I..anger, If they shall enter into my full-rest.'

12. TAKE HEED,] *or* 'see, brethren, lest at any time there shall be..of unstedfastness ..in the standing off from the living God.'

13. EXHORT,] *or* 'call upon yourselves through every day..lest any one of you be dried up with the.'

14. ARE MADE,] *or* 'have become joint-holders of the Christ,, if we may hold thoroughly the beginning (*or* chief-part) of the confidence,' *lit.* a thing 'standing *or* set under' one.

15. WHILE,] *lit.* 'in (its) being said, To-day, if ye may hear his voice, may ye not dry up ..the great bitterness.'

16. SOME,] *or* 'certain having heard made (him) very bitter..through Moses.'

17. GRIEVED,] *or* 'very vexed.. whose limbs.'

18. ENTER,] *lit.* 'enter for themselves to his full-rest.. those unfaithful,' *or* disobedient.

19. SO,] *lit.* 'and we..were not able to enter in because of unstedfastness.'

Chapter IV. may be divided into four parts; v. 1—5 fear of coming short of the promised rest; v. 6—10 a sabbatic rest; v. 11—13 diligence because of God's reckoning; v. 14—16 confidence because of our high priest.

1. LET,] *or* 'May we..being fully left of suffering into his full-rest..may seem to have been late,' *or* behind.

2. UNTO US,] *lit.* 'for we also are having good-news proclaimed, even as these, but the word of the hearing did not..not having been mixed together with the faith.'

3. WHICH,] *lit.* 'who believed do enter with a view to the full-rest, even as he has said: As I sware in my anger, If..full-rest, though indeed the works were made from the laying-down of the world,' *Gr.* kosmos.

4. SPAKE,] *lit.* 'has said somewhere concerning the seventh (day) thus: And God rested fully in the.'

6. SEEING,] *or* 'since then it is left over for certain to enter into it, and those first having good-news proclaimed did not enter in through unfaithfulness.'

7. LIMITS,] *lit.* 'marks out..as it has been said..may hear his voice, may ye not dry up your hearts.'

8. JESUS,] i.e. Joshua, as in Acts 7. 45.

HAD,] *lit.* 'gave them full-rest..after these things have been speaking about.'

9. REMAINETH,] *lit.* 'is left over then a cessation (*lit.* sabbatism) to the people of God,'—after death, as in Rev. 14. 13.

10. IS,] *lit.* 'who entered into his full-rest (i.e. Jesus), he also rested fully from his works, as God (did) from his own.'

11. LABOUR,] *lit.* 'may we be hasting..may fall in the same under-showing of the unfaithfulness.'

12. WORD,] *or* 'reckoning of God (with sinners) is living and energetic, and more cutting than any double-cutting sword, and coming through unto the division both of soul and spirit, both of joints and marrow, and a judge (*Gr.* critic) of the inner-desires, and inner-thoughts of the heart.'

13. NEITHER,] *lit.* 'and there is no created thing un-manifested before Him,..and laid bare to..we have the reckoning.'

14. SEEING,] *lit.* 'having then a great chief-priest, himself gone through the heavens.. may we keep hold of the confession,' *lit.* speaking the same thing.

15. WHICH,] *lit.* 'unable to suffer together with (us) in our strengthlessnesses, but one tried in all things in like manner—apart from sin.'

16. LET,] *lit.* 'may we come forward then with full-speech to the throne of the grace, that we may receive kindness, and may find grace, with a view to a seasonable help.'

Chapter V. may be divided into three parts; v. 1—4 character and qualifications of a priest like Aaron; v. 5—9 and of the Christ; v. 10—14 called after Melchisedec, whom the Hebrews could not appreciate.

1. TAKEN,] *lit.* 'who is taken out of men is set down in behalf of men in the things relating to God that he may bear forward.. in behalf of sins.'

2. CAN,] *lit.* 'who is able to bear in some measure with the ignorant and those going astray, since he himself also is laid around with strengthlessness.'

3. BY REASON HEREOF,] *lit.* 'because of this.'

OFFER,] *lit.* 'bear forward in behalf of sins.'

4. MAN,] *lit.* 'no one receives *or* takes.'

OF,] *lit.* 'by God, as also Aaron was.'

5. CHRIST,] *lit.* 'the Christ..to become chief-priest.'

6. A PRIEST,] *or* 'priest to (*or* with a view to) the age, according to the arrangement of Melchisedec,' i.e. by which he was appointed, viz. God's will, not by hereditary descent.

MELCHISEDEC,] i.e. 'king of righteousness.'

7. OFFERED UP,] *lit.* 'having brought forward both wants and supplications..to him who is able to save him out of death, and was hearkened to because of the easy *or* good reception *or* acceptance.'

8. THOUGH,] *lit.* 'and truly being a Son, he learned the obedience from.'

9. BEING MADE,] *lit.* 'having been perfected he became to all those hearkening-submissively to him a cause of salvation age-during.'

10. CALLED,] *lit.* 'publicly declared by God chief-priest according to the arrangement of Melchisedec.'

11. MANY THINGS,] *or* 'much discourse *or* matter, and hard of interpretation to say, since ye have become sluggish in the ears.'

12. FOR,] *lit.* 'when because of the times ..need of one teaching you again which are the steppings of the beginning of the words of God, and have become in need of milk, and not of solid nourishment.'

13. USETH,] *lit.* 'is partaking of milk, is untried.'

14. STRONG,] *lit.* 'the solid nourishment is for those perfect (*lit.* ended), who because of the use (*lit.* having) are having the perceptions exercised (*lit.* made naked) towards a thorough judgment both of good and of evil.'

Chapter VI. may be divided into two parts; v. 1—9 warning against apostacy; v. 10—20 encouragement to perseverance.

1. LEAVING,] *lit.* 'having left the word (i.e. doctrine) of the beginning of the Christ may we be borne on upon the perfection, not laying down again a foundation of a new (*or* another) mind, and of faith upon God, of (the) teaching of baptisms (e.g. such as John's and Christ's,) of placing on also of hands, and of (the) upstanding of (the) dead and of a judgment age-during.'

3. PERMIT,] *lit.* 'turn it over upon us.'

4. IMPOSSIBLE,] i.e. in the eyes of men, humanly speaking, but 'with God all things are possible.'

TASTED,] *lit.* 'tasted for themselves of.. and having become partakers of holy spirit.'

5. TASTED,] *lit.* 'tasted for themselves the good word (*or* saying, matter) of God, (the) powers also of (the) age about to be, and having fallen aside to renew (them *or* themselves) with a view to another mind, having crucified again to themselves the Son of God, and made (him) a false show,' *or* example, *or* spectacle.

7. THE EARTH,] *lit.* 'for earth, that has drunk in the rain coming many times upon it, and is bringing forth herbage well-set (*or* fitted) to those because (*or* on account) of whom also it is worked, receives again (*or* with it) a good word (*Gr.* eulogy) from God.'

8. BEARETH,] *lit.* 'but bringing forth..is disapproved (*or* unaccepted), and nigh to a thorough curse..is for a burning.'

9. ARE,] *lit.* 'have been persuaded concerning you, beloved, (as to) the things better and having salvation.'

10. FORGET,] *lit.* 'let lie hid for himself your work, and the labours of the love, which ye showed inwardly for yourselves with a view to his name, having been deacons to the hallowed ones, and being deacons.'

11. DESIRE,] *lit.* 'greatly desire each of you to show inwardly the same speed towards the full-bearing of the hope till (the) end.'

12. BE,] *or* 'become..imitators of those through faith and long-suffering inheriting.'

13. WHEN,] *lit.* 'for God having made promise to Abraham, since he had none greater to swear by.'

14. SURELY,] *or* 'truly indeed speaking-well I will speak-well of thee,' i.e. very well.

15. ENDURED,] *or* 'suffered, he fully obtained.'

16. AN,] *lit.* 'the oath is to them a limit of all gainsaying (*or* contradiction) in relation to confirmation.'

17. WILLING,] *lit.* 'counselling..shew fully to the heirs of the promise..mediated with (*or* in, by) an oath.'

18. BY,] *lit.* 'through..God to be false to himself, we may have strong comfort who fled down to lay..laid before (us).'

19. STEDFAST,] *or* 'firm, and entering in to the inner place of the full-extended veil.'

20. THE,] *lit.* 'a fore-runner entered in our behalf—Jesus—who became a chief-priest to the age according to the arrangement of Melchisedec.'

Chapter VII. may be divided into five parts; v. 1—10 Melchisedec greater than Abraham and the Levitical priesthood; v. 11—14 which was changed as to order, law, tribe; v. 15—21 Christ made priest by oath; v. 22—25 and excels others by his unchangeableness; v. 26—28 his sinlessness and perfection.'

1. MELCHISEDEC,] i.e. 'king of righteousness.'

SALEM,] i.e. 'peace,' supposed to be Jerusalem; but see Ge. 33. 18; John 3. 23.

PRIEST,] *or* 'a priest,' like Job, Abraham, &c.

RETURNING,] *lit.* 'turning round quietly from the smiting;' Ge. 14. 17, 18.

BLESSED,] *lit.* 'spake well of *or* to him.'

2. OF ALL] the spoils, as in v. 4.

RIGHTEOUSNESS,] i.e. 'righteous king.'

PEACE,] i.e. a 'peaceful king.'

3. WITHOUT,] *lit.* 'fatherless, motherless, un-genealogized..but having been made thoroughly like.'

ABIDETH,] *lit.* 'remaineth a priest in reference to the thorough continuity (of his priesthood).' Levitical priests required 'fathers,' and 'mothers,' and 'genealogies,' to become priests, but Melchisedec required none of these things, having apparently no predecessor or successor in his offices.

4. CONSIDER,] *lit.* 'see..this one (is)..a tenth of the spoils,' *lit.* 'top of the heaps.'

5. VERILY,] *lit.* 'and those, indeed, out of the sons of Levi, receiving the priesthood.. from the people..they themselves have come forth out of.'

6. WHOSE DESCENT,] *lit.* 'but he who is not reckoned genealogically out of them has tithed Abraham, and eulogized him having the promise.'

7. WITHOUT,] *or* 'apart from all..lesser is well-spoken of by the stronger.'

8. HERE,] *lit.* 'here indeed men dying away take (*or* receive) tithes, but there, he who is testified to, that he lives.'

9. I,] *lit.* 'and so to speak, even Levi, who is receiving tithes, has been tithed.'

11. IF,] *lit.* 'if, indeed, then, perfection were through..for (upon) it the people had been put under law..for another (*or* different) priest to set himself up (*or* stand up for himself) according to the arrangement of Melchisedec, and not to be spoken of, according to the arrangement of Aaron.'

12. FOR,] *or* 'therefore the..there comes of necessity a change also of law.'

13. OF,] *lit.* 'about whom..has partaken of another (*or* different) tribe, from which no one has held towards the altar,' *lit.* place of sacrifice.

14. EVIDENT,] *lit.* 'publicly known that our Lord has risen up out of Judah, in reference to which.'

15. FAR,] *lit.* 'more abundantly publicly known, if according to the likeness of Melchisedec another (*or* a different) priest sets himself up (*or* stands up for himself).'

16. IS MADE,] *lit.* 'has come not according to a law of a fleshly precept, but according to (the) power of a thoroughly indissoluble life.'

17. THOU,] *lit.* 'that, thou art a priest to the age, according to the arrangement of Melchisedec.'

18. THERE IS,] *lit.* 'there comes a putting away indeed of the precept leading-forward because of the strengthlessness'

19. BUT,] *or* 'and the leading in also of a better hope, through which.'

20. WITHOUT,] *lit.* 'apart from oath-swearing.'

21. THOSE,] *lit.* 'for they indeed apart from oath-swearing have become priests, but he with oath-swearing, through him.. not be careful (*or* concerned) afterwards.'

22. WAS,] *lit.* 'has Jesus become surety of a better covenant.'

23. TRULY,] *lit.* 'indeed have become many priests, because they were hindered from remaining by the death.'

24. THIS,] *lit.* 'but he, because of his remaining to the age has the priesthood not going by;' i.e. it is not transmitted to any other, as the supporters of 'apostolical succession' pretend. See Harrison's '*Whose are the Fathers?*' for an elaborate exposure of this popish and prelatic fiction.

25. WHEREFORE,] *or* 'whence..save to the full-end those coming forward to God through him, always living to be (*or* come) in in our behalf.'

26. BECAME,] *lit.* 'was proper for us, kind, un-evil, undefiled, having been apart from the sinful, and become higher.'

27. NEEDETH,] *lit.* 'has no necessity daily, as the (other) chief-priests, first in behalf of his own sins to bear up sacrifices, then (in behalf) of the people; for this he did once for all, having borne up himself.'

28. MAKETH,] *lit.* 'sets men down chief-priests..oath-swearing, which is after the law..having been perfected to the age.'

Chapter VIII. may be divided into two parts; v. 1—6 position and duties of our chief priest; v. 7—13 the New Covenant contrasted with the Old.

1. OF,] *lit.* 'but about the things (that are being) spoken, a chief point is: We have.. who sat down in the right hand of the throne of the greatness in the heavens.'

2. MINISTER,] *lit.* 'public worker of the hallowed things.'

3. ORDAINED,] *lit.* 'set down with a view to the bearing forward both of gifts..whence (it is) necessary (for) this one to have something which he might bear forward.'

4. IF,] *lit.* 'if indeed he..not even be a priest—there being the priests who are bearing forward the gifts according to the law.'

5. SERVE,] *lit.* 'who tremble (*or* go tremblingly) to the example (*lit.* 'under-shew) and shadow of the..has been divinely told being about to end fully the tabernacle..thou mayest do (*or* make) all according to the type that was shown to thee.'

6. MORE EXCELLENT,] *or* 'thoroughly different public work..he is middle-man..one which has been legalized (*or* made law) upon.'

7. HAD BEEN,] *lit.* 'were blameless, place would not have been sought (*or* desired) for a second.'

8. FINDING FAULT,] *lit.* 'attaching blame to them, he says, Behold, days come, saith the Lord, and I will complete (*lit.* end together) a new covenant over the house of Israel, and over the house of Judah.'

9. WITH,] *or* 'to their fathers in (the) day of my taking..lead them forth out of..remained not..I was careless of them.'

10. FOR,] *lit.* 'because this..will covenant to (*or* with)..Lord, giving my laws to their thorough (*or* different) mind, and upon their hearts I will write them fully..them for a God..for a people.'

11. EVERY MAN,] *lit.* 'each..each..know thou..because all..little one of them unto the great one of them.'

12. FOR,] *lit.* 'because..kind (*or* gentle).. lawlessnesses will I not.'

13. IN THAT,] *lit.* 'in the saying 'new' he has..which is becoming old and antiquated is nigh disappearance.'

Chapter IX. may be divided into five parts; v. 1—5 contents of the first and second tabernacles; v. 6—10 what was done there, and its meaning; v. 11—14 superiority of Christ's work; v. 15—22 reasons for frequent blood-shedding; v. 23—28 sufficiency of the one sacrifice once for all.

1. VERILY,] *or* 'indeed also (*or* even) the first had righteous acts of service (*lit.* much trembling), also the hallowed place worldly.'

2. THERE WAS,] *lit.* 'for a tabernacle was made thoroughly ready *or* prepared, the first in which were both the lampstand and the table, and the setting forth of the bread, which is called 'Hallowed place.'

3. VEIL,] *lit.* 'full-extended veil, a tabernacle..called Holy of Holy.'

4. WHICH HAD,] *lit.* 'having a golden censer (*lit.* 'place of incense,')..covered all round..a golden pot having the manna.. tablets.'

5. OVER,] *lit.* 'over above it cherubim of glory thoroughly shadowing the place of gentleness; of which things it is not (for us) now to speak concerning every part.'

6. WHEN,] *lit.* 'these things having been thus made thoroughly ready, the priests ending fully the services, (*lit.* much trembling) go into the first tabernacle.'

7. YEAR,] on the 10th day of the 7th month.

OFFERED,] *lit.* 'bears near in behalf of himself and of the ignorant-errors of the people.'

8. SIGNIFYING,] *lit.* 'making known the way of the hallowed places to have been not yet manifested, the first tabernacle having yet a standing.'

9. WAS,] *or* 'which is a simile (*Gr.* parable) in reference (*or* with a view) to the time which has set in, according to (*or* in) which both gifts and sacrifices are borne forward, which are not able, according to (*or* in) conscience, to perfect him who is coming-very-tremblingly.'

10. WHICH] sacrifices are 'only over victuals, and drinks (Lev. 10. 9; 11. 4), and different baptisms, even righteous acts of (the) flesh, till the season of thorough-rectification laid upon (them).'

11. COME,] *lit.* 'being come along-side, chief priest of the good thing about to be, through the greater..that is, not of this creation,' *or* formation.

12. BY,] *lit.* 'through blood..but through ..once for all into the hallowed places, hav

ing himself found an age-during ransom,' *lit.* 'loosing-price.'

13. THE,] *lit.* 'and ashes of a tame-heifer sprinkling those having become common (like the Gentiles), halloweth towards the purification of the flesh.'

14. OF CHRIST,] *lit.* 'of the Christ..age-during Spirit bore himself forward unblemished to God..with a view to go-very-tremblingly to (the) living God.'

15. THE,] *lit.* 'is middle-man of a new covenant, that, death having come, with a view to a loosing away of the transgressions over the first covenant, those called may receive the promise of the age-during inheritance,' *lit.* distribution by lot.

16. TESTAMENT,] *lit.* 'covenant is, the death of the covenant-victim is necessary to be brought (into court).'

17. TESTAMENT,] *lit.* 'covenant is firm over dead-victims, since it has no strength at all while the covenant-victim lives.'

18. WHEREUPON,] *lit.* 'whence not even the first has been made thoroughly new apart from blood.'

19. WHEN,] *lit.* 'for every precept having been spoken, according to law, by Moses, to all the people, having taken the blood of the calves and goats..he sprinkled both the book itself, and all.

20. TESTAMENT,] *lit.* 'covenant which God enjoined (*or* raised inwardly) for himself toward you.

21. MOREOVER,] *lit.* 'and also the tabernacle, and all the vessels of the public-work, he sprinkled with the blood, in like manner.

22. BY,] *lit.* 'according to the law cleansed in blood, and apart from a pouring forth of blood, a letting go (of sins) comes not.'

23. IT WAS,] *or* 'is necessary, therefore, (for) the under-showings indeed of the things in the heavens to be cleansed.'

24. CHRIST,] *lit.* 'for the Christ entered not into hallowed places made by hands, anti-types of the true, but into the heaven itself, now to be fully-manifested in the face of God in our behalf.'

25. NOR YET,] *lit.* 'nor even that he may bear himself forward many times..hallowed places each year with (*lit.* in) blood of others.'

26. FOR,] *lit.* 'since it were behoving him to suffer many times from (the) laying-down of the world, but now, once for all, on the full-end of the ages, has he been manifested with a view to a putting away of sin, through his own sacrifice.'

27. AS,] *lit.* 'and according as it is laid-off to men, once for all to die-fully, but after this—judgment.'

28. SO,] *lit.* 'so also the Christ, having once for all bore-himself-forward to bear-up sin in reference to the many, shall show himself a second time, apart from a sin-offering, to those receiving him fully with a view to salvation.'

Chapter X. may be divided into seven parts; v. 1--4 legal sacrifices not sufficient; v 5--11 but the one offering of Christ is; v. 12—18 results of his offering; v. 19—25 practical conclusions; v. 26—31 danger of wilful sin; v. 32—34 former attainments; v. 35—39 prayer for endurance.

1. GOOD,] *lit.* 'of the good things about to be, not the very image of the matters, by the same sacrifices which they bear-forward each year, to the full continuity, is at no time able to perfect those coming forward.'

2. FOR,] *lit.* 'since would they (not) have ceased themselves to be borne forward, because of those coming tremblingly, having no more conscience of sins, having been once for all cleansed.'

3. THOSE,] *or* 'in them is a reminding of sins each year.'

4. NOT,] *lit.* 'impossible (for) blood of bulls and goats to lift away sins.'

5. WHEN,] *lit.* 'entering into..offering (*lit.* a thing borne forward), thou didst not wish, but a body thou didst thoroughly complete to me.' See Ps. 40. 6 where the Hebrew is: 'Ears thou hast prepared for me,' i.e. thou hast prepared for me the means of '*hearing*' thy law, and of course, of *doing* it, which he could not have done (for man) without a bodily organization. The Psalmist specially instances the 'ears,' which Paul (following the Septuagint) amplifies (quite correctly) into the whole '*body*.' Elsewhere Paul does the very reverse of what he does here; he reduces the Psalmist's: 'a little lower than God,' into a 'little lower than the angels:' see 2. 7. Both statements are true.

6. BURNT-OFFERINGS,] *Gr.* holocausts, i.e. 'about whole burnt-offerings and sin-offerings thou didst not think well.'

7. LO,] *or* 'behold, I am come (in the volume, *lit.* head of the Roll (of Psalms) it has been written concerning me).'

8. WHEN,] *lit.* 'saying, that Sacrifice..and whole burnt-offerings..thou didst not wish, nor think well of, which are brought forward according to the law.'

9. LO,] *or* 'behold, I am come .he lifts up the first, that he may set down the second.'

10. BY,] *lit.* 'in the which will we are hallowed persons..once for all.'

11. STANDETH,] *lit.* 'has stood every day a public worker, and bearing forward many times the same sacrifices, which are at no time able perfectly to lift up sins.'

12. MAN,] *lit.* 'this one, having borne forward one sacrifice in behalf of sins to the full continuity, sat down at (*lit.* in) the right-hand of God.'

13. FROM HENCEFORTH,] *lit.* 'as to the thing left over *or* behind fully-receiving till his enemies may be set (as the) footstool of his feet.'

14. FOR EVER,] *lit.* 'to the full continuity those being hallowed.'

15. WHEREOF,] *lit.* 'and the Holy Spirit doth witness also to us, for after that said before.'

16. MAKE,] *lit.* 'I will covenant towards them..Giving my laws upon their hearts, and upon their full-minds will I write them fully.'

17. INIQUITIES,] *lit.* 'their lawless acts.'

18. NOW,] *or* 'and where a sending-away.'

19. BOLDNESS,] *or* 'full speech in reference to the entrance of the hallowed places in the blood.'

20. NEW,] *or* 'recent, *or* shining.'

HAS,] *lit.* 'did make inwardly new to us, through the thoroughly-extended vail, that is, of his flesh.'

21. HIGH,] *lit.* 'great priest.'

22. DRAW NEAR,] *lit.* 'come forward..full-bearing of faith, having the heart sprinkled from (*or* because of) an evil conscience, and the body washed with clean water.'

23. PROFESSION,] *Gr.* homologation, i.e. confession, speaking the 'same word.'

OF FAITH,] *lit.* 'of the hope.'

WITHOUT WAVERING,] *lit.* 'un-inclined.. is steady.'

24. CONSIDER,] *or* 'know one another thoroughly, with a view to a paroxysm (*lit.* over-sharpness) of love and good works.'

25. FORSAKING,] *lit.* 'leaving thoroughly the full-synagogue of ourselves ..behold the day drawing nigh,' when Jerusalem would be destroyed.

26. IF,] *lit.* 'for we yieldingly not attaining (the mark) after the receiving the full-knowledge..is left over no longer a sacrifice for sins.'

27. LOOKING FOR,] *lit.* 'full-reception.'

INDIGNATION,] *or* 'zeal, about to eat up the opposers.'

28. HE,] *lit.* 'any one having put aside a law of Moses, dies, apart from mercies, upon (the testimony of) two or three witnesses.'

29. WORSE PUNISHMENT,] *lit.* 'seeing of weight,(honour,*or* vengeance),think ye,shall he be reckoned worthy who trampled down the Son of God, and esteemed for himself (as) common the blood of the covenant in which he was hallowed, and insulted the Spirit of the grace.'

30. KNOW,] *lit.* 'have known him who said, Full-justice is for me, I will give back again.'

31. THE,] *lit.* 'into hands of a living God.'

32. CALL,] *lit.* 'be calling to remembrance of yourselves..which, having been enlightened, ye remained under a great (*or* heavy) contest of sufferings.'

33. PARTLY,] *lit.* 'this, indeed, being made theatrical exhibitions, both with reproaches and tribulations, and this, having become sharers *or* partners of those being so turned round again.'

34. FOR,] *lit.* 'for ye also suffered with (me) in my bonds, and the robbery *or* seizure of your substance ye received forward for yourselves with joy, knowing (your) having to yourselves in the heavens a better substance and an abiding one.'

35. CAST,] *lit.* 'may ye not cast away then, your full-speech.'

36. AFTER,] *lit.* 'having done..may bring to yourselves the promised thing.'

37. A LITTLE,] *lit.* 'a very very little, He who is coming will come and will not make *or* spend time.'

38. JUST,] *or* 'righteous one out of (*or* from) faith shall live, but if he send himself back (*lit.* under), my soul has no good-thought in him.'

39. WE,] *lit.* 'but we, we are not of a sending-ourselves back to a full-loss, but of faith to a thorough making of soul.'

Chapter XI. may be divided into seven parts; v. 1—3 description of faith; v. 4—7 in Abel, Enoch, Noah; v. 8—19 Abraham and Sarah; v. 20—22 Isaac, Jacob, Joseph; v. 23—28 Moses; v. 29—31 Israel; v. 32—40 and many others.

1. SUBSTANCE,] *lit.* 'under-standing, i.e. basis, *or* sure confidence.

THE EVIDENCE,] *lit.* 'a conviction..not beheld.'

2. BY IT,] *lit.* 'in this the elders were witnessed to *or* testified of.'

3. THROUGH,] *or* 'by faith we understand the ages to have been made thoroughly perfect by a saying of God, in reference to the things beheld not having come of things manifesting themselves.'

4. OFFERED,] *lit.* 'bore forward a ..through which he was testified to be just..concerning his..through it he having died fully, yet speaks,' *or* is spoken of.

ABEL,] i.e. 'vanity.'

CAIN,] i.e. 'acquisition.'

5. ENOCH,] i.e. 'initiated, dedicated.'

TRANSLATED,] *lit.* 'put over'—not to see (i.e. experience) death..God put him over, for before his (being) putting over he has been testified to, to have been well-pleasing to God.'

6. WITHOUT,] *lit.* 'apart from..to be well-pleasing,for he that is coming forward to God it behoves to believe..he becomes a recompenser of reward to those seeking him out.'

7. BEING,] *lit.* 'having been divinely-warned concerning the things not yet beheld, having received it well, made an ark thoroughly ready with a view to (the) salvation of his house, through which he judged-down the world, and of the righteousness according to faith he became heir,' *or* inheritor, *lit.* 'one who receives a distribution by lot.

8. WHEN,] *lit.* 'being called to go forth to the place which he was about to receive for inheritance, hearkened submissively, and went forth, not fully knowing where he goes

9. SOJOURNED,] *lit.* 'housed-near to the land of the promise as a stranger place, having housed-wholly in tabernacles..joint-heirs,' *or* inheritors.

10. LOOKED,] *lit.* 'was expecting the city having the foundations, whose artificer and public-worker is God.'

11. THROUGH,] *lit.* 'by faith..power for a casting-down of seed, and bore (a child) much beyond (the due) season; seeing she reckoned him stedfast who promised.'

12. SPRANG,] *lit.* 'there were begotten even of one, and that of one having become dead ..along the lip of the sea—the innumerable.'

13. IN,] *lit.* 'according to *or* through faith, not having received the things promised, but..from afar, and having been persuaded *or* confident, and having drawn (them) near

and having confessed (*Gr.* homologated), that *or* because they are strangers and pilgrims,' (*lit.* those 'near upon a people').

14. THEY,] *lit.* 'those saying such things make (it) inwardly-manifest that they seek after a fatherland.'

15. TRULY,] *lit.* 'and if, indeed, they were mindful of that from which they came forth, they would have had a season to bend back again.'

16. DESIRE,] *lit.* 'stretch out the arms for themselves for a better..ashamed of them, to be called of (them) their God, for he made ready a city to them.'

17. WHEN,] *lit.* 'being tried, has borne Isaac forward, and he who received back to himself the promises bore forward the only-begotten one,' i.e. Isaac.

18. OF,] *lit.* 'in reference to whom..that, In Isaac shall a seed be called to thee.'

19. ACCOUNTING,] *or* 'reasoning that even out of (the) dead God is able to raise (him), whence also he himself brought him in a parable,' i.e. simile, *lit.* a 'thing laid alongside' of another.

20. TO COME,] *lit.* 'about to be.'

21. BOTH,] *lit.* 'each of the sons.'

WORSHIPPED,] *lit.* 'kissed forward (the hand), upon the point of his rod.'

22. WHEN HE DIED,] *lit.* 'ending (his life) made mention concerning the out-going of the sons..and gave a precept for himself concerning his bones.'

23. HID,] *or* 'concealed..under his parents, because they saw the boy comely, and they did not fear the different-arrangement of the king.'

24. WHEN,] *lit.* 'having become great, refused for himself to be called Son of (the) daughter of Pharaoh.'

25. CHOOSING,] *lit.* 'lifting up for himself rather to have evil along with..to have an enjoyment of sin for a season.'

26. ESTEEMING,] *or* 'reckoning for himself the reproach of the Christ (i.e. the anointed one) greater wealth..for he looked from (these) to the recompence of reward.'

27. FORSOOK,] *lit.* 'left Egypt thoroughly ..for he strengthened himself as seeing the Unseen One.'

28. THROUGH,] *lit.* 'by faith he has made the passover, and the pouring forth of the blood..first-born (of man and cattle) might touch them.'

29. PASSED,] *or* 'went..through dry land, which the Egyptians having received (*or* accepted the) temptation, were drunk down,' i.e. swallowed up.

30. AFTER,] *lit.* 'having been encircled during.'

31. HARLOT,] *or* 'fornicatress,' *lit.* one who 'sells' herself.

PERISHED,] *lit.* 'destroyed not herself with the untrustful..spies (*lit.* thorough-viewers) with peace.'

32. MORE,] *lit.* 'yet say? for the time will leave me fully, leading through concerning Gideon, Barak also, and Samson, and Jephthah, David also, and Samuel, and the prophets.'

33 SUBDUED,] *lit.* 'agonized against kingdoms, they worked out for themselves righteousness, openly obtained promised things, shut (*lit.* hedged in) mouths of lions.'

34. VIOLENCE,] *lit.* 'power.. escaped mouths of (the) sword, from strengthlessness were made inwardly powerful, became strong in battle, caused camps of strangers (*or* aliens) to give way.'

35. RAISED TO LIFE AGAIN,] *lit.* 'out of (*or* from) an upstanding.'

AND,] *lit.* 'but.'

TORTURED,] *lit.* 'struck (to death) with clubs, not receiving to them the loosing-away ..better upstanding.'

36. HAD,] *lit.* 'received a temptation of.'

37. SAWN,] *lit.* 'cut asunder, they were tempted, they died away in (the) slaughter of (the) sword, they went about in. being behind, troubled, suffering evil.'

38. WANDERED,] *lit.* 'they were being led astray in.'

39. OBTAINED,] *lit.* 'having been testified to through the faith received not to themselves the promised thing.'

40. PROVIDED,] *lit.* 'beheld beforehand something better concerning us, that they might not be perfected apart from us.'

Chapter XII. may be divided into six parts; v. 1—3 exhortation to run the contest from the sight and consideration of Jesus; v. 4—11 the loving chastisement of God; v. 12—17 renewed exhortations to perseverance, peace, separation, watchfulness; v. 18—21 terrors of the old-law-giving; v. 22—24 happiness of the new; v. 25—29 prayer for grace not to refuse to hear the voice from heaven.

1. SEEING,] *lit.* 'we also having so great a cloud of witnesses (i.e. testimony-bearers) laid (*or* set) around us, every weight (*or* swelling, pride) putting off, and the easily-set-around sin, may we run through endurance the contest (*Gr.* agony) laid before us.'

2. LOOKING,] *lit.* 'looking away to Jesus the chief-leader and perfector of the faith, who, on account of the joy laid before him, remained under a cross, having thought-down shame, and has sat down.'

3. CONSIDER,] *lit.* 'reason back for yourselves (concerning) him who has remained submissively under such contradiction (*or* gainsaying) of the sinful in reference to himself, that, being loosed out, ye may not be wearied.'

4. HAVE,] *lit.* 'did not yet stand fully in opposition—unto blood, agonizing (i.e. contending) with the sin,'—of apostacy.

5. FORGOTTEN,] *lit.* 'been utterly hid from the exhortation (*or* comfort, *lit.* calling alongside), which speaks thoroughly to you as to sons: My son, be not caring little for (the) instruction of the Lord, nor be loosed out, being convicted by (*lit.* under) him.'

6. CHASTENETH,] *or* 'instructeth..receiveth alongside (of himself).'

7. ENDURE,] *lit.* 'remain under instruction God bears forward to you as to sons.'

8. BE WITHOUT,] *lit.* 'are apart from instruction, of which all have become sharers *or* partakers.'

9. FURTHERMORE,] *lit.* 'then, indeed, we were having the fathers of our flesh (as) instructors, and we were turning in for ourselves, shall we not rather be arranging ourselves under the Fathers of the spirits, and we shall live?'

10. VERILY,] *lit.* 'indeed, with reference to a few days according to what appeared to them, were instructing, but He, over the full-bearing, with a view to the partaking of his holiness,' *lit.* un-earthliness.

11. NOW,] *or* 'but no instruction, indeed, with reference to the present seems to be matter of joy, but of sorrow, but at last it giveth back the peaceable fruit of righteousness to those having been exercised (*lit.* naked) through it.'

12. LIFT UP,] *lit.* 'make right again the laid-aside hands and the loosed-aside knees.'

13. STRAIGHT,] *or* 'right roads (*lit.* running-places) to your feet, that the lame (in faith) may not be turned-out, but rather healed.'

14. FOLLOW,] *lit.* 'pursue..and the separation, apart from which no one.'

15. LOOKING DILIGENTLY,] *lit.* 'acting as overseers (i.e. bishops) that no one being behind of (*lit.* from) the grace of God—that no root of bitterness springing up—may crowd in, and through this many be defiled.'

16. LEST,] *lit.* 'that no one (being) a whoremonger, or a common (minded) person, as Esau, who in exchange for one meal gave away for himself his first-born-ship.'

17. HOW THAT,] *lit.* 'that even after this, wishing to receive by lot the good-word, he was thoroughly disapproved of, for he found no place for a change of mind (in his father), even though he sought it out with tears.'

18. ARE NOT COME,] *lit.* 'did not come forward (when ye first believed) to a mount.. and burnt with fire, and a thick cloud, and darkness, and a rushing wind.'

19. THE,] *lit.* 'and a trumpet's sound, and a voice of sayings, which they who heard asked off for themselves that a word be not put forward to them.'

20. COULD,] *lit.* 'were not bearing what was sent through (the camp): And if a beast may touch..or shot down with a missile.'

21. TERRIBLE,] *or* 'fearful was that being made apparent..I am greatly fearing and trembling inwardly.'

22. ARE COME,] *lit.* 'came forward to..a city of a living God, a heavenly Jerusalem, and to myriads—of messengers a full collection, and to an assembly of first-born ones, having written themselves away among heavenly ones, and to God, judge of all, and to spirits of just ones, having been perfected,' *or* 'having perfected themselves,'—by faith.

24. THE,] *lit.* 'a middleman of a new (*or* fresh) covenant, and to blood..speaking better things than Abel'—spake of in his sacrifice.

25. SEE,] *or* 'behold, may ye not be asking off from him who is speaking, for if these fled not who asked off from themselves him who upon the earth (*or* land) was divinely-speaking, much more we turning away round for ourselves from him who (is) from heaven.'

26. ONCE MORE,] *lit.* 'once for all..the heaven.'

27. ONCE MORE,] *lit.* 'yet once for all, evidences the change (*lit.* placing-over) of the things shaken as of things made, that the things not being shaken may remain.'

28. WHICH,] *lit.* 'unshaken, may we have grace (*or* joy), through which we may go very tremblingly well-pleasing to God with modesty (*lit.* un-seen-ness) and good reception,' *or* acceptance.

29. FOR,] *lit.* 'for even (*or* also) our God is a thoroughly consuming fire,'—purging his people, and punishing his enemies.

Chapter XIII. may be divided into four parts; v. 1—6 brotherly and personal duties; v. 7—16 remembrance of leaders, and imitation of Christ; v. 17—19 also trustfulness, yieldingness, prayer; v. 20—25 concluding prayer, and praise, entreaty, information and salutation.

1. LET,] *lit.* 'let the brotherly friendship remain.'

2. TO,] *lit.* 'about the stranger's friendship, for through this certain receiving strangers (received) messengers unawares,' *lit.* lain hid.

3. REMEMBER,] *lit.* 'be mindful of those bound, as being justly bound, of those having (i.e. receiving) evil.'

4. MARRIAGE,] *lit.* 'let the marriage-state be honourable, (*lit.* weighty), and let the bed.'

5. CONVERSATION,] *lit.* 'turning round about (i.e. behaviour) without the love (*or* friendship) of money, being sufficed with the things present (*lit.* being alongside), for he has said, No, I may not send thee back, no, nor may I leave thee thoroughly.'

6. MAY,] *lit.* 'are bold to say, The Lord is to me a helper.'

7. REMEMBER,] *lit.* 'be mindful of those leading you on, who spake..be imitating, beholding again (*or* looking up to) the outcoming of the behaviour,' *lit.* turning round again.

8. THE SAME,] *or* 'is the same,' in his doctrine, person, and character.

9. CARRIED ABOUT,] *or* 'borne aside by manifold and strange teachings, for it is good (*or* right) for the heart to be confirmed with grace..in which they who walked about did not profit.'

10. ALTAR,] *or* 'place of sacrifice.. authority.. are serving,' *lit.* 'going very tremblingly.'

11. FOR,] *lit.* 'for of those animals whose blood is borne in for sin to the hallowed places through the chief-priest—of these the bodies are thoroughly burned without the camp.'

12. SANCTIFY,] *or* 'hallow *or* set apart the people through.'

13. LET,] *lit.* 'now, then, may we go forth towards him.'

14. CONTINUING,] *lit.* 'remaining city, but we seek after the one about to be.'

15. BY,] *lit.* 'through him, therefore, may

we bear up a sacrifice of praise through all (time), to God, that is, fruit of lips (i.e. words) confessing *or* homologating his name.'

16. TO DO,] *lit.* 'but of well-doing and communion (*or* fellowship) be not forgetful.'

17. OBEY,] *lit.* 'have confidence in those leading you, and yield somewhat, for they are wakeful in behalf of your souls, as those giving back an account..do this..not constrained.'

18. PRAY,] *lit.* 'be pouring forth in our behalf, for we have been confident for ourselves, that we have..wishing to behave (*or* turn round) ourselves well.'

19. BESEECH,] *or* 'call alongside (of you) the more abundantly to do this, that I may be set thoroughly away to you the more speedily.'

20. PEACE,] *lit.* 'the peace, who led up out of the dead..the great..in (the) blood of an age-during covenant.'

21. MAKE,] *or* 'to make you thoroughly complete in every good work, with a view to do his will, doing in (*or* among) you that which is well-pleasing before him..is the glory to the ages of the ages. Amen.'

22. BESEECH,] *lit.* 'call upon you, brethren, be holding up the word of the exhortation, for I wrote a letter to you through few (words).'

23. OUR,] *lit.* 'the brother Timotheus has been loosed away..speedily.'

24. SALUTE,] *lit.* 'draw near all those leading you, and all the hallowed ones; they of (*lit.* from) Italy draw you near.'

25. GRACE,] *lit.* 'the grace is with you all. Amen.'

JAMES' LETTER TO THE TWELVE TRIBES

The author of this Letter was probably son of Alphaeus or Cleopas, surnamed 'the less,' and 'the just,' and 'the Lord's brother;' after the murder of James the son of Zebedee, he appears to have been foremost in Jerusalem, where he was martyred A.D. 68. This Letter (written about A.D. 67) has always formed a part of the Syriac Peshito Version, (which omits 2d Peter, 2d and 3d John, Jude and Revelation, executed before A.D. 200), and is found in all complete MSS. of the Greek Testament. It is quoted or referred to by Clement of Rome (A.D. 108), Hermas (A.D. 108), Origen (A.D. 230), Irenaeus (A.D. 178), Clement of Alexandria (A.D. 194), &c., but none of the Latin fathers before A.D. 300 quote it.

It is an address by a Jewish believer, chiefly to his fellow-believers in Christ belonging to what is here called 'the Twelve Tribes,' because remnants from each of these had mingled themselves with those of the two tribes, who had returned from Babylon. By the time this Letter was written hundreds of thousands of Jews had embraced the gospel, but the zeal of the unbelieving Jews and the practical errors of the Gnostics and Judaising false brethren rendered his position important and perilous, hence the pre-eminently practical character of his teaching in cautions, censures, and exhortations.

It may be divided into three parts; *first*, ch. 1. 1—27; *second*, ch. 2. 1—5. 6; and *thirdly*, ch. 5. 7—20.

Chapter I. may be divided into seven parts; v. 1 introductory salutations; v. 2—8 call to rejoice because of trials, to ask of God unwaveringly; v. 9—12 exhortation to the low, the rich, and the tried; v. 13—15 whence temptations; v. 16—18 and every perfect gift come; v. 19—25 to be doers not hearers only; v. 26, 27 vain and true religion.

1. JAMES,] *Gr.* Jacob, i.e. 'one who takes by the heel.'

SERVANT,] *lit.* 'bondsman.'

TWELVE TRIBES] of Israel, as in Acts 26. 7; the S S. no where recognizes the modern notion of 'the ten tribes' being 'lost,' the N.T. name 'Jews,' or 'Israelites,' including the whole of the 'seed of Jacob.'

WHICH,] *lit.* 'who are in the dispersion,' in different lands, whether of a voluntary or of an involuntary nature, by war, commerce, or pleasure.

GREETING,] *lit.* 'to hail!' 'to rejoice!'

2. COUNT,] *lit.* 'count it for yourselves.. may fall around manifold trials.'

3. TRYING,] *or* 'proof..thoroughly worketh endurance,' *lit.* a 'remaining under.'

4. PATIENCE,] *lit.* 'the endurance have a perfect work..and whole-loted, being left behind in nothing.'

5. IF,] *lit.* 'but if any one of you be left behind in wisdom, let him ask from God, who is giving to all simply (*or* with simplicity) and is not reproaching.'

6. WAVERING,] *lit.* 'judging differently, for he who is judging differently has been like (*or* yielded) for himself to a wave (*lit.* washer) of a sea driven by a wind and tossed.'

7. OF,] *lit.* 'from the Lord.'

8. A DOUBLE-MINDED,] *lit.* 'a two-souled man, (he is) not set down in any of his ways.'

9. OF LOW DEGREE,] *lit.* 'who is low boast in his exaltation.'

10. RICH,] *or* 'wealthy in his becoming low, because as a flower of grass he shall go along.'

11. IS,] *lit.* 'sun rose up with the burning hot-wind, and it dried up the grass..falleth off, and the comeliness of its presence (*lit.* face) fell off for itself..be faded in his ways.'

12. BLESSED,] *lit.* 'happy is a man who remaineth under trial, because, becoming approved . . of the life which the Lord promised for himself to those loving him.'

13. MAN,] *lit.* 'no one say, being tempted (*lit.* tried, i.e. with evil), that, I am tempted from God, for God is untempt (*or* untried) of evils, and Himself tempts no one.'

14. EVERY MAN,] *or* 'each one is tempted, being drawn out from his own over-desires and bribed by himself.'

15. THEN,] *or* 'afterwards, the over-desire having taken (it) together, beareth sin, and the sin having been fully ended begetteth death.'

16. DO NOT ERR,] *or* 'be not led astray.'

17. GOOD GIFT,] *or* 'giving..of the lights, alongside of whom there is not one change or even shadow of turning.'

18. OF HIS OWN WILL,] *lit.* 'having taken counsel he begat us with a word of truth, with a view to our being a certain first-fruit of his creatures,' or formations.

19. WHEREFORE,] *lit.* 'so that..speedy, with a view to the hearing, heavy to the speaking, heavy to anger.'

20. THE WRATH,] *lit.* 'for anger of man doth not work out at all (the) righteousness of God.'

21. LAY APART,] *lit.* 'having put away for yourselves all..abundance of evil, and receive to yourselves in meekness the engrafted (*or* implanted) word.'

22. BE,] *lit.* 'become ye..reckoning *or* reasoning to yourselves amiss.'

23. FOR,] *lit.* 'because if any one is a hearer ..he was like..considering fully the face of his birth.'

24. BEHOLDETH,] *lit.* 'considered himself fully and went away..forgot for himself of what sort he was.'

25. WHOSO LOOKETH,] *lit.* 'he who bent

along with a view to..the liberty, and remained alongside, he becoming not..a doer of work, he shall be happy in his doing.'

26. MAN,] *lit.* 'any one among you thinks himself..not leading his tongue by a bridle.'

27. BEFORE,] *or* 'alongside of *or* with the God and Father is this: To over-look orphans and bereaved ones in their tribulation.'

Chapter II. may be divided into six parts; v. 1—4 exhortation against respect of persons; v. 5—7 from the doings of God and of the rich; v. 8—13 also from the royal law; v. 14—19 faith without works unprofitable and dead; v. 20—23 contrasted with that of Abraham; v. 24—26 and of Rahab.

1. WITH,] *lit.* 'in acceptances of faces.'

2. COME,] *lit.* 'may come to your synagogue a man with a gold-ring, in shining apparel, and there may come in.'

3. HAVE RESPECT,] *lit.* 'may look upon him bearing the shining apparel, and may say to him, Thou—be thou seated here well, and may say..Thou—stand thou there, or be seated here.'

4. ARE YE,] *lit.* 'and were ye not judged diversely (*or* thoroughly) among (*or* in) yourselves, and became judges of (i.e. with) evil reasonings.'

5. HEARKEN,] *or* 'give ear..Did not God lay out for himself..he promised for himself to those loving him.'

6. HAVE,] *lit.* 'ye dishonoured the poor one; do not the rich use power against you, and themselves drag you to places of judgment?'

7. THEY,] *lit.* 'they themselves speak injuriously of that right (*or* good) name which was called over upon you.'

8. IF,] *lit.* 'if indeed, then, ye fulfil (*lit.* end) a kingly law.'

9. HAVE,] *lit.* 'ye accept faces, ye work sin, being convicted under.'

10. OFFEND,] *lit.* 'stumble in one, he has become held-in of all.'

11. DO,] *lit.* 'thou mayest not..Thou mayest not kill, but if thou shalt..but shall kill, thou hast become a transgressor of law.'

12. THEY,] *lit.* 'as being about to be judged through a law of freedom.'

13. FOR,] *lit.* 'for the judgment without-kindness (is) to him not doing kindness, and kindness boasts against judgment.'

14. WHAT,] *lit.* 'what is the profit..if any one may speak of having faith, but may have no works? is the faith (alone) able to save him?'

15. IF,] *lit.* 'but if..begin to be naked, and may be lacking of the daily nourishment.'

16. ONE,] *lit.* 'any one of you may say, Go away (*or* quietly) in peace..but may not give to them the very-sweet (*or* soothing) things of the body; what is the profit?'

17. EVEN,] *or* 'so also the faith (of such a one), if it may have no works, is dead by itself.'

18. YEA,] *lit.* 'but some one may say..out of (i.e. from) thy works..out of (i.e. from) my works.'

19. THERE IS,] *lit.* 'that God is One..the demons..shudder.'

20. WILT,] *lit.* 'dost thou wish to know.. the faith apart from the works.'

21. JUSTIFIED,] *or* 'declared righteous out of (i.e. from) works, having borne up.'

22. SEEST THOU,] *or* 'thou seest that the faith was working with his works, and out of (i.e. from) the works the faith was perfected.'

23. SCRIPTURE,] *lit.* 'writing, that is saying, And Abraham believed (i.e. remained stedfast to) God, and it was reckoned to him with a view to righteousness, and he was called Friend of God.'

24. YE SEE,] *or* 'see ye, then, that out of works is man justified, and not out of faith alone,' *or* only.

25. BY,] *lit.* 'out of (i.e. from) works, having secretly received the messengers (*Gr.* angels), and cast them forth by another way.'

26. WITHOUT,] *lit.* 'apart from..the faith apart from the works.'

Chapter III. may be divided into three parts; v. 1—6 warning against becoming teachers and talkative; v. 7—12 because of the power of the tongue; v. 13—18 heavenly and earthly wisdom.

1. BE,] *lit.* 'become not many masters, having known..a greater judgment.'

2. FOR,] *lit.* 'for we all stumble many times; if any one stumbles..he is.'

3. PUT,] *lit.* 'cast bridles into..for their obeying us, we lead on.'

4. SHIPS,] *lit.* 'sailing vessels, being so great, and driven by hard winds, are led on under the smallest rudder, wheresoever the impulse of the leader (*lit.* straightener) counsels.'

5. GREAT THINGS,] *or* 'greatly; behold, a little fire how much wood it lights up.'

6. AND,] *lit.* 'and the tongues, the world of the unrighteous (is) a fire, thus the tongue, which is spotting the whole body, and inflaming the running of the birth (origen, descent), and is inflamed by the gehenna, is set down among our members.'

7. KIND,] *lit.* 'nature, both of wild beasts and of flying creatures, both of creeping creatures, and of those in the salt waters.. tamed by the human nature.'

8. CAN,] *lit.* 'is no one of men able to tame,' *or* 'of men is no one able to tame, an un-held-down evil, full of death-bearing poison.'

9. THEREWITH,] *lit.* 'in it we speak well of the God and Father, and in it we curse for ourselves the men who have been made in the likeness of God.'

10. THE SAME,] *lit.* 'his mouth cometh good-speech..need not so to be.'

11. A,] *lit.* 'the fountain out of its opening gush forth the sweet and the bitter.'

12. CAN,] *lit.* 'is a..able to make olive-fruit..fountain make salt and sweet water.

13. A WISE MAN,] *lit.* 'is wise and intelligent..the good behaviour (*lit.* turning round up and down)..in meekness of wisdom.'

14. ENVY,] *lit.* 'zeal..boast not at all, and be (not) lying.'

DESCENDETH,] *lit.* 'is not coming down from above, but is earthly (*lit.* upon earth), sensual, (*lit.* physical, natural-like,) demon-like.'

16. ENVY,] *lit.* 'zeal..is un-settled-downness and every foul work.'

17. WISDOM,] *lit.* 'wisdom from above is first, indeed, pure, then peaceable, very yielding, easily persuaded, full of kindness, and good fruits, without judging diversely, and unhypocritical.'

18. THE,] *lit.* 'and fruit of the righteousness..to those making peace.'

Chapter IV. may be divided into four parts; v. 1—5 warning against wars and worldly friendship; v. 6—10 pride and impurity; v. 11, 12 judging a brother; v. 13—16 reckoning on the future.

1. COME,] *or* 'are wars..among (*or* in) you ..your pleasures that are (as) soldiers in your members?'

2. LUST,] *or* 'desire fully..kill (inwardly) and are zealous, and are not able to obtain fully, but..of your not asking.'

3. YE ASK,] *or* 'ask ye and receive not, because ye are asking evilly for yourselves, that ye may spend it in your pleasures.'

4. YE ADULTERERS.] Some MSS. omit.

KNOW,] *lit.* 'have ye not known..with (*lit.* of) God..may counsel to be a friend of the world is set (*or* sets himself) down an enemy of God.'

5. SAITH,] *or* 'speaketh emptily? Did the Spirit that dwelt in us desire fully towards envy?' *or* withering.

6. MORE,] *or* 'greater..God arranges himself against over appearing ones, but to lowly ones he gives grace,' *lit.* cause of leaping for joy.

7. SUBMIT,] *lit.* 'be arranged (*or* arrange yourselves) under God; stand against the Devil.'

8. DOUBLE-MINDED,] *lit.* 'double-souled.'

9. BE AFFLICTED,] *lit.* 'sustain affliction and suffer..turned round again to affliction, and the joy to a down-cast eye.'

10. HUMBLE YOURSELVES,] *lit.* 'be low before the Lord.'

11. EVIL,] *lit.* 'be not speaking against one another, brethren, he who is speaking against a brother, and judging his brother, speaks against law, and judges law, but if thou judgest law, thou art not a doer of law.'

12. THERE IS,] *lit.* 'the law-giver (*lit.* law-placer) is One; thou—who art thou who judgest the other?'

13. GO TO,] *or* 'come on, now, ye who are saying, To-day and to-morrow we may go on for ourselves to that city, and make (i.e. use) one year there, and go on in (it), and make gain.'

14. WHEREAS,] *lit.* 'ye who know not at all the thing of the morrow, for of what kind is your life? for it is a vapour which is apparent for a little, and afterwards is not apparent.'

15. FOR,] *lit.* 'instead of your saying, If the Lord may will *or* wish, and we may live, and may do this or that.'

16. REJOICE,] *lit.* 'boast in your assumptions; every such boast is evil.'

17. KNOWEST,] *lit.* 'knowing..and not doing.'

Chapter V. may be divided into seven parts; v. 1—6 warnings for the rich; v. 7—9 exhortation to patience; v. 10, 11 from the example of Job; v. 12 against swearing; v. 13—15 directions for the suffering and the joyful; v. 16—18 mutual confessions and power of prayer; v. 19, 20 value of a straying one.

1. GO TO,] *lit.* 'come on now, ye rich, weep ye, howling over your sustaining of afflictions that are coming over (you).'

2. RICHES,] *or* 'wealth has corrupted itself..have become moth-consumed.'

3. IS CANKERED,] *lit.* 'has been thoroughly rusted..to you..as fire..ye treasured (it) up in the last days,'—of Judaism.

4. LABOURERS,] *lit.* 'workers who mowed your fields (*or* places), which has been unsettled (*lit.* un-confirmed) by you cries, and the loud cries of those who reaped have gone for themselves.'

5. YE HAVE,] *lit.* 'ye luxuriated upon the earth and adorned yourselves, ye nourished.'

6. HAVE,] *lit.* 'ye judged down, ye murdered the righteous one; he does not array himself in opposition to you.'

7. PATIENT,] *or* 'long-suffering..presence of..earth-worker receives fully the weighty (*or* honourable) fruit of the earth, being long-suffering over it, till it may receive rain—early and latter.'

8. PATIENT,] *lit.* 'long-suffering, confirm your hearts, because the presence of the Lord has drawn nigh,'—the Roman armies beginning to encompass Jerusalem.

9. GRUDGE,] *lit.* 'be not constrained against one another, brethren, that ye may not be judged down; behold, the Judge has stood before the doors.'

10. TAKE,] *or* 'receive..who spake..as an under-exhibition of the suffering of evils, and of the long-suffering.'

11. COUNT,] *or* 'declare those remaining under (trial) happy; ye heard of the endurance..very pitiful (*lit.* has many bowels) and of tender mercies.'

12. ABOVE,] *lit.* 'before all things..be not swearing, neither by the heaven, neither by the earth,..no, no, that ye may not fall under judgment.'

13. ANY,] *lit.* 'doth any one among you suffer evil? let him be pouring forth before (God); has any one a good-mind? let him psalm,' (i.e. play the psaltery).

14. ANY,] *lit.* 'is any one strengthless among you? let him call forward the elders (*Gr.* presbyters) of the assembly, and let them pour forth for themselves before (God) over him, having anointed him.'

15. PRAYER,] *lit.* 'pouring forth of the faith shall save the labouring (*or* tried one), and the Lord shall raise him, and if he may have committed sins, they shall be let go to him.'

16. CONFESS,] *lit.* 'be confessing for yourselves the fallings-aside to one another, and

be pouring forth in behalf of one another, so that ye may be healed; a supplication of a righteous one is very strong, working in for itself.'

17. SUBJECT,] *lit.* 'like-passioned to us, and with pouring forth he poured forth before (God) for himself—not to rain, and it rained not upon the land three years and six months.'

18. AND,] *lit.* 'and again he poured forth before (God) for himself..land sprouted up her fruit.'

19. ANY,] *lit.* 'any one among you may go astray..any one may turn him round about.'

20. CONVERTETH,] *lit.* 'who turned a sinner round about, out of the straying of his way, shall save a soul out of death, and shall cover a multitude of sins,' i.e. 'missings' of the mark on the part of the person converted.

GENERAL LETTER OF PETER
(THE FIRST)

PETER, originally called Simon (*or* Symeon), was son of Jonas, and brother of Andrew, who first brought him to Jesus, when he received the name Peter or Cephas, i.e. 'a (man-of-the) rock,' on account of his determination. He was a fisherman in Bethsaida or Capernaum, with a wife, whose mother was healed by Jesus. His forward outspoken character procured him the foremost place among the apostles, and led him into many stumbles. The last intimation we have of him, is that he resided at Babylon (on the Euphrates, though some absurdly enough explain it as Rome), whence he addressed his believing Jewish brethren in Asia Minor, A.D. 66. His object in this (first) Letter is to comfort, prepare, and exhort them to stand fast under trials, and so to discharge their relative duties to each other, that the gainsayer may be won; his style is earnest and practical, and 'glory' and 'hope' are pre-eminent; he seems acquainted with James' Epistle, and his language here is very similar to his own speeches in the 'Acts.'

It is quoted or referred to by Polycarp (A.D. 108), Papias (A.D. 116), Irenaeus (A.D. 178), Theophilus (A.D. 181), Clement of Alexandria (A.D. 194), Origen (A.D. 230), Tertullian (A.D. 200). It is found in the Syriac Peshito Version, but is wanting in Muratori's Canon.

There appear to be allusions in this Letter to Ge. 6. 7; 18. 12; Exod. 19. 5, 6; De. 7. 6; Isa 10. 12; 28. 16; 40. 6—8; 48. 8, 9; 53. 57. 15; 61. 6; Jer. 23. 22; Ezek. 9. 6; 19. 5, 6; 34. 4; Da. 2. 44; 8. 13; 9. 26; Hos. 1. 9, 10; Hag. 2. 7; Zec. 13. 9.

Chapter I. may be divided into seven parts; v. 1, 2 address and salutation; v. 3—5 thanksgiving to God for his kindness; v. 6—9 joy in trials; v. 10—12 searching of prophets; v. 13—17 call to hope, obedience, holiness, fear; v. 18—21 redemption through blood of believers; v. 22—26 call to love, being begotten through God's word.

1. PETER,] i.e. a 'rock-man,' *or* 'rock-like man.'

APOSTLE,] *lit.* one 'sent forth.'

JESUS CHRIST,] i.e. an 'anointed saviour.'

STRANGERS,] *lit.* 'to elect (*or* select, choice, excellent) ones, to sojourners of the dispersion (Jo. 7. 35; Jas. 1. 1) of Pontus,' &c.

PONTUS,] on the Euxine, north of Cappadocia.

GALATIA,] west of the river Halys, in the interior of Asia Minor, south of Bithynia.

CAPPADOCIA,] separated from Phrygia by the Halys.

ASIA,] i.e. proconsular Asia.

BITHYNIA,] north of Phrygia and Galatia.

2. ELECT,] i.e. elect strangers *or* sojourners

ACCORDING TO.] Cyril, Ecumenius, Theophylact, &c., all connect this phrase with 'an apostle,' i.e. 'Peter, an apostle according to a fore-knowledge;' comparing 2 Tim. 1. 1; Tit. 1. 4.

FORE-KNOWLEDGE,] *or* 'public recognition.'

THROUGH,] *lit.* 'in sanctification of spirit, with a view to a submissive hearkening and a sprinkling of.'

GRACE,] *lit.* what 'causes leaping for joy.'

PEACE,] *lit.* what 'brings into unity.'

3. BLESSED,] *lit.* 'well-spoken of is the God..who according to his much kindness begat us again to a living hope (*lit.* a hope living) through (the) up-standing of Jesus Christ out of dead men.'

4. TO,] *or* 'with a view to..and unfading, having been kept in (the) heavens (*or* among heavenly things *or* persons) with a view to you.'

5. KEPT,] *or* 'who are being guarded in.. with a view to salvation, ready to be uncovered in the last season.'

6. YE GREATLY REJOICE,] *or* 'greatly rejoice ye for yourselves, being made sorry a little now, if it is needful, in the manifold trials.'

7. TRIAL,] *lit.* 'your proving of the faith, much more precious than of gold that is lost (*or* loosed away), but through fire being proved..in the uncovering of Jesus Christ'

8. YE LOVE,] *or* 'love ye, *or* ye may love; in reference to whom, not now seeing, but believing, greatly rejoice ye for yourselves with joy unexpressible made glorious.'

9. RECEIVING,] *lit.* 'bringing to yourselves ..faith—salvation of souls.'

10. OF,] *lit.* 'concerning which salvation prophets who prophesied concerning the grace to you sought out and searched out.'

11. SEARCHING,] in reference to what or what sort of season the Spirit of Christ in them was evidencing, testifying beforehand (*or* openly) the sufferings in relation to Christ, and the glory after these.'

12. REVEALED,] *or* 'uncovered..they were deaconizing these things, which were now told again to you through those who proclaimed good-news for themselves to you in holy spirit sent forth from heaven, in reference to which messengers (men *or* spirits) desire fully to bend alongside of.'

13. GIRD,] *lit.* 'have girded up for yourselves the loins of your full mind, being not-drinking, hope perfectly upon the grace being borne to you in an uncovering of Jesus Christ.'

14. OBEDIENT,] *lit.* 'children of a submissive-hearkening, not being formed together with the former over-desires.'

15. HATH,] *lit.* 'who called you is holy become ye yourselves also holy in every turning round up and down.'

16. IT IS,] *lit.* 'it has been written, Become ye holy, because.'

17. CALL,] *lit.* 'call for yourselves upon a Father who without acceptance of faces is judging according to the work of each, turn round again for yourselves the time of the sojourning in fear.'

18. FORASMUCH AS,] *lit.* 'having known that ye were not loosed with corruptible things, with silver or with gold, out of the vanity (*or* emptiness) of your turning round again, given from fathers.'

19. BUT,] *lit.* 'but with precious blood of Christ, as of a lamb unblemished and unspotted.'

20. WHO VERILY,] *lit.* 'fore-known (*or* publicly known) indeed, before the foundation of the world,' *Gr.* cosmos, i.e. order, arrangement, beauty, of nature or of grace.

WAS,] *lit.* 'but manifested during the last of the times on your account.'

21. BY,] *lit.* 'through him are believing in reference to God..for your faith and hope to be in reference to God.'

22. SEEING,] *lit.* 'having purified..in the submissive hearkening of the truth, through spirit, with a view to unhypocritical brotherly love..out of a pure heart intensely.'

23. BEING,] *lit.* 'having been begotten again, not out of..through a word of God, living and remaining to the age.'

24. FOR,] *lit.* 'because..every glory of a man is as a flower of grass, the grass dried up..fell off.'

25. WORD,] *or* 'saying..remains to the age ..saying which was told as good news to you.'

Chapter II. may be divided into five parts; v. 1—5 exhortation to desire the milk of the Word, if built up on Christ; v. 6—10 advantages of belief, and disadvantages of disbelief; v. 11, 12 to avoid fleshly desires, and have a right behaviour; v. 13—17 to be subject, loving, fearing, honouring; v. 18—25 to submit to crosses after Christ's example.

1. WHEREFORE,] *or* 'therefore, having put away for yourselves every evil, and every guile..and all down-speakings.'

2. NEW-BORN,] *lit.* 'now-born,' i.e. just-born.

DESIRE,] *lit.* 'desire greatly the rational guileless milk, that ye may grow *or* increase in it with a view to salvation.'

3. IF SO BE,] *or* 'if indeed, ye tasted for yourselves that the Lord is useful *or* good.'

4. TO WHOM,] *lit.* 'coming forward towards whom—a living stone, having been disapproved of indeed by men, but alongside of God elect, (*or* select, choice), inwardly weighty *or* honourable.'

5. LIVELY,] *lit.* 'living stones, ye are being built (*or* be ye build) up..to bear up..through Jesus Christ.'

6. IT IS CONTAINED,] *or* 'he *or* it holds round about *or* everywhere in the Writing, Behold, I set in Zion a top corner stone, elect, (*or* select, choice), inwardly weighty *or* honourable, and he who is believing upon him may not be at all ashamed.'

7. BELIEVE,] *lit.* 'who are believing is the weightiness *or* honour, but to the untrustful—a stone which those building disapproved of, this became for head of a corner.'

8. STUMBLING,] *lit.* kicking at, and a rock of lameing, who kick at the word, being untrustful, in reference to which also they were set'—by God, that they might be built up, God set them as it were face to face with the top-corner stone, even Christ, but they were untrustful, and neglected him. Or it may be read: 'they set themselves.'

9. CHOSEN,] *lit.* 'elect, (*or* choice, select, excellent) generation, a kingly priesthood, a hallowed nation, a people for an over (*or* thorough) making, that ye might tell forth the pleasing features of him who called you out of darkness with a view to his astonishing light.'

10. WHICH,] *lit.* 'who once were not a people, but are now a people of God, who had not found kindness, but have now found kindness.'

11. DEARLY.] Omit this word as unnecessary.

BESEECH,] *lit.* 'call upon *or* exhort, as sojourners..to hold off for yourselves from the fleshly over-desires, which are themselves soldiers against the soul.'

12. CONVERSATION,] *lit.* 'turning round (i.e. behaviour) right *or* good among the nations, that in that which they..they may, out of the good *or* right works they have looked upon, glorify God in a day of inspection.'

13. SUBMIT YOURSELVES,] *lit.* 'be arranged under, then, every human creation, because of the Lord, whether to a king, as to one holding superiority,' *or* excellence.

14. OR,] *lit.* 'whether to leaders, as to those being sent through him with a view to justice indeed from evil-doers, but (the) full praise of good-doers.'

15. FOR,] *or* 'because..wish of God, doing

good, to silence (*lit.* muzzle) the ignorance of the thoughtless men.'

16. AS FREE,] *lit.* 'loosed, and not having the looseness as an over-covering of the badness, but as bondsmen of God.'

17. FEAR,] *lit.* 'be fearing God; be honouring.'

18. SERVANTS,] *lit.* 'the domestics, being arranging themselves under the despots in all fear..and very yielding, but also to the sharp,' *or* thorny.

19. THANKWORTHY,] *lit.* 'grace (*or* a cause of joy), if because of a conscience of God (i.e. a godly conscience) any one bears up under grief, suffering unjustly.'

20. WHAT,] *lit.* 'for what kind of celebrity (is it), if sinning (*or* 'missing' the mark') and being buffeted, ye shall remain-submissive? but if doing good and suffering ye shall remain-submissive, this is grace (*or* a cause of joy) alongside of God.'

21. FOR,] *lit.* 'for with a view to this ye were called, because Christ also suffered in our (*or* your) behalf, leaving behind to us (*or* you) an under-writing that ye may follow upon his tracts,' *or* footsteps.

23. WHEN,] *lit.* 'who, being reviled was not reviling in return, suffering, was not threatening, but was giving (it) along to him who is judging justly.'

24. HIS OWN SELF,] *lit.* 'who himself bore up our sins in his body on the tree, that we coming away from the sins may live to the righteousness, by whose stripe (*or* scar) ye were (*or* may be) healed.'

25 GOING ASTRAY,] *or* 'wandering, erring, but ye were turned round upon the shepherd and overseer of your souls.'

Chapter III. may be divided into four parts; v. 1—6 exhortation to wives; v. 7 to husbands; v. 8—15 and to all; v. 16—22 with a good conscience to suffer, doing good like Christ, who was spiritually strengthened and glorified.

1. LIKEWISE,] *or* 'in like manner (as the 'servants' in 2. 18) the wives (*or* O wives) be arranged (*or* being arranging yourselves) under your own husbands, that even if any are untrustful to the word, they may without a word be gained through the behaviour of the wives,' *or* women.

2. WHILE,] *lit.* 'having looked upon your chaste behaviour in fear.'

3. ADORNING,] *Gr.* kosmos, *lit.* turning, order.

THAT OUTWARD,] *lit.* 'that which is outward—of plaiting of hair, and of putting around of gold..garments.'

4. A,] *lit.* 'of the meek ..face of God very precious,' *or* great end *or* result.

5. AFTER THIS MANNER,] *lit.* 'for so once also (*or* even) the holy women who are hoping upon God, were adorning themselves, who are arranged under their own husbands.'

6. OBEYED,] *lit.* 'hearkened submissively to..Sir, of whom ye became children, doing good and not fearing any terror.'

7. LIKEWISE,] *or* 'in like manner (as the 'servants' and the 'wives') the husbands (*or* men), dwelling according to knowledge with the wife, as with a weaker vessel, distributing forth honour, as also joint-heirs of the grace of life, with a view to your pourings forth before (God) being not struck in.'

8. FINALLY,] *lit.* 'but the end (is that ye be) all like-minded, suffering together (*Gr.* sympathizing) friendly as brethren, compassionate, (*lit.* well-bowelled), friendly-minded.'

9. RENDERING,] *lit.* 'giving away evil in return for evil, or reproach in return for reproach, but on the contrary, speaking well (of all), having known that ye were called with a view to this, that ye may inherit (*lit.* receive by lot) a good word.'

10. WILL,] *lit.* 'who is wishing (*or* willing) to love life, and to see..lips, not to speak guile.'

11. ESCHEW,] *lit.* 'decline from..pursue it.'

12. FOR,] *lit.* 'because the..upon righteous ones, and his ears toward their supplication ..upon those doing evil things.'

13. WILL HARM,] *lit.* 'will be using you evilly, if ye may become for yourselves imitators of the Good One.'

14. BUT AND IF,] *lit.* 'but, if ye would also suffer because of righteousness, happy ye! but may ye not be afraid of their fear, nor may ye be troubled.'

15. SANCTIFY,] *or* 'hallow,' i.e. set apart.

TO GIVE,] *lit.* 'with *or* towards an apology to every one asking you a word *or* account about the hope in (*or* among) you.'

16. WHEREAS,] *lit.* 'in that which they speak against you as evil-doers, they may be thoroughly ashamed who are openly traducing (*or* calumniating) your good behaviour in Christ.'

17. BE SO,] *lit.* 'will (it), to suffer, doing good, than doing evil.'

18. FOR,] *lit.* 'because Christ also suffered once for all about (*or* concerning) sins, a just one in behalf of unjust ones, that he might lead us forward to God, put to death, indeed, as to flesh, but made alive as to spirit, in which also, having gone on, to the spirits in guard he had cried (as a herald,) to those once *or* formerly untrustful, when the long-suffering of God was waiting, in days of Noah, the ark being made thoroughly ready, in which few, that is, eight souls (i.e. persons) were thoroughly saved through (the medium of) water.'

21. THE LIKE FIGURE,] *lit.* 'to which also baptism an anti-type, doth now save us, not a putting away of filth of flesh, but a good conscience's open-question in reference to God, through (the) up-rising of Jesus Christ.'

22. WHO,] *lit.* 'who having gone on to heaven is in the right-hand (place) of God, messengers..having been arranged under him.'

Chapter IV. may be divided into three parts; v. 1—6 exhortation to arm ourselves with the mind of Christ and be done with sin; v. 7—11 because the end is nigh, to be as good stewards; v. 12—19 to rejoice in trials, avoid evil-doing, and trust in God.

1. FORASMUCH,] *lit.* 'Christ then having suffered in our behalf in flesh, ye also arm yourselves with the same inner mind, because he who suffered in flesh.'

2. THAT,] *lit.* 'with a view to the living no longer the rest of time in flesh to over-desires of men.'

3. PAST,] *lit.* 'having come alongside for itself of the life is sufficient to have wrought thoroughly for ourselves the will of the nations, having passed on in lasciviousnesses, over-desires, boilings of wine, revelries, drinking, and unlawful idolatries.'

4. WHEREIN,] *lit.* 'in which they think (it) strange your not running with (them), with a view to the same pouring forth again of unsavingness, speaking injuriously.

5. GIVE,] *lit.* 'give back a reckoning to him having readily to judge living and dead.'

6. FOR,] *lit.* 'for with a view to this were good news proclaimed even to dead (men), that..judged indeed..in flesh..in spirit.'

7. IS AT HAND,] *lit.* 'has drawn nigh.. sound-minded, and not drunk with a view to the pourings forth before (God).'

8. ABOVE,] *lit.* 'and before all things having the intense love to yourselves (*or* each other), because the love shall cover a multitude of sins,' so as to induce us to forgive and forget them.

9. USE HOSPITALITY,] *lit.* 'acting to one another (as) friends of strangers, without (*or* apart from the assent of) murmuring.'

10. EVERY,] *or* 'each one received a gracious gift, be deaconizing the same in reference to yourselves, as good (*or* honest, right) house-distributors.'

11. MAN,] *lit.* 'if any one speaks—as oracles (*or* words) of God; if any one deaconizes—as out of strength which God supplies, (*lit.* as leader of the chorus,)..is the glory and the might to the ages of the ages. Amen.'

12. THINK,] *lit.* 'be not strange at the fiery trial coming among you for a test to you, as at a strange thing coming through to you.'

13. REJOICE,] *lit.* 'leap for joy, according as ye have communion with the sufferings of the Christ, that also, in the uncovering of his glory, ye may leap for joy, being glad,' *or* exulting.

14. BE,] *lit.* 'are reproached in the name of Christ, happy ye! because the spirit of the glory and (the Spirit) of God rests again upon you; among them, indeed, he is injuriously spoken of, but among you he is glorified.'

15. BUT,] *lit.* 'for (*or* therefore) let no one of..or thief, or evil-doer, or as looking over other men's affairs.'

16. YET,] *lit.* 'but if as a Christian (see Acts 11. 26: 26. 27, 28)..in this respect,' Vulg. 'name.'

17. FOR,] *lit.* 'because (it is) the season to begin for oneself the judgment from the house of God, and if first from us, what the end of those untrustful to the good-news of God?'

18. RIGHTEOUS,] *or* 'just one is scarcely (*or* with labour) saved, where shall the irreverent and sinful one appear for himself?'

19. WHEREFORE,] *lit.* 'so that let those also suffering..be putting for themselves their own souls alongside in well-doing as to a stedfast Creator,' *or* builder, former.

Chapter V. may be divided into five parts; v. 1—4 exhortation to elders; v. 5—7 to younger persons; v. 8, 9 to be sober, vigilent; v. 10, 11 prayer and praise; v. 12—14 closing address and salutation.

1. THE ELDERS,] *Gr.* 'the presbyters among you I call upon, who am a fellow-presbyter and witness of the sufferings of the Christ, and who am partaker of the glory about to be uncovered.'

2. FLOCK,] *lit.* 'little flock of God among you, being overseers, not constrainedly, but yieldingly, nor for shameful gain, but of a forward mind.

3. NEITHER,] *or* 'nor as being at all lords of the inheritances (*lit.* lots), but becoming types of the little flock.'

4. WHEN,] *lit.* 'and the chief-shepherd (*lit.* feeder) having been manifested, ye shall bring to yourselves the unfading crown of glory.'

5. SUBMIT,] *lit.* 'be arranged under elders (*Gr.* presbyters); yea all be arranging yourselves under one another, gird (*or* knot) in for yourselves the lowlymindedness, because God arranges himself against over-manifest ones, but gives grace to lowly ones.'

6. HUMBLE YOURSELVES,] *lit.* 'be lowly.. due season.'

7. CASTING,] *lit.* 'having cast over upon him all your anxiety, (division *or* partings of mind), because there is carefulness to him concerning you.'

8. BE SOBER,] *lit.* 'be not-drinking, be wakeful, because the Devil (*lit.* thruster through), your opponent (in law), as a lion roaring for himself walks round about, seeking whom he may swallow down.'

9. RESIST,] *lit.* 'be set against, firm.. having known the same sufferings (are) to be fully ended in your brotherhood in the world.'

10. ALL,] *or* 'every grace, who called you, ye having suffered a little with a view to his age-during glory in Christ Jesus, (is) Himself thoroughly to perfect, to confirm, to strengthen, to settle you,' as on a 'foundation.'

11. BE,] *lit.* 'is the glory and the might to the ages of the ages. Amen.'

12. BY,] *lit.* 'through Silvanus (i.e. Silus, a forester) the stedfast brother, as I reckon to you, I wrote through few (words) calling along and openly witnessing this to be a true grace of God in reference to which ye have stood,' *or* set ye yourselves.

13. CHURCH,] *or* 'the jointly-elect assembly in Babylon (on the Euphrates) draws you near, also Marcus (i.e. Mark) my son,' natural or spiritual.

14. GREET,] *lit.* 'draw ye one another near in a friendship of love; peace (is) to you, to all those in Christ Jesus. Amen.'

GENERAL LETTER OF PETER
(THE SECOND)

THIS EPISTLE is wanting in the Syriac Peshito Version, and is not mentioned by Tertullian (A.D. 160—200), Clement of Alexandria (A.D. 194), Cyprian (A.D. 200—258), or the fragment of Muratori (A.D. 200). The first who expressly mentions it, (which he does as S.S.), is Origen (A.D. 182—254), while he states that some doubted its canonicity. Clement of Rome (A.D. 108), Hermas (A.D. 108), Justin-Martyr (A.D. 140), Athenagorus (A.D. 178), Irenaeus (A.D. 140—200), &c. appear to have several allusions to certain phrases that appear in it. The style is somewhat different from that of Peter's First Epistle, but this is too indefinite a criterion to decide so weighty a point, and not a few verbal coincidences between them have been pointed out, and Jude's language is in many verses almost indentical.

The date and place of its composition are alike uncertain; it has apparently allusions to Gen. 1. 6—9; 7. 1—11, 16, 22, 23; 19. 16, 24, 25; Nu. 22. 5, 7, 21, 23, 28; Jos. 23. 14; 2 Sa. 23. 2; Ps. 102. 26; Isa, 5. 19; 65. 17—19; Mat. 17. 1—5; Rev. 21.

It may be divided into three parts; ch. i. Exhortations, ch. ii. False Teachers, ch. iii. Scoffers.

Chapter I. may be divided into five parts; v. 1, 2 address and salutation; v. 3, 4 divine gifts and promises; v. 5—11 encouragement to abound in graces; v. 12—15 reasons for reminding them; v. 16—21 of the truthfulness of the apostolic and scripture testimony to Christ.

1. SIMON,] *Gr.* Symon, i.e. (in *Heb.*) 'hearing;' comp. Ge. 29. 33.

PETER,] i.e. a 'rock,' a firm, unbending man.

SERVANT,] *lit.* 'bondsman and apostle (i.e. one sent forth) of Jesus Christ (i.e. the 'anointed saviour,') to those who obtained by lot like precious (*or* honourable, weighty) faith with us in (the) righteousness of our God and Saviour Jesus Christ.'

2. GRACE,] *lit.* what 'causes leaping for joy.'

THROUGH,] *lit.* 'in (the) full-knowledge (*or* open-knowledge, i.e. acknowledgment) of God, and (*or* even) of Jesus our Lord.'

3. ACCORDING AS,] *or* 'seeing that, by his Divine Power, all things relating to life and reverence have been freely given to us, through the full knowledge (*or* acknowledgment) of him who called us through glory and pleasingness.'

4. WHEREBY,] *lit.* 'through which have been freely given to us the exceeding great and precious (honourable *or* weighty) promises, that, through these ye may become partakers of a divine nature, having fled from the corruption in the world in over-desire.'

5. BESIDE,] *lit.* 'but also for this very thing, having brought in along-side all diligence, supply also in your faith the pleasingness, and in the pleasingness the knowledge, and in the knowledge the inward-strength, and in the inward-strength the endurance (*lit.* remaining under), and in the endurance the reverence, and in the reverence the brotherly friendship, and in the brotherly friendship the love.'

8. IF,] *lit.* 'for these things subsisting to you, and becoming more abundant, set you down neither idle nor unfruitful in reference to the full-knowledge.'

9. LACKETH,] *lit.* 'for he to whom these things are not present is blind, shutting the eyes, having accepted a hiding of the cleansing of his former sins.'

10. GIVE DILIGENCE,] *or* 'be diligent to make for yourselves your calling and election firm, (*or* for your calling and election to be made firm) for doing these things, ye may not stumble at any time.'

11. AN,] *lit.* 'the entrance *or* introduction shall be over-supplied to you richly.'

12. NEGLIGENT,] *lit.* 'careless always to remind you a little concerning these things, even though ye have known them, and have been.'

13. YEA,] *lit.* 'but I reckon (it) right..to rouse (you) thoroughly in a little remembrance.'

14. KNOWING,] *lit.* 'having known that speedily shall be the putting off of my tabernacle even as..Christ made evident to me.'

15. ENDEAVOUR,] *lit.* 'be diligent also, on each occasion, for you to have after my departure (*Gr.* exodus) to make for yourselves this remembrance.'

16. HAVE,] *lit.* 'did not follow out wisely devised myths..and presence of..but became eye-witnesses of that one's greatness.'

17. HE,] *lit.* 'for having received..such a voice having been borne to him under the greatly-becoming glory..in reference to whom I thought well.'

18. CAME,] *lit.* 'was borne..heard, being with him.'

19. A MORE,] *lit.* 'also the prophetic word more firm, to which ye do well holding forward as to a lamp shining (*or* appearing) in a dry (*or* squalid) place, till the day may shine through, and a light bearer may rise up, in your hearts.'

20. THE,] *lit.* 'of scripture comes of one's (i.e. a prophet's) own solution (*or* 'loosing out' of probable events).'

21. THE,] *lit.* 'for prophecy was not borne on at any time by (the) will of man, but being borne on under a holy spirit (*or* divine influence the) holy men of God spake (it).'

Chapter II. may be divided into four parts; v. 1—3 prediction of false teachers; v. 4—8 God's conduct towards sinful messengers, the old world, the cities of Sodom and Gomorrah; v. 9—16 and those following Balaam; v. 17—22 their awful corruption and depravity.

1. WERE,] *lit.* 'came also false..who shall bring in along-side destructive sects, and denying for themselves the Despot that bought them, bringing upon themselves a speedy destruction,' *or* loosing away.

2. FOLLOW,] *lit.* 'follow out their dissolute (*or* lascivious) ways, because of whom the way of the truth shall be injuriously spoken of.'

3. THROUGH,] *lit.* 'in covetousness shall they with framed words pass in for themselves among you, with whom the judgment (pronounced) of old is not idle, and their destruction (*lit.* loosing away) does not nod,' *or* slumber.

4. SPARED,] *lit.* 'did not flee-from-giving-up for himself messengers who sinned, (*lit.* 'missed' the mark,) but in chains (*or* dens) of gloom, having tartarized he gave (them) over—reserved with a view to judgment.'

5. SPARED,] *lit.* 'did not flee from giving up for himself (the) ancient world, but guarded Noah (the) eighth, a crier (*or* herald) of righteousness, having led in upon (the) world of the irreverent ones a thorough washing.'

6. TURNING,] *lit.* 'having reduced..to ashes, he judged (them) down to a full overturn, having set them an under-shew of those about to be irreverent.'

7. DELIVERED,] *lit.* 'freed for himself just Lot, labouring for himself under the behaviour of the unsettled in lasciviousness.'

8. THAT,] *lit.* 'for the just one, dwelling inwardly among them, was trying (*or* oppressing, violating, forcing) a just soul.. with lawless works.'

9. KNOW,] *lit.* 'has known to free reverent ones out of trial, and to keep unjust ones being punished (*lit.* cut off, mutilated, restrained) with a view to a day of judgment.'

10. CHIEFLY,] *or* 'especially those passing on after (the) flesh, in an over-desire of defilement, and thinking down upon lordship; daring ones! self-pleased! speaking injuriously of glories they tremble not.'

11. ANGELS,] *lit.* 'messengers, being greater in strength and might, bear not against them an injurious-speaking judgment near (*or* because of) the Lord.'

12. NATURAL,] *lit.* 'as irrational animals, physical, having been made with a view to capture and corruption) speaking injuriously in *or* among the things they are ignorant of, shall utterly corrupt themselves in their own corruption.'

13. RECEIVE,] *lit.* 'be bringing to themselves (the) hire of injustice, reckoning (as) pleasure the riot in (the) day, spots and blemishes! inwardly rioting in their deceits, holding-well-inwardly with you.'

14. ADULTERY,] *lit.* 'of an adulteress, and not thoroughly ceasing from sin, using baits for unconfirmed souls, having a heart exercised (*lit.* made naked) in covetousness, children of a curse!'

15. FORSAKEN,] *lit.* 'having utterly left the right way, they were led astray, following on in the way of..a hire of injustice.'

16. WAS REBUKED,] *lit.* 'had a conviction of his own lawlessness (*or* going aside from law), a voiceless ass (*lit.* one under yoke) in man's voice sounding for itself, restrained the wrong-mind of the prophet.'

17. THAT ARE CARRIED,] *lit.* 'clouds being driven by (*lit.* under) a tempest, to whom the blackness of the darkness has been kept for an age.'

18. WHEN,] *lit.* 'for sounding forth overswellings of vanity, they use baits in overdesires of flesh, in lasciviousnesses, for those having really (*or* scarcely) fled from those turning themselves round again in error.'

19. WHILE,] *lit.* 'promising for themselves liberty *or* freedom to them, themselves are subsisting bondsman of the corruption, for to whom any one is inferior, even to this one has he been a bondsman.'

20. AFTER,] *lit.* 'having fled from the pollutions of the world in the full-knowledge ..and being folded in again by these, are inferior, the last things have become worse to them than the first.'

21. HAD BEEN,] *lit.* 'were better to them not to have fully-known the way of the righteousness, than having fully-known (it) to turn round fully out of the hallowed precept given along to them.'

22. IT IS HAPPENED,] *lit.* 'come together to them has the true by-word, A dog having turned round fully upon its own vomit, and A sow having bathed itself—to a rolling of mud,' *or* 'food.'

Chapter III. may be divided into five parts; v. 1, 2 exhortation to be mindful of former sayings; v. 3—7 prediction of coming scoffers and their folly; v. 8—10 certainty of the coming of the day of the Lord; v. 11—16 and what we ought to be and to do; v. 17, 18 final warning, exhortation and doxology.

1. THIS,] *lit.* 'this now, beloved, a Second Letter I write to you, in both which I stir up thoroughly your clear judging full-mind, in a little reminding.'

2. THAT YE,] *lit.* 'to be mindful of the before (*or* publicly) spoken words by (*lit.* under) the holy prophets, and of the precept.'

3. LAST DAY,] *lit.* 'last of the days (of the Jewish dispensation, as always,) scoffers (*lit.* those acting inwardly as boys) passing on according to their own over-desires.'

4. COMING,] *lit.* 'being alongside,' i.e. present.

FELL ASLEEP,] *lit.* 'were laid (*or* laid themselves) down, all things remain thoroughly thus from (the) beginning of creation,' *or* formation.

5. FOR,] *lit.* 'for this lies willingly hid (from) them..were from of old, and earth has been standing together out of water and through water.'

6. WHEREBY,] *lit.* 'through which things the then kosmos (*lit.* 'order' of things)—having been washed thoroughly with water, loosed itself away.'

7. HEAVENS,] *lit.* 'the new heavens..are having been treasured up (*lit.* set for to-morrow), being kept for fire with a view to a day of judgment and of a loosing-away of the irreverent men.'

8. BE NOT,] *lit.* 'let not this one thing lie hid (from) you.'

9. SLACK,] *or* 'slow,' as being under a 'burden.'

SOME MEN,] *lit.* 'certain reckon.'

NOT WILLING,] *lit.* 'not counselling (i.e. taking or giving counsel) certain ones to be loosed (*or* loose themselves) away, but—all to have place (*or* be open) in reference to another mind.'

10. THE,] *lit.* 'in which..go aside whizz-ingly, and steppings (i.e. first principles) being burnt (*or* set on fire) shall be dissolved, and earth and the works in it shall be burnt down.'

11. SEEING,] *lit.* 'all these things, then, being (in the act of) dissolving themselves (already), what kind of persons doth it be-hove you to be (*or* exist, submit) in hallowed behaviours (*or* acts of conduct, *lit.* turnings round again) and reverences,' i.e. reveren-tial acts.

12. LOOKING FOR,] *lit.* 'looking toward and hasting the presence of the day of God, because of which heavens.. and elements being burnt (*or* set on fire) shall wither,' *or* melt.

13. NEVERTHELESS,] *lit.* 'but we look..to-ward new heavens and a new earth.'

14. SEEING,] *lit.* 'looking towards these things, be diligent to be found by him spot-less and blameless in peace.'

15. ACCOUNT,] *lit.* 'be reckoning the long-suffering of our Lord (to be) salvation,' i.e. a time of it.

GIVEN,] *lit.* 'that was given to him wrote to you.'

16. OF,] *lit.* 'concerning these things, a-mong which things are certain hard for the mind, which those untaught and uncon-firmed wrest,' *or* turn round.

TO,] *lit.* 'towards their own loosing-away.'

17. SEEING,] *lit.* 'knowing beforehand, (*or* publicly), be guarding yourselves, lest being led away with the straying of the un-settled, ye may fall out of your own firm-ness.'

18. GROW,] *lit.* 'be growing (*or* increasing) in (the) grace and knowledge..To him (is) the glory both now and to (the) day of (the) age. Amen!

GENERAL LETTER OF JOHN

THIS EPISTLE is quoted or referred to by Hermas (A.D. 108), Polycarp (A.D. 108), Papias (A.D. 116), the Churches of Vienna and Lyons (A.D. 177), Irenaeus (A.D. 178), Clement of Alexandria (A.D. 194), Tertullian (A.D. 200), Origen (A.D. 230), Cyprian (A.D. 248), Dionysius of Alexandria (A.D. 247), Eusebius (A.D. 320), Athanasius (A.D. 326), Jerome, &c., and was not doubted to be John's (save by Marcion) till the 6th century. The internal evidence in his favour is as powerful as the external.

To whom it was written, and when, are alike uncertain, probably to the Christians in Syria and Asia Minor, and before the destruction of Jerusalem; see 2. 13, 14, 18. It is full of aphorisms and repetitions, contrasts of 'spirit' and 'flesh,' of 'light' and darkness,' of 'life' and 'death,' of 'love' and hate.'

It may be divided into six parts; 1. 1—7; 1. 8—2. 2; 2. 3—17; 2. 18—29; 3. 1—24; 4. 1—21; 5. 1—21; and has allusions to Gen. 4. 4—8; De. 13. 13; 1 K. 8. 46; Job 19. 26; 42. 8; Ps. 16. 11; 41. 9; Ecc. 7. 20; Isa. 9. 6; 53. 55. 7; 61. 1; Jer. 31. 33, 34; Mic. 6. 7; Rom. 3. 24.

Chapter I. may be divided into two parts; v. 1—4 of what and why the author writes; v. 5—10 what God is, and what we should be and do.

1. BEGINNING] of the gospel history (*or* perhaps, of the creation)—concerning the Word of Life, even Christ.

HEARD,] *lit.* 'heard for ourselves.'

LOOKED UPON,] *lit.* 'viewed for ourselves.'

HAVE,] *lit.* 'did touch.'

OF,] *lit.* 'concerning the Word (*Gr.* Logos) of the life.'

2. FOR,] *lit.* 'and the Life was manifested *or* manifested itself..and tell fully to you the age-during life, which was towards (*or* with) the Father, and was manifested (*or* manifested itself) to us.'

3. HEARD,] *lit.* 'heard for ourselves tell we fully to you..fellowship (*or* communion).. and also our communion is.'

4. FULL,] *or* 'made full.'

5. THIS THEN,] *lit.* 'and this is the message (*or* full-tale) which we have heard for ourselves from him, and tell again to you.. is not even one thing darkness.'

6. WE SAY,] *lit.* 'we may say..communion ..may walk-about in the darkness, we lie (*or* are false) for ourselves, and do not do (i.e. act) the truth.'

7. WE WALK,] *lit.* 'we may walk about in ..communion with one another..cleanseth (i.e. is able to do so) us from every sin,' *or* 'missing' of the mark.

8. WE SAY,] *lit.* 'we may say..we lead ourselves astray.'

9. WE CONFESS,] *lit.* 'we may confess (*Gr.* homologate, i.e. say the same thing)..just that he may send away to us the sins, and may cleanse us from every unrighteousness.'

10. WE SAY,] *lit.* 'we may say..make (i.e. declare) him false.'

Chapter II. may be divided into seven parts; v. 1—6 we may not sin, but if we do we have an advocate, who is a propitiation for sin, whom we know if we obey him; v. 7—11 a new, yet old, command to love our brother; v. 12—14 reasons for writing to little children, fathers, little boys, young men; v. 15—17 not to love the world; v. 18, 19 the last hour (of the Jewish dispensation); v. 20—23 the liar and anti-christ; v. 24—29 to let truth remain in us, and we in Christ.

1. YE SIN,] *lit.* 'ye may not sin (*or* 'miss' the mark, i.e. not-attain to it) at all, and if any one may sin at all, we have a righteous caller-alongside (of us) towards the Father, Jesus Christ.'

2. AND HE,] *lit.* 'and himself is a propitiation (*lit.* what makes 'mild,') for our sins ..all the world.' Comp. 4. 14; 5. 19; John 1. 29; 4. 42; 11. 51, 52; 1 Tim. 4. 10; 2 Pet. 2. 1.

3. HEREBY,] *lit.* 'in this..we have known him, if we may keep his precepts.'

4. THAT SAITH,] *lit.* 'who is saying, I have known him, and is not keeping his precepts.'

5. KEEPETH,] *lit.* 'may keep..truly has the love of God been perfected.'

6. SAITH,] *lit.* 'is saying to remain in him ..to walk about, according as he walked about.'

7. BRETHREN.] Many MSS. Versions, and Fathers, read 'Beloved.'

HAVE HEARD,] *lit* 'ye heard.'

8. IS PAST,] *lit.* 'led away *or* leads itself away..is already manifest.'

9. SAITH,] *lit.* 'is saying to be in the light, and is hating his brother, is in the darkness till now.'

10. LOVETH,] *lit.* 'is loving..remaineth in ..no stumbling-block.'

11. HATETH,] *lit.* 'is hating..in the darkness, and walketh about in the darkness, and has not known for himself when he goes away, because the darkness blinded his eyes.'

12. ARE FORGIVEN,] *lit.* 'have been sent away because of his name.'

13. OVERCOME,] *lit.* 'not yielded (to) the evil.'

CHILDREN,] *lit.* 'little boys.'

14. HAVE WRITTEN,] *lit.* 'I wrote..I wrote ..remains in you, and ye have not yielded (to) the evil.'

15. LOVE NOT,] *or* 'ye may not love, *or* ye do not love..if any one loves.'

16. LUST,] *lit.* 'over-desire..assumption

of the (things of) life, is not out of..out of the world.'

17. PASSETH AWAY,] *or* 'is led away, *or* leads itself away, and the over-desire of it, but he who is doing the will of God remains to the age.'

18. THE LAST TIME,] *lit.* 'a last hour, and even as ye heard that the anti-christ comes, even now anti-christs have become many, whence we know that it is a last hour,'—with unbelieving Jerusalem.

19. OUT,] *lit.* 'went forth out of us (i.e. out of our midst), but they were not out of us (in regard to spirit) for if they were out of us (in this respect) they would have remained with us, but—that they might be manifested, because all (in our midst) are not out of us (in regard to spirit).'

20. BUT,] *lit.* 'and ye—ye have an anointing..ye have known for yourselves all.'

21. HAVE,] *lit.* 'I wrote not..have not known for yourselves..have known it for yourselves, and because no lie.'

22. A LIAR,] *lit.* 'the liar, except he who is denying..this one is the anti-christ, who is denying.'

23. WHOSOEVER,] *lit.* 'every one who is denying..is homologating the Son.'

24. ABIDE,] *lit.* 'remain..ye heard..ye heard..may remain..shall remain.'

25. HATH,] *lit.* 'he himself promised for himself to us—the age-during life.'

26. HAVE I WRITTEN,] *lit.* 'I wrote..those leading you astray.'

27. BUT,] *lit.* 'but ye, the anointing which ye received from him, remains in you,..any one may teach you..you concerning all, and is true..it taught you, ye shall remain (*or* remain ye) in him,' *or* it.

28. ABIDE,] *lit.* 'remain..may be manifested, we may have full-speech, and may not receive shame from him in his presence.'

29. YE KNOW,] *lit.* 'if ye may know (*or* perceive)..know ye that every one who is doing the righteousness has been begotten out of *or* by him.'

Chapter III. may be divided into seven parts: v. 1—3 children of God not known, but purifying themselves; v. 4—6 sin not in Christ, nor the sinful; v. 7—9 who are of the devil, whose works Christ came to destroy; v. 10—12 how the children of God and of the devil are manifested; v. 13—17 love and hatred of the brethren; v. 18—20 call to love in truth; v. 21—24 our boldness and acceptance with God, and their grounds.

1. BEHOLD,] *or* 'see ye, what kind of love the Father has given to us, that we may be called children of God;' the oldest MSS. add, 'and we are so.'

2. THE SONS,] *lit.* 'we are children of God, and it was not hitherto manifested what we shall be, but we have known for ourselves that, if he (*or* it) may be manifested.'

3. MAN,] *lit.* 'every one who is having (*or* holding) this hope upon him.'

4. WHOSOEVER,] *lit.* 'every one who is doing the sin, does also the lawlessness, and the sin is the lawlessness.'

5. YE,] *lit.* 'ye have known for yourselves that..that he might lift away.'

6. WHOSOEVER,] *lit.* 'every one who is remaining does not sin, every one who is sinning.'

7. DECEIVE,] *or* 'lead you astray; he who is doing the righteousness.'

8. COMMITTETH,] *lit.* 'he who is doing the sin, is out of the devil, because..might loose the works.'

9. WHOSOEVER,] *lit.* 'every one who has been begotten by (*lit.* out of) God does not do sin, because..he is not able to sin, because he has been begotten by (*lit.* out of) God.'

10. WHOSOEVER,] *lit.* 'every one who is not doing..out of God; also he who is not loving.'

11. FOR,] *or* 'because..may love one an other.'

12. WHO,] *lit.* 'of the evil one he was.'

13. MARVEL,] *lit.* 'be not wondering..hates you.'

14. WE KNOW,] *lit.* 'we, we have known for ourselves that we have gone over out of the death to the life..he who is not loving the brother remains in the death.'

15. WHOSOEVER,] *lit.* 'every one who is hating the brother is a manslayer, and ye have known for yourselves that no manslayer has age-during life remaining in him.'

16. HEREBY,] *lit.* 'in this we have known the love, that he..in our behalf..in behalf of the brethren.'

17. HATH,] *lit.* 'may have the (means of) livelihood of the world, and may view his brother having need, and may close his.. how doth the love of God remain in him?'

18. IN WORD,] *lit.* 'with word, nor with the tongue.'

19. HEREBY,] *lit.* 'in this..are out of the truth and shall persuade.'

20. FOR,] *lit.* 'because if the heart may know (anything) against us.'

21. CONDEMN,] *lit.* 'may not know (anything) against us we have full-speech toward God.'

22. ASK,] *lit.* 'may ask, we receive from him,'—if agreeable to his will.

23. SHOULD,] *or* 'might believe in..may love.'

24. KEEPETH,] *lit.* 'is keeping..remains in him..and in this we..remains in us, from (*lit.* out of) the spirit which he gave to us' —at our conversion.

Chapter IV. may be divided into six parts; v. 1—3 warning against and *first* test for false prophets; v. 4—6 a second test; v. 7, 8 a third test; v. 9—13 God's love to men should increase our love; v. 14—16 apostle's testimony to God's love; v. 17—21 love with fear of God, or hate of a brother.

1. BELIEVE NOT,] *lit.* 'be not believing (*or* trusting to) every spirit, but be testing the spirits, if they are out of God..have gone out for themselves.'

2. HEREBY,] *lit.* 'in this know ye (*or* ye know)..homologates Jesus Christ having come for himself in flesh, is out of God.'

3. CONFESSETH,] *lit.* 'homologates Jesus

Christ having come for himself in flesh is not out of God, and this is the spirit of the anti-christ, which ye have heard for yourselves that it comes, and now it is in the world already.'

4. YE ARE,] *lit.* 'ye—ye are out of God.'

5. THEY ARE,] *lit.* 'they—they are out of.'

6. WE ARE,] *lit.* 'we (the apostles)—we are out of God; he who is knowing God..In this we..of the truth..of the error,' *lit.* leading astray.

7. LET US,] *or* 'may we love..the love is out..is loving has been begotten out of God.'

8. LOVETH NOT,] *lit.* 'is not loving did not know God, because.'

9. TOWARD,] *lit.* 'in (*or* among) us, that God has sent forth.'

10. HEREIN,] *lit.* 'in this is the love..sent forth his Son—a propitiation.'

12. MAN,] *lit.* 'no one has viewed for themselves God at any time; if we may love..remains in us..and the love of him has been perfected in us.'

13. HEREBY,] *lit.* 'in this..we remain..out of his spirit.'

14. SEEN,] *lit.* 'viewed for ourselves..has sent forth the Son—Saviour of the world.'

15. SHALL,] *lit.* 'may homologate that.. God remains.

16. TO US,] *lit.* 'in us..is remaining in the love remains in God.'

17. HEREIN,] *lit.* 'in this the love has been perfected with us, that we may have full-speech in the day of the judgment.'

18. IN LOVE,] *lit.* 'in the love, but the perfect love casts the fear without, because the fear has punishment (*or* restraint), and he who is fearing for himself has not been perfected in the love.'

19. LOVE,] *or* 'we may love him.'

20. A MAN,] *lit.* 'if any one may say, that, I love God, and may hate his..is not loving his.. how is he able to love God.'

21. LOVETH,] *lit.* 'is loving God may love.

Chapter V. may be divided into five parts; v. 1—5 believers are begotten by God and they love all such, showing this by keeping God's commands; v. 6—8 the three witnesses; v. 9—12 God's testimony regarding Christ; v. 13—15 object of the present writing and full-speech toward God; v. 16—21 prayer for a sinning brother, and purity and knowledge in Christ.

1. WHOSOEVER,] *lit.* 'every one who is believing..has been begotten out of God..is loving him..loves (*or* may love) him also who has been begotten out of him.'

2. BY,] *lit.* 'in this we know that we love (*or* may love)..may love God, and may keep his precepts.'

3. KEEP,] *lit.* 'we may keep..not heavy.'

4. FOR,] *lit.* 'because every thing that has been begotten out of God..that overcome the world.'

5. OVERCOMETH,] *lit.* 'is overcoming..except he who is believing.'

6. BY,] *lit.* 'through..Jesus the Christ, not in the water only, but in the water and the blood..that is witnessing..is the truth.'

7. FOR,] *lit.* 'because there are three who are bearing witness [*omit* 'in heaven, the Father, the Word, and the Holy Ghost, and these three are (with a view to) one (testimony), and there are three who are bearing witness in the earth].' These words are wanting in all the Greek MSS. except *two*, in all the *oldest* Ancient Versions, and in all the quotations of v. 6—8 in the ancient Fathers before A.D. 475; it is undoubtedly a mere gloss written thoughtlessly on the margin.

THESE THREE,] *lit.* 'and the three are with a view to the one (testimony).'

9. FOR,] *lit.* 'because..concerning his Son.'

10. BELIEVETH,] *lit.* 'is believing (*or* trusting to) the Son..is not believing (*or* trusting to) God has made (i.e. pronounced) him a liar, because he has not believed (*or* trusted to) the witness which God has testified concerning his son.'

11. RECORD,] *lit.* 'witness, that God gave to us life age-during.'

12. HATH,] *lit.* 'is having the Son has the life, he who is not having the Son has not the life.'

13. HAVE I WRITTEN,] *lit.* 'wrote I to you [some MSS. and Versions *omit* who are believing (*or* trusting to) the name of the Son of God.']

14. CONFIDENCE,] *lit.* 'full-speech..toward him, that if we may ask anything for ourselves.'

15. KNOW,] *lit.* 'we have known for ourselves that he hears us, whatever we may ask for ourselves, we have known for ourselves that we have the things asked for, which we have asked from him.'

16. MAN,] *lit.* 'if any one may see his brother sinning sin not to death,—he shall ask, and he shall give to him life, for those sinning not to death; there is sin to death, I do not speak concerning that (sin), that he may make request.'

17. A SIN,] *lit.* 'there is sin.'

18. WE KNOW,] *lit.* 'we have known for ourselves that every one who has been begotten out of God does not sin, but he who was begotten out of God keeps himself, and the evil one does not himself touch him.'

19. WE KNOW,] *lit.* 'we have known for ourselves that we are out of God..lies (*or* is laid) in the evil one.'

20. WE KNOW,] *lit.* 'we have known for ourselves..a full-mind..and the life age-during.'

21. KEEP,] *lit.* 'guard yourselves from the idols. Amen.'

JOHN'S LETTER TO KYRIA

THERE is no good reason for questioning the generally received opinion that the writer of this Letter (as well as the following one to GAIUS) was the Apostle John; out of the thirteen verses of which it consists, not less than eight are found substantially in his first Letter, while it was attributed to him by Irenaeus (A.D. 167), Clement of Alexandria (A.D. 192), Origen (A.D. 230), Cyprian (A.D. 248), Eusebius (A.D. 315), Aurelius (A.D. 256), Alexander of Alexandria (A.D. 313), Dionysius of Alexandria (A.D. 247), Ephraim Syrus (A.D. 370), &c. The only other person to whom these two letters have been attributed is one John, surnamed 'the Presbyter,' but beyond the circumstance that the writer of both Letters calls himself 'the presbyter' there is nothing to recommend or prove the hypothesis, since Peter in his first letter (5. 1) assumes the same title, it being in reality the highest permanent title of office in the early Christian church: unfortunately also we have no writings of John the Presbyter which we could compare with these, while their whole tone, style, and sentiments are in thorough accordance with all we know of the 'beloved disciple.'

The dates of the composition of the so-called 'second' and 'third' Letters are altogether unknown; Lardner fixes both about A.D. 68, while others fix them at A.D. 90, a very unlikely date, every thing considered; they are supposed to have been both written in Ephesus.

The party to whom the 'Second' Letter is addressed has been a matter of dispute. The Common Version speaks of an 'elect lady,' others render it the 'lady Electa,' the 'elect Kyria,' is decidedly preferable. Some again, consider the word *kyria* as equivalent to *ecclesia*, and think that some particular church is meant, e.g. of Jerusalem, Antioch, Rome, Babylon, &c., but Neander, Alford, &c. agree in regarding the 'elect Kyria,' as literally a Christian Lady of that name.

The Letter to Kyria may be divided into four parts; 1—3 address and salutation; v. 4—7 call to love and obedience; v. 8—11 warning against losing the reward and encouraging transgressors; v. 12,13 joyful hope and salutation.

1. THE ELDER,] *Gr.* 'the presbyter;' a title of age or office; see 1 Pet. 5. 1, 5; Acts 15, 2.

ELECT,] i.e. select, excellent, choice, as in Rom. 16. 13; Mat. 20. 16.

LADY.] *Gr.* 'Kyria;' *Heb.* 'Martha.'

THE,] *lit.* 'love in truth..those having known (*or* approved of) the truth.'

2. SAKE,] *lit.* 'because of (*or* through) the truth that is remaining in (*or* among) us (*or* you)..us (*or* you) to the age.'

3. GRACE,] *lit.* what 'causes leaping for joy.'

BE,] *lit.* 'shall be with you (*or* us) to the age, kindness, peace from (*or* alongside of) God the Father, and alongside of the Lord.'

4. REJOICED,] *lit.* 'I was caused to leap much for joy, that *or* because I have found out of thy children (some) walking about in truth, as we received.'

5. BESEECH,] *lit.* 'request thee, Kyria, not as writing a new precept..we were having ..we may love.'

6. LOVE,] *lit.* 'the love, that we may walk about..ye heard..ye may walk.'

7. FOR,] *lit.* 'because many leading-astray went into the world, who are not homolo gating (*lit.* speaking the same thing with) Jesus Christ coming in flesh; this is the leader-astray and the anti-christ;' as in Mat. 24. 5, 12.

8. LOOK,] *lit.* 'behold yourselves, that we (*or* ye) may not fully lose the things which we ourselves (*or* ye yourselves) wrought..we (*or* ye) may fully-receive a full hire.'

9. WHOSOEVER,] *lit.* 'every one who is going beyond, and is not remaining in the teaching of the Christ..he who is remaining in the teaching of the Christ, this one has.'

10. IF,] *lit.* 'if any one comes towards you, and does not bear this teaching,..and say (*or* tell) not to him to rejoice,' *or* leap for joy.

11. BIDDETH,] *lit.* 'is saying (*or* telling) to him to rejoice *or* leap for joy has communion with his evil works.'

12. WOULD,] *lit.* 'I did not counsel *or* intend (to do so) through paper and ink, but *or* for I hope to come to *or* be with you, and to speak mouth to mouth, that our (*or* your) leaping with joy may be filled full.'

13. ELECT,] as in v. 1.

GREET,] *lit.* 'draw thee near,' to salute.

JOHN'S LETTER TO GAIUS

THIS Letter is quoted by the same ancient fathers as quote the preceding one, and rests on the same kind of evidence. This Gaius (*or* Caius) is supposed by some to be the same as Gaius of Macedonia (Acts 19. 29), by others as Caius of Corinth (1 Cor. 1. 14), by others as Gaius of Derbe (Acts 20. 4), and by others as Gaius of Rome (Rom. 16. 23), but nothing is certain on this point. He appears to have been a man of substance and influence.

This Letter may be divided into five parts; v. 1—4 address and salutation; v. 5—8 approval and encouragement; v. 9, 10 a complaint and promise; v. 11, 12 a warning and testimony; v. 13—15 a hope and salutation.

1. THE ELDER.] *Gr.* 'the presbyter;' a title of age, or of office; see 1 Pet. 5. 1, 5, &c.

WELL-BELOVED,] *lit.* 'beloved;' as in v. 2.

GAIUS,] i.e. *Lat.* Caius.

IN THE,] *lit.* 'in truth,' i.e. truly.

2. I WISH,] *lit.* 'concerning (*or* above) all things I pour myself forth well for thee to have a good journey and to be in health, according as thy soul has a good journey.'

3. I REJOICED,] *lit.* 'I was caused to leap much with joy, brethren coming and testifying of thee as to the truth, according as thou walkest about in truth.'

4. JOY,] *lit.* 'cause of leaping for joy than these, that I hear of my own children walking about in truth.'

5. FAITHFULLY,] *or* 'stedfastly..mayest work in reference to the brethren, and to the strangers.'

6. WHICH,] *lit.* 'who testified of thee, as to the love, before an assembly, whom having set forward worthily of God thou dost well.'

7. BECAUSE,] *lit.* 'for in behalf of the Name ..from the nations.'

8. RECEIVE,] *lit.* 'fully receive..become fellow-workers in the truth.'

9. CHURCH,] *lit.* 'assembly.'

DIOTREPHES,] i.e. 'nourished by Jove.'

LOVETH,] *lit.* 'is loving a foremost place of them, receives us not fully.'

10. WHEREFORE,] *lit.* 'because of this, if I may come, I will cause him to remember somewhat (*or* shortly)..flooding us with evil words..fully receive..restrains those counselling (to do so), and casts forth out of the assembly.'

11. FOLLOW,] *lit.* 'be not imitating the evil things but the good, he who is doing good is out of God, but he who is doing evil.'

12. DEMETRIUS,] i.e. 'belonging to mother earth.'

HATH,] *lit.* 'to Demetrius testimony has been borne by all, and by..ye have known for yourselves that.'

13. WILL,] *lit.* 'I do not wish to write to thee through ink and pen.'

14. TRUST,] *lit.* 'hope straightway to see thee..mouth to mouth..the friends..be embracing the friends by name.'

LETTER OF JUDAS

JUDE—or rather JUDAS—the writer of this Letter was probably that one of the twelve apostles referred to in John 14. 22, and elsewhere called Lebbeus and Thaddeus (*lit.* one with a heart, i.e. a bold man). His brother James, to whom he refers in the opening of his Letter, was doubtless the one who spoke at the Jerusalem Council. This Letter is quoted or referred to by Clement of Alexandria (A.D. 194), Tertullian (A.D. 200), Origen (A.D. 230), Eusebius (A.D. 320), Jerome (A.D. 392), Ephraim Syrus (A.D. 370). It was evidently written a little before the destruction of Jerusalem.

This Letter may be divided into eight parts; v. 1, 2 address and salutation; v. 3—7 exhortation to contend for the faith, against certain impious men, from God's past dealings; v. 8—11 their presumption and carnality; v. 12, 13 their dangerous character and end; v. 14, 15 like those to whom Enoch prophesied; v. 16—19 and they themselves spoken of beforehand by the apostles; v. 20—23 call to build themselves up, to wait for the kindness of Christ, and to help others; v. 24, 25 ascription of praise to God.

1. JUDE,] *Gr.* Judas, same as *Heb.* Judah, 'praise, confession.'

THE SERVANT,] *lit.* 'a bondsman' of

JESUS CHRIST,] i.e. an 'anointed saviour.'

BROTHER,] *lit.* 'one from the same womb.'

JAMES,] *Gr.* Jacobus, same as *Heb.* Jacob, 'one who takes by the heel,' i.e. supplants; he is called the Less *or* Little (Mark 15. 40; Luke 6. 16; Jas. 1. 1), probably because of his stature.

ARE,] *lit.* 'to those having been set-apart (*lit.* 'not of the earth,' but many MSS. read, 'beloved,') in God the Father, and in Jesus Christ having been kept—called.'

2. MERCY,] *lit.* 'kindness.'

PEACE,] *lit.* what 'brings into unity.'

BE,] *or* 'oh that it may be multiplied.'

3. WHEN,] *lit.* 'making all haste to write

(at once) to you about the common salvation (*or* safety) I had a necessity to write to you, exhorting to agonize-openly for the faith once-for-all given-over to the saints,' i.e. those 'out of the earth.'

4. FOR,] *lit.* 'for there came in along-side certain men who of old have been publicly described (v. 17, 18), in reference to this judgment, irreverent ones, putting over the grace of our God into lasciviousness, and the only despot, God and Lord of us —Jesus Christ—disowning for themselves.'

5. I WILL,] *lit.* 'and I intend (*or* am counselled) to remind you somewhat *or* a little, ye having once for all known this, that . . a people . . at last loosed away those.'

6. AND,] *lit.* 'messengers also, those who kept not their own principality *or* first estate, but left fully their proper place of dwelling, he has kept to a judgment of a great day, in perpetual bonds, under blackness.'

7. MANNER,] *lit.* 'manner to these having committed excessive whoredom, and gone away after other flesh, are laid forth (as) an example, being under the justice of age-during fire.'

8. ALSO,] *lit.* 'likewise nevertheless these also, putting themselves in a sleep, defile indeed, flesh, and put away lordship, and speak injuriously of glories.'

9. YET,] *lit.* 'but Michael (i.e. who is like God?) the chief-messenger, when judging-diversely with the Devil he was speaking-diversely about the body of Moses, (i.e. the Jewish church, comp. the 'body of Christ,') did not dare to bear against (him) a judgment of evil speaking, but said, The Lord put a weight upon thee!'

10. THESE,] *lit.* 'of as many things as they have not known for themselves, but as many things as they know about physically (*or* naturally), as irrational beings, in these they are corrupted.'

11. FOR,] *lit.* 'because they passed on for themselves in . . and poured themselves forth in the going astray of . . and loosed themselves away in the contradiction of Kore.'

12. SPOTS,] *or* 'craggy rocks in your love-feasts, holding themselves well together fearlessly, shepherding themselves, waterless clouds, being borne about (*or* along) by (*lit.* under) winds, trees withered of autumnal fruit, fruitless, twice dead, uprooted.'

13. RAGING,] *or* 'wild (*lit.* field) waves of a sea, foaming up their own shameful things, stars going astray, to whom has been kept the gloom of the darkness to the age.'

14. OF,] *lit.* 'to (such as) these, saying, Behold, the Lord came (*not* cometh) in his saintly myriads.'

15. EXECUTE,] *lit.* 'to do judgment against all, and to convict-fully all their irreverent ones concerning all their irreverent works which they irreverently committed, and concerning all the dry things which irreverent sinners speak against him.'

16. MURMURERS,] *or* 'grumblers, fault-finders, passing on according to their own over-desires . . admiring faces (*or* persons) because of profit.'

17. BUT,] *lit.* 'but ye, beloved, remember the sayings spoken before by (*lit.* under) the apostles.'

18. HOW THAT,] *lit.* 'that they laid out to you, that there shall be scoffers (*lit.* those acting inwardly as boys) in (the) last time (of the Jewish dispensation), passing on according to their own over-desires of the irreverencies.'

19. BE,] *lit.* 'these are those making themselves thoroughly out, physical (*or* natural), not having (the) spirit.'

20. PRAYING,] *lit.* 'pouring yourselves forth well in (the) holy Spirit.'

21. LOOKING FOR,] *lit.* 'holding yourselves towards the kindness of . . with a view to life age-during.'

22. OF SOME,] *lit.* 'and some, indeed, be kind to, judging thoroughly.'

23. OTHERS,] *lit.* 'and some be saving (i.e. trying to save) in fear, snatching out of . . coat spotted from the flesh.'

24. KEEP,] *lit.* 'guard you unstumbling, and to set (you) down unblemished in the presence of His glory in gladness,' *lit.* much leaping.

25. BE,] *or* 'is glory and greatness, strength and authority, both now and to all the ages Amen.' See 1 Tim. 1. 17.

BOOK OF REVELATION

THIS BOOK is not quoted by any Christian writer till the time of Justin Martyr (A.D. 140), who expressly declares it to be the work of 'JOHN, one of the apostles of Christ;' Melito (A.D. 171), is said by Eusebius to have written a Commentary on it; Theophilus (A.D. 160—180) is said by the same to have quoted Rev. 12. 9 in answer to a heretic; Apollonius (A.D. 186) is also said to have quoted it in his public Apology; Irenaeus (A.D. 175) quotes it twenty times; Clement of Alexandria (A.D. 192—220) alludes to it four times; Tertullian (A.D. 200) everywhere quotes it, and so does Hippolytus, Origen, &c. Papias, a hearer of the apostle John, and father of millenarianism, wrote (about A.D. 110—116) a book unfortunately now lost, referring to it. About A.D. 200 doubts regarding the authorship and the public utility of the Book began to rise; some attributed it (most gratuitously) to 'John the Presbyter,' others refused to read it publicly in the churches. These doubts arose entirely from the absurdities foisted upon it by millenarians, and the want of proper principles of interpretation. It is wanting in the Peshito Syriac Version, but is often quoted by Ephraim Syrus (A.D. 300—375) in his Syriac Commentaries.

It was written in Patmos (about A.D. 68), whither John had been banished by Domitius Nero, as stated in the title of the Syriac Version of the Book; and with this concurs the express statement of Irenaeus (A.D. 175), who says it happened in the reign *Domitianou*,' i.e. Domitius (Nero). Sulpicius Severus, Orosius, &c., stupidly mistaking Domitian*ou* for Domitian*ikos*, supposed Irenaeus to refer to *Domitian*, A.D. 95, and most succeeding writers have fallen into the same blunder. The internal testimony is wholly in favour of the earlier date. The temple at Jerusalem was still standing (ch. 11. 1—10); the exact duration of the siege is foretold, viz., 42 months, 3½ years, or 1260 days; the two witnesses are to be slain in the city where our Lord was crucified; Nero was reigning at that time, for it is said of the seven kings of Rome; 'five are fallen, *and one is*, and the other is not yet come, and when he cometh, he must continue a short space.' The five kings are Julius Caesar, Augustus, Tiberius, Caligula, Claudius. The '*one who is*' is Nero; the one who 'must continue a short space' is Galba, who reigned only *seven* months. Everywhere the events are 'to come quickly,' *lit.* 'with haste,' *or* speed (ch. 1. 1; 2. 16; 3. 11; 11. 14; 22. 7, 12, 20). The escape of the Christian Jews from Jerusalem to Pella is undoubtedly referred to in ch. 7. 1—8, compared with Mat. 24. 30.

The Book may be divided into three parts; 1) the Prefatory Matter; 2) the Principal Visions; and 3) the Conclusion of the Whole

I. The Prefatory Matter occupies ch. i. ii. iii. viz.—
- i. Introductory manifestation of Christ.
- ii. iii. His Addresses to seven Churches.

II. The Principal Visions occupy ch. iv—xx. viz.—
- iv. v. Introductory manifestations.
- vi.—xi. First Catastrophe, describing the Overthrow of Judaism, as the first great enemy of Christianity.
- xii—xix. Second Catastrophe, describing the overthrow of Paganism, as the second great enemy.
- xx. Third Catastrophe, describing the Overthrow of all Future Enemies, of whatever kind, and age, they may be.

III. The Conclusion occupies ch. xxi. xxii. describing the future glory of the church on earth, with a last warning.

This book is full of symbols and imagery taken from earthly kingdoms and events to typify the spiritual struggles of the church with the opposing powers of Judaism and Paganism in the first place, and with all contrary principles that may rise hereafter, in any age, or country. It must be interpreted on the same principles as Psalm ii. xvi. xviii. xlv. cx. Song of Songs, Isa. xiii. xiv. and the whole book of Ezekiel, and is thus fitted for all ages alike.

Chapter I. may be divided into four parts; v. 1—3 title of the Book, and happiness of its readers; v. 4—8 John's salutation; v. 9—16 his vision of Christ; v. 17—20 Christ's title, dignity, and directions.

1. THE REVELATION,] *lit.* 'an uncovering.'

JESUS CHRIST,] i.e. an 'anointed saviour.'

SERVANTS,] *lit.* 'bondsmen what things it behoves to come to pass in haste; and he signified (it), having sent (it) forth through his messenger to his bondsman John,' i.e. 'Jah is gracious.'

2. RECORD OF,] *or* 'who testified the word ..as many things also as he saw.'

3. BLESSED,] *lit.* 'happy is he who is reading (*or* knowing again), and those hearing.. those keeping the things written in it, for the season is nigh;' within 3½ years.

4. JOHN] the apostle, not John the presbyter, as some suppose; he was a person of no note, and of doubtful existence; the simple name 'John,' in the latter half of the first century, could only have been understood of the beloved disciple.

CHURCHES,] *lit.* 'assembles.'

ASIA,] i.e. proconsular Asia, comprising Phrygia, Mysia, Caria and Lydia.

GRACE,] *lit.* what 'causes leaping for joy.'

PEACE,] *lit.* what 'brings into unity.'

WHICH,] *lit.* 'who Is, and who Was, and who is Coming.'

SEVEN SPIRITS,] i.e. perhaps 'the Holy Spirit;' otherwise it may mean 'the full number of spirits;' compare 1 Tim. 5. 21.

5. FAITHFUL,] *lit.* 'stedfast witness, the first-born out of the dead, and the chief of the kings of the land..washed (*lit.* loosed) us..his blood.'

6. HATH,] *lit.* 'and made us kings (*or* a kingdom) and priests to God, even His Father, to him is the glory and the might to the ages of the ages. Amen.'

7. CLOUDS,] *lit.* 'with the clouds..who pierced him through..tribes of the land (of Israel) shall smite themselves over it. Yes! Amen.'

8. ALPHA,] *lit.* 'the Alpha and the Omega, [the beginning and ending], saith the Lord [God], who Is, and who Was, and who is Coming, the Almighty.'

9. COMPANION,] *lit.* 'joint-partaker in the tribulation..endurance of Jesus Christ, I came (not necessarily against his will) into the Isle,' *lit.* place for swimming.

PATMOS,] one of the Cyclades in the Ægean Sea, now called Palmosa, a barren rock, south of Samos, in the Archipelago.

FOR,] i.e. through *or* on account of.

10. WAS,] *lit.* 'I came into (the) spirit in the Lord's day,' the first day of the week no doubt, on which the first Christians systematically met together to worship God, and observe divine ordinances, as is everywhere testified to in the New Testament and the writers of the first and second centuries. They never in a single case call it 'Sabbath,' but either 'Sunday' or 'the Lord's Day,' and this they did on principle, viewing the name 'Sabbath' as applicable only to the Jewish day; while the Lord's day is emphatically a *day of work*—spiritual work of course—in commemoration of Christ's rising from *rest* to *work* in a higher sphere, as Intercessor, and King in Zion. Some have weakly confounded this 'Lord's day' with the 'day of the Lord,' so often spoken of, but the phrases in Greek are entirely distinct.

VOICE,] *lit.* 'a voice, great, as of a trump.'

11. I AM..LAST, AND.] Oldest MSS. omit.

SEEST,] *or* 'shalt see (*or* behold), write (at once) for a little book, and send (at once) to the seven assemblies.'

WHO ARE IN ASIA.] Oldest MSS. omit.

EPHESUS,] i.e. 'beloved, desired;' a city of Ionia, in proconsular Asia, destroyed A.D. 1401, and now almost unknown.

SMYRNA,] i.e. 'myrrh,' 45 miles N.W. of Ephesus; still large and flourishing.

PERGAMOS,] i.e. 'castle, tower;' in Mysia, north of Smyrna; now called Bergamos, famous for its library.

THYATIRA,] i.e. 'unwearied about sacrifices;' in Lydia, now called Akhissar, famous for cotton; south of Pergamos.

SARDIS,] capital of Lydia; now almost unknown.

PHILADELPHIA,] i.e. 'brotherly love,' in Lydia, 28 miles S.E. of Sardis.

LAODICIA,] in Phrygia, S. of Colosse, now called Ladik.

12. TURNED,] *lit.* 'turned round upon (it) to behold which spake (*or* was speaking) with me, and having turned round upon (it) I perceived seven gold lampstands.'

13. CANDLESTICKS,] *lit.* 'lampstands one like to a son of man (i.e. a human being), clothed in a long robe, and girded round about towards the breasts with a golden girdle,' *lit.* zone.

14. WHITE,] *lit.* 'seen, visible,' like 'white wool, like snow.'

SNOW,] *lit.* a thing 'poured forth.'

15. FINE BRASS,] *or* 'white brass,' *or* 'brass and frankincense.'

THEY BURNED,] *lit.* 'as having been fired in a furnace.'

THE,] *lit.* 'as a sound.'

16. HE HAD,] *lit.* 'and having in his..is going forth a sharp two-mouthed sabre (i.e. a long Thracian sword)..his power,' *or* ability.

17. SAW,] *or* 'perceived..laid over his..Be not fearing for thyself.'

18. I AM,] *lit.* 'and the Living One, and I became dead..am living to the ages of the ages, [Amen]..of the Hades (*lit.* 'unseen' world) and of the Death.'

19. WRITE] at once [therefore], the things thou didst perceive..are about to happen after (*or* with) these.'

20. MYSTERY,] *or* 'secret of..upon my right..lampstands..are messengers of..are seven assemblies.'

Chapter II. may be divided into four parts; v. 1—7 address to the Ephesian; v. 8—11 the Smyrnean; v. 12—17 the Pergamos; v. 18—29 the Thyatirean assembly.

1. ANGEL,] *lit.* 'messenger,' i.e. minister whom the assembly in Ephesus had probably sent along with messengers from six other churches to visit John in Patmos, as their representatives, to ask direction in the day of trial.

CHURCH,] *lit.* 'assembly in (*or* of) Ephesus,' where Paul laboured three years.

WRITE] at once, as in 1. 19, &c.

HOLDETH,] *lit.* 'is holding fast the..is walking about in..lampstands.'

2. KNOW,] *lit.* 'I have known for myself thy..toil..endurance, and that thou art not able to bear evil (men)..laying themselves out (*or* affirming themselves) to be apostles didst find.'

3. BORNE,] *lit.* 'and hast endurance, and didst bear, because of my name, and hast not been toiled,' *or* wearied out.

4. NEVERTHELESS,] *or* 'but I have (this) against thee, that thou didst send away (*or* let go) thy first love.'

5. REMEMBER,] *lit.* 'be remembering [therefore], whence thou hast fallen, and have another mind (at once), and do (at once) the first work, but if not, I come to thee speedily, and will move thy lampstand..if thou mayest not have another mind.'

6. DEEDS,] *lit.* 'works of the Nicolaitanes, a sect according to Irenaeus and Tertullian, called after Nicolaus, (Acts 6. 3. 5.) Very weak is the idea that *Nicolaus* (i.e. conqueror of the people) is equal to *Balaam* (i.e. swallower up of the people), and that the name is symbolic of covetous, unclean persons.

7. HATH,] *lit.* 'is having an..assemblies..is overcoming..from the tree of the life.'
8. ANGEL,] *lit.* 'messenger of the assembly in (*or* of) Smyrna write (at once).. who became dead and lived.'
9. KNOW,] *lit.* 'have known for myself (thy works and) the tribulation and the poverty .. injurious speaking from those laying themselves out to be.. a synogogue (i.e. an assembly led together) of the adversary,' *Gr.* Satan, i.e. one 'who shuts up' the way.
10. FEAR NOT,] *lit.* 'be not fearing for thyself the things thou art about to suffer, behold, the Devil (*lit.* thruster through) is about to cast (some) of you into guard.. become thou for thyself stedfast.. the crown of the life.'
11. HATH,] *lit.* 'is having.. is overcoming (*lit.* not yielding) may not be injured from (*lit.* out of) the second death.'
12. ANGEL,] *lit.* 'messenger.. who is having the sharp two mouthed sword.'
13. KNOW,] *lit.* 'I have known for myself ..thou housest-down, where the throne of the adversary (as in v. 9) is.. didst not disown for thyself.. the days in which Antipas (i.e. Antipater), my stedfast witness, who was killed outright.'
14. BECAUSE,] *or* 'that thou hast there those holding fast the teaching of Balaam (i.e. swallower up of the people), who was teaching Balak (i.e. a breaker off, destroyer) to cast a stumbling-block (*Gr.* scandal, i.e. a thing for 'laming' man or beast), before the sons of Israel, to eat idol-sacrifices and to commit whoredom,' *lit.* a 'selling' of oneself. Nu 24. 14; 25. 1; 31. 16.
15. THEM,] *lit.* 'those holding fast the teaching of the Nicolaitans;' see v. 6.
WHICH THING I HATE.] Best MSS. read 'likewise, in like manner.'
16. REPENT,] *lit.* 'have another mind (therefore), but if not, I come to thee speedily and will war with thee with (*lit.* in) the sword.'
17. HATH,] *lit.* 'is having.. is overcoming (*lit.* not yielding).. white pebble, and upon the pebble.. no one knew (*or* has perceived for himself) except he who is receiving,' or accepting the pebble which was used in lots.
18. ANGEL,] *lit.* 'messenger.. is having his eyes as a.. feet like to whitened brass;' comp. 1. 14, 15.
19. KNOW,] *lit.* 'have perceived for myself .. the love, and the deaconship, and the faith, and the endurance of thee.'
20. BECAUSE,] *or* 'that thou lettest go the woman.'
JEZEBEL,] i.e. 'without cohabitation;' 1 K. 16. 31; 2 K. 9. 22. 30.
CALLETH,] *lit.* 'is laying herself out (as) a prophetess.. lead astray for herself my bondsmen, to commit whoredom and to eat idol-sacrifices.'
21. SPACE,] *lit.* 'time that she might have another mind (because) of her whoredom, and she had not another mind.'
22. WILL,] *lit.* 'I cast her into a couch, and those committing.. they may have another mind because of.'
23. KILL,] *lit.* 'kill outright.. in death.. know for themselves.. who is searching out reins and heart, and I will give to you, to each.'
24. REST,] *lit.* 'those left over..this teaching, and who knew not the depths of the adversary, as they lay (it) out; I will cast.. weight.'
25. THAT WHICH,] *lit.* 'what things.. I may *or* shall come.'
26. OVERCOMETH,] *lit.* 'is not yielding, and is keeping.. authority.'
27. SHALL,] *lit.* 'he rules (*or* feeds) them in a.. as I also have received from.'
28. MORNING,] *lit.* 'early star.'
29. HATH,] *lit.* 'he having an..assemblies.'

Chapter III. may be divided into three parts; v. 1—7 address to Sardis; v. 8—14 to Philadelphia; v. 15—22 to Laodicea.
1. ANGEL,] *lit.* 'messenger.. assembly.. is having.. I have perceived for myself that thou hast the name.'
2. BE,] *lit.* 'become thou wakeful for thyself, and confirm the things left, which are about to die away.. perfected,' *or* made full.
3. REMEMBER,] *lit.* 'be remembering.. didst hear, and be keeping, and have a new mind; if therefore thou mayest not be wakeful, I may come..mayest not know what hour I may come upon thee.'
4. HAVE,] *lit.* 'who did not defile.. walk about.. white (garments).'
5. OVERCOMETH,] *lit.* 'is not yielding, this one shall be arrayed in white garments .. blot (*lit.* smear).. of the life, and I will confess for myself.. messengers.'
6. HATH,] *lit.* 'is having an ear.' Mat. 11. 15; 13. 9; Mark 4. 9, 23; 7. 16; Luke 8. 8; 14. 35.
7. ANGEL,] *lit.* 'messenger..is having the key of David, he who is opening up, and no one closes, and closes, and no one opens up.'
8. KNOW,] *lit.* 'I have perceived for myself..have given..opened up door, and no one is able to close it, because..didst keep my word, and didst not disown for thyself my name.'
9. WILL MAKE,] *lit.* 'I give (some) out of the synagogue of the adversary (i.e. Satan, the 'shutter up,') of those laying themselves out to be Jews..but lie for themselves..that they may come and kiss forward (the hand) ..I loved thee.'
10. HAST,] *lit.* 'didst keep..endurance.. out of the hour of the trial that is about to come upon the whole inhabited land, to try (at once) those dwelling (*lit.* housing-down) upon the land.'
11. QUICKLY,] *lit.* 'speedily *or* hastily; be holding fast what thou hast, that no one may receive thy crown.'
12. OVERCOMETH,] *lit.* 'is not yielding.. habitation of..he may go no more forth without..is coming down out of the heaven.'
13. HATH,] *lit.* 'is having an..assemblies.'
14. ANGEL,] *lit.* 'messenger of the assembly of (*or* in) Laodicia write (at once)..the stedfast..the chief (*or* first) of the creation of God.'
15. KNOW,] *lit.* 'I have perceived for myself..hot (*or* fervent, living).'
16. I WILL,] *lit.* 'I am about to spue.'

17. SAYEST,] *lit.* 'layest down, that, I am rich (*or* wealthy) and have become rich.. hast not perceived for thyself that thou, thou art the sustainer of wretchedness, and (the one) needing kindness, and trembling.'

18. COUNSEL,] *lit.* 'I counsel thee fully to buy (at once) from me gold fired out of fire ..raiments that thou may cast around thyself..may not be manifested (*or* manifested itself), and anoint inwardly with collyrion thine eyes that thou mayest behold.'

19. LOVE,] *or* 'I am friend to, I convict and instruct (*lit.* use as children); be zealous (at once), therefore, and have another mind.'

20. STAND,] *lit.* 'I have stood at (*lit.* upon) ..any one may hear..may open up the door, I will come in for myself to him.'

21. TO HIM,] *lit.* 'He who is not yielding, to him will I give..also did not yield, and sat down..throne,' *lit.* seat.

22. HATH,] *lit.* 'is having..assemblies.'

Chapter IV. may be divided into three parts; v. 1—3 vision of an opened door in heaven, a voice, a throne, and One sitting on it; v. 4—7 with twenty-four elders and four living creatures; v. 8—11 and their employment.

1. THIS,] *lit.* 'after these things I perceived, and behold, a door opened up in the heaven ..heard (in 1. 10) is as of a..me, saying.. what behoves to come to pass after these.'

2. IMMEDIATELY,] *lit.* 'straightway I came in spirit..laid down in the heaven, and (one) is sitting.'

3. SAT,] *lit.* 'is sitting was in appearance (*or* sight) like to jasper and sardine stone, and a rainbow is around.'

4. ROUND ABOUT,] *lit.* 'around the throne are twenty and four thrones, and upon the thrones I perceived the twenty and four elders (*Gr.* presbyters) sitting, arranged in white garments..golden crowns.'

5. PROCEEDED,] *lit.* 'pass forth do flashings, and roarings, and voices, and seven torches of fire are kindled (*or* kindling themselves).'

6. THERE WAS,] *lit.* 'a transparent sea.. are four living creatures.'

7. BEAST,] *lit.* 'living creature is like to a lion..living creature..living creature is having the face as a (*or* of) man..living creature (is) like to an eagle flying for itself.'

8. BEASTS,] *lit.* 'living creatures, each by itself severally, were having a-piece six wings around, and rest again they have not: the Almighty, who Was, and Is, and who is Coming.'

9. THOSE,] *lit.* 'the living creatures.'

THANKS,] *lit.* 'much leaping for joy to him sitting, to him who is living to the ages of the ages.'

10. FALL,] *lit.* 'shall cast themselves down before him who is sitting..shall kiss forward (the hand) to him who is living to the ages of the ages, and shall cast.'

11. RECEIVE,] *or* 'take the glory, and the honour, and the power, because thou—thou didst create (*or* form, build) the all things, and because of thy will they are (*or* exist,) and they were created.'

Chapter V. may be divided into four parts; v. 1—3 vision of an unopened scroll; v. 4—7 which a Lamb takes; v. 8—10 amid the praises of the living creatures and the elders; v. 11—14 and of every other creature.

1. SAW,] *or* 'perceived upon the right hand of him who is sitting..a little roll..and behind, sealed down with.'

2. SAW,] *or* 'perceived..crying (as a herald) in a great voice.. to open up the little roll, and to loose (at once) its seals?'

3. MAN,] *lit.* 'no one in the heaven, nor upon the earth..open up the little roll, nor to behold it.'

4. WEPT,] *lit.* 'was breaking forth much (with anguish) because no one..open up and to read the little roll, nor to behold it.'

5. OF,] *lit.* 'out of the presbyters..Be not breaking forth; behold the Lion who is out of..overcame (*lit.* did not yield) to open up the little roll and to loose (at once) its seals.'

6. BEHELD,] *lit.* 'perceived..living creatures..presbyters, has stood a little Lamb, as having been slain..that have been sent forth to all the land.'

7. TOOK,] *lit.* 'has taken (*or* received) the little roll..is sitting.'

8. HAD TAKEN,] *lit.* 'he took (*or* received) the little roll,..living creatures..presbyters..having each harps (*or* guitars)..of incense, which are the pourings forth before (God) of the saints.'

9. SUNG,] *lit.* 'use a new ode..little roll, and to open up..didst buy us..in thy blood, out of every tribe.'

10. HAST,] *lit.* 'didst make..upon (*or* over) the earth.'

11. BEHELD,] *lit.* 'perceived..a voice of.. living creatures and the presbyters..was myriads of myriads.'

12. LOUD,] *lit.* 'great .little Lamb has been slain..the power.'

13. CREATURE,] *or* 'created thing..the heaven, and in..and those that are upon the sea, and the all things in them..The eulogy and the honour, and the glory, and the might, is to..is sitting..little Lamb to the ages of the ages.'

14. BEASTS,] *lit.* 'living creatures..presbyters..kissed forth (the hand) to him who is living to the ages of the ages.'

Chapter VI. may be divided into six parts; v. 1, 2 first seal, a white horse; v. 3, 4 second seal, a red horse; v. 5, 6 third seal, a black horse; v. 7, 8 fourth seal, a pale horse; v. 9—11 fifth seal, souls of the slain; v. 12—17 sixth seal, a great earthquake.

1. SAW,] *or* 'perceived when the little Lamb opened up one out of the (seven) seals .. as a voice of thunder (*lit.* roaring).. living creatures, saying, Be coming and behold (at once).'

2. SAW,] *or* 'perceived .is sitting on it is having a bow..unyielding, and that he might not yield.'

3. HAD,] *lit.* 'he opened up..saying, Be coming, and behold (at once).'

4. OUT,] *or* 'forth another horse—red (*or* fire-coloured), and there was given to him sitting on it to take the peace from the land, and that they might slay.'

5. HAD,] *lit.* 'he opened up..living creature saying, Be coming and behold (at once). And I perceived, and behold..is sitting on it is having a balance.'

6. BEASTS,] *lit.* 'living creatures saying, A choenix of wheat for a denary, and three choenixes of barley, for a denary, and Thou mayest not injure the oil and the wine.'

7. HAD,] *lit.* 'he opened up..a voice of the fourth living creature saying, Be coming, and behold (at once).'

8. LOOKED,] *or* 'perceived..pale (*lit.* sallow, *or* green)..is sitting on it is The Death, and The Hades follows with him..authority ..to kill utterly in sword, and in famine, and in death, and by (*lit.* under) the wild beasts of the land.'

9. HAD,] *lit.* 'he opened up..I perceived under the place of sacrifice the souls of those having been slain because of the word of God, and because of the witness which they were holding.'

10. CRIED,] *lit.* 'were crying with a great voice, saying, Till when, O Despot, the holy and the true..take vengeance (for) our blood from those dwelling upon the land.'

11. EVERY,] *or* 'each one..said (*lit.* lifted up)..may rest themselves again yet a little time, till their fellow-bondsmen..who are about to be killed outright even as they, shall make themselves full.'

12. BEHELD,] *lit.* 'perceived when he opened up..behold, there came a great shaking.'

13. HEAVEN,] *lit.* 'of the heaven..her dissolved fruit, being shaken under a great wind.'

14. THE,] *lit.* 'and heaven was withdrawn (*or* withdrew itself) as a little roll being rolled up (*or* rolling itself up)..were moved (*or* moved themselves).'

15. EARTH,] *or* 'land..the captains of thousands..dens,' *or* caves.

16. SAID,] *lit.* 'and they say..and to the rocks..is sitting..anger (*lit.* stretching out of the hand) of the little Lamb.'

17. FOR,] *lit.* 'because the day, the great one, of his anger came, and who is able to station himself?'

Chapter VII. may be divided into five parts; v. 1—3 the four winds restrained; v. 4—8 a perfect number of Israel are sealed; v. 9, 10 praise by a great multitude; v. 11, 12 and by the messengers, the presbyters, and the four living creatures; v. 13—17 happiness of the saved.

1. SAW,] *or* 'perceived..having stationed themselves..land, holding fast..land..may not blow..against any tree.'

2. SAW,] *or* 'perceived..having come up from the uprising of the sun, having a seal ..great voice..messengers..to injure the land.'

3. HURT NOT,] *lit.* 'ye may not injure the land, till we may seal the bondsmen of our God upon their foreheads.'

4. THEM,] *lit.* 'those having been sealed, 144 thousands, they having been sealed out of every tribe of the sons of Israel.'

5. OF,] *lit.* 'out of the tribe of Juda 12,000 were having been sealed.'

6. MANASSES.] Put instead of Dan.

9. BEHELD,] *or* 'perceived, and behold, a great crowd, which no one was able to number, out of every nation and tribe and peoples, having stationed themselves..little Lamb, having cast around themselves white robes.'

10. CRIED,] *lit.* 'crying (*or* they cry) with a great voice, saying, The salvation (is) to him who is sitting..little Lamb.'

11. ANGELS,] *lit.* 'messengers had stationed themselves..presbyters..living creatures..face, and kissed forward (the hand) to God.'

12. BLESSING,] *lit.* 'the eulogy, and the glory, and the wisdom (*lit.* soundness of speech) and the much leaping for joy, and the honour, and the power, and the strength is to our God, to the ages of the ages Amen.'

13. OF,] *lit.* 'out of the presbyters answered (*lit.* judged off for himself)..have cast round themselves the white robes.'

14. SAID,] *lit.* 'have said..Lord, thou, thou hast known for thyself..are coming out of the great tribulation, and washed..little Lamb.'

15. THEREFORE,] *lit.* 'because of this..and tremble much to him..his habitation, and he who is sitting on the throne shall tabernacle over them.'

16. SHALL,] *lit.* 'may the sun fall..burning heat.'

17. FOR,] *lit.* 'because the little Lamb.. doth feed (*or* tend) them, and shall lead them in the way by (*lit.* upon) living wells of waters, and God shall wipe off every tear.'

Chapter VIII. may be divided into six parts; v. 1—5 opening of the seventh seal; v. 6, 7 sounding of the first trumpet; v. 8, 9 of the second; v. 10, 11 of the third; v. 12 of the fourth; v. 13 announcement of the fifth.

1. HAD,] *lit.* 'he opened up..there came silence in the heaven as (if) half-an-hour.'

2. STOOD,] *lit.* 'have stationed themselves,' *or* stood.

3. STOOD,] *or* 'stationed himself by (*lit.* upon) the place of sacrifice..frankincense vessel..might give (it) to the good-pourings forth before (God) of all the saints upon the golden place of sacrifice which is.'

4. WHICH CAME,] *or* 'added to the good pourings forth before (God) of the saints came up, out of the hand of the messenger before God.'

5. TOOK,] *lit.* 'has taken (*or* received) the frankincense-vessel, and filled it out of the fire of the place of sacrifice, and cast it to the land, and there came voices and roarings and flashings and a shaking.'

6. ANGELS,] *lit.* 'messengers, those having ..that they might sound the trumpets.'
7. THE,] *lit.* 'and the first messenger sounded the trumpet, and there came.. having been mingled in blood, and it was cast to the land, [and the third part of the land was burnt down], and the third part of the trees was burnt down.. was burnt down.'
8. ANGEL,] *lit.* 'messenger sounded the trumpet.. being burnt [with fire].'
9. HAD LIFE,] *lit.* 'and having life (*lit.* souls) died away.. was thoroughly corrupted.'
10. ANGEL,] *lit.* 'messenger sounded the trumpet.. out of the heaven, burning as a lamp (*or* torch).. fountains (*or* wells) of (the) waters?'
11. WORMWOOD,] *lit.* 'undrinkable.. becomes undrinkable, and many of the men died away by (*lit.* out of, from).'
12. ANGEL,] *lit.* 'messenger sounded the trumpet.. that the third part of them might be darkened, and the day might not manifest (itself).'
13. BEHELD,] *lit.* 'perceived a messenger (*or* eagle) flying in mid-heaven.. great voice .. those dwelling upon the land, from (*lit.* out of) the remaining voices.. messengers, who are about to sound the trumpets.'

Chapter IX. may be divided into five parts; v. 1, 2 sounding of the fifth trumpet, and opening of the abyss; v. 3—6 authority given to locusts; v. 7—12 their likeness and king; v. 13—16 sounding of the sixth trumpet, and loosing of four messengers; v. 17—21 appearance of the horses and horsemen.

1. ANGEL,] *lit.* 'messenger sounded the trumpet, and I perceived a star having fallen (*or* cast himself) to the land..pit of the abyss,' i.e. a very deep *or* bottomless place.
2. OPENED,] *lit.* 'opened up the pit of the abyss, and there came up..as smoke..darkened from,' *lit.* out of.
3. CAME,] *lit.* 'came forth out..to the land..authority..authority.'
4. COMMANDED,] *lit.* 'said to them, that they may not injure..but [only] the men.. upon their foreheads.'
5. SHOULD,] *lit.* 'may not kill them utterly, but that they may be tried.. trial is as the trial.. he may strike.' The word *trial* in Greek is derived from the stone *Basanos*, used in Lydia for *testing* gold. See Mat. 4. 24; 8. 6; 18. 34; Luke 16. 23, 28, &c.
6. MEN,] *lit.* 'the men seek (*or* desire) the death.. and they shall greatly-desire to die fully, and the death shall flee for itself from them.'
7. SHAPES,] *lit.* 'likenesses.. having been prepared.. as crown like to gold.. as faces of men.'
8. THE,] *lit.* 'as hair of woman.'
9. BREASTPLATE,] *or* 'cuirasses as cuirasses of iron..as a sound of.'
10. HAD,] *lit.* 'have tails..authority is to injure the men.'
11 HAD,] *lit.* 'have a king over them—the messenger of the abyss—whose name Hebraistically is Abaddon (i.e. a separator, destroyer), and in the Hellenistic (language) he has a name Apollyon,' i.e. a looser away.
12. ONE,] *lit.* 'the one wo went away, behold, there cometh yet two woes after these.'
13. ANGEL,] *lit.* 'messenger sounded the trumpet..one voice out of.'
14. ANGEL,] *lit.* 'messenger, who is having ..Loose (at once)..messengers who have been bound by (*lit.* upon).. Euphrates,' i.e. very fruitful one.
15. ANGELS,] *lit.* 'messengers, who have been prepared for the hour, and day, and month, and year, that he might slay-fully the third of the men.'
16. ARMY,] *or* 'forces *or* soldiers.. two myriads of myriads.'
17. SAW,] *or* 'perceived..and these sitting ..cuirasses fiery and purple and sulphurous .. as heads.. passes forth.. sulphur.'
18. BY,] *lit.* 'from.. the men killed fully, from (*lit.* out of) the fire, and from (out of) the smoke, and from (out of) the sulphur that is passing forth.'
19. AND HAD,] *lit.* 'having in them they injure.'
20. THE REST,] *lit.* 'those remaining of.. killed outright, in the plagues (*or* smitings) neither had another mind out of the.. may not kiss forward (the hand) to the demons, and the idols—the golden, and the silvern, and the brazen, and the stone, and the wooden, which are neither able to behold, nor to hear, nor to walk about.'
21. NEITHER,] *lit.* 'and they had not another mind because of (out of) their murders, nor of their drugs, nor of their whoredom, nor of their thefts.'

Chapter X. may be divided into four parts; v. 1—4 vision of a messenger forbidding further writing; v. 5—7 and swearing that time shall not be yet; v. 8, 9 John directed to eat a little roll; v. 10, 11 which is at first sweet, but afterwards bitter.

1. SAW,] *or* 'perceived another strong messenger coming down out of the heaven, having been arrayed (*or* having arrayed himself) with a cloud, and the rainbow (is) upon his head, and his face as the sun.'
2. HAD,] *lit.* 'he is having in his hand a little roll opened up..left (*lit.* well-named) upon the land.'
3. LOUD,] *lit.* 'great voice.. roars for itself, and when he cried, the seven thunders (*lit.* roarings) spake out their own voices,' *or* sounds.
4. HAD,] *lit.* 'spake their own voices (*or* sounds)..out of the heaven.. Seal up (at once) the things the seven thunders spake, and, Thou mayest not write these things.'
5. ANGEL,] *lit.* 'messenger, which I perceived having stationed himself..land.. his [right] hand to the heaven.'
6. BY,] *lit.* 'in the Living one to the ages of the ages, who created (*or* formed, built) the heaven and the things in it, and the land and the things in it, and the sea and

the things in it, that (*or* because) the time shall not be yet'—to reveal the whole.

7. ANGEL,] *lit.* 'messenger, when he may be about to sound the trumpet, and the secret of God was ended, as he told good-news to his own bondsmen the prophets'—then shall be the time.

9. WENT,] *lit.* 'went away towards the messenger, saying to him to give to me the little roll; and he says to me, Take and eat it wholly.'

10. BOOK,] *or* 'roll..messenger..eat it wholly..and when I ate it, my belly was made bitter.'

11. SAID,] *lit.* 'says to me, Again it behoves thee to prophesy (at once) concerning.'

Chapter XI. may be divided into five parts; v. 1—6 the measurement of the habitation of God and the two witnesses; v. 7—10 their death and the enemy's joy; v. 11—14 their ascent and the enemy's fear; v. 15—18 sounding of the seventh trumpet and the praise of the presbyters; v. 19 vision of the ark, &c.

1. ANGEL,] *lit.* 'messenger had stood saying, Raise thyself and measure (at once) the habitation of God and the place of sacrifice, and those kissing forward (the hand) in it.'

2. TEMPLE,] *lit.* 'habitation cast forth without, and, Thou mayest not measure it, because it was given to the nations..tread down 42 months,' i.e. 1260 days or 3½ years, the exact time the Romans besieged Jerusalem.

3. 1260 DAYS,] i.e. 42 months, or 3½ years. See my 'Biblical Tracts' for an exposure of the monstrosity of supposing that 'a day' in prophetic language means 'a year.' Among all the Old Testament prophecies that have already been fulfilled *not one* has been, or *can* be, adduced as supporting such a hypothesis.

TWO WITNESSES,] i.e. a sufficient number; two being required by law.

4. CANDLESTICKS,] *or* 'lampstands.'

5. MAN,] *lit.* 'any one wishes to injure them, fire passeth forth out of their mouth, and eats down their enemies, and if any one wishes to injure them, it behoves him thus to be fully killed.'

6. POWER,] *lit.* 'authority to close the heaven, that it may not rain in their days of the prophecy, and they have authority over the waters..land with every plague..they may wish.'

7. SHALL HAVE,] *lit.* 'may end..wild beast that is coming up out of the abyss (i.e. very deep place)..with them..kill them fully.'

8. DEAD BODIES,] *lit.* 'fallen carcases are upon the broad place of the great city, which is called spiritually (i.e. by the prophets) Sodom (Isa. 1, 10), and Egypt, and where our Lord was crucified,'—even Jerusalem.

9. THEY,] *lit.* 'some of the peoples and tribes..behold their fallen carcase..let away their fallen carcases to be put into a monument.'

10. THEY,] *lit.* 'those dwelling upon the land shall leap for joy over them, and shall have a good mind..tried those dwelling upon the land.'

11. THREE,] *lit.* 'the three days..a spirit of life out of God went in upon them..those viewing them.'

12. FROM,] *lit.* 'out of the heaven..went up to the heaven in the cloud..viewed them.'

13. THE,] *lit.* 'and in that hour there came a great shaking..shaking there were fully-killed—names of men seven thousand, and those remaining became inwardly fearful, and gave glory to the God of the heaven.'

14. IS PAST,] *lit.* 'went away; behold..comes speedily,' *or* hastily.

15. ANGEL,] *lit.* 'messenger sounded the trumpet, and there came..the heaven..the world became..reign to the ages of the ages.'

16. ELDERS,] *Gr.* 'presbyters who are sitting..their thrones..kissed forward (the hand) to God.'

17. GIVE THEE THANKS,] *or* 'leap much with joy before thee, O Lord God, the Almighty, who Is, and who Was, [and who is Coming], because thou hast taken (*or* received) thy great power, and didst reign.'

18. WERE ANGRY,] *or* 'were angered, and thy anger came, and the season of the dead, to be judged, and to give the hire to the bondsmen..to those fearing thy name—the little and the great, and to thoroughly corrupt those thoroughly corrupting the land.'

19. TEMPLE,] *lit.* 'habitation of God was opened up in the heaven, and the ark of his (*or* the) covenant (of the Lord) was seen in his habitation, and there came flashings, and voices and roarings, and a shaking, and great hail.'

Chapter XII. may be divided into five parts; v. 1, 2 sign of a woman in child-birth; v. 3—6 and of a dragon seeking to destroy her child and herself; v. 7—9 war in the heaven and some cast out; v. 10—12 causing joy therein; v. 13—17 the dragon pursues the woman and her seed.

1. APPEARED,] *or* 'was seen a great sign in the heaven, a woman having been arrayed with the sun.'

2. SHE,] *lit.* 'having in the womb she cries, being pained and tried to bring forth.'

3. APPEARED,] *lit.* 'was seen another sign in the heaven..fiery dragon..diadems upon his heads.'

4. DREW,] *lit.* 'draws..of the heaven..has stood..who is about to bring forth, that when she may bring forth he may eat up her child.'

5. MAN CHILD,] *lit.* 'a son, a male, who is about to tend (*lit.* feed) all the nations in an iron rod..snatched away to God.'

6. PREPARED,] *lit.* 'having been prepared from God, that they may nourish her there.'

7. WAS,] *lit.* 'came war in the heaven.'

MICHAEL,] i.e. 'who is like God?'

ANGELS,] *lit.* 'messengers..messengers.'

8. PREVAILED,] *lit.* 'and were not strong ..not even.. in the heaven.'

9. THAT,] *lit.* 'the old serpent, who is called Devil (*lit.* 'thruster through,') and the Shutter-up (*Heb.* Satan), who is leading astray (i.e. trying to do so) the whole inhabited earth, he was cast to the land.'

10. LOUD,] *lit.* 'great voice saying in the heaven, Now did the salvation and the power.. authority of his Christ come, because the accusor (*lit.* him who is 'making (anything) public against' one).. was cast down, who is making public against them.'

11. BY,] *lit.* 'on account of the blood of the little Lamb, and on account of the word .. life (*lit.* soul) unto death.'

12. THEREFORE,] *lit.* 'because of this be of a good mind, ye heavens, and those tabernacling in them. Wo to those dwelling in the land and the sea, because the Devil went down to you having great fury, having perceived that he has a short season.'

13. SAW,] *or* 'perceived.. caused the woman who brought forth the male to flee.'

14. A,] *lit.* 'the great eagle.. whither she is nourished a season and seasons and half a season.'

15. FLOOD,] *or* 'river.. may cause her to be borne away by the river.'

16. EARTH,] *or* 'land..opened fully.. drank up the river.'

17. WROTH,] *lit.* 'made angry over the.. went away.. those left of her seed, who are keeping.. and having.'

Chapter XIII. may be divided into four parts; v. 1—4 appearance of a little wild beast coming up out of the sea; v. 5—10 its authority and conduct; v. 11—17 a second little wild beast; v. 18 its number.

1. I STOOD.] Some MSS. read 'He stood,' i.e. the dragon of 12. 17.

SAW,] *or* 'perceived a wild beast coming up.. ten diadems.. a name (*or* names) of injurious speaking.'

2. BEAST,] *lit.* 'little wild beast which I perceived.. as a mouth.. and his throne.'

3. SAW,] *lit.* 'perceived.. as having been slain to death, and the stroke of his death.'

4. WORSHIPPED,] *lit.* 'kissed forward (the hand) to the dragon who (*or* because he) gave authority.. kissed forward (the hand) to the little wild beast.'

5. BLASPHEMIES,] *lit.* 'injurious speaking, and authority.. make war.'

6. IN,] *or* 'for injurious speaking towards God, to speak injuriously of his name.. and those tabernacling in the heaven.'

7. POWER,] *lit.* 'authority over every tribe and people and tongue and nation.'

8. THAT,] *lit.* 'those dwelling upon the land shall kiss forward (the hand) to him, whose names have not been written (in the roll of the life of the little slain Lamb) from the laying down of the kosmos.'

9. MAN,] *lit.* 'if any one.'

10. BE,] *lit.* 'if any one brings a captivity (*lit.* what is taken by a spear) together, he goes away into captivity; if any one kills outright with (*lit.* in) a sword, it behoves him with (*lit.* in) a sword to be killed out right.. the endurance.'

11. BEHELD,] *or* 'perceived another little wild beast, coming up out of the land, and he was having.. was speaking.'

12. EXERCISETH,] *or* 'useth.. authority .. little wild beast, and he uses the land. and those dwelling in it, that they may kiss forward (the hand) to the.. the stroke of whose death was healed,' *lit.* cherished.

13. WONDERS,] *lit.* 'signs, that even fire he may make to come down out of the heaven to the land before the men.'

14. DECEIVETH,] *or* 'leadeth astray those dwelling.. on account of the signs which were given to him.. to those dwelling.. to make an.. the wild beast, which has the stroke of the sword and lived.'

15. HE HAD POWER,] *lit.* 'and there was given to him to give spirit to.. wild beast .. wild beast may both.. as may not kiss forward (the hand) to the.. may be killed outright.'

16. CAUSED,] *lit.* 'causes all, the small and the great, and the rich and the poor, and the freeman and the bondsmen, that they may give to them (selves) an impressed mark upon.. upon their forehead.'

17. MAN,] *lit.* 'no one may be able to buy .. is having the impressed mark.. wild beast.'

18. WISDOM,] *lit.* 'the wisdom.. is having (the mind) calculate.. wild beast, for it is (the) number of a man,'—yet most expositors treat it as that of a *system!* others as a chronological *era!*

SIX HUNDRED THREESCORE AND SIX.] The Greek here (as in 7. 4—18) gives the number not in words but in letters, viz., χξς, i.e. 600 + 60 + 6=666. Another reading mentioned by Irenaeus is 616. For a fuller account of this number, see my 'Biblical Tracts,' where it is shown to refer to *Nero*, whose character is entirely in accordance with the description here given, and whose name, when spelt in the full Hebrew form *Neron*, yields the number 666, and in the shorter Greek form *Nero* gives 616, thus accounting satisfactorily for the variation as noticed by Irenaeus.

Chapter XIV. may be divided into three parts; v. 1—5 vision of a Lamb and 144,000 redeemed singers; v. 6—13 four voices speak v. 14—20 vision of the two reapers.

1. LOOKED,] *lit.* 'beheld, and behold, (the) Lamb having stood,' *or* stationed himself.

SION.] *Heb.* 'dry *or* sunny place.'

IN,] *lit.* 'upon their foreheads.'

2. FROM,] *lit.* 'out of the heaven, as a voice of many (i.e. mighty) waters, and as a voice of great roaring, and I heard a voice ..in (*or* among) their harps.'

3. SUNG,] *lit.* 'ode a new ode.. living creatures.. presbyters, and no one was able to learn the ode.. have been brought.'

4. WERE NOT DEFILED,] *or* 'did not defile themselves with women, (comp. Ge. 6. 2) for they are virgins;' the word is *mas.* not feminine here.

FOLLOW,] *lit.* 'are following.. he may gc

away, these were bought from (among) the men—a first-fruit.'

5. GUILE.] Some MSS. read 'falsehood.'

WITHOUT FAULT,] *lit.* 'unblemished.'

6. SAW,] *or* 'perceived another messenger flying in mid-heaven, having age-during good-news to tell as good news to those dwelling..tribe.'

7. WITH,] *lit.* 'in a great voice, Fear God for yourselves..because..did come; and kiss ye forward (the hand) to..the heaven and the land, and (the) sea, and fountains of waters.'

8. ANGEL,] *lit.* 'messenger, saying, Fall, fall did Babylon the great (city), because she has caused all nations to drink (some) of the wine of (the wrath of) her whoredom.'

9. THE,] *or* 'and (another) third messenger ..in a great voice, If any one kisses forward (the hand) to the little wild beast..receives an impressed mark upon..upon.'

10. THE SAME,] *lit.* 'he also shall drink for himself (some) of..has been mixed unmixed in the cup of his anger..tried in fire.'

11. TORMENT,] *lit.* 'trial go up to ages of ages, and they have not rest again..are kissing forward (the hand) to the little wild beast.'

12. THE,] *lit.* 'is endurance..those keeping.'

13. FROM,] *lit.* 'out of the heaven..Happy henceforth are the dead who are fully dying away in the Lord; yes..they may rest themselves again from (*lit.* out of) their toils, but their works do follow with them.

14. LOOKED,] *lit.* 'perceived..is (one) sitting like to a son of man,' i.e. a human being, as in 1. 13; evidently the 'Lord of angels' could not receive a *command* from one, as here in v. 15, 'Send forth at once!' as the *aorist* imperative implies.

15. CAME OUT,] *lit.* 'came forth out of the Habitation, crying in a great voice to him sitting..Send forth (at once) thy reaping-hook, and bring in the harvest, because the hour of the harvesting came, because the harvest of the earth was dried up,' i.e. ready for cutting down.

16. SAT,] *lit.* 'is sitting..cast his reaping-hook over the earth.'

17. ANGEL,] *lit.* 'messenger came forth out of the Habitation that is in the heaven.'

18. ANGEL,] *lit.* 'messenger came forth out of the place of sacrifice having authority over the fire; and he sounded with a great cry to him having..Send forth (at once).. because..were matured.'

19. THRUST,] *lit.* 'cast his reaping-hook.'

20. CAME,] *lit.* 'came forth out of the wine-press, unto the horses' bridles, a thousand six hundred stadium (*or* furlongs) off.'

Chapter XV. may be divided into two parts; v. 1—4 vision of seven messengers, a sea of glass, and the song of the victors; v. 5—8 also of seven vials and the sanctuary filled with smoke.

1. SAW,] *lit.* 'perceived..in the heaven.. because in them was ended.'

2. SAW,] *lit.* 'perceived as a glassy (i.e. transparent) sea..and the victors over (*lit.* out of) the little wild beast..having stationed themselves upon the glassy sea, having harps of God.'

3. SING,] *lit.* 'ode the ode of Moses, bondsman of God, and the ode of the little Lamb, ..O Lord, the Almighty God..O (*or* the) king of the saints,' *or* nations, *or* ages.

4. SHALL,] *lit.* 'who may not..may glorify ..because..because all the..kiss forward the hand..because thy righteous acts were manifested,' *or* manifested themselves.

5. THAT,] *lit.* 'these things I beheld..habitation of the tabernacle..in the heaven was opened up.'

6. CAME OUT,] *lit.* 'came forth out of the habitation, those having..having been clothed.'

7. BEASTS,] *lit.* 'living creatures..wrath of the living God—to the ages of the ages.'

8. TEMPLE,] *lit.* 'habitation..from (*lit.* out of)..from (*lit.* out of)..no one..habitation..may be ended.'

Chapter XVI. may be divided into seven parts; v. 1, 2 pouring out of the vials upon men; v. 3 upon the sea; v. 4—7 upon the rivers and the fountains; v. 8, 9 upon the sun; v. 10, 11 upon the throne of the wild beast; v. 12—16 upon the Euphrates; v. 17 —21 upon the air.

1. TEMPLE,] *lit.* 'habitation..Be going away and pour forth fully the (seven) vials ..to the earth.'

2. WENT,] *lit.* 'went away and poured forth fully..there came a bad and evil ulcer to the men, those having the impressed mark of the little wild beast, and those kissing forward the hand to his image.'

3. OUT,] *lit.* 'poured forth fully..to the sea, and it became blood, as of a dead (man) and every living soul (i.e. breathing creature) died away in the sea.'

4. OUT,] *lit.* 'poured out fully..to the rivers, and to the fountains of the waters, and it became blood.'

5. SAY,] *lit.* 'saying, Righteous art thou, (O Lord), who art, and who was, and [who shall be *or*] who is kind, because thou didst judge these things.'

6. FOR,] *lit.* 'because they poured forth blood of..didst give to them.'

7. ANOTHER OUT OF.] Some MSS. omit.

SAY,] *lit,* 'saying, Yes, O Lord, the Almighty God.'

8. ANGEL.] Some MSS. omit.

OUT,] *lit.* 'poured forth fully..and there was given to it to scorch the men in fire.'

9. MEN,] *lit.* 'and the men..and spake injuriously of the..is having authority.. and they had not another mind.'

10. ANGEL.] Some MSS. omit.

OUT,] *lit.* 'poured out fully..throne of the little wild beast..became darkened and they were gnawing..from (*lit.* out of) the.'

11. BLASPHEMED,] *lit.* 'spake injuriously of the God of the heaven from (*lit.* out of) ..from (*lit.* out of) their ulcers, and they had not a new mind from (*lit.* out of) their works.'

12. ANGEL.] Some MSS. omit.
OUT,] *lit.* 'poured forth fully.'
OF,] *lit.* 'from the uprising of the sun may be made ready.'
13. SAW,] *or* 'perceived.'
14. THE,] *lit.* 'are spirits of demons doing signs.'
GO,] *lit.* 'passing forth.' The nominative to this verb is in v. 13, 'three unclean spirits like frogs,' the intermediate words being parenthetical.
UNTO,] *lit.* 'upon *or* over the kings of the land and of the whole inhabited world, to lead them together.'
15. BLESSED,] *lit.* 'happy is he who is working and keeping..that he may not walk about naked, and they may behold his unseemliness.'
16. GATHERED,] *lit.* 'led them..called Hebraistically Armageddon,' i.e. hill of Mageddon, where Sisera was overthrown and Josiah was killed, Jud. 5. 19; 2 K. 23. 29. The name is symbolic of lamentation and wo.
17. ANGEL.] Some MSS. omit.
OUT,] *lit.* 'poured forth fully into (*or* upon) the air, and there came forth a..from the Habitation of the heaven..It has happened!'
18. WERE,] *lit.* 'there came voices and roarings and flashings, and there came a great shaking, such as came not since the men came upon the land.'
19. WAS,] *lit.* 'came into three..was remembered..fury of his anger.'
20. THE,] *lit.* 'and mountains.'
21. FELL,] *lit.* 'comes down upon the men out of the heaven, as of a talent weight (i.e. 93¾ lb. avoirdupois), and the men spake injuriously of God from (*lit.* out of) the..is exceeding great.'

Chapter XVII. may be divided into four parts; v. 1—5 vision of a great whore; v. 6—11 uncovering of the secret of the wild beast carrying her with its seven heads; v. 12—14 and of its ten horns, warring with the little Lamb; v. 15—18 and of the waters on which she sits, which with the horns at last hate and consume her, who is now reigning over the kings of the land.

1. OF,] *lit.* 'out of the seven messengers, of those having..spake..is sitting upon the many waters,' i.e. peoples, as in v. 15.
2. HAVE,] *lit.* 'earth committed whoredom, and those inhabiting the earth were made drunk out of the wine of her whoredom.'
3. SO,] *lit.* 'and he bore me away in spirit to a wilderness, and I perceived a woman sitting upon a..being full of names of injurious-speech.'
4. WAS,] *lit.* 'was having been arrayed with..and having been gilded..stone..being full of..whoredom.'
5. MYSTERY,] i.e. a thing formerly unknown, now known.
BABYLON,] a symbolic name of any great oppressor of the church, as explained in v. 18.
HARLOTS,] *lit.* 'of the whores and of the abominations of the earth.'
6. SAW,] *or* 'perceived..out of the blood ..of the blood..and having beheld her..wonder.'
7. MARVEL,] *or* 'wonder..tell (*lit.* lift up) to thee..is bearing her, having the seven..the ten horns.'
8. SAWEST,] *or* 'didst perceive, it was, and it is not, and it is about to come up out of the abyss, and to go away to disolution; and those dwelling upon the earth shall wonder for themselves, whose names have not been written from the laying-down of the kosmos upon the little roll of the life, beholding the beast that it was, and is not.'
9. AND,] *lit.* 'here is the mind that is having wisdom..seats herself.'
10. THERE,] *lit.* 'and they are seven kings.'
FIVE,] *lit.* 'the five fell, and the one is, the other did not yet come, and when he may come, it behoves him to remain a little.'
11. THE,] *lit.* 'he is eighth, and is out of (*or* from) the seven, and goes away to a loosing away,' or disolution.
12. SAWEST,] *or* 'perceivedst..which received..authority.'
13. MIND,] *lit.* 'knowledge,' i.e. opinion.
SHALL GIVE,] *or* 'do give their own power.'
14. LAMB,] *lit.* 'little Lamb..choice and stedfast.'
15. SAWEST,] *or* 'didst perceive..seats herself down..and crowds.'
16. UPON.] Best MSS. read 'and.'
EAT,] *lit.* 'eat for themselves her masses-of-flesh, and shall burn her thoroughly in fire.'
17. HATH PUT,] *lit.* 'gave to their hearts to do his knowledge (i.e. opinion), and to make one opinion, and to give..sayings (*or* words)..may be ended.'
18. SAWEST,] *or* 'didst perceive is the great city that is having a kingship over the kings of the land,' i.e. Rome.

Chapter XVIII. may be divided into eight parts; v. 1—3 announcement of Babylon's fall and its cause; v. 4—6 call to come out of her; v. 7, 8 her self-glorification; v. 9, 10 kings bewail her; v. 11—16 and merchants; v. 17—19 and those on the sea; v. 20 call to heaven to rejoice over it; v. 21—24 its violent and final end.

1. SAW,] *or* 'perceived (another) messenger coming down out of the heaven,..authority,..out of his glory.'
2. WITH,] *lit.* 'in strength with a (great) voice, saying, Fall, fall did Babylon the great, and it became a place for settling down of demons, and a ward of every unclean spirit, and a ward of.'
3. FOR,] *lit.* 'because all the nations..out of (the wine of) the..whoredom..earth committed whoredom..earth became rich out of the power of her licentiousness.'
4. FROM,] *lit.* 'out of..Come forth out of her..may not have fellowship with..may not receive out of.'
5. HAVE REACHED,] *lit.* 'did follow, *or* followed for themselves unto the heaven, and God remembered her unrighteous acts.'
6. REWARD,] *lit.* 'give away *or* back..gave away *or* back (to you)..she mixed mix ye.'

7. HOW MUCH,] *or* 'as much as she glorified herself, and was licentious, so much trial and suffering (*or* mourning) .. because .. I seat myself down .. not bereaved, and may perceive no suffering' *or* mourning.

8. THEREFORE,] *lit.* 'because of this .. suffering and failure, .. in fire, because .. is judging her.'

9. HAVE,] *lit.* 'who committed whoredom and were licentious with her, shall themselves break forth and smite themselves over her .. behold .. fiery trial.'

10. STANDING,] *or* 'having stationed themselves .. because of the fear of her trial .. Oh! oh! the great city, Babylon the strong city, because in one hour came thy judgment.'

11. MERCHANTS,] *or* 'passers-in of the land .. their fulness.'

12. THE,] *lit.* 'fulness of gold .. stone .. thyine (i.e. perfume) wood (*or* tree) .. ivory (*Gr.* elephantine) .. marble,' *lit.* 'shining.'

13. ODOURS.] Some MSS. read 'and amomium and incense and myrrh (*or* ointment) and frankincense, .. cattle .. bodies and lives (*lit.* souls) of men.'

14. FRUITS,] *lit.* 'autumnal fruits of the over-desire of thy soul went away .. all the fat and the shining things departed (*or* loosed themselves off) from thee, and thou mayest.'

15. BY,] *lit.* 'from her .. shall stand for themselves afar off, on account of the fear of her trial.'

16. ALAS,] *lit.* 'oh! oh! the great .. arrayed with .. gilded in gold and precious stone.'

17. FOR,] *lit.* 'because in .. was made bare.' SHIP-MASTER,] *or* 'pilot, steersman, and all the crowd upon the ships, and seamen, and as many as work the sea.'

18. CRIED,] *lit.* 'were crying, beholding the .. fiery trial, .. the great city.'

19. CAST,] *lit.* 'were casting .. were crying .. Oh! oh! the great .. those having ships .. out of her preciousness, because .. was she made bare.'

20. REJOICE,] *lit.* 'be of a good mind over her, O heaven, and ye holy apostles and ye prophets, because God judged your judgment out of her.'

21. A MIGHTY,] *or* 'one strong messenger lifted up .. violence (*or* excitement) shall the .. cast .. may be found.'

22. THE,] *lit.* 'and voice of .. may be heard .. artisans of any art, may be found .. a sound of .. may be heard.'

23. THE,] *lit.* 'and light of a lamp may shine .. and voice of bridegroom (*lit.* one of a new appearance) and bride may be heard .. because .. because in thy sorcery (*Gr.* pharmacy) were all the nations led astray.'

24. THE,] *lit.* 'was found blood of (N. T.) prophets and saints .. those having been slain upon the land.'

Chapter XIX. may be divided into seven parts; v. 1—4 praises because of the punishment of the harlot; v. 5—8 of the marriage of the Lamb; v. 9, 10 order to write, and refusal of homage; v. 11—13 appearances of the Word of God; v. 14—16 his followers, work, and name; v. 17, 18 call to devour; v. 19—21 the beast and false prophet and followers defeated and ruined.

1. MUCH PEOPLE,] *or* 'a numerous crowd in the heaven, saying, Alleluia (in *Heb.* Hallelujah, i.e. praise ye Jah,) the safety, and the glory, and the honour (*or* weightiness), and the power (is) to (the Lord) our God.'

2. HATH,] *lit.* 'he judged .. in her whoredom, and arranged thoroughly .. bondsmen out of her hand.'

3. AGAIN,] *lit.* 'a second time they have said .. goes up to the ages of the ages.'

4. ELDERS,] *Gr.* 'presbyters .. living creatures .. kissed forward (the hand) to the God who is seating himself.'

5. CAME,] *lit.* 'came forth out of .. Be praising .. bondsmen, and ye who are fearing him, both the small and the great.'

6. AS IT WERE,] *lit.* 'as of a numerous crowd, and as a voice .. as a voice of strong roarings .. because .. did reign.'

7. LET,] *or* 'may we leap for joy .. give the glory to him, because .. came, and his wife made herself ready.'

8. GRANTED,] *lit.* 'given that she may be arrayed .. and shining for the fine linen are the righteous acts of the saints.'

9. WRITE,] *lit.* 'write (at once), Happy are those who have been called to the supper of the marriage of the Lamb .. true words.'

10. AT,] *lit.* 'before .. kiss forward (the hand) to him. . See no! .. fellow-bondsmen .. are having (*or* holding) .. kiss forward (the hand) at once to God .. of the prophecy'—that I am now declaring.

11. SAW,] *lit.* 'perceived the heaven having been opened up (*or* opening itself up), and he who is seating himself upon it, is called stedfast.'

12. HIS,] *lit.* 'but his eyes are as .. are many diadems, having .. no one has known for himself.'

13. WAS,] *lit.* 'is arrayed in a garment having been bathed with blood,' i.e. covered or sprinkled with his own and his enemy's blood.

14. WHICH WERE,] *or* 'that are in the heaven were following.'

15. GOETH,] *lit.* 'goeth forth a sharp sword, that with (*lit.* in) it he himself may .. rule (*lit.* feed) them in a rod .. and himself treads the press of the wine of the fury and of the anger (*lit.* 'stretching out' of the arms) of the Almighty God.'

16. VESTURE,] *or* 'garment.'

17. SAW,] *or* 'perceived one messenger having stationed himself in .. great voice .. birds flying in mid-heaven, Come and be led together to the supper, the great one, of God.'

18. THE,] *lit.* 'eat masses of flesh .. and flesh of chiefs of thousands, and flesh of strong (men), and flesh of horses, and of those seating themselves upon them, and flesh of all—both freedmen and bondsmen, both of small and great.'

19. SAW,] *or* 'perceived the little wild beast .. led together to make war with him who is sitting .. with his army.'

20. TAKEN,] *or* 'seized.. who did the signs .. in which he led astray those who received the impressed mark of .. kissing forward (the hand) to his .. living they were cast—the two—into the lake of the fire that is burning in (the) sulphur.'

21. THE REMNANT,] *lit.* 'those left were utterly slain in the sword of him who is sitting.. which is passing forth out of .. birds were filled out of their flesh.'

Chapter XX. may be divided into four parts; v. 1—3 vision of the binding of the Devil; v. 4—6 the thousand years' reign; v. 7—10 ruin of Gog and Magog; v. 11—13 vision of a great white throne and final judgment.

1. SAW,] *or* 'perceived a messenger coming down out of the heaven .. abyss .. upon his hand.'

2. LAID HOLD ON,] *or* 'held fast the dragon, the ancient serpent (12. 9) who is Devil, (*lit.* 'thruster through,') and Satan,' *lit.* 'shutter up.'

3. BOTTOMLESS PIT,] *Gr.* 'abyss, and closed (him) up .. he may led astray .. may be filled out, and after these things it behoved him to be loosed a little time.'

4. SAW,] *or* 'perceived .. even the souls of those beheaded (*lit.* made so with an 'axe,') on account of .. and on account of .. did not kiss forward (the hand) to the wild little beast, nor to his image, and did not receive the impressed mark upon (their) forehead, or upon their hand, and they lived (*or* revived, in seeing the downfall of Satan), and reigned with Christ a thousand years,'—a round number being used to indicate its greatness, as in Rev. 7. 4—8; 9. 16; 21. 16, &c.

5. DEAD,] i.e. the *wicked* dead lived not, i.e. had no spirit or power during the 1000 years, till their chief was freed again.

RESURRECTION,] *lit.* 'upstanding.'

6. BLESSED,] *lit.* 'happy.. who is having a part in the first upstanding, over such .. authority.'

7. ARE,] *lit.* 'may be ended, the Shutter-up shall be loosed out of his ward.'

8. OUT,] *lit.* 'go forth to lead astray .. corners of the earth—the Gog and (the) Magog, to lead them together.'

9. ON,] *or* 'over.. encircled.. of the heaven, and devoured them thoroughly.'

10. DEVIL,] *lit.* 'thruster through, who is leading them astray.. of the fire and sulphur ..tried.. to the ages of the ages.'

11. SAW,] *lit.* 'perceived .. is sitting .. fled.'

12. SAW,] *lit.* 'perceived.. having stationed themselves before God (*or* the throne), and rolls were opened up, and another little roll was opened up, which is (that) of the Life.. rolls.'

13. DEATH,] *lit.* 'the death and the unseen state (*Gr.* Hades) gave up.. each one.'

14. DEATH,] *lit.* 'the death and the unseen state.. of the fire.'

15. WHOSOEVER,] *lit.* 'and if any one.. roll of the life, he was cast.. of the fire.'

Chapter XXI. may be divided into five parts; v. 1—4 visions of a new heaven, earth, and city; v. 5—8 God's promises and warnings; v. 9—14 vision of the Lamb's wife—holy Jerusalem; v. 15—21 its measurements and its foundations; v. 22—27 its glory and purity.

1. SAW,] *or* 'perceived.. earth went along, and there is no more sea.'

2. I JOHN.] Omitted in many MSS., Versions, &c.

SAW,] *or* 'perceived.. out of the heaven, made ready.'

3. HEAVEN,] *lit.* 'of the heaven.. with the men.. tabernacle.'

4. AWAY,] *lit.* 'wipe off every tear.. because the first things went away.'

5. SAT,] *lit.* 'is sitting.. says to me, Write (at once) that *or* because.. and stedfast.'

6. IT IS DONE,] *lit.* 'it has happened, *or* come to pass; I am the Alpha and the Omega.. I—I will give to him who is thirsting out of.. of the life freely,' *or* gratis.

7. OVERCOMES,] *lit.* 'is overcoming.. all (*or* these) things, and I will be a God to him, and he shall be to me—the Son.'

8. UNBELIEVING,] *lit.* 'unstedfast, and (sinful, and) abominable.. sorcerers (*lit.* users of pharmacy), and idol-tremblers, and all the liars, have.. is burning.'

UNTO ME.] Best MSS. omit these words.

ANGELS,] *or* 'messengers having.. that are full.. spake.'

10. CARRIED,] *lit.* 'bore me away in spirit over a .. the (great) city.. the heaven.'

11. LIGHT,] *or* 'light-giver.. made like crystal.'

12. AND HAD,] *lit.* 'having also a.. having twelve.. and over the.. sons of.'

13. ON,] *lit.* 'from (the) uprising (of the sun).. from (the) north .. from (the) south.. from (the) west.'

14. HAD,] *lit.* 'is having.. them (are) names.'

15. TALKED,] *lit.* 'is speaking.. is having ..reed-measure, that he may measure.'

16. FOURSQUARE,] *lit.* 'four-cornered.. of it is as great.. equal,' i.e. proportionate.

17. THE,] *lit.* 'of an angel,' *or* messenger.

18. BUILDING,] *lit.* 'in building of.. clear gold.'

19. GARNISHED,] *lit.* 'adorned with every precious stone.'

21. EVERY SEVERAL,] *lit.* 'each one severally of the gates.. broad place of.. clear gold.'

22. SAW,] *or* 'perceived no Habitation (of God).. its Habitation.

23. HAD,] *lit.* 'has no.. that they may shine.. is its Lamp.'

24. OF THEM WHICH ARE SAVED.] MSS. omit.

WALK,] *lit.* 'walk about.. do bear.'

25. SHALL,] *lit.* 'may not be closed.'

26. BRING,] *lit.* 'bear.'

27. SHALL,] *lit.* 'may not.. anything (making) common, or doing an abomination or a lie.. roll of the life of the Lamb.'

Chapter XXII. may be divided into eight parts; v. 1—5 vision of the river of life and its fruits; v. 6, 7 a double assurance; v. 8, 9 refusal of obeisance; v. 10—13 coming of the end; v. 14, 15 happiness and misery; v. 16, 17 invitation to come; v. 18—20 warning; v. 21 salutation.

1. PURE.] Some MSS. and Versions omit.

CLEAR,] *or* 'shining..passing forth out of.'

2. STREET,] *lit.* 'broad place of it (i.e. the city) and of the river, on this side and on that, a tree of life, making twelve (kinds of) fruits, according to each several month giving away its fruit, and the leaves (*or* produce) of the tree is for a.'

3. CURSE,] *lit.* a thing 'put up' *or* 'put down' upon the altar of God, as devoted.

BUT,] *lit.* 'and the..bondsmen shall go very tremblingly to him.'

4. IN,] *lit.* 'upon their foreheads.'

5. CANDLE,] *lit.* 'lamp or light of a sun, because..gives light over them..to the ages of the ages.'

6. SAYINGS,] *lit.* 'words are stedfast (19. 9; 21. 5)..holy (*or* spirits of the) prophets sent forth his messenger..bondsmen the things which behove to happen in haste.'

7. BEHOLD,] *lit.* 'and behold, I come hastily; happy is he who is keeping..little roll.'

8. SAW,] *or* 'am he who is beholding these things and hearing; and when I heard and beheld, I fell to kiss forward (the hand) before..messenger who is shewing me.'

9. THEN,] *lit.* 'and he says to me, See! not!..of those keeping the words of this little roll; kiss forward (the hand) to God This appears a repetition of 19. 10.

10. SEAL NOT,] *lit.* 'thou mayest not seal the words..little roll; because the season is nigh.' This shews that the book relates to the contests of the church with ancient Judaism and Paganism.

12. QUICKLY,] *or* 'hastily, speedily, and my hire is with me, to give away to each as.'

13. THE,] *lit.* 'beginning and end.'

14. BLESSED,] *lit.* 'happy those doing.. that their authority shall be over the tree of the life.'

15. FOR,] *lit.* 'but without are the dogs, and the users of pharmacy, and the whoremongers, and the murderers, and the idolworshippers, and every one who is befriending and doing (i.e. acting) a lie.'

16. HAVE,] *lit.* 'did send..about the assemblies..shining and early star.'

17. COME,] *lit.* 'be coming (from time to time)..is hearing say, Be coming, and let him who is thirsting be coming, and let him who is willing *or* wishing take.'

18. TESTIFY,] *lit.* 'testify fully to every one hearing the..little roll, If any one may ..have been written in this little roll.'

19. MAN,] *lit.* 'any one may lift up..lift up..book (*or* tree) of the life.'

20. TESTIFETH,] *lit.* 'is testifying..Yes, I come speedily! Amen! yes, be coming.'

21. OUR.] Some MSS. omit; for 'you' others read 'is with all the saints. Amen.'

www.ingramcontent.com/pod-product-compliance
Ingram Content Group UK Ltd.
Pitfield, Milton Keynes, MK11 3LW, UK
UKHW022002270726
14060UKWH00006B/731

9 781589 602618